A Concise
Dictionary of
Middle English
from 1150 to 1580

By

Anthony Lawson Mayhew

and

Walter William Skeat

Revised by

Michael Everson

evertype
2009

Published by Evertype, Cnoc Sceichín, Leac an Anfa, Cathair na Mart, Co. Mhaigh Eo, Éire. *www.evertype.com*.

This edition © 2009 Michael Everson.

First edition Oxford: Clarendon Press, 1888.

A catalogue record for this book is available from the British Library.

ISBN-10 1-904808-23-9
ISBN-13 978-1-904808-23-7

Typeset in Baskerville and 𝔦𝔫 𝔅𝔞𝔰𝔱𝔞𝔯𝔡𝔢 Ⓜ𝔞𝔫𝔲𝔞𝔩 by Michael Everson.

Cover design by Michael Everson.

Printed and bound by LightningSource.

For
Sigmund Eisner,
scholar, mentor,
builder of astrolabes,
and friend,
who encouraged a 16-year-old
to pursue a love of languages,
and whose expectations of excellence
remain an inspiration 30 years on.

Ich habbe boþe luue ⁊ þonc
Þat ich her com ⁊ hider swonk.

M.E.

CONTENTS

PREFACE TO THE 2009 EDITION

Although in the age of the Internet we have access to the magnificent
Middle English Compendium hosted by the University of Michigan, few
students of Middle English would question the usefulness of a desktop copy
for day-to-day reference. There has been no handy, reliable edition of such
a dictionary for many years. The 1888 edition of Mayhew and Skeat's
Concise Dictionary of Middle English can sometimes be found in
antiquarian bookshops, but it is scarce, and available copies vary in both
condition and cost. This new edition of Mayhew and Skeat has been
revised and completely reset for the modern reader. It offers in a concise
form more than 11,000 headwords with source references, cross references,
and etymologies.

Free online digital editions of the dictionary are now available at two
major archives, and these too are useful for online searching. Some of these
have been edited into legible formats; some are more or less raw ASCII texts.
A few "publishers" have released printed versions which are little more
than dumps of those plain-text files—and I use the scare quotes advisedly
here, feeling sorry for those students who have bought those editions
thinking that they were, in fact, buying proper dictionaries.

This edition has been set in Baskerville, a clear and accessible font, which
it is hoped, will increase the legibility of the book. Further choices made in
typesetting have led to additional changes in format, both for aesthetic
reasons and to modernize the text in line with the contemporary reader's
expectations.

- Headwords begin with lower-case letters, apart from a fairly small
  number of proper nouns (**Fri-dæi**, **Þorr**, etc.).
- Alphabetical order is *a b c d e f g h i j k l m n o p q r s t þ u v w x y ȝ z*. The
  1888 edition gave *i* [*vowel*] and *i* [*consonant*] instead of *i* and *j*, treated *ð*
  and *þ* as variants of *th* within the letter *t*, and gave *u, v* [*vowel*] and *v, u*
  [*consonant*] instead of *u* and *v*.
- Citation forms follow the manuscript spellings, as in the 1888 edition.
  In the guide-words at the top of each page, however, and in cross

references, consonantal *i* [dʒ] is rewritten as *j*, consonantal *u* [v] is rewritten as *v*, vocalic *v* [u] is rewritten as *u*, and *ð* and *th* [θ]~[ð] are rewritten as *þ*.

- The letter *æ* is sorted as *ae*.
- Consonantal *i* and *j* [dʒ] are interfiled under *j*.
- The letters *ð*, *th*, and *þ* are all interfiled under *þ*. Where *th* represents [t], it is found between *te* and *ti* (as **rethoryke**, rhetoric).
- Vocalic *u* and *v* [u] are interfiled under *u*.
- Consonantal *u* and *v* [v] are interfiled under *v*.
- A section for words beginning in *z-* has been added.
- Superscript numbers are used to distinguish homonymous headwords (as **meten**[1], to dream; **meten**[2], to paint; **meten**[3], to meet; **meten**[4], to measure).
- Cross references point to the correct headword based on the superscript number.
- Danish etymologies use *ø* and *å* instead of *ö* and *aa*.
- Gothic etymologies use *þ* and *ƕ* instead of *th* and *hw*.
- Sanskrit etymologies conform to modern Brahmic transliteration.
- The mixed usage of *cf.* and *cp.* for 'compare' has been normalized to *cf.*
- Current Modern English spellings are used in definitions (such as *show* for *shew*, *ache* for *ake*).
- Errors in cross references have been corrected, so s.v. **must**, new wine, "cf. **moiste**" now reads "cf. **moyste**".
- Other errors have been corrected where discovered (*cf.* "**hong** *pt. s.* hung" alongside "**hongede** *pt. s.* hung"; the latter has been corrected to "**hongede** *pt. s.* hanged").

I would like to thank Greg Lindahl, Anzia Kraus, and Louise Hope for the extensive and painstaking work which they and their Distributed Proofreaders team did to prepare what became the source files for this dictionary. Since I have extensively revised those sources, I alone bear the final responsibility for any errors that persist. I am confident nonetheless that this book will prove a welcome and useful tool for students of Middle English.

Michael Everson

PREFACE TO THE 1888 EDITION

The present work is intended to meet, in some measure, the requirements of those who wish to make some study of Middle-English, and who find a difficulty in obtaining such assistance as will enable them to find out the meanings and etymologies of the words most essential to their purpose.

The best Middle-English Dictionary, that by Dr Mätzner of Berlin, has only reached the end of the letter H; and it is probable that it will not be completed for many years. The only Middle-English Dictionary that has been carried on to the end of the alphabet is that by the late Dr Stratmann, of Krefeld. This is a valuable work, and is indispensable for the more advanced student. However, the present work will still supply a deficiency, as it differs from Stratmann's Dictionary in many particulars. We have chosen as our Main Words, where possible, the most typical of the forms or spellings of the period of Chaucer and Piers Plowman; in Stratmann, on the other hand, the form chosen as Main Word is generally the oldest form in which it appears, frequently one of the twelfth century. Moreover, with regard to authorities, we refer in the case of the great majority of our forms to a few, cheap, easily accessible works, whereas Stratmann's authorities are mainly the numerous and expensive publications of the Early English Text Society. Lastly, we have paid special attention to the French element in Middle-English, whereas Stratmann is somewhat deficient in respect of words of French origin.[1] The book which has generally been found of most assistance to the learner is probably Halliwell's Dictionary of Archaic and Provincial Words; but this is not specially confined to the Middle-English period, and the plan of it differs in several respects from that of the present work.

The scope of this volume will be best understood by an explanation of the circumstances that gave rise to it. Some useful and comparatively inexpensive volumes illustrative of the Middle-English period have been issued by the Clarendon Press; all of which are furnished with glossaries, explaining all the important words, with exact references to the passages wherein the words occur. In particular, the three useful hand-books containing Specimens of English (from 1150 down to 1580) together supply

---

1 A new and thoroughly revised edition of Stratmann's Dictionary is being prepared by Mr Henry Bradley, for the Delegates of the Clarendon Press.

no less than sixty-seven characteristic extracts from the most important literary monuments of this period; and the three glossaries to these books together fill more than 370 pages of closely-printed type in double columns. The idea suggested itself that it would be highly desirable to bring the very useful information thus already collected *under one alphabet*, and this has now been effected. At the same time, a reference has in every case been carefully given to the *particular* Glossarial Index which registers each form here cited, so that it is perfectly easy for any one who consults our book to refer, not merely to the particular Index thus noted, but to the references given in that Index; and so, by means of such references, to find every passage referred to, with its proper context. Moreover the student only requires, for this purpose, a small array of the text-books in the Clarendon Press Series, instead of a more or less complete set of editions of Middle-English texts, the possession of which necessitates a considerable outlay of money. By this plan, so great a *compression* of information has been achieved, that a large number of the articles give a summary such as can be readily expanded to a considerable length, by the exercise of a very little trouble; and thus the work is practically as full of material as if it had been three or four times its present size. A couple of examples will show what this really means.

At p. 21 is the following entry:

> **bi-heste**, *sb.* promise, S, S2, C2, P; **byheste**, S2; **beheste**, S2; **byhest**, S2; **bihese**, S; **biheest**, W; **bihese**, *pl.*, S.—AS. *be-hǽs*.

By referring to the respective indexes here cited, such as S (= Glossary to Specimens of English, Part I), and the like, we easily expand this article into the following:

> **bi-heste**, *sb.* promise, S (9. 19); S2 (1*a*. 184); C2 (B 37, 41, 42, F 698); P (3. 126); **byheste**, S2 (18*b*. 25); **beheste**, S2 (14*a*. 3); **byhest**, S2 (12. 57, 18*b*. 9, [where it may also be explained by *grant*]); **bihese**, S (where it is used as a plural); **biheest**, W (promise, command, Lk. 24:49, Rom. 4:13; pl. *biheestis*, Heb. 11:13); **bihese**, S (*pl.* behests, promises, 4*d*. 55).— AS. *behǽs*.

In order to exhibit the full meaning of this—which requires no further explanation to those who have in hand the books denoted by S, S2, etc.— it would be necessary to print the article at considerable length, as follows:

biheste, *sb.* promise; "dusi *biheste*" a foolish promise, (extract from) Ancren Riwle, l. 19; "and wel lute wule hulde þe *biheste* þat he nom", (extract from) Robert of Gloucester, l. 184; "holdeth your *biheste*", Chaucer, Introd. to Man of Law's Prologue, l. 37; "*biheste* is dette", same, l. 41; "al my *biheste*", same, l. 42; "or breken his *biheste*", Chaucer, sequel to Squieres Tale, l. 698; "þorw fals *biheste*", Piers Plowman, Text B, Pass. iii, l. 126; "to vol-vulle (fulfil) þat *byheste*", Trevisa (extract from), lib. vi. cap. 29, l. 25; "the lond of promyssioun, or of *beheste*", Prol. to Mandeville's Travels, l. 3; "wiþ fair *by-hest*", William and the Werwolf, l. 57; "þe *byhest* (promise, *or* grant) of oþere menne kyngdom", Trevisa, lib. vi. cap. 29, l. 9; "y schal sende the *biheest* of my fadir in-to 3ou", Wyclif, Luke 24:49; "not bi the lawe is *biheest* to Abraham", Wycl. Rom. 4:13; "whanne the *biheestis* weren not takun", Wycl. Heb. 11:13; "longenge to godes *bihese*", Old Eng. Homilies, Dominica iv. post Pascha, l. 55.

We thus obtain fifteen excellent examples of the use of this word, with the full context and an exact reference (easily verified) in every case. And, in the above instance, all the quotations lie within the compass of the eleven texts in the Clarendon Press Series denoted, respectively, by S, S2, S3, C, C2, C3, W, W2, P, H, and G.

The original design was to make use of these text-books only; but it was so easy to extend it by including examples to be obtained from other Glossaries and Dictionaries, that a considerable selection of interesting words was added from these, mainly for the sake of illustrating the words in the Clarendon text-books. These illustrative words can be fully or partially verified by those who happen to possess all or some of the works cited, or they can safely be taken on trust, as really occurring there, any mistake being due to such authority.

A second example will make this clearer.

brant, *adj.* steep, high, MD, HD; **brent**, JD; **brentest**, *superl.* S2.—AS. *brant* (*bront*); cf. Swed. *brant*, Icel. *brattr*.

Omitting the etymology, the above information is given in two short lines. Those who possess the 'Specimens of English' will easily find the example of the superlative *brentest*. By consulting Mätzner's, Halliwell's, and Jamieson's Dictionaries, further information can be obtained, and the full article will appear as follows:

brant, *adj.* steep, high, MD [**brant, brent**, *adj.* ags. *brand*, arduus, altus, altn. *brattr*, altschw. *branter*, schw. *brant, bratt*, dän. *brat*, sch. *brent*, nordengl. Diall. *brant*: cf. "*brant*, steepe", Manipulus Vocabulorum, p. 25: steil, hoch.—"Apon the bald Bucifelon *brant* up he sittes", King Alexander, ed. Stevenson, p. 124; "Thir mountaynes ware als *brant* uprit3e as thay had bene walles", MS quoted in Halliwell's Dict., p. 206; "Hy3e bonkkes & *brent*", Gawain and the Grene Knight, l. 2165; "Bowed to þe hy3 bonk þer *brentest* hit wern", Alliterative Poems, ed. Morris, Poem B, l. 379]; HD [**brant**, steep. *North*: "Brant against Flodden Hill", explained by Nares from Ascham, "up the steep side"; cf. Brit. Bibl. i. 132, same as *brandly*?—"And thane thay com tille wonder heghe mountaynes, and it semed as the toppes had towched the firmament; and thir mountaynes were als *brant* upri3te as thay had bene walles, so that ther was na clymbyng upon thame", Life of Alexander, MS Lincoln, fol. 38]; JD [**brent**, *adj.* high, straight, upright; "My bak, that sumtyme *brent* hes bene, Now cruikis lyk are camok tre", Maitland Poems, p. 193; *followed by a discussion extending to more than 160 lines of small print, which we forbear to quote*]; **brentest**, *superl.* S2. 13. 379 ["And bowed to þe hy3 bonk þer *brentest* hit were (MS wern)", Allit. Poems, l. 379; *already cited in* Mätzner, *above*].

The work, in fact, contains a very large collection of words, in many variant forms, appearing in English literature and in Glossaries between 1150 and 1580. The glossaries in S2, S3 (Specimens of English, 1298–1393, and 1394–1579) have furnished a considerable number of words belonging to the Scottish dialect, which most dictionaries (excepting of course that of Jamieson) omit.

The words are so arranged that even the beginner will, in general, easily find what he wants. We have included in one article, together with the Main Word, all the variant spellings of the glossaries, as well as the etymological information. We have also given in alphabetical order numerous cross-references to facilitate the finding of most of the variant forms, and to connect them with the Main Word. In this way, the arrangement is at once etymological and alphabetical—adapted to the needs of the student of the language and of the student of the literature.

The meanings of the words are given in modern English, directly after the Main Word. The variant forms, as given in their alphabetical position, are frequently also explained, thus saving (in such cases) the trouble of a cross-reference, if the meaning of the word is alone required.

A Concise Dictionary of Middle English

An attempt is made in most cases to give the etymology, so far at least as to show the immediate source of the Middle-English word. Especial pains have been taken with the words of French origin, which form so large a portion of the vocabulary of the Middle-English period. In many cases the AF (Anglo-French) forms are cited, from my list of English Words found in Anglo-French, as published for the Philological Society in 1882.

The student of English who wishes to trace back the history of a word still in use can, in general, find the Middle-English form in Skeat's Etymological Dictionary, and will then be able to consult the present work in order to obtain further instances of its early use.

The relative share of the authors in the preparation of this work is easily explained. The whole of it in its present form (with the exception of the letter N) was compiled, prepared, and written out for press by Mr Mayhew. The original plan was, however, my own; and I began by writing out the letter N (since augmented) by way of experiment and model. It will thus be seen that Mr Mayhew's share of the work has been incomparably the larger, involving all that is most laborious. On the other hand, I may claim that much of the labour was mine also, at a much earlier stage, as having originally compiled or revised the glossaries marked S2, S3, C2, C3, W, W2, P, and G, as well as the very full glossarial indexes cited as B, PP, and WA, and the dictionary cited as SkD. The important glossary marked S was, however, originally the work of Dr Morris (since re-written by Mr Mayhew), and may, in a sense, be said to be the back-bone of the whole, from its supplying a very large number of the most curious and important early forms.

The material used has been carefully revised by both authors, so that they must be held to be jointly responsible for the final form in which the whole is now offered to the public.

NOTE ON THE PHONOLOGY OF MIDDLE-ENGLISH

One great difficulty in finding a Middle-English word in this, or any other, Dictionary is due to the frequent variation of the symbols denoting the vowel-sounds. Throughout the whole of the period to which the work relates the symbols i and y, in particular, are constantly interchanged, whether they stand alone, or form parts of diphthongs. Consequently,

xiii

words which are spelt with one of these symbols in a given text must frequently be looked for as if spelt with the other; i.e. the pairs of symbols *i* and *y*, *ai* and *ay*, *ei* and *ey*, *oi* and *oy*, and *ui* and *uy*, must be looked upon as likely to be used indifferently, one for the other. For further information, the student should consult the remarks upon Phonology in the *Specimens of English (1150 to 1300)*, 2nd ed., p. xxv. For those who have not time or opportunity to do this, a few brief notes may perhaps suffice.

The following symbols {i.e., graphs} are frequently confused, or are employed as equivalent to each other because they result from the same sound in the Oldest English or in Anglo-French:

i, y	*ai, ay*	*ei, ey*	*oi, oy*	*ui, uy*	
a, o		*a, æ, e, ea*	*e, eo, ie*	*o, u, ou*	(all originally short).
a, æ, ea, e, ee		*e, ee, eo, ie*	*o, oo, oa*	*u, ou, ui*	(all long).

These are the most usual interchanges of {graphs}, and will commonly suffice for practical purposes, in cases where the cross-references fail. If the word be not found after such substitutions have been allowed for, it may be taken for granted that the Dictionary does not contain it. As a fact, the Dictionary only contains a considerable number of such words as are most common, or (for some special reason) deserve notice; and it is at once conceded that it is but a small hand-book, which does not pretend to exhibit in all its fulness the extraordinarily copious vocabulary of our language at an important period of its history. The student wishing for complete information will find (in course of time) that the New English Dictionary which is being brought out by the Clarendon Press will contain all words found in our literature since the year 1100.

Of course variations in the vowel-sounds are also introduced, in the case of strong verbs, by the usual "gradation" due to their method of conjugation. To meet this difficulty in some measure, numerous (but not exhaustive) cross-references have been introduced, as when, e.g. "**bar,** bare" is given, with a cross-reference to "**beren**". Further help in this respect is to be had from the table of 183 strong verbs given at pp. lxix-lxxxi of the Preface to Part I of the *Specimens of English* (2nd edition); see, in particular, the alphabetical index to the same, at pp. lxxxi, lxxxii. The same Preface further contains some account of the three principal Middle-English dialects (p. xl), and Outlines of the Grammar (p. xlv). It also explains the meaning of the symbols *thorn* þ and *eth* ð (both used for *th* {[θ] and [ð], alongside **th**}), and *yogh* ʒ (used for *y* {[j]} initially, *gh* {[ɣ]} medially, and *gh* or *z* {[ɣ] or [z]} finally), with other necessary information.

THE CLARENDON PRESS GLOSSARIES

This work gives *all* the words and *every* form contained in the glossaries to eleven publications in the Clarendon Press Series, as below:—

S.—Specimens of Early English, ed. Morris, Part I: from A.D. 1150 to A.D. 1300. This book contains extracts from:—**1.** Old English Homilies, ed. Morris, E.E.T.S. 1867-8, pp. 230-241; **2.** The Saxon Chronicle, A.D. 1137, 1138, 1140, 1154; **3.** Old Eng. Homilies, ed. Morris, First Series, pp. 40-53; **4.** The same, Second Series, pp. 89-109; **5.** The Ormulum, ed. White, ll. 962-1719, pp. 31-57; **6.** Layamon's Brut, ed. Madden, ll. 13785-14387 [*add* 13784 *to the number of the line in the reference*]; **7.** Sawles Warde, from Old Eng. Homilies, ed. Morris, First Series, pp. 245-249, 259-267; **8.** St. Juliana, ed. Cockayne and Brock; **9.** The Ancren Riwle, ed. Morton, pp. 208-216, 416-430; **10.** The Wooing of our Lord, from Old Eng. Homilies, ed. Morris, First Series, pp. 277-283; **11.** A Good Orison of our Lady, from the same, pp. 191-199; **12.** A Bestiary, the Lion, Eagle, and Ant, from An Old Eng. Miscellany, ed. Morris; **13.** Old Kentish Sermons, from the same, pp. 26-36; **14.** Proverbs of Alfred, from the same, pp. 102-130; **15.** Version of Genesis and Exodus, ed. Morris, ll.1907-2536; **16.** Owl and Nightingale, from An Old Eng. Miscellany, ed. Morris, ll. 1-94, 139-232, 253-282, 303-352, 391-446, 549-555, 598-623, 659-750, 837-855, 905-920, 1635-1682, 1699-1794; **17.** A Moral Ode (two copies), from An Old Eng. Miscellany and Old Eng. Homilies, 2nd Series, ed. Morris; **18.** Havelok the Dane, ed. Skeat, ll. 339-748; **19.** King Horn (in full).

S2.—Specimens of English, Part II, ed. Morris and Skeat; from A.D. 1298-1393. This book contains extracts from:—**1.** Robert of Gloucester's Chronicle (William the Conqueror and St. Dunstan); **2.** Metrical Psalter, Psalms 8, 14(15), 17(18), 23(24), 102(103), 103(104); **3.** The Proverbs of Hendyng; **4.** Specimens of Lyric Poetry, ed. Wright (Alysoun, Plea for Pity, Parable of the Labourers, Spring-time); **5.** Robert Mannyng's Handlynge Synne, ll. 5575-5946; **6.** William of Shoreham, De Baptismo; **7.** Cursor Mundi, ed. Morris, ll. 11373-11791 [*add* 11372 *to the number in the reference*]; **8.** Eng. Metrical Homilies, ed. Small (Second Sunday in Advent, Third Sunday after the Octave of Epiphany); **9.** The Ayenbite of Inwyt, ed. Morris, pp. 263-9, and p. 262; **10.** Hampole's Prick of Conscience, ll. 432-9,

464-509, 528-555, 662-707, 728-829, 1211-1292, 1412-1473, 1818-29, 1836-51, 1884-1929, 2216-2233, 2300-11, 2334-55, 2364-73, 7813-24; **11.** Minot's Songs, Nos. 3, 4, 7; **12.** William of Palerne, ed. Skeat, ll. 3-381; **13.** Alliterative Poems, ed. Morris, Poem B, ll. 235-544, 947-972, 1009-1051; **14.** Mandeville's Travels, Prologue, part of Chap. 12, and Chap. 26; **15.** Piers the Plowman, A-text, Prologue, Passus 1, part of Pass. 2, Pass. 3, Pass. 5, parts of Pass. 6 and 7; **16.** Barbour's Bruce, ed. Skeat, Book VII. ll. 1-230, 400-487; **17.** Wyclif's translation of St. Mark's Gospel, Chapters 1-6; Hereford's version of the Psalms, Ps. 14(15), 23(24), 102(103); **18.** Trevisa's translation of Higden's Polychronicon, lib. i. c. 41, c. 59, lib. vi. c. 29; **19.** Chaucer, Man of Law's Tale; **20.** Gower's Confessio Amantis, part of Book V.

S3.—Specimens of English, Part III, ed. Skeat; from A.D. 1394-1579.

This book contains extracts from:—**1.** Pierce the Ploughman's Crede, ll. 153-267, 339-565, 744-765, 785-823; **2.** Hoccleve's De Regimine Principum, stanzas 281-301, 598-628; **3.** Lydgate, London Lickpenny, and the Storie of Thebes, bk. ii. ll. 1064-1419; **4.** James I (of Scotland), the King's Quair, stanzas 152-173; **5.** Pecock's Represser, pt. i. c. 19; pt. ii. c. 11; **6.** Blind Harry's Wallace, bk. i. ll. 181-448; **7.** Chevy Chase (earlier version); **8.** Malory's Morte Darthur, bk. xxi. c. 3-7; **9.** Caxton's History of Troy; **10.** The Nut-brown Maid; **11.** Dunbar, Thistle and Rose, and Poem on being desired to be a Friar; **12.** Hawes, Pastime of Pleasure, c. 33; **13.** G. Douglas, Prol. to Æneid, book xii; **14.** Skelton, Why Come Ye Nat to Courte, ll. 287-382, 396-756; Philip Sparrow, ll. 998-1260; **15.** Lord Berners, tr. of Froissart, c. 50, c. 130; **16.** Tyndale, Obedience of a Christian Man; **17.** More, Dialogue Concerning Heresies, bk. iii. c. 14-16; Confutation of Tyndale, bk. iii; **18.** Sir T. Elyot, The Governor, bk. i. c. 17, 18; **19.** Lord Surrey, tr. of Æneid, bk. ii. ll. 253-382, 570-736, and minor poems; **20.** Sir T. Wiat, Three Satires, and minor poems; **21.** Latimer, Sermon on the Ploughers; **22.** Sir D. Lyndesay, The Monarchy, bk. iii. ll. 4499-4612, 4663-94, 4709-38; bk. iv. ll. 5450-5639; **23.** N. Udall, Ralph Roister Doister, Act iii. sc. 3-5; **24.** Lord Buckhurst, The Induction; **25.** Ascham, The Schoolmaster, bk. i; **26.** Gascoigne, The Steel Glas, ll. 418-470, 628-638, 750-893, 1010-1179; **27.** Lyly, Euphues and his Ephœbus; **28.** Spenser, Shepherd's Calendar, November, December.

The remaining eight publications in the Clarendon Press Series which have also been indexed are those marked C, C2, C3, W, W2, P, H, and G; i.e. three books containing extracts from Chaucer, two books containing parts of Wyclif's Bible, part of Piers Plowman, Hampole's Psalter, and Gamelyn; the full titles of which are given below.

A Concise Dictionary of Middle English

We also give all the important words occurring in CM (Chaucer, ed. Morris); and in addition to this, and for the purpose of illustration, forms are given from various texts and Dictionaries, and from the Glossaries to B (Bruce), PP (Piers Plowman), and WA (Wars of Alexander).

Walter W. Skeat

FULL LIST OF AUTHORITIES, WITH EXPLANATIONS OF ABBREVIATIONS

Note.—The abbreviations referring to the authorities for the forms of English words (1150–1580) are printed in italics. (CP = Clarendon Press.)

1. *Alph.*: Alphita, a Medico-Botanical Glossary, ed. Mowat, 1887. CP.
2. Anglo-Saxon Gospels, in AS. and Northumbrian Versions, ed. Skeat.
3. Apfelstedt: Lothringischer Psalter (des XIV Jahrhunderts), 1881.
4. *B*: Barbour's Bruce, ed. Skeat, 1870, EETS. (Extra Series xi).
5. *Bardsley*: English Surnames, 1875.
6. Bartsch: Chrestomathie de l'ancien français (glossaire), 1880.
6*. BH: Bartsch and Horning, Langue et Littérature françaises, 1887.
7. Bosworth: Anglo-Saxon Dictionary, 1838.
8. Brachet: French Dict., 1882. CP.
9. Brugmann: Grundriss, 1886.
10. BT.: Bosworth-Toller AS. Dict. [A-SAR]. CP.
11. *C*: Chaucer; Prol., Knight's Tale, Nun's Priest's Tale. CP.
12. *C2*: Chaucer; Prioress, Sir Thopas, Monk, Clerk, Squire. CP.
13. *C3*: Chaucer; Man of Law, Pardoner, Second Nun, Canon's Yeoman. CP.
14. *Cath.*: Catholicon Anglicum (A.D. 1483), ed. Herrtage, 1881. EETS (75).
15. Chron.: Two Saxon Chronicles, ed. Earle, 1865. CP.
16. *CM*: Chaucer, ed. Morris, 1880.
17. Constans: Chrestomathie de l'ancien français (glossaire), 1884.
18. Cotg.: Cotgrave, French and English Dict., 1611.
19. Curtius: Greek Etymology, ed. Wilkins and England, 1886.
20. CV: Icelandic Dictionary, Cleasby and Vigfusson, 1874. CP.
21. *DG*: Davies, Supplementary English Glossary, 1881.
22. Diez: Etymologisches Wörterbuch, 1878.
23. Douse: Introduction to the Gothic of Ulfilas, 1886.
24. Ducange: Glossarium, ed. Henschel, 1883-7.
24*. Ducange: Glossaire Français, ed. 1887.
25. *EDS*: English Dialect Society.
26. *EETS*: Early English Text Society.
27. Fick: Wörterbuch der indogermanischen Sprachen, 1874.
28. Florio: Italian and English Dict., 1611.
29. *G*: Tale of Gamelyn, ed. Skeat, 1884. CP.
30. Godefroy: Dictionnaire de l'ancienne langue française [A-LIS].
31. Grein: Glossar der angelsächsischen Poesie, 1861.
32. Grimm: Teutonic Mythology, ed. Stallybrass, 1883.

33. *H*: Hampole, Psalter, ed. Bramley, 1884. CP.

34. *HD*: Halliwell, Dict. of Archaic and Provincial Words, 1874.

35. Heliand, ed. Heyne, 1873.

36. *JD*: Jamieson, Scottish Dictionary, 1867.

37. Kluge: etymologisches Wörterbuch der deutschen Sprache, 1883.

38. Leo: angelsächsisches Glossar, 1877.

39. *Manip.*: Manipulus Vocabulorum, Levins, ed. Wheatley, EETS, 1867.

40. *MD*: Mätzner, altenglisches Wörterbuch [A-H], 1885.

41. Minsheu: Spanish and English Dict., 1623.

42. *ND*: Nares, Glossary, 1876.

43. *NED*: New English Dictionary, ed. Murray [A-BOZ]. CP.

44. *NQ*: Notes and Queries.

45. OET: Oldest English Texts, ed. Sweet, 1885, EETS (83).

45*. *ONE*: Oliphant, The New English, 1886.

46. Otfrid: Evangelienbuch, glossar, ed. Piper, 1884.

47. *P*: Piers the Plowman (B-text), ed. Skeat. CP.

48. *Palsg.*: Palsgrave, Lesclaircissement de langue francoyse, ed. 1852.

49. *PP*: Piers the Plowman, glossary by Skeat, 1885, EETS (81).

50. *PP. Notes*: by Skeat, 1877, EETS (67).

51. *Prompt.*: Promptorium Parvulorum, ed. Way, Camden Soc., 1865.

52. Ps.: (after French forms), see Apfelstedt.

53. *RD*: Richardson's English Dictionary, 1867.

54. Roland: Chanson de Roland, ed. Gautier, 1881.

55. *S*: Specimens of Early English, Part I, ed. Morris, 1885. CP.

56. *S2*: Specimens of Early English, Part II, ed. Morris and Skeat, 1873. CP.

57. *S3*: Specimens of English Literature, ed. Skeat, 1879. CP.

58. *SB*: Sinonoma Bartholomei, 14th Cent. Glossary, ed. Mowat, 1882. CP.

59. Schmid: Gesetze der Angelsachsen (glossar), 1858.

60. *SD*: Stratmann, Dict. of the Old English Language, 1878.

61. *Sh.*: Shakespeare Lexicon, by Schmidt, 1875.

62. Sievers: Grammar of Old English, ed. A. S. Cook, 1885.

63. *SkD*: Skeat, Etymological Dict. of Eng. Lang., 1884. CP.

64. Skeat, English Words in Norman-French, 1882, Phil. Soc.

65. Skeat, Mœso-gothic Glossary, 1868.

66. *SPD*: Smythe Palmer, Dictionary of Folk-Etymology, 1882.

67. *Spenser*: Faery Queene, glossaries to Books I and II, 1887. CP.

68. Sweet: AS. Reader, 1884. CP.

69. Tatian: Evangelienbuch, ed. Sievers, 1872.

70. *TG*: Trench, Select Glossary, 1879.

71. *Trevisa*: version of Higden, Rolls' Series (41).

72. *Voc.*: Wright's Vocabularies, ed. Wülcker, 1884.

73. VP: Vespasian Psalter, as printed in OET., see 45.

74. Vulg.: the Vulgate Version of the Bible.

75. *W*: Wycliffe, New Testament (Purvey's revision), ed. Skeat, 1879. CP.

76. *W2*: Wycliffe, Job, Psalms, etc. (revised by Hereford and Purvey), ed. Skeat, 1881. CP.

77. *WA*: Wars of Alexander, ed. Skeat, 1887, EETS (Extra Series xlvii).

78. Weigand: deutsches Wörterbuch, 1878.

79. Windisch: Glossary added to Old Irish Texts, 1882.

80. *WW*: Wright, The Bible Word-Book, 1884.

81. ZRP: Zeitschrift für romanische Philologie, ed. Gröber.

LANGUAGE ABBREVIATIONS
WITH REFERENCES TO AUTHORITIES

AF.: Anglo-French, see 64.

AS.: Anglo-Saxon, see 10, 31, 45, 62.

Church Lat.: Ecclesiastical Latin, see 24, 74.

Goth.: Gothic, see 23, 65.

Gr.: Greek, see 9, 19, 27.

Icel.: Icelandic, see 20.

It.: Italian, see 28.

Lat.: Latin.

Late Lat.: Post-classical Latin, of Latin origin, see 24, 72, 74.

Low Lat.: Latin derived from the later European languages, see 1, 14, 24, 51, 58.

ME.: Middle English.

North.E.: Northern English, see 4, 36.

OF.: Old French, see 3, 6, 17, 18, 22, 24, 30, 48, 54.

OHG.: Old High German, see 37, 46, 69, 78.

OIr.: Old Irish, see 19, 79.

OMerc.: Old Mercian, see 2 (Rushworth version), 45, 73.

ONorth.: Old Northumbrian, see 2.

OS.: Old Saxon, see 35.

OTeut.: Old Teutonic (as restored by scholars), see 27, 43.

Skt.: Sanskrit.

Sp.: Spanish, see 41.

SYMBOLS

In the etymological part three stops are used as symbols in connexion with the cognate forms cited, namely the comma, the semi-colon, and the colon. The comma is used to connect various spellings of a word, as well as parallel forms cited from nearly connected languages; for instance, s.v.

daunger, the OF. forms are so connected. The semi-colon between two forms denotes that the two forms are phonetically equivalent, and that the preceding one is directly derived from, and is historically connected with the one following this symbol; for instance, s.v. **bugle**, the OF. *bugle* is the phonetic equivalent of the Lat. *buculum*, and is immediately derived therefrom. The colon between two forms denotes that the two forms are phonetically equivalent, and that the form following this symbol is an earlier, more primitive form than the one preceding, without an immediate interborrowing between the languages being asserted; for instance, s.v. **demen**, the Goth. *dómjan* is an older form than the AS. *déman*, but *déman* is not borrowed from the Gothic. The abbreviation 'cf.' introduces other cognate forms, and has the same value as the symbol + in Skeat's Dictionaries.

The asterisk * at the beginning of a word denotes a theoretical form, assumed (upon scientific principles) to have formerly existed. The sign = is to be read 'a translation of'. '(*n*)' after Prompt., Cath. and other authorities refers to foot-notes or other notes citing the form in question.

A

a-,[1] *prefix*, adding *intensity* to the notion of the verb.—AS. *á* for *ar-*, OHG. *ar-*, Goth. *us-*. For the quantity of the *á* see Sievers, 121. Cf. **or-**.

a-,[2] *prefix*, standing for **a**, *prep.*, and for Icel. *á*; see **on-**[1].

a-,[3] *prefix*, standing for **of**, *prep.*; see **of**[1].

a-,[4] *prefix*, standing for AS. *and-*, against, in return, toward.—AS. *and-, ond-, on-* (proclitic). Cf. **on-**[2].

a-,[5] *prefix*, standing for **at**, *prep.*, and Icel. *at*, used with the infin. See **at-**[1].

a-,[6] *prefix*, standing for AS. *ge-*; see **зе-**.

a-,[7] *prefix*, standing for OF. *a-* and Lat. *ad-*.

a-,[8] *prefix*, standing for OF. *a-* and Lat. *ab-*.

a-,[9] *prefix*, standing for AF. *a*, OF. *e-, es-* from Lat. *ex-, e-*.

a-,[10] *prefix*, standing for AF. *an-*, OF. *en-* from Lat. *in-*. See **in-**[2].

a-,[11] *prefix*, standing for Gr. α- privative.

a,[1] *interj.* oh! ah! expressing surprise, pain, S, MD.

a,[2] *prep.* on, in, PP, S, S2, C2; see **on**[1].

a,[3] *prep.* of, S2, S3, PP; see **of**[1].

a,[4] *adv.* ever, S; **aa**, S; **a buten**, ever without, S; see **o**[2].

a-bac, *adv.* backwards, S, W2; **abec**, S; **abak**, C2, W; **obak**, S2.—AS. *on-bæc*. (**a-**[2].)

abasshen, *v.* to abash, S3; **abasshed**, *pp.* abashed, ashamed, alarmed, C3, PP; **abashed**, S2; **abasshid**, S3; **abasched**, PP; **abaisshed**, PP; **abaischid**, W; **abaischt**, S2; **abaissed**, PP; **abaist**, S3; **abayste**, S2, C2.—OF. *esbahiss-* stem of pr. p. of *esbahir*, to astonish; Lat. *ex + *badire* for *badare*, to open the mouth. (**a-**[9].)

abaten, *v.* to beat down, bring down, calm down, P, NED.—AF. *abatre* (pr. p. *abatant*); Late Lat. **adbatere*. (**a-**[7].)

abaue, *v.* to put to confusion, to be confounded, NED, HD, JD; **abawed**, *pp.* HD; **abaued**, HD.—OF. **abavir*: *esbahir* (with *v* in place of lost *h*, see Brachet, s.v. *glaive*). (**a-**[9].). See **abasshen**.

abaye, *sb.* barking; *phr.* **at þe abaie**, **at abaye**, at bay, S2.—OF. *abai*, barking, from *abaier*; cf. F. *aboi* in phr.: *être aux abois*.

abbay, *sb.* abbey, C2; **abbeis**, pl., S2.—AF. *abbeie* (*abeie*); Church Lat. *abbādia, abbātia*, from *abbātem*. See **abbod**.

abbesse, *sb.* abbess, PP.—OF. *abbesse*; Church Lat. *abbatissa*.

abbod, *sb.* abbot, MD, S2; **abbot**, S, PP; **abbodes**, *pl.* S2.—Church Lat. *abbātem*

(pronounced *abbādem*), nom. *abbas*; Gr. ἀββάς; Syriac, *abba*, father.

abbodesse, *sb.* abbess, PP.

abbot-rice, *sb.* abbacy, S.—AS. *abbod-ríce*, the rule of an abbot.

a.b.c; see **abece**.

abeah, abeh; see **abuзen**.

abece, *sb.* the alphabet, Cath. (*n*); **a.b.c.**, P; **abcy**, Cath.; **abce**, Cath. (*n*), PP; **abcee**, Cotg.; **apece**, Prompt.—Cf. OF. *abece*, the crosse rowe (Cotg.).

abeggen, abeien; see **abyen**.

a-bernen, *v.* to burn; **abernð**, *pr. s.* S.—AS. *á-beornan*. (**a-**[1].)

abhominacioun, *sb.* abomination, NED, C2.

abhomynable, *adj.* abominable, S3, C3.—AF. *abhominable*; Lat. *abominabilem*.

a-biden, *v.* to abide, remain, await, endure, S, S2, W2; **habide**, S, S2; **abyde**, C2; **abid**, *imp.*, S, S2; **abid**, *pr. s.*, S; **abit**, S, S2, C3; **abod**, *pt. s.*, S; **abood**, W2; **abide**, *pt. pl.*, S2; **abididen**, W2; **abide**, *pp.*, G.—AS. *á-bídan*. (**a-**[1].)

a-biding, *sb.* expectation, W2.

abiggen; see **abyen**.

abil, *adj.* able, CM; **able**, C; **hable**, S3, MD.—OF. *able*, *hable* (mod. F. *habile*); Lat. *habilem*.

abilite, *sb.* ability, NED; **habilitie**, S3.—OF. *habilité*.

abilзeit, *pp.* apparelled, S3.—OF. *habiller*.

abilзement, *sb.* clothing, S3.—OF. *habillement*.

abit, *sb.* dress, a monk's clothing, habit, PP, CM, HD; **abite**, W.—AF. *abit* (*habit*); Lat. *habitum* (acc.).

a-biten, *v.* to bite, S.—AS. *á-bítan*. (**a-**[1].)

abject, *pp.* and *adj.* cast out, NED.

abjecte, *v.* to cast aside, S3.

a-blawen, *v.* to blow, MD; **ableow**, *pt. s.*, S.—AS. *á-bláwan*. (**a-**[1].)

a-blenden, *v.* to blind, MD; **ablent**, *pr. s.*, S; *pl.*, S; **ablende**, *pt. s.*, MD; **ablend**, *pp.* MD.—AS. *á-blendan*. (**a-**[1].)

a-bouten, *adv.* and *prep.* about, C2, P, MD; **abuten**, S; **abuuten**, S; **abuton**, S; **abute**, S; **aboute**, S, G; **oboute**, MD; **obout**, S2.—AS. *on-bútan* (= *on-be-útan*). (**a-**[2].)

a-bouen, *adv.* and *prep.* above, C2, PP, MD; **aboue**, PP; **abufen**, S; **abuuen**, MD; **abowen**, MD; **abone**, S3, JD; **oboven**, MD; **obowen**, MD; **oboune**, MD. *Phr.*: **at**

1

here aboue, S2.—AS. *on* + *bufan* (= *be* + *ufan*). (**a-²**.)

abregge, *v.* to abridge, shorten, C; **abreggide**, *pp.*, W; **breggid**, W.—OF. *abreger, abregier*: Prov. *abrevjar*; Lat. *abbreviare*. (**a-⁸**.)

a-breiden, *v.* to start up, to draw (sword), to thrust out, to blame, S; **abreyden**, NED; **abraid**, *pt. s.*, S; **abreyde**, C2; **abrayde**, C; **abroden**, *pp.*, S; **abruden**, S.—AS. *á* + *bregdan*. (**a-¹**.)

a-brode, *adv.* abroad, PP; **abrood**, C2; **abrod**, widely apart, PP. (**a-²**.)

abusioun, *sb.* deceit, S2, C3.—OF. *abusion* (Cotg.).

abute, abuton, abuten; see **abouten**.

a-bu3en, *v.* to bow, MD; **abuen**, MD; **abouwen**, MD; **abowe**, NED; **abeah**, *pt. s.*, MD; **abeh**, S.—AS. *á-bugan*. (**a-¹**.)

a-byen, abye, *v.* to buy, to pay for, S3, C2, C3, PP; **abygge**, PP; **abiggen**, PP; **abuggen**, S, PP; **abeggen**, MD, G; **abeien**, S; **abie**, PP; **abuiþ**, *pr. s.*, S; **abugeð**, *pr. pl.*, S; **abouhte**, *pt. s.*, S; **aboughte**, G; **abought**, *pp.* C3.—AS. *ábycgan*. (**a-¹**.)

abyme, *sb.* abyss, S2, HD.—OF. *abime, abisme*; Low Lat. **abyssimum*, superl. of Lat. *abyssus*; Gr. ἄβυσσος, bottomless. (**a-¹¹**.)

ac, *conj.* but, S, S2, P; **acc**, S; **ah**, S, S2; **ak**, S2, PP; **hac**, S; **ach**, MD; **auh**, MD, S; **auch**, MD; **oc**, S; **occ**, S.—AS. *ac*.

acc-; see also words beginning in **ac-**.

accident, *sb.* accident (a term of the schoolmen), C3.—Lat. *accidentem*.

accidie, *sb.* sloth, indolence, S, CM, PP.— AF. *accidie* (NED); Low Lat. *accidia, acedia*; Gr. ἀκηδία, heedlessness, torpor. (**a-¹¹**.)

accompt, *sb.* account, S3; see **acounte²**.

accompted, *pp.* accounted, S3; see **acounte¹**.

ace, *sb.* a jot, S3; see **as**.

a-cennen, *v.* to bring forth, to beget, MD; **acenned**, *pp.* MD; **accenned**, S; **akenned**, MD; **akennet**, S; **acende** (for **acend**), S.—AS. *á-cennan*. (**a-¹**.)

a-cennende, *sb.* begetting, birth, S.

a-cenneng, *sb.* birth, S.

a-chape, *v.* to escape, NED; **achaped**, *pt. s.*, S2.—OF. *achaper*; cf. AF. *ascaper*. (**a-⁹**.) Cf. **eschapen, ascapie**.

achate¹, *v.* to purchase, NED.—OF. *achater* (F. *acheter, acater*; Late Lat., *accaptare*.

achate², *sb.* purchase, provisions purchased, NED, C; **achat**, HD; **acate**, NED; **acates**, *pl.*, HD.—OF. *achat*, AF. *acate*. See **achate¹**.

achatour, *sb.* a purchaser of provisions, purveyor, C, NED, HD; **acatour**, NED.— AF. *achatour, acatour*; Late Lat. *accaptatorem*.

ache¹, *sb.* pain, Prompt.; **eche**, MD; **hache**, HD.—AS. *æce* (*ece*). See **aken**.

ache², *sb.* wild celery, parsley, NED, Voc.— OF. *ache*; Lat. *apium*; Gr. ἄπιον.

achesoun, *sb.* occasion, motive, HD, MD, NED.—OF. *achoison, ocoison*; Lat. *occasionem*. Cf. **anchesoun, enchesoun, chesoun**.

achtande, *ord.* eighth, S2, NED.—Icel. *áttandi*; cf. OHG. *ahtande*. Cf. **eighte²**.

a-colien, *v.* to wax cold; **acolede**, *pt. s.*, S; **acoled**, *pp.*, S.—AS. *á-cólian*. (**a-¹**.)

acombren, *v.* to encumber, PP; **acumbrid**, *pp.*, S2.—OF. *encombrer*. (**a-¹⁰**.)

acomplesshen, *v.* to accomplish, NED; **accomplice**, C; **accompliced**, *pp.* NED. —AF. *acomplir* (*acomplice*, pr. s. subj.); Late Lat. *accomplere*; see Brachet. (**a-⁷**.)

acord, *sb.* accord, agreement, MD; **accord**, S2; **acorde**, S.—AF. *acord*.

acordaunce, *sb.* agreement, PP.

acorden, *v.* to reconcile, to agree, MD, S2, P; **accordyng**, *pr. p.*, S3; **accorded**, *pp.*, S2; *pt. s.*, S3.—OF. *acorder*; Late Lat. *accordare*, from Lat. *ad* + *cord-*, stem of *cor*, heart. (**a-⁷**.)

acorse; see **acursien**.

acounte¹, *v.* to count, to calculate, NED, C2, PP; **acompte**, NED, PP; **accompted**, *pp.*, S3.—AF. *acounter*, OF. *acunter, aconter*; Late Lat. *accomptare*; Lat. *ad* + *computare*. (**a-⁷**.)

acounte², *sb.* account, reckoning, PP; **acompte**, PP; **accompt**, S3; **accomptes**, *pl.*, S3.—AF. *acounte, acunte*.

acoupen, *v.* to accuse, NED, HD; **acoupede**, *pt. s.*, NED, PP; **acopede**, NED; **acoulped**, NED; **acouped**, *pp.*, S2.—OF. *acouper, acolper*, for *encouper, encolper*; Lat. *inculpare*. (**a-¹⁰**.)

acoyen, *v.* to quiet, coax, tame, NED, Palsg.; **acoyed**, *pt. s.*, S2.—OF. *acoyer*, to calm; Lat. *ad* + *quietare*. (**a-⁷**.)

acumbrid; see **acombren**.

a-cursien, *v.* to curse, NED; **acursi**, S, NED; **acorse**, PP; **acorsed**, *pp.* MD. (**a-¹**.)

acustumaunce, *sb.* customary use, NED, C2.—OF. *acostumance*. (**a-⁷**.)

acwenchen; see **aquenchen**.

adamant, *sb.* adamant, very hard metal, a fabulous rock or mineral, the diamond, the loadstone or magnet, NED; precious stone, Prompt.; **ademaunt**, C; **adamounde**, Prompt. (*n*); **admont**, NED; **athamant**, NED; **athamaunte**, C; **attemant**, NED; **aymont**, NED.—AF. *adamant* (*aimant*); Lat. *adamantem*; Gr. ἀδάμας (-αντα), lit. invincible, untamable, from ἀ- + δαμάω, I tame. (**a-¹¹**.)

2

adaunten, *v.* to subdue, NED; **adauntede**, *pt. s.*, S2.—OF. *adanter, adonter*; Lat. *ad + domitare*, to tame. (**a-**⁷.)

a-dawe, out of life, NED, HD.—AS. *of dagum*, from days. (**a-**³.)

a-dawen, *v.* to rise from sleep, also, to arouse, NED; **adawed**, *pp.* S3.—Cf. MHG. *er-tagen*, to dawn. (**a-**¹.)

a-day, *adv.* at morn, by day, S2, P; **adai**, S. (**a-**².)

addledd, *pp.* earned, S; see **adlen**.

a-diliȝen, *v.* to be lost, to perish, S; **adiliȝede**, *pt. s.*, S; **adiligde**, S.—AS. *á-diligan*, to destroy. (**a-**¹.)

a-diȝten, *v.* to appoint, order, prepare, compose, clothe, treat, MD, S; **adyȝt**, *pp.*, MD; **adight**, G; **adyght**, MD, HD. (**a-**¹.)

adlen, *v.* to earn, MD; **addle**, Manip., MED; **addledd**, *pp.*, S.—Icel. *öðla*, refl. *öðla-sk*, to acquire for oneself property, from *óðal*, property, patrimony, from **aþal*, race, see Fick, 7. 14; cf. OHG. *uodil*, 'praedium' (Tatian). See **aþel**.

admirald, *sb.* a Saracen commander, S; see **amirail**.

admod, *adj.* humble, gentle, S; **ædmod**, MD; **edmod**, MD.—AS. *éadmód, éaðmód*. See **eþ**.

admoded, *pp.* as *adj.* lowly; see **eadmodien**.

admodie, *adj. pl.* humble, MD; **edmodi**, MD.

admodliche, *adv.* humbly, gently, MD; **ædmodliȝ**, S.—AS. *éadmódlice*.

admodnesse, *sb.* humility, gentleness, MD, S; **edmodnesse**, S; **æddmodnesse**, S.—AS. *éadmódnes*.

a-do, *sb.* fuss, trouble, difficulty, S3, Prompt., WW; = to do, PP, WW; **adoe**, ND, (**a-**⁵.)

a-doun, *adv.* down, S, S2, C2, C3, G; **adun**, S; **adune**, S.—AS. *of dúne*, off the hill. (**a-**³.)

a-drad, *pp.* frightened, put in dread, NED, S2, G, C, PP; **adred**, S; **adrede**, NED.—AS. *of-drad* (**a-**³.) Cf. **ofdreden**.

a-drawen, *v.* to draw out, S2; **adroh**, *pt. s.*, NED; **adrou**, NED; **adraȝe**, *pp.* NED. (**a-**¹.)

a-dreden, *v.* to fear greatly, S, NED; **adrade**, *reflex.*, S.—OMerc. *and-drǽdan* (Rushw.); see NED. (**a-**⁴.)

a-drenchen, *v.* to drown, to be drowned, MD, S, PP; **adreynten**, *pt. pl.*, PP; **adreynt**, *pp.* drenched, PP; **adreint**, MD; **adrent**, S, PP; **adreynched**, PP.—AS. *á-drencan*. (**a-**¹.)

adressen, *v.* to make straight, to direct, NED, H.—OF. *adressier, adrecier* Late Lat. *addrictiare*, from Lat. *directum*, straight. (**a-**⁷.)

a-drinken, *v.* to be drowned, MD, S; **adronc**, *pt. s.*, MD; **adronken**, *pl.*, MD; **adrunken**, *pp.*, MD.—AS. *á-drincan*. (**a-**¹.)

a-drye, *v.* to endure, bear, HD; **adriȝen**, S (19. 1047), MD.—AS. *á-dréogan*. (**a-**¹.)

a-dun, *adv.* down, S; see **adoun**.

a-dunien, *v.* to din; **adunest**, *2 pr. s.*, **adenyd**, *pp.* MD. (**a-**¹.)

adun-ward, *adv.* downward, NED; **adon-ward**, S2.

adversarie, *sb.* adversary, C3.—OF. *adversarie*; Lat. *aduersarius*.

advertence, *sb.* mental attention, C3.—Late Lat. *advertentia*.

advocat, *sb.* advocate, intercessor, C3; **vokate**, PP; **vokyte**, *causidicus*, Voc.; **vokettus**, *pl.* PP.—OF. *advocat*; Lat. *aduocatum* (acc.).

æ, *sb.* law, MD.—AS. *ǽw* (*ǽ*), law, divine law, the Mosaic law, marriage; Goth. *aiws*, an age, eternity; cf. OHG. *éwa*, the law of God, eternity (Otfrid). Cf. **æ-vez**, **eu-bruche**, **eche**.

ædmod, *adj.* humble, gentle, MD; see **admod**.

ædmodliȝ, *adv.* humbly, S; see **admodliche**.

ædmodnisse, *sb.* humility, MD; **æddmodnesse**, S; see **admodnesse**.

æhte, *num.* eight, MD; see **eighte**¹.

æhtene, *num.* eighteen, S; see **eightene**.

æn, *num.* and *indef. art.* one, S; **ænne**, S; see **oon**.

æness, *adv.* once, S; see **oones**.

æoure, *pron.* your, S; see **ȝoure**.

ærd, *sb.* native land, home, S; see **erd**.

ærfeð-telle, *adj.* difficult to count, S. See **arfeþ**.

ærnde, *sb.* errand, MD; see **erende**.

ærnd-race, *sb.* messenger, S; **ærnd-raches**, *pl.*, S.—AS. *érend-raca*.

ærnen, *v.* to run, S; see **rennen**.

æ-uez, *adj.* pious, fast in the law, S.—AS. *á-fest*. See **æ**.

afaiten, *v.* to affect, to prepare, array, dress, to train, tame, subdue, NED, PP; **affaiten**, P; **fayten**, S2, PP; **faiten**, PP.—OF. *afaiter, afeiter*; Lat. *affectare*, freq. of *afficere*; *ad + facere*. (**a-**⁷.)

a-fallen¹, *v.* to fall, MD; **auallen**, MD; **afeol**, *pt. s.*, MD; **afallen**, *pp.*, MD.—AS. *á-feallan*. (**a-**¹.)

a-fallen², *v.* to fell, NED; **afal**, *imp.*, S; **aual**, S.

a-felde, *adv.* a-field, to the field, PP. (**a-**².)

a-fellen, *v.* to fell, NED; **auellen**, MD.—AS. *á-fellan, á-fyllan.* (**a-**¹.)

a-fer, *adv.* afar, W, W2; **afeer**, NED; **of feor**, S (s.v. *feor*). (**a-**³.) Cf. **aferre**.

afere, *sb.*, affair, bustle, appearance, demeanour, S2, NED; **effere**, S2; **effeir**, S2, S3; **effer**, S2; **afferes**, *pl.*, PP.—OF. *afere = a + fere*; Lat. *facere*, to do. (**a-**⁷.)

a-feren, *v.* to frighten, terrify, S, PP; **afferen**, MD; **affeare**, *2 pr. s. subj.*, S; **afered**, *pp.* afraid, S, C, P; **aferd**, S, C, P, W2; **afeerd**, W; **afert**, PP; **aferde**, S3, P, W; **afferde**, S3.—AS. *á-féran*. (**a-**¹.)

a-ferre, *adv.* afar, Prompt.; **oferrum**, S2; **onferrum**, S2; **onferre**, NED; **onferr**, NED. (**a-**².) Cf. **afer**.

aff-; see also words beginning in **af-**.

affamysit, *pp.* famished, S3, NED. Cf. OF. *afamer*; Late Lat. *affamare*.

affectuosly, *adv.* passionately, HD, NED.

affectuouse, *adj.* hearty, affectionate, NED, H; **affectuse**, NED.—Lat. *affectuosus*.

affray, *sb.* terror, S3, C2, C3. Cf. **effray**.

affrayen, *v.* to frighten, C2; **affrayed**, *pp.* S2, C, C3, W; see **afrayen**.

afile, *v.* to file down, NED; **affyle**, C.—OF. *afiler*.

afingret, *pp.* an-hungered, starving, NED, HD; see **of-hungred**.

a-flemen, *v.* to drive away, MD; **aulem**, *imp. s.*, S.—AS. *á-fléman (á-flýman)*. (**a-**¹.)

afolen, *v.* to befool; **afoled**, *pp.*, S; **afoild**, NED, HD.—OF. *afoler* (Bartsch); Low Lat. **adfolare*, to make foolish. (**a-**⁷.)

a-fon, *v.* to receive, S; **afeoh**, *imp.*, S; **avoþ**, *pr. pl.*, S; **auenge**, *pt. pl.*, S2.—AS. *á-fón, on-fón* (for *ond-fón*), see Sievers, 198, 5. 1. (**a-**⁴.) Cf. **onfon**.

aforce, *v.* to force, constrain, NED, H; **afforce**, H; **aforsed**, *pt. pl.*, H.—OF. *aforcer, efforcer, esforcier*; Late Lat. *exfortiare*, from Lat. *fortis*, strong. (**a-**⁹.)

a-fore, *adv. prep.*, before, PP, WW; **affore**, PP; **afor**, PP; **affor**, PP; **aforn**, NED.—AS. *on-foran*. (**a-**².)

a-forthen, *v.* to further, promote, to achieve, to manage to do, to manage to give, to afford; P, NED, SkD, HD; **aforde**, NED.—AS. *ge + forðian*. (**a-**⁶.)

a-fote, *adv.* on foot, PP; **afoote**, S3, W; **auote**, S2. (**a-**².)

afrayen, *v.* to disturb from peace and quiet, to frighten, NED; **affraye**, C2 (E. 455); **afreyd**, *pp.* alarmed, afraid, NED; **affrayed**, W, S2, C, C3; **affrayd**, S3; **affrayt**, S3; **frayd**, S3, **fraid**, S3.—AF. *affrayer, effrayer*, OF. *esfreer*: Prov. *esfredar*; Low Lat. *ex-fridare*, from *fridum*; cf. OS. *friðu*, peace. (**a-**⁹.) See **affrayen**.

a-fright, *pp.* terrified, C; **afriȝt**, NED, HD; **afryȝte**, HD.—AS. *á-fyrht, á-fyrhted*. (**a-**¹.)

after, *prep.* and *adv.* after, according to, S, HD, S2, C3; **efter**, S, S2; **eftir**, S3;

eafter, MD; **aftir**, S2.—*Æf-ter* is a comp. form, see SkD.

after-clap, *sb.* an evil consequence or result, HD; **after-clappys**, *pl.*, MD.

after-del, *sb.* disadvantage, MD; **after-dele**, HD.

a-fure, *adv.* on fire, S2; **auere**, S2; **afiere**, W2. (**a-**².)

afyngred; see **ahungerd**.

afyrst, *pp.* athirst, PP; **afurst**, PP; **afrust**, PP; see **ofþurst**.

a-gasten, *v.* to terrify, MD, PP; **agesten**, S; **agaste**, *pt. s.*, C2, C; **agast**, *pp.*, PP, S2, S3, C2, C3, G; **agazed**, S3; **agaste**, *pl.*, S2, W.—AS. *á + gǽstan*, to frighten. (**a-**¹.)

a-gen, *prep.* and *adv.* towards, back, again, S; see **aȝein**.

agenes, *prep.* against, S; see **aȝeines**.

agenst, *prep.* against, NED; see **aȝeinst**.

Agenst-Christ, *sb.* Antichrist, S3.

a-gessen, *v.* to reckon, calculate, S. (**a-**¹.)

aghe, *sb.* awe, H; **agh**, NED; see **awe**.

aghe-ful, *adj.* awful, H; **aghful**, H.

a-gon¹, *v.* to obtain, PP.—AS. *of-gangan*, to require. (**a-**³.)

a-gon², *pp.* and *adv.* gone away, ago, S2, C3; **agoon**, C2, C3; **agone**, S3; **agoo**, PP; **ago**, C2.—AS. *a-gán*, pp. of *á-gán*, to go forth. (**a-**¹.)

a-graythen, *v.* to make ready, to dress, NED; **agreþed**, *pp.*, S2; **agrayþed**, NED.—From Icel. *greiða*: Goth. *ga-raidjan*. (**a-**¹.)

a-graythinge, *sb.* apparel, S2, NED.

agreable, *adj.* pleasant, NED; **aggreable**, favourable, S3.—AF. *agreable*. (**a-**⁷.)

a-gref, in grief, NED; **agrief**, C; **ogrefe**, NED. *Phr.*: **takes not agreve**, takes it not unkindly, NED. (**a-**².)

agreggen, *v.* to make heavy, to be heavy, to aggravate, HD; **agreggid**, *pp.*, W2.—OF. *agregier*: Prov. *agreujar*; Late Lat. *aggreuiare*, from **greuis* for Lat. *grauis*. (**a-**⁷.)

agreþed, *pp.* made ready, S2; see **agrayþen**.

agreuen, *v.* to bear heavily on, to grieve, oppress, HD; **agreued**, *pp.*, C2, PP.—OF. *agrever*; Lat. *aggrauare*; *ad + grauare*, from *grauis*. (**a-**⁷.)

agrimony, *sb.* agrimony, Prompt.; **agre-moine**, Voc.; **egrimony**, Prompt.; **egremoin**, C3; **egremounde**, NED; **ogremoyne**, Voc.—Lat. *agrimonia*; Gr. ἀγρεμώνη cf. F. *aigremoine*.

a-grisen, *v.* to be horrified, to terrify, to loathe, HD, MD, S; **agryse**, S2, C3.—AS. *á-grísan*. (**a-**¹.)

a-grounde, on the ground, S2, PP; on this earth, PP. (**a-**².)

agte, *sb.* possession, S; see **auhte**¹.

a-gulten, *v.* to sin, to offend, MD, PP, S; **agilten**, MD; **agelten**, MD; **aȝulten**, S; **agulte**, *pt. s.*, PP; **agult**, *pp.*, S; **agilt**, HD, PP.—AS. *á-gyltan*. (**a-**[1].)

ah[1], *conj.* but, S, S2; see **ac**.

ah[2], *pr. s.* owes (as a duty), S; **ahen**, *pr. pl.*, are obliged, S; see **owen**[1].

a-honge, *pp.* hanged up, S. (**a-**[1].)

aht[1], *adj.* worthy, valiant, NED; see **auht**.

aht[2], *sb.* aught, anything; **ahte**, S; **ahct**, S; see **ought**.

ahte, *sb.* possession, S2; **ahhte**, S; see **auhte**[1].

ahtlice, *adv.* valiantly, NED; **ohtliche**, NED. See **auht**.

a-hungerd, *pp.* a-hungered, hungry, PP, S3; **ahungred**, NED; **afyngred**, PP.—AS. *oftyngred*. (**a-**[3].) See **ofhungred**.

aihte, *sb.* property, S; **ayhte**, S; see **auhte**[1].

air, *sb.* air, S2; **aire**, NED; see **eyre**[1].

airtis, *sb. pl.* quarters of the sky, S3; see **art**.

aisille, *sb.* vinegar, S; **eisil**, MD; **eisel**, MD; **eyselle**, MD; **esylle**, Prompt.; **aselle**, MD; **eysell**, Sh.; **aysel**, H.—OF. *aisil* (*eisil*), also, *aisi*, Ps. 68. 21 (Metz); Late Lat. *acitum* (cf. OF. *azet*); Lat. *acētum*; see Schuchardt, *Vokalismus*, i. 294.

aisliche, *adv.* timorously, S3; see **eisliche**.

ak[1], *conj.* but, S2, PP; see **ac**.

ak[2], *sb.* oak, Voc.; **akis**, *pl.*, S3; see **ook**.

a-kelen, *v.* to make cold, to grow cold, S, MD.—AS. *á-célan*. (**a-**[1].)

aken, *v.* to ache, to throb with pain, C2, S2, Prompt., NED; **eken**, MD; **ȝaik**, NED; **oc**, *pt. s.*, MD; **ok**, MD; **oke**, MD, NED; **akide**, NED; **oken**, *pt. pl.*, PP.—AS. *acan*, *pt. óc*, *pp. acen*; cf. Icel. *aka*, to drive, Lat. *agere*. Cf. **ache**[1].

akennet, *pp.* born, S; see **acennen**.

aketoun, *sb.* a jacket of quilted cotton worn under the mail, a jacket of leather plated with mail, NED, Voc., C2; **acketoun**, HD; **acton**, NED, HD, JD; **hakatone**, HD; **haqueton**, NED; **haketon**, ND; **hacqueton**, ND.—OF. *auqueton*; Sp. *alcoton*; Arab. *al-quṭn*, the cotton.

a-kneon, on knees, S, NED; **aknen**, HD; **aknewes**, HD. (**a-**[2].)

al[1], *adj., sb., adv.* all, MD, S, S2, C2, C3; **all**, S, S3; **hal**, S2; **alle**, *dat.*, S; **ælle**, *pl.*, S; **alle**, S2; **halle**, S; **ealre**, *gen.*, S; **allre**, S; **alra**, S; **alre**, S.—AS. *eall, all, al*.

al[2], *adv.* (with conjunctions); **al if**, although, NED.

al[3], *adv.* (with subj. mood), although, NED, C, C3; **al be it**, even though it be that, C.

alabastre, *sb.* alabaster, W (Mt. 26. 7); **alabaustre**, S3; **alablaster**, Sh.—OF. *alabastre*; Lat. *alabastrum* (nom. *-ter*); Gr. ἀλάβαστρος, ἀλάβαστος.

a-lang, *adv.* along, MD; **along**, MD; **olong**, MD (**a-**[4].) See **endlang**.

alange, *adj.* tedious, strange, foreign, Prompt.; **alenge**, HD; see **elenge**.

alarge, *v.* to enlarge, to give largely, HD; **alargid**, *pp.*, W, W2.—OF. *alargir*. (**a-**[7].)

a-last, *adv.* at last, S2, NED. (**a-**[5].)

alaun, *sb.* a large dog used for hunting; **alan**, NED; **alant**, NED; **alauntz**, *pl.*, C; **allaundes**, NED.—OF. *alan* (*allan* in Cotg.); It. *alano* (Florio); Low Lat. *alanus*.

alay, *sb.* alloy, PP; **alayes**, *pl.*, C2.—AF. *alay*.

alayen, *v.* to mix metals, to alloy, NED, PP; **alayed**, *pp.*, PP.—AF. *alayer, aleyer* (F. *aloyer*); Lat. *alligare*, to bind. (**a-**[7].)

albe, *sb.* a vestment worn by priests, and by some kings; NED.—Church Lat. *alba*, an alb; Lat. *alba* (*vestis*), a white garment.

albificacioun, *sb.* the process of making white (in alchemy), C3.—Late Lat. *albificationem*.

alblastrye, *sb.* the use of cross-bows, S3. See **arblaste**.

ald, *adj.* old, S, S2; **alder**, *comp.*, MD; **aldreste**, *superl.*, S; see **old**.

al-day, *adv.* always, continually, C2, PP.

alde-like, *adv.* with solemn, venerable mien, S.

alder[1], *sb.* elder, ancestor, also, prince, chief, MD, PP; **aldren**, *pl.*, S; **ælderen**, S; **elderne**, S2; **ealdren**, MD; **ealdrene**, *gen.*, S.—AS. *ealdor* (*aldor*). See **ald**.

alder[2], *gen. pl.* of all, C2, H; see **alre-**.

alder-best, *adj.* best of all, H; see **alrebest**.

alder-first, *adj.* first of all, C2; see **alrefyrst**.

alder-mon, *sb.* a prince, also, the principal officer in the shire, MD, Voc.; **elldernemanness**, *gen.*, S; **aldermen**, *pl.*, PP, AS. *ealdormann*.

aldire-, *gen. pl.* of all, H; see **alre-**.

aldire-mast, *adj.* most of all, H; see **alremest**.

ale, *sb.* ale, S2, C; ale-house, S2; an ale-drinking, NED. *Comb.*: **ale-stake**, a stake before an alehouse as a sign, C, C3, NED.—AS. *ealu, alu*; OTeut. stem **alut-*. Cf. **nale**.

a-leggen, *v.* to lay down, to lay aside, to put down, confute, S, NED (*allay*[1]).—AS. *á-lecgan*. (**a-**[1].)

alemaunde, *sb.* almond, NED, W2; **almaundes**, *pl.*, NED; **almoundes**, NED.—OF. *alemande, alemandre, alemandle* (cf. Sp. *almendra*); Late Lat. *amendola* (cf. Pg. *amendoa*); Lat. *amygdala*; Gr. ἀμυγδάλη.

alemaunde-tre, *sb.* almond-tree, W2.

alembyk, *sb.* a retort (used in alchemy), C3; **alambic**, NED; **limbeck**, ND, Sh.; **lymbecke**, (Minsheu).—OF. *alambic*, Sp. *alambique* (Minsheu); Arab. *al-anbíq*; Gr. ἄμβῖκ-, stem of ἄμβιξ, a cup.

a-lemen, *v.* to illumine, S; **alimen**, S; **aleomen**, S.—AS. *á + léoman*. (**a-**¹.)

a-lesednesse, *sb.* redemption, MD.

a-lesen, *v.* to loose, deliver, S; **alesde**, *pt. s.*, S; **alesed**, *pp.*, S, HD.—AS. *á-lésan, álýsan.* (**a-**¹.)

a-lesendnesse, *sb.* redemption, MD.

a-lesnesse, *sb.* redemption, S, MD.—AS. *á-lésnis.*

al-gate, *adv.* every way, always, in any case, NED, S3, C, C2, C3; **allegate**, S; **algates**, S2, C2, C3; **algatis**, W.—Cf. Icel. *alla götu*, every way.

algorisme, *sb.* the Arabic or decimal system of numeration, arithmetic, NED; **algrim**, MD; **augrim**, S. *Phr.*: **cipher in algorisme**, the figure **0**, a mere cipher, NED.—OF. *algorisme (augorime)*; Low Lat. *algorismus* (cf. Span. *guarismo*, arithmetic, Minsheu); from Arab. *al-Khowarazmi*, the surname of an Arab mathematician of the 9th cent.

al-halowen, *sb. pl.* all saints, NED; **alhalowes**, NED; **halalwes**, S2.

Al-Halowen Day, *sb.* All Saints' Day, NED.—AS. *ealra halgena dæg.*

aliance, *sb.* alliance, NED; **alliaunce**, C2.—AF. *aliance.*

a-liche, *adv.* alike, PP, NED.—AS. *ge-líce.* (**a-**⁶.) See **iliche**¹.

alie, *sb.* ally, relative, PP; **allye**, C2.

alien, *v.* to combine, unite, ally, NED; **allyed**, *pp.*, C2.—OF. *alier*; Lat. *alligare.* (**a-**⁷.)

a-liri, *adv.* across (said of the legs), P; **alyry**, PP.—AS. *on + lira*, the fleshy part of the leg (Voc.). (**a-**².)

a-liȝten¹, *v.* to alight, get lightly down from a horse, to descend, also, to lighten, MD; **alyghte**, C2; **alyghte**, *pt. s.*, PP; **alyȝte**, PP; **alihte**, MD; **aliȝte**, S; **alyhte**, S2; **aliȝt**, *pp.*, S2.—AS. *á-líhtan.* (**a-**¹.)

a-liȝten¹, *v.* to enlighten, illuminate, to light (a fire), NED.—AS. *on-líhtan.* (**a-**².)

a-liȝtnen, *v.* to enlighten, NED; **alichtyn**, S3; **alyctnyng**, *pr. p.*, S3. (**a-**¹.)

al-kaly, *sb.* alkali, C3.—Arab. *al-qalīy*, calcined ashes; from *qalay*, to roast in a pan.

alkamistre, *sb.* alchemist, C3, NED. OF. *alkemiste.*

al-kamye, *sb.* medieval chemistry, PP.— OF. *alcamie, alquimie*; Sp. *alquimia*; Arab. *al-kīmīā*; Late Gr. χημία, of doubtful origin, prob. from χυμεία, pouring.

al-karon, *sb.* the Koran, S2.—OF. *al-coran*; Ar. *al-qur'ān*, the reading, from *qara'a*, to read aloud.

al-katran, *sb.* the resin of fir trees, pitch, also, bitumen, NED, S2.—OF. *alketran*; Sp. *alquitran*; Ar. *al-qatran*, from *qatara*, to drop.

al-kin, *adj.* of every kind, MED, PP; **alkyn**, S2, PP; **alkynnes**, PP; **alle kynez**, S2.— AS. *alles cynnes*, gen.

al-kynd, *adj.* of every kind, S3.

all-; see also words beginning in **al-**.

allunge, *adv.* altogether, S, MD; **allynge**, MD; **allinge**, MED.—AS. *eallunga, eallunge.*

allure, *sb.* a place to walk in, a gallery, a walk by the parapets of a castle, a cloister, S3; **alure**, Prompt., NED.—OF. *alure* (now *allure*), walk, going, a gallery, also, *aleüre* (= Low Lat. **alatura*), from *aler*, to go (F. *aller*).

Almain¹, *adj.* German, NED; **Almaines**, *pl.* Germans, NED; **Almaygnes**, S3.—OF. *aleman* (F. *allemand*).

almain², *sb.* a kind of dance, NED; **almond**, NED. *Comb.*: **almain-leap**, ND; **almond-leape**, Cotg. (s.v. *saut*).

Almaine, *sb.* Germany, H; **Almayne**, NED; **Alemaine**, S; **Almeyne**, NED; **Almen**, NED; **Alamanie**, S.—OF. *Alemaigne*; Lat. *Allemannia*, the country of the *Allemanni.*

almes-dede, *sb.* deed of mercy, S2.

almesse, *sb.* alms, charity, S, PP, Prompt., S2, C3; **ælmes**, S; **elmesse**, MD; **almes**, S, S2, W; **almous**, S2; **almessis**, *pl.*, W.—AS. *ælmysse*; Church Lat. **alimosina* (cf. OF. *almosne*); *eleemosyna* (Tertullian); Gr. ἐλεημοσύνη alms, Lu. 12. 33; orig. pity.

al-mest, *adv.* almost, S2, C2, W, W2; **almeest**, W2; **almost**, PP.

al-miȝt, *adj.* all-powerful, MD; **almight**, NED, G.—AS. *ælmiht.*

al-miȝti, *adj.* almighty, NED; **almichti**, S; **allmahhtiȝ**, S; **almyȝty**, S2; **almihti**, S.—AS. *ælmeahtig.*

al-miȝtin, *adj.* almighty, NED; **almihten**, NED; **almihtin**, S.

alne-way; see **alweye**.

a-lofte, *adv.* on high, aloft, PP; **aloft**, PP; **on-lofte**, S2, C2; **o lofte**, NED; **o loft**, NED.—Icel. *á lopt* (of motion), *á lopti* (of position); *lopt*, air, sky, loft; cf. AS. *on þá lyft*, into the air, (**a-**².)

a-londe, on land, in the land, S2, HD; **alond**, S2.

al-one, *adj., adv.* alone, MED. *Phr.*: **hym allane**, S2. See **oon**.

a-longen, *v.* to seem long to, to long, NED; **alonged**, *pp.* filled with longing, G, HD; **alonget**, S2.—AS. *of-langian.* (**a-**³.)

a-long on, *prep.* on account of, S2, NED.— AS. *ge-lang*, along. (**a-**⁶.) See **ilong**.

al-only, *adv.* merely, S2; **alle only**, S2.

a-loofe, *adv.* aloof, more nearly to the wind, NED; **alofe**, S3; **aluffe**, HD. Probably from Du. *loef*, in *te loef*, to windward. (**a-**².)

a-losen, *v.* to praise, PP; **alosed**, *pp.* notorious, S2, NED, HD. (**a-**⁷.)

al-out, *adv.* entirely, NED: **all out**, H.

a-louten, *v.* to bow down, S3, NED; **alowtid**, *pt. s.*, PP.—AS. *á-lútan*. (**a-**¹.)

a-low, on the low ground, on earth, ED, PP; **alawe**, S3; **alowe**, PP. (**a-**².)

alowable, *adj.* praiseworthy, PP.

alowaunce, *sb.* praise, PP.

alowen¹, *v.* to praise, commend, to approve of, sanction, to admit (intellectually), S3, PP; **allowen**, C2, G, PP.—OF. *alouer*; Late Lat. *allaudare; Lat. *ad* + *laudare*. (**a-**⁷.)

alowen², *v.* to assign, bestow, to give an allowance to, NED, Palsg.; **allow**, Sh.—AF. *alower*, OF. *alouer*, *aloer*; Lat. *allocare*, to place. (**a-**⁷.)

a-loyne, *v.* to remove far off, NED, HD, AF. *aloyner*, from *loin*; Lat. *longe*. (**a-**⁷.)

alre, *gen. pl.* of all, used as an intensifying prefix **alre-** with a superlative, NED (*all*, see sect. D. II, p. 227), MD (p. 56); **allere**, H; **aller**, G, C; **alder**, C2, H; **alther**, G, C, W2; **aldire-**, H.—AS. *ealra*.

alre-best, best of all, S2; **alderbest**, H; **altherbest**, NED, HD, C; **altherbeste**, S, HD.

alre-fyrst, first of all, NED; **altherfirst**, NED, HD; **alderfirst**, C2, C3.

alre-mest, most of all, S; **aldiremast**, H; **althermoost**, HD.

als, *adv.* and *conj.* also, as, S, S2, S3, C2; see **also**.

als-as, *conj.* just as if, S3.

al-so, *adv.* and *conj.* (1) even so, likewise, also, (2), as, MED, PP, S, S3, C3; **allswa**, S; **alswo**, MED; **alse**, S; **alsse**, S; **als**, S, S2, S3, C2; **alls**, S; **ase**, S, S2; **as**, S, S2, S3, C2; **es**, PP; **alsswa**, S2; **alsua**, S2; **als-so**, 32, **alswa**, 3, 32, MED.—AS. *eal-swá*.

Al Solne Day, All Souls' Day, NED; **Alle Soule Day**, S2.—AS. *ealra sawlena dæg*.

als-tite, *adv.* as quick, immediately, MED, S2.

al-suic, *adj.* all such, S.

al-swithe, *adv.* as fast, immediately, MED; **alswythe**, PP; **als-suith**, S2; **aswithe**, S2; **asswythe**, S2.

al-to, *adv.* entirely, S, NED (s.v. *all*, see C, sect. 15), W, W2, H; **all-to**, H.

al-togidere, *adv.* altogether, G; **alte-gædere**, S.

alther-, *gen. pl.* of all, C, G, W2, PP; see **alre-**.

alther-best, *adj.* best of all, S, C; see **alrebest**.

alther-feblest, *adj.* feeblest of all, S2, HD.

alther-first, *adj.* first of all, HD; see **alrefyrst**.

alther-moost, *adj.* most of all, HD; see **alremest**.

al-wat, *conj.*, *adv.* all the while, till, S, MD (s.v. *al*, p. 57); **alwet**, MD; **alhuet**, NED (s.v. *all what*). See **what**².

al-weldand, *adj.* all-wielding, S2; **alweald-ent**, S.—AS. *al-wealdend*.

al-weye, *adv.* all along, at all times, perpetually, at any rate, NED; **alne-way**, S2; **alwey**, C2, C3, PP; **alwais**, S2; **alleweyes**, NED.—AS. *ealne weg*.

alynen, *v.* to besmear; **alyned**, *pp.*, S2.—Lat. *allinere*. (**a-**⁷.)

a-lyue, *adv.*, *adj. as pred.* alive, C2, S2, PP; **onlyue**, C2, G; **onliue**, S.—AS. *on life*. (**a-**².)

am, *1 pr. s.* am, S, C3; **æm**, S, MD; **ham**, S; **eam**, MD; **eom**, MD.—ONorth. *am*, OMerc. *eam* (VP), AS. *eom*.

a-mad, *pp. as adj.* distracted, mad, MD, S; **amed**, MD; **amadde**, *pl.* MD.—AS. *ge-méd*, *pp.* of *ge-médan*, to madden; cf. OHG. *ga-meit*, foolish. (**a-**⁶.)

amaistrien, *v.* to master, teach, PP; **amaistrye**, P, HD.—OF. *amaistr(i)er*; Lat. *ad* + *magistrare*. (**a-**⁷.)

amalgame, *sb.* a soft mass, mixture of metal with mercury, NED; **malgam** NED.—OF. *amalgame*; Low Lat. *amalgama*.

amalgaming, *sb.* the formation of an amalgam, C3.

amang; see **amonge**.

a-mansien, *v.* to curse, to excommunicate, MD; **amansi**, MD; **amansy**, MD; **amonsi**, HD; **amawns**, HD; **amansed**, *pp.*, S.—Contracted from AS. *á-mánsumian*, to put out of intimacy, from *mánsum*, familiar, intimate; *pp. á-mánsumod*, also *ámánsod*; see Schmid. (**a-**¹.)

a-masen, *v.* to amaze, stupefy, NED; **amased**, *pp.*, C3. (**a-**¹.)

ambassade, *sb.* the function of ambassador, an ambassador and suite, NED; **embas-sades**, *pl.*, S3.—OF. *ambassade*, *ambaxade*; OSp. *ambaxada*, from Low Lat. *ambaxia*, *ambactia*, office, employment, from *ambactus*, vassal, retainer, a Celtic word found in Caesar.

ambassadrie, *sb.* ambassadorship, NED; **embassadrie**, S2, C3.—F. *ambassaderie*.

ambassage, *sb.* embassy, NED; **ambas-sages**, *pl.*, S3.

amblen, *v.* to move at an easy pace, NED.—OF. *ambler*; Lat. *ambulare*, to walk.

amblere, *sb.* an ambling horse or mule, C, NED.

amellen, *v.* to enamel, MD; **ammell**, Palsg.; **amelled**, *pp.*, Palsg.; **amelyd**, HD; **amiled**, HD; **ameled**, NED.—AF. *aymeler*, OF. *esmailler*; OHG. *smalzjan*, to smelt, liquefy; cf. It. *smaltare*, to enamel (Florio). Cf. **enamelen**, **mute**.

amenden, *v.* to amend, mend, MD, S, S2, C2, W; **amended**, *pp.* S2; **amendid**, W2.—OF. *amender*; Lat. **ē-mendare*, from *ex* + *mendum*, fault. (**a-**⁹.)

amene, *adj.* pleasant, S3, NED; **ameyn**, S3.—OF. *amene*; Lat. *amoenum*.

amerant, *sb.* amaranth, a fadeless flower, S3.—OF. *amarante*; Lat. *amarantum* (acc.); Gr. ἀμάραντος (**a-**¹¹.)

amercy, *v.* to amerce, fine, P, NED.—AF. *amercier*; from OF. *estre a merci* came *estre amercie*, then *amercier*.

amete, *sb.* ant, emmet, NED; **amte**, W2; **emete**, Voc.; **emote**, NED; **ematte**, Voc.; **amtis**, *pl.*, W2; **amptis**, NED.—AS. *émete*, *émete*. Cf. OHG. *ámeiza*; from OHG. *á*, off + *meizan*, to cut, as if 'the cutter or biter off'.

ametist, *sb.* amethyst, NED; **ametistus**, W (Rev. 21. 20); **amatyste**, HD; **amaste**, HD; **amaffised**, MD.—OF. *ametiste*; Lat. *amethystum* (acc.); Gr. ἀμέθυστος (**a-**¹¹.)

ameuen, *v.* to be moved, NED; **ameued**, *pt. s.*, C2.—OF. *esmeuv-*, accented stem of *esmover*; Lat. *exmouēre*. (**a-**⁹.)

ameyn; see **amene**.

a-midde, *adv.* and *prep.* amid, S2, C2, PP; **amidden**, S; **amydde**, PP.—AS. *on middan*, *on middum*. (**a-**².)

amirail, *sb.* a Saracen ruler or commander, an emir, an admiral, MD; **amerel**, Prompt.; **amyralle**, MD; **amrayl**, HD; **admirald**, S.—OF. *amirail*, *amiral*; cf. Arab. *amīr-al-bahr*, commander of the sea, *amīr-al-mūminīm*, commander of the faithful.

a-mis, *adv.* amiss, C2; **amys**, G; **onmys**, NED. (**a-**².)

amome, *sb.* an odoriferous plant, amomum, NED; **amonye**, W, HD.—OF. *amome* (Cotg.); Lat. *amomum*; Gr. ἄμωμον, a name applied to several spice plants.

amoneste, *v.* to admonish, warn, HD.—OF. *amonester*; Late Lat. **admonitare*, from Lat. *admonitus*, pp. of *admonere*, see Constans. (**a-**⁷.)

amonestement, *sb.* admonishment, S, HD.—OF. *amonestement*.

amonestyng, *sb.* admonishing, CM.

a-monge, *prep.* and *adv.* among, in, at intervals, PP; **amange**, NED; **omang**, MD; **amang**, S, S2; **among**, S, PP. *Phr.*:

eure among, ever among, every now and then, S; **ever and among**, NED.—AS. *onmang*, *on-gemang*. (**a-**².)

a-monges, *prep.* among, S2, S3, C2, C3 G, PP.

a-morewe, on the morrow, S2, W; **amor we**, HD, PP, S2; **amoreʒe**, S; **amorʒe**, S (16. 432).—AS. *on morgen*. (**a-**².)

amountance, *sb.* amount, NED; **mountouns**, S2, HD.

amounten, *v.* to ascend, rise, amount, mean, S2, C2, PP; **amunten**, S.—AF. *amunter*, from Lat. *ad* + *montem*. (**a-**⁷.)

ampole, *sb.* a vessel for holding consecrated oil, or for other sacred uses, NED; **ampulles**, *pl.*, P; **ampolles**, S2, PP; **hanypeles**, PP.—OF. *ampole*; Lat. *ampulla*.

ampre, *sb.* a tumour, flaw, blemish; **amper**, HD; **ampres**, *pl.*, S.—AS. *ampre*, 'varix' (Voc.).

amte; see **amete**.

a-murðrin, *v.* to murder, S; **amorthered**, *pp.*, MD.—AS. *á-myrðrian* (Schmid). (**a-**¹.)

amyable, *adj.* friendly, lovely, NED; **amyabill**, S3; **amiable**, WW.—OF. *amiable*; Lat. *amicabilem*.

an¹, *1 pr. s.* I grant, allow, S; on, *pr. s.*, S. See **unnen**.

an², *num.* and *indef. art.* one, an, S, S2, PP; see **oon**.

an³, *prep.* on, upon, in, PP, S, S2; see **on**¹.

an⁴, *conj.* and, if, PP, S, S2; see **and**.

anaunter, for **an aunter**, a chance, S2; see **aventure**.

anchesoun, *sb.* occasion, MD; **ancheisun**, MD; **anchaisun**, HD.—AF. *anchesoun*. See **achesoun**.

ancre, *sb.* an anchorite, recluse, hermit, a monk, a nun, NED, S, S2; **auncre**, S2; **anker**, S2; **ancres**, *pl.*, P.—AS. *ancra*, m. (**ancre*, f.); Church Lat. *anachoreta*; Gr. ἀναχωρητής.

and, *conj.* and, also, if, G, S, S2, S3, C2 **ant**, S, S2; **an**, S, S2; **a**, MD.—*Phr.*: **and if**, MD.

ande, *sb.* breath, H; see **onde**.

anefeld, *sb.* anvil, W2; **anefelt**, NED.—AS. *onfilti* (Voc.).

an-ent, *prep.* and *adv.* on a level with, among, opposite, towards, in respect of, NED; **anont**, MD; **onont**, S; **onond**, S; **anende**, MD; **anonde**, MD; **ononde**, MD; **anendes**, MD; **anentes**, NED; **anentis**, W, W2; **anemptis**, MD; **anempst**, NED; **anence**, H; **anens**, H; **ynentes**, H.—AS. *on efen*, *on efn*, *on emn*, on even ground with.

anentesch; see **anientise**.

aner-ly, *adv.* only, alone, S2, NED, JD.

anete, *sb.* the herb dill, Voc., W, NED.—OF. *anet*; Lat. *anethum* (Vulg.); Gr. ἄνηθον, dial, form of ἄνισον. See **anise**.

a-netheren, *v.* to lower, humiliate, NED; **anethered**, *pp.*, HD. (**a-¹**.) See **aniþerien**.

anew¹, *sb.* ring, wreath; **anewis**, *pl.*, S3; **aneus**, links of a chain, NED.—OF. *aniaus*, pl. of *anel*, ring; Lat. *anellus*, dim. of *ānulus*, dim. of *annus*, a circuit, year.

anew², enough, S3. (**a-⁶**.) See **ynow**.

a-newe, *adv.* anew, NED. (**a-³**.) See **ofnewe**.

anfald, *adj.* single, simple, S, HD; see **oonefold**.

angel, *sb.* angel; **ongel**, S; **angles**, *pl.*, S; **ængles**, S; **anglene**, *gen.* S.—Lat. *angelus.* See **engel²**.

an-gin, *sb.* beginning, MD; **angun**, S, NED.

an-ginnen, *v.* to begin; **on gon**, *pt. s.*, S.—AS. *an-(on-)ginnan.*

angle, *sb.* a name given to the four astrological 'houses', NED, S2.—OF. *angle*; Latin *angulum* (acc.).

Angles, *sb. pl.* the English, the people of 'Angul', a district of Holstein, S, NED; **Englis**, S.—AS. *Angle*, pl.

angre, *sb.* affliction, sorrow, wrath, pain, inflammation, NED, S2, PP; **angers**, S2.—Icel. *angr.*

angren, *v.* to annoy, injure, make angry, NED; **angre**, PP.—Icel. *angra.*

angwisch, *sb.* anguish, W2; **anguyssh**, PP; **angoise**, S, MD; **anguise**, MD; **anguisse**, MD.—OF. *angoisse*, AF. *anguisse*; Lat. *angustia*, tightness, from *angere*, to squeeze.

anhed, *sb.* unity, H; see **oonhed**.

an-hei3, *adv.* on high, S2, PP; **an hei**, S2; **an hey**, S2; **an hi3**, W.

an-heten, *v.* to heat, to become hot; **anhet**, *pr. s.* S; **anhéét**, *pp.* S.—AS. *onhætan.*

an-he3en, *v.* to exalt, NED; **anhe3ed**, *pp.*, S2.

an-hitten, *v.* to hit against, S, MD.

an-hon, *v.* to hang (*tr.*), MD; **anhoð**, *pr. pl.*, S; **anhonge**, *pp.*, MD.—AS. *on-hón.*

an-hongen, *v. tr.* and *intr.* to hang, S, MD; **anhonged**, *pp.*, MD; **anhanged**, C2.

aniente, *v.* to bring to nought, NED; **anyente**, PP.—OF. *anienter*, from *a*, to + *nient*; Late Lat. **necentem* = *nec* + *entem*. (**a-⁷**.)

anientise, *v.* to bring to nought, to destroy, NED; **anientice**, PP; **anentisen**, CM; **anentesch**, PP; **anyntische**, W2; **neentishe**, NED; **annentissched**, *pp.* CM; **anyntisschid**, W2; **enentyscht**, H; **enentist**, H.—OF. *anientir* (variant of *anienter*), pr. p. *anientissant.* (**a-⁷**.)

anise, *sb.* anise, also dill, NED; **anys**, NED; **aneyse**, Voc.—OF. *anis*; Lat. *anisum*; Gr. ἄνισον. Cf. **anete**.

a-niðerien, *v.* to lower, humiliate, MD; **aneðered**, *pp.* MD, HD.—AS. *á + niðerian.* (**a-¹**.)

anker, *sb.* anchor, S.—AS. *ancor*; Lat. *ancora*; Gr. ἄγκυρα.

anlas, *sb.* a kind of dagger, anlace, MD, C; **anelace**, HD; **anelas**, MD, NED.—Cf. Low Lat. *anelacius* (Ducange), OWelsh *anglas.*

an-leth, *sb.* face, countenance, MD, HD, NED; **onndlæt**, MD; **onlete**, MD.—Icel. *andlit* (Swed. *anlete*): AS. *and-wlíta.*

ann-; see also words beginning in **an-**.

annamyllit, *pp.* enamelled, S3; see **enamelen**.

annuel, *adj.* yearly; *sb.* a mass said either daily for a year after, or yearly on the anniversary of a person's death, NED; **anuell**, S3.—AF. *annuel*; Late Lat. *annualem*, for Lat. *annālem*, from *annus*, year.

annueler, *sb.* a priest who sang an annual, PP, C3, HD.

an-on, *adv.* at once, instantly, soon, in a short time, S, S2, C3, PP; **anan**, S, NED; **onan**, S2; **onon**, S, S3; **anoon**, S3, C2, G, W.—AS. *on án*, into one; *on áne*, in one (moment).

anonder; see **anunder**.

anon-ryght, *adv.* immediately, C3, G; **anonrihtes**, S; **ananriht**, S.

an-ouen, *adv.* above, S, NED; **onuuen**, NED.—AS. *on ufan.*

a-nough, *adj.* (as *pred.*) enough, CM; **anew**, S3. (**a-⁶**.) See **ynow**.

anoy, *sb.* discomfort, vexation, trouble, MD, S2, PP; **anoye**, W2; **anui**, MD; **enuye**, S.—OF. *anoi*: OSp. *enoyo*: OIt. *inodio*, from the Lat. phrase *est mihi in odio*; see Diez. Cf. **noye**.

anoyen, *v.* to annoy, PP, W2, S2, C2, C3; **anoiede**, *pt. s.*, W; **noyede**, W; **anoyed**, *pp.* W; **anuyed**, PP; **anuid**, MD; **anud**, S; **anuy3ed**, S2; **ennuyed**, P.—AF. *ennuyer.* Cf. **noyen**.

answere, *sb.* answer, MD; **ondswere**, S; **answare**, S; **onswere**, S; **andsware**, S.—AS. *and-swaru.*

answeren, *v.* to give an answer, S, PP; **ondswerien**, S; **andswarede**, *pt. s.* S; **andswerede**, S; **ontswerede**, S; **onswerde**, S; **answarede**, S; **answerede**, S.—AS. *and-swarian.*

ant, *conj.* and, also, if, S, S2. See **and**.

antem, *sb.* anthem, C2; **antefne**, MD.—AS. *antefne*; Church Lat. *antífona* (cf. Prov. *antífena*, It. *antífona*); for older *antiphōna*; Gr.

anticrist   appel

ἀντίφωνα lit. things sounding in response. Cf. **antiphone**.

anticrist, *sb.* antichrist, MD; **antecrist**, W (1 John 4. 3); **ancrist**, MD; **ancryst**, Voc.—Church Lat. *antichristus* (Vulg.); Gr. ἀντίχριστος.

antiphone, *sb.* antiphon, NED; Church Lat. *antiphōna*; see **antem**.

antiphonere, *sb.* anthem-book, C2; **antyphonere**, Voc.; **anfenare**, Voc.; **amfanere**, Voc.—Church Lat. *antiphonarius*.

anum, *adv.* at once, S.—AS. *ánum*, dat. of *án*, one. [The MS. has *anú*, put for *anū* (= anu*m*)]. See **oon**.

an-under, *prep.* under, S; **anonder**, S.

an-uppe, *prep.* and *adv.* upon, MD; **onuppe**, S.

an-uppon, *prep.* upon, S, MD; **anuppen**, S.

anwalde, *sb. dat.* power, S; **anwolde**, S; see **onwald**.

a-nyghte, *adv.* by night, C2; **aniȝt**, S; **onigt**, S. (**a-²**.)

a-nyghtes, *adv.* at night, nightly, S3.

apalled, *pp.* made pale, NED; **appalled**, C, C2.—OF. *apalir, apallir*; Lat. *ad + pallire* for *pallere*. (**a-⁷**.)

aparail, *sb.* apparel, PP; **apparaille**, C2, PP.

aparailen, *v.* to make ready, to fit up, furnish, to dress, attire, PP; **apparayleden**, *pt. pl.* S2; **aparailed**, *pp.* S; **apparailled**, P.—OF. *apareiller*; Late Lat. **adpariculare*, to make equal or fit, from Lat. *par*, equal. (**a-⁷**.)

aparaunce, *sb.* appearance, NED; **apparence**, C2.—AF. *apparence*. (**a-⁷**.)

apart¹, *adv.* apart, aside, C2; **aparte**, separately, PP, NED.—OF. *a part*. (**a-⁷**.)

apart², *v.* to set aside, separate, NED; **aparte**, S3 (24. 14).

apartie, *adv.* in part, partly, PP, NED. (**a-²**.)

apayen, *v.* to satisfy, please, to requite, HD, PP; **apayd**, *pp.* S3, C2, C3; **apayed**, C2, W; **apaied**, W, PP.—OF. *apaier (apayer)*: Prov. *apagar*; Lat. *ad + pacare*, from *pacem*, peace. (**a-⁷**.)

ape, *sb.* ape, MD, C2, C3, P; fool, HD. *Phr.*: **þe olde ape**, i.e. the devil, MD; **wyn of ape** (= OF. *vin de singe*), wine which makes the drinker pleasant, wanton, or boyish, Cotg., MD, HD.—AS. *apa*.

apece, *sb.* the alphabet, Prompt.; see **abece**.

apenden, *v.* to belong, S2, PP; **appenden**, S2, PP. OF. *ap(p)endre*; Lat. *ad + pendere*. (**a-⁷**.)

aperceyue, *v.* to perceive, C2, PP; **aperseyue**, PP.—OF. *aperçoiv-*, accented stem of *aperceveir*; Late Lat. *appercipēre*; Lat. *ad + percipere*. (**a-⁷**.)

aperceyuinges, *sb. pl.* observations, C2.

aperen, *v.* to appear, S, PP; **apeeren**, PP; **aper**, S2; **appiere**, P; **apperand**, *pr. p.* S3.—AF. *aper-*, stem of *apert*, pr. s. of *aparoir*; Lat. *apparere (ad + parere)*. (**a-⁷**.)

apert¹, *adj.* clever, expert, NED; **aspert**, S3.—OF. *aspert, espert*; Lat. *expertus*. (**a-⁹**.) See **expert¹**.

apert², *adj.* open, NED, H, HD; *adv.* C2. *Phr.*: **in to apert** (= Lat. *in palam*), S2.—OF. *apert*; Lat. *apertus*, pp. of *aperire*, a verb with *ā = ab*, prefix. (**a-⁸**.)

aperteliche, *adv.* openly, S2; **apertly**, P, H; **appertly**, P.

apertenaunt, *pr. p.* appertaining, C2.—OF. *apertenant*.

apertene, *v.* to appertain, NED, C3.—OF. *apertenir*; Lat. *ad + pertinere*. (**a-⁷**.)

apertinent, *pr. p.* appertaining, C2.—Late Lat. *adpertinentem*.

apesen, *v.* to appease, NED, S3 (3b. 1352), C2, C3; **appease**, S3 (19a. 295).—OF. *apeser*, from *a + pes*; Lat. *pacem*, peace. (**a-⁷**.)

apeyren, *v.* to harm, diminish, impair, PP, W; **apeyre**, P, W; **appayre**, S2, P; **apeyred**, *pp.* S2.—OF. *ampeirer, empeirer*; Lat. *in + peiorare*, to make worse, from *peior*, worse. (**a-¹⁰**.)

apeyryng, *sb.* injuring, S2, W; **appairing**, S3.

a-piken, *v.* to trim, adorn, MD; **apiked**, *pp.*, C. See OF. *piquer* (Cotg.).

aplien, *v.* to apply, devote one's energies to, NED; **apply**, S3.—OF. *aplier*; Lat. *applicare*.

apointen, *v.* to come or bring matters to a point, to agree, arrange, to prepare, equip, NED.—OF. *apointer*, from *a point*.

apointment, *sb.* agreement, NED; **poyntemente**, S3.—OF. *apointement*.

aposen, *v.* to question, S2, PP, Prompt.; **apposen**, C3, PP. Cf. **opposen**.

apostel, *sb.* apostle, S; **appostel**, NED; **appostil**, NED; **apostle**, W; **postlis**, *pl.* NED.—AS. *apostol*; Church Lat. *apostolus* (Vulg.); Gr. ἀπόστολος, one sent forth, messenger; cf. AF. *apostle* (OF. *apostre*).

apostil-hed, *sb.* office of apostle, W.

apotecarie, *sb.* apothecary, C; **potekary**, NED.—OF. *apotecaire*; Late Lat. *apothecarium* (acc.), from *apotheca*; Gr. ἀποθήκη, storehouse.

apoyson, *v.* to poison, PP; **apoysoned**, *pp.*, PP.—OF. *apoisoner*, for *empoisoner*. (**a-¹⁰**.)

app-; see also words beginning in **ap-**.

appairen, *v.* to injure; **appayre**, S2, P; see **apeyren**.

appairing, *sb.* injuring, S3.

appel, *sb.* apple, PP; **eppel**, MD; **applis**, *pl.* W2.—AS. *æppel*.

apple-garnade, *sb.* pomegranate, S2 (*garnade*). Cf. **garnet-appille.**
aprentis, *sb.* apprentice, NED; **prentis,** S2, PP; **aprentys,** *pl.* PP.—OF. *aprentis* (AF. *aprentiz*), nom. of *aprentif,* from *aprendre,* to learn; Lat. *apprehendere = ad + prehendere.* (**a-**7.)
a-quenchen, *v.* to quench, PP; **acwenchen,** S; **aqueynte,** *pt. s.* S2; **aqueynt,** PP.—AS. *á-cwencan.* (**a-**1.)
aquerne, *sb.* squirrel, S, NED; **acquerne,** S.—AS. *ácwern* (Voc.); cf. Icel. *íkorni,* G. *eichhorn,* MDu. *éncoren.*
aqueyntaunce, *sb.* acquaintance, S2, CM, MD.—OF. *acointance,* AF. *aqueyntance.* (**a-**7.)
aqueynten, *v.* to become known, MD; **aquointe,** *pp.* acquainted, NED; **aquente,** NED; **aquynt,** S2.—OF. *acointer* (*acuinter*); Late Lat. *adcognitare,* from Lat. *ad + cognitum,* pp. of *cognoscere.* (**a-**7.)
ar1, *prep., conj.* and *adv.* before, S, S2, G, H, P; see **er**2.
ar2, *pr. pl.* are, S2, PP; see **aren**2.
arace, *v.* to pull up by the roots, C2, CM; **arache,** NED.—AF. *aracer,* OF. *esrachier;* Lat. *e(x)radicare.* (**a-**9.)
aranye, *sb.* spider, Prompt.; **arain,** HD; **aranee,** HD; **eranye,** Prompt.; **erayne,** Prompt.; **erayn,** H; **arane,** H; **erane,** Voc.; **yreyne,** W2; **aran,** H; **irain,** NED; **arrans,** *pl.,* HD; **yreyns,** W2.—OF. *araigne* (*iraigne*); Lat. *aranea.*
arate, *v.* to correct, blame, rate, PP. Probably a variant of **aretten.** Cf. OF. *aratter = aretter* (Godefroy).
aray, *sb.* array, PP; **array,** S2 (19. 393), C2, C.—OF. *arei* (*arroi*).
arayen, *v.* to array, NED, PP; **arayed,** *pp.* W; **arrayed,** C2, C3.—AF. *arayer;* OF. *areier, areer:* It. *arredare* (Florio); from Lat. *ad + Low Lat. *rēdo* (OF. *rei*), preparation, of Teutonic origin. (**a-**7.)
arblaste, *sb.* a military engine for throwing missiles, MD, S2; **alblast,** S2.—OF. *arbaleste;* Late Lat. *arcuballista.*
arblaster, *sb.* an arblast-man, S2.
arch, *sb.* arch, Prompt.; **arches,** *pl.* court of Arches, P.—OF. *arche* (Cotg.).
arch-, *prefix,* chief; **erche-,** Church Lat. *archi-;* Gr. ἀρχι-, ἀρχ-.
arch-angel, *sb.* archangel, S, PP; **arch-angles,** *pl.* S.—Church Lat. *archangelus;* Gr. ἀρχάγγελος.
arche-biscop, *sb.* archbishop, S; **erche-bissop,** S2.—AS. *ærce-biscop* (S); Lat. *archi- + AS. biscop.*
archer, *sb.* archer, S2; **archeer,** C2; **harchere.** Voc.—AF. *archer.* See **ark**2.
archi-deken, *sb.* archdeacon, PP; **erche-dekene,** S2.

archi-flamyn, *sb.* high-priest, S2.—Church Lat. *archiflamen,* archbishop (Ducange), from Lat. *flamen.*
archi-triclin, *sb.* the ruler of the feast, S; **architriclyn,** W.—Church Lat. *architriclinus* (Vulg.); Gr. ἀρχιτρίκλινος.
arch-wyfe, *sb.* a wife who rules; **arche-wyues,** *pl.* C2, CM.
are1, *sb.* honour, reverence, also, grace, clemency, MD, NED, S; **ore,** S, S2, G, HD; happy augury, MD, S.—AS. *áre* (*ár*); cf. OHG. *éra,* honour (Otfrid).
are2, *sb.* oar, MD; see **ore**1.
a-recchen, *v.* to explain, expound, to speak, NED.—AS. *á-reccan.* (**a-**1.)
a-rechen, *v.* to reach, to strike, to reach in thought, to imagine, to be sufficient, NED, S, S (ii. 47), S2, W, PP.—AS. *á-récan.* (**a-**1.)
a-reden, *v.* to declare, to interpret, NED, W; **areede,** W.—AS. *á-rédan;* cf. G. *errathen.* (**a-**1.)
a-redy, *adj.* ready, P, HD, NED; **ȝe-redi,** MD. (**a-**6.)
are-full, *adj.* compassionate, MD, S.—AS. *ár-full.*
are-les, *adj.* merciless, MD; **oreleas,** S; **oreles,** S.—AS. *ár-léas.*
aren1, *v.* to show mercy to, S, MD.—AS. *árian.*
aren2, *pr. pl.* are, S, PP; **arn,** MD, C2, PP; **are,** MD; **ar,** MD, S2, PP; **ere,** MD, S2; **er,** H.—ONorth. *aron.*
arende, *sb.* errand; HD, PP; see **erende.**
arerage, *sb.* the state of being in arrear, indebtedness, NED, PP; **arrerage,** C, PP.—OF. *arerage,* AF. *arrerage.*
arere, *adv.* to the rear, in the rear, PP; **arrere,** PP.—AF. *arere;* Late Lat. *ad retro,* backward. (**a-**7.)
a-reren, *v.* to raise, build, to arise, to rear, S2, PP; **arearen,** S; **areride,** *pt. s.,* W; **arerde,** S; **arerd,** S; **arerdon,** *pl.,* S; **arered,** *pp.,* S2, W, W2; **arerd,** S2.—AS. *á-réran:* Goth. *ur-raisjan.* Causal of **arisen.** (**a-**1.)
a-rest, at rest, PP. (**a-**2.)
arest, *sb.* stop, S2; **arreest,** custody, C. Phr.: **spere in arest,** in rest, C.—OF. *areste,* stoppage, AF. *arest,* act of arresting. (**a-**7.)
aresten, *v. int.* and *tr.* to stop, cause to stop, NED, C.—AF. *arester;* Lat. *ad + restare.* (**a-**7.)
aretten, *v.* to reckon, count, accuse, NED, W, W2; **aretted,** *pp.* C; **arettid,** W, W2; **rettid,** W.—AF. *aretter,* OF. *areter; a + reter:* OSp. *reptar,* to challenge (Minsheu); Lat. *reputare,* to count; cf. Late Lat. *reptare* (Ducange). (**a-**7.) Cf. **retten.**
a-reysen, *v.* to raise, to arouse, NED; **areysed,** *pt. s.,* S3; **areisid,** *pp.,* W. (**a-**1.)

areȝth, *sb.* cowardice; **areȝthe**, *dat.*, S. See **arwe²**.

arfeð, *adj.* difficult, MD; **arefeð**, S; **earfeð**, MD; **arueð**, NED; **erfeð**, MD.—AS. *earfeðe*; cf. *earfeðe*, *earfoþ*, labour, toil: Goth. *arbaiþs*.

argoile, *sb.* the tartar deposited from wines, C3, NED; **arguyll**, NED; **argall**, Cotg. (s.v. *tartre*), ND.—AF. *argoil*.

arguen, *v.* to prove, to reason, PP.—OF. *arguer*; Late Lat. *argutare*, from Lat. *arguere*.

arguere, *sb.* reasoner, PP.

argument, *sb.* proof, clear proof, proof presumptive, NED; **argumens**, *pl.*, PP.—AF. *argument*; Lat. *argumentum*.

argumenten, *v.* to argue, C3, S2.

a-risen, *v.* to arise, MD; **aryse**, PP; **aris**, *imp. s.* S; **arys**, PP; **arist**, *pr. s.*, S, S2, C3; **aros**, *pt. s.*, S, PP; **aroos**, PP; **arisen**, *pp.*, MD; **arise**, S2.—AS. *á-rísan*. (**a-¹**.)

a-rist, *sb.* rising, resurrection, NED; **aristes**, *gen.*, S; **ariste**, *dat.*, S.—AS. *é-ríst*. (**a-¹**.)

ariue¹, *v.* to arrive, to come to shore, S; **aroue**, *pt. s.*, NED; **ariuede**, *pl.* S2; **aryue**, *pp.*, S; **aryven**, NED.—AF. *ariver*; Late Lat. *arribare*, *arripare*, *adripare*, from Lat. *ad* + *ripa*, shore. (**a-⁷**.)

ariue², *sb.* landing, arrival, C, NED.

a-rixlien, *v.* to rule; **arixlye**, S. (**a-¹**.)

a-riȝt, *adv.* in a right way, straightway, S2; **aryght**, C2; **ariȝte**, S; **origt**, S. (**a-²**.)

ark¹, *sb.* an ark, chest, MD; **arrke**, S; **arc**, S2.—Lat. *arca*; cf. OF. *arche*.

ark², *sb.* segment of a circle, C2, MD.—OF. *arc*; Lat. *arcum* (acc.), a bow.

arles, *sb.* an earnest, NED, JD, HD.—Probably a plural in form from an OF. **erle*, **arle*; Lat. **arrhula*, dim. of *arrha*, for *arrhabo*; Gr. ἀρραβών; Heb. *'érábón*. Cf. OF. *erres*, *arres*: Sp. *arras* (Minsheu); Lat. *arrhas*, pl. acc. of *arrha*. See **ernes**.

arly, *adj.* and *adv.* early, S2, H; see **erly**.

arm¹, *sb.* arm, MD; **earmes**, *pl.*, S, MD; **armes**, *interj.* arms! (an oath) by God's arms!, S3, NED. *Phr.*: **Gog's arms**, S3.—AS. *earm*: Icel. *armr*: Goth. *arms*.

arm², *adj.* poor, wretched, MD; **ærm**, MD; **erme**, *dat.* S; **arme**, *pl.* S; **earme**, MD.—AS. *earm*: Icel. *armr*: Goth. *arms*.

armen, *v.* to arm, C3, PP; **i-armed**, *pp.*, S.—AF. *armer*; Lat. *armare*.

armes, *sb. pl.* weapons, coat-armour, MD, P.—AF. *armes*.

arm-heorted, *adj.* tender-hearted, S.—Cf. AS. *earm-heort*.

arm-hertnesse, *sb.* compassion, S.

arminge, *sb.* the act of arming, putting on of armour, C2.

armipotent, *adj.* mighty in arms, C.—Lat. *armipotentem*.

armony, *sb.* harmony, S3.—F. *harmonie*; Lat. *harmonia*; Gr. ἁρμονία.

armure, *sb.* armour, weapons, P, C2, C3, G; **armoure**, C2; **armuris**, *pl.*, W, W2.—AF. *armure* (*armoure*), *armeure*; Lat. *armatura*.

arn, *sb.* eagle, HD; **aryn**, H; see **ern**.

arnde, *pt. s.* ran, S; see **rennen**.

a-rode, on the rood (the cross), NED, S, S2. (**a-²**.)

a-rowe, *adv.* in a row, one after another, S; **areawe**, S; **arewe**, NED. (**a-²**.)

arr-; see also words beginning in **ar-**.

arr, *sb.* scar, wound, NED, JD; **ar**, HD; see **erre**.

arred, *pp.* scarred, JD.

arsenik, *sb.* arsenic, C3.—OF. *arsenic*; Lat. *arsenicum*; Gr. ἀρσενικόν, yellow orpiment, orig. the masculine, male, from ἄρσην, a male.

arskes, *pl.* newts, S2; see **ask**.

arsmetike, *sb.* arithmetic, NED; **arsmetrike**, C.—OF. *arismetique*: Prov. *arismetica*; Lat. *arithmetica*; Gr. ἀριθμητική (τέχνη), the art of counting.

arst, *adj.* and *adv. superl.* first, G, P; see **er²**.

art, *sb.* a quarter of the heaven, point of the compass, NED, S3; **airt**, NED, JD; **airth**, NED; **airtis**, *pl.*, S3.—Gael. *ard*; OIr. *aird*, top, height, point.

artou, art thou, S2; **artow**, S2, C2, C3. See **ert**.

arwe¹, *sb.* arrow, NED; **arewe**, S2; **arwes**, *pl.* S2, C2, P; **arewis**, W2; **arowis**, W2.—AS. *arwe* for **arhwe*; cf. Goth. *arhwazna*, arrow, the thing belonging to the bow, from **arhw* = Lat. *arcus*.

arwe², *adj.* cowardly, timid, lazy, sluggish, vile, base, Prompt.; **areȝ**, S; **arh**, MD; **arȝ**, NED; **erewe**, S; **arewe**, *sb.* betrayer, enemy, S, MD.—AS. *earg* (*earh*); Icel. *argr*; cf. OHG. *arg* (Otfrid).

arwed, *pp.* made cowardly, PP.

arȝen, *v.* to be timid, to frighten, NED.

as, *sb.* unit, a single bit, a jot, ace, NED, C2; **ace**, S3; **ase**, PP. *Phr.*: **ambes as**, double aces, C2.—OF. *as*; Lat. *as*.

asailen, *v.* to leap upon, assail, PP; **assaile**, PP, S; **assaille**, C2, PP; **asailid**, *pp.*, PP; **assalȝeit**, S2.—AF. *assailir*, OF. *asalir*; Late Lat. *adsalire*. (**a-⁷**.)

a-saken, *v.* to deny, renounce; **asoke**, *pt. s.*, S.—AS. *of-sacan* (Schmid). (**a-³**.) Cf. **of-saken**.

asaut, *sb.* assault, S2; **assaut**, C, PP.—OF. *asaut*. (**a-⁷**.)

ascapie, *v.* to escape, PP; **askapie**, PP; **ascapen**, PP.—OF. *escaper* (Picard). Cf. **achape**.

ascaunce, *conj.* as though, C3, NED.

asche, *sb.* ash, *cinis*; **aische**, W, W2; **aske**, H; **asken**, *pl.*, S; **axen**, S; **asshen**, C2; **asskess**, S; **asshes**, C3; **aschis**, W2; **askes**, S2, P; **askis**, H; **askez**, S2.—AS. *asce (axe)*: Icel. *aska*: Goth. *azgo*.

ascrien, *v.* to cry out, NED; **escrien**, MD.—OF. *escrier*; Late Lat. *ex + quiritare*, see Diez.

ascrive, *v.* to ascribe, H.—OF. *ascriv-* stem of pr. p. of *ascrire*: It. *ascrivere*; Lat. *adscribere*. (**a-⁷**.)

ascry, *sb.* outcry, S2.

asegen, *v.* to besiege, C.—OF. *asegier*: It. *assediare* (Florio). (**a-⁷**.)

aselen, *v.* to seal up, to set one's seal to, NED; **aseele**, W2; **asselen**, PP, S2.—OF. *anseler*, *enseler*; Late Lat. *insigillare*, from *sigillum*, seal. (**a-¹⁰**.) Cf. **ensele**.

a-senchen, *v.* to cause to sink, S; **aseynt**, *pp.*, MD. (**a-¹**.)

asent, *sb.* assent, S2, PP; **assent**, C3, PP.—OF. *as(s)ent*. (**a-⁷**.)

a-setnesse, *sb.* appointed order, S.—AS. *á-setnis*, institute (Schmid).

a-setten, *v.* to set up, appoint, NED.—AS. *á-settan*. (**a-¹**.)

aseth, *sb.* satisfaction, PP, HD; **aseeth**, W; **asethe**, Cath., HD; **assyth**, JD; **assetz**, PP; **asseth**, NED, HD.—OF. *aset*, *asset*; from Late Lat. *ad satis*. For the final *-t* in OF. = *þ* in English, cf. OF. *feit* with ME. *feiþ*, faith. Hence our *assets*. (**a-⁷**.)

asise, *sb.* decree, edict, judgement, S2; **assise**, C, G; **assises**, *pl.* assizes, PP.—OF. *as(s)ise*, a sitting down, settlement of imposts, from *as(s)is*, pp. of *as(s)eeir*, to sit at, to settle; Lat. *assidere*. (**a-⁷**.)

asisour, *sb.* juror, PP; **acisoure**, PP; **sisour**, PP; **sysour**, PP.

ask-; see also words beginning in **asc-**.

ask, *sb.* a newt or eft, a lizard, NED, HD, JD; **aske**, NED; **asker**, HD, JD, DG; **askis**, *pl.*, NED; **arskes**, S2.—AS. *áðexe*: OS. *egithassa*; cf. OHG. *egidehsa* (G. *eidechse*).

aske, *sb.* ash, H; **askes**, *pl.*, S2, P; **askis**; H; see **asche**.

aske-baðie, *sb.* one who sits among the ashes, S; **askebathe**, NED.

aske-fise, *sb.* one who blows the ashes, Prompt.; **askfist**, NED. Cf. Sw. *askefis* and G. *aschenfister* (Grimm).

asken, *v.* to ask, S, S2; **eskien**, MD; **aschen**, MD; **eschen**, MD; **esse**, MD, S2; **ocsien**, MD; **acsien**, MD, S2; **axien**, MD, S2; **axen**, S, S2, S3, C2, C3, W, W2;

escade, *pt. s.*, S; **easkede**, S; **haxede**, S; **esste**, S2.—AS. *áscian*: OHG. *eiscón* (Otfrid); cf. G. *heischen*.

a-slaken, *v.* to diminish, to become slack, C, NED. (**a-¹**.)

a-slawe, *pp.* slain, S2; **asla3e**, S; **asla3en** S.—AS. *á-slagen*, pp. of *á-sléan*, see Sievers, 378. (**a-¹**.)

a-slepe, *adv.* asleep, S, PP.—AS. *on slǽpe*. (**a-²**.)

a-slepid, *pp.* gone to sleep, W2.

a-sonder, *adv.* asunder, C, C3.—AS. *on sundran*. (**a-²**.)

a-soylen, *v.* to absolve, to answer (a question), PP, S2; **assoile**, S3, C3, P, G; **asoyly**, NED; **asoilede**, *pt. s.*, S2; **asoylede**, S2; **assoylid**, *pp.*, W.—OF. *asoiler*, *assoiler*; Late Lat. *absoluere* (= Lat. *absolovere*). (**a-⁸**.)

aspaltoun, *sb.* asphalt, S2.—OF. **aspaltoun*; from Late Lat. *asphalton*; Gr. ἄσφαλτον.

aspect, *sb.* a term in astrology; the relative positions of the heavenly bodies as they appear at a given time, NED, SkD, Sh.; **aspectis**, *pl.*, S3.—Lat. *aspectus*. (**a-⁷**.)

aspert, *adj.* expert, clever, S3; see **apert¹**.

aspie, *sb.* spy, W, W2; **aspye**, C3; **aspy**, S3.—OF. *espie*.

aspien, *v.* to look after, to watch, S, S3, W, W2.—OF. *espier*. See **espye**.

a-spillen, *v.* to destroy, kill, S. (**a-¹**.)

aspiyng, *sb.* ambush, W.

aspre, *adj.* rough, cruel, fierce, NED.—OF. *aspre*; Lat. *asprum*, rough, harsh.

asprely, *adv.* roughly, fiercely, S3; **asperliche**, NED.

a-squint, *adv.* obliquely, out at the corner of the eyes, S.

ass-; see also words beginning in **as-**.

assay, *sb.* trial, experiment, an attempt, attack, tested quality, NED, S2, S3, C2, C3; **asaie**, W.—AF. *assai (asai)*; It. *assaggio*; Lat. *exagium*, a weighing, from *ex-agere (exigere)*, to weigh, prove, to drive out the tongue of the balance.

assayen, *v.* to examine, to attack, S2, S3, C2, P; **asaien**, W2; **asayen**, S3; **assaied**, *pp.*, W.—AF. *assayer (asayer)*: It. *assaggiare*.

assemble, *sb.* assembly, P.—OF. *asemblee*.

assemblen, *v.* to bring together, to come together, NED; **assembled**, *pp.*, C3.—OF. *asembler*; Lat. *assimulare*.

assiduel, *adj.* continual, H; **asseduel**, H.—OF. *assiduel*.

assiduelly, *adv.* continually, H.

assoilen, *v.* to loosen, absolve, explain, PP, S3, C3; see **asoylen**.

assoillyng, *sb.* absolution, acquittal, C.

13

astate, *sb.* state, estate, S3; see **estat.**

a-sterten, *v.* to start up, to happen, to escape, NED, S2, S3, C3, C; **astart**, S3; **asterted**, *pt. s.*, S2, C3. (**a-**¹.)

a-sti3en, *v.* to proceed, ascend, descend, MD; **astighð**, *pr. s.*, S; **astah**, *pt. s.*, S.—AS. *á-stígan.* (**a-**¹.)

astonen, *v.* to stupefy, amaze, NED; **astony**, NED, C2; **astonyed**, *pp.*, W, PP; **astoynde**, S3.—OF. *estoner*; Late Lat. **extonare*, to stupefy as with a thunderbolt. (**a-**⁹.)

astore, *v.* to repair, to provide, store, NED; **astorede**, *pt. s.*, S2; **astored**, *pp.*, C; **astorid**, W2.—AF. *estōrer*, OF. *estaurer*; Lat. *instaurare.* (**a-**¹⁰.) Cf. **enstore.**

a-strangeled, *pp.* suffocated, S2, (**a-**⁶.) See **strangelyn.**

astronomye, *sb.* astronomy, PP.—OF. *astronomie*; Lat. *astronomia*; Gr. ἀστρονομία.

astronomyen, *sb.* astronomer, astrologer, PP; **astromyenes**, *pl.* (= Lat. magi), W; **astrymyanes**, PP.—OF. *astronomien.*

asure, *sb.* azure, NED, C2, C.—OF. *asur*, *azur*; Low Lat. *lazur (lazulus)*; Pers. *lajward.*

aswagen, *v.* to assuage, C2, PP.—AF. *as(s)uager*: Prov. *assuaviar*; from Lat. *suauis.* (**a-**⁷.)

a-swelten, *v.* to die, S, NED. (**a-**¹.)

aswithe, *adv.* as quickly as possible, S2, PP; **asswythe**, S2; see **alswiþe.**

a-swowne, *pp.* as *adv.* aswoon, C2; **assowe**, HD.—AS. *ge-swógen*, see NED (s.v. *aswoon*) and SkD (s.v. *swoon*). (**a-**⁶.)

a-syde, *adv.* aside, C2. (**a-**².)

at-¹, *prefix*, at; **et-**; **a-.**—AS. *æt-.*

at-², *prefix*, from, away; **et-.**—AS. *æt-* for *oð-* proclitic form of **úð-*, away: Goth. *unþa-*; cf. Du. *ont-*, OHG. *int-* (G. *ent-*).

at¹, *pron. rel.* and *conj.* that, S2, S3, H, NED; see **þat.**

at¹, *prep.* at, in, with, from, of, amongst, PP, S, S2, C2; **et**, S; **æt**, S; **ed**, S; **at**, *used with the infin. mood*, S2, NED (vi), H. *Comb.*:—**atte**, at the, PP, S, S2, C2; **ate**, S, S2; **ette**, S; **eter**, S; **atten**, S2, PP; **at-after**, after, C2; **att-alle**, in every way, S2; **at-foren**, before, MD; **et-foren**, S; **at-uore**, S2; **at-om**, at home, S2, PP; **at-on**, at one, in accord, NED, S; **at oon**, G (s.v. *oon*), C2; **at-ones**, at once, together, PP, C2, C3; **attonis**, S3; **attonys**, S3; **attones**, S3.

atache, *v.* to arrest, indict, S2, PP; **attache**, PP; **atteche**, S3, NED; **atachet**, *pp.*, S2, PP.—AF. *attacher*; cf. It. *attaccare.* (**a-**⁷.)

a-take, *v.* to overtake, catch, C3, HD, NED. *Phr.*: **wel atake**, well caught, NED. (**a** 1.)

atamen, *v.* to cut into, broach, open (a vessel), NED, PP, HD; **attamen**, HD,

Prompt., C2.—OF. *atamer*: Prov. *(en)- tamenar*; Lat. *attaminare.* (**a-**⁷.)

atazir, *sb.* influence (astrological term), S2, S3. Cf. Sp. *atazir*; Arab. *at-tâthîr*, *'al + tâthîr*, influence, see Steingass, *Arab. Dict.*, p. 157, and Dozy's *Glossary*, s.v. *atacir.*

at-beren, *v.* to bear away, NED; **atbar**, *pt. s.*, HD.—AS. *æt-beran.* (**at-**².)

at-breken, *v.* to break away, escape, NED. (**at-**².)

at-bresten, *v.* to burst away, escape, NED.—AS. *(æt-bærstan.* (**at-**².)

ate, *sb.* eating, S. See **eten.**

atel, *adj.* terrible; **atell**, NED.—AS. *atol*; cf. Icel. *atall.*

atelich, *adj.* horrible, S; **eatelich**, S.—AS. *atelic.*

ateliche, *adv.* horribly, S.—AS. *atelice.*

atempre, *pp.* as *adj.* temperate, H; **attempre**, C, HD.—OF. *atempré*; Lat. *attemperatus.* (**a-**⁷.)

atemprely, *adv.* temperately, H, HD.

a-tenden, *v.* to set on fire, kindle, MD; **atend**, *pr. s.*, S. (**a-**².) Cf. **ontenden.**

at-ewen, *v.* to show; to appear; **atewede**, *pt. s.*, NED; **atywede**, S; **atawed**, *pp.*, MD.—AS. *æt-éawan (æt-ýwan)*: Goth. *at-augjan*, from *augo*, the eye; cf. OHG. *ougen*, to show (Otfrid). Cf. **awnen.** (**at-**¹.)

ateynt, *pp.* convicted, affected with sorrow, PP; **atteynt**, S3; **attaynt**, S3.—OF. *ateint*, pp. of *ateindre*, to attain; Lat. *attingere.* (**a-**⁷.)

at-fallen, *v.* to fall away, NED.—AS. *æt- feallan.* (**at-**².)

at-fleon, *v.* to flee away, NED; **atfliþ**, *pr. s.*, S.—AS. *æt-fléon.* (**at-**².)

at-fore, *prep.* before, NED; **atuore**, S2; **etforen**, S; **afore**, NED.—AS. *æt-foran.* (**at-**¹.) Cf. **afore.**

at-gangen, *v.* to go away, MD; **atgo**, MD, NED. (**at-**².)

at-holden, *v.* to withhold, retain, S; **athælde**, S; **ethalden**, S; **athalde**, S; **etholden**, S; **ethalt**, *pr. s.*; S; **atheold**, *pt. s.*, S; **atholde**, *pp.*, S.—AS. *óð-healdan.* (**at-**².)

atiffen, *v.* to adorn, deck the person, S.—OF. *atiffer*, cf. *atifer* (Cotg.) (**a-**⁷.)

atisen, *v.* to stir up, urge, entice, NED; **attyse**, HD; **attice**, NED.—OF. *atiser*, to kindle (Bartsch); Late Lat. *attitiare*, from *ad + titium* (for *titio*) a brand (Voc.), see Ducange, s.v. *atticinari.* For the change of *ti* into soft *s* as well as into *ç* see Brachet, s.v. *agencer.* (**a-**⁷.)

atlien, *v.* to think, suppose, intend, to direct one's way, to go, MD; **attle**, MD; **attele**, S2; **etlien**, MD; **etteleden**, *pt. pl.*, S2.—Icel. *ætla (etla)*; related to OHG. *ahtón*, to consider.

atlinge, *sb.* purpose, conjecture, MD; **etlunge**, S.

at-reden, *v.* to outdo in counsel, C, NED. (**at-**[2].)

at-rennen, *v.* to run away, to surpass in running, C, MD; **att-rann**, *pt. s.*, S; **atornde**, NED. (**at-**[2].)

at-rinen, *v.* to touch, to befall, NED; **attryne**, MD.—AS. *æt-hrínan.* (**at-**[1].)

at-routen, *v.* to rush away, escape, S2; **atruten**, NED. From AS. *hrútan.* (**at-**[2].)

at-scheoten, *v.* to shoot away, MD; **atschet**, *pt. s.*, S; **atschote**, *pp.* NED. (**at-**[2].)

at-stonden[1], *v.* to withstand, S; **edstonden**, S, NED. (**at-**[2].)

at-stonden[1], *v.* to remain, to stop, NED, S2; **etstonden**, NED; **atstonde**, *pp.*, S.—AS. *æt-standan.* (**at-**[1].)

att-; see also words beginning in **at-**.

attame, *v.* to broach, to cut into, HD, C2; see **atamen**.

atteir, *sb.* attire, S3; see **ayre**.

atter, *sb.* poison, venom, esp. of reptiles, NED, S; **hatter**, NED.—AS. *attor*, for *ātor*, *átr*, (Voc.); cf. OHG. *eitar, eittar* (Otfrid).

atter-coppe, *sb.* spider, NED, S; **attercop**, HD.—AS. *attor-coppa.*

atter-lich, *adj.* venomous, bitter; **atter-luche**, NED.

atter-liche, *adv.* bitterly, NED.

atter-lothe, *sb.* an antidote to poison, applied spec. to various plants, NED, Voc., HD.—AS. *attor-láðe.*

attern, *adj.* venomous, cruel, HD, NED; **hatterne**, NED.—AS. *ættern, ættren.* See **atter**.

attice, *v.* to stir up, NED; see **atisen**.

attour, *sb.* array, dress, head-dress, HD; **atour**, NED; **aturn**, S.—OF. *atour, aturn*, from *aturner, atorner*; Lat. *ad + tornare*, to round off.

attri, *adj.* venomous, S, HD; **attriȝ**, NED; **wattri**, S2.—AS. *ættrig.* See **atter**.

a-tweyne, in twain, PP. (**a-**[2].)

at-witen[1], *v.* to reproach, twit, S.—AS. *æt-wítan.* (**at-**[1].)

at-witen[2], *v.* to depart, NED; **atwot**, *pt. s.*, MD. (**at-**[2].)

a-two, in two, S2, C2, C3, PP; **ato**, S2. (**a-**[2].)

a-twynne, in two, apart, W, G, PP; **atwinne**, C3; **atwynny**, W; **otwinne**, S; **otwyn**, H. (**a-**[2].)

atyre, *sb.* equipment, dress, head-dress, PP, Cath.; **atir**, S2; **atteir**, S3; **atyr**, HD.

atyren, *v.* to attire, NED; **atyred**, *pp.*, PP; **atired**, PP; **tyred**, S2.—OF. *atirer.* (**a-**[7].)

ath, *sb.* oath, S; see **oþ**[2].

athamant, *sb.* adamant, NED; **athamaunte**, C; see **adamant**.

athel, *adj.* and *sb.* of good birth, noble, a lord, NED, S, S2; **hathel**, NED, S2; **hathill**, NED; **hatell**, NED.—AS. *æðele, eðele*: OS. *eðili*: OTeut. *apalis*, of good family, from *apal*, race, family; cf. OHG. *adal* (Otfrid).

apeling, *sb.* a member of a noble family, a noble, a prince of the blood royal, NED; **eþelyng**, S.

a-þestrien, *v.* to darken, S.—AS. *á-þéostrian.* (**a-**[1].)

a-þet, *conj.* until that, S. See **oþ**[1].

auchtene, *num.* eighteen, S3; see **eightene**.

aucte, *sb.* property, S; see **auhte**[1].

auctoritee, *sb.* authority, C2, C3; **autorite**, S3; **auctorite**, C.—AF. *autorite, auctorite*; Lat. *auctoritatem.*

auctour, *sb.* author, C, C2, HD; **auctor**, S3; **autour**, S3, NED.—AF. *autour*; Lat. *auctorem*, from *augere*, to make to grow, to originate.

augrim, *sb.* arithmetic, S; see **algorisme**.

auh, *conj.* but, S; see **ac**.

auht, *adj.* worthy, valiant, doughty, NED (s.v. *aught*); **aȝt**, S2, MD; **oht**, S; **aht**, NED; **æht**, MD.—AS. *áwiht (áht)*. Cf. **ought**.

auhte[1], *sb.* possessions, NED; **auht**, S2; **ahte**, S2; **eahte**, MD; **ahhte**, S; **agte**, S, S (15. 2090); **eihte**, MD, S; **echte**, S; **ehte**, S; **eyhte**, S; **aihte**, S; **ayhte**, S; **aucte**, S; **aght**, S2.—AS. *æht*: Goth. *aihts*. See **owen**[1].

auhte[2], *pt. s.* ought, S; **aucte**, owned, S; see **owen**[1].

aul, *sb.* an awl; **aule**, NED; **owel**, S; **aules**, *pl.*, S.—AS. *awel* (Voc.); cf. OHG. *ala* (G. *ahle*).

aulf, *sb.* elf, SkD; **auph**, SkD; **awf**, HD; **ouphe**, Sh.; **oaf**, SkD.—Icel. *álfr*. Cf. **elf**.

aumener, *sb.* an alms-purse, a purse, NED, HD.—OF. *aumoniere*; Low Lat. *almosinaria* (*bursa*).

aumoner, *sb.* almoner, alms-giver, NED; **aumonere**, S2, NED; **aumenere**, HD; **amner**, HD.—OF. *aumoner*; Church Lat. *almosinarius*, from *alimosina*. See **almesse**.

aun-; see also words beginning in **an-**.

auncel, *sb.* a kind of balance and weight, NED, S2, PP; **auncer**, PP; **auncere**, P, HD.—AF. *auncelle* for *launcelle*; Late Lat. *lancella* (cf. It. *lancella*), 'a kind of measure', (Florio); dim. of Lat. *lanx (lancem)*, a plate, a scale of a balance.

auncessour, *sb.* ancestor, NED; **ancessour**, NED, HD.—AF. *ancessur*; Lat. *antecessorem.*

auncetre, *sb.* predecessor, ancestor, NED, S2, CM; **ancestre**, NED; **auncestre**, NED; **aunsetters**, *pl.*, NED, HD; **aunceteres**, HD.—AF. *auncestre, ancestre*; Lat. *ante-cessor.*

auncien, *adj.* old, whilom, ex-; *sb.* an old man, an elder (title of dignity), a senior member of an Inn of Court, NED; **auncient**, S3 (25. 136), HD.—AF. *auncien*, OF. *ancien*; Late Lat. *antianum* (cf. It. *anziano*), for *ante-anum*, from Lat. *ante*, before.

auncre, *sb.* anchoress, nun, S2; see **ancre**.

aunder, *sb.* afternoon, HD; see **undern**.

aunders-meat, *sb.* afternoon's collation, Cotg. (s.v. *reciné*), HD. Cf. Goth. *undaurnimats*.

aungel, *sb.* angel, messenger, W; **aunge**, HD; **aungeles**, *pl.*, S2, C3; **aungels**, W2 (Ps. 90. 11).—AF. *angele*. Cf. **angel**, **engel**[2].

auntour, *sb.* chance, adventure, S2; **aunter**, S3. *Comb.*: **anaunter**, for **an aunter**, in case, S2; see **aventure**.

auntren, *v.* to adventure, S3, G, PP.—OF. *aventurer*.

auntrous, *adj.* adventurous, C2, PP.

auter, *sb.* altar, S, S2, C, C2, C3, P, W, W2; **awter**, S3, HD.—OF. *auter, alter*; Lat. *altare*.

autorite, *sb.* authority, C; see **auctoritee**.

autour, *sb.* author, S3; see **auctour**.

au- (av-); see also words beginning in **af-**.

auailen, *v.* to avail, PP; **auailȝe**, B; **auaille**, C2, PP, S2; **auayle**, PP, Prompt.; **awayled**, *pt. s.*, S2.—Cf. OF. *vail(l)e*, from *valoir*; Lat. *ualere*.

aual, *imp. s.* fell, cause to fall, S; see **afallen**.

aualen, *v.* to descend, to lower, MD, S2, S3, B; **availl**, B; **availed**, *pp.*, S3.—OF. *avaler*, from phr. *à val*; Lat. *ad uallem*, to the valley. (**a-**[7].)

auarous; see **averous**.

auaunce, *v.* to advance, NED, S3, C, C3, P; **awance**, S3; **avaunset**, *pp.*, S2; **auanced**, S2.—OF. *avancer*.

auauncement, *sb.* advancement, G; **auancement**, S2.

auaunt[1], *adv.* forward, away, NED.—AF. *avaunt*, OF. *avant*; Late Lat. *ab-ante*.

auaunt[2], *interj.* away! begone! NED.

avaunt[3], *sb.* boast, vaunt, C, NED. See **avaunten**.

auauntage, *sb.* superiority, advantage, NED, S3, C; **auantage**, S2, C3.—AF. *avantage*, from *avant*, before.

avaunten, *v.* to speak proudly of, to commend, to boast, NED, W2.—OF. *avanter*; Lat. *ad* + Late Lat. *vanitare*, to boast. (**a-**[7].)

avauntour, *sb.* boaster, C; **auaunter**, NED.—OF. *avanteur*. (**a-**[7].)

auentaille, *sb.* the moveable front of a helmet, C2, HD.—AF. *aventaille*, OF. *esventail*; Late Lat. **exventaculum*, airhole. (**a-**[9].)

auente, *v.* to get air by opening the aventaille, HD, NED.

auenture, *sb.* chance, a chance occurrence, jeopardy, S, S3, C, C3, G, PP; **auentur**, S2; **auntour**, S2; **aunter**, S3, PP; **antur**, MD; **eventour**, HD. *Comb.*: **an auenture**, lest perchance, PP; **on auenture**, in case, PP; **anaunter**, for **an aunter**, S2; **in auenture**, PP.—AF. *aventure*; Lat. *aduentura*, a thing about to happen. (**a-**[7].)

auer, *sb.* property, a beast of burden, HD.—AF. *aver* (pl. *avers*); OF. *aveir* (*avoir*); Lat. *habere*, to have.

auere; see **afure**.

auerous, *adj.* greedy, H, HD, CM; **auerouse**, W, W2, PP; **auarous**, S2, PP, NED.—OF. *averus*. See **aver**.

Auerylle, *sb.* April, NED; **Aueril**, S2; **Auerel**, PP.—OF. *avril*; Lat. *aprilis*, from *aperire*. See **apert**[2].

a-ulem, *imp. s.* drive away, S; see **aflemen**.

auoide, *v.* to empty, to make of no effect, to make void, to remove, to move away, retire, to avoid, NED, W; **auoyde**, W; **auoyd**, WW, Sh.; **auoided**, *pp.*, W, W2.—AF. *avolder*; OF., *esvuidier*; *es*, out + *vuidier*, to empty. (**a-**[9].)

auote, *adv.* on foot, S2; see **afote**.

avouter, *sb.* adulterer, W2; **avowtere**, Prompt.—OF. *avoutre, aöutre*; Lat. *adulterum*. For intercalated *v*, see Brachet (s.v. *corvée*).

avoutrer, *sb.* adulterer, HD; **auoutreris**, *pl.*, W; **avowtreris**, W2.

avoutresse, *sb.* adulteress, W.—OF. *avoutresse*.

avoutrie, *sb.* adultery, PP, CM, W, HD; **avoutry**, Cath.; **avowtrie**, NED, W; **avowtery**, NED; **auowtries**, *pl.*, W.—OF. *avoutrie, aöuterie, aülterie*; Lat. *adulterium*.

auowe, *sb.* vow, S3, PP, Prompt.; **auow**, S2, C, C3, G; **auou**, PP; **auowis**, *pl.*, W, W2.

avowen[1], *v.* to bind with a vow, NED, W (Acts 23. 14), P.—OF. *avoer*; Late Lat. *advotare*, from Lat. *uotum*; from *uouere*. (**a-**[7].)

avowen[1], *v.* to call upon or own as defender, patron, or client, to avow, acknowledge, NED, S3, C3, PP.—AF. *avower*, OF. *avouer*; *avoer*; Lat. *ad-vocare*. (**a-**[7].)

avowry, *sb.* patronage, a patron saint, NED; **vorie**, NED.—AF. *avouerie*, from OF. *avoeor*; Lat. *aduocatorem*.

avoy, *interj.* oh! oy!, exclamation of surprise, fear, remonstrance, NED, C, HD.—OF. *avoi*.

auys, *sb.* opinion, advice, C3; **avise**, PP.—OF. *avis*.

auyse, *v.* to observe, consider, give advice, S2, C2, C3, H, PP; **auisen**, PP, S2.—AF. *aviser*; Late Lat. *advisare*. (**a-**[7].)

auysely, *adv.* advisedly, H; **auisili**, W.

auysement, *sb.* consideration, C2; **auisement**, S2.

auysyon, *sb.* vision, S3; **auision**, C, S2.—OF. *avision* (Bartsch).

aw-; see also words beginning in **au-**.

a-wakenen, *v. intrans.* to awake, S; **awakenin**, S; **awakened**, *pp.*, S.—AS. *onwæcnan*. (**a-²**.)

a-wakien, *v. intrans.* to awake, S; **awalk** (*for* **awakk**?), *imp.*, S3; **awoik**, *pt. s.*, S3; **awoilk** (*for* **awoikk**?), S3.—AS. *awacian* (for *on-wacian*). (**a-²**.)

awarien; see **awerien**.

a-way, *adv.* on way, onward, along, away (from a place), NED; **awai**, PP; **awezz**, S; **awei**, S; **ewei**, S2; **owai**, S2; **aweye**, C3, PP; **away**, *interj.* away!, S2, NED.—AS. *aweg, on weg*. (**a-²**.)

awayte¹, *v.* to await, watch, S2, S3, PP; **awaite**, PP; **awaitie**, NED.—AF. *awaitier*; OF. *aguaitier*. (**a-⁷**.)

awayte², *sb.* a lying in wait, watching, NED, C.—AF. *await*; OF. *aguait*.

away-ward, *adv.*, *adj.* turned away, wayward, NED, PP **awaywarde** passing away, H.

awe, *sb.* awe, C, C2; **aʒe**, NED.—Icel. *agi* (OTeut. **agon*). Cf. **eʒe¹**.

a-wecchen, *v.* to arouse out of sleep, NED, HD; **aweihte**, *pt. s.*, NED; **aweightte**, HD; **aweht**, *pp.*, NED.—AS. *á-weccan*; cf. OHG. *ar-wekkan* (Tatian): Goth. *uswakjan*. (**a-¹**.)

a-weden, *v.* to become mad, S2, NED.—AS. *á-wédan*. (**a-¹**.)

a-wei, *interj.* ah woe! alas! S.

a-welden, *v.* to control, S, NED.—AS. *gewealdan*. (**a-⁶**.)

a-wenden¹, *v.* to go away, NED.—AS. *á-wendan*. (**a-¹**.)

a-wenden², *v.* to change to, NED; **awente**, *pt. s.*, S.—AS. *on-wendan*. (**a-²**.)

a-werien, *v.* to curse, S; **awariede**, *pt. s.*, S.—AS. *á-wergian*. (**a-¹**.)

a-weʒen, *v.* to weigh out, NED; **awiðhst**, *2 pr. s.*, S.—AS. *á-wegan*. (**a-¹**.)

a-winnen, *v.* to win, NED; **awynne**, S.—AS. *á-winnan*. (**a-¹**.)

awke, *adj.* turned the wrong way, sinister, perverse, NED, Prompt.—Icel. *afugr*.

awke-ward, *adv.* in the wrong direction, NED; **awkwart**, S3.

awnen, *v.* to show, NED; **awwnenn**, S.—Related to OHG. *ougen*, to show (Otfrid); from *ougá*, eye. See **atewen**.

a-wondrien, *v.* to be astonished, NED; **awondered**, *pp.*, S2.—AS. *of-wundrian*. (**a-³**.)

a-wreken, *v.* to take vengeance, to avenge, NED, S2, P; **awreke**, *pp.*, S, G, PP; **awroke**, P.—AS. *á-wrecan*. (**a-¹**.)

axen¹, *sb.* ashes, S. *Comb.*: **axe-waddle**, an indolent stay-at-home, HD; see **asche**.

axen², *v.* to ask, S, S2, S3, C2, C3, W, W2; **axien**, S2; see **asken**.

axer, *sb.* asker, W. *Phr.*: **maistirful axer** (= Lat. *exactor*), W; **axere**, W2.

axinge, *sb.* Asking, C3; **axyngis**, *pl.*, W, W2.

ay¹, *adv.* ever, S, S2, S3, C2, H; **ai**, S, S2; **aʒʒ**, S.—Icel. *ei*. Cf. **o²**; cf. **a⁴**.

ay², *sb.* egg, G, HD; **ayren**, *pl.*, MD; see **ey**.

ayel, *sb.* grandfather, forefather, C; **ayeles**, *pl.*, PP.—OF. *aïel*, *aïol*: Pr. *aviol*; Late Lat. *aviolus*, dimin. of Lat. *auus*; see Brachet.

ayen, *prep.*, *adv.* against, back, S; see **aʒein**.

ayen-wende, *v.* to return, S.

aynd, *sb.* breath, B; see **onde**.

aynding, *sb.* smelling, B; see **ondyng**.

ayr, *sb.* oar, B; see **ore¹**.

ay-where, *adv.* everywhere, S2, NED; **aywhere**, H; **aywhore**, S2; **aiware**, S; **aihware**, S; **aihwer**, SD.—AS. *é-g-hwǽr*. Cf. **owher**.

a-ʒefen, *v.* to give, give up, give back, MD, S; **aʒeuen**, MD; **aʒiuen**, MD; **aʒeoue**, S; **aʒaf**, *pt. s.*, S; **a-iauen**, *pl.*, S.—AS. *á-gifan*. (**a-¹**.)

a-ʒein, *prep.*, *adv.*, *conj.*, opposite to, towards, against, in return for, again, PP, S, S2, G; **aʒeuen**, PP, S2; **aʒen**, PP, S, S2, G, W, W2; **agayn**, S2, S3, C2, PP; **agen**, S; **agen**, W, W2, PP; **aʒeins**, PP; **aʒeyns**, PP; **ayeins**, C2; **ageyns**, S3, C2; **agayns**, C2, C3, PP; **igaines**, S; **oʒeines**, S; **oganis**, S2; **ogaines**, S2; **ogaynes**, S2; **onn-ʒænness**, S. (**a-²**.)

a-ʒeines, *prep.* and *conj.* against, contrary to, in return for, PP, S; **aʒeynes**, PP; **aʒenes**, S, S2; **agenes**, S; **agænes**, S; **aʒens**, S2, W, W2, PP; **aʒeins**, PP; **aʒeyns**, PP; **ayeins**, C2; **ageyns**, S3, C2; **agayns**, C2, C3, PP; **igaines**, S; **oʒeines**, S; **oganis**, S2; **ogaines**, S2; **ogaynes**, S2; **onn-ʒænness**, S. (**a-²**.)

a-ʒeinst, *prep.* and *conj.* against, MD; **aʒeynst**, PP.

aʒen¹, *v.* to have, to be obliged, to owe, S; see **owen¹**.

aʒen², *adj.* own, S; see **owen²**.

aʒen³, *prep.*, *adv.* against, back, S; see **aʒein**.

aʒen-bien, *v.* to buy back, NED, W2; **aʒeenbieth**, *pr. s.*, NED, W2, S2; **aʒenbouʒt**, W2.

aʒen-biere, *sb.* redeemer, NED, W, W2.

aʒen-biyng, *sb.* redemption, NED, W.

aʒen-clepe, *v.* to recall, W, W2.

aʒen-fiʒtinge, *pr. p.* fighting against, W.

aʒen-risyng, *sb.* resurrection, NED.

aʒen-seyen, *v.* to say nay, to contradict, NED; **aʒenseie**, W, W2.

aȝen-stonden, *v.* to withstand, NED, W; **aȝenstood**, *pt. s.*, W2.

aȝen-ward, *adv.* backward, in reply, over again, NED, W, S3; **aȝeinward**, S2; **agaynward**, S2, C3.

a-ȝer, in the year, S2. (**a-**[2].)

aȝte, *num.* eight, S2; **aȝt**, S2; see **eighte**[1].

aȝt-sum, *adj.* eight in all, S2.

B

ba, *adj.* and *conj.* both, S.—AS. *bá*, both.
baar, *pt. s.* bare, carried, C, W; see **beren**[1].
babelen, *v.* to babble, P.
babelyng, *sb.* babbling, S3.
baber-lipped, *adj.* having thick lips, P, Prompt.
babishe, *adj.* babyish, S3.
bacheler, *sb.* a bachelor, an unmarried man, C, C2; a novice in the church, or arms, young knight, P.—OF. *bacheler*.
bachelerie, *sb.* state of bachelor, CM, MD; **bachelrye**, company of young men, C2.—OF. *bachelerie*.
bacin, *sb.* basin, cymbal, a light helmet, MD; **bacyn**, helmet, MD.—OF. *bacin*.
bacinet, *sb.* helmet, MD; **bacenett**, Prompt.; **basnetes**, *pl.*, S3.—OF. *bacinet*.
bacoun, *sb.* bacon, C, PP; **bacon**, PP.—OF. *bacon*.
bad[1], *pt. s.* prayed, S; see **bidden**.
bad[2], *pt. s.* bade, C2; see **beden**.
badde, *adj.* bad, PP; **badder**, *comp.* worse, C2.
baddeliche, *adv.* badly, PP, HD.
bade, *pt. s.* remained, S3; see **biden**.
bagage, *sb.* dregs, refuse, S3; **baggage**, ND.
baid, *pt. pl.* remained, S3; see **biden**.
baie, *in phr.*: **to baie**, at bay, S2; see **bay**.
baili[1], *sb.* stewardship, *villicatio*, W; **baillye**, power of a bailiff, G.—OF. *bailie*, power.
baili[2], *sb.* steward, *villicus*, W; **baillif**, bailiff, C; **bailliues**, *pl.*, bailiffs, P; **bayllyues**, P.—OF. *baillif*.
baill, *sb.* sorrow, S3; see **bale**.
bair, *adj.* bare, S3; see **bare**[4].
bairnis, *sb. pl.* bairns, S3; see **barn**.
baiten, *v.* to feed, C2, S3; **bayte**, S2, C3.—Icel. *beita*.
bak, *sb.* back, PP, C; cloth for the back, cloak, coarse mantle, C3; **bac**, S.—AS. *bæc*.
bak-biten, *v.* to backbite, slander, P.
bak-bitere, *sb.* backbiter, S.
bak-bitynge, *sb.* backbiting, P.
baken, *v.* to bake, MD; **boke**, *pt. s.*, MD; **book**, MD; **baken**, *pp.*, P; **bakenn**, S; **bake**, C, C2, P; **y-baken**, P; **y-bake**, P.—AS. *bacan*.
bakere, *sb.* baker, MD; **bakers**, *pl.*, PP.
bakestere, *sb.* baker, P; **baxter**, NED, P.—AS. *bæcestre*, woman-baker (also used of men).
bald; see **bold**.
balde, *pt. s.* encouraged, S; see **bolden**.

bale, *sb.* sorrow, misfortune, death, S, C3; destruction, S2; **baill**, S3; **bales**, *pl.*, evils, torments, H; **balys**, S3.—AS. *bealu*.
bale-drinch, *sb.* a deadly drink, S.
bale-ful, *adj.* baleful, evil, MD.—AS. *bealoful*.
bale-fully, *adv.* miserably; **balfully**, S2, MD.
balene, *sb.* whale, S2, Voc.—Lat. *balaena*.
bali, *adj.* grievous, S, NED.—AS. *bealu*, baleful: Goth. *balws* (in compounds).
balies, *sb. pl.* bellies, S2, PP; see **bely**.
balke, *sb.* balk, beam, ridge, MD; **balks**, *pl.* ridges, divisions of land, S3; **balkes**, P.—AS. *balca*.
balled, *adj.* bald, C, PP; **ballede**, S2, PP.
baly; see **bely**.
ban, *sb.* bone, S, S2; **banes**, *pl.*, S2; see **bon**[1].
band, *pt. s.* bound, S; see **binden**.
bane, *sb.* destruction, death, bane, poison, PP, C; **bone**, PP.—AS. *bana, bona*.
banere[1], *sb.* banner, S, PP, Prompt.; **baner**, S2, C, PP.—OF. *baniere*.
banere[2], *sb.* banner-bearer, NED.—OF. *banere*; Low Lat. *bannator*; from *bannum*, *bandum*, standard.
baneur, *sb.* banner-bearer, S2; see **banyour**.
bank, *sb.* a bank, tumulus, PP; **bonk**, S2; **bonkis**, *pl.*, S3; **bonkez**, S2.
bannen, *v.* to ban, curse, summon, S2, S3, P; to forbid, prohibit severely, P; **bonnen**, MD; **i-banned**, *pp.*, S.
bannyng, *sb.* cursing, H.
ban-wort, *sb.* bone-wort, S3, MD; see **bon**[1].
banyour, *sb.* banner-bearer, MD, S2; **banyowre**, Prompt.; **banyer**, MD; **baneur**, S2, NED; **baneoure**, PP.—AF. *baneour*, OF. *baneor*; Low Lat. *bannatorem*.
baptym, *sb.* baptism, S2, W; **baptimys**, *pl.* W. OF. *baptismo*.
bar, *pt. s.* bare, S, S2, C2; see **beren**[1].
barayn, *adj.* barren, S3; see **bareyne**.
barbarik, *sb.* barbarian, W.
barbarus, *sb.* barbarian, W.
barberyns, *sb. pl.* heathen men, W.
barbour, *sb.* barber, C, NED; **barboure**, Prompt.—AF. *barbour*, OF. *barbeor*; Late Lat. *barbatorem*.
barbre, *adj.* barbarous, S2, C3.
bare[1], *sb.* bier, S; see **beere**.
bare[2], *sb.* a wave, billow, NED, S2 (8b. 38); **beres**, *pl.*, NED; **bieres**, MD; **beares**, MD.—Icel. *bára*.
bare[3], *sb.* boar, S2; see **boor**.

bare⁴, *adj.* bare, simple, single, sheer, S, C; **bair**, bare, worn alone, S3. *Comb.*: **baruot**, barefoot, S.

bare⁵, *sb.* the open country, S; naked skin, W.

barel, *sb.* barrel, C2.—OF. *baril.*

baren, *v.* to make bare, uncover, S, MD; **y-bared**, *pp.*, S3.—AS. *barian.*

baret, *sb.* deceit, strife, NED; **barrat**, confusion, S3.—OF. *barat*, fraud; cf. Icel. *barátta*, a contest.

bareyne, *adj.* barren, C, C2, PP; **bareyn**, W2; **barayn**, S3.—OF. *baraigne.*

bareʒ, *sb.* a barrow-pig, S; see **barowe**.

bargane, *sb.* business, strife, combat, S2; **bargayn**, bargain, PP; **bargeynes**, *pl.*, PP.—OF. *bargaine.*

barly, *sb.* barley, MD, PP; **barlic**, S.

barm, *sb.* bosom, S3, C2; **berm**, S.—AS. *bearm.*

barmkyn, *sb.* rampart, S3; **barnekin**, the outermost wall of a castle, HD; **barnekynch**, MD.

barmkyn-wall, *sb.* rampart-wall, S3.

barn, *sb.* bairn, child, S, S2, H, PP; **bern**, S; **barne**, S3, P; **bearnes**, *pl.*, S; **bairnis**, S3.—AS. *bearn.*

barnage, *sb.* childhood, S2, MD.

barnen, *v.* to burn, S, S2; see **bernen**, **brennen**.

barnhede, *sb.* childhood, H, PP.

barn-site, *sb.* sorrow felt for a child, S2, NED.—Icel. *barn-sút.*

barn-team, *sb.* offspring, a family of children, MD; **barntem**, S2.—AS. *bearn-téam.*

baronage, *sb.* the men, vassals of a feudal chief, S; assembly of barons, S2, C3; **barnage**, MD.—OF. *barnage*, Low Lat. *baronagium.*

baroun, *sb.* baron, lord, PP; **baronys**, *pl.* PP.—OF. *baron*, acc. of *bers*, a man, a male.

barowe, *sb.* barrow-pig, MD; **bareʒ**, S, NED.—AS. *bearh.*

barrat, *sb.* confusion, S3; see **baret**.

barre, *sb.* bar of a door, C; bar of justice, G, PP; **barres**, *pl.*, ornament of a girdle, C, PP.—OF. *barre.*

barste, *pt. s.*, burst, S2, PP; see **bresten**.

baselarde, *sb.* dagger, MD, PP, Prompt.; **baslard**, PP.—AF. *baselarde*. OF. *basalart* (cf. Low Lat. *bassilardus*). Probably from Late Lat. *badile*, a billhook; see NED.

basnetes, *sb. pl.*, helmets, S3; see **bacinet**.

bataille, *sb.* battle, S, PP; **bataile**, PP; **batayle**, S2, C, PP; **batayls**, *pl.* battalions, S3.—OF. *bataille.*

bataillen, *v.* to embattle, fortify, MD; **batailed**, *pt.s.*, PP; **bataylld**, *pp.* embattled, C.—OF. *bataillier.*

baten, *v.* to bate, abate, grow less, S2, MD; see **abaten**.

bateren, *v.* to batter, beat, pat, PP.—OF. *bat-*, stem of *batre*, with freq. suffix *-er*.

batte, *sb.* club, staff, bat, Prompt., Voc.; **battis**, *pl.*, W.—OF. *batte.*

battill, *adj.* rich for pasture, S3, JD; **battle**, HD.

baþe, *adj.* and *conj.* both, S, S2; see **boþe**.

baþiere, *sb.* water-pot, S.

baudekyn, *sb.* a gold-embroidered stuff named from Baghdad, MD; **bawdekyn**, Prompt.; **baudkin**, S3.—OF. *baudequin*; Low Lat. *baldakinus*, from It. *Baldacco*, Baghdad.

bauderye, *sb.* unchastity, foul conversation, MD; pandering, CM; **bawdry**, S3.

bauderyk, *sb.* baldric, MD; **bawderyke**, Prompt.; **bawdryk**, C, Voc.

baudry, *sb.* baldric, NED.—OF. *baudrei*, *baldrei.*

baudy, *adj.* dirty, C3, P, Palsg.

bauld; see **bold**.

baundoun, *sb.* discretion, freewill, power, S2; **baundon**, CM.—OF. *bandon*; Low Lat. **bandonem*, from *bandum* for*bannum*, public proclamation.

bausand, *adj.* marked with white, NED.—OF. *bausant*; cf. Prov. *bausan*, It. *balzano.*

bauson, *sb.* badger, MD; **bawsone**, Prompt.; **bawsyn**, Voc.; **bausenez**, *pl.* S2; **baucynes**, MD. See **bausand**.

bawd, *pt. s.* bade, commanded, S3; see **beden**.

bawe-lyne, *sb.* bowline, HD, S2; see **bowe-lyne**.

baxtere, *sb.* female baker, PP; see **bakestere**.

bay, *sb.* noise made by the united songs of birds, S3; barking of dogs, MD, HD. *Phr.*: **to baie**, at bay, S2.—Cf. OF. *abaier*, to bark.

bayard, *sb.* a bay horse, a horse, P, CM; **baiardes**, *pl.*, P. *Phr.*: **blynde bayardes**, i.e. foolish people, lit. blind horses, HD, S3, MD, ND.—Cf. Low Lat. *baiardus.*

bayn, *adj.* ready, willing, obedient, fair, pleasant, easy, good, NED; **bayne**, Manip.; **beyn**, Prompt., S3.—Icel. *beinn.*

bayne, *sb.* bath, S3.—OF. *bain.*

bayske, *adj.* bitter, H, MD; **bask**, MD, HD, JD; **beʒʒsc**, MD.—Icel. *beiskr.*

be-, *prefix.* See in many cases **bi-** words.

beade; see **bidden**.

bearnen; see **bernen**.

bearyng in hand, *sb.* cajolery, false assurances, S3; see **beren**¹.

be-bedden, *v.* to supply with a bed, S.

beche

beche, *sb.* valley, S; **bæch**, MD; **bache**, NED.
be-cheche, *v.* to choke, stifle, S, NED.
bedde, *sb.* bed, PP.—AS. *bedd.*
bedde-strawe, *sb.* bed, couch, *stratum*, Voc.; **bedstre**, W2.
bede, *sb.* prayer, S, H, PP; **beode**, S; **beyde**, S3; **bedes**, *pl.* S2, S3, P; beads, C; **beades**, S3.—AS. *(ge)bed.*
bedel, *sb.* messenger, herald, crier, beadle, H, P; **bedeles**, *pl.* S, H; **bedelles**, P.—OF. *bedel*; cf. AS. *bydel.* Cf. **budele**.
bede-man, *sb.* beadsman, one who prays for another, P; **beodemon**, S2, NED; **beodeman**, PP.
beden, *v.* to command, to offer, S, S2, S3, C2; **beode**, S2; **bedden**, S; **bidden**, S; **beot**, *pr. s.* S; **byt**, C; **bet**, S; **bead**, *pt. s.*, **bed**, S, S2; **bawd**, S3; **bad**, C2, S2; **boden**, *pl.* S; **beden**, S3; **bode**, S2; **bede**, *pp.* S2; **bode**, **bodun**, invited, W; **bodyn**, S2; **bidde**, C3.—AS. *béodan.* {Note that many of the above forms are confused with those of the verb **bidden**.}
bede-sang, *sb.* the singing of the prayers, S, NED.
bedred, *adj.* lying in bed, bed-ridden, CM, PP; **bedreden**, S2, P; **bedrede**, PP.—AS. *bedreda* and *bedrida* (Voc.).
be-drenchen, *v.* to drench completely; **bedreynt**, *pt. pl.*, S3; *pp.* MD.
bed-roll, *sb.* catalogue, ND. See **beyderoule**.
bee-; see also words beginning in **be-**.
bee, *sb.* bee, Voc.; **been**, *pl.* S3, C2, W2; **beys**, S3 (13. 244); **bees**, C2.—AS. *béo.*
beek, *sb.* beak, C2; **bec**, S; **beekis**, *pl.* PP.—OF. *bec.*
beem, *sb.* beam, C, PP; **beom**, S; **bem**, MD.—AS. *béam*, tree, plank.
beere, *sb.* bier, W, CM, MD; **beer**, C; **bare**, S, MD; **beare**, S3; **bere**, HD, MD; **byears**, *pl.* S3.—AS. *bær*; cf. OF. *biere.*
beest, *sb.* beast, C, PP; **best**, PP, C, S, S2; **bestes**, *pl.* S, S2; **beestes**, S2.—OF. *beste*; Lat. *bestia.*
beestli, *adj.* animal, W.
beeten, *v.* to beat, W2, CM; **beten**, S, C; **bet**, *pr. s.* P; **bet**, *imp. s.* S2; **beot**, *pt. s.* P; **beet**, PP; **bet**, S3, PP; **bette**, P; **beten**, *pl.* S; **beeten**, W2; **beten**, *pp.* C2, G; **bete**, C2; **betun**, W2; **y-beten**, C2; **y-bete**, C; **y-bette**, P; **i-beaten**, S; **ibete**, C.—AS. *béatan*, pt. *béot*, pp. *béaten.*
bege, *sb.* collar, S; see **beiȝ.**
beggen, *v.* to beg, PP, C2, Prompt., W (John 9. 8).
beggere, *sb.* beggar, C, PP, W (John 9. 8).
beggestere, *sb.* beggar, C, NED.

benden

be-grime, *v.* to smear, daub all over, S3.
beild; see **belde**[1].
beiȝ, *sb.* a ring, collar, P; **byȝe**, PP; **bege**, collar, S; **bie**, W2; **beies**, *pl.* circlets of metal, S; **biȝes**, P; **behes**, PP.—AS. *béah*: Icel. *baugr.*
bek, *sb.* brook, H, Voc., Prompt., MD; **beckis**, *pl.* H.—Icel. *bekkr.*
bekken, *v.* to nod, C3; **beken**, Prompt.; **beks**, *pr. s.* S3.
beknen, *v.* to beckon, show, S; **bikenen**, W2.—OMerc. *bécnian* (VP).
bel, *adj.* beautiful, PP.—OF. *bel.*
belamp; see **bilimpen.**
belde[1], *sb.* protection, shelter, MD, HD; **beld**, S2; **beild**, S3, JD.—AS. *byldo*, boldness, from *beald.* See **bold.**
belde[2], *adj.* big, blustering, S; see **bold.**
belden, *v.* to build, S3; see **bilden.**
beldinge, *sb.* building, S3.
belle, *sb.* bell, S, C2, PP.—AS. *belle.*
bellyche, *adv.* beautifully, S3, MD. See **bel.**
belphegor, *sb.* Baal Peor, H (p. 376).—Lat. *Belphegor* (Vulg.).
belt, *pp.* built, S3; see **bilden.**
bely, *sb.* belly, bellows, MD, P; **baly**, S3; **below**, *follis*, Voc.; **balies**, *pl.* S2, PP.—AS. *bælg.*
bely-ioye, *sb.* belly-joy, appetite, PP.
belȝen, *v.* to swell, to be angry, MD; **bollȝhenn**, MD; **i-bolȝe**, S.—AS. *belgan*, pt. *bealh*, (pl. *bulgon*), pp. *bolgen.*
bemare, *sb.* trumpeter, S.—AS. *bémere.*
beme, *sb.* trumpet, MD, Voc.; **bemen**, *pl.* S; **beemes**, C; **beamous**, S3.—OMerc. *béme* (VP).
bemen, *v.* to sound a trumpet, S, NED.
bemyng, *sb.* humming of bees, S3, JD.
ben, *v.* to be, PP, S, S2; **been**, C; **bien**, **bienn**, S; **buen**, S2; **beo**, S, S2; **bi**, S, S2; **bue**, **by**, S2; **beonne**, **bienne**, *ger.* S; **beoþ**, *pr. s.* S; **beþ**, **buð**, **byð**, **bið**, S; **beis**, S3; **bes**, S2; **beoþ**, *pl.* S; **bieþ**, S; **buð**, S, S2; **beth**, S2, **buð**, S; **bes**, S2; **bi**, *pr. s. subj.* S; **bie**, S (s.v. *Ibie*); **beo**, *pl.* S; **beth**, *imp. pl.* C2, S2, S3; **byeþ**, S2; **ben**, *pp.* S; **been**, C; **bue**, S2; **be**, S3, C; **y-be**, S2; **iben**, S; **ibeon**, S; **ibeo**, S, S2; **ibe**, S, S2; **ibi**, S.—AS. *béon.*
benam; see **binimen.**
benche, *sb.* bench, Prompt., PP.—AS. *benc.*
benched, *pp.* furnished with benches, SD; **y-benched**, S3.
bend, *sb.* bond, MD; **bendes**, *pl.* S, G; **bende**, *dat.* S, S2, G.—AS. *bend*: Goth. *bandi.*
benden, *v.* to bend, Prompt., MD; **bende**, *pt. s.* MD; **bent**, MD; **bend**, *pl.* S2; **y-bent**,

21

bene

pp. S3; **ye-bent**, S3.—AS. *bendan*, to fasten a band or string to a bow.

bene[1], *sb.* a prayer, S, S2, NED; **benes**, *pl.* S2.—AS. *bén*: OTeut. **bóni-z*, see Sievers, 268.

bene[2], *adj.* pleasant, S, NED.

benefet, *sb.* benefit, PP, MD; **bynfet**, PP; **benfait**, P; **bienfetes**, *pl.* P.—OF. *bienfet*; Lat. *benefactum*.

bent[1], *sb.* coarse grass, small rushes, Manip., Voc., MD, HD.—Cf. OHG. *binuz* (G. *binse*).

bent[2], *sb.* a moor, an open grassy place, NED, S, S3, C. See **bent**[1].

benumde; see **binimen**.

beo-, *prefix*; see **bi-** words.

beo, beoþ; see **ben**.

beode, *v.* to pray, S; see **bidden**.

beodele; see **budele**.

berd, *sb.* beard, S, S2, C; **berde**, P, G; **berdes**, *pl.* S3.—AS. *beard*.

bere[1], *sb.* beer, Prompt.; **ber**, S, MD.—AS. *béor*.

bere[2], *sb.* noise, S, S2, MD, HD; **ber**, S2.—AS. *(ge)bére*; see **ibere**.

bere[3], *sb.* bear, C, MD, PP; **beres**, *pl.* C2; **beores**, PP.—AS. *bera*: OHG. *bero*.

bere[4], *sb.* bier, HD, MD. See **beere**.

bere[5], *sb.* barley, MD; **beir**, S3; **beris**, *gen.*, S3.—AS. *bere*.

bere-lepe, *sb.* basket, H; **berlepe**, H; **barlep**, basket for keeping barley in, HD. See **lepe**.

beren[1], *v.* to bear; **bere**, S, W; **berþ**, *pr. s.*, S2; **beoreð**, *pl.*, S; **bar**, *pt. s.*, S, S2, C2; **bare**, S2; **ber**, S2, C3; **baar**, W; **bure**, S3; **beore**, *pl.*, S; **boren**, *pp.* born, S2; **borun**, W2; **iboren**, S; **iborn**, S; **ibore**, S, S2; **y-boren**, C2; **y-born**, C2; **y-bore**, S2, C2, *Phr.* **bereth on hand**, persuades, makes (him) believe, assures, S3; **berth hir on hond**, beareth false witness against her, C3.—AS. *beran*.

beren[2], *v.* to cry, make a noise, MD, HD; **bere**, to low as a cow, PP; see **bere**[2].

bergh, *sb.* hill, PP; **berghe**, PP; **beruh**, PP; **berwe**, PP; **berghe**, *dat.*, P.—AS. *beorg*; cf. OIr. *bri* (Windisch).

beriall, *adj.* bluish-green, beryl-coloured, S3. See **beril**.

berie, *sb.* berry, C; **bery**, Prompt.; **beries**, *pl.* grapes, S, PP.—AS. *berige*.

berien, *v.* to pierce, strike, MD; **bery**, to thresh, Cath.—Icel. *berja*, to strike; cf. Lat. *ferire*.

beril, *sb.* beryl, MD; **berel**, MD.—OF. *beril*; Lat. *beryllus*; Gr. βήρυλλος.

beringe, *sb.* birth, behaviour, bearing, C2, S; **berynge**, PP; see **beren**[1].

beten

berken, *v.* to bark, S2, PP; **berkyd**, *pt. s.*, S2.—AS. *beorcan*.

berkere, *sb.* watch-dog, PP.

berkyng, *sb.* barking, C.

berme, *sb.* harm, Prompt., S; **berm**, C3.—AS. *beorma*.

bern[1], *sb.* a man, PP, HD; **berne**, PP; **burn**, S2; **burne**, S2; **beorn**, MD; **burnes**, *pl.*, S2; **biernes**, P.—AS. *beorn*.

bern[2], *sb.* barn, C2, MD; **beren**, S (12. 263), MD; **berne**, S; *dat.*, C3, W; **bernes**, *pl.*, W, W2, P.—AS. *bern*: ONorth. *ber-ern*, i.e. barley-house.

bern[3]; see **barn**.

bernacle, *sb.* a snaffle for a horse, W2; **barnacle**, Voc., NED.

bernake[1], *sb.* an instrument set on the nose of unruly horses, Voc.; **bernak**, Prompt.—OF. *bernac*.

bernake[2], *sb.* barnacle, a fabulous kind of goose, S2, MD, NED.—OF. *bernaque*; cf. Low Lat. *bernaca*.

bernen, *v.* to burn, MD, S, S2; **barnen**, MD, S; **bearnen**, S; **beornen**, S; **birnen**, S; **barnde**, *pt. s.*, S2; **barnd**, *pp.*, S2.—AS. *beornan*. Cf. **brennen**.

bersten, *v.* to burst, S, C; see **bresten**.

berstles, *sb. pl.* bristles, C; see **brystylle**.

berwe; see **bergh**.

berynes; see **burinisse**.

ber3en, *v.* to help, deliver, preserve, NED; **berwen**, S; **berr3henn**, S; **beregeð**, *pr. s.*, S; **iborhen**, *pp.*, S; **ibore3e**, S; **iboruwen**, S.—AS. *beorgan*.

besaunt, *sb.* a gold coin named from Byzantium, W, MD; **besauntes**, *pl.*, S3; **besauntis**, W.—OF. *besant*.

besene, besie; see **bisen**.

be-slombred, *pp.* dirtied, bedaubed, S3; **beslombered**, NED.

besme, *sb.* besom, rod, Prompt.; **besmes**, *pl.*, S; **besyms**, W; **besmen**, *dat.*, S.—AS. *besma*.

best, *adj.* and *adv. superl.* best, PP; **beast**, S; **bezste**, S.

beste, *sb.* advantage, S.

be-steriinge, *sb.* bestirring, emotion, S2.

be-swapen, *pp.* convicted, S.—AS. *be-swápen*, pp. of *be-swápan*, to persuade.

bet, *adv. comp.* better, S, C, C2, S2, G; **bette**, P. *Phr.*, **go bet**, go as fast as you can, C3; **betere**, S, S2; **betre**, S, S3; **bettre**, S.

betaken, *v.* to betoken, S2; see **bitoknen**.

beten[1], *v.* to amend, S, S2, P, S3; **beete**, to kindle, C; **beyt**, S3; **bet**, *pr. s.*, S; **beeten**, *pt. pl.*, kindled, C3; **bet**, *pp.*, S, S2; **ibet**, S.—AS. *bétan*, pt. *bétte*, pp. *béted*. See **bote**[2].

beten[2], *v.* to beat, S, C, PP; see **beeten**.

22

be-thenchinge, *sb.* thinking upon, meditation, S2. See **biþenken.**
beuer, *sb.* beaver, S, Voc.; **beuveyr**, S.—AS. *befer* (*beofer*); cf. OHG. *bibar.*
beyde-roule, *sb.* bead-roll, prayer-roll, catalogue of persons for whom prayers are to be said, S3; **beadroll, bedroll**, ND. See **bede.**
beye[1], *v.* to buy, CM, C3; see **biggen**[2].
beye[2], *adj.* both, S2; **beien**, S; **beyne**, S.—AS. *begen.*
beyer, *adj. gen.* of both, PP; **beire**, PP, MD; **beyre**, MD.—AS. *begra.*
beyn, *adj.* pliant, flexible, pleasant, S3, Prompt.; see **bayn.**
bi-, *prefix*, also **be-, by-, beo-, b-.**
bi-bled, *pp.* covered with blood, C; **bybled**, MD; **bebledd**, S2, S3.
bi-burien, *v.* to bury, MD; **be-byrieden**, *pt. pl.* S; **bebyried**, *pp.*, S; **bebered**, S2.—AS. *bi-byrgan.*
bi-cacchen, *v.* to catch, ensnare, MD; **bicauhte**, *pt. s.*, MD; **bi-keihte**, S; **bicought**, *pp.*, MD.
bi-callen, *v.* to accuse, summon, MD, S; **becallen**, MD, HD.
bi-cause, *conj.* because, MD; **by-cause**, C.
bicche, *sb.* bitch, PP; **bycche**, PP.
bicched, *pp.* a word of doubtful meaning, applied to the basilisk, and to bones used for dice, NED, CM, C3; **byched**, MD; **bichede**, NED.
bi-chermen, *v.* to scream at, S.
bi-cherren, *v.* to entice, mislead, betray, S; **bicharre**, S; **bicherd**, *pp.*, S.—AS. *becerran.*
bi-clappen, *v.* to lay hold of suddenly, C3; **beclappe**, Palsg.
bi-clarten, *v.* to defile, make dirty, S, NED.
bi-clepien, *v.* to accuse, S; **bicleopien**, S; **bicleoped**, *pp.*, S.—AS. *be-cleopian.*
bi-clippen, *v.* to embrace, W, W2; **biclipped**, *pt. s.* wrapped (him) round, S3; **by-clypped**, *pp.* surrounded, S2; **biclippid**, W.—AS. *bi-clippan.*
bi-clusen, *v.* to enclose, S.—AS. *be-clýsan.*
bi-colmen, *v.* to blacken with soot, S, NED (p. 722a), MD. See **culme.**
bi-comen, *v.* to come, go to, to befall, to become, befit, suit, PP, S2, S; **bycome**, PP, S2; **bicom**, *pt. s.*, S; **bycam**, PP; **bicome**, *pp.*, S2; **bycome**, S2; **becomen**, S3; l'·ı ılı ı ı ı ,f Af fı ıııı ıı
bi-cumelich, *adj.* comely, becoming, MD; **bicumeliche**, *adv.* becomingly, S.
bi-daffed, *pp.* befooled, C2; **bedaffed**, NED.
bidden, *v.* to beg, pray, ask, S, S2, PP; **bydde**, S2; **beode**, S; **bit**, *pr. s.*, S, P; **byd**,

S2; **bad**, *pt. s.*, S, S2, PP; **bede**, *subj.*, PP; **beade**, S; **beden**, *pp.* S; **ibeden**, S.—AS. *biddan.* {Note that some of the above forms are due to a confusion with those of the verb **beden.**}
biddere, *sb.* asker, PP; **bidders**, *pl.* beggars, S2, P.
biddinge, *sb.* prayer, S; **biddynge**, begging, P.
biden, *v.* to bide, remain, PP; **byden**, S2, PP; **bod, bode**, *pt. s.*, S2; **bade**, S3; **baid**, *pl.* abode, lived, S3.—AS. *bídan.*
bidene, *adv.* together, S; at once, S2; **bedene**, NED; **bydene**, S2.
bi-draueled, *pp.* slobbered, covered with grease, P.
bie, *sb.* collar, W2; see **bei3.**
bienfet; see **benefet.**
biennales, *sb. pl.* biennials, biennial commemorations of the dead, P.
bierne, *sb.* man, PP, HD; see **bern**[1].
bi-fallen, *v.* to befall, C; **biualle**, S; **biful**, *pt. s.* befell, S; **byfyl**, S2; **befyl**, S2; **byfel**, **byfil**, C; **bifil, bifel**, C2; **bifelde**, W2; **bifalle**, *pp.* befallen, S, S2, C; **bifelde**, W2; **biualle**, S.—AS. *be-feallan.*
bi-flen, *v.* to fly from, S.—AS. *be-fléon.*
bi-fleten, *v.* to flow round; **biflette**, *pt. s.*, S, NED (p. 721 a).
bi-foren, *prep.* before, S, C2; **biuoren**, S; **byuoren**, S; **beforen**, S; **biforn**, S2, C2, C3; **bifore**, S; **bifor**, S; **befor**, S2; **beforne**, S3.—AS. *biforan.*
big, *adj.* big, C2; **byg**, PP; **bigg**, wealthy, S2, MD; **bygge**, *pl.*, PP.
bigat; see **bi3eten.**
biggen[1], *v.* to till, dwell, build, MD, PP, S (5. 1611); **byggen**, PP; **biggand**, *pr. p.*, H.—Icel. *byggja*; cf. AS. *búgian.*
biggen[2], *v.* to buy, S3, P; **buggen**, S, S2, PP; **bygge**, PP; **beggen**, MD; **beye**, C3; **bij**, S2; **bye**, S2; **by**, C3; **bie**, W2; **buyeþ**, *pr. s.*, PP; **buþ**, S; **bies**, redeems, S2; **bohte**, *pt. s.*, S; **bouhte**, S; **bo3te**, S2; **bohton**, *pl.*, S; **bo3te**, S; **bogt**, *pp.*, S; **y-bou3t**, P.—AS. *bycgan.*
biggere, *sb.* buyer, W; **biere**, W2.
bi-gilen, *v.* to beguile, S, P; **bigyle**, C2, C3.
bi-ginnen, *v.* to begin, S, S2; **bigan**, *pt. s.*, C2; **bigon**, S2; **bigonne**, 2 *pt. s.*, C3; **bigunnen**, *pt. pl.*, S; **begouth**, *pt. s.*, S2, S3; **bigunnen**, *pp.*, S; **begunnen**, S.—AS. *be-ginnan.*
bi-gon, *pp.* surrounded, provided, set round, MD; **be-gon**, filled, S2.—AS. *begán*, pp. of *begán*, to go round, surround.
bi-greden, *v.* to cry out at, to lament, S; **begredde**, *pt. pl.*, MD.

bi-gripen, *v.* to seize, MD; **be-gripe**, *pp.*, S.—AS. *be-grípan*, to chide.

bi-growe, *pp.* overgrown, S; **begrowe**, MD.

bi-grucchen, *v.* to begrudge, murmur at, P; **bygrucche**, PP.

bi-gurdel, *sb.* a purse, PP.—AS. *bí-gyrdel* (Matt. 10.9).

bi-gynandly, *adv.* at the beginning, H. See **biginnen**.

bi-hangen, *v.* to deck, clothe, MD; **bi-hengen**, *pt. pl.* hung about, S.—AS. *be-hón*.

bi-healde, *v.* to behold; **bihalden**, S2; see **biholden**.

bi-heden, *v.* to behead, MD; **bi-hedide**, *pt. s.*, W; **biheedid**, *pp.*, W.—AS. *be-héafdian*.

bi-heste, *sb.* promise, S, S2, C2, P; **byheste**, S2; **beheste**, S2; **byhest**, S2; **bihese**, S; **biheest**, W; **bihese**, *pl.*, S.—AS. *be-hǽs*.

bi-heten, *v.* to promise, S, C3, W; **bihote**, S, S2, P; **byhote**, C; **beohote**, S2; **bihat**, *pr. s.*, S; **bihet**, *pt. s.*, S, S2; **bihiȝte**, W; **behighte**, S2; **behihte**, S2; **bihight**, P; **biheyhte**, S; **bihoten**, *pp.*, S; **byhote**, S; named, S3.—AS. *be-hátan*. See NED (s.v. *behight*).

bi-heue, *adj.* profitable, S, MD.—AS. *be-héfe*, necessary; from *bihóf, utility (in *behóflic*). See **bihovely**.

bi-hinde, *prep.* behind, S; *adv.* S2; **bihynde**, backwards, W2; = to come, future, C3.

bi-holden, *v.* to hold, to behold, PP, C, MD; **bi-healde**, S; **bihalden**, S2; **bihalt**, *pr. s.*, S; **biheold**, *pt. s.*, S; **beoheold**, S2; **bihuld**, S2; **biheolt**, S; **biholde**, *pp.*, W2, C3; **beholdinge** *wrongly used for* **beholden**, indebted, S3.—AS. *be-healdan*.

bihote; see **biheten**.

bi-houe, *sb. dat.* advantage, MD; **biofþe**, S2. Cf. **biheve**.

bi-houely, *adj.* behoveful, necessary, CM, MD; **behouelich**, S2.—AS. *be-hóflic*.

bi-houeþ, *pr. s.* behoveth, needs, S, C2, P; **behoueþ**, S2; **byhoueþ**, S2; **bihoues**, S; **byhoues**, *pr. pl.*, are obliged to, S2; **behoued**, *pt. s.*, S; **bihofte**, W.—AS. *be-hófian*.

bi-huden, *v.* to hide, MD; **by-hud**, *imp. s.*, S.—AS. *be-hýdan*.

bi-iapen, *v.* to deceive, befool, MD; **byiaped**, *pp.*, C, C3, PP.

bijs; see **bisse**.

~~bikeihte; see bicacchen.~~

bikenen, *v.* to beckon, W2; see **beknen**.

bi-kennedd, *pp.* begotten, MD.

bi-kennen, *v.* to commit, commend, to signify, MD; **bikenned**, *pt. s.* recommended, S2; **bekenned**, S2.

biker, *sb.* a fight, MD, HD.

bikeren, *v.* to fight, PP, HD; **bekeryn**, Prompt.; **byckarte**, *pt. pl.* skirmished, S3.

bi-knowen, *v.* to acknowledge, know, P, C3; **byknowe**, C; **beknowe**, S2; **biknew**, *pt. s.*, C; **biknewe**, *pl.*, S; **biknowen**, *pp.*, favourably received, P.

bilæde, *pt. s.* enclosed, S; see **bileggen**.

bilæuen, *v.* to remain, S; see **bileven**[3].

bild, *sb.* building, S3.

bilden, *v.* to build, PP, W, CM, MD; **bulden**, MD; **belden**, MD, S3; **bulde**, *pt. s.*, C, MD; **bildide**, W; **bildiden**, *pt. pl.*, W; **bilden**, W2; **belt**, *pp.*, S3; **y-buld**, S2, S3; **y-beld**, S3.—Probably from AS. *bold*, dwelling.

bile, *sb.* a boil, a festering sore PP; **bilis**, *pl.*, W; **byles**, PP; **boilus**, PP.—AS. *býle*; cf. G. *beule* (Weigand).

bi-leden, *v.* to use, treat, MD; **biledet** (*for* biledeþ), *pr. pl.*, S.—AS. *be-lǽdan*.

bi-lefful, *adj.* believing, S, MD.

bi-leggen, *v.* to lay (something) on, cover, to prove, explain, MD; **bileist**, *2 pr. s.*, glozest (glossest), S, MD; **bilæde**, *pt. s.*, enclosed, S.—AS. *bi-lecgan*, to cover.

bi-leue[1], *sb.* belief, S, S2, PP, C3; **beleaue**, S; **byleue**, PP; **belaue**, S; **bileaue**, S; **biliaue**, S; **beoleeue**, S2, PP; **bilefues**, *pl.*, S.—Cf. AS. *(ge)léafa*.

bi-leue[2]; see **bilive**[1], **bilive**[2].

bi-leuen[1], *v.* to believe, PP, MD, S; **beleue**, S; **bilefeð**, *pr. pl.*, S; **biliueð**, S; **bilefden**, *pt. pl.*, S.

bi-leuen[2], *v.* to leave, forsake, renounce, HD, MD; **bilef**, *imp. s.*, S, MD.—Cf. AS. *lǽfan*, to leave.

bi-leuen[3], *v.* to remain, be left, MD, CM, C2, S2, HD; **byleue**, HD; **bilæuen**, S; **bileaue**, S; **bilefue**, S; **bleuen**, S2; **blefþ**, *pr. s.*, S2; **bileued**, *pp.* left remaining, G; **byleued**, G.—AS. *be-léfan*.

bilfoder, *sb.* food, sustenance, S2, MD; **bilfodur**, NED.

bi-liggen, *v.* to belong to, MD; **bi-lien**, *pr. pl.*, S.—AS. *bi-licgan*, to lie round.

bi-likien, *v.* to make pleasing, MD; **bi-liked**, *pp.* made pleasing, S.

bi-limpen, *v.* to happen, to belong to, S; **belimpen**, S; **belamp**, *pt. s.*, S.—AS. *be-limpan*.

bi-linnen, *v.* to cease, to be silent, to make to cease, MD; **by-linne**, G; **blinnen**, S, S2, C3; **blyne**, S3; **blynne**, S2; **blin**, S2; **blan**, *pt. s.*, MD; **blane**, S3.—AS. *blinnan* (= *be* + *linnan*, to cease, to be deprived of), *pt. blann* (pl. *blunnon*), p. *blunnen*.

bi-liue[1], *adv.* quickly, S, S2; **bylyue**, S2; **belyue**, S2, S3; **bliue**, S, S2; **blyue**, S3.—AS. *be lífe*, with life.

bi-liue[2], *sb.* food, sustenance, S (4b.102), MD; **bylyue**, PP; **bileoue**, MD; **bileue**, S, SD.—AS. *bigleofa*; cf. OHG. *bilibi*.

bi-liuen, *v.* to live by, S.—AS. *bi-libban*.

bille[1], *sb.* papal bull, petition, PP; see **bulle**.

bille[2], *sb.* bill, beak, S, C; **bylle**, Voc.—AS. *bile*.

billen, *v.* to peck with the bill, S.

billet, *sb.* a piece of firewood; **byllets**, *pl.*, S3 (26. 785).

bi-loken, *v.* to look upon, regard, MD; **belocest**, *2 pr. s.*, S.

bi-long on, *prep.* pertaining to, S.

bi-luken, *v.* to enclose, lock up, imprison, include, MD; **biloken**, *pp.*, S; **beloken**, S; **bilouked**, S2, MD.—AS. *be-lúcan.*

bi-lyen, *v.* to lie against, accuse falsely, MD; **belye**, P; **bilowen**, *pp.*, S2, P, MD.—AS. *be-léogan*, pp. *belogen.*

bi-masen, *v.* to confuse, SkD (s.v. *maze*).

bi-menen, *v.* to mean, to bemoan, MD, HD; **bymenen**, P; **bemenen**, S2, P; **biment**, *pp.*, S.—AS. *bi-ménan.*

bi-mening, *sb.* bemoaning, S.

bi-mong, *prep.* among, S, MD.

bi-mornen, *v.* to mourn over, MD, W; **bimurnen**, S.—AS. *bi-murnan.*

bi-mowe, *v.* to mock, W2.

binam; *pt. s.* took from; see **binimen**.

binden, *v.* to bind, S; **band**, *pt. s.*, S; **bond**, S2, G, C2; **bunden**, *pl.*, S; **bunden**, *pp.*, S; **bundyn**, S2; **bunde**, **ibunde**, S; **bounden**, S, C2; **y-bounde**, S2, S3, C2; **y-bound**, S3; **ibunde**, S.—AS. *bindan.*

bi-nemnen, *v.* to declare, stipulate; **bynempt**, *pt. s.* promised, S3.—AS. *be-nemnan.*

bi-neðe, *prep.* and *adv.* beneath, S2; **byneþe**, C; **bineþen**, S.—AS. *be-neoðan.*

bi-nimen, *v.* to take from, MD; **bynymen**, S; **benymen**, S2; **bineome**, *pr. s. subj.* deprive, S; **binam**, *pt. s.*, P; **binom**, S2; **benam**, S; **bynome**, *pp.*, P; **benumde**, S3.—AS. *be-niman.*

binne[1], *adv.* and *prep.* within, S; **bynne**, S2; **bine**, S.—AS. *binnan* (for *be-innan*).

binne[2], *sb.* bin, chest, MD; **bynne**, C, Voc.—AS. *binn*, manger.

binom; *pt. s.* took from; see **binimen**.

bi-queste, *sb.* bequest, P, MD.—A deriv. of *cweðan*, see NED.

bi-quethen, *v.* to bequeath, MD, CM, PP; **byquethen**, C, G; **bi-queth**, *pt. s.*, S2; **biquath**, PP, G.—AS. *bi-cwéðan.*

bi-quide, *sb.* bequest, 82; **bequide**, MD.—Cf. AS. *cwide*, a will.

birafte; see **bireven**.

bird[1], *pt. s. impers.* (it) behoved, S2; **birrde**, S; see **bureþ**.

bird[1], *sb.* a young bird, MD; see **brid**.

birded, *pt. pl.* laid snares for birds, S3.

bire, *sb. dat.* force, impetus, W; see **bur**[1].

bi-reden, *v. reflex.* to take counsel, MD; **byrad**, *pp.* determined, resolved, S2.

bi-reinen, *v.* to rain upon, bedew, MD; **berayne**, *pr. pl.* berain, S3; **birine**, *subj.* S; **beraynde**, *pt. pl.* S3.

bi-reusien, *v.* to lament, regret, MD, S; **bireused**, *pp.* S.—AS. *be-hréowsian*, to feel remorse.

bireusunge, *sb.* contrition, S.

bi-reuen, *v.* to bereave, C3, P; **birafte**, *pt. s.* C2; **bireued**, *pp.*, S; **byreued**, G; **byraft**, C.—AS. *bi-réafian*, to deprive of.

bi-rinnen, *v.* to run with moisture, MD; **birunne**, *pp.* bedewed with tears, S.—AS. *birinnan*, to run as a liquid, *bi-runnen*, pp.

birle, *sb.* cup-bearer, MD, HD.—AS. *byrle*, *byrele.*

birlen, *v.* to pour out drink, to give to drink, MD, JD, H, HD; **bryllyn**, Prompt.—AS. *byrlian*; cf. Icel. *byrla.*

birlynge, *sb.* a giving to drink; pouring out liquor, H.

bi-rolled, *pp.* rolled about, S2.

birth, *sb.* birth, offspring, natural disposition, nation, MD; **burþ**, MD; **birþes**, *pl.* nations, S2, MD.—Icel. *burðr*; cf. Goth. *gabaurþs*, birth, native country.

birth-tonge, *sb.* native tongue; **burþtonge**, S2.

bisay; see **bisen**.

bi-sched, *pp.* besprinkled, W2.

bi-schetten, *v.* to shut up; **bessette**, S2; **bischetten**, *pt. pl.*, PP; **bishetten**, P; **bishette**, *pp.*, PP.

bi-schinen, *v.* to shine upon, MD; **byschyne**, *pp.* shone upon, S2.

bischop, *sb.* bishop, S, PP; **bisscopp**, the Jewish high priest, S; **bischopis**, *pl.* chief priests, W; **bissopes**, S2.—AS. *biscop*; Lat. *episcopus.*

bi-schrewen, *v.* to corrupt, to curse, MD; **byschrewed**, *pp.* cursed, P.

bi-schrichen, *v.* to shriek at, S.

bi-schunien, *v.* to shun, MD; **bisunien**, S.

bise, *sb.* the north-wind, S.—OF. *bise*; cf. OHG. *bísa.*

bi-sechen, *v.* to beseech, S; **biseke**, C2; **beseken**, C, S; **besech**, *imp. s.*, S; **bisohte**, *pt. s.* besoght, S2; **bisoȝte**, S2; **bisouȝten**, *pl. pl.*, S2.

bi-segen, *v.* to besiege, MD; **bi-segiden**, *pt. pl.*, W2; **bi-seged**, *pp.*, C2.

bi-semen, *v.* to beseem, to appear, MD; **bi-semeþ**, *pr. s.*, him bisemeþ, he appears, S; **bisemyde**, *pt. s.*, beseemed, fitted, W; **ibsemed**, *pp.* made seemly, plausible, S (16. 842).

bi-sen

bi-sen, *v.* to look, to behold, consider, to arrange, appoint, to manage, MD, S; **besie**, S; **biseo**, S2; **bisið**, *pr. s.*, S; **bise**, *imp.*, W; **byse**, S2; **biseh**, *pt. s.*, S; **bisay**, S2; **beseyn**, *pp.* arranged; **beseyne**, decked; **besene**, equipped, S3; **biseye**, *as in phr.* **yuel biseye**, ill to look at, C2, **richely biseye**, splendid in appearance, C2.—AS. *biséon*, to look about.

bisenen, *v.* to give an example, MD; **bisend**, *pp.* likened, signified, S2.—AS. *bysnian.* See **bisne**.

bisening, *sb.* example, S.—AS. *bys-nung.*

bi-setten, *v.* to fill, occupy, to surround, beset, to set, place, to employ, MD, C, P; **bisettiden**, *pt. pl.*, W.—AS. *bi-settan.*

bisi, *adj.* busy, S; see **busy**.

bisily, *adv.* busily, C2; **bisili**, W; **bisiliche**, S.

bi-sitten, *v.* to sit close to, to press hard, MD, P; **be-sæt**, *pt. s.* besieged, S; **be-sætte**, S.—AS. *be-sittan.*

bi-slabered, *pp.* beslobbered, P.

bi-smeoruwed, *pp.* besmeared, S.

bi-smer, *sb.* scorn, reproach, P; **bisemar**, S; **busemare**, S2; **bismare**, HD; **bissemare**, CM; **bismeres**, *pl.*, PP; **bismares**, PP.—AS. *bi-smer*, insult; cf. OHG. *bismer*, ridicule (Otfrid).

bi-smitten, *v.* to dirty, MD; **bismitted**, *pp.* dirtied, S; **besmet**, MD.

bi-smotered, *pp.* spotted, smutted, C.

bisne, *sb.* example, parable, S, MD.—AS. *bysn*; Goth. *busns* (in *anabusns*); from *biudan*; see Douse, p. 60.

bi-soken, *sb.* request, petition, MD; **bisokne**, NED; **bi-socne**, *dat.*, MD; **bisocnen**, *dat. pl.*, S.

bi-soȝte, *pt. s.* beseeched; see **bi-sechen**.

bi-speken, *v.* to speak to, to speak, blame, to decide, resolve, MD; **byspack**, *pt. s.*, G; **bespayke**, S3; **bispeke**, *pp.* S.—AS. *be-sprecan.*

bi-spel, *sb.* parable, S.—AS. *bigspell*, example, proverb, parable.

bi-speten, *v.* to spit upon, W; **bispatten**, *pt. pl.*, W; **bispat**, *pp.*, W.

bi-sprengen, *v.* to besprinkle, MD; **bi-spreynde**, *pt. s.* W; **besprent**, *pp.* bedewed, S3; **bysprent**, S3; **besprint**, S3; **bispreynt**, W2.—AS. *be-sprengan.*

bisse, *sb.* a stuff of fine texture, MD; **bis**, MD; **bys**, S2; **bles**, **bijs**, fine linen, W; **bijs** (= *byssus* = Heb. *shésh*, fine linen, also Egyptian cotton), W2.—OF. *bisse*; Lat. *byssus*; Gr. βύσσος; Heb. *búts*, fine Egyptian cotton.

bissyn, *sb.* fine linen (= *byssinum*), W.—Lat. *byssinum*, a garment made of byssus.

bi-toknen

bi-stad, *pp.* placed, circumstanced, bestead, hard bestead, sorely imperilled, overcome, MD, S2, C3; **bystad**, G; **bistadde**, CM; **bistaðed**, MD; **bistaðet**, S; **bisteaðet**, S. Probably from Icel. *staðr*, place, see NED.

bi-standen, *v.* to surround, to be busy about, to attack, MD; **bi-stod**, *pt. s.*, S; **bistode**, S2; **bistonden**, *pp.*, S.—AS. *bestandan.*

bi-steken, *v.* to shut out, MD; *pp.*, S.

bi-striden, *v.* to bestride, S; **bistrood**, *pt. s.*, C2; **bystrood**, G.

bi-sunien, *v.* to shun, S; see **bischunien**.

bi-swiken, *v.* to betray, deceive, S, S2; **beswike**, S; **besuiken**, S.—AS. *be-swícan.*

bi-swinken, *v.* to obtain by work, to, earn by labour, MD; **biswynke**, P.—AS., *be-swincan.*

bisy, *adj.* busy, C2, P; see **busy**.

bisyhed, *sb.* busyhood, MD; **bysyhede**, S2.

bisynesse, *sb.* business, W2; see **busynesse**.

bi-taken, *v.* to commit, entrust, S, C2, W, NED; **betake**, PP; **beotake**, PP; **bytake**, PP; **bitaak**, W; **bitak**, *imp. s.*, S; **bitok**, *pt. s.*, S2; **bitook**, C3; **bytokist**, 2 *pt. s.*, W; **betoke**, *1 pt. s.*, S; **bitoken**, *pl.*, W; **bitakun**, *pp.* W; **bitake**, S2.

bi-techen, *v.* to entrust, assign, S; **beteche**, HD; **byteche**, PP; **biteache**, S; **bitache**, *imp. s.*, S; **bitæhte**, *pt. s.*; **bitahte**; **bitagte**; **bitaucte**, S; **bitaughte**, G; **bytaȝt**, S2; **bitæht**, *pp.*; **bitaht**; **biteiht**; **bitagt**; **beteht**, S.—AS. *be-técan*, pt. *betǽhte*, pp. *betǽht.*

bitel, *adj.* sharp, biting, MD.

bitel-browed, *adj.* with shaggy, prominent eye-brows, S2, P; **bytelbrowed**, PP.

bi-tellen, *v.* to clear, justify, to express, show, to claim, to set free, to persuade, deceive, MD, S; **bitald**, *pp.*, H, MD.—AS. *be-tellan.*

biten, *v.* to bite, PP; **byte**, PP; **bot**, *pt. s.*, S2, PP; **bote**, P.—AS. *bítan*, pt. *bát* (pl. *biton*), pp. *biten.*

bi-teon, *v.* to draw over, to cover, to employ, NED; **biten**, MD; **bitowen**, *pp.*, S; **bitoȝen**, NED; **bitogen**, MD.—AS. *be-téon.*

bi-tiden, *v.* to happen, betide, MD; **bityde**, C2, C3; **beotyde**, PP; **bitit**, *pr. s.*, PP; **bitid**, S; **bitide**, *pt. s.*, S2; **betydde**, PP; **bitid**, *pp.*, S; **betight**, *pp.*, S3; NED.

bi-tilden, *v.* to cover; **bi-tild**, *pp.*, S.—AS. *be-teldan.* See **overtild**.

bi-time, *adv.* betimes, S, S2; **bityme**, PP; **bitimes**, C3.

bi-toknen, *v.* to betoken, C2; **bitocknen**, S; **bytoknen**, PP; **betoknen**, S, PP; **betaken**, S2; **bitacnedd**, *pp.*, S.

26

bi-trayen, *v.* to betray, PP, C2; **bitraide**, *pt. s.*, S. From OF. *traïr*: It. *tradire*; Lat. *tradere*.

bitter[1], *adj.* bitter, MD; **bittur**, PP; **bittere**, *adv.* bitterly, P.—AS. *bitor.*

bitter[2], *sb.* bitterness, S2, P.

bittur-browed, *adj.* having prominent brows, PP. See **bitel-browed.**

bituhhe, *prep.* between, S; see **bitwiȝe.**

bi-turnen, *v.* to turn; **biturnde hom**, *pt. pl.*, turned themselves about, S2.

bi-twenen, *prep.*, between; **bitwine**, **bitwen**, **betwenen**, **betuene**, S.—AS. *betwéonan.*

bi-twix, *prep.* betwixt, S2, C2; **bitwixe**, C2; **bitwixen**, C2; **betwyx**, **betwux**, S; **bitwex**, S; **bythuixte**, S2.—AS. *be-tweox.*

bi-twiȝe, *prep.* between, MD; **betwe**, S2; **bituhhe**, S.—AS. *be-twih, be-twuh.*

bityl, *sb.* beetle, NED.—AS. *bitula.*

bi-þenken, *v.* to think, bethink, S, W; **biþenchen**, S; **biþohte**, *pt. s.*, S; **biþoȝte**, planned, S2; **biþouhte**, S; **beþout**, S2; **biþoht**, *pp.* repented, S; **biþouht**, S; **bythought**, called to mind, C.—AS. *biþencan.*

biuien, *v.* to tremble, NED; **biueð**, *pr. s.*, S.—AS. *bifian (beofian)*; OHG. *bibēn*, see NED.

bi-wailen, *v.* to bewail, lament, C2; **biwaille**, MD; **biweile**, MD, W; **biwailled**, *pp.*, C2.

bi-welden, *v. refl.* to wield oneself, i.e. to have full and free use of one's limbs, MD; **bywelde**, S3; **bewelde**, Palsg.; **beweld**, to wield, HD.

bi-wenden, to turn, MD; **biwente**, *pt. s.*, turned round, S.

bi-wepen, *v.* to beweep, S, W.—AS. *bewépan.*

bi-werien, *v.* to defend, S.—AS. *be-werian.*

bi-winden, *v.* to wind about, S; **bewinden**, to enwrap, cover, S; **bewunden**, *pp.*, S.—AS. *be-windan.*

bi-winnen, *v.* to obtain, MD; **biwon**, *pt. s.*, S.

bi-witen, *v.* to guard, MD; **bywite**, S; **biwiste**, *pt. s.*, MD; **biwisten**, *pl.*, S.

bi-wlappe, *v.* to wrap round, W2.

bi-wreyen, *v.* to accuse, to reveal, disclose, C2, C3; **bywreye**, C; **biwreie**, S; **bewreye**, C, S2; **bewraye**, NED.

biȝes, *sb. pl.* collars, S; see **beiȝ.**

bi-ȝete, *sb.* profit, S, S2; offspring, P.

bi-ȝetel, *adj.* profitable, S.

bi-ȝeten, *v.* to obtain, possess, beget, S; **biȝiten**, S; **bigat**, *pt. s.* S; **bigæt**, S; **begæt**, S; **bygeten**, *pp.* S2; **biȝetenn**, S; **biyete**, **biȝite**, **biȝute**, **bigotten**, **biȝoten**, S.—AS. *bi-gitan (bigietan).*

bi-ȝonde, *prep.* beyond, S, S2, PP; **biȝende**, W; **biȝunde**, P; **biyond**, S2; **beionde**, S; **biȝendis**, W.

blaberen, *v.* to blabber, to talk idly, HD, Prompt.; **blaberde**, *pt. s.*, PP.

bladder, *sb.* bladder, MD; **bladdre**, C3; **bledder**, S3; **bleder**, Voc.—AS. *blédre*, OMerc. *blédre* (OET.)

blak[1], *adj.* pale, MD; **blake**, wan, Palsg. *Phr.*: **blak and blo**, pale and livid, MD, NED (s.v. *black*, 13).—AS. *blác.* Cf. **bleike.**

blak[2], *adj.* black, MD.—AS. *blæc.*

blake, *sb.* smut, black, S; blackness, S2.

blake-beryed, *sb.* blackberrying, i.e., wandering hither and thither purposely, C3.

blanchet, *sb.* a white powder used as a cosmetic, S.—OF. *blanchet.*

blanc-mangere, *sb.* a kind of cheese-cake, PP; **blammanger**, PP.

blane (*for* **blan**), *pt. s.* ceased; see **bi-linnen.**

blank, *adj.* white, S3.—OF. *blanc.*

blase, *sb.* blaze, flame, PP.—AS. *blæse.*

blasen[1], *v.* to blaze, flare, PP; **blasie**, *pr. s. subj.*, S; **blesand**, *pr. p.*, S3.

blasen[2], *v.* to blow (with trumpet), to proclaim, publish, NED, CM. Cf. OHG. *blásan.*

blasen[3], *v.* in heraldry to blaze arms, i.e. to describe them, MD, S3, Prompt., Palsg.; **blaze**, Cotg. (s.v. *blasonner*).

blasfeme, *adj.* and *sb.* blasphemous, blasphemer, MD, W.—Lat. *blasphemus*; Gr. βλάσφημος.

blaundissen, *v.* to flatter, H; **blaundiss**, *pr. s.*, H; **bloundisand**, *pr. p.*, H.—OF. *blandir* (pr. p. *blandisant*).

blawen; see **blowen**[1].

bledder; see **bladder.**

blee, *sb.* colour, complexion, MD, HD; **ble**, MD, JD; **bleo**, S, S2; **blie**, JD.—AS. *bléo.*

blefþ; see **bileven.**

bleike, *adj.* pale, S, NED; **bleyke**, Prompt.; **blayke**, NED; **bleyk**, S3; **bleke**, wan, Palsg. *Phr.*: **blaike and blo**, pale and livid, NED (s.v. *black*, 13).—Icel. *bleikr.* Cf. **blak**[2].

blenchen, *v.* to flinch, turn aside, S, P; **bleynte**, *pt. s.*, C; **bleinte**, NED.—AS. *blencan*, to deceive.

blenden[1], *v.* to mix together, MD; **blende**, *pp.*, S2.—Cf. Icel. *blanda.*

blenden[2], *v.* to blind, deceive, MD, PP; **blent**, *pr. s.*, C3; **blente**, *pt. s.*, PP; **blent**, *pp.* blinded, C3, HD.—AS. *blendan.*

blenk, *sb.* a gleam, blink, glance, S3; **blenkis**, *pl.*, NED; **blinkes**, MD.

blenken, *v.* to glitter, to glance, NED; **blynke**, to open the eyes, NED; **blenkit**, *pt. s.*, looked, S2; **blencheden**, *pl.*, MD.

blere, *adj.* blear, dim, NED.

27

bleren, *v.* to make dim, to be blear-eyed, MD, S2, P; **blered**, *pp.* dimmed, S2, C3, P.

blesen, *v.* to blaze, S3; see **blasen**[1].

blessen, *v.* to bless, PP, S; **blesseth hir**, *pr. s.*, crosses herself, C3; **blesced**, *pp.* S; **bletcæd**, consecrated, S; **y-blessed**, S3, C3, P; **i-blessed**, S; **iblescede**, S; **iblesset**, S2.—AS. *blétsian*, *blédsian* ONorth. *blóedsian* (NED); from *blód*, blood.

blete, *adj.* bare, exposed, miserable, S, MD; **blait**, JD; **blout**, JD.—AS. *bléat*, wretched, miserable; cf. Icel. *blautr*, Du. *bloot* G. *bloss*.

bleten, *v.* to bleat, Prompt.; **blæten**, S.— AS. *blétan*.

bleuen; see **bileven**[3].

blewe[1], *adj.* blue, livid, C2, PP; black, MD; **blew**, MD.—OF. *bleu*. See **blo**.

blewe[2], *sb.* blue, MD; **bluȝ**, S2.

bleynte; see **blenchen**.

blinnen, *v.* to cease, S, S2, C3; see **bilinnen**.

blis, *sb.* bliss, S.—AS. *bliss* (= *blíðs*), see Sievers, 202(7). See **bliþe**.

blissien, *v.* to rejoice, be glad, to gladden, MD; **blissin**, S, S2.—AS. *blissian* (= *blíðsian*). See **blis**.

bliþe, *adj.* blithe, cheerful, S, S2; **blyþe**, S2, C2.—AS. *blíðe*.

bliðe-liche, *adv.* gladly, S; **bluðeliche**, S; **bloðeliche**, S; **bliþeliȝ**, S; **bleþely**, S2.—AS. *blíðelice*.

bliue, *adv.* quickly, S, S2; see **bilive**[1].

blo, *adj.* livid, S2, PP; black, MD.—Icel. *blá(r)*. See **blewe**.

blod, *sb.* blood, S, S2, PP; **blode**, *dat.*, S2.— AS. *blód*.

blode, *sb.* a blood-relation, a person, living being, MD, CM; **blod**, MD.

blok, *adj.* pale, NED. *Phr.* **blok and blo**, NED. See **blak**[1].

blo-man, *sb.* negro, MD; **blamon**, MD; **blewe-men**, *pl.*, MD.—Cf. Icel. *blá-maðr*, negro. See **blo**.

blome, *sb.* flower, S2, MD.—Icel. *blóm*, flower, blossom.

blosme, *sb.* blossom, S, PP, Prompt., CM; **blostme**, S; **blosmen**, *pl.*, S2; **bloosmes**, S3.—AS. *blóstma*.

blosmen, *v.* to blossom, W2, Prompt.; **blosmed**, *pt. pl.*, P.—AS. *blóstmian*.

bloundisen, *v.* to flatter, H; see **blaundissen**.

bloundisynge, *sb.* blandishing, H.

blowen[1], *v.* to blow, PP; **blawe**, S; **blou**, *imp. s.*, S; **bloaweð**, *pr. s.*, S; **bleu**, *pt. s.*, S; **bleowen**, *pl.*, S; **blawen**, *pp.*, S2; **blowe**, C3.—AS. *bláwan*, pt. *bléow*, pp. *bláwen*.

blowen[2], *v.* to blow, to bloom, MD; **i-blowe**, *pp.* S.—AS. *blówan*, pt. *bléow*, pp. *geblówen*.

blubren, *v.* to bubble, MD; **blubrande**, *pr. p.*, S2.

blustren, *v.* to rush about aimlessly, NED; **blustreden**, *pt. pl.*, P.

bluȝ, *sb.* blue, S2; see **blewe**.

blyn-hede, *sb.* blindness, H.

blynke; see **blenken**.

bo-; see also words beginning in **bou-**, **bu-**.

bobbe, *sb.* a knock, jerk, jog, S3; **bobbes**, *pl.*, S3.

bobben, *v.* to knock, strike, MD.

bocche, *sb.* tumour, boil, PP; **botche**, W2, Prompt.; **boche**, CM; **boce**, CM.—AF. *boche*, OF. *boce*, bump.

bocher, *sb.* butcher, S2, S3, P, C.—OF. *boucher*.

bocherie, *sb.* shambles, W, Prompt.—OF. *boucherie*.

bod[1], *sb.* abiding, waiting, delay, S.

bod[2], *pt. s.* waited, S2; **bode**, waited for, S2; see **biden**.

bode, *sb.* message, command, S, PP; **bodes**, *pl.*, S, S2.—AS. *(ge)bod*, command.

boden; see **beden**.

bode-word, *sb.* command, S; **bodworde**, message, S2.

bodien, *v.* to announce, S; **bodeden**, *pt. pl.*, S.—AS. *bodian*.

body, *sb.* body, person, PP; **bodie**, S; **bodi**, S, PP; **bodiȝ**, S. *Phr.*: **my ioly body**, my jolly self, C2.—AS. *bodig*.

body-half, *sb.* the front part (of a dress), PP.

boile; see **bile**.

boistous, *adj.* boisterous, noisy, S3; **boustious**, S3; **bustuus**, **busteous**, S3; **buystous**, W.

boistously, *adv.* loudly, C2.

bok, *sb.* book, S, S2, PP; **boc**, S, S2; **boke**, P.—AS. *bóc*; cf. OHG. *buoh* (Tatian).

bokele, *sb.* buckle, MD; **bokle**, MD.—OF. *bocle*.

bokeler, *sb.* buckler, shield, C, G; **bocler**, Palsg.—OF. *bocler*.

boket, *sb.* bucket, C; **bokett**, Prompt.

bold, *adj.* fierce, bold, daring, PP, S; **bauld**, **bawld**, S3; **belde**, big, blustering, S; **bald**, S2; **balder**, *comp.*, P.—AS. *beald*; OHG. *bald* (Otfrid).

boldeliche, *adv.* boldly, S; **baldly**, S2; **boldely**, C2.

bolden, *v.* to make bold, encourage, MD; **bolded**, *pt. s.*, P; **balde**, S.—AS. *bealdian*.

bole[1], *sb.* a kind of clay, C3. *Comb.*: **bole armoniak**, Armenian clay, C3, NED (s.v. *ammoniac*).—Lat. *bolus*; Gr. βῶλος, clod.

bole[2], *sb.* bull, S, C, C3; **bule**, S; **bulez**, *pl.*, S2; **bolis**, W; **boolis**, W.—Icel. *boli*.

bolle, *sb.* bowl, S, S2, C3, P; a rounded seed-vessel, NED (s.v. *boll*), HD; **boll**, rounded top (of barley), S3.—AS. *bolla.*

bollen[1], *v.* to swell, S2, PP; **bolled**, *pp.*, S2, PP.

bollen[2], *pp.* swollen, NED; **bollen**, W; **bolne**, S3; **bowlne**, S3.

bollyng, *sb.* swelling, P.

bolnen, *v.* to swell, S2, P, H; **bolned**, *pt. s.*, S2; **bolnyde**, W2; **bolnyd**, W.

bolnyng, *sb.* swelling, H, W.

bolt, *sb.* arrow, S; **bolte**, Prompt.—AS. *bolt* (Voc.).

bolȝen, *v.* to puff up, MD; **boluweð**, *pr. s.*, S.—AS. *belgan*, pt. *bealg* (pl. *bulgon*), pp. *bolgen.*

bon[1], *sb.* bone, PP., S2; **boon**, W2; **ban**, S; **banes**, *pl.*, S, S2; **bon**, S; **boonys**, W2; **bannes**, S2. *Phr.*: **to make bones**, to hesitate, S3.—AS. *bán.*

bon[2], *pp.* prepared, S2; see **boun.**

bonayre, *adj.* kind, gentle, MD; **bonere**, MD; **bonair**, *adv.*, MD; **bonure**, S2. See **debonaire.**

bonayrelyche, *adv.* reverently, S2.

bonchen, *v.* to strike, bump, S2, P; see **bunchen.**

bond; see **binden.**

bonde, *sb.* a peasant serf, slave, NED, S2; *pl.*, PP.—AS. *bonda, bunda*, a householder; Icel. *bóndi*, for *búandi*, a tiller of the soil.

bonde-man, *sb.* tiller of the soil, NED; **bondman**, P; **bondemen**, *pl.*, S2, P, G, PP.

bone[1], *sb.* pain, poison, PP; see **bane.**

bone[2], *sb.* prayer, petition, S, S2, C3, G, PP; **bon**, S2; **boone**, C, G; **bonen**, *pl.*, S.—Icel. *bón.* Cf. **bene**[1].

bonen, *adj.* made of bone, S2.

bonet, *sb.* additional sail, PP, Cath.—OF. *bonet*, bonnet.

bonk, *sb.* bank, shore, S2, S3; see **bank.**

boo-; see also words beginning in **bo-.**

boor, *sb.* boar, C, W2; **bare**, S2; **bore**, S, PP; **bor**, S2, PP; **bores**, *pl.*, P.—AS. *bár.*

boot, *sb.* boat, S2, W, CM; **bot**, PP.—AS. *bát.*

boras, *sb.* borax, C, C3.—OF. *boras*: It. *borace*; Arab. *bōraq.*

bord, *sb.* board, table, S, S2, C, NED; **borde**, S; **boord**, W; **bordes**, *pl.*, S.—AS. *bord*, plank. Cf. **bred**[2].

borgounen, *v.* to bud, S2; see **burjounen.**

borne; see **burne.**

bornen, *v.* to burnish, S3; see **burnen.**

borwe, *sb.* pledge, surety, W2, C, C2, G; **borgh**, H; **borghe**, P; **borewe**, S2; **borwes**, *pl.*, sponsors, S2; pledges, P.—AS. *borh.*

borwen, *v.* to deliver, to borrow, MD, PP, C2, G; **borewe**, W2; **borowe**, NED; **borwede**, *pt. s.*, PP.—AS. *borgian.*

borwynge, *sb.* borrowing, Prompt.; **borewyng**, S2.

boske; see **busch.**

bosken; see **busken.**

bost, *sb.* boast, noise, MD, C3, PP; **boost**, C2; **boste**, PP; **bostus**, *pl.*, H.

bosten, *v.* to boast, PP; **booste**, NED.

bosum, *sb.* bosom, S, W (John 13. 23); **bosem**, MD.—AS. *bósm.*

bote[1], *prep.* and *conj.* without, except, unless, but, S, S2, PP; **bot**, CM, S2; **bute**, S; **butt**, S; **boute**, S, S2; **buten**, S; **buton**, S; *Comb.*: **bote-ȝef**, except that, unless, S2, C.—AS. *be-úton* (*búton*).

bote[2], *sb.* remedy, succour, amendment, S, S2, C2, G, P; **boote**, S3, C, G. *Phr.*: **to bote**, to advantage, in addition, NED.—AS. *bót*; cf. Goth. *bota.*

botelees, *adj.* without remedy, PP; **bootelesse**, useless, S3; **botles**, S2.

botelere, *sb.* butler, Voc.; **botiler**, C; **butler**, S.

botelle, *sb.* bottle, MD; **botel**, CM.—OF. *boutelle*, also *botel.*

boterace[1], *sb.* buttress; **boteras**, Prompt.; **butterace**, SkD (p. 789); **butteras**, *pl.*, SkD; **buttrace**, SkD; **butteraces**, SkD.—ME. *boterace* for OF. *bouterets*, i.e. (pillars) bearing a thrust, *pl.* of *bouteret.*

boterace[2], *v.* to buttress; **butteras**, Palsg.; **boteraced**, *pp.*, PP.

botme, *sb.* bottom, C, C3, Prompt.; **boþom**, a vale, S2, NED; **boþem**, S2.—AS. *botm.*

botme-les, *adj.* bottomless, CM.

botnen, *v.*, to heal, to recover, MD; **botened**, *pp.* bettered, P. See **bote**[2].

botun, *sb.* button, bud, Prompt., Voc.; **bothom**, MD, CM; **buttonys**, *pl.*, S3.—OF. *bouton*, button, bud (Cotg.).

bothe, *adj.* both, PP, S; **baþe**, S, S2; **beoðe**, S; **beðe**, S; **buoðe**, S2.—Icel. *báði*, both (*neut.*).

bouel, *sb.* bowel, MD; **bouele**, S2.—OF. *boel* (and *boele*); Lat. *botellus.*

bouge, *sb.* a leathern bottle or wallet, *uter*, W2 (Ps. 77. 13); **bowge**, W2, Prompt.—OF. *bouge*, budget, leather-case; Low Lat. *bulga*, leathern vessel (Voc.).

bouhte; see **biggen**[2].

bouk, *sb.* the belly, trunk, body, C, JD; **buc**, S.—AS. *búc*: Icel. *búkr.*

boun, *sb.* prepared to go, ready to start, S3, CM, PP; **bon**, ready, S2; **bun**, S2; **bown**, P, H.—Icel. *búinn*, prepared, *pp.* of *búa*, to get ready, to till; cf. AS. *ge-bún*, pp. of *gebúan*; cf. E. *bound* (said of a ship.)

bounden, *pp.* bound, S, C2; see **binden**.

bounen, *v.* to get ready, to go, also to make ready, NED; **bowneth**, *pr. s.*, NED; **bownd**, *pt. s.*, prepared himself, got ready, S3.

bour, *sb.* bower, chamber, women's chamber, C, G; **bur**, *dat.*, S; **boure**, S, S2, P; **bowre**, P; **bourez**, *pl.* sleeping-places, S2.—AS. *búr*, a dwelling.

bourde, *sb.* jest, PP, C3, G; **bourd**, S2, S3; **bord**, NED.—OF. *bourde*.

bourden, *v.* to jest, C3, PP; **borde**, NED.—OF. *bourder*.

bourding, *sb.* jesting, 83.

bourdon, *sb.* pilgrim's staff, CM, HD; **bordun**, S2, PP; **burdon**, S, HD; **burdoun**, P, MD; **bordon**, MD, PP; **bordoun**, HD.—OF. *bourdon* (Cotg.); Low Lat. *burdonem*; see **burdon**.

boustious, *adj.* noisy, S3; see **boistous**.

bouȝ, *sb.* bough, PP; **boh**, S; **bogh**, S2; **bowh**, PP; **boȝe**, *dat.*, S; **boges**, *pl.*, S; **buges**, S; **bughes**, S2; **bewis**, S3; **bewys**, S3; **bowes**, PP, S3; **boowes**, C; **boȝe**, *dat.*, S.—AS. *bóg*, *bóh*, Icel. *bógr*, shoulder, bow of a ship; cf. Gr. πᾶχυς.

bowe, *sb.* bow, W2, PP; **bouwe**, W2; **bowes**, *pl.*, PP; **boys**, S3.—AS. *boga*.

bowe-lyne, *sb.* bowline, MD; **bawelyne**, S2.

bowen, *v.* to bow, bend, submit, to direct one's course, turn away, PP, S2, C2, W; **bouwe**, W2, PP; **boghen**, S2, H; **buwen**, S; **buȝen**, S; **buhen**, S; **bugen**, S; **beien**, S; **bowande**, *pr. p.* obedient, S2; **bues**, *pr. s.*, S2.—AS. *búgan*.

boydekyn, *sb.* poniard, bodkin, NED, Prompt.; **bodekyn**, Prompt.; **boydekins**, *pl.*, C2.

boyste, *sb.* box, PP, Prompt., Cath.; **boyst**, MD; **boist**, C3.—OF. *boiste* (F. *boîte*).

boȝte; see **biggen**[2].

brac, *sb.* a, crashing sound, *fragor*, **brace**, outcry, S.—Icel. *brak*; cf. AS. *(ge)bræc*.

brace, *sb.* couple of hounds, Prompt.—OF. *brace*, the two arms, a grasp; Lat. *brachia*, pl.

bracer, *sb.* a guard for the left arm in archery, C; **braser**, Voc. See Ascham, Toxophilus, ed. Arber, p. 108.

brade, *sb.* roast flesh, S; **brede**, S.—AS. *bréde*.

bradit; see **brayden**.

brak; see **breken**.

brand, *sb.* brand, firebrand, sword, MD; **brond**, brand, S2, C; **brondes**, *pl.*, S; **brands**, i.e. fire-side, S2; **brondis**, torches, W.—AS. *brand* (*brond*).

brant, *adj.* steep, high, MD, HD; **brent**, JD; **brentest**, *superl.*, S2.—AS. *brant* (*bront*); cf. Swed. *brant*, Icel. *brattr*.

bras, *sb.* brass, C2; **bres**, S; **breas**, S.—AS. *bræs*.

brasten; see **bresten**.

bratful; see **bretful**.

braȡ, *sb.* violence, MD; **braþþe**, *dat.*, S.—Cf. Icel. *bráȡ*. See **broþ**.

braun, *sb.* brawn, CM; boar's flesh, PP; **brawnes**, *pl.*, muscles, C2.—OF. *braon*, Prov. *bradon* (*brazon*); Low Lat. *bradonem*; see Ducange.

brayde, *sb.* a quick movement, a start, a while, moment, MD, CM; **braid**, S3; **braydes**, *pl.* grimaces, S2; **breides**, cunning tricks, MD. *Phr.*: **at a brayde**, in a moment, S2.—Icel. *bragȡ*, quick movement.

brayden, *v.* to draw, pull, to draw away quickly, to twist, braid, to start, to move quickly, hasten (intr.), to wake up, MD, Prompt., S2, CM; **breyde**, CM, C2; **breide**, W2; **breyde**, *pt. s.*, PP, CM, C2; C3; **brayde**, MD; **bradit**, S3; **broiden**, *pp.*, MD; **broydyn**, *laqueatus*, Prompt.; **brayden**, MD; **browden**, MD, JD; **browded**, C, HD; **brouded**, C2; **broyded**, WW; **brayded**, MD.—AS. *bregdan*, pt. *brægd* (pl. *brugdon*), pp. *brogden*.

brea-; see als words beginning in **bre-**.

breas, *sb.* brass, S; see **bras**.

bred[1], *sb.* bread, S, PP; **breed**, C2, W2; **bræd**, S; **bread**, S; **brad**, S; **brede**, S2; **breade**, *dat.*, S.—ONorth. *bréad*.

bred[2], *sb.* board, tablet, MD, S (s.v. *wax*); **brede**, Prompt.—AS. *bred*.

bred-ale, *sb.* bride-feast, S; see **bryd-ale**.

brede[1], *sb.* bride, PP; see **bryde**.

brede[2], *sb.* roast-flesh, S; see **brade**.

brede[3], *sb.* breadth, S, S2, S3, C2, H; **breede**, C, W2. *Phr.*: **on breid**, on breadth, abroad, S3; **did on breid**, did abroad, unfolded, S3.—AS. *brédu*.

breden[1], *v.* to spread, S, Prompt.—AS. *brédan*.

breden[2], *v.* to roast, MD; **bret**, *pr. s.*, S.—AS. *brédan*.

breden[3], *v.* to breed, to produce, to be produced, MD, PP; **bredden**, *pt. pl.*, PP; **i-bred**, *pp.*, S.—AS. *brédan*, to nourish. See **brode**[2].

bred-gume; see **brydegome**.

bred-wrigte, *sb.* bread-wright, baker, S. See **bred**[1].

breech, *sb. pl.* breeches, drawers, C2, C3; **brech**, S; **breche**, PP; **brek**, Voc.—AS. *bréc*, pl. of *bróc*; cf. Icel. *brækr*, pl. of *brók*.

breed; see **bred**[1].

breels, *sb. pl.* wretches, HD, MD (p. 343).

breggid, *pt. s.* shortened, W; see **abregge**.

breken, *v.* to break, S, S2, PP; **breoken**, S; **brecð**, *pr. s.*, S; **brac**, *pt. s.*, S; **brek**, S; **brec**, S2; **brak**, S2, PP; **breken**, *pl.*, S; **y-broke**, *pp.*, S2; **ibroke**, S2.—AS. *brecan*, pt. *bræc* (pl. *brǽcon*), pp. *brocen*.

brek-gurdel, *sb.* a breech-girdle, MD; **brek-gyrdylle**, *lumbare*, Voc.; **brechgerdel**, MD; **breigirdel**, MD; **brigirdil**, MD; **brygyrdyll**, Prompt.; **breigerdlis**, *pl.*, purses, PP. See **breech**.

breme[1], *sb.* bream, Prompt.; **brem**, C.—OF. *bresme* (F. *brème*); OHG. *brahsema*.

breme[2], *adj.* fierce, angry, S, S2, S3, H, PP; **brem**, S2; **breme**, *adv.*, S2; **breeme**, C.—AS. *bréme* famous, noble.

bremely, *adv.* fiercely, furiously, loudly, S2; **bremly**, S2.

bremstoon; see **brynston**.

bren, *sb.* bran, S2, C, P.—OF. *bren* (F. *bran*).

brene; see **brune**.

brenke; see **brink**.

brennen, *v.* to burn, S2, S3, C, C2, PP, W; **bren**, S2; **brinnen**, S, S2; **brende**, *pt. s.*, S, S2, C2; **brent**, S2; **brendon**, *pl.*, S; **brenneden**, W; **brende**, **brenned**, **brend**, S2; **brende**, C; **brenten**, W2; **brend**, *pp.*, S, S2, C; **brent**, C2, S3, W; **y-brend**, C3; **y-brent**, C.—Icel. *brenna*; cf. Goth. *brinnan*, Cf. **bernen**.

brenningly, *adv.* ardently, fiercely, C.

brent, *adj.* steep, high, S2, JD; see **brant**.

breo-; see also words beginning in **bre-**.

brerd, *sb.* brim, margin, surface, top, S3, MD; **brurd**, MD; **brerde**, MD.—AS. *brerd*, brim, top of a vessel; shore; cf. OHG. *brort*, also Icel. *broddr*, the front.

brerd-ful, *adv.* brimful, MD; **brurdful**, S2. Cf. **bretful**.

brere, *sb.* briar, S3, W2; **brer**, S3; **breres**, *pl.*, S, S3, C; **breris**, W.—AS. *brér*, also *brǽre*, pl. (OET).

bres; see **bras**.

bresil, *adj.* brittle, H; see **brisel**.

brest, *sb.* breast, C; **breost**, MD; **breast**, voice, S3; **breste**, PP; **bryst**, MD.—AS. *bréost*.

bresten, *v.* to burst, S2, C2, W, MD; **brasten**, S3, MD; **bersten**, S, C; **brast**, *pt. s.*, C3, PP; **barste**, P; **braste**, *pl.*, C3, S2; **brest**, S3; **brusten**, *pp.*, damaged, hurt severely, S2, MD.—Icel. *bresta*, pt. *brast*, pp. *brostinn*; cf. AS. *berstan*.

bretful, *adj.* brimful, S3, C, PP, HD; **bratful**, S2, PP; **bredful**, PP. Cf. Swed. *bräddful*. See **brerdful**.

breð, *sb.* breath, vapour, voice, word, MD, PP, CM; **breðe**, *dat.*, S.—AS. *brǽð*.

brethe, *sb.* anger, wrath, H; **breth**, H.—Icel. *brǽði*, anger, from *bráðr*, hasty. See **broþ**.

brethir; see **broþer**.

breuet, *sb.* brief, letter of indulgence, P; **breuettes**, *pl.*, P.—Late Lat. *brevetum*.

brewen, *v.* to brew, MD; **brew**, *pt. s.* contrived, C2, PP; **breuh**, S2, PP.—AS. *bréowan*, pt. *bréaw*, pp. *browen*.

brewestere, brewster, P; **breusters**, *pl.* ale-wives, female-brewers, S2, PP.

breyden; see **brayden**.

brid, *sb.* a young bird, PP, C2, C3, W; **bridd**, S; **bridde**, PP; **bred**, PP; **bredde**, PP; **berd**, MD; **bird**, MD; **briddes**, *pl.*, S2, C; **bryddez**, S2; **briddis**, W, H; **birds**, S3 (26. 1150).—AS. *bridd*.

brigge, *sb.* bridge, PP, S, CM; **brugge**, PP; **bregge**, MD; **brygge**, PP; **brig**, S2.—AS. *brycg*; cf. Icel. *bryggja*.

briggen, *v.* to bridge, S.

brike, *sb.* calamity, C2; see **bryk**.

bringen, *v.* to bring, S; **brohte**, *pt. s.*, S; **brochte**, S; **brouȝte**, S2; **brouhte**, S; **broȝte**, S, S2; **broght**, *pl.*, S2; **broht**, *pp.* S2; **broght**, S2; **brouȝt**, S2; **ibrȝt**, S2; **y-broȝt**, S2; **y-brought**, C; **ibroht**, S; **ibrouht**, S2; **ibrocht**, S.

brink, *sb.* brink, margin, MD; **brenke**, *dat.*, W; **brynke**, MD.—Cf. Swed. *brink*, Icel. *brekka*.

brinnen; see **brennen**.

brisel, *adj.* brittle, H; **bresil**, H; **brissal**, JD. See **brisen**.

brisen, *v.* to crush, MD; **brisse**, MD; **bresen**, MD; **brisid**, *pp.*, W.

brisokis, *sb. pl.* wild cabbage, H.

britel, *adj.* brittle, fragile, MD; **britil**, S2, W; **brutel**, MD; **brutil**, CM; **brotel**, MD.—From base of AS. *bruton*, *pt. pl.* of *bréotan*, to break.

britnen, *v.* to break, break up, MD; **bruttenet**, *pp.* destroyed, slain, S2; **bretynyd**, HD.—AS. *brytnian*, to distribute, dispense.

Britoner, *sb.* a man of Brittany, a Frenchman, P; **Brytonere**, P; see **Brutiner**.

briȝt, *adj.* bright, S, PP; **bricht**, S; **brict**, S; **briht**, S; **brigt**, S; **bryht**, S2; **bryȝt**, S2; **brihtre**, *comp.*, S; **briȝter**, S; **brictest**, *superl.*, S.—AS. *beorht*.

briȝte, *adv.* brightly, MD; **bryghte**, C2.

briȝtnesse, *sb.* brightness, W2; **brichtnesse**, S; **brihtnesse**, S; **brictnesse**, S.—AS. *beorhtnes*.

brocage, a treaty by an agent, PP; **brokages**, *pl.*, P.—OF. *brocage*, 'exprime l'idée de ruse et de perfidie' (Godefroy).

broche

broche, *sb.* brooch, match, spear, spit, MD; **brouch**, S2; **broch**, C; **broches**, *pl.*, C2, PP.—OF. *broche*.

brochen, *v.* to spur, pierce through, put on the spit, broach a cask, MD; **brochede**, *pt. s.*, S2, PP.—OF. *brocher*, Prov. *brocar*.

brocket, *sb.* a stag in its second or third year, HD, MD, Cotg.; **broket**, MD; **brokkettis**, *pl.*, S3.—Cf. OF. *brocart* (Cotg.).

brocour, *sb.* broker, P; **brokour**, P.—AF. *abrocour*; Low Lat. *abrocatorem* (Ducange), from *abrocare*, to broach a cask, from *broca*. See **broche**.

brod, *adj.* broad, S, S2, PP; **brood**, C; **braid**, S3; **brode**, C, PP; **brade**, S, S2, H; **broddeste**, *superl.*, W2.—AS. *brád*.

brode[1], *adv.* broadly, wide awake, C3; widely, PP; **broode**, broadly, plainly, C.

brode[2], *sb.* brood, S, Prompt.—Cf. OHG. *bruot* (Weigand).

broiden; see **brayden**.

brok[1], *sb.* brock, badger, Prompt.; **broc**, W; **brockes**, *pl.*, P; **brokkys**, PP.—AS. *broc*; OIr. *brocc*.

brok[2], *sb.* brook, PP; **broke**, P.—AS. *bróc*.

brol, *sb.* a brat, child, MD, S3, PP; **brolle**, P; **brawl**, ND.—Cf. Low Lat. *brollus*, 'miserculus' (Prompt., p. 50).

brond; see **brand**.

broð, *adj.* violent, MD; **braþ**, MD; **braith**, JD.—Icel. *bráðr*. Cf. **braþ**.

broþeful, *adj.* violent, MD; **braithful**, JD.

brothel, *sb.* a wretch, PP, MD, HD; **brothell**, Palsg.

broþeliche, *adv.* violently, MD; **broþely**, hastily, quickly, S2; **braithly**, JD.

broðer, *sb.* brother, PP; *gen. s.*, C2; **broðere**, *pl.*, S; **breðere**, S; **brethir**, S3; **breðre**, S; **briðere**, S; **bretheren**, C2, PP.—AS. *bróðor*.

broðer-hed, *sb.* brotherhood, MD; **bretherhede**, C; **britherhed**, W; **britherhod**, W.

broðer-rede, *sb.* fraternity, MD (p. 354).—AS. *bróðorrǽden*.

brouded, *pp.* braided, C2; see **brayden**.

broudster, *sb.* embroiderer, JD.

broudyng, *sb.* embroidery; **browdyng**, C, CM.

brouken, *v.* to use, enjoy, eat, PP, C, G; **bruken**, S; **breken**, S; **brooke**, to endure, S3; **bruc**, *imp. s.* use, S; **ibroken**, *pp.*, 3.—AS. *brúcan*, *pt. bréac* (*pl. brucon*), *pp. brocen*.

broun, *adj.* brown, C, PP; **brun**, *sb.* brown horn, S.—AS. *brún*.

bru-; see also words beginning with **bry-**, **bri-**, and **brou-**.

brugge; see **brigge**.

bule

bruk, *sb.* locust (= *bruchus*), W2, H; **bruyk**, H.—Gr. βροῦχος, βροῦκος.

brune, *sb.* burning, S, MD; **brene**, S2.—AS. *bryne*.

brunie, *sb.* corslet, coat of mail, S; **brinie**, MD; **brini**, HD, MD; **burne**, MD; **bryniges**, *pl.*, S; **brenyes**, HD.—Icel. *brynja*: Goth. *brunjo*; cf. AS. *byrne*.

brurd; see **brerd**.

brusten; see **bresten**.

Brut, *sb.* Briton; **Bruttes**, *pl.*, S.

Brutayne, *sb.* Brittany, S2.

brutil; see **britel**.

Brutiner, *sb.* a man of Brittany, a Frenchman, a swaggerer, PP; **Brytonere**, P; **Britoner**, P.

brutnen, *v.* to hew in pieces, MD; **bruttenet**, *pp.* slain, S2; see **britnen**.

bryche, *adj.* reduced, poor, S2.—AS. *bryce*, frail.

bryd-ale, *sb.* marriage-feast, MD; **bridale**, P, W; **bredale**, S; **bruydale**, P; **brudale**, S.—AS. *brýd-ealo*, a bride-ale, bride-feast.

bryde, *sb.* bride, *domiduca*, Voc., PP; **brede**, PP; **bruyd**, CM; **brud**, MD, S; **brid**, MD.—AS. *brýd*: OS. *brúd*; cf. OHG. *brút* (Otfrid).

bryde-gome, *sb.* bridegroom, MD; **bredgume**, S; **brudgume**, MD.—AS. *brýdguma* (*brédguma*); cf. OHG. *brútigomo* (Otfrid).

bryk, *sb.* misery, calamity, MD; **brike**, C2; **bruche**, injury, MD.—AS. *bryce*.

bryllyn; see **birlen**.

brymme, *sb.* margin, shore, S, MD.—AS. *brim*, surf, the sea; cf. Icel. *brim*.

bryn-ston, *sb.* sulphur, Voc., PP, S2; **brymston**, W2; **bremstoon**, C, PP; **brimstoon**, C3; **brunstan**, H.—Cf. Icel. *brennisteinn*.

brystylle, *sb.* bristle, Prompt., Voc.; **berstles**, *pl.*, C.—From AS. *byrst*: OHG. *burst*.

bryttlynge, *sb.* breaking up, S3. See **britel**.

bu-; see also words beginning in **bou-**, **bo-**.

budele, *sb.* beadle, officer, PP; **budeles**, *pl.*, S; **beodeles**, S2.—AS. *bydel*; cf. OHG. *butil*. Cf. **bedel**.

bue, **buð**; see **ben**.

bulde, *pt. s.* built, C; see **bilden**.

buggen, *v.* to buy, S, S2, PP; see **biggen**[2].

bugle, *sb.* wild ox, S2, Prompt.; **bugill**, S3; **buwgle**, S3, **bugle**, buffalo-horn, bugle, MD.—OF. *bugle*; Lat. *buculum* (acc.).

builen, *v.* to boil, S2; **buylith**, *pr. s.*, W2; **buylyng**, *pr. p.*, PP; **buyliden**, *pt. pl.*, W2.—OF. *buillir*; Lat. *bullire*.

bule[1]; see **bile**.

bule[2]; see **bole**[2].

32

bulle

bulle, *sb.* bull, papal rescript, P; **bille**, PP; petition, PP; **bylle**, PP.—Lat. *bulla*, boss, stud, hence Late Lat. *bulla*, seal, document with seal; see Ducange.

bulten, *v.* to boult, sift, C, Prompt.; **boulte**, Palsg.; **bultedd**, *pp.*, S.—OF. *buleter, bureter,* to sift through coarse cloth, from *bure*, coarse cloth; Late Lat. *burra*; see Ducange (s.v. *buratare*).

bult-pele, *sb.* a sifter, Voc.

bumbase, *v.* to quilt with bombast, i.e. cotton wadding, Florio (p. 234a); **bumbast**, *pr. pl.*, S3.—From Milanese *bombás*; Low Lat. *bombacem*, cotton; from Gr. βόμβυξ.

bummen, *v.* to taste, take a draught, MD; **bummede**, *pt. s.* tasted, S2, P.

bun, *pp.* prepared, S2, MD; see **boun**.

bunchen, *v.* to strike, MD, Prompt.; **bonchede**, *pt. s.*, S2; **bonched**, P.

bunden; see **binden**.

bur[1], *sb.* wind, storm, force, impetus, MD; **bir**, MD; **birr**, HD; **hire**, *dat.*, W, MD; **birre**, W; **byrre**, HD.—Icel. *byrr*, wind, storm.

bur[2], *sb.* the broad ring of iron behind the place for the hand on a tilting-spear, S3; **burr**, HD.

burde, *sb.* maiden, virgin, lady, S, S2, PP; **birde**, P; **berde**, PP; **buirde**, PP; **buyrde**, S2, PP; see **bryde**.

burden, *sb.* burden, Manip.; see **burþene**.

burdenous, *adj.* burdensome, S3.

burdon, *sb.* mule; **burdones**, *pl.*, MD; **burdowns**, MD.—Lat. *burdonem* (Vulg.).

burdoun, *sb.* droning sound, bass, MD, C.—OF. *bourdon*, a drone, the humming of bees, the drone of a bag-pipe (Cotg.).

bureth, *v.* it behoves, MD; **birrþ**, *pr. s.*, S; **burth**, MD; **birs**, MD; **bers**, MD; **birrde**, *pt. s.*, S; **bird**, S2, MD; **burd**, MD.—AS. *ge-byrian*; cf. OHG. *gi-burren*, to happen (Otfrid).

burgage, *sb.* an estate held of a lord of a borough; **burgages**, *pl.*, P; **borgages**, PP.—Low Lat. *burgagium*; OF. *bourgage* (Cotg.).

burgeis, *sb.* burgess, MD; **burgeys**, C, CM; **burgeis**, *pl.*, S2, P; **burgeyses**, P.—OF. *burgeis*; Low Lat. *burgensis*.

burgh, *sb.* borough, town, fortress, shelter, MD; **burghe**, PP, CM; **borghe**, PP; **borw**, PP; **borugh**, PP; **borowe**, PP; **borh**, S; **burch**, S; **burh**, S; **bureh**, MD, S; **biri**, MD, S; **berie**, S; **borwȝ**, S2; **borwes**, *pl.*, PP, MD.—AS. *burh*; gen. *byrig*.

buriel, *sb.* tomb, S2; **buryel**, S2; **biriel**, W; **biryel**, S2; **buriels**, *pl.* the Catacombs, C3; **biriels**, W2; **birielis**, W.—AS. *byrgels*.

burien[1], *v.* to bury, MD, S, PP; **birien**, MD, W2; **berien**, C3; **bery**, MD, C3; **byrien**, S; **i-burred**, *pp.*, S2.—AS. *byrigan*.

burien[2], *sb.* grave, MD; **berien**, S.—AS. *byrgen*.

burinisse, *sb.* burial-place, MD; **berynes**, H.—AS. *byrignes*.

burjoun, *sb.* burgeon, bud, MD; **burioyn**, H; **burgon**, HD; **burgionys**, *pl.*, S3; **burioyns**, H.—OF. *borjon*, in Cotg. *bourgeon*.

burjounen, *v.* to bud, MD; **buriowne**, W2; **burgionys**, *pr. s.*, S3; **borgouneȝ**, *pr. pl.*, S2; **burioneþ**, PP; **burionand**, *pr. p.*, H; **buriownynge**, W.

burn, *sb.* man, S2, HD; **burne**, S2; see **bern**[1].

burne, *sb.* spring of water, MD, S; **bourne**, S2; **borne**, S2; *burn, stream*, S2.—AS. *burna*.

burnen, *v.* to burnish, MD; **burned**, *pp.*, C; **borned**, S3.—OF. *brunir*, to burnish, polish, to make brown (Cotg.). See SkD. p. 789.

burnet[1], *adj.* brown, S3.—OF. *brunet*, brownish (Cotg.).

burnet[2], *sb.* cloth of brown colour, CM, MD.—OF. *brunette* (Cotg.); cf. Low Lat. *brunetum*.

burðene, *sb.* burden, MD; **birthin**, W; **birthun**, W2; **burden**, Manip.—AS. *byrðen*.

busch, *sb.* bush, wood, W, W2, MD; **buysch**, W; **busk**, the head or tuft of a stalk of wheat, S; bush, S2, MD; **boske**, S2; **boskez**, *pl.*, S2.

buschement, *sb.* ambush, MD; **busshement**, S3. Cf. OF. *en-buschement*, an ambuscade NED, (s.v. *ambushment*).

busken, *v.* to prepare oneself, to get ready, to go, to hasten, to prepare, dress, MD, H, S2, P; **buschen**, S2; **bosken**, S2. Icel. *búask* (reflex.), to get oneself ready.

buskinge, *sb.* equipment, dress, MD, S3; **bosking**, MD.

busteous, *adj.* noisy, S3; **buystous**, W; see **boistous**.

busy, *adj.* busy, MD; **bisi**, S, W2; **bisie**, S; **bisy**, C2, P; **besy**, C.—AS. *bysig*.

busyen, *v.* to busy, *occupare*, MD; **bisien**, C3, W.

busynesse, *sb.* business, activity, care, industry, MD, C, C3; **bisinesse**, C3; **besynesse**, S3; **besynes**, H; **bisynesses**, *pl.*, W2.

buþ[1]; see **ben**.

buþ[2]; see **biggen**[2].

buuen, *prep.* and *adv.* above, S; **buue**, S; **boue**, MD; **bufon**, S.—AS. *be-ufan*.

buxum, *adj.* obedient, ready, willing, courteous, PP; **boxum**, S2, PP; **buxom**, CM; **buhsum**, S. See **bowen**.

buxumliche, *adv.* obediently, PP; **boxumly**, S2; **buxomly**, C2.

buxumnesse, *sb.* obedience, PP; **buxomnes**, P; **boxumnes**, S2.

by-, *prefix.* See **bi-** words.

by[1], **bi**, *prep.* by, at, according to, S, S2, with regard to, PP, S, S2, S3; **bie**, S; **be** S, S2. *Phr.*: **by and by**, *adv.* immediately, S3; in order, separately, C, Prompt., MD.

by[2], *v.* to dwell, build, C2; see **biggen**[1].

bye, *v.* to buy, S2; **by**, C3; see **biggen**[2].

byggyng, *sb.* building, S2.

byȝe; see **beiȝ**.

34

C

For words in which initial **c-** *has the sound of* **k-**, *see also under* **K** *and* **Q** *below.*

caas[1], *sb.* case, circumstance, chance, C; **kas**, S2; **cass**, S3; **cas**, S2, C2.—AF. *cas*; Lat. *casum* (acc.), a fall, from *cadere*, to fall.

caas[2], *sb.* case, quiver, C; see **casse**.

caban, *sb.* hut, small room, MD, PP; **cabin**, MD.—OF. *cabane*; cf. Low Lat. *cabanna*, *capanna*; see Brachet.

cabine, *sb.* a shed made of boughs, Cotg. (s.v. *cabane*); **cabin**, small enclosed place, Sh.

cabinet, *sb.* small shed, arbour, S3.—OF. *cabinet*, an arbour in a garden, Cotg.; cf. It. *cabinetto* (Florio).

cacchen, *v.* to catch, to chase, MD, C3, P; **katchen**, MD; **kecchen**, MD; **chacche**, S2; **chacen**, MD; **chaci**, MD; **caucht**, S3; **cacces**, *pr. s.*, S2; **cahte**, *pt. s.*, MD; **caȝte**, S2; **caughte**, C2; **cauȝt**, MD; **cought**, MD; **caght**, MD; **cahten**, *pl.*, MD; **keiȝt**, MD; **caht**, *pp.* MD; **kauȝt**, W2.—OF. *cachier, cacier* (also *chacier, chasser*); Late Lat. *captiare*, from Lat. *captare*, freq. of *capere*, to take, to hold; see Constans.

cache-pol, *sb.* a tax-gatherer, constable, bailiff, MD, PP; **cahchpolle**, Prompt.; **catchepollis**, *pl.*, W.—AF. *cacchepole*, OF. *chacepol, chassipole*; cf. Low Lat. *cachepollus, cacepollus, chacepollus, chassipullus*. The form *cacepollus* is met with in the *Leges Ethelredi*, see Schmid and Ducange. The word probably meant at first the officer who collected from the tenant the fowls (*pullos*) paid as rent.

cacherel, *sb.* an inferior officer of justice, MD; **kachereles**, *pl.*, S2.—OF. *cacherel*; cf. Low Lat. *cacherellus*.

cæse; see **chese**.

cæste, *sb. dat.* chest, S; see **chest**[1].

caf, *sb.* chaff, H; see **chaf**.

caitif, *adj. and sb.* captive, miserable wretch, MD, W, C3, H; **caytif**, C2; **caytiue**, P; **caitifes**, *pl.*, S3; **caytiues**, S3; **kaytefes**, S2.—AF. *caitif*; Prov. *captiu*; Lat. *captiuum* (acc.); see Brachet (s.v. *chétif*).

caitifte, *sb.* wretchedness, S2, W, W2, H; **caytefte**, S2.—OF. *caitivete*; Lat. *captiuitatem*.

calabre, *sb.* Calabrian fur, P, S2 (p. 200); NQ. (5. 12. 232); **calabere**, P (*n*). *Comb.*: **calaber amyse**, a person wearing an amice trimmed with calabre, P (*n*).

cald; see **cold**.

calengen, *v.* to accuse, to charge, W2; see **chalengen**.

calewe, *adj.* bald, without hair, MD, S2.—AS. *calwo-*, stem of *calu*; cf. OHG. *chalo* (gen. *chálawes*), and Lat. *caluus*.

caliz, *sb.* chalice, S, MD, SkD; **chalis**, MD; **chalys**, Voc.; **calice**, *dat.* S, SkD.—OF. *caliz*; Lat. *calix*; also OF. *calice*; Lat. *calicem*.

calle, *sb.* a caul, net for the hair (worn by women), MD, CM, SkD (s.v. *caul*).

callen, *v.* to call, S, C2; **kalle**, MD, S2.—AS. *ceallian*; cf. Icel. *kalla*.

callour, *adj.* cool, fresh, healthy, JD, S3; **caller**, JD; **cauler**, JD.

calme, *adj.* calm, MD.—OF. *calme* (Cotg.), It. *calma* (Florio); Low Lat. *cauma*, heat (Vulg.); Gr. καῦμα.

calmen, *v.* to become calm, MD; **cawmyt**, *pp.*, S3.—OF. *calmer*; to quiet.

cal-stocke, *sb.*, cabbage-stalk, S3; **calstok**, 38 Voc.; **calstoke**, Palsg.; **castock**, JD; **custoc**, JD. See **cole**[1].

camamelle, *sb.* camomile, Voc.; **camemille**, Voc.; **camamyle**, Prompt.; **cammamyll**, Palsg.; **camomylle**, MD; **camamyld**, S3; **camamy**, Voc.—Late Lat. *camamilla*; Gr. χαμαίμηλον.

camel, *sb.* camel, MD; **camelle**, Prompt.; **camaille**, C2; **chamelle**, Prompt.; **chamayle**, MD.—OF. *camel*; Lat. *camelum* (acc.); Gr. κάμηλος; Heb. *gāmāl*. {The regular OF. equivalent for Lat. *camēlum* was *chameil*. In OF. *camel* the termination *-el* is due to analogy with French forms derived from *-ālem*. See BH, § 43.}

cameline, *sb.* camlet, MD.—OF. *cameline*; Low Lat. *camelinum*.

camelot, *sb.* camlet, SkD; **chamelot**, S3; **chamlet**, Cotg.—OF. *camelot* (Cotg.); cf. Low Lat. *camelotum*.

cammamyld, *sb.* camomile, S3; see **camamelle**.

camp, *sb.* contest, MD; **comp**, S; **kemp**, JD; **kampe**, *dat.*, MD.—AS. *camp* (*comp*); cf. Icel. *kapp*.

campe, *adj.* See **kempe**[2].

campen, *v.* to contend, contest, esp. at football, MD, Prompt.—AS. *campian*.

campynge, *sb. pedipiludium*, game of football, Prompt.

can, *pr. s.* can, knows, S, S2. *Phr.*: **can þanc**, S; see **kunnen**.

canceler, *sb.* chancellor, S; see **chaunceler**.

candel, *sb.* candle, MD; **kandel**, S; **candlen**, *pl.* S2.—AS. *candel (condel)*; Lat. *candela*; cf. Icel. *kyndill*, candle, torch.

candel-messe, *sb.* Candlemass, MD; **candel-masse**, *dat.*, S, S2.—Cf. Icel. *kyndill-messa*, in Church Lat. *candelaria*, the feast of the Purification.

canelle, *sb.* cinnamon, S2, Voc., Cath. (*n*); **canylle**, Cath.; **canel**, W, W2.—AF. *canelle*; Late Lat. *canella*, cinnamon, also, a reed (Ducange), from Lat. *canna*. See **canne**[1].

canevas, *sb.* canvas, C3; **canvas**, Voc.; **canwas**, Voc.—AF. *canevas, canevace*; Late Lat. *canabacius*, hempen cloth; from OF. *canve* (F. *chanvre*), hemp; Late Lat. *cannabum*, Lat. *cannabis*; Gr. κάνναβις.

cang, *adj.* foolish, lustful, MD; **canges**, *sb. gen.*, fool's, S; **kanges**, *pl.*, MD. See PP; Notes, (p. 241).

cangen, *v.* to befool, MD.

cang-liche, *adv.* foolishly, MD.

cang-schipe, *sb.* foolishness, MD.

canker, *sb.* cancer, a disease, MD, W; **cankyr**, Voc.; **cankere**, Voc.—Lat. *cancer*, crab, an eating tumour, also, in *pl. cancri*, lattice-work.

cankerd, *pp.* corrupted, S3.

canne[1], *sb.* cane, reed, MD; **cane**, Voc.—Lat. *canna*; Gr. κάννα, κάννη, cane, reed; Heb. *qāneh*.

canne[2], *sb.* can, MD, W; **cane**, Voc. Cf. Late Lat. *canna*, a measure for liquids; see Weigand (s.v. *Kanne*).

canon, *sb.* a rule, MD, PP; **canoun**, MD; canon-law, PP.—Lat. *canon*; Gr. κανών, a rule, standard, from κάνη, κάννη, a cane, reed. See **canne**[2].

canonisen, *v.* to admit into the canon of the Mass, to canonize, MD; to consecrate, admit to the dignity of the papacy, MD.—Late Lat. *canonizare*.

canonistres, *sb. pl.* men skilled in canon-law or ecclesiastical law, PP.—OF. *canoniste*; Late Lat. *canonista*.

canoun, *sb.* a canon of a chapter, MD; **kanun**, S; **chanoun**, S, Voc., C3, G; **chanon**, C3.—OF. *canone, canoine (chanoine)*; Church Lat. *canonicum* (acc.) one on the church-roll or list (*canon*). {Church Lat. *canonicus* did not mean originally 'one on the church-roll or list', but one who was bound to observe a certain rule of life (*canon*, κανών). OF. *chanoine* is not the precise equivalent of *canonicum*, but represents a Latin type **canonium*. See Scheler's Dict. (ed. 3).}

cant[1], *adj.* lively, brave, cheerful, MD, S2, JD.

cant[2], *sb.* a portion, S3; corner, SkD, ND.—OF. *cant*; cf. It. *canto*, corner (Florio).

cantel, *sb.* edge, piece, bit, MD, C, Prompt., Palsg.; **kantel**, MD; **cantle**, Sh., ND.—OF. *cantel* (F. *chanteau*).

caper-cailye, *sb.* capercailyie, JD.—Ir. *capull-coille*, lit., the horse of the forest. See **capul**.

capitain, *sb.* captain, C2; **capitayne**, S3.—OF. *capitain*; Late Lat. *capitaneum* (acc.) captain, from Lat. *caput*.—Cf. **chevetayn**.

capitle, *sb.* the sum, the chief point, W; see **chapitre**.

cappe, *sb.* cap, MD; **keppen**, *pl.*, S.

capret, *sb.* a wild goat, W2; **capretis**, *pl.*, W2.—Late Lat. *capretus*; cf. F. *chevrette*.

capul, *sb.* horse, nag, MD, Prompt., PP, HD; **capil**, MD; **capel**, C3; **caple**, MD, PP, HD.—Icel. *kapall*; Lat. *caballus*; cf. Ir. *capull*, Wel. *ceffyl*.

caracter, *sb.* a mark, sign, character, W; **carecter**, W; **carracte**, Palsg.; **carecte**, PP; **carect**, W; **caractes**, *pl.*, HD; **carectes**, PP.—Lat. *character*; Gr. χαρακτήρ, an engraved mark; cf. Prov. *caracta*.

carayne, *sb.* carrion, S2; see **caroigne**.

carboncle, *sb.* a precious stone, MD; **carbokyl**, Voc.; **charboncle**, MD; **charbucle**, MD; **charbocle**, C2.—OF. *carboncle* (*carboucle, charboucle*); Lat. *carbunculum* (acc.).

carde, *sb.* teasel, Prompt.; —OF. *carde*; Late Lat. *cardum* (acc.), from Lat. *carduus*, thistle.

carden, *v.* to card wool, MD, Prompt., S3.—OF. *carder*, It. *cardare* (Florio).

cardiacle, *sb.* pain about the heart, PP, Cath. (*n*), C3; **cardyacle**, Prompt.; **cardiakylle**, Cath., Voc.; **cardiake**, Cath.—OF. *cardiaque*, a malady of the heart (Cotg.); Late Lat. *cardiaca*, 'cordis passio'; Gr. καρδιακός, from καρδία, the heart. For the intrusive *l*, see **cronique**.

care, *sb.* grief, S, C3, G; **cayr**, S3; **kare**, S2.—AS. *cearu*: OS. *kara*; cf. OHG. *chara*.

care-full, *adj.* full of grief, S3, C; **karful**, S2; **carefullich**, *adv.* anxiously, P; **carfuli**, S2.

caren, *v.* to be anxious, MD; **karien**, S; **cared**, *pt. s.*, G; *pl.*, P.—AS. *cearian*.

carf, *pt. s.* cut, C2; see **kerven**.

carited, *sb.* charity, S; see **charitee**.

cark, **carke**; see **charge**.

carl, *sb.* a man, *rusticus, colonus, maritus*, MD, C3.—Icel. *karl*; cf. OHG. *karl* (Otfrid).

carl-man, *sb.* a man; **carman**, MD; **caremane**, MD; **carlmen**, *pl.*, S.—Icel. *karlmaðr (karmaðr)*, a man, male.

carme, *sb.* a Carmelite friar; **karmes**, *pl.*, S3.—OF. *Carme* (Bartsch); from Church Lat. *Carmelus*; Heb. *Carmel*, 'cultivated land'.

caroigne

celle

caroigne, *sb.* carrion, MD, PP, C; **caroyne**, MD, PP; **caroin**, S2; **careyne**, MD, PP; **careyn**, W2; **carayne**, MD, S2; **caraing**, MD; **karyun**, H; **carion**, MD; **caren**, MD; **karyn**, MD; **careyns**, *pl.* W.—OF. *caroigne* (F. *charogne*); cf. It. *carogna*; from Lat. *caro*, flesh. See **crone**.

carole, *sb.* a round dance, singing, MD; **karole**, a chain, MD; **caroles**, *pl.*, C; **carolles**, MD.—OF. *carole* (*carolle*); It. *caróla*, a dance, song (Florio); Low Lat. *carola*, *karola*, a dancing, also, a chain (of pearls), see Ducange; Lat. *corolla*, a wreath; dimin. of *corona*.—ALM. For another account of this word see SkD.

carolen, *v.* to dance in a ring, to sing, MD, PP.

carolinge, *sb.* carolling, C3.

carpen, *v.* to talk, to speak, to say, MD, C, S3; to rebuke, S3; **carpede**, *pt. s.*, S2; **carped**, S2, P.—Icel. *karpa*, to boast.

carpyng, *sb.* talking, P.

carre, *sb.* car, cart, Prompt.; **charre**, MD; **chare**, Voc., S3, W; **schare**, *carpentum*, Voc.; **char**, S2, S3, C, C2; **chaar**, MD; **charis**, *pl.*, W, W2, H.—OF. *carre*, also *car* (*char*); Lat. *carrum* (acc.). A Celtic word, cf. OIr. *carr* (Windisch).

carry, *v.* *carro vehere*, to carry, MD; **carien**, C2; to drive, ride, travel, S2; **y-caried**, C2.—AF. *carier* (OF. *charier*, *charroier*); Late Lat. *carricare* (*carrigare*), see Ducange. See **chargen**.

carte, *sb.* chariot, cart, MD; **kart**, H (Ps. 67. 18).

cary, *sb.* a rough material, S3; see **cauri-maury**.

casse, *sb.* box, chest, cover, Prompt.; **kace**, Prompt.; **caas**, C.—OF. *casse* (AF. *chasse*); Lat. *capsa*; cf. Gr. κάψα.

cast, *sb.* a throw, plan, intention, plot, MD, C, G; **caste**, P; **kastis**, *pl.*, H.—Icel. *kast*.

castel[1], *sb.* village, small town (= *castellum*), W; **castels**, *pl.*, camp (= *castra*), W2; **kastels**, H (Ps. 77. 32).—Late Lat. *castellum*, village (Vulg.), Lat. *castellum*, fortress.

castel[2], *sb.* castle, S.—OF. *castel* (*chastel*). See **castel**[1].

castel-weorces, *sb. pl.* fortifications, S, MD.

casten, *v.* to cast, throw, to consider, imagine, purpose, design, S, S2, S3, C; **kasten**, MD, H; **kesten**, MD, S2; **caste**, *pt. s.*, MD, S2, S3, C2, C3, G; **kast**, S2; **kest**, S3; **casten**, *pl.*, P, W; **kesten**, S2, W; **castiden**, W; **casten**, *pp.*, MD, C2; **i-cast**, S; **y-cast**, C3; **ikest**, S2; **kest**, S2; **cast**, C3. *Phr.*: **caste tornes**, tried tricks, G.—Icel. *kasta*.

castyng, *sb.* a vomiting, W.

cat, *sb.* cat, Voc., MD; **catt**, Voc.; **kat**, S.

catapuce, *sb.* name of a purgative plant, euphorbia, C; **catapus**, CM.—OF. *catapuce* (*petite*), garden spurge (Cotg.); Low Lat. *catapotium*, 'medicamentum quod non diluitur, pillula' (Ducange); Gr. καταπό-τιον, that can be gulped down, a pill, from πότος, drink. Cf. Low Lat. *cathapucia*, 'semen spurgie', SB.

cat-cluke, *sb.* trefoil, S3, JD; **catluke**, JD; **ketelokes**, *pl.*, H (Ps. 36. 2).

catel, *sb.* capital, property, wealth, CM, MD, S2, C2, C3, W; **kateyl**, S2; **catelle**, S2; **catele**, S2; **chatel**, MD; **chetel**, MD.—OF. *catel*, *chatel*; Late Lat. *captale*, *capitale*, property, principal; from Lat. *capitalis*, from *caput*, the head.

catour, *sb.* a buyer of provisions, caterer, Palsg., G; **cater**, S3.—OF. *acateur*, buyer, from *acater* (F. *acheter*), *achapter*; Late Lat. *accaptare*.

caucion, *sb.* security, surety, account, MD; **caucioun**, W.—Lat. *cautionem*, security, bond, warranty, from *cautus*, pp. of *cauere*, to be on one's guard.

caudron, *sb.* cauldron, W2.—AF. *caudron*, OF. *chaudron*. See **chaud**.

cauri-maury, *sb.* the name of a coarse rough material, PP; **caurimauri**, S2; **kaury-maury**, PP; **cawrymawry**, PP (*n*). Cf. **cary**.

cautele, *sb.* caution, deceit, MD, Prompt.; **cawtele**, S3; **cautel**, ND, Sh.—OF. *cautele* (*cautelle*); Lat. *cautela*.

cautelous, *adj.* sly, deceitful, MD, ND, Sh.; **cautelouse**, W2.—OF. *cautelos*; Late Lat. *cautelosum* (Ducange).

cavell, *v.* to divide by lot, JD; see **kevel**.

cawmyt, *pp.* calmed, S3; see **calmen**.

caȝte; see **cacchen**.

cedre, *sb.* cedar, MD, W2 (Job 40. 12); **cedres**, *pl.*, S2.—AF. *cedre*; Lat. *cedrum* (acc.); Gr. κέδρος.

cedyr-tre, *sb.* cedar-tree, Voc.; **sydyre-tre**, Voc.

ceelen, *v.* to line the walls or roof of a room, Prompt., MD; **selyn**, Prompt.; **seeled**, *pp.*, WW (s.v. *cieled*).

ceinte, *sb.* girdle, MD; **seynt**, C.—OF. *ceinte*; Lat. *cincta*, pp. f. of *cingere*.

celer, *sb.* cellar, *promptuarium*, Prompt., W (Lu. 12. 24), MD; **celler**, MD; **seller**, G; **selleer**, G; **celere**, *dat.* S, H; **celeris**, *pl.*, W2; **selers**, W2.—AF. *celer*, OF. *celier*; Lat. *cellarium*.

celerer, *sb.* cellarer, C2.

celicall, *adj.* heavenly, S3.

celle, *sb.* cell, a religious house, C, C2; **selle**, C; **selles**, *pl.*, P.—OF. *celle*; Lat. *cella*.

37

celure

celure, *sb.* canopy, ceiling; see **selure**.

cementing, *sb.* hermetically sealing, C3. See **syment**.

cendal, *sb.* a fine stuff (linen or silk), S, MD; **sendal**, PP, ND, C; **cendel**, MD, HD, Prompt.; **sendel**, PP, H; = Lat. *sindon*, W, Voc.; **cendell**, Palsg.; **sendalle**, Cath.; **sendylle**, *sandalium, sindo*, Cath.—OF. and AF. *cendal* (cf. Low Lat. *cendalum, sendalum*); perhaps an adaptation of Gr. σινδών, orig. Indian muslin, from Skt. *Sindhu*, India.

centaure, *sb.* centaury, name of a plant, C; **centorye**, Alph.—OF. *centaure*; Lat. *centaurea, centaureum*; Gr. κενταύρειον, from κένταυρος, a centaur.

ceptre, *sb.* sceptre, C2, MD, Palsg.; **ceptyr**, Prompt.; **ceptire**, H (Ps, 44. 8).—AF. *ceptre*; Lat. *sceptrum*; Gr. σκῆπτρον, staff.

cerchen, *v.* to search, MD; **cergyn**, Prompt.; **serchen**, MD; **sherch**, S3; **seirsand**, *pr. p.*, S3; **sherched**, *pt. pl.*, S3.—OF. *cercher* (*sercher*); Lat. *circare*, to go round, from *circus*, a circle.

cercle, *sb.* circle, MD, C; **sercle**, Prompt., W2.—OF. *cercle*; Lat. *circulum* (acc.), dimin. of *circus*.

cerclen, *v.* to circle, MD; **sirculit**, *pp.*, S3.—OF. *cercler*; Lat. *circulare*.

circulat, *adj.* revolving, S3.

cere, *v.* to cover with wax, SkD, C3; **cered**, *pp.* shrouded in waxed cloth, SkD.—Lat. *cerare*, to wax, from *cera*, wax.

cere-cloth, *sb.* waxed linen (for dead bodies), Sh.; **searcloth**, SkD.

cerements, *sb. pl.* burial cloth, Sh. See **cere**.

cerge, *sb.* wax taper, MD; **serge**, MD, JD, Cath.; **cerges**, *pl.*, S.—OF. *cerge, cierge*; Late Lat. *ceria*, fem. from Lat. *cereus*, from *cera*, wax.

cerial, *adj.* sacred to Ceres, C.—Lat. *Cerialis, Cerealis*.

ceriously, *adv.* minutely, with full details, S2, C3; see **seryowsly**.

certes, *adv.* certainly, S, C2, C3; **sertes**, S2, PP; **certis**, S3, P.—OF. *certes*, (Constans): OSp. *certas*; Lat. *certas*, pl. f. of *certus*, certain.

ceruse, *sb.* ceruse, white lead, with which women painted their faces, MD; **ceruce**, C.—OF. *ceruse* (Cotg.); Lat. *cerussa*; cf. Gr. κηρωτόν, a cerate or salve used as a cosmetic, from κηρός, bees-wax.

cessen, *v.* to cease, C2, C3; **cesen**, MD.—AF. *cesser*; Lat. *cessare*.

cetewale, *sb.* zedoary, a root resembling ginger, MD, C2, Prompt., SB; **setewale**, MD, HD; **setwale**, Prompt.; **setuale**, Prompt.; **sedewale**, MD; **sedwale**, MD; **zedewale**, Alph.—AF. *cetewale*; cf. *citoual*,

champion

citouart; Low Lat. *zedoarium*; Arab. *jadwár* (from the Persian).

ceðen, *sb. pl.* countries, S; see **cuþþe**.

chaf, *sb.* chaff, straw, MD; **chaff**, MD; **chaffe**, W, Prompt.; **chef**, MD; **caf**, H; **cafe**, H.—AS. *ceaf*.

chaffare, *sb.* business, selling, merchandise, S2, C2, C3; **chaffar**, C3; **chafare**, S; **cheffare**, S; **chapfare**, MD; **cheapfare**, MD.—AS. *céap + faru*, a journey, business; cf. Icel. *kaupför*.

chaffaren, *v.* to chaffer, S2, C3, P, W.

chaflet, *sb.* a small stage or platform, S3, HD.—A dimin. of OF. *chafaut, chaffaut*, see Ducange (s.v. *chaaffallum*). See **skaffaut**.

chaine, *sb.* chain; **chayne**, MD; **cheyne**, Prompt., C2; **chyne**, MD.—AF. *chaine* (*cheine*); OF. *chaäine, cadene*; Lat. *catena*.

chaire, seat, chair, MD; **chayere**, MD; **chaier**, W2; **chaere**, S, MD.—AF. *chaïère, chayère*, seat, throne; Lat. *cathedra*; Gr. καθέδρα.

chald, *adj.* cold, S; see **cold**.

chalenge, *sb.* false claim, accusation, claim, MD, W2; **calenge**, MD; **chalaunge**, MD.—AF. *chalenge, chalange*, OF. *calenge*; Lat. *calumnia*.

chalengen, *v.* to accuse, charge, claim, MD, W, S2, P; **chalange**, H; **calengynge**, *pr. p.*, W2; **chalangede**, *pt. s.*, S2; **chalanged**, *pp.* accused, P.—AF. *chalenger, chalanger*, 'calumniate'.

chalengere, *sb.* accuser, W2.

chamber, *sb.* chamber, MD; **chambur**, MD; **schambyr**, Voc.; **chambre**, C2, C3, PP; **chombre**, MD; **chaumbre**, MD, PP; **chawmere**, MD; **chamer**, Voc.; **chalmer**, S3.—AF. *chambre*; Lat. *camera*.

chamberere, *sb.* handmaid, MD, S2, C2; **chambrere**, MD; **chomberier**, MD.—OF. *chamberiere*.

chamberling, *sb.* chamberlain; **chaumberling**, MD; **chamberlein**, MD; **schamberleyne**, Voc.; **chamberlayn**, MD; **chamerlane**, Voc.—OF. *chamberlenc* (cf. It. *camerlengo* in Florio); OHG. *chamarlinc*; Lat. *camera* + OHG. *-linc*. On the suffix see SkD.

chamelle; see **camel**.

chamelot, *sb.* camlet, S3; see **camelot**.

champaine, *adj.* and *sb.* level, level country, CM, S3.—AF. *champaigne*.

champarde, *sb.* share in land, partnership in power, C; **chanpartye**, S3.—OF. *champart*, field-rent, see Cotg.; Lat. *campi partem*.

champion, *sb.* a fighter in the duel, a champion, MD; **champioun**, C, G.—AF. *champion*; Late Lat. *campionem*.

chan-; see also words beginning in **chaun-**.

chanoun; see **canoun**.

chape, *sb.* the locket of a scabbard, Cotg., Cath.; **schape**, Cath. (*n*).—OF. *chappe* (Cotg.).

chapele, *sb.* chapel, S, MD; **chapelle**, MD; **schapelle**, Voc.—AF. *chapele*, OF. *capele*; Church Lat. *capella*.

chapelein, *sb.* chaplain, MD; **chapeleyne**, MD, C; **chapeleyns**, *pl.*, S2.—AF. *chapelein*; Church Lat. *capellanus*.

chapiter, *sb.* the capital of a column, SkD.—OF. *chapitel*; Lat. *capitellum*, dimin. of *caput*.

chapitre, *sb.* a chapter, division of a book, a meeting of clergy, MD, PP; **chapiter**, S3; **chapitere**, PP; **chapitle**, PP; **chapitele**, PP; **capitle**, summary, W.—OF. *chapitre*, *chapitle*; Lat. *capitulum*, dimin. of *caput*.

chapitre-hous, *sb.* chapter-house, PP; **chapitel-hous**, PP.

chapman, *sb.* merchant, C, PP; **chapmon**, S2, PP; **chepmon**, S; **chapmen**, *pl.*, S, S2, C3, PP.—AS. *céapman*.

chapmanhode, *sb.* trade, S2, C3.

chapolory, *sb.* a kind of scarf, S3; see **scaplorye**.

char, **chare**, *sb.* car, S3; see **carre**.

charbocle, *sb.* carbuncle (stone), C2; see **carboncle**.

charen, *v.* to turn, S; see **cherren**.

charge, *sb.* a load, injunction, responsibility, MD, S2, C3, C, W; **charche**, MD; **carke**, S3; **karke**, MD; **cark**, MD, G.—AF. *charge*, also *kark*.

chargen, *v.* to put a load on, to enjoin, MD, S2; to care for, W, W2; **charchyng**, *pr. p.*, S3; **y-charged**, *pp.*, S2; **charged**, S2.—AF. *charger*; OF. *cargier*; Late Lat. *carricare*. See **carry**.

chargeouse, *adj.* burdensome, W; **chariouse**, W2.

charitee, *sb.* charity, C2; **charyte**, S2; **charite**, MD, S2, G; **carited**, S; **kariteþ**, MD.—AF. *charite*, OF. *caritet*, Prov. *caritat*; Lat. *caritatem*. Cf. **cherte**.

chariȝ, *adj.* sad, S.—AS. *cearig*; cf. OS. *karag*. See **care**.

charnel, *sb.* charnel-house, P, SkD.—AF. *charnel*, *carnel*; Lat. *carnalem*.

chartre¹, *sb.* prison, S, MD.—OF. *chartre*, Ps. 141. 7; Lat. *carcerem*, see Brachet. For *tr* from original *cr*, compare OF. *veintre*; Lat. *vincere*.

chartre², *sb.* charter, S, PP.—AF. *chartre*; Lat. *chartula*, dimin. of *charta*.

chase, *sb.* hunting, pursuit, also, hunting-ground, MD; **chas**, MD; **chays**, S3.—AF. *chace*, hunting-ground.

chaser, *sb.* hunter (horse), chaser, MD; **chaseris**, *pl.*, S2.

chastelet, *sb.* little castle, domain, P.—OF. *chastelet* (Cotg.). See **castel²**.

chasteleyne, *sb.* castellan, MD.—AF. *chasteleyn*.

chastien, *v.* to chastise, MD, S; **chaste**, S2, C2, P.—AF. *chastier*, OF. *castier*; Lat. *castigare*.

chastisen, *v.* to chastise, MD; **chastyse**, C2.

chastyng, *sb.* chastisement, P.

chaud, *adj.* hot, S2, PP.—OF. *chaud*, *chald*; Late Lat. *caldum*; from Lat. *calidus*.

chaunce, *sb.* chance, S2, C2, C3; **cheance**, MD; **cheaunce**, MD; **chans**, MD; **chance**, S3.—OF. *cheance*; Late Lat. *cadentia*, a falling, from *cadere*.

chauncel, *sb.* chancel, Prompt.; **chauncell**, Palsg.; **chawnsylle**, Voc.—OF. *chancel*; Late Lat. *cancellus*, chancel, screen; cf. Lat. *cancetti*, *pl.*, latticework, dimin. of *cancri*, lattice work, from *cancer*, a crab. See **canker**.

chaunceler, *sb.* chancellor, Prompt.; **chanceler**, MD; **cancaler**, S.—AF. *chanceler*, OF. *cancelier*; Late Lat. *cancellarius*.

chauncellerie, *sb.* chancery, MD; **chancelerie**, MD.—AF. *chauncelerie*.

chauncerye, *sb.* chancery, MD.—AF. *chancerie*.

chaunge, *sb.* change, C2.

chaungen, *v.* to change, MD, S2; **chaungi**, S; **chongen**, S2; **i-changet**, *pp.*, S.—AF. *changer*; OF. *changier*, *cangier*; Low Lat. *cambiare*, to barter.

chaunger, *sb.* money-changer, W.

chaungyng, *sb.* changing, W2.

chaunterie, *sb.* chantry for singing masses for the dead, C.—AF. *ckaunterie*, OF. *chanterie*; Late Lat. *cantaria*, from Lat. *cantare*, to sing.

chavel, *sb.* the jaw; **chavyl**, MD; **chawle**, MD; **chaul**, MD; **choule**, MD; **chol**, S3; **choll**, MD.—AS. *ceafl*. See further in SkD (s.v. *jowl*).

chavyl-bone, *sb.* jaw-bone, Prompt.; **chavylbon**, MD.

che-; see also words beginning in **chi-**.

cheap, *sb.* bargain, S; see **chepe¹**.

cheap-ild, *sb.* a female trader, S. See **-ild** suffix.

chearre, *v.* to turn, S; see **cherren**.

cheas, *pt. s.* chose, S; see **chesen**.

cheast; see **chest¹**.

checker, *sb.* exchequer, S3; see **escheker**.

cheef, *sb.* and *adj.* head, upper part, chief, MD, PP; **chief**, MD; **cheff**, PP; **chef**, MD; **chyf**, PP.—OF. *chef* (AF. *chief*) *cheve*; Late Lat. *capum* (acc.); cf. It. *capo*, Sp. *cabo*.

cheef-mete

cheef-mete

cheef-mete, *sb.* chief meat, PP, S2.

chees; see **chesen**.

cheffare, *sb.* business, S; see **chaffare**.

chekelew, *adj.* suffocating, HD; see **-lewe**.

cheken, *v.* to choke, suffocate, MD, Prompt., SkD. See NED (s.v. *achoke*).

cheker, *sb.* exchequer, PP; see **escheker**.

cheld, *adj.* cold, S2; see **cold**.

chelde, *sb.* cold, PP.

chelden, *v.* to grow cold, S; **kelde**, MD.— AS. *cealdian.*

chĕle[1], *sb.* chill, S, S2; see **chil**.

chĕle[2], *sb.* throat, fur made up from the fur about the marten's throat, S; **cheole**, MD; **chelle**, MD.—AS. *ceole*, the throat; cf. OHG. *chĕla* (G. *kehle*). See **meþeschele**.

chelle, *sb.* bowl, incense-vessel, S.—AS. *ciella* (*cylle*), a vessel for drinking; cf. OHG. *chella*.

chemys, *sb.* chief mansion, JD; see **chymmys**.

chene; see **chyne**.

cheosen; see **chesen**.

chepe[1], *sb.* bargain, business, MD; **cheap**, S. *Phr.*: **good chepe**, cheap, MD; **gret chep**, plenty, cheapness, MD; **to good cheep**, too cheaply, G.—AS. *céap*, business, purchase, price, also, cattle; Icel. *kaup*, bargain; cf. OHG. *kouf* (Otfrid).

chepe[2], *sb.* Cheapside, S3, P.

chepen, *v.* to transact business, buy or sell, MD, S; **chepet**, *pp.*, S.—AS. *céapian*, to bargain.

cheping, *sb.* market, W; **chepynge**, S2, P.—AS. *céapung*, trade, commerce.

chepmon; see **chapman**.

cher, *adj.* dear, PP; **chere**, MD. *Phr.*: **cher ouer**, careful of, PP.—OF. *cher*; Lat. *carum*.

cherarchy, *sb.* an assembly of holy rulers, a hierarchy, S3; **yerarchy**, SkD (p. 810).— OF. *hierarchie*; Gr. ἱεραρχία; cf. It. *gerarchía*, a hierarchy of angels (Florio).

cherche, *sb.* church, S2, C3; see **chirche**.

chere[1], *sb.* a time, S; see **cherre**.

chere[2], *sb.* face, friendly welcome, S, MD, S2, S3, C3, G, C2; **chiere**, S3; **cheare**, S3; **cheere**, G; **cher**, S2; **cheer**, W; **cheres**, *pl.*, wry faces, S.—AF. *chere*, countenance, OF. *chere*, head (Roland); Low Lat. *cara*, the face, head; Gr. κάρα; see Ducange. Cf. E. *cheer*.

cheren, *v.* to make good cheer, to make glad, MD, Prompt., S.

cheriche, *v.* to cherish, PP; **cheryce**, C2.— OF. *cherir* (pr. p. *cherissant*).

cherissing, *sb.* cherishing, PP.

cherl, *sb.* peasant, S, S2, C2, C3; **chorle**, Prompt.; **churle**, Voc.—AS. *ceorl*; cf. MHG. *kerl*. Cf. **carl**.

chesunabile

cherliche, *adv.* dearly, fondly, PP; **cherli**, S2. See **cher**.

cherre, *sb.* a turn, space of time, business, affair, job, MD; **chere**, S; **char**, MD; **chore**, SkD (p. 792).—AS. *cerr* (*cirr, cyrr*); cf. OHG. *chér*.

cherren, *v.* to turn, MD; **chearre**, S; **churren**, S; **charen**, S; **cherde**, *pt. pl.*, S.—AS. *cerran* (*cirran*); cf. OHG. *kéren* (Otfrid).

cherte, *sb.* charity, MD: friendship, S3.— OF. *cherte*; Lat. *caritatem*. Cf. **charitee**.

cherubim, *sb. pl.* cherubim; **cherubym**, W2 (Ps. 17. 12); **cherubin**, S2; **cherubyn**, H.—Church Lat. *cherubim* (Vulg.); Heb. *cherubim*, pl. of *cherub*. Cf. OF. *cherubins*, PS. 17. 10.

chervelle, *sb.* chervil, PP; **cherefelle**, Alph.; **chiruylles**, *pl.*, PP.—AS. *cærfille* (Voc.); Lat. *caerifolium*; Gr. χαιρέφυλλον; cf. OF. *cerfueil* (Cotg.).

chery, *sb.* cherry, Voc.; **chere**, Voc.; **chiries**, *pl.* cherries, S2, P.—OF. *cerise*; Late Lat. *cerasea*, adj. from *cerasum*, cherry; from Gr. κέρασος, cherry-tree; see Diez.

chesbolle, *sb.* a small onion, poppy-head, Voc.; **chesebolle**, HD; **chessebolle**, HD; **chespolle**, Voc.

chese, *sb.* cheese, MD, Voc., S (18. 643); **schese**, Voc.; **cæse**, S.—OMerc. *cése* (OET), AS. *cése*; Lat. *caseus*.

chesen, *v.* to choose, S, S2, C2, C3, G; **cheosen**, S, S2, MD; **ches**, *imp. s.*, S2; **chees**, C3; **choyss**, S3; **cheas**, *pt. s.*, S; **ches**, MD, S2; **chees**, MD, S2, C2, C3; **chesit** (*weak*), S3; **curen**, *pl.*, MD; **cusen**, S; **icoren**, *pp.*, S; **ychose**, PP; **cosan**, S.— AS. *céosan*, pt. *céas* (pl. *curon*), pp. *coren*.

chesible, *sb.* chasuble, P; **chesibylle**, Voc.; **chesyble**, Palsg.; **chesypyl**, Voc.; **chesypylle**, Prompt.—OF. **chasible*, cf. Church Lat. *casibula, casubula* (OF. *chasuble*); from *casula*, a sacerdotal vestment, from Lat. *casa*, a cottage.

chesun, *sb.* cause, account, MD; **chesun**, S2, H; **cheson**, H. See **achesoun**.

chest[1], *sb.* jangling, strife, MD, P; **cheast**, MD; **cheaste**, MD; **cheste**, G, S; **cheestis**, *pl.*, W.—AS. *céast*.

chest[2], *sb.* chest, ark, coffin, PP, MD; **chæst**, MD; **cæste**, *dat.*, S. Cf. **kist**.

chesten, *sb.* chestnut-tree, Manip.; **chesteyn**, C, MD; **cheston**, Voc.—AF. *chestaine*, OF. *chastaigne*; Lat. *castanea*; from Gr. κάστανον.

chesten-tre, *sb.* chestnut-tree, MD; **chestantre**, Voc.

chesun, *sb.* cause, occasion, account, S2, H; see **chesoun**.

chesunabile, *adj.* open to an accusation, H.

40

cheðen, *sb. pl.* countries, S; see **cuþþe.**

cheuaunce, *sb.* gain, profit, MD.

cheuen, *v.* to succeed, to attain one's end, MD, C3, P; **cheeuen,** S2.—OF. *chevir,* from *chef.* See **cheef.**

cheuesance, *sb.* success, profit, agreement, MD, PP; **cheuisaunce,** agreement, bargain, PP, C.—OF. *chevisance.*

cheuesen, *v.* to procure, to get, MD; **chevisen,** MD; **cheviss,** to achieve one's purpose, S2; **cheuyce,** to lend, S3.—OF. *chevir* (pr. p. *chevissant*).

cheuetayn, *sb.* captain, S2; **cheueteyn,** MD; **cheventeyn,** S2, PP, C; **cheuentayn,** MD, PP; **chefetayn,** MD; **chiveteyn,** MD; **chiftaigne,** PP.—AF. *chevetayn* (*cheventeyn*); Late Lat. *capitaneum,* from Lat. *capit-* stem of *caput,* head. Cf. **capitain.**

chewen, *v.* to chew, S, S2; **cheowen,** MD.—AS. *céowan,* pt. *céaw* (pl. *cuwon*), pp. *cowen.*

cheyne, *sb.* chain, C2; see **chaine.**

chibolle, *sb.* a small kind of onion, MD, S2, P; **chebole,** a young onion, Palsg.; **chibole,** PP; **schybbolle,** Voc.; **chesbolle,** Voc.—OF. *ciboule*; Late Lat. *caepulla* from Lat. *caepa,* onion. Cf. It. *cipolla,* cyboll (Florio) and G. *zwiebel,* onion (Weigand).

chiden, *v.* to chide, dispute, MD; **chid,** MD; *imp. s.,* S; **chit,** *pr. s.,* MD, C3; **chidden,** *pt. pl.,* S, W.—AS. *cídan,* pt. *cídde.*

chil, *sb.* chill, coolness, MD, SkD; **chele,** S, S2, P.—AS. *ciele* (Voc.), *cyle.*

chilce, *sb.* childishness, S. *Chilc*; for AS. *cild + s*; see Sievers, 258. For the French spelling, cf. **milce.**

child, *sb.* child, the child of a noble house, a title of honour, young knight, S; **cild,** S, MD; **childre,** *pl.,* S, S3; **childer,** MD, S, S2; **cyldren,** S; **cheldren,** S; **childrene,** *gen.,* S.—AS. *cild,* pl. *cild,* also *cildru,* and in**ONorth.** *cildo, cildas.*

childen, *v.* to bring forth children, W2.

child-had, *sb.* childhood, S; **childhede,** *dat.,* C2.—AS. *cildhád.*

chimney, *sb.* furnace, oven, also, fireplace, Sh., PP (*n*); **chymney,** W; **chymneye,** PP.—AF. *chimenee,* OF. *cheminee*; Late Lat. *caminata,* a room with a stove; from Lat. *caminus,* a furnace; Gr. κάμινος, a furnace.

chinche, *adj.* and *sb.* niggardly, a niggard, MD, CM; **chiche,** MD; **chynchis,** *pl.,* H.—OF. *chiche,* miserable, niggardly (Cotg.): Sp. *chico,* small; Lat. *ciccum* (acc.), the core of a pomegranate, a mere trifle.

chinchen, *v.* to be niggardly, Prompt.

chincherie, *sb.* miserliness, Prompt.

chirche, *sb.* church, S, S2, W2, PP, CM; **churche,** S, S2, PP; **cherche,** S2, C3; **kirke,** S, S2, P; **kyrke,** P, Voc., S3; **kirc,** S2; **circe,** S, Voc.; **cyrce,** S.—AS. *cyrce*; cf. OHG. *kirichâ* (Tatian).

chirche-gong, *sb.* churching of women, S2, MD.—Cf. Icel. *kirkju-ganga.*

chirche-haie, *sb.* cemetery, MD; **chyrchehaye,** Voc.

chirche-ʒeard, *sb.* church-yard, MD; **chyrcheʒarde,** Prompt.; **kyrkeʒerde,** Voc.; **kyrgarth,** Voc.; **cyrce-iærd,** S.— Icel. *kirkju-garðr.*

chirch-socne, *sb.* congregation, S.—AS. *ciric-sócn* (Schmid); cf. Icel. *kirkju-sókn.*

chiries, *sb. pl.* cherries, S2, P. See **chery.**

chiri-tyme, *sb.* cherry-time, P.

chirken, *v.* to twitter, chirp, MD, CM.

chirkyng, *sb.* a grating, stridulent, hissing sound, C, CM; **chyrkynge,** *sibilatus,* Prompt.

chirm, *sb.* noise of birds, MD; **charm,** ND; **chirme,** *dat.,* S.—AS. *cirm, cyrm.*

chirmen, *v.* to chirp and twitter, MD; **cherme,** Palsg.; **chyrmys,** *pr. s.,* S3. See SkD (s.v. *chirp*), and Brugmann, § 420.

chisel, *sb.* chisel, MD; **chysel,** Prompt.; **chyssell,** S3; **chesyll,** MD; **scheselle,** Voc.; **sceselle,** Voc.—North F. *chisel,* OF. *cisel,* It. *cesello,* see SkD (p. 793).

chit, *pr. s.* disputes, C3; see **chiden.**

chiteren, *v.* to twitter, MD, CM; to chatter, C3.

chitering, *sb.* twittering, MD; **chyteryng,** S2.

chivache, *sb.* riding, expedition, CM, MD, C3; **chivachie,** C; **chevache,** CM.—AF. *chivauche, chevauchee,* OF. *chevalchee,* from *chevalchier,* to ride on horseback, from *cheval,* horse; Lat. *caballum,* (acc.). See **capul.**

chiualer, *sb.* chevalier, knight, PP; **cheualere,** MD.—AF. *chevaler.*

chivalrie, *sb.* the knights of Christendom, S2; **chevalrye,** MD; **chyvalrie,** knightly deeds, MD; **chiualrye,** C2.—AF. *chivalrie, chevalerie.*

chiueren, *v.* to shiver, tremble, Prompt., SkD (s.v. *shiver*); **cheueren,** PP; **sheeuering,** *pr. p.,* S3.—Cf. Du. *huiveren,* to shiver.

chiueringe, *sb.* shivering, trembling, **chyuerynge,** Prompt., p. 75; **chyueryng,** Palsg., Prompt.

chois, *sb.* and *adj.* choice, MD, C2; **choys,** MD, C, C2.—OF. *chois, cois,* from *choisir, coisir,* to choose. Of Teutonic origin. See **chesen.**

choisly, *adv.* choicely, MD; **chysly,** S2.

chol; see **chavel.**

chold, *adj.* cold, S; see **cold.**

choppen, *v.* to chop, cut, mince, MD; **chappyd,** *pp.,* MD.

chorle; see **cherl.**

chrisolyte, *sb.* chrysolite, 3; **crysolyt**, SkD.—Lat. *chrysolithus* (Vulg.); Gr. χρυσό-λιθος, 'gold stone'.

chronique, *sb.* chronicle, C; see **cronique**.

churren, *v.* to turn, S; see **cherren**.

chymmys, *sb.* chief mansion, S3; **chemys**, JD.—OF. *chef* + *mes* (Bartsch.), *chefmois*, chief manor house (Cotg.); Late Lat. *capmansum* (acc.); see Ducange (s.v. *caput mansi*). See **cheef**.

chymney, *sb.* furnace, W; see **chimney**.

chynchis, *sb. pl.* niggards, H; see **chinche**.

chyne, *sb.* chink, fissure, W2; **chenes**, *pl.*, S2, MD; **chynnes**, S3.—AS. *cínu*.

chynnyng, *sb.* chink, S3.

chyp, *v.* to chip, S3. See **choppen**.

chyrmen, *v.* to chirp, S3; see **chirmen**.

chysly, *adv.* choicely, S2; see **choisly**.

chyssell, *sb.* chisel, S3; see **chisel**.

ciclatun, *sb.* a costly silk texture, S; **ciclatoun**, MD, C2; **siclatoun**, MD; **ciclatuns**, *pl.*, S.—OF. *ciclatun* in Roland (cf. Icel. *siklatun*); cf. Arab. *siqlát*, a fine cloth.

cipres, *sb.* cypress, MD; **ciprees**, C2; **cypres**, Palsg.; **cipresse**, MD.—OF. *cypres*; Lat. *cupressus*, *cyparissus*; Gr. κυπάρισσος.

circe, *sb.* church, S, Voc.; see **chirche**.

circe-wican, *sb. dat.* church-dwelling, S.

cisterne, *sb.* cistern, Joseph's pit, MD, Cath.; **sisterne**, MD; **sesterne**, Prompt.—Lat. *cisterna*, (Vulg.).

cisternesse, *sb.* Joseph's pit, S.

citee, *sb.* city, MD, C2, C3; **cyte**, MD; **syte**, Prompt.; **scite**, S; **citee**, MD, C2, C3; **cite**, S, S2, Cath.—AF. *cite*, OF. *citet*; Lat. *ciuitatem*, a community of citizens.

citesein, *sb.* citizen, MD; **citeseyn**, W (Acts 22. 26); **cytezeyne**, Prompt.—AF. *citeseyn*, *citezein*: Prov. *ciutadan*, *ciptadan*; Late Lat. **civitadanum*.

citiner, *sb.* citizen, JD; **cyttenere**, Voc.

citole, *sb.* cithern, C, MD, CM; **cytole**, Voc.—AF. *citole*, OF. *cytholle* (= Lat. *cithara*), Ps. 56. 8; cf. Low Lat. *citola*, (Voc.); Lat. *cithara*; Gr. κιθάρα, also κίθαρις; cf. Chaldee *qīthārōs*, Dan. 3. 5. See **giterne**.

citolerer, *sb.* a player on the cithern; **cytolerer**, Voc.

citrinacioun, *sb.* the turning to the colour of citron (in alchemy), C3, CM.

citrine, *adj.* citron-coloured, MD.—OF. *citrin*; Lat. *citrinus*.

citur, *sb.* citron-tree, MD. *Comb.*: **cytyr-tre**, Prompt.; **citur tree**, MD.—OF. *citre*; Lat. *citrum* (acc.).

clam¹, *adj.* sticky, H, MD.

clam², *pt. s.* climbed, S2; **clamb**, C2; see **climben**.

clanlych, *adv.* purely, S2; see **clene**.

clappen, *v.* to make a noise like the clapper of a mill, MD, Palsg.; to chatter, C2, C3.—Icel. *klappa*.

clapping, *sb.* chatter, idle talk, C2.

clapsen, *v.* to clasp, C, CM; see **claspen**.

claret, *sb.* a spiced wine, MD, Prompt.

clare, MD; **clarre**, C, MD; **clarry**, MD.—OF. *claret* (AF. *clare*); Late Lat. *claretum* and *claratum*. See **clere**.

clarifien, *v.* to glorify, MD, W, H (Ps. 19, 1).—OF. *clarifier*; Lat. *clarificare* (Vulg.).

clarioun, *sb.* clarion, C, MD; **claryone**, Prompt.—OF. *clarion* (F. *clairon*). See **clere**.

clarre, *sb.* a spiced wine, C, CM; see **claret**.

claspen, *v.* to clasp, Palsg.; **clapsen**, C, CM.

clauster, *sb.* cloister, MD; **closter**, MD; **claustres**, *pl.*, S2.—Lat. *claustrum* (*clostrum*), whence Icel. *klaustr*, AS. *clúster*. Cf. **cloister**.

claver, *sb.* clover, *trifolium*, Voc., MD; **clavyr**, S3; **clovere**, Voc.—AS. *cláfre* (OET.), also *clæfre*, (Voc.); cf. Dan. *kløver*.

claw, *sb.* hoof, Voc.; **clau**, Voc.; **clawwess**, *pl.*, S; **cluvis**, S3; **clawes**, claws of bird, C2.—AS. *clávu*, hoof; cf. Icel. *klauf*, see Weigand (s.v. *klaue*).

clawen, *v.* to scratch, stroke, MD; **clowe**, to scratch, PP. *Phr.*: **to claw the back**, to flatter, S3. *Comb.*: **claw-back**, *sb.* flatterer, sycophant, Cotg. (s.v. *flateur*).

cleche, *sb.* hook, MD; **cleek**, HD.

clechen, *v.* to seize, MD, HD; **cleke**, MD; **cleikis**, *pr. s.*, S3; **clahte**, *pt. s.*, MD; **claucht**, *pp.*, MD.

cled, *pt. s.* clothed, S3; see **cloþen**.

clee, *sb.* hoof, W2.—AS. *cléo*. See **claw**.

clef, *pt. s.* split, S2; see **cleven¹**.

clei, *sb.* clay, W2, MD; **cley**, Prompt.; W (John 9. 6), Voc.—AS. *clæg*.

clemen, *v.* to plaster with clay, to, daub, to smear, MD, S2; **clemyd**, *pp.*, glued, H.—AS. *cléman*, from *clám*, clay.

clenchen, *v.* to clench, seize, PP; to twang the harp, S; **clenten**, *pt. pl.*, embraced, S; **cleynt**, *pp.*, fixed, MD.—Cf. OHG. *klenken* (in *in-klenken*), to fasten (Otfrid).

clene, *adj.* clean, MD, S; *adv.* entirely, *penitus*, MD, S, S2; **clenner**, *comp.*, W2.—AS. *cléne*; cf. OHG. *kleini*, fine, tender, *kleino*, 'penitus' (Otfrid).

clengen, *v.* to cling, S2; see **clingen**.

clenlich, *adj.* cleanly, MD; **clenliche**, *adv.* purely, S; **clanlych**, C2; **clennlike**, S; **clenli**, entirely, S.—AS. *clénlic*.

clennes, *sb.* purity, S2; **clennesse**, W2; **clenesse**, S.—AS. *clénnis*.

clensien

clensien, *v.* to cleanse, MD; **clansi**, S; **clennsenn**, S; **y-clense**, S3.—AS. (ge) *clénsian*, see Sievers, 185.

clensinge, *sb.* cleansing, S.

cleo; see **clyffe**.

clepen, *v.* to call, S2, C2, W, W2; **clepien**, S; **cleopien**, S; **clupien**, MD, S2 **cleopede**, *pt. s.*, S; **clupede**, S; **clepide**, S2, W; **clepte**, S2; **clepud**, S2; **clepet**, S2; **clepit**, S3; **i-cleopet**, *pp.*, S; **i-cleped**, S; **y-clepud**, S2; **y-cleped**, C3; **cleped**, S2, C2; **clept**, S2; **y-clept**, C3; **iclepet**, S2; **icluped**, S2; **iclyped**, S3.—AS. *cleopian*.

clepyng, *sb.* a calling, W.

clere, *adj.* clear, bright, glorious, C2 W, W2; **cleer**, MD; **cler**, MD; **clier**, MD.—AF. *cler*; Lat. *clarum*.

clerenesse, *sb.* brightness, W; **cleernes**, C3.

clerete, *sb.* brightness, W.

clergeon, *sb.* a chorister, little priest, young scholar, MD, C2.—AF. *clergeon*; cf. Sp. *clerizon* (Minsheu).

clergial, *adj.* learned, C3; **clergealy**, *adv.* in clerkly wise, P.

clergie, *sb.* (1) the clergy, (2) the clerical profession, (3) book-learning, MD; **clargy**, H.—OF. *clergie*: Sp. *clerecia*, clergy; Late Lat. *clericia*, the clergy, learning; see Constans.

clerk, *sb.* clergyman, scholar, secretary, C2; **clerc**, S, MD; **clerkes**, *pl.*, S, C2, C3, P; **clerekes**, S; **clerken**, *gen. pl.*, S2.—OF. *clerc* (AF. *clerk*); Church Lat. *clericum* (acc.); Gr. κληρικός from κλῆρος a lot, in eccl. writers, the clergy.

cler-matin, *sb.* a kind of corn for grinding, MD, S2, PP.

cleue, *sb.* dwelling, bedroom, bed, MD, S; **kleue**, MD.—AS. *cléofa*, a recess, den, bed, chamber; cf. Icel. *klefi*, a closet, bedroom.

cleuen[1], *v.* to split asunder, MD, P; **cleoue**, MD; **cleues**, *pr. s.*, S; **claf**, *pt. s.*, MD; **clef**, MD, S2; **cleef**, MD; **clevede**, G; **clouen**, *pl.*, S2; **clofenn**, *pp.*, S; **cloue**, W.—AS. *cléofan*, pt. *cléaf* (pl. *clufon*), pp. *clofen*.

cleuen[2], *v.* to cleave, adhere, MD, W2, PP; **cliuyn**, Prompt.; **cliuen**, S; **clyuen**, PP; **cliued**, *pt. s.*, S; **cleuede**, W2.—AS. *clifian* (*cleofian*); OHG. *klebên* (Otfrid).

cleuering, *pr. p.* clinging, holding on by claws, S3. See **cliver**[2].

cleynt, *pp.* fixed, MD; see **clenchen**.

clicche; see **clochen**.

cliket, *sb.* a kind of lock or fastening, PP, CM; **clyket**, PP, Voc.; **clykyt**, Voc.—OF. *cliquette* (Bartsch), from *cliquer*, to click, snap; cf. Low Lat. *cliquetus*.

cliketed, *pp.* fastened with a latch, PP.

climben, *v.* to climb, MD; **clymben**, C2; **clam**, *pt. s.*, S2, MD; **clamb**, C2; **clomb**,

MD; **clomben**, *pp.*, C; **clombe**, C2.—AS. *climban*, pt. *clamb* (pl. *clumbon*); pp. *clumben*.

clingen, *v.* to shrivel up, wither, to cling, MD, S, ND, Sh.; **clengen**, S2; **clyngen**, S2; **clang**, *pt. s.*, MD; **clonge**, *pl.*, MD; **clungen**, *pp.*, MD.—AS. *clingan*, pt. *clang* (pl. *clungon*), pp. *clungen*.

clippe; see **cluppen**.

clippen, *v.* to clip, shear, S, C2, MD.—Icel. *klippa*.

cliue, *sb.* cliff, S; see **clyffe**.

cliuen, *v.* to cleave, adhere, S; see **cleven**[2].

cliuer[1], *adj.* eager, sharp, MD, SkD.

cliuer[2], *sb.* claw, S; **clivres**, *pl.*, S.—AS. *clifer*.

clobbed, *adj.* like a club, rough, C2; **clubbed**, MD. See **clubbe**.

cloche, *sb.* claw, PP; **cloke**, HD; **cluke**, S3 (s.v. *cat*), JD; **cleuck**, JD; **clokis**, *pl.*, H.

clochen, *v.* to clutch, PP; **clucchen**, PP, HD, SkD; **clouche**, PP; **clycchen**, PP; **clicche**, PP.

clocken, *v.* to limp, hobble, PP; **clokke**, PP.—OF. *cloquer* (*clocher*), to limp (Cotg.), also *cloper*: Prov. *clopchar*; Low Lat. **cloppicare*, from *cloppus*; see Diez (P. 550).

clodde; see **clot**.

clofenn; see **cleuen**[1].

cloister, *sb.* cloister, MD; **cloistre**, C3; **cloystre**, C; **cloystyr**, Prompt.—AF. *cloister* OF. *cloistre* (F. *cloître*). Cf. **clauster**.

cloisterer, *sb.* cloister-monk, C2.

clom, *sb.* silence, S2; see **clum**.

clomben, *pp.* climbed, C; see **climben**.

clomsen, *v.* to be benumbed, stupified, PP, H. See **clum**.

clomstnes, *sb.* numbness, fixedness, H.

cloos, *adj.* close, C3; **clos**, MD.—AF. *clos*, closed, pp. of *clore*; Lat. *claudere*.

clos, *sb.* an enclosure, a locked-up place, MD; **cloos**, Prompt., S2; **cloyss**, S3.

closen, *v.* to close, to enclose, MD.—From AF. *clos*, pp.; Lat. *clausum*. See **cloos**.

closter, *sb.* cloister, MD; see **clauster**.

closures, *sb. pl.* enclosures, fastenings, S3.

closyngis, *sb. pl.* gates, W2.

clot, *sb.* a clod, MD; **clotte**, Cath.; **clodde**, Prompt., Palsg., Manip.; **clottes**, *pl.*, lumps, S2; **clottis**, W2. See Weigand (s.v. *kloss*).

clote, *sb.* burdock, Voc., MD, Prompt., Alph.; **cloote**, MD.—AS. *cláte*.

clote-bur, *sb.* burr of the burdock, C3.

clote-leef, *sb.* leaf of the burdock, C3.

cloteren, *v.* to clot, coagulate, Prompt.; **cloderen**, Prompt.; **clothred**, *pp.*, C.

cloth, *sb.* cloth, clothing, S, S2; **cloþe**, S2; **cloþt**, S2; **clað**, S; **claðes**, *pl.*, S; **cloðes**, S.—AS. *cláð*.

cloþ

43

cloþen   cointise

clothen, *v.* to clothe, S; **claðen**, S; **cled**, *pt. s.*, S3; **cloðeden**, *pl.*, S2; **y-clothed**, *pp.*, PP; **y-clad**, C3; **cled**, S3.

cloude, *sb.* a mass of rock, a hill, clod, S2, MD; **clude**, MD; **clowdys**, *pl.*, MD (s.v. *clot*); **cluddis**, masses of cloud, S3; **cloudis**, H (Ps. 67. 37).—AS. *clúd*.

clout, *sb.* clout, rag, W; **clowt**, C3; **clutes**, *pl.*, S; **cloutes**, S2, S3, C3; **clowtes**, S2.— AS. *clút* (OET.).

clouten, *v.* to patch, mend, S3; **clouȝtand**, *pr. p.*, S2; **clouted**, *pp.*, provided with an iron plate, S3.

cloue, *pp.* split, W; see **cleven**[1].

clowe[1], *v.* to scratch, P; see **clawen**.

clowe[2], *sb.* a clove, pink, Prompt.; **clowes**, *pl.*, MD.—OF. *clou*, *clo*, a nail; Lat. *clauum* (acc.).

clow-gilofre, *sb.* a clove-gilly-flower, C2; **clowe-gylofres**, *pl.*, S2.—AF. *cloue de gilofre*. See **gerraflour**.

clubbe, *sb.* club, MD; **clobbe**, MD.—Icel. *klubba*, *klumba*.

clubbed, *adj.* club-shaped, rough, MD, Prompt.; **clobbed**, C2.

clucche, *v.* to clutch, PP; see **clochen**.

cluddis, *sb. pl.* masses of cloud, S3; see **cloude**.

cluke; see **cloche**.

clum, *sb.* stillness, silence, MD, CM; **clom**, S2.

clumsen, *v.* to be benumbed, stupified, MD; **clomsen**, PP; **clomsed**, *pp.*, set fast, H; **clumst**, H; **clumsyd**, 'enervatus', Cath.

clumst-hede, *sb.* numbness, H.

clupien, *v.* to call, S2; see **clepen**.

cluppen, *v.* to embrace, S, MD; **clyppe**, S2; **clippe**, S2, MD; **cleppen**, MD; **clupte**, *pt. s.*, S.—AS. *clyppan*.

cluster-loc, *sb.* enclosure, S.—AS. *clúster-loc*. See **clauster**.

clute; see **clout**.

cluvis, *sb. pl.* hoofs, S3; see **claw**.

clyffe, *sb.* cliff, MD; **clyfe**, MD; **cliue**, *dat.*, S; **cleoue**, MD; **cleo**, S; **cliues**, *pl.*, MD; **cleues**, MD.—AS. *clif* (OET), pl. *cleofu*, *cliofu*; see Grein, Sievers, 241.

clymbare, *sb.* climber, S3.

clymben, *v.* to climb, C2; see **climben**.

clyngen, *v.* to wither, to shrink, S2; see **clingen**.

cnawen, *v.* to know, S; see **knowen**.

cnawlechen, *v.* to acknowledge, MD.

cnawlechunge, *sb.* acknowledgment, S.

cnelinng, *sb.* kneeling, S.

cneowe, *sb. dat.* knee, S; see **kne**.

cniht, *sb.* knight, S; see **kniȝt**.

cnotted, *pp.* knotted, S; **i-knotted**, S; see **knotte**.

cnouwe, *sb. dat.* knee, S; see **kne**.

cnowen, *v.* to know, S; *pp.*, S2; see **knowen**.

co-arten, *v.* to compel, constrain, HD; **coarted**, *pp.*, S3.—Lat. *co-arctare*, to constrain, compress.

cocatrice, *sb.* a serpent (= Lat. *basiliscus* = Heb. *pethen*, an adder or cobra), W2; **cocatryse**, *basiliscus*, *cocodrillus*, Prompt.; **kokatrice**, MD; **cockatrice**, WW.—OF. *cocatriz*, crocodile: Sp. *cocadriz*, basilisk, cocatrice (Minsheu). Cf. **cokedrill**.

cocke, *sb. in phr.*: **by cocke** (a profane oath), S3, ND; **by cock**, Sh.; **Cock's passion**, Sh.; **Cox my passion**, Sh.; **by cock and pie**, Sh., ND, SkD (s.v. *pie*); **for cokkes bones**, C3; **for cocks body**, 'de par Dieu', Palsg.—Cf. Grimm, p. 15 (*n*).

cocow; see **cukkow**.

cod[1], *sb.* cod, pod, husk, MD; **codde**, Prompt., Palsg.; **coddis**, *pl.*, W.—AS. *codd*, bag (Mark 6. 8).

cod[2], *sb.* pillow, Cath., MD; **coddis**, *pl.*, HD.—Icel. *koddi*, pillow.

cof, *adj.* quick, MD; **kof**, MD; **coue**, MD; **cofe**, *adv.*, S; **cofer**, *comp.*, S.—AS. *cáf*; cf. Icel. *á-kafr*, vehement.

coffes, *sb. pl.* cuffs, P; see **cuffe**.

cofin, *sb.* basket, MD; **coffyn**, W2; **cofyne**, paste, crust of a pie, MD; **coffyns**, *pl.*, baskets, S2; **cofyns**, W; **cofynes**, W.— OF. *cofin*; Lat. *cophinus* (Vulg.); Gr. κόφινος (NT).

cofre, *sb.* box, coffer, MD, C2, C3, P; **cofer**, S2; **cofres**, *pl.*, S2.—AF. *cofre*; Lat. *cophinum* (acc.); see Brachet.

cofren, *v.* to put into a coffer, S3.

cog, *sb.* cog, tooth on the rim of a wheel, MD; **kog**, Voc.; **cogge**, *dat.*, S.

cognisaunce, *sb.* knowledge, MD; **cognizance**, that by which something is known, Sh.; **conisantes**, *pl.*, badges, S3.—AF. *conisaunce*, knowledge, OF. *cognoissance*, from *cognoissant*, pr. p. of *cognoistre*; Lat. *cognoscere*.

coife, *sb.* coif, cap, MD; **coyfe**, S3, Prompt., Palsg.—OF. *coiffe*; Low Lat. *cofea*. Cf. **cuffe**.

coint, *adj.* knowing, prudent, skilful, sly, neat, fine, quaint, MD; **koynt**, MD; **quoynte**, MD; **queynte**, MD, S3, C2; **quaynte**, MD; **queynt**, MD; **quaynt**, H.—OF. *cointe*, prudent, trim, friendly; Lat. *cognitum*.

cointeliche, *adv.* skilfully, neatly, quaintly, MD; **quoynteliche**, MD; **queyntelich**, MD; **queynteli**, S3; **queinteliche**, S2; **quaintelye**, S2.

cointise, *sb.* art, skill, cunning, MD; **quointise**, MD, S2; **quantise**, H; **queyntise**, MD, S3; **quaintis**, H.—OF. *cointise*.

44

coite

coite, *sb.* quoit; **coyte**, Prompt., Palsg., Manip.; **coitis**, *pl.*, S3. Cf. the v. *coit*, JD; OF. *coitier*, to push, press (Bartsch).

coiten, *v.* to play quoits, Prompt., Palsg.

cok, *sb.* cook, S2; **cokes**, *pl.*, C3, PP; **kokes**, PP.—AS. *cóc*; Lat. *coquus*, from *coquere*, to cook.

cokedrill, *sb.* crocodile, HD, MD; **coca-drylle**, Voc.; **cokodrilles**, *pl.*, HD; **coco-drilly**, Trev. 1. 131, MD.—Low Lat. *cocodrillus*; cf. It. *cocodrillo*, a crocodile (Florio), Sp. *cocodrillo*, a serpent, crocodile (Minsheu); Lat. *crocodilus*; Gr. κροκόδειλος. Cf. **cocatrice**.

cokeney, *sb.* cook's assistant, scullion, undercook, petted child, cockney, MD, PP, S2; **cocknaie**, MD; **coknay**, Prompt., Cath.; **cokenay**, CM; **cocknaye**, Palsg. (s.v. *bring*); **cockney**, Sh.; **kokeney**, PP; **coknayes**, *pl.*, S3.

coker, *sb.* quiver, also a kind of half-boots or gaiters, MD; **koker**, MD; **cocur**, Prompt. (see *n.*); **cokeres**, *pl.*, PP; **cockers**, HD, ND.—AS. *cocer*, a quiver.

coket[1], *sb.* a seal with which bread sold in London was stamped by a public officer, Ducange; **cocket**, Cath. (*n*); certificate, S3, ND.

coket[2], *sb.* a kind of fine bread stamped, PP, S2. Cf. Low Lat. *panis de coket*, see Ducange (s.v. *coket*). See **coket**[1].

cokewold, *sb.* cuckold, CM; **kokewolde**, P; **kukwald**, Voc.; **cockewold**, MD; **kuke-weld**, MD; **cokolde**, MD, SkD.—Cf. Prov. *cugol*; Lat. *cuculum*, cuckoo. See **cukkow**.

col-, *prefix*, expressing depreciation, contempt. *Comb.*: **col-fox**, a crafty fox, C; **col-knif**, a big knife, MD; **col-prophet**, false prophet, ND; **cold-prophet**, ND; **cole-prophet**, ND; **colle-tragetour**, false juggler, CM (5. 248. 187).

cold, *adj.* cold, PP; **chald**, S; **kald**, S; **cald**, S2, MD; **kold**, S; **chold**, S; **cheld**, S2; **cold**, evil, G.—AS. *ceald*, *cald*: Goth. *kalds* from OTeut. **kalan*, to freeze, cf. Icel. *kala* (pt. *kól*, pp. *kalinn*).

colde, *v.* to grow cold, C3, MD.—AS. *cealdian*.

cole[1], *sb.* cabbage, cale, kail, Voc., MD; **cool**, MD; **kale**, MD, H.—AS. *cole* (OET); cf. Icel. *kál*; Lat. *caulis*, stalk, cabbage; see Weigand (s.v. *kohl*).

cole[2], *sb.* charcoal, coal, S, S2; **coole**, MD; **coylle**, MD; **coles**, *pl.*, C2, C3; **coolis**, W; **koles**, S2.—AS. *col* (OET).

cole[3], *adj.* cool, somewhat cold, Prompt., MD.—AS. *cól*; cf. OHG. *kuali* (Otfrid).

combren

colen, *v.* to cool, MD, Prompt., G, H.—AS. *cólian*; cf. OHG. *kualen* (Otfrid).

coler, *sb.* collar, MD; **coller**, *torques*, Prompt.; **colers**, *pl.*, P.—OF. *coler* (F. *collier*); Lat. *collare*, from *collum*, neck.

colere, *sb.* anger, C, MD.—OF. *colere*; Lat. *cholera*; Gr. χολέρα, an affection of the bile.

colerik, *adj.* choleric, passionate, C2, MD; **coleryke**, Cath.—Lat. *cholericus*, having one's bile affected; Gr. χολερικός, from χολή, gall.

coles, *sb. pl.* (?); *in phr.*: **swearing precious coles**, S3.

collacioun, *sb.* conference, CM.—OF. *collacion*, discourse, harangue; Lat. *collationem*, a bringing together, conferring.

collen, *v.* to embrace, W2, MD; **kollen**, S2. *Der.*: **collyngis**, *sb. pl.*, W2.—Cf. OF. *collée*, a neck-embracement (Cotg.). See **coler**.

collerie, *sb.* eye-salve, W; **colirie**, MD; **colorye**, HD.—Lat. *collyrium*; Gr. κολλύριον.

colloppe, *sb.* a slice of flesh, *carbonella*, Prompt., MD, Palsg.; **collop**, Cath., Cotg. (s.v. *riblette*); **colope**, Voc.; **colop**, Cath. (*n*); **coloppe**, PP; **colhoppe**, PP, Voc.; **collip**, Manip.; **colopus**, *pl.*, PP, S2.

colour, *sb.* colour, pretext, S3, C2; **colur**, S, MD.—AF. *colur*; Lat. *colorem*.

col-plontes, *sb. pl.* cabbages, PP, S2; **kole-plantes**, PP; **cale-plantes**, PP. See **cole**[1].

coltre; see **culter**.

columbine, *sb.* columbine (flower), Alph., MD, Sh.; **columbyne**, Voc., Prompt.; **columby**, S3.—OF. *columbine*; Late Lat. *columbina*.

colvyr; see **culver**.

colwie, *adj.* grimy, S.

colwyd, *pp.* blackened with coal or soot, *carbonatus*, Prompt. See **cole**[2].

comaunde, *v.* to command, PP, C; **co-manden**, MD; **comaundet**, *pt. s.*, S2; **comande**, S2, MD; **cumand**, S2.—OF. *comander*, *commander*; Late Lat. *commendare*, to order. Cf. **comenden**.

comaundement, *sb.* commandment, C, PP; **comandement**, C2.

comaundour, *sb.* commander, C3, PP; **comandour**, S2.—OF. *commandeor*; Late Lat. *commendatorem*.

combe, *sb.* comb for hair, comb of a bird, Prompt., Voc.; **komb**, MD.—AS. *camb*.

combren, *v.* to encumber, overwhelm, MD, S3; **comeren**, S3; **combrez**, *pr. s.*, S2; **cumrit**, *pt. s.*, S2; **cummerit**, S3; **cum-bred**, *pp.*, S2.—OF. *combrer* to hinder, from *combre*, a heap, see Ducange (s.v. *cumbra*); Lat. *cumulum* (acc.).

45

combre-world

combre-world, *sb.* cumberer of the world, S3.

combust, *pp.* burnt, MD, C3.—Lat. *combustus*, pp. of *comburere*, to burn.

come, *sb.* a coming, S, S2, C3; **kume**, S; **kime**, S; **cume**, S; **comes**, *pl.*, S.—AS. *cyme*.

comelyng, *sb.* stranger, W, W2; **kumeling**, MD; **comling**, W; **comlyng**, S2; **comelingis**, *pl.*, W; **cumlyngis**, H.

comen, *v.* to come, S; **cumen**, S; **kumen**, S; **cum**, S2; **com**, S2; **cuminde**, *pr. p.*, S; **comynde**, S2; **cominde**, S2; **comste**, comest thou, S2; **comþ**, *pr. s.*, S2; **com**, *pt. s.*, S, S2, G; **cam**, S, G, P; **kam**, S; **come**, *2 pt. s.*, S, G; **coman**, *pt. pl.*, S; **coomen**, C2; **comen**, MD, S, G; **come**, S2; **i-cumen**, *pp.*, S; **i-kumen**, S; **i-cume**, S; **i-comen**, S; **i-come**, S, S2; **comen**, S2, S3, G; **come**, S2.—AS. *cuman*; cf. Goth. *qiman*.

comenden, *v.* to commend, C2, PP; **commended**, *pp.*, PP.—Lat. *commendare*. Cf. **comaunde**.

comers, *sb. pl.*, strangers, visitors, passersby, S2, PP; **comeres**, PP.

commoditie, *sb.* advantage, profit, S3, ND, Sh.—OF. *commodité* (Cotg.); Lat. *commoditatem*.

comp, *sb.* contest, S; see **camp**.

compainoun, *sb.* companion, MD.—OF. *compagnon*; Late Lat. *companionem*.

companable, *adj.* sociable, PP, C; **companabile**, H.—OF. *compaignable* (Cotg.).

companie, *sb.* company, MD, C2; **compaynye**, S; **compainie**, S2.—OF. *companie*, from *compain*, an associate at meals; from Lat. *cum + panis*, bread.

comparisoun, *sb.* comparison, MD, C2.—OF. *comparison*; Late Lat. *comparationem*.

comparisounen, *v.* to compare, MD, W (Mark 4. 30), S2.

compas, *sb.* circle, circuit, device, craft, MD, C3, G; **compaas**, C; **compasse**, S3; **cumpas**, W2.—OF. *compas*; Late Lat. *compassum* (acc.).

compassen, *v.* to go round, to devise, contrive, MD; **cumpas**, W2; **conpassed**, *pp.*, S3.—AF. *compasser*.

compassyng, *sb.* craft, contrivance, C.

compeir, *v.* to appear, S3.—OF. *comper-*, tonic stem of *compareir*; Lat. *comparere*.

comper, *sb.* compeer, comrade, C, S2; **compere**, Prompt.; **cumpers**, *pl.*, MD.—Of OF. origin; Lat. *comparem*, (acc.).

complie, *sb.* the last church-service of the day, compline, MD; **cumplie**, S, MD.—OF. *complie*; Church Lat. *completa (hora)*.

confiture

compline, *sb.* compline, MD; **complyn**, MD; **cumplyne**, *completorium*, Prompt. See **complie**.

composicion, *sb.* arrangement, agreement, C, C2.—AF. *composicion*; Lat. *compositionem*.

comptroller; see **controller**.

comsen, *v.* to commence, S2, PP, MD; **cumsen**, S2, PP.—OF. *comencer*; Lat. *com + initiare*.

comune[1], *adj.* common, PP; **comun**, MD; **comyn**, MD; **comen**, S2.—AF. *commun*; Lat. *communem* (acc.).

comune[2], *sb.* the commons, commonalty, PP; **commune**, C2; **comunes**, *pl.*, PP; **comyns**, S2, PP.

comunlych, *adv.* commonly, S2; **comunliche**, PP; **comunly**, C2.

comyn, *sb.* cummin, C2, MD, Prompt.; **cummyn**, W.—OF. *comin*; Lat. *cyminum* (Vulg.); Gr. κύμινον.

comynalte, *sb.* community, W2.—AF. *comunalte*; OF. *communaulte*; Late Lat. *communalitatem*, from *communalis*.

comyne, *v.* to commune, W, W2; **commune**, C3.—OF. *communier*; Lat. *communicare*.

comynere, *sb.* participator, W.

comynte, *sb.* community, W2; **comunete**, PP.—Lat. *communitatem*.

con, *pr. s.* can, know, S. *Phr.*: **con-þonk**, thanks, S; see **kunnen**.

conabill, *adj.* suitable, convenient, B.—OF. *covenable, convenable*; Late Lat. *convenabilem*.

conand, *sb.* covenant, B; **connand**, B; **cunnand**, B.—OF. *convenant*, agreeing, befitting, also, a covenant, *pr. p.* of *convenir*; Lat. *convenire*. See **covenaunt**.

conandly, *adv.* befittingly, S3.

conceipt, *sb.* imagination, fancy, idea, MD; S3; **conceit**, C3; **conceits**, *pl.*, fantastic patterns, S3.

conceiven, *v.* to comprise, to conceive, to imagine, MD; **conceyue**, PP.—OF. *concevoir*; Lat. *concipere*.

conduit, *sb.* guidance, conduit, MD; **condut**, MD; **condite**, MD; **conduyte**, S3; **cundyth**, Voc.; **condeth**, MD; **kundites**, *pl.*, S3.—OF. *conduit* (Bartsch); Lat. *conductum*, from *conducere*.

confessen, *v.* to confess, to receive a confession, MD.—AF. *confesser*; from Lat. *confessus*, pp. of *confiteor*.

confessor, *sb.* a confessor of Christianity before the heathen, a hearer of confessions, MD, S; **cunfessurs**, *pl.*, S.—AF. *confessor*; Church Lat. *confessorem*.

confiture, *sb.* an apothecary's mixture, C3.—OF. *confiture* (Cotg.); Late Lat. *confectura*.

46

confort

confort, *sb.* comfort, C3, C, PP.—AF. *confort*.
conforten, *v.* to strengthen, comfort, MD, C, P; counforte, S2, PP.—AF. *conforter*; Late Lat. *confortare*; Lat. *con + fortis*, strong.
confounden, *v.* to bring to confusion, C3; confoundet, *pp.*, PP.—AF. *confoundre*; Lat. *confundere*.
confus, *pp.* put to confusion, C3, C, PP.—AF. *confus*, pp.; Lat. *confusum*.
congie, *v.* to bid farewell to, dismiss, get rid of, PP; congeye, PP, MD; cunge, PP.—OF. *congier*, to dismiss, from *congié*, *cumgiet*; Late Lat. *commiatum*, Lat. *commeatum*, permission to go.
conisantes, *sb. pl.* badges, S3; see cognisaunce.
conjecten, *v.* to guess, suppose, MD, S3.—Lat. *conjectare*.
coniectere, *sb.* diviner, W2.
conjoignen, *v.* to conjoin, MD; coniunit, *pp.*, S3.—From OF. *conjoignant*, pr. p. of *conjoindre*; Lat. *conjungere*.
con-ioyninge, *sb.* conjoining, C3.
conne[1], *v.* to know, to be able, S2, S3; see kunnen.
conne[2], *v.* to test, examine, con, C2, P; kun, H; cunnien, SkD.—AS. *cunnian*, to try to know.
conning[1], *sb.* science, skill, C2, C3; konning, C2; coninge, S2; kunnyng, W.
conning[2], *adj.* skilful, C2.
conningly, *adv.* skilfully, C2.
conrey, *sb.* division of troops, also provision, MD; conrai, S2.—OF. *cunrei* (*conroi*), equipage, arrangement, a division of troops (Bartsch); It. *corredo*, equipage, paraphernalia (Florio); Low Lat. *corredium*, *conredium*, equipage, provision, entertainment (Ducange); *con + redium*, a word of Teut. origin.
conseil, *sb.* counsel, S, S2, C2; counseil, G, C; consail, PP.—OF. *conseil*; Lat. *consilium*.
conseili, *v.* to advise, S2; conseille, PP.—OF. *conseillier*.
constable, *sb.* constable, warden, officer, C3, PP; conestable, MD; cunstable, PP; cunestable, S.—OF. *conestable*; Late Lat. *comes stabuli*, see Brachet.
constablesse, *sb.* constable's wife, S2, C3.
constance, *sb.* constancy, C2, MD.—OF. *constance* (Cotg.); Lat. *constantia*.
constorie, *sb.* an ecclesiastical court, PP, S2; consistorie, PP, CM.—Church Lat. *consistorium*, a place of assembly, from Lat. *consistere*, to stand together.
contek, *sb.* strife, contention, C, G, H, MD, CM; contumely, MD; contak, MD; conteke, HD; conteck, HD, ND; contakt, HD.—AF. *contek*.

coper

conteken, *v.* to strive, MD.
contekour, *sb.* one who quarrels, HD.
contenance, *sb.* look, gesture, outward appearance, encouragement, favour, MD, S2, C2; contenaunce, PP, C3; cuntenaunce, S2; countenance, S3; continaunce, G.—OF. *contenance*; Late Lat. *continentia*, mien.
contesse; see countesse.
contrarie, *adj.* contrary, C2, C3.—AF. *contrarie* (OF. *contraire*); Lat. *contrarium*.
contrarien, *v.* to oppose, C2.—OF. *contrarier*; Late Lat. *contrariare*.
contree, *sb.* country, MD, C2, C3; contre, MD, C; contreie, S2; contreye, S2; cuntre, S2, MD, C; contrai, S2, MD.—OF. *contree* (AF. *cuntree*), Prov. *contrada*; Late Lat. *contrata*, from Lat. *contra*, see SkD.
control[1], *sb.* restrictive authority, Sh.—OF. *contre-rôle*, *contre-rolle*, a duplicate roll, used for verification, see Brachet, Cotg. (s.v. *controlle*).
control[2], *v.* to restrain, check, Sh.
controller, *sb.* superintendent, overseer of accounts, Sh.; comptroller, S3.
controven, *v.* to contrive, MD, PP; controeven, MD, S2; contreven, PP; contriven, MD.—AF. *controver*; *con + OF. trover*, to find, compose poetry; Low Lat. *tropare*, from *tropus*, a song, lit. a trope, turn of speech; Gr. τρόπος, a turn.
conventiculis, *sb. pl.* assemblies, W2.
conveyen, *v.* to accompany, also to bring, MD.—AF. *cunveier*; Late Lat. *conviare*, to accompany.
conyng, *sb.* cony, rabbit, MD, S2, S3, P; konyng, S; cunin, S; conig, MD, HD; cony, Prompt., HD; conies, *pl.*, S3.—AF. *conyng*, *conyn*, *conil* (pl. *conis*); Lat. *cuniculum* (acc.).
conyngere, *sb.* rabbit-warren, MD, HD; connyngere, Prompt.
coosted, *pt. pl.* went past, S3; see costey.
coostez, *sb. pl.* properties, qualities, S2; see cost[2].
coote; see cote[2].
cop, *sb.* top, head, MD, S2, C, W, W2; coppe, *dat.*, MD, W2; coppis, *pl.*, W2.
cope, *sb.* cape, cope, Voc., S2, C; kope, S; coope, Prompt., MD; copis, *pl.*, P.—Cf. Icel. *kápa*; Late Lat. *cāpa*, *cappa*.
copen[1], *v.* to cover with a cope, provide with a cope, PP, S2; i-copet, *pp.*, S2.
copen[2], *v.* to barter, to meet, to have to do with, to encounter, S3, Sh.—Cf. Du. *koopen*, to buy.
coper, *sb.* copper, C3, MD; copyr, Voc., Prompt.; copper, MD.—Du. *koper*; Late

47

Lat. *cuper, cuprum*, for Lat. *cyprium (aes)*; from *Cyprus*; Gr. Κύπρος.

coppe, *sb.* cup, S2, P; see **cuppe**.

corage, *sb.* heart, spirit, MD, C, C2.—AF. *corage*.

corageus, *adj.* courageous, S2, MD; **corageous**, C2.—OF. *corageus*.

coral, *sb.* coral, MD; **coralle**, Prompt.; **corall**, Palsg., Manip.; **curall**, S3.—OF. *coral*; Lat. *corallum, corallium*; Gr. κοράλλιον.

corasiue, *sb.* a corrosive, S3; see **corosif**.

coraye, *v.* to curry a horse, MD; see **curry**.

corbel, *sb.* raven, MD; **corbyal**, S2; **corby**, S3.—OF. *corbel* (F. *corbeau*); Late Lat. *corvellum* (acc.), from Lat. *coruus*.

cordewane, *sb.* Spanish leather, C2; **cordewan**, MD; **cordewayne**, Voc.; **cordwane**, Prompt.; **corduane**, Voc.; **corden**, MD.—OF. *cordouan, corduan*, Prov. *cordoan*, Sp. *cordován*, cordovan leather (Minsheu), from *Cordova*, name of a town in Andalusia.

cordwaner, *sb.* a worker in leather, Prompt.; **cordwainer**, SkD.—AF. *cordewaner*. See **cordewane**.

core, *sb.* the heart, central part of fruit, Prompt., MD.—OF. *cor*; Lat. *cor*.

coriour, *sb.* currier, W; **curiour**, W. See **curry**.

corn, *sb.* a grain, corn, MD, S, C3; **coren**, S; **cornys**, *gen.*, S3; **corns**, *pl.*, S2; **cornes**, S2, PP, C2, W.—AS. *corn*, Goth. *kaurn*; cf. Lat. *grānum*; see Brugmann, § 306.

corny, *adj.* strong of the corn or malt (applied to ale), C3.

corone, *sb.* crown, MD, C2, C3; **coroune**, MD, C2; **corowne**, C; **corune**, MD; **croune**, S; the tonsure, G; **crune**, S; **krune**, S; **crun**, S; **crounis**, *pl.*, S3.—AF. *corone (coroune)* Lat. *corona*.

coronen, *v.* to crown, MD; **corounen**, S2, C2; **crouni**, MD, S2; **y-corouned**, *pp.*, S2; **y-crouned**, S3; **y-coroned**, PP; **i-kruned**, S; **cruned**, S.—OF. *coroner (coruner)*.

corosif, *adj.* corrosive, C3; **corrosive**, *sb.*, a corrosive, a caustic, ND; **corsive**, ND; **corasiue**, S3; **corsye**, S2; **corzie**, ND.— OF. *corrosif*, biting away.

corour, *sb.* runner, W2; see **currour**.

cors[1], *sb.* curse, S3, G; see **curs**.

cors[2], *sb.* a body, a dead body, MD, S, C2, C3, PP; **corps**, S3, C2; **corpis**, S3.—AF. *cors, corps*; Lat. *corpus*.

cors[3], *sb.* course, S2; see **cours**.

corsaint, *sb.* the body of a saint, a relic, MD; **corseynt**, S2; **corseint**, CM, PP.—AF. *corsaint*; Lat. *corpus sanctum*.

corser, *sb.* horsedealer, MD, S3, HD; see **courser**[2].

corsing, *sb.* exchange, barter, S2; horse-dealing, HD.

corsye, *sb.* a corrosive, S2; see **corosif**.

cort, *sb.* court, MD; see **court**.

corteis, *adj.* courteous, S2; **corteys**, S2; **curteis**, S3, C.—AF. *curteis*; Late Lat. *cortensem, curtensem*.

corteisliche, *adv.* courteously, PP; **curteisly**, C2.

cortesye, *sb.* courtesy, PP; **curtesy**, S2; **curteisie**, S2, C2, C3.—AF. *curteisie*.

corumpable, *adj.* corruptible, C.

corumpen, *v.* to corrupt, MD; **corrumpen**, C.—OF. *corrumpre*; Lat. *corrumpere*.

corupcions, *sb. pl.* sores, illnesses, PP.

coruen, *pp.* carved, S3, C; see **kerven**.

cos, *sb.* kiss, S, W, W2; see **cus**.

cosan, *pp.* chosen, S; see **chesen**.

cosset, *sb.* a lamb brought up without her dam, S3, ND.

cosshe, *sb.* a little house, Prompt., Palsg.

cost[1], *sb.* rib, side of a human body, shore, coast, MD, S2; **coste**, C2; **costes**, *pl.*, S2, P.—AF. *coste*; Lat. *costa*.

cost[2], *sb.* nature, property, condition, manner, MD; **costez**, *pl.*, properties, S2; **coostez**, S2. Cf. **cust**.

costage, *sb.* expense, C2, HD.—OF. *costage*. See **costen**.

costard, *sb.* a kind of apple, Prompt., ND; humorous expression for the head, Sh., ND; **costarde**, S3; **costard**, a cap, ND. It probably means the 'ribbed apple'.—OF. *coste + ard*, see SkD (p. 796).

costard-jagger, *sb.* costermonger, ND.

costard-monger, *sb.* seller of apples, costermonger, SkD; **costard-mongar**, Palsg.; **costerd-monger**, SkD; **costar-monger**, ND.

coste, *sb.* cost, P; **coust**, MD; **cost**, C2.— AF. *cust, coust*.

costen, *v.* to cost, MD; **coste**, *pt. s.*, C2; **costed**, P; **costed**, *pp.*, P.—OF. *coster (couster)*; Lat. *constare*.

costey, *v.* to coast, also to come near, approach, MD; **coosted**, *pt. pl.* went past, S3.—OF. *costoier* (F. *côtoyer*). See **cost**[1].

costlewe, *adj.* costly, CM, MD; **costelewe**, Prompt. See **-lewe** *suffix*.

cosyn, *sb.* cousin, C, PP; **cosin**, S, S2; **cusyng**, S3; **cosyns**, *pl.* kinsmen, W; **cousyns**, W.—AF. *cosin (cousyn)*; cf. Late Lat. *cosinus* (Brachet); Lat. *consobrinus*.

cosynage, *sb.* kindred, fellowship, H; **cusynage**, H.

cote¹, *sb.* cottage, S, Voc., C, C2; **cotes**, *pl.* sheep-cotes, S3; **coates**, S3.—AS. *cot*, also *cyte* (Grein); cf. OHG. *cutti*, 'grex' (Tatian).

cote², *sb.* garment, coat, S2, PP, S3, C2, C; **coote**, C, W.—AF. *cote*, OF. *cotte*, PS. 21. 18; MHG. *kotte*, *kutte*.

cote-armure, *sb.* coat-armour, linen coat with armorial bearings worn over armour, body-armour, S3, C2, C.

coten, *v.* to provide with coats, S2; **cotyd**, *pp.* clothed, S3.

couche, *sb.* chamber, W.

couchen, *v.* to lay, place together, to lie down, MD, S2, C2, C3; **cowchyn**, Prompt.; **cowchen**, C.—AF. *cucher*, *cocher*, OF. *colcher*; Lat. *collocare*.

coude, *pt. s.* could, S2. See **kunnen**.

counforte, *v.* to comfort, S2, PP. See **conforten**.

counte, *sb.* county, shire, P, MD; **countee**, MD, PP.—AF. *counte*; Late Lat. *comitatum*.

countesse, *sb.* countess, C2; **contesse**, S2; **cuntesse**, S.—AF. *contesse*, from OF. *conte*, *comte*; Late Lat. *comitem*, a count (a court dignity), in Lat. a companion.

countrefete, *v.* to counterfeit, C, C2; **contrefete**, MD; **counterfeted**, *pp.*, C3.—From OF. *contrefet*, *contrefeit*, pp. of *contrefeire*, *contrefaire*; Lat. *contra* + *facere*.

countre-taille, *sb.* correspondence (of sound); *in phr.*: **at the countretaille**, with corresponding sound, C2.—OF. *contretaille*, the one part of a tally, the counter-tenor part in music (Cotg.).

countryng, *sb.* countering in music, S3; the plain chant, S3 (*n*).—See S3 (p. 453).

coupable, *adj.* culpable, PP; **cupabil**, H.—OF. *coupable*.

coupe¹, *sb.* fault, PP; **culpe**, PP, ND.—OF. *coupe*, *colpe*; Lat. *culpa*.

coupe², *sb.* cup, S2; **cupe**, S.—AF. *cupe*; Lat. *cupa*. Cf. **cuppe**.

courben, *v.* to bend, MD; **courbed**, *pt. s.*, P.—OF. *courber*; Lat. *curuare*.

courche, *sb.* kerchief, S3; see **coverchief**.

cours, *sb.* running, course, MD, C2, C3; **cors**, S2.—AF. *cours*; Lat. *cursum* (acc.).

courser¹, *sb.* a steed, MD, C2; **coursour**, MD; **cowrcer**, Prompt.—OF. *coursier*; Late Lat. *cursarium* (acc.).

courser², *sb.* horse-dealer, Palsg.; **corser**, MD, S3 (s.v. *horse*); **scorser**, ND.

court, *sb.* court, enclosure, yard, PP, MD; **curt**, S; **kurt**, S; **cort**, MD; **courte**, PP.—AF. *curt*; Late Lat. *cortem*; Lat. *cohortem*, an enclosure.

courteislich, *adv.* courteously, PP; see **corteisliche**.

courte-py, *sb.* short coat or cloak, PP, S2, C; **cowrteby**, Voc.; **kourteby**, P; **courtepies**, *pl.*, PP; **court-pies**, PP.—Cf. Du. *kort*, short + *pije*, rough coat; cf. E. *pea* in *pea-jacket*.

couthe¹, *v.* to make known, PP; see **kyþen**.

couthe², *pt. s.* could, knew, S, S2, S3; *pp.*, S2; **couth**, C2; see **kunnen**.

couthe³, *sb.* kith, PP; see **kyþ**.

coue, *sb.* den, S2.—ONorth. *cófa*, 'spelunca' (John II.38).

coveiten, *v.* to covet, MD, PP; **coueitiden**, *pt. pl.*, W2.—AF. *coveiter*, OF. *cuveitier*; Late Lat. **cupiditare*. See Constans.

coveitise, *sb.* greed, avarice, PP; **coueityse**, C3; **couetise**, PP; **couetyse**, S2, S3; **coueitisis**, *pl.*, W.—OF. *coveitise*.

coveitous, *adj.* covetous, MD; **coueytous**, S2; **couetous**, S2.—OF. *coveitus*, AF. *cuveitus*; Late Lat. **cupiditosum*.

couenable, *adj.* proper, fit, agreeing, W, MD, S2, H; **cuuenable**, S; **conabill**, H; **conable**, Prompt.; **cunabil**, H.—AF. *cuvenable*; Late Lat. *convenabilem*.

couenaunt, *sb.* a covenant, PP; **couenant**, PP; **covand**, MD; **conant**, MD.—AF. *covenant*, OF. *convenant*, pr. p. of *convenir*, to agree; Lat. *conuenire*.

couent, *sb.* an assembly, a convent, MD, PP, C2, C3; **couant**, PP.—OF. *covent*, *convent*; Church Lat. *conventus*, from Lat. *conuenire*, to come together.

couerchief, *sb.* kerchief, MD; **keuerchief**, MD; **kerchef**, C3; **kyrchefe**, Prompt.; **courchef**, HD; **courche**, S3; **kerche**, Prompt.—OF. *couvre-chef*, covering for the head (Cotg.).

coueren¹, *v.* to cover, MD, C2; **keueren**, MD, S3, P, W; **kuueren**, MD; **kyueren**, MD, W.—AF. *covrir*; Lat. *cooperire*.

coveren², *v.* to gain, to heal, to recover one's health, MD, S2, W; **keueren**, MD, CM, PP; **kuueren**, MD, S2; **keuord**, *pt. s.*, H.—OF. *covrer*, (in *recovrer*) *coubrer*, to seize (Bartsch); Lat. *-cuperare* (in *recuperare*); cf. Late Lat. *cuperamentum*, acquisition (Ducange).

couert, *adj. and sb.* covert, hidden, a covert, MD; **cowart**, S3.—OF. *covert*, pp. of *covrir*.

couerture, *sb.* bed-clothes, horse-cover, covering, MD, S; **kuuertur**, S.—OF. *coverture*.

couine, *sb.* conspiracy, craft, deceit, trickery, S3, MD, HD; **covyne**, C; **covin**, MD, ND; **coven**, ND.—AF. *covine*, from OF. *covenir*, *convenir*; Lat. *conuenire*.

cow, *sb.* cow, Voc.; **ku**, S, MD, Voc.; **cou**, MD; **kues**, *gen. s.*, S; **ky**, *pl.*, MD, S3; **kie**, MD; **kye**, H; **kyn**, MD, S2, C; **kyne**,

S3, P; **ky3n**, S2; **kyen**, PP; **kien**, W2; **ken**, MD, S2, PP.—AS. *cú*, pl. *cӯ* (gen. *cína*).

coward, *adj.* and *sb.* cowardly, a coward, MD, C2.—AF. *coward, cuard*, cf. the heraldic term *lion couard*, a lion with his tail between his legs, and the name for the hare in the old terms of hunting 'la *cowarde* ou la court *cowe*', i.e. short-tail.—Formed with the suffix *-ard* from OF. *coe*, tail; Lat. *cauda*. Cf. It. *codardo*, from *coda*, a tail.

cowardie, *sb.* cowardice, C; **cowardy**, MD.—OF. *couardie*.

cowart, *sb.* covert, S3; see **covert**.

cowde, cowthe, *pt. s.* could, knew, G; see **kunnen**.

cowschet, *sb.* cushat, wood-pigeon, S3; **cowscott**, Voc.; **cowshot**, SkD.—AS. *cúsceote* (Voc.), *cúscute* (OET.).

coy, *adj.* still, quiet, MD, C, C2; sober, *modestus*, Prompt.—AF. *coy*, quiet, OF. *coi*, Ps. 77. 13, also *coit*; Lat. *quietum*.

crabbe, *sb.* crab, S, Voc., Prompt.; also (in building) an arch, *fornix, cancer*, MD.—AS. *crabba*; cf. AF. *crabbe*.

crabbed, *adj.* shrewish, cross, bitter, C2, Palsg., MD, PP; **crabbyd**, 'awke or wrawe, *cancerinus*' Prompt.

cracchen, *v.* to scratch, MD, PP, C; **crechen**, S; **cark**, JD.

craft, *sb.* might, power, ability, art, craft, deceit, MD, S, S2, C2; **creft**, MD; **craftes**, *pl.* trades, P.—AS. *cræft*; cf. OHG. *kraft* (Otfrid).

crafti, *adj.* skilful, sly, MD, S2; **crafty**, C, P; **crefti**, S.

crafti-man, *sb.* artificer, W.

crage, *sb.* the neck, throat, S3, JD; **crawe**, the craw of fowls, Prompt., MD.—Cf. Du. *kraag*, neck, collar.

crak, *sb.* a thunder-peal, MD. *Phr.*: **crakkis of wer**, cannon, B.

craken, *v.* to crack (like thunder), to cry out, to chatter, to break with a noise, MD, PP; **crakede**, *pt. s.*, S.—AS. *cracian*.

crammasyn, *sb.* and *adj.* crimson, S3; see **crimosine**.

crammen, *v.* to cram, stuff, MD; **crommen**, MD; **cremmyn**, Prompt.; **i-crommet**, *pp.*, S2.—AS. *crammian*.

crampe, *sb.* the cramp, Voc., Prompt., PP; **craumpe**, CM.—OF. *crampe* (Cotg.); ODu. *krumpe*.

crane, *sb.* crane (bird), MD, Voc.; **kranes**, *pl.*, MD; **crennis**, S3; **cronez**, MD.—AS. *cran* (Voc.).

crasen, *v.* to break, MD; **crased**, *pp.*, S3, C3; **crasid**, PP. Cf. Swed. *krasa*, to break in pieces.

cratche, *sb.* manger, W, W2; **cratch**, HD, Cotg. (s.v. *creiche*); **cracche**, Voc., Prompt.; **creche**, MD.—OF. *creche*: Prov. *crepcha, crepia*; OHG. *crippea* (Tatian). Cf. **cribbe**.

crauen, *v.* to crave, beg earnestly, S, MD, to prosecute, accuse, MD.—AS. *crafian*, 'petere, postulare'; cf. Low Lat. *cravare*, in judicium mittere (also written *gravare*), see Schmid, Ducange.

crawand, *pr. p.* crowing, S3; see **crowen**.

creat, *pp.* created, MD.—Lat. *creatus*, pp. of *creare*.

creatour, *sb.* Creator, C3.—OF. *creatour*; Lat. *creatorem*.

creature, *sb.* creature, MD; **creatour**, MD; **creator**, S2.—OF. *creature*; Lat. *creatura*.

creaunce, *sb.* belief, MD, C3; **creance**, S2, C3.—OF. *crëance, credence*; Late Lat. *credentia*.

creauncen, *v.* to borrow, MD.

creaunt, *pr. p.* and *adj.* submitting as conquered, MD, PP; *in phr.*: **cry 'creaunt'**, MD.—OF. *crëant*; Lat. *credentem*.

crechen, *v.* to scratch, S; see **cracchen**.

crede, *sb.* the Creed, S, C3, PP; **credo**, S, PP.—Lat. *credo*, I believe.

credensynge, *sb.* believing, S3.

crefti, *adj.* crafty, S; see **crafti**.

creme, *sb.* the sacred oil used in anointing, chrism, Voc., HD, MD; **cream**, HD; **creame**, Palsg.; **creyme**, S2, Voc.; *Phr.*: **hille of creme**, i.e. the Mount of Olives, MD.—OF. *cresme*; Church Lat. *chrisma*; Gr. χρίσμα. Cf. **crisme**.

cremelen, *v.* to anoint with oil or fat, MD; **y-crymyled**, *pp.*, PP; **kremelyd**, MD; **crymailed**, PP.—OF. *cresmeler*, to anoint with holy oil.

crempe, *v.* to draw in, S. Cf. G. *krämpfen*. See **crampe**.

crennis, *sb. pl.* cranes, S3; see **crane**.

crepen, *v.* to creep, S, C2; **crope**, MD; **creap**, *pt. s.*, MD; **crep**, MD; **crope**, MD; 2 *pt. s.*, P; **crupen**, *pl.*, MD; **crepte**, *pt. s.* (weak), MD; **cropen**, *pp.*, MD.—AS. *crēopan*, pt. *crēap* (pl. *crupon*), pp. *cropen*.

creste, *sb.* crest (of bird, helmet), summit, MD, Prompt.; **creistis**, *pl.*, S3.—OF. *creste*; Lat. *crista*.

Cresten, *adj.* Christian, S2; see **Cristen**.

creyme, *sb.* the sacred oil, S2; see **creme**.

cribbe, *sb.* crib, manger; **crib**, MD; **crybbe**, Prompt.; **cribbe**, S, MD. Cf. OHG. *crippea* (Tatian).

crike, *sb.* creek, MD; **krike**, MD, S; **cryke**, C, Prompt.—Icel. *kriki*.

crimosine, *sb.* and *adj.* crimson, S3; **crimosin**, SkD; **crammasyn**, S3.—OF. *cramoisin* (*cramoisi*); Low Lat. *carmesinum*;

from Pers. *qirmisi*, crimson; from Skt. *kṛmi*, a worm, insect, (i.e. the cochineal insect).

crisme, *sb.* consecrated oil for anointing, MD; **crysme**, oil, Prompt.—Church Lat. *chrisma*, sacred oil; Gr. χρίσμα Cf. **creme**.

crisme-child, *sb.* the child anointed at baptism, MD.

crisme-cloð, *sb.* the chrisom, the cloth tied round the head of the anointed child, S. Cf. Church Lat. *chrismalis pannus*.

crisome, *sb.* the chrisom-cloth, *crismale*, Voc.; **crysome**, Palsg.; **crisom**, Cotg. (s.v. *cresmeau*).

Crist, *adj.* and *sb.* anointed, Christ, MD, S2, W, W2.—Lat. *Christus*; Gr. χριστός, anointed.

Cristen, *adj.* and *sb.* Christian, S, C2, C3; **Christen**, S, S2; **Cresten**, S2.—Lat. *Christianus*.

Cristendom, *sb.* Christianity, S, S2, C3; **Crystendom**, S2.—AS. *cristendóm*.

Cristenly, *adv.* in a Christian manner, C3.

Cristes-messe, *sb.* Christmas, MD; **Cristemasse**, C2.

Cristiente, *sb.* Christendom, MD; **Cristiante**, S3; **Cristianyte**, S2, C3.—OF. *crestiente, cristientet*; Church Lat. *Christianitatem*.

cristnien, *v.* to make Christian, to baptize, MD, S2; **i-cristned**, *pp.*, S2; **y-cristned**, *pp.*, S2; **cristned**, C3.—AS. *cristnian*.

critouns, *sb. pl.* refuse of the frying-pan, W2.—OF. *cretons* (Cotg.).

crochette, *sb.* a small hook, crotchet (in music), MD; **crochettes**, *pl.* crockets, S3.—OF. *crochet* (Bartsch).

croft, *sb.* field, enclosure, PP, S2, MD.—AS. *croft*; cf. ODu. *crocht*, a field on the downs.

croh, *sb.* a crock, waterpot, MD; **cróós**, *pl.*, S.

crois, *sb.* cross, PP, S, S3; **croys**, PP, S2, C2, C3; **croiz**, MD; **croice**, MD, S2.—OF. *crois, croiz*; Lat. *crûcem*, see Brachet. Cf. **crouche, cros**.

crok, *sb.* a hook, curl, a crooked way, wile, deceit, MD, Voc.; **crokes**, *pl.*, S; **crocks**, HD. *Phr.*: **went on croke**, went astray, H.—Icel. *krókr*.

croken, *v.* to bend, to curl hair, to turn aside, MD, W2; **crokid**, *pp.* curved, W2; **i-croked**, S.

croket, *sb.* curl, MD, HD.

crokke, *sb.* crock, pot, S2, PP; **crocke**, S, Voc.—AS. *crocca*.

crom-bolle, *sb.* crumb-bowl, S3.

cromme, *sb.* crumb, C3; **crumme**, MD; **crume**, MD; **crome**, MD; **crowm**, Voc.—AS. *cruma*.

crommen, *v.* to cram, MD, S2; see **crammen**.

crone, *sb.* an old hag, S2, MD, C3; **crony**, SkD. Cf. ODu. *kronie, karonie*, an old sheep; Picard *carone* = F. *charogne*, see SkD (p. 797). See **caroigne**.

cronicle, *sb.* chronicle, MD.—OF. *cronique*. For the intrusive *l*, cf. *manciple, participle, principle, syllable, canticle, treacle, cardiacle*.

cronique, *sb.* chronicle, S2; **chronique**, C.—OF. *cronique*; Late Lat. *chronica*; Gr. χρονικά, annals.

croos, *sb. pl.* water-pots, S; see **croh**.

crop, *sb.* top, upper part of a tree, crop of corn, Voc., PP, S2; **croppe**, Prompt., Palsg.; **croppes**, *pl.*, young shoots, C; **croppis**, S3.—AS. *crop*.

crope[1], *2 pt. s.* didst creep, P; **cropen**, *pp.*, MD; see **crepen**.

crope[2], *sb.* crupper, HD; **croupe**, CM, SkD.—OF. *crope* (F. *croupe*).

croper, *sb.* crupper, the hinder part of a horse, C3.—OF. *croupiere* (Cotg.).

cropiers, *sb. pl.* the housings on a horse's back, HD.

cropone, *sb.* the buttock, HD.—AF. *cropoun*.

cros, *sb.* cross, PP, MD; **crosse**, P, MD.—ONorse, *cros (cors)*; cf. Ir. *cros*, Prov. *cros*. Cf. **crois**.

crosselet, *sb.* a small crucible, C3; **croslet**, C3. See SkD (s.v. *crucible*).

crouche, *sb.* the cross of Christ, crucifix, sign or representation of the cross, MD, PP, HD; **cruche**, PP; **crowch**, S.—Cf. OHG. *crûci (krûzi)* in Otfrid; Lat. *cruci-* (stem of *crux*). Cf. **crois**.

crouchen, *v.* to sign with the cross, MD; **cruchen**, MD; **crowche**, MD; **crouched**, *pt. s.*, MD.

croud, croude, *sb.* a musical instrument (stringed), H, W; see **crowde**[1].

crouken[1], *v.* to croak, MD; **crowken**, Prompt.; **croak**, Sh.

crouken[2], *v.* to bend down, S3, MD; see **croken**.

croune, *sb.* crown, the tonsure, S, G; see **corone**.

crouni; see **coronen**.

crouning, *sb.* crowning, S2; the tonsure, P. See **corone**.

crowch, *sb.* cross, S; see **crouche**.

crowd, *v.* to coo as a dove, S3; **croud**, JD.

crowde[1], *sb.* a musical instrument (stringed), Prompt., Cath., Voc.; **crouthe**, MD; **croud**, H; **croude** (= *chorus*), W, H; **crowd**, ND; **crouth**, MD.—Wel. *crwth*, a fiddle: Ir. *cruit*: OIr. *crot*; cf. Low Lat. *chrotta* (Ducange). Cf. **rote**[2].

crowde[2], *sb.* wheelbarrow, Prompt.

crowden, *v.* to push, HD, S2, C3; **crouden**, MD, HD, C3; **crude**, to press forward, S; **crowdyn**, Prompt.; **crud**, *pt. s.*, MD, HD.—AS. *crúdan, to press, drive, pt. *créad* (pl. *crudon*), pp. *croden*; cf. Du. *kruyden*, to push (Hexham). See Sievers, 384, 385.

crowdyng, *sb.* pressure, S2, C3.

crowen, *v.* to crow; **crawand**, *pr. p.*, S3; **him croweth**, *pr. s. reflex.*, C3.—AS. *cráwan*, pt. *créow*, pp. *crawen*.

crownell, *sb.* corolla, small crown, S3. See **corone**.

crucchen, *v.* to crouch, MD; **cruchen**, S3. **cruche**; see **crouche**.

crud, *sb.* curd, MD; **curde**, Prompt.; **cruddes**, *pl.*, S2, PP; **croddes**, PP; **crouds**, JD; **curddys**, Voc.

cruddid, *pp.* curded, W2.

crude, *v.* to press forward, S; see **crowden**.

cruel, *adj.* cruel, MD; **cruwel**, MD; **crewell**, MD.—OF. *cruel*; Lat. *crudelem*.

cruelnesse, *sb.* cruelty, MD; **cruwelnes**, S2.

crueltee, *sb.* cruelty, C2.—AF. *cruelte*; Lat. *crudelitatem*.

crulle, *adj.* curly, C; **krulle**, MD; **crolle**, MD.—Cf. G. *krolle*, curl; see Weigand.

crune, *v.* crown, S; see **corone**.

cry, *sb.* cry, MD; **crye**, Prompt.; **crei**, S.—AF. *cri*, *crie*.

cryen, *v.* to cry, MD, PP; **crie**, PP; **criȝinge**, *pr. p.*, S2; **criȝed**, *pt. s.*, S2; **crieden**, *pl.*, S; **criede**, S2.—AF. *crier*, *cryer*, for older *cridar*; cf. It. *gridare*.

crymailed, *pp.* anointed, PP; **y-crymyled**, PP; see **cremelen**.

crystal, *sb.* ice, crystal, MD; **cristal**, W2.—AF. *cristal*; Lat. *crystallum*, ice (Vulg.), also, mountain-crystal; Gr. κρύσταλλος, ice.

cubit, *sb.* elbow, a cubit (measure), MD; **cubytes**, *pl.*, C2; **cupydez**, S2.—Lat. *cubitum*.

cucurbite, *sb.* a gourd-shaped chemical vessel.—Lat. *cucurbita*, gourd.

cudde, *pt. s.* made known, S; see **cuþen**, **kyþen**.

cude, *sb.* cud, S, MD; **code**, MD; **cudde**, Prompt., Palsg.; **quide**, MD; **quede**, MD; **quid**, HD, SkD.

cuen, *sb.* queen, S; see **quene**.

cuffe, *sb.* cuff, PP, Prompt., Palsg.; **coffes**, *pl.*, PP.—Cf. MHG. *kuffe*, coif. Cf. **coife**.

cukkow, *sb.* cuckoo, MD, Prompt.; **cocow**, Voc.; **cocowe**, Palsg.; **cucko**, Voc.; **gukgo**, S3.—OF. *coucou*; Lat. *cuculum* (acc.).

culle, *v.* to strike, to kill, P; see **kulle**.

culme, *sb.* soot, Prompt.

culorum, *sb.* end, conclusion, PP.—For Lat. *seculorum* in the phr. *in secula seculorum*, for ever and ever, at the end of the Gloria Patri.

culpon, *sb.* slice, shred, MD, C; **culpown**, Prompt.; **culpen**, Manip.—AF. *colpoun*; Low Lat. *colponem*; cf. F. *coupon*.

culter, *sb.* coulter, the fore-iron of a plough, PP, Voc., Prompt.; **kulter**, PP; **coltre**, PP.—Lat. *culter*.

culuer, *sb.* dove, MD, W, W2; **cullfre**, S; **colvyr**, Voc.; **culuere**, S2.—AS. *culfre* (OET.).

culuer-briddis, *sb. pl.* young pigeons, W.

cum-; see also words beginning in **com-**.

cumen, *v.* to come, S; see **comen**.

cumlyng, *sb.* stranger, H; see **comelyng**.

cumplie, *sb.* compline, S; see **complie**.

cumrit, *pt. s.* encumbered, S2; **cummerit**, S3; see **combren**.

cumsen, *v.* to commence, S2, PP; see **comsen**.

cun-; see also words beginning in **con-**.

cun[1], *v.* to know how to, H; see **kunnen**.

cun[2], *sb.* kin, kind, nature, S; **cunne**, *dat.*, S; see **kyn**[2].

cunde[1], *adj.* natural, kind, MD; see **kynde**[1].

cunde[2], *sb.* kind, nature, S; see **kynde**[2].

cundeliche, *adv.* naturally, S; see **kyndely**.

cunes-mon, *sb.* kinsman, S; see **kynes-man**.

cunin, *sb.* cony, rabbit, S; see **conyng**.

cunnen, *v.* to know, to be able, S, S2; see **kunnen**.

cunreadnes, *sb. pl.* kindreds, S; see **kynrede**.

cupabil, *adj.* culpable, H; see **coupable**.

cuppe, *sb.* cup, S, C2, C; **kuppe**, S; **coppe**, S2, P.—AS. *cuppe*; Lat. *cupa*. Cf. **coupe**[2].

cuppe-mel, *adv.* by cupfuls, S2, PP; **in cupmel**, P.

cupydez, *sb. pl.* cubits, S2; see **cubit**.

curace, *sb.* cuirass, S3, SkD; **curat**, HD.—OF. *cuirace*; Late Lat. *coracium*, from Lat. *corium*, leather.

curall, *sb.* coral, S3; see **coral**.

curat, *sb.* curate, C.—Late Lat. *curatus*.

curatour, *sb.* curate, priest who has cure of souls, PP, S2.

cure, *sb.* a charge, cure of souls, PP, C3; **cures**, *pl.*, pursuits, C2.—Church Lat. *cura*.

curiour, *sb.* currier, W; see **coriour**.

curious, *adj.* busy, zealous, eager to know, dainty, fine, MD, S3; careful, C.

curlew, *sb.* curlew, *coturnix*, Prompt., W2 (Ps. 104. 40); **curlu**, H; **kurlu**, MD; **corlew**, MD; **curlowyr**, Voc.—OF. *corlieu*, curlew (Cotg.).

currour, *sb.* runner, courier, W2; **corour**, W2; **currours**, *pl.* light-armed troops, S3.

52

curry, *v.* to prepare leather, to curry horses, to rub down, flatter, S3, MD; **currayyn**, Prompt.; **coraye**, MD.—OF. *couraër, coureer* (F. *courroyer*); It. *corredare*; from Low Lat. *conredium.* See **conrey**.

curs, *sb.* curse, C, G; **cors**, S3, G.

cursedly, *adv.* wickedly, C2.

cursednes, *sb.* malice, wickedness, C2; **cursednesse**, C2; **cursidnesse**, misery, W2.

cursen, *v.* to curse, MD; **corse**, S2; **cursede**, *pt. s.*, S; **corsed**, *pp.*, S2.—AS. *cursian.*

curt, *sb.* court, S; see **court**.

curteis, *adj.* courteous, S3, C; see **corteis**.

curteisly, *adv.* courteously, C2; see **corteisliche**.

curteisye, *sb.* courtesy, PP; see **cortesye**.

cus, *sb.* kiss, Prompt.; **coss**, W; **cos**, S, W, W2; **kosses**, *pl.*, MD; **cossis**, W2.—AS. *cos*; cf. OHG. *cus* (Tatian).

cusen; see **chesen**.

cussen, *v.* to kiss, S, MD; **kussen**, S; **kesse**, S, C2; **custe**, *pt. s.*, S; **keste**, C2; **kiste**, S, C2; **kest**, S2; **cusseden**, *pl.*, S2.—AS. *cyssan*; cf. OHG. *cussan* (Tatian).

cust, *sb.* choice, moral excellence, character, MD; **custe**, *dat.*, S.—AS. *cyst*; cf. OHG. *kust* (Otfrid). See **chesen**.

custome, *sb.* custom, a public due, MD, S; **custume**, S; **costom**, MD.—AF. *custume, coustume*; Late Lat. **consuetunimem, *consuetuninem*; Lat. *consuetudinem*; see Constans, and SkD (p. 798).

custome-house, *sb.* custom-house, S2.

cut, *sb.* a cut twig, a lot, C, C3, H, Prompt., MD; **kut**, H, MD; **cutte**, Palsg.; **kuttis**, *pl.*, H. *Phr.*: **to draw cuts**, HD. See **kutten**.

cut-purs, *sb.* cut-purse thief, PP; **kittepors**, PP. See **kutten**.

cuth[1], *sb.* race, people, PP; see **kyþ**.

cuth[2], *pp.* known, S; see **kunnen**.

cuðe, *pt. s.* could, knew, S; see **kunnen**.

cuðen, *v.* to make known, S; see **kyþen**.

cuðmon, *sb.* acquaintance, kinsman, S.—AS. *cúðman.*

cuðreden, *sb.* familiarity, MD.

cuððe, *sb.* relationship, one's native land, S, MD; see **kyþ**, **ceþen**, **cheþen**.

cwakien, *v.* to quake, S; see **quaken**.

cwalm, *sb.* death, pestilence, MD; see **qualm**.

cwalm-hus, *sb.* prison, place of torment, MD.

cwalm-stow, *sb.* place of execution, S, MD.—AS. *cwealm-stów* (Schmid).

cwað, *pt. s.* quoth, S; see **queþen**.

cwead-schipe, *sb.* wickedness, S; see **quedschipe**.

cwellen, *v.* to kill, S; see **quellen**.

cweme, *adj.* pleasing, S; see **queme**.

cwemen, *v.* to please, S; see **quemen**.

cwennkenn, *v.* to quench, S; see **quenchen**.

cweðen, *v.* to speak, S; **cweð**, *pt. s.*, S; see **queþen**.

cwic, *adj.* living, S; see **quik**.

cwidden, *v.* to speak, announce, MD; **i-cwiddet**, *pp.*, S.—AS. *cwiddian.*

cwide, *sb.* speech, bequest, S; see **queþen**.—AS. *cwide*, a saying.

cyll, *sb.* a canopy, SkD (s.v. *ceil*).—OF. *ciel*, canopy, inner roof, ceiling (Cotg.); Lat. *caelum*, see Brachet, p. lv.

cyne-rice, *sb.* kingdom, rule, S; see **kine-**.

cyrce-iærd, church-yard, S; see **chirche-ȝeard**.

D

dade, *sb.* deed, S; see **dede**[2].
dæd, *adj.* dead, S; see **deed**.
dæde, *sb. pl.* deeds, S; see **dede**[2].
dæi, *sb.* day, S; **dæȝe**, *pl.*, S; see **day**.
dære, *adj.* dear, S; see **dere**[3].
dæð, *sb.* death, S; see **deeþ**.
daft, *adj.* apt, fit, SkD (p. 799); **deft**, fit, mild, gentle, innocent, foolish, MD; **daffe**, a fool, S2, PP; **deffe**, *obtusus, agrestis*, Prompt.; **defte**, *dat.*, S.—AS. *dæft*.
dafte-like, *adv.* fittingly; **deftly**, MD; **defly**, MD; **dafftelike**, S.
dage, *sb. pl.* days, S; see **day**.
dagen, *v.* to become day, S; see **dawen**.
dagge, *sb.* a jag of cloth, Prompt., MD, HD, CM; **dagges**, *pl.* jagged edges, PP.
daggen, *v.* to pierce, to notch, to jag, to cut at the edges, MD, PP, SkD (p. 150), CM, HD; **daggyn**, *fractillo*, Prompt.; **daggyde**, *pp.*, Prompt.—Cf. ODu. *daggen*, to stab. See **jagge**[1].
dagger, *sb.* dagger, *pugio*, CM; **daggar**, Voc.; **daggare**, Prompt.
daghynge, *sb.* dawning, H; see **dawing**.
dagoun, *sb.* a jag of a blanket, CM; **dagon**, HD. See **daggen**.
daheð, *sb.* dawn; **daheðes**, *gen.*, S. See **dawen**.
dai, *sb.* day, S, W; see **day**.
dai-gang, *sb.* day's journey, S2.
dai-liht, *sb.* daylight, MD; **dai-liȝt**, S.
dai-rawe, *sb.* day-break, MD.
dai-red, *sb.* the flush of morn, MD.
dai-rime, *sb.* the edge of dawn, MD; **dai-rim**, S.—AS. *dæg-rima*.
dai-sterre, *sb.* day-star, S, W2; **day-sterre**, PP.—AS. *dæg-steorra*, morning-star.
dale, *sb.* dale, valley, S, PP; **dele**, S; **dalen**, *dat.*, S; **dales**, *pl.*, MD; **deales**, MD.—AS. *dæl*: Goth. *dal*; see Sievers, 49.
dalf, *pt. s.* dug, W; see **delven**.
daliaunce, *sb.* talk, C, C2, C3; **daliance**, MD.—AF. *daliaunce*, interference.
dalien, *v.* to talk, Prompt.; **dalye**, to play and sport, Palsg., MD.—AF. *dayler*, to dally.
dal-neominde, *pr. p.* as *sb.* partaker, sharer, S.—OMerc. *dæl-niomend*, Ps. 118. 63 (VP.).
dalte, *pt. s.* dealt, G; see **deelen**.
damage, *sb.* damage, loss, Prompt., MD; **domage**, S3.—AF. *damage* (also OF. *damage*); Late Lat. **damnaticum*, from Lat. *damnum*.
dame, *sb.* dame, lady, dam, S, C3, MD; **dam**, MD.—AF. *dame*; Lat. *domina*.

damesele, *sb.* damsel, S, W2, MD; **damoysele**, C.—AF. *damoysele*; Late Lat. *domicella*, for **dominicella*; see Constans.
dan, *sb.* a title of respect placed before personal names, MD, C2, CM; **danz**, MD; **daun**, MD, CM; **dene**, S3.—OF. *danz*, *dans*; Lat. *dominus*; in oblique case OF. *dam*; Lat. *dominum*, see Bartsch and Roland.
dang, *pt. s.* beat, S3; see **dyngen**.
dar, *1 pr. s.* I dare, MD; **dear**, MD; **der**, MD; **darst**, *2 pr. s.*, S, C3; **dærst**, MD; **derst**, MD; **dar**, *pr. s.*, MD, C2, C3, P; **durren**, *pl.*, MD; **duren**, S; **doren**, W; **durre**, *pr. subj. s.*, MD; *pl.*, S; **durste**, *pt. subj. s.*, S; **durst**, MD, P; **durste**, *pl.*, S; **dorste**, S, S2, C2; **dorst**, S2, P; **durren**, *v.*, MD.—AS. *dear*, I dare, 2 pr. s. *dearst*, pl. *durron*, subj. *durre*, pt. s. *dorste*.
dare, *adj.* dark, S; see **derk**.
darked, *pt. s.* lay hid, S; see **derken**.
darklyng, *adv.* in the dark, S3, Sh.
dasewen, *v.* to be dim, MD; **daswen**, C3; **dasewide**, *pt. s.*, W2.—Cf. E. *daze*.
daun, *sb.* a title of respect, CM; see **dan**.
daunger, *sb.* absolute control, power, also difficulty, MD, PP, C; **daungere**, refusal, denial, S3; power to harm, PP.—OF. *dangier*, *dongier*, power, lordship, refusal, danger, (Bartsch); Late Lat. **dominiarium*, from Lat. *dominium*, see Brachet.
daungerous, *adj.* haughty, difficult to please, MD, C2, C.
daunten, *v.* to force, tame, MD, S2, S3, P.—AF. *danter*, OF. *donter* (F. *dompter*); Lat. *domitare*.
daw[1], *sb.* dew, S; see **dew**.
daw[2], *sb.* day, S2; see **day**.
dawen, *v.* to become day, C2, PP, Prompt., Palsg., MD, JD; **dagen**, S, Prompt.; **daȝede**, *pt. s.*, MD.—AS. *dagian*.
dawing, *sb.* dawning, S3; **dagheynge**, H; **daghynge**, H.
dawnen, *v.* to dawn, Prompt.
dawning, *sb.* dawning, MD; **dawenynge**, C.
day, *sb.* day, SkD; **dæi**, S; **dai**, S, W (1 Cor.4. 3); **daȝȝ**, S; **dei**, S; **dæies**, *gen.*, S; **deies**, S; *phr.*: **be dæies**, by day, S; **now a dayes**, C2; **daie**, *dat.*, S; **daw**, S2; **daȝes**, *pl.*, S; **dayes**, S; **dawes**, S, PP; **dage**, S; **daga**, *gen.*, MD; **daȝa**, MD, **daȝene**, MD; **dawene**, MD; **dahene**, S; **dæȝen**, *dat.*, S; **dæȝe**, S; **daiȝe**, S; *phr.* **to give day**, to give trust, S3; **bring of daw**, to kill,

dayerie

S2.—AS. *dæg, dæges, dæge*; pl. *dagas, daga* (and *dagena*), *dagum*.

dayerie, *sb.* dairy, C; **deyry**, Voc., Prompt. See **deye**.

dayesie, *sb.* daisy, CM; **dayesye**, CM; **dais-eie**, Voc.; **dayes-eȝes**, *pl.*, S2.—AS. *dæges-éage*, i.e. day's eye (Voc.).

daynen, *v.* to deign, S2; see **deynen**.

dayntethis, *sb. pl.* dainties, H, MD.—OF. *deintet*; Prov. *dentat, dintat*; Lat. *dignitatem*. Cf. **deyntee**[1].

dayre, *sb.* dairy-maid, *androchia*, Voc. See **deye**.

de-; see also words beginning in **dis-**.

de, *v.* to die, S3; see **deyen**.

deað, *pr. s.* doeth, S; see **don**.

deawes, *sb. pl.* dews, S2; see **dew**.

debat, *sb.* strife, discord, C2; **debate**, S3, P; **debaat**, C3.—AF. *debat*.

de-baten, *v.* to contend, fight, MD, C2.—OF. *debatre* (pr. p. *debatant*), It. *dibattere*, (Florio).

debonaire, *adj.* mild, gentle, MD, C; **debonere**, S2; **deboner**, W2, H; **deboneire**, MD; **dubonure**, S2; **debonayr**, S3; **debonur**, H.—OF. *debonaire*; cf. OIt. *di bon aire*. Cf. **bonayre**.

debonerte, *sb.* gentleness, MD, H.—OF. *debonerete, debonnaireteit* (Ps. 44. 4).

de-breiden, *v.* to tear apart, W.—This is a hybrid form: *de* + ME. *breiden*.

de-breken, *v.* to break asunder, to tear, S2; **debroken**, *pp.*, MD.—A hybrid form.

debrusen, *v.* to bruise; **debrise**, MD; **debrusede**, *pt. s.*, MD; **debrused**, S2.—AF. *debruser*, OF. *debriser*.

deburs, *v.* disburse, pay, S3; see **disburse**.

deceit, *sb.* deceit, MD; **disseit**, W2.—AF. *deceit*; Late Lat. *decepta*.

deciple, *sb.* disciple, S; see **disciple**.

ded[1], *adj.* dead, S, PP; see **deed**.

ded[2], *sb.* death, S2, PP.—Cf. Swed. *död*, Dan. *död*, death. See **deeþ**.

dede[1], *pt. s.* did, S, S2; **deden**, *pl.*; see **don**.

dede[2], *sb.* deed, S, S2, PP; **dade**, S; **dede**, *pl.*, S; **dæde**, S; **dedes**, S, S2; **deades**, MD.—AS. *déd*, (*dǽd*); cf. Goth. *ga-dēþs*, see Brugmann, § 75.

dede[3], *pt. pl.* died, S3; see **deyen**.

dede[4], *sb.* death, PP, S, S2, S3; see **ded**[2], **deeþ**.

dede-stoure, *sb.* death-struggle, S2.

dedeyn, *sb.* disdain, W, H; see **disdeyn**.

dedeyne, *v.* to deign, S3. See **deynen**.

dedly, *adj.* liable to death, H; see **deedli**.

deduit, *sb.* delight, pleasure, MD, HD; **deduyt**, C; **dedut**, MD; **dute**, MD.—AF. *deduit*; cf. Late Lat. *deductus*, 'animi

defoulen

oblectatio' (Ducange); from OF. *deduire*, (refl.) to rejoice; Late Lat. *deducere*.

dee, *sb.* a die, MD; **die**, Sh.; **dees**, *pl.* dice, PP, C2, C3; **dys**, PP, C.—OF. *de* (pl. *dez*): It. *dado*, Prov. *dat*; Lat. *datum*.

deed, *adj.* dead, S2, C2; **ded**, S, PP; **dæd**, S; **dyad**, S2; **deade**, *pl.*, S.—AS. *déad*; cf. Icel. *dauðr*, Goth. *dauþs*.

deedli, *adj.* mortal, subject to death, deadly, W, W2; **dedly**, H, PP; **diadlich**, S; **dedlich**, MD, PP.—AS. *déadlic*.

deef, *adj.* deaf, MD, C; **def**, MD; **deue**, *pl.*, C3.—AS. *déaf*: Goth. *daubs*.

deel, *sb.* deal, share, MD, G; **del**, S, S3; **deal**, MD; **deyl**, S2. *Phr.*: **neuer a deyl**, not a bit, S2; **euery deyl**, S2.—AS. *dǽl*; cf. Goth. *dails* (*daili*-); see Douse, p. 94.

deelen, *v.* to deal, share, divide, MD; **delen**, S2, G; **delte**, *pt. s.*, C3; **dalte**, G; **deled**, *pp.*, G.—AS. *délan*: Goth. *dailjan*, from *daili*-; see Douse, p. 113.

deep, *adj.* deep, C; **dep**, S; **deop**, S, MD; **dyep**, MD; **dup**, MD; **depe**, *sb.*, S2, C3; **deopre**, *comp.*, S; **deope**, *adv.*, S; **deoppre**, *comp.*, S; **depper**, C3.—AS. *déop*; cf. Goth. *diups*, Icel. *djúpr*.

deer, *sb.* wild animal, C2; **der**, S; **diere**, *dat.*, S; **deer**, *pl.*, C2.—AS. *déor*; cf. Goth. *dius*, wild beast.

deeþ, *sb.* death, C2; **dæð**, S, MD; **deð**, S; **diath**, S; **dyaþ**, S2; **dead**, S; **ded**, S2, PP; **deaðe**, *dat.*, S; **deðe**, S, S2; **dede**, S, S2, S3.—AS. *déaþ*; cf. Icel. *dauði, dauðr*: Goth. *dauþus*.

defame; see **diffame**.

defaute, *sb.* defect, fault, S2, C2, PP; **defalte**, S2; **defautis**, *pl.*, S3, W2.—AF. *defaute, defalte*.

defenden, *v.* to protect, to forbid, S2, MD, C3, H.—AF. *defendre*; Lat. *defendere*.

defense, *sb.* protection, prohibition, MD; **defence**, S2.—AF. *defense, defence*.

defet, *pp.* defeated, MD.—AF. *defet, aefait*, pp. of *defaire*.

defien[1], *v.* to digest, MD, PP, HD; S2; **defy**, Cath.

defien[2], *v.* to mistrust, to defy, PP; **defye**, *despicere*, Cath.—AF. *defier*, OF. *defier*: It. *disfidare*, to defy, (Florio).

defigure, *v.* to disfigure; **defygurd**, *pp.*, S2.—AF. *desfigurer*.

defless, *sb. pl.*, devils, S; **deflen**, S; **devel**.

defoulen[1], *v.* to tread down, MD, W, W2, H, SkD (s.v. *defile*); **defoilen**, MD, SkD; **defoulid**, *pp.*, W.—OF. *defouler*, to trample on, rebuke (Cotg).; cf. *fouler* (Bartsch), *foller*, Ps. 138. 11; It. *follare*, to

55

press, to full clothes (Florio); Lat. *fullare*, to full cloth; cf. *fullo*, a fuller.

de-foulen[2], *v.* to make foul, *inquinare*, MD; **defowlyn**, Prompt.; **defoulid**, *pp.*, W.—A hybrid form, *de* + ME. *fulen*. See **foulen**.

defte, *adj.* gentle, S; see **daft**.

deghe, *v.* to die, S2; see **deyen**[1].

degoutit, *pp.* spotted, S3. Cf. OF. *degoutter* (Cotg.), and Lat. *gutta*, a drop, a spot, speck on an animal.

degyse, *adj.* fashionable, finical, H.—OF. *desguisé*, dissembled, sophisticated (Cotg.). See **disgysen**.

degyset, *pp.* disguised, S2; see **disgysen**.

deh, *sb.* dye, colour, SkD.—AS. *déah*.

dehtren, *sb. pl.* daughters, S; see **dohter**.

dei, *sb.* day, S; see **day**.

deide; see **deyen**[1].

deih, *pr. s.* profits, S; see **duȝen**.

dei-hwamliche, *adv.* every day, S.—AS. *dæg-hwamlice*.

deir, *v.* to harm, S3; see **dere**[2].

deken, *sb.* deacon, MD; **diakne**, MD; **deakne**, MD; **dekene**, W; **deknes**, *pl.*, S2, C3.—AS. *diacon*; Church Lat. *diaconus*; Gr. διάκονος (NT).

del[1], *sb.* deal, share, S, S3; see **deel**.

del[2], *sb.* grief, S2; see **dole**.

dele, *sb.* dale, S; see **dale**.

delen, *v.* to deal, S2, G; see **deelen**.

delfin, *sb.* dolphin, Voc.; **delfyne**, Prompt.; **delfyn**, SkD; **delfyns**, *pl.*, MD; **delphyns**, S2.—Lat. *delphinus*; Gr. δελφιν- (stem of δελφίς). Cf. **dolfin**.

delful, *adj.* doleful, S2; see **dolefulle**.

delfulli, *adv.* dolefully, MD; see **dolfully**.

delices, *sb. pl.* delights, H, C3, W2; **delicis**, W, H.—OF. *delices*; Lat. *delicias*.

delit, *sb.* delight, MD; **delyt**, S3, C2, C3.—OF. *delit, deleit*.

delitable, *adj.* delightful, PP, S3, W2, H; **delytable**, S2, C2; **dilitable**, S2.—AF. *delitable*; Lat. *delitabilem*.

delite, *v.* to delight, Cath., PP, W2; **delyting**, *pr. p.*, C2.—AF. *deliter*; Lat. *delectare*.

delitingis, *sb. pl.* delights, W2.

deliuer, *adj.* quick, active, MD; **delyuere**, C.—OF. *delivre*, quick, literally 'freed'.

deliueren, *v.* to set free, MD; **deliuery**, S2; **delyuery**, PP.—AF. *deliverer*; Late Lat. *deliberare*; Lat. *de* + *liberare*.

deliuerly, *adv.* quickly, nimbly, S2; **delyuerly**, S2, C.

deluen, *v.* to delve, dig, S, C2, P, W; **dalf**, *pt. s.*, MD, W; **dalfe**, W; **doluen**, *pl.*, MD, P; **delueden** (*weak pt.*), W2; **dolue**, *subj.*, S2; **i-doluen**, *pp.*, S; **y-dolue**, S2; **doluen**,

buried, S, P; **i-doluen**, S2.—AS. *delfan*, pt. *dealf* (pl. *dulfon*), pp. *dolfen*.

deluers, *sb. pl.* diggers, S2; **delueres**, P.

deme, *sb.* judge, S.—AS. *déma*.

demen, *v.* to give doom, to judge, decree, S, S2, S3, C2; **deeme**, S2; **demde**, *pt. s.*, S; **i-demed**, *pp.*, S; **y-demed**, S; **y-demd**, S2; **i-demd**, S; **demet**, S; **dempt**, S.—AS. *déman*: OS. *dómian*, Goth. *domjan*. See **doom**.

demenen, *v.* to manage, to behave (*refl.*), MD; **demenyng**, *pr. p.* showing, S3.—OF. *demener*, to carry on, make; *demener joie*, to rejoice, also *demener dol*, to grieve, Bartsch; cf. Cotg., and the phrase *demener dolor* in Roland.

demere, *sb.* judge, S; **demare**, S.—AS. *démere*.

demeyne, *sb.* power, possession, C2; **demayn**, MD; **demeigne**, MD.—OF. *demeine*, property, that which belongs to a lord; Lat. *dominicum*, from *dominus*; see Roland.

dene[1], *sb.* a title of respect, S3; see **dan**.

dene[2], *sb.* din, noise, PP, MD; see **dyn**.

deneis, *sb. pl.* Danes, S2.—OF. *Deneis*; Low Lat. *Denensis*, a Dane, see Brachet, lvii.

denie, *v.* to din; see **dinnen**.

denne, *sb.* den, MD; **den**, S; **dennes**, *pl.*, S2, W, H; **dennys**, H.—AS. *denn*.

dennen, *v.* to dwell; **dennede**, *pt. s.*, S.

denounce, *v.* to command, W (= Lat. *denunciare*).—OF. *denoncer*, to declare.

dent, *sb.* blow, S, S2, PP, CM; **dynt**, S3; **dint**, S, S2; **dunt**, S, S2.—AS. *dynt*.

deofell, *sb.* devil, S; see **devel**.

deol, *sb.* grief, S, S2; see **dole**.

deop, *adj.* deep, S; see **deep**.

deopliche, *adv.* deeply, S.

deopnesse, *sb.* deepness, S; see **depnesse**.

deore[1], *v.* to last, S2; see **duren**.

deore[2], *adj.* dear, S; see **dere**[3].

deore-wurðe, *adj.* precious, S; see **dere-wurþe**.

deorling, *sb.* darling, S; see **derling**.

deorne, *adj.* secret, dark, S; see **derne**.

deouele, *sb.* devil, S; see **devel**.

dep, *adj.* deep, S; see **deep**.

departen, *v.* to separate, divide, PP, S3, C3, W, W2; to become separated, S2; **depart**, *pp.*, S3.—AF. *departir*; OF. *despartir*; It. *dispartire* (Florio).

departere, *sb.* a divider, W.

departyng, *sb.* division, W; **departyngis**, *pl.*, W2.

depaynt, *pp.* painted, S3; **depeynted**, C; **depaynted**, S3; **depeynt**, *pt. pl.*, S3.—OF. *depeindre* (pp. *depeint*).

depayntar, *sb.* painter, S3.

depe, *sb.* depth, S2, C3.—AS. *dȳpe.*

depen, *v.* to dip, S2.

deplike, *adv.* deeply, MD; **deopliche**, S.—AS. *déoplice.*

depnesse, *sb.* deepness, depth, MD; **depnes**, S2; **deopnesse**, S.—AS. *déopnes.*

depraue, *v.* to slander, depreciate, W2, PP.—Lat. *deprauare*, to distort.

depuren, *v.* to purify, S3, MD.—OF. *depurer*; Late Lat. *depurare.*

der, *sb.* wild animal, S; see **deer.**

derby, *in phr.*: **father Derbies bands**, handcuffs, S3; **Darbies bands**, DG; **darbies**, DG.

dere[1], *sb.* harm, injury, MD; **darr**, MD; **der**, S3.—AS. *daru.*

dere[2], *v.* to harm, S, S2, C2; **derien**, S, MD; **deir**, S3; **ders**, *pr. pl.*, S2.—AS. *derian*; cf. OHG. *derien (derren)* in Otfrid.

dere[3], *adj.* and *adv.* dear, S, PP; **diere**, S; **duere**, S2; **dære**, S; **dure**, MD; **deore**, S; **der**, S2; **deir**, MD; **derre**, *comp.*, C; **derrest**, *superl.*, P.—AS. *déore*, *dýre*: OS. *diuri*, costly, loved.

dereliche, *adv.* dearly, MD; **derelych**, S2; **derli**, S2.—AS. *déorlice.*

dere-wurðe, *adj.* precious, S; **dereworth**, W; **dierewurth**, S; **derworþe**, S2, P; **deorewurðe**, S.—AS. *déorwurðe.*

derewurðlice, *adv.* respectfully, S.

dereynen, *v.* to answer to an accusation, to maintain a right in a judicial contest, CM, S2; **dereyni**, S2; **derreyne**, C; **darreyne**, C; **dereyned**, *pp.*, S2.—AF. *dereiner*, OF. *desresnier*; Late Lat. *disrationare* (also *derationare*); see Ducange.

derf[1], *adj.* brave, powerful, difficult, hard, MD; **derfe**, *pl.*, MD; **derue**, MD, S; **derfre**, *comp.*, S; **derure**, S.—Cf. OS. *derbi.*

derf[2], *sb.* affliction, hardship, S.—AS. *(ge)deorf.*

derfliche, *adv.* severely, cruelly, S.

derk, *adj.* dark, MD, S2, PP; **deork**, MD; **dorc**, S; **darc**, S; **dirk**, MD; **durk**, MD; **derke**, *dat.*, S.—AS. *deorc.*

derken, *v.* to make dark, to become dark, MD, S3; **dirken**, MD; **darken**, S2.

derkful, *adj.* dark, W.

derkhed, *sb.* darkness, MD.

derknesse, *sb.* darkness, MD, W.

derling, *sb.* darling, S, W2; **durlyng**, S, MD; **deorling**, S; **derlyngis**, *pl.*, chosen ones, W, W2.—AS. *déorling.* See **dere**[3].

derne, *adj.* secret, dark, S, S2, P, H; **deorne**, S; **dærne**, MD; **durne**, MD; **dern**, S2.—AS. *derne*; cf. OS. *derni* and MHG. *tarn* in *tarn-kappe*, the mantle of darkness, Grimm, p. 870.

dernel, *sb.* a kind of weed, rye-grass, *lollium*, Prompt.; **dernell**, Palsg.; **darnel**, S3, MD.

derring-doe, *sb.* daring enterprise, ND, S3. See **dar.**

dert, *sb.* dirt, S3; see **drit.**

derðe, *sb.* dearth, S, P. See **dere**[1].

derue, *adj.* bold, S; **derure**, *comp.* more severe, S; see **derf**[1].

deruen, *v.* to afflict, S. See **derf**[2], *sb.*

des-; see also words beginning in **dis-.**

desaly, **desselic**, *adv.* foolishly, S2; see **dusiliche.**

desarayen, *v. reflex.* to fall into disorder, S2.—OF. *desarroyer.*

desauauntage, *sb.* disadvantage, S2; **disauauntage**, MD; **disadvauntages**, *pl.*, MD.—OF. *desavantage.*

descenden, *v.* to go down, SkD.—AF. *descendre*; Lat. *descendere.*

descensorie, *sb.* vessel used for extracting oil *per descensum*, C3.

descriuen, *v.* to describe, MD; **descryue**, S3; **descryfe**, S2; **discryue**, S2, S3, C2; **discreue**, S2; **discriued**, *pp.*, S2; **discryued**, W.—OF. *descrivre* (pr. p. *descrivant*; Lat. *describere.*

deserited; see **disheriten.**

desert, *sb.* merit, C2.—AF. and OF. *deserte*, see Ducange (s.v. *deservire*).

deserven, *v.* to merit, MD; **disserued**, *pp.*, well served, W.—AF. *deservir*; Late Lat. *deservire.*

desi, *adj.* foolish, MD; see **dusi.**

despeir, *sb.* despair, MD.—AF. *despeir.*

despeiren, *v.* to despair, MD; **despeired**, *pp.*, C2.—OF. *desperer*, Lat. *desperare.*

desperate, *adj.* outrageous, S3.—Lat. *desperatus.*

despisabil, *adj.* despicable, H; **dispisable**, W2.

despit, *sb.* contempt, injury, S2, C3; **despyt**, C2; **despite**, WW; **dispit**, W.—AF. *despit*; Lat. *despectum* (acc.).

de-spiteful, *adj.* full of contempt, WW.

despitous, *adj.* ignominious, MD, C; **dispitous**, contemptuous, S3; **despitus**, H.

despitously, *adv.* contemptuously, spitefully, S2, C2, C3; **dispitously**, C.

despoilen, *v.* to despoil, to strip, MD; **dispoilen**, C2; **dispoyled**, *pp.*, S3.—OF. *despoiller*; Lat. *despoliare.*

dest, *2 pr. s.* doest, S; see **don.**

destrer, *sb.* a courser, war-horse, MD; **dextrer**, C2.—AF. *destrer*; Late Lat. *dextrarium* (from Lat. *dextra*, the right hand), the horse led by the squire on the right of his own horse.

destroyen, *v.* to destroy, MD; **destruien**, MD, C; **destrue**, S2; **distruen**, S2;

destrie, MD, W, W2; **dysstrye**, S2; **distruyede**, *pt. s.*, W; **distried**, *pp.*, W, W2.—AF. *destruire*. (pr. p. *destruyant*); Lat. *destruere*.

destroyere, *sb.* destroyer, Prompt., MD; **distrier**, W.

dette, *sb.* debt, C2; **dett**, *adj.* due, H.—AF. *dette*; Lat. *debita*.

deð[1], *pr. s.* doeth, S, S2; see **don**.

deð[2], *sb.* death, S; see **deeþ**.

deð-vuel, *sb.* death-evil, S2.

deuh; see **dew**.

deue, *adj. pl.* deaf, C3; see **deef**.

deuel, *sb.* devil, S, S2, W2; **deofel**, MD; **deofell**, S; **diuel**, S; **dyeuel**, S2; **dewill**, S3; **dewle**, Prompt.; **dwylle**, MD; **deouele**, S; **diefles**, *gen.*, S; **dieule**, *dat.*, S; **deofles**, *pl.*, MD; **defless**, S; **deoules**, S; **deoflen**, S; **deflen**, S; **deoflene**, *gen. pl.*, S.—AS. *déofol*; Lat. *diabolus* (Vulg.); Gr. διάβολος; cf. OHG. *diufal* (Otfrid).

deuin, *sb.* prophesying, divinity, theology, MD; **diuyn**, S2.

deuine, *sb.* theologian, augur, soothsayer, MD; **dyuynes**, *pl.*, MD.—OF. *devin*; Lat. *diuinum*.

deuinen, *v.* to foretell, guess, suspect, MD; **deuyne**, PP.

deuinourr, *sb.* interpreter, explainer, theologian, MD, PP; **dyuynour**, PP.

deuise, *sb.* tale, narrative, S3; **deuys**, order, C.

deuisen, *v.* to divide, arrange, order, decide, tell, relate, MD, S2; **deuyse**, C2, C3; **deuice**, MD, S2; **diuise**, S2.—AF. *deviser*, It. *divisare*; formed from Lat. *diuidere* (pp. *diuisus*).

deuisynge, *sb.* narration, S2.

deuoid, *pp.* as *adj.* destitute of, SkD.

deuoiden, *v.* to quit, leave, also to annihilate, exterminate, MD; **deuoyden**, S2.—OF. *desvoider, desvuidier*.

devoir, *sb.* duty, knightly duty, PP, C2; **deuoyr**, S3; **devor**, ND, PP; **deuer**, PP, CM.—OF. *devoir* (sb. orig. v.); Lat. *debere*.

deuouren, *v.* to devour, MD; **devoir**, S3.—AF. *devourer*; Lat. *deuorare*.

dew, *sb.* dew, PP; **dæw**, MD; **daw**, S; **deu**, S; **deuh**, PP; **deawes**, *pl.*, S2.—AS. *déaw*.

dewill, *sb.* devil, S3; see **devel**.

dewite, *sb.* duty, S3; see **duete**.

dewle, *sb.* grief, S3; see **dole**.

dextrer, *sb.* a war-horse, C2; see **destrer**.

deye, *sb.* a female servant, esp. one who looks after the cows and dairy, *androchia*, Voc., Prompt., C; **deye**, a cow-boy, *androchius*, MD, Cath.—Icel. *deigja*, see CV.; cf. AF. *deye*.

deyen[1], *v.* to die, S2, PP; **deʒen**, MD, S2; **deghe**, S2; **deie**, S; **dey**, S3; **dye**, PP; **diʒe**, PP; **dyʒe**, S2, PP; **de**, S3; **deide**, *pt. s.*, S, S2; **deiʒede**, MD; **deyde**, C2; **deid**, S2; **deit**, S3; **dede**, *pl.*, S3; **deyed**, *pp.*, C2.—Icel. *deyja*: OS. *dóian*.

deyen[2], *v.* to dye, MD; **dyyn**, Prompt.; **dyed**, *pt. s.*, C2.—AS. *déagian*, from *déah*. See **deh**.

deyere, *sb.* dyer, C.

deyl, *sb.* deal, share, S2; see **deel**.

deynen, *v.* to deign, to appear good, to please, MD, CM, S2; **deignen**, MD; **daynede**, *pt. s.*, S2; **dæyned him**, (*refl.*) C2.—AF. *deigner*; Lat. *dignare*.

deynous, *adj.* proud, disdainful, MD, CM, Cath. (p. 95, *n.*).

deyntee[1], *sb.* worth, pleasure, liking, S2, C2, C3; **deynte**, S2; **deinte**, MD; **deyntees**, *pl.*, S2, C2, C3.—OF. *daintie, deintet*, Prov. *din-tat*; Lat. *dignitatem*. Cf. **daynteþis**.

deyntee[2], *adj.* dainty, C2, C3.

deynteuous, *adj.* choice, dainty, C2.

deys, *sb.* daïs, high table in hall, C, C2, PP; **deyes**, PP; **deis**, PP; **dese**, PP; **deyse**, PP; **dees**, MD; **des**, MD; **day**, canopy, JD.—OF. *deis* (AF. *dois*); Lat. *discum* (acc.), see Brachet, p. lxv. Cf. **disshe**.

deʒter, *sb. pl.* daughters, S2; see **dohter**.

di-; see also words beginning in **de-, dis-**.

dia, *sb.* A term set before medicinal confections or electuaries that were devised by the Greeks, Cotg.; **dya**, HD; **dyas**, *pl.* remedies, medicines, PP.—Gr. διά. See **diapenidion**.

diadlich, *adj.* mortal, S; see **deedli**.

diamant, *sb.* diamond, PP, Cath.; **dyamand**, MD; **dyamaunt**, C.—OF. *diamant*, a diamond, the loadstone (Cotg.). See **adamant**.

dia-penidion, *sb.* a kind of sweet stuff like barley-sugar used to relieve coughs, PP; **diapenydion**, PP; **diopendion**, S2.—OF. *diapenidion*, It. *diapenídio*, cf. *diapiéde*, 'a diapedon or confection made of *Penids*' (Florio). See **dia** and **penid**.

diaper[1], *sb.* a kind of figured cloth; **dyaper**, MD; **diapery**, MD.—OF. *diaspre, diaspe*, diapered cloth; Lat. *iaspidem*, jasper; from Gr. ἴασπις, probably of Semitic origin; see Diez, p. 119.

diaper[2], *v.* to variegate, adorn with figures and colours, ND; **diapred**, *pp.*, ND; **dyapred**, C.

diath, *sb.* death, S; see **deeþ**.

dicht, *pp.* prepared, S2; see **dihten**.

diciples, *sb. pl.* disciples, S; see **disciple**.

dide, *pt. s.* did, caused, put, S; see **don**.

diefles, *sb. gen.* devil's, S; see **devel**.

dier, *sb.* wild animal, beast; **diere**, *dat.*, S; see **deer**.

dier-chin, *sb.* deer-kind, beasts, S.

diere, *adj.* dear, S; see **dere**[3].

diere-wurð, *adj.* precious, S; see **dere-wurþe**.

diete, *sb.* diet, food, MD, C; **dyetis**, *pl.*, PP.—OF. *diete*; Late Lat. *dieta*, Lat. *diæta*; Gr. δίαιτα.

dieten, *v.* to diet; **diʒete**, *pr. subj.* S2, PP.

dieð, *pr. s.* doeth, S; see **don**.

dieule, *sb. dat.* devil, S; see **devel**.

diffacen, *v.* to deface, MD; **deface**, to obliterate, C2; **defaste**, *pp.*, S3.—OF. *deffacer*.

dif-faden, *v.* to fade away, MD; **defade**, to cause to fade, S3; **defadide**, *pp.*, HD.

diffame, *sb.* dishonour, disgrace, MD, S3, C2; **defame**, C3.—OF. *diffame*.

diffamen, *v.* to spread abroad a rumour, also to slander, MD, S2; **defame**, C2; **diffameden**, *pt. pl.*, W; **defamed**, *pp.*, W, C3.—AF. *diffamer*, to slander; Lat. *diffamare*, to spread abroad a report.

digne, *adj.* worthy, proud, MD, C, C2, C3, S2, S3; **dygne**, S2. *Phr.*: **digne as dich-water**, i.e. making people keep their distance, S3.—OF. *digne*; Lat. *dignum*.

dignelich, *adv.* worthily, P; **dyngneliche**, S2.

dignete, *sb.* worth, dignity, high office, MD; **dignitee**, C2; **dingnetes**, *pl.*, S2.—AF. *dignete*; Lat. *dignitatem*. Cf. **deyntee**[1].

dihten, *v.* to order, rule, prepare, adorn, MD, S2; **diʒten**, MD; **diʒtti**, S2; **diht**, *pr. s.*, **dightes**, S2; **dihte**, *pt. s.*, S; **diʒte**, S2; **diht**, *pp.*, S2; **diʒt**, MD, S2; **dight**, MD, S3; **ydiʒt**, S2, S3; **dyʒt**, S2; **dicht**, S2; **ydyʒt**, S3; **dygth**, H.—AS. *dihtan*; Lat. *dictare*.

dilatacioun, *sb.* extension, diffuseness, S2, C3.—Lat. *dilatationem*.

dilitable, *adj.* delightful, S2; see **delitable**.

dim, *adj.* dim, MD; **dym**, C; **dymme**, MD; **dimme**, *pl.*, S.—AS. *dim*.

dimliche, *adv.* dimly, softly (of sound), MD; **dimluker**, *comp.*, S.

dimnes, *sb.* dimness, S2.

dinnen, *v.* to din, MD; **dunien**, MD; **denie**, S; **dinede**, *pt. s.*, MD; **donyd**, MD; **dynnit**, MD.—AS. *dynian*; cf. Icel. *dynja*. See **dyn**.

dint, *sb.* blow, S, S2; see **dent**.

dinten, *v.* to strike, S.

diopendion, *sb.* a kind of barley-sugar, S2; see **diapenidion**.

dirige, *sb.* the name of an anthem in the office for the dead beginning with the words from Ps. 5. 8, '*Dirige*, Dominus meus', MD, S3; **dyrge**, MD; **dorge**, MD.

dis-; see also words beginning in **des-**.

disburse, *v.* to pay out of a purse, Sh.; **deburs**, S3.—OF. *desbourser*.

dischargen, *v.* to unload, MD; **deschargen**, MD; **dischargiden**, *pt. pl.*, W.—AF. *descharger*.

dischevele, *pp.* with hair in disorder, MD, C.—OF. *deschevelé*, pp. of *descheveler*, to dischevel (Cotg.).

disciple, *sb.* disciple, W (John 20. 2); **disciplis**, *pl.*, PP, W; **diciples**, S; **deciples**, S; **decipelis**, S2.—AF. *disciple*; Lat. *discipulum* (acc.).

disciplesse, *sb.* a woman-disciple, W.

discipline, *sb.* chastisement, MD; **disceplines**, *pl.* flagellations, S.—OF. *discipline* (Cotg.); Church Lat. *disciplina* (Ducange).

disclaundre, *sb.* evil fame, S2, PP; **desclandre**, MD; **dislander**, ND. See **sclaundre**[1].

disclaundre, *v.* to slander, S2, C3. See **sclaundre**[2].

disclose, *v.* to disclose, S3; **desclosen**, S2.—OF. *desclore* (subj. *-close*); Lat. *disclaudere*.

discomfiten, *v.* to defeat, to put to the rout, MD; **dyscowmfytyn**, Prompt.; **disconfet**, *pt. s.*, MD; **disconfite**, MD; *pp.*, MD; **discumfyst**, S3; **dysconfited**, S3.—OF. *desconfire* (pp. *desconfit*); Lat. *dis* + *conficere*.

discomfiture, *sb.* defeat, MD; **disconfiture**, C.—AF. *descumfiture*, *desconfiture*.

disconfort, *sb.* discomfort, C; **discomfort**, W.

disconforten, *v.* to trouble, discomfort, C; **disconfort**, S3; **discomforten**, MD.—OF. *desconforter*.

discoueren, *v.* to discover, uncover, MD, C3; **diskeuer**, MD; **discure**, S3.—OF. *descovrir*, *descuvrir*.

disdeyn, *sb.* disdain, C2; **desdayn**, CM; **desdeyn**, C; **dedeyn**, MD, W, H; **dedeyne**, HD.—AF. *dedeigne*, OF. *desdein*.

disdeyne, *v.* to disdain, C2; **desdainen**, MD.—AF. *desdeigner*, It. *disdegnare*.

disese, *sb.* lack of ease, MD, S2, C2, C3, W; **desese**, S3.—OF. *desaise*.

diseseful, *adj.* troublesome, W2.

disesid, *pp.* troubled, W.

disgysen, *v.* to disguise, MD; **degisen**, PP, MD; **degyset**, *pp.*, S2; **disguised**, S3.—AF. *degiser*, *degyser*, OF. *desguiser*. Cf. **degyse**.

disheriten, *v.* to disinherit, S2; **deseritede**, *pt. s.*, MD; **deserited**, *pp.*, S2; **disheryt**, C.—AF. *desheriter*, OF. *deseriter*.

disjoint, *sb.* perplexity, MD; **disjoynt**, C.—OF. *desjoinct*, pp. of *desjoindre*; Lat. *disjungere*.

dismayen, *v.* to dismay, G; **desmayen**, MD.—OF. **desmayer*; cf. Sp. *desmayar*, also (with different prefix), OF. *esmaier*, Prov. *esmagar*, It. *smagare*.

disour, *sb.* professional story-teller, minstrel, MD; **disoures**, *pl.*, P.—OF. *disour, diseor*: Sp. *dicedor*, It. *dicitore*, from Lat. *dicere*.

disparage, *sb.* a want of parity or equality, especially in birth or station, disparagement, disgrace, C2. See **parage**.

disparagen, *v.* to disparage, disgrace; **desparaged**, *pp.*, MD.—AF. *desparager*.

disparplen, *v.* to become scattered, also to scatter, W; **desparplen**, MD, S2; **dysparplyn**, Prompt.; **sparplyn**, Prompt.; **disperpelde**, *pt. s.*, H; **deperpeyld**, H; **disparpoilid**, *pp.*, S2; **disparplid**, **disparplit**, W.—OF. *deparpillier*, Ps. 21. 14 (cf. It. *sparpagliare*, Florio); from OF. **parpille*, butterfly; Lat. *papilio*, see Brachet (s.v. *éparpiller*), and Diez, p. 236.

dispence, *sb.* expenditure, C, C2, S3; **despense**, C2, MD; **dispenses**, *pl.*, S3.—OF. *despense*.

dispenden, *v.* to spend, S3, C2, H; **despenden**, C2, MD; **dispent**, *pp.*, S3.—AF. *despendre*; Late Lat. *dispendere*, to weigh out.

dispendour, *sb.* steward, W; **dispendere**, W.

dispers, *pp.* dispersed, S3, MD.—Lat. *dispersus*.

displesance, *sb.* annoyance, C3.—OF. *desplaisance*.

disport, *sb.* pleasure, recreation, S2, S3, C2, C3; **desport**, C3, MD.—AF. *desport*, mirth; cf. OF. *deport* (Bartsch).

disporten, *v.* to cheer, amuse, MD.—OF. *se desporter*, *se deporter*; cf. It. *diportare* (compounded with Lat. *de-*).

disposed, *pp.*; *in phr.*: **wel disposed**, in good health, C3.

disputen, *v.* to dispute, MD; **desputen**, MD.—AF. *desputer*; Lat. *disputare*.

disputeson, *sb.* disputation, MD; **disputisoun**, C; **desputisoun**, MD.—OF. *desputeson*; Lat. *disputationem* (for *-eson* = *-tionem*, see Ps. Introd. xxx).

disseit; see **deceit**.

disseueren, *v.* to separate, C3.—AF. *desseverer*; Lat. *dis + separare*.

disshe, *sb.* dish, PP; **disch**, S; **dysche**, *discus*, Voc.; **dysshe**, discus, Prompt.; **dishe**, disc, quoit, MD; **disse**, S; **dysshes**, *pl.*, S2.—AS. *disc*; Lat. *discus*; Gr. δίσκος, quoit. Cf. **deys**.

dissheres, *sb.* a female dish-seller, P.

dissimulen, *v.* to pretend a thing is not so, MD, C3; **dissymilide**, *pt. s.*, W2.—Lat. *dissimulare*.

dissimulinge, *sb.* dissembling, C2, C3.

distaf, *sb.* distaff, C2; **dystaf**, Voc.; **dysestafe**, Voc.

distinguen, *v.* to distinguish, MD; **destingeþ**, *pr. pl.*, MD; **distyngis**, *imp. pl.*, H; **distingwed**, *pp.*, MD; **distyngid**, H.—OF. *distinguer*.

distrier, *sb.* destroyer, W; see **destroyere**.

distraught, *pp.* distracted, tormented, S3; **distrauhte**, MD; **destrat**, SkD.—OF. *destrait* (F. *distrait*); Lat. *distractum*, pp. of *distrahere*.

distresse, *sb.* distress, misery, S2; **destresse**, MD.—AF. *destresse, destresce*; Late Lat. **districtitia* from Lat. *districtus*, pp. of *distringere*, to pull asunder, to punish.

distreynen, *v.* to vex, S3; **destreyne**, C; **distrayne**, S3.—AF. *destreindre* (pr. p. *destreignant*); Lat. *distringere*.

disturben, *v.* to disturb; **destourbe**, C3; **distourbe**, MD; **desturbi**, MD.—AF. *desturber*; Lat. *disturbare*.

disturblen, *v.* to disturb, trouble, MD, W, W2; **disturblid**, *pp.*, S2, W, W2. Cf. OF. *tourbler, torbler* (F. *troubler*); Late Lat. **turbulare*, from Lat. *turbare*.

disturblyng, *sb.* disturbance, W, W2.

diten, *v.* to indict for trespass, Prompt.—OF. *dicter*; Lat. *dictare*. Cf. **dihten**.

diuel, *sb.* devil, S; see **devel**.

diueren, *v.* to tremble, S, MD.

diuise, *v.* to tell of, describe, S2; see **devisen**.

diuulgate, *pp.* divulged; **dy-wlgat**, S3.—Lat. *diuulgatus*.

diuyn; see **devin**.

diyngis, *sb. pl.* dyes, colours, W2; see **deyen**[2].

diȝe, to die; see **deyen**[1].

diȝel, *adj.* secret, MD; **diȝele**, *dat.*, S.—AS. *dígol, dégol, déogol, déagol*; cf. OHG. *tougali* (Tatian), also with different suffix, *dougan* (Otfrid).

diȝte, *pt. s.* ordained, S2; **diȝt**, *pp.* prepared, S2; see **dihten**.

doale, *sb.* dole, portion, S3; see **dool**.

docken, *v.* to cut away the tail, *decaudare*, MD; to cut short, C; **dokkyn**, Prompt. See **dok**.

dodden, *v.* to crop, lop branches, MD, Prompt.; **i-dodded**, *pp.*, S; **doddyd** (as trees), Prompt.

doddit, *adj.* without horns, JD; **doddy**, JD; **doddie**, *sb.* cow without horns, JD.

dogge, *sb.* dog, MD, S2, Voc., Prompt., W2 (Ps. 21. 21), PP, C2.—AS. *docga*.

dohter, *sb.* daughter, S; **do3ter**, S, S2; **dou3ter**, P, W2; **dowter**, S; **douhtres**, *pl.*, S; **dou3tres**, P; **dou3tris**, W2; **doutres**, S; **de3ter**, S2; **do3tren**, S2; **doughtren**, C; **dehtren**, *dat.*, S.—AS. *dohtor* (*dehter*, dat. s.); cf. Goth. *dauhtar*; see Sievers, 93.

dok, *sb.* a tail, MD, JD.—ONorse *dockr*; see MD.

doke, *sb.* duck, S2, Voc., PP, C; **douke**, PP; **docke**, Prompt.; **duke**, Voc.; **duk**, PP.

dole, *sb.* grief, P, CM; **deol**, S, MD, S2; **duel**, MD; **doel**, P; **diol**, MD; **dol**, MD; **dool**, S2, CM; **dul**, MD; **del**, MD, S2; **dewle**, S3; **dule**, S3.—OF. *doel, duel, deol, dol, del*; Late Lat. **dolium*, from *dol-*, stem of Lat. *dolere*, to grieve; see Constans, supplement, p. 23.

dolefulle, *adj.* doleful, MD; **delful**, S2, MD.

dolfin, *sb.* dolphin, MD; **doulphyn**, Palsg.—OF. *doulphin* (Palsg.), *daulphin* (Cotg.), Prov. *dalfin*; Lat. *delphinum*. Cf. **delfin**.

dolfully, *adv.* dolefully, G; **delfulli**, MD.

doluen, *pt. pl.* dug, P; *pp.* buried, S, P; see **delven**.

dom, *sb.* judgement, S, S2, W; **dome**, S2, G; see **doom**.

domage, *sb.* damage, loss, S3; see **damage**.

domb, *adj.* dumb, MD, C3; **doumb**, MD; **dum**, Prompt.; **dom**, MD; **dumbe**, Manip.; **doumbe**, S, S2; **dome**, S3.—AS. *dumb*; cf. Goth. *dumbs*, OHG. *dumb*, foolish (Otfrid).

dome, *sb.* doom, S2; **domes**, *pl.*, S2, G; see **doom**.

domes-day, *sb.* dooms-day, P; **domesdai**, S; **domesdei**, S.—AS. *dómes-dæg*.

domes-man, *sb.* judge, S, W, W2; **domys-men**, *pl.* H.

domlen, *v.* to be dull; **domland**, *pr. p.* clouding over, S2.

dom-place, *sb.* judgement-hall, W.

don, *v.* to do, put, make, cause, S; **do**, S, S2; **donne**, *ger.*, S, S2; **done**, S2, MD; **doand**, *pr. p.*, S2; **doande**, CM; **doing**, S3; **doð**, *imp. pl.* S; **dest**, *2 pr. s.*, S; **deð**, *pr. s.*, S, S2; **dieð**, S; **deað**, S; **doð**, S, S2; **doð**, *pl.*, S, S2; **done**, S2; **dude**, *pt. s.*, S2; **dide**, S; **dede**, S, S2; **ded**, S2; **duden**, *pl.*, S; **deden**, S; **dyden**, S; **dude**, S2; **ydoon**, *pp.*, C2; **idon**, S, S2; **idone**, S, S2; **ydon**, S2; **ydo**, S2; **don**, S2; **doon**, MD; **do**, S2, MD.—AS. *dón*, pt. s. *dyde*, pp. *gedón*.

donet, *sb.* grammar, primer, elementary instruction, PP, S2.—From *Donatus*, the grammarian; see Cotg. (s.v. *donat*).

dong, *pt. s.* beat, MD; **dongen**, *pp.*, S2, H; see **dyngen**.

donjoun, *sb.* the highest tower of a castle, also the dungeon or underground prison, MD; **dongeon**, P; **dongoun**, MD; **dungun**, S2.—AF. *dongoun*, OF. *dongon, donjon*: Prov. *dompnhon*; Late Lat. *domnionem*, a tower that dominates (Ducange), *dominionem*, lordship, from Lat. *dominium*.

donk, *adj.* moist, S3, JD; **danke**, MD.—Cf. Icel. *dökkr*, obscure (stem **danku*).

donken, *v.* to moisten, MD, S2.

don-ward, *adv.* downward, S2; see **dounward**.

doo, *sb.* doe, Voc., Palsg., W2; **do**, MD; **da**, MD; **days**, *pl.*, S3.—AS. *dá*.

dool, *sb.* dole, share, portion, MD; **dole**, MD; **doale**, S3.—AS. *dál* (see OET).

doom, *sb.* doom, judgement, sentence, W; **dom**, S, W, S2; **dome**, S2; **domes**, *pl.*, S2, G.—AS. *dóm*: Goth. *doms*.

dorc, *adj.* dark, S; see **derk**.

dore, *sb.* door, MD, S2, C3; **dur**, MD, S3; **dure**, S.—AS. *duru*; cf. Gr. θύρα; see Brugmann, § 51.

dore-tre, *sb.* bar of a door, P.

dore-ward, *sb.* porter, door-keeper, S2; **durewart**, S.

dorren, *pr. pl.* dare, MD; **doren**, W; **dorste**, *pt. subj. pl.*, S, S2, C2; see **dar**.

dortour, *sb.* dormitory, MD, S3, CM; **dorture**, Voc.; **dorter**, Voc.—OF. *dortour, dortoir*; Lat. *dormitorium*.

dosc, *adj.* dusk, S; **deosc**, MD.

doseyn, *num.* dozen, C; see **dozein**.

dotard, *sb.* dotard, MD, Sh.

dote, *sb.* fool, S, MD; **dotest**, *adj. superl.*, very foolish, S2.

dotel, *sb.* fool, MD; **dottel**, Manip.

doten, *v.* to dote, to be foolish, childish, MD, S2, C2.

doucte, *pt. s.* had value, S; see **du3en**.

doughtren, *sb. pl.* daughters, C; see **dohter**.

doughty, *adj.* brave, C2, G; see **du3ti**.

douhtres, *sb. pl.* daughters, S; see **dohter**.

doumbe, *adj.* dumb, S, S2; see **domb**.

doun, *sb.* a down, hill, MD; **dun**, MD; **doune**, S2; **dune**, *dat.*, MD; **downes**, *pl.*, MD; **dounes**, S2; **dun**, *adv.*, down, S; **don**, S2; **doun**, S2, W.—AS. *dún*.

doun-right, *adv.* right down, S2.

doun-ward, *adv.* downward, MD; **don-ward**, S2; **dunward**, S.

doute, *sb.* fear, doubt, MD, S2, C2, G; **dute**, MD, S2; **dout**, S2.—OF. *dute, doute, doubte*.

doute-lees, *adv.* doubtless, S2, C2.

douten, *v.* to fear, to doubt, MD, S3; **duten**, MD, S; **dowte**, S3; **dowt**, *imp. s.*, G; **doutede**, *pt. s.*, S; **doutiden**, *pl.*, G.—AF. *duter*, OF. *douter*; Lat. *dubitare*.

douthe; see **duheþe**.

douȝter, *sb.* daughter, P, W2; **doutres**, *pl.*, S; see **dohter**.

douene, *sb. f.* dove, S2; **doune**, S2; **downe**, S2. See **dowve**.

dowaire, *sb.* dower, C2; **dower**, C2.—AF. *douayre* (and *dowere*); Late Lat. *dotarium*.

dowen[1], *v.* to endow, MD.—OF. *douer*, *doer*; Lat. *dotare*.

dowen[2]; see **duȝen**.

doweþe, *sb.* army, host, S. *Phr.*: **doweþes louerd**, Lord of Hosts, S; see **duheþe**.

dowter, *sb.* daughter, S; see **dohter**.

dowue, *sb.* dove, MD, C3, W; **douve**, MD; **dow**, S3.—Icel. *dúfa*; cf. OS. *dúba*, Goth. *dubo*. Cf. **dovene**.

doȝter, *sb.* daughter, S, S2; see **dohter**.

dozein, *adj.* dozen, S2; **doseyn**, C.—AF. *dozeine*, from *doze*, twelve; Lat. *duodecim*.

drad, *pp.* dreaded, C2; **dradde**, *pt. pl.*, S; see **dreden**.

dræm, *sb.* joyful sound, S; see **dreem**.

draf[1], *pt. s.* drove, S2; see **driven**.

draf[2], *sb.* draff, husks, dregs, MD, C3, PP, Cath.; **draff**, JD; **draffe**, PP; **draft**, W2.—Icel. *draf*.

dragen, *v.* to draw, S; **drah**, *imp. s.*, S, S2; **drahen**, *pp.*, S; see **drawen**.

dragge, *sb.* a comfit or digestive sweetmeat, *dragetum*, Prompt., Voc.; **dragges**, *pl.*, C.—AF. *dragge*, OF. *dragée* (Cotg.), Prov. *dragea*, It. *treggéa*, an adaptation of Late Gr. τραγήματα, sweetmeats; see Diez, p. 326, Ducange (s.v. *tragemata*).

drah, *pt. s.* suffered, S; see **dreȝen**.

drapen, *pt. pl.* slew, S; see **drepen**.

drast, *sb.* dregs, W2; **drastys**, *pl. feces*, Voc.; **drestys**, Prompt.—OMerc. *derste*, PS. 39, 3 (VP).

drasty, *adj.* trashy, worthless, MD, C2; **dresti**, Prompt.; **dresty**, Palsg.

drawen, *v.* to draw, S, S2, CM; **draȝen**, S, S2; **dragen**, S; **dreaien**, S; **dreihen**, S; **drah**, *imp. s.*, S, S2; **drawand**, *pr. p.*, S2; **droh**, *pt. s.*, S; **droȝ**, S, S2; **drou**, S, S2; **drow**, S2, C2; **drouȝ**, S2; **drouh**, S2; **dreuch**, S2; **drough**, S2; **droȝen**, *pl.*, S; **drowen**, W; **droȝe**, S; **drowe**, S2; **dragen**, *pp.*, S; **drahen**, S; **ydrawe**, C2.—AS. *dragan*, pt. *dróh* (pl. *drógon*), pp. *dragen*.

dre, *v.* to suffer, S2, S3; see **dreȝen**.

drecchen, *v.* to vex, torment, also to tarry, MD, S, S3, C; **drechen**, S, S2; **draihte**, *pt. s.*, MD; **drechede**, MD; **draiht**, *pp.*, MD; **drecched**, MD.—AS. *dreccan*, pt. *drehte*, pp. *dreht*.

drede, *sb.* dread, MD, S, S2, C2, W2; **dreid**, S3; **dred**, S.

dreden, *v.* to dread, S, S2, C2; **dredand**, *pr. p.*, S2; **dradde**, *pt. s.*, MD, C2; **dredde**, MD, C2, W; **dredden**, *pl.*, MD, W; **dradde**, S; **drad**, *pp.*, C2.—AS. (*on*)-*drǽdan*, pt. *dreord*, *drǽdde*, see Sievers, 394, 395.

dredful, *adj.* dreadful, MD; timid, C; **dredfule**, *dat.*, S.

drednes, *sb.* dread, MD; **drednesse**, S; **dridnes**, S2.

dreem, *sb.* a joyful sound, dream, MD; **dream**, S; **dræm**, S; **dreme**, *dat.*, S; **drem**, MD, S; **dremes**, *pl.*, S.—AS. *dréam*, joyful sound, Icel. *draumr*, dream; cf. OS. *dróm*, joy, also dream.

drehen, *v.* to suffer, S; see **dreȝen**.

dreid, *sb.* dread, S3; see **drede**.

dreihen, *v.* to draw, S; see **drawen**.

drem, *sb.* dream, S; see **dreem**.

dremels, *sb.* dream, PP.

dremen, *v.* to make a joyful sound, to dream, S; **dreamen**, S; **drempte**, *pt. s.*, S; **dremden**, *pl.*, S.—AS. *dréman*, to rejoice: OS. *drómian*; cf. Icel. *dreyma*, to dream.

drench, *sb.* drink, S, MD.

drenchen, *v.* to drown, S, S2, C3, W; **drinchen**, S; **dreinchen**, S; **dreynt**, *pp.*, W, C, C2; **drent**, S3; **drenched**, C3; **drenchid**, W.—AS. *drencan*; cf. Icel. *drekkja*.

drenchyng, *sb.* drowning, S2.

dreng, *sb.* servant, retainer, MD; **dring**, S; **drenches**, *pl.*, MD; **dringches**, S.—Icel. *drengr*, brave man, also bachelor; hence AS. *dreng*.

drepen, *v.* to slay, S, S2; **drap**, *pt. s.*, MD; **drapen**, *pl.*, S; **drape**, MD.—AS. *drepan*, pt. *dræp* (pl. *drǽpon*), pp. *drepen*.

drere, *sb.* grief, S3, ND.

dreriment, *sb.* sadness, ND; **dreeriment**, S3.

drery, *adj.* sad, dreary, C2; **dreriȝ**, MD; **drury**, MD.—AS. *dréorig*.

dreryhead, *sb.* sorrow, ND.

dressen, *v.* to make straight, direct, reach, prepare, dress, S2, S3, C2, C3, W, W2; **y-dressed**, *pp.*, C2.—OF. *dresser*, *drescier*; Late Lat. **dirictiare* (It. *dirizzare*); from Lat. *directus*, pp. of *dirigere*. Cf. Late Lat. *drictum* (Ducange).

dressyngis, *sb. pl.* directions (= Lat. *directiones*), W2.

dreuen, *v.* to trouble, afflict, MD; **dreued**, *pt. s.*, S2; **drefedd**, *pp.*, MD; **dreofedd**, MD; **i-dreaued**, S.—AS. *dréfan*: OS. *dróbian*; cf. OHG. *druaben* (Otfrid), *truoben* (Tatian), G. *trüben*. See **drovy**.

drewery, *sb.* darling, P; see **druerie**.

dreye, *adj.* dry, C, C2; see **drye**[1].

dre3, *adj.* continuous, great, powerful, MD; **dry3**, patient, S2.—Icel. *drjúgr.*

dre3en, *v.* to endure, suffer, continue, MD; **dregen**, S; **dre3henn**, S; **drehen**, S; **dreye**, S; **drye**, CM; **dreghe**, H; **dri3en**, S, MD; **dry3e**, S2; **drie**, S, PP; **dree**, JD; **dre**, S2, S3; **drah**, *pt. s.*, S; **dreg**, MD; **dry3ed**, continued, S2; **druhen**, *pl.*, MD; **drogen**, *pp.*, MD.—AS. *dréogan*, pt. *dréah* (pl. *drugon*), pp. *drogen*.

dre3-ly, *adv.* continuously, earnestly, S2, MD; **dry3ly**, patiently, S2.

dridnes, *sb.* dread, S2; see **drednes**.

drihten, *sb.* Lord (only used for God, Christ), S; **dryhtin**, S; **dryhten**, S; **drigten**, S; **drigtin**, S; **drightin**, S2; **dryhte**, S; **drihte**, S; **dry3te**, PP; **dri3te**, S, PP; **dry3tyn**, S2.—AS. *dryhten*: OS. *drohtin*; cf. Icel. *dróttinn* and OHG. *truhtin* (Tatian). From AS. *dryht*, men, warriors, retainers: OS. *druht*; cf. OHG. *truht* and Icel. *drótt.*

driht-ful, *adj.* noble, S.

dring, *sb.* servant, S; **dringches**, *pl.*, S; see **dreng.**

drink, *sb.* drink, MD; **drinch**, S; **drinnch**, S; **drinc**, S2.

drinken, *v.* to drink, S; **drincken**, S; **dring**, *imp. s.*, S; **dranc**, *pt. s.*, S; **dronc**, S; **dronk**, S; **drunken**, *pl.*, S; **dronken**, C2; **drongken**, S; **dranc**, S2; **i-drunke**, *pp.*, S; **dronke**, C2. *Phr.*: **drinc-hail**, drink, hale! S.—AS. *drincan*, pt. *dranc* (pl. *druncon*), pp. *druncen.*

drinkere, *sb.* drinker, MD; **drinckares**, *pl.*, S.

drit, *sb.* dirt, MD, W, W2; **dert**, S3.

drit-cherl, *sb.* dirt-churl (term of abuse), S.

driuen, *v.* to drive, rush, pass, go, S; **dryuen**, S; **drif**, S2; **draf**, *pt. s.*, MD, S2; **drof**, S, S2; **droof**, MD, W, W2; **drofe**, S2; **driuen**, *pl.*, S, MD; **dryuen** MD; **driueden**, W2; **driuen**, *pp.*, MD; **driue**, C2; **dryuun**, W2.—AS. *drífan*, pt. *dráf* (pl. *drifon*), pp. *drifen.*

dri3en, *v.* to suffer, S; see **dre3en.**

dri3te; see **drihten.**

drof, *pt. s.* drove, S, S2; **droof**, W, W2; see **driuen.**

drof-lic, *adj.* painful, MD. Cf. **drovy.**

drogen; see **dre3en.**

drogges, *sb. pl.* drugs, PP; **droggis**, S3.

droh, *pt. s.* drew, S; see **drawen.**

dronk, *pt. s.* drank, MD; **drone**, S; **dronke**, *pp.*, C2; see **drinken.**

dronkelewe, *adj.* given to drink, C3; see **drunkelew.**

dronkenesse, *sb.* drunkenness, C3.

drought, *sb.* drought, MD, C (p. 1); **droughte**, C2; **drouhþe**, S2; **drugte**, S; **drythe**, S2.—AS. *drugoðe.* See **drye**[1].

drounen, *v.* to be drowned, to drown, MD; **drune**, MD; **drund**, *pt. pl.*, S2. Cf. **drunknen.**

droupen, *v.* to droop, *vultum dejicere*, MD, Palsg.; **drowpen**, C.—Icel. *drúpa.*

droupnen, *v.* to be cast down, MD; **drupnin**, S.

drouen, *v.* to trouble, MD; **druuy**, H; **droues**, *pr. pl.*, MD; **droued**, *pp.*, MD; **drouyd**, H; **druuyd**, H. Cf. **dreven.**

drouing, *sb.* trouble, S2, MD; **druuynge**, H.

drouy, *adj.* turbid, troubled, CM, S2; **droui**, MD.—Cf. AS. *dróf*, OS. *dróbi*, OHG. *truobi*, G. *trübe.* Cf. **idreaved.**

dro3, *pt. s.* drew, S, S2; **drou**, S, S2; **drow**, S2, C2; **drou3**, S2; **drouh**, S; **drough**, C2; see **drawen.**

drubild, *adj.* disturbed, H.

drublen, *v.* to disturb water, to trouble; **drubblyn**, Prompt.; **drobyl**, MD. Cf. **droven.**

drubly, *adj.* turbid, H; **drobly**, Prompt.

drublynesse, *sb.* turbulencia, Prompt.

drublynge, *sb.* disturbance, H.

druerie, *sb.* love, affection, also the object of affection, also a jewel, PP, MD, C2 (s.v. *love*); **drurye**, MD; **drurie**, S2, PP; **druery**, HD; **druwery**, PP; **drewrye**, MD; **drewery**, P; **drowryis**, *pl.*, HD; **druries**, HD.—AF. *druerie*; Prov. *drudaria*, from OHG. *drút*, dear, beloved (Otfrid). See NQ. (6. 4. 270).

druggar-beste, *sb.* the animal that has to pull forcibly, S3.

druggen, *v.* to pull with force, CM, C.—Cf. E. *drudge.*

drui3est, *2 pr. s.* art dry, S2; see **drye**[3].

drund, *pt. pl.* drowned, S2; see **drounen.**

drunk, *sb.* draught, MD; **drunc**, S; **drunch**, S.—Cf. Icel. *drykkr.*

drunkelew, *adj.* given to drinking, W, Prompt.; **dronkelewe**, C3, PP; **dronke-leuh**, PP; **dronkenlewe**, PP; **drunkenlewe**, MD. See **-lewe.**

drunken, *sb.* drinking, S, MD.

drunkennesse, *sb.* drunkenness, MD; **dronkenesse**, C3, PP.

drunknen, *v.* to be drowned, to cause to drown, MD; **drunkenes**, *pr. s.*, S2; **dronkenes**, S2.—AS. *druncnian*, to be drowned, to be drunk. Cf. **drounen.**

drupnin, *v.* to be cast down, S; see **droupnen.**

drurie; see **druerie.**

druuy, *v.* to trouble, H; see **droven.**

druuynge, *sb.* trouble, H.

drye[1], *adj.* dry, MD, PP; **druye**, MD, S2; **drue**, MD; **dru**, S; **driȝe**, MD; **drie**, MD; **dreye**, C2, C. *Phr.*: **drui fot**, dry foot, S.—AS. *dryge*; cf. Du. *droog*.

drye[2], *v.* to dry, to be dry, MD, G; **druiȝest**, *2 pr. s.*, S2.—AS. *drygan*.

drye[3], *v.* to suffer, CM; **dryȝed**, *pt. s.* continued, S2; see **dreȝen**.

drythe; see **drought**.

dryȝ, *adj.* patient, S2. Cf. **dreȝen**.

dryȝly, *adv.* patiently, S2.

dryȝte, **dryȝtyn**; see **drihten**.

dubben, *v.* (1) to dress, arm for battle, (2) to dub a knight by the stroke with the flat of the sword, MD, S, PP; **dubbed**, *pp.*, S, S2, PP; **dobbed**, PP; **doubed**, PP.—AF. *dubber*, to dress; cf. Icel. *dubba*, to arm, dress, also to dub, AS. *dubban*, to dub a knight, in Chron. ann. 1085; cf. OF. *aduber*, *adouber*, to arm (Roland).

dubbing, *sb.* decoration, adornment, S; the conferring of knighthood, S.

dubonure, *adj.* mild, gentle, S2; see **debonaire**.

dude, *pt. s.* did, S2; **duden**, *pl.*, S; see **don**.

duelle, *v.* to stay, S, W2; see **dwellen**.

duere, *adj.* dear, S2; see **dere**[3].

duete, *sb.* duty, MD; **dewtee**, MD; **dwete**, CM; **dewite**, S3.—AF. *duete*, debt, obligation, from OF. *dĕu*, owed; Lat. *debitum*, pp. of *debere*.

duhen, *v.* to get on well, S; see **duȝen**.

duheðe, *sb.* body of retainers, people, might, worth, dignity, S; **doweþe**, S; **douþe**, S2.—AS. *duguð*, worth, help, body of men, host.

duk, *sb.* leader, prince, duke, MD; **duc**, S2; **duyk**, W, W2; **douc**, MD; **duykis**, *pl.*, W2.—AF. *duc*; Lat. *ducem*.

dulce, *adj.* sweet, S3.—Lat. *dulcem*.

dule, *sb.* grief, S3; see **dole**.

dully, *adj.* dull, S3, DG; **dolly**, JD; **dowie**, JD.

dumel, *sb.* a stupid man, Manip.; **dummel**, a dumb man, Manip.; **dumble**, HD. See **domb**.

dun[1]; see **doun**.

dun[2], **dunne**, *adj.* dun, dull brown, MD, Manip.; **donne**, MD.—AS. *dunn*; OIr. *donn*, *dond* (Windisch).

dun[3], *sb.* a dun horse; *Proverb*: Dun is in the myre, C3.

dunchen, *v.* to batter, S, Prompt.; **dunch**, to push, JD.—Cf. Dan. *dunke*, to thump.

dune, *sb.* din; see **dyn**.

dungon, *sb.* dungeon, S2; see **donjoun**.

dunt, *sb.* blow, S, S2; see **dent**.

dun-ward, *adv.* downward, S; see **doun**.

dup, *adj.* deep, MD; see **deep**.

duppen, *v.* to dip, S2, MD; **dippen**, MD.—AS. *dyppan*, for *dup-ian, see SkD (p. 800), Sievers, 400.

durance, *sb.* endurance, S3; imprisonment, Sh.

dure[1], *adj.* dear, MD; see **dere**[3].

dure[2], *sb.* door, S; **dur**, S3; see **dore**.

duren, *v.* to last, C2, S2, S3, H; **dury**, MD; **duyre**, MD; **deore**, S2; **duyryng**, *pr. p.*, S2; **durede**, *pt. s.*, S2.—AF. *durer*; Lat. *durare*, from *durus*, hard, unyielding.

duresse, *sb.* hardship, severity, MD, S3; **duresce**, MD.—AF. *duresse*, *duresce*; Lat. *duritia*, from *durus*.

durlyng, *sb.* darling, S; see **derling**.

durren, *pr. pl.* dare, MD; **durre**, S; **duren**, S; see **dar**.

dusi, *adj.* foolish, S, MD; **dysy**, MD; **desi**, MD.—AS. *dysig*.

dusiliche, *adv.* foolishly, MD; **desaly**, dizzily, S2; **desselic**, S2.

dusken, *v.* to grow dark, C.

dusten, *v.* to throw, toss, S; **duste**, *pt. s.*, MD; **deste**, fell headlong, MD.

dutchkin, *adj.* German-like, S3.

dute, *sb.* doubt, fear, S, S2; see **doute**.

dutten, *v.* to shut, close, MD; **dittenn**, MD; **dutande**, *pr. p.*, S2; **dutt**, *pp.*, MD; **dit**, MD.—AS. *dyttan*; see OET (p. 573).

duyk, *sb.* leader, prince, W, W2; see **duk**.

duȝen, *v.* to get on well, to be fitting, to be worth, to avail, *valere*, MD; **duhen**, S; **dowen**, MD; **deah**, *pr. s.*, MD; **deh**, MD; **deih**, S; **dugen**, *pl.*, MD; **doucte**, *pt. s.*, S; **dought**, MD; **dowed**, S2.—AS. *dúgan*, pret. pres. *déag* (*déah*, *dég*), pl. *dugon*, pt. *dohte*; cf. OHG. *tugan*.

duȝeðe, *sb.* nobles, S, MD; see **duheþe**.

duȝti, *adj.* fit, excellent, brave, doughty, MD; **doughty**, C2, G; **douȝtiore**, *comp.*, S2.—AS. *dyhtig*, strong.

dwal, *adj.* foolish, dull, erring, apostate, MD, SkD (p. 801); **dwales**, *sb. pl.* fools, S.—Cf. Goth. *dwals*, foolish.

dwale, *sb.* error, MD; **duale**, MD; **dwole**, MD, S (16. 1777.).—ONorth. *duala*, error (Mt. 24. 24); cf. AS. *dwola*.

dwellen, *v.* (1) to err, wander, (2) to loiter, stay, dwell, MD, G; **duelle**, S, W2; **dwelland**, *pr. p.*, S2.—AS. *dwellan*, to err, also to make to err, to deceive; also *dwellan*, to deceive, to hinder, delay, also to remain, dwell; cf. Icel. *dvelja*, to tarry.

dweole, *sb.* error, MD; **dwele**, MD; **dwelle**, MD.—AS. *(ge)dweola*.

dweoluhðe, *sb.* error, foolishness, S.

dwergh, *sb.* dwarf, MD; **dwerk**, MD; **dwerf**, MD; **dwarfe**, MD; **dwerþ** (for **dwerȝ**), S2.—AS. *dweorh*; cf. Icel. *dvergr*.

dwilde, *sb.* error, S, MD.—AS. *dwild*. See **dwellen**.

dwindle, *v.* to waste away, Sh.

dwinen, *v.* to vanish away, to waste away, MD, HD; **dwynyn**, Prompt.; **dwynen**, S2; **dwynede**, *pt. s. (weak)*, MD.—AS. *dwínan*, pt. *dwán* (pl. *dwinon*), pp. *dwinen*.

dwole; see **dwale**.

dyad, *adj.* dead, S2; see **deed**.

dyed, *pt. s.* coloured, C2; see **deyen**[2].

dyeuel, *sb.* devil, S2; see **devel**.

dyk, dyke, *sb.* dike, ditch, S3; **dic**, S; **dich**, MD; **diche**, MD; *pl.*, S; **dichen**, S.—AS. *díc*.

dyken, *v.* to make a ditch, to dig, S2; **idyket**, *pp.*, S2.

dyker, *sb.* ditcher, S2, P; **dikere**, P.

dyn, *sb.* din, H, MD; **dynne**, H; **dene**, MD; **dyne**, PP; **dine**, MD; **dune**, MD.—AS. *dyne, dyn*.

dyngen, *v.* to beat, PP, H; **dang**, *pt. s.*, MD, 83; **dong**, MD; **dange**, *pl.*, S3; **dongen**, *pp.*, S2; **dongyn**, H; **dongene**, HD.

dyngis, *sb. pl.* blows, H.

dyngynge, *sb.* beating, H.

dys, *sb. pl.* dice, C, P; see **dee**.

dys-playere, *sb.* dice-player, P.

dyttay, *sb.* indictment, S3.—AF. *dite*; Lat. *dictatum*.

dyvers, *adj. pl.* divers, MD; **diverse**, MD.—AF. *divers* (pl. *diverses*); Lat. *diuersum*.

dyuerseli, *adv.* in diverse directions, W2.

dyversen, *v.* to make difference, to diversify, also to be different, MD, Prompt.; **dyuersith**, *pr. s.*, W; **diuerside**, *pt. s.*, W.—OF. *diverser*.

dyversitee, *sb.* divers colours, W2.

dyuynistre, *sb.* a divine, C.—Late Lat. **divinista*. See **devine**.

dyȝe, *v.* to die, S2; see **deyen**[1].

dyȝt; see **dihten**.

E

e-, *prefix*; see ȝe-. Cf. **eliche**.
e[1]; see **eȝe**[2].
eadiȝ, *adj*. wealthy, precious, happy, blessed, MD; **eadi**, S; **ædie**, S; **edie**, S; **eddi**, S; **edy**, S; **edye**, S.—AS. *éadig*: Goth. *audags*. From AS. *éad*, a possession, happiness, also, rich, happy: Icel. *auðr*, wealthy; cf. OS. *ód*, property.
eadmodien, *v*. to humble, MD; **eadmode**, *pt. s.*, MD; **admoded**, *pp.* as *adj.* lowly, S, MD.—AS. *éaðmódian*, from *éaðmód* humble. Cf. **edmod**, **eþemoded**.
ealde[1], *adj.* old, S; see **old**.
ealde[2], *sb.* an age, age, S; see **elde**[1].
ealdren, *pl.* elders, chiefs; see **alder**[1].
ealre, *gen.* of all, S; see **al**[1].
eam, *1 pr. s.* am; see **am**.
earding-stowe, *sb.* dwelling-place, S; see **erdingstouwe**.
earm, *sb.* arm (of the body), S, MD; see **arm**[1].
earme, *adj. pl.* poor; see **arm**[2].
earming, *sb.* a wretched being, S; see **erming**.
earnynge, *sb.* earning, S; see **ernen**[1].
eatelich, *adj.* horrible, S; see **atelich**.
eað, *adj.* easy, S; see **eþ**.
eaðe, *adv.* easily, S; see **eþe**.
Ebrayk, *adj.* Hebrew, S2.
Ebrisse, *adj.* Hebrew, S.—AS. *ebreisc*.
ecclesiaste, *sb.* a preacher, C.—OF. *ecclesiaste* (Cotg.); Church Lat. *ecclesiastes* (Vulg.); Gr. ἐκκλησιαστής (LXX), from ἐκκλησία, an assembly.
eche[1], *adj.* each, S, S2, W; **ælche**, S, MD; **elc**, MD, S; **elch**, S; **elche**, MD; **alc**, MD, S; **alche**, MD, S; **eilc**, MD; **ilc**, MD, S; **ilk**, S (12. 97), S2, H; **ilch**, S; **ulc**, MD; **ulch**, S; **ulche**, MD; **æche**, MD; **ache**, S; **ech**, MD, S, S2; **ich**, MD, S, S3; **ych**, S2; **ewc**, MD; **euch**, MD, S; **uch**, S, S2; **uche**, P, H; **uich**, S; **uych**, S.—*Comb.*: **eche dayes**, daily, on each day, S2; **eche deyl**, every bit, entirely, S2; **ech on**, each one, S2, S3, C2; **ech oon**, C2, W; **ech one**, S2; **ich on**, S3; **ich a**, S3; **uch one**, S2, P; **ilk an**, S2; **ilc kines**, of every kind, MD; **ilkines**, S; **ich wer**, everywhere, S.—AS. *ǽlc*, *elc*, ONorth. *ǽlc*, OMerc. *ylc*. The form *ǽlc = á + ge + líc*; cf. OHG. *io-gi-líh* (Tatian), G. *jeglich*. See Sievers, 347.
eche[2], *adj.* eternal, S; **echeliche**, *adv.*, S.—AS. *éce*, *écelíce*; cf. OHG. *éwic*, also *éwig* (Otfrid). See **æ**.

eche[3], *sb.* increase, addition, S2, MD.—AS. *éaca*.
eche[4], *sb.* pain, MD; see **ache**[1].
echen, *v.* to increase, add, HD, CM, MD; **eken**, S, S3, H; **ayked**, *pt. s.*, MD.—AS. *écean (écan)*: OS. *ókian*.
echte, *sb.* possessions, S; see **auhte**[1].
eclipse, *sb.* eclipse, PP; **eclypse**, Manip.; **enclips**, PP; **clips**, PP; **clyps**, S3.—Lat. *eclipsis*; Gr. ἔκλειψις, failure.
ecnesse, *sb.* eternity, MD; **ecenisse**, *dat.*, S; **ecenesse**, S; **echenesse**, MD; **ecchenesse**, S.—AS. *écnis*. See **eche**[2].
ed-, *prefix*.—AS. *ed-*, cf. Goth. *id-*, back, again, OHG. *it-*, *ita-* (Tatian, Otfrid), as in *it-lón*, retribution; *it-máli*, feast (Tatian).
ed-grow, *sb.* after-math, *regermen*, Prompt.; **edgrew**, HD.
ed-len, *sb.* retribution, MD.—AS. *ed-léan*.
edmod, *adj.* humble, MD; see **admod**.
edmodi, *adj.* humble, MD; see **admodie**.
edmodnesse, *sb.* humility, S; see **admodnesse**.
ed-wit, *sb.* reproach, S2.—AS. *ed-wít*; cf. OHG. *it-uuizzi*, a twitting (Otfrid). See **ed-**.
ed-witen, *v.* to blame, S, P; **eadwiten**, S; **edwited**, *pt. pl.*, PP.—AS. *ed-wítan*; cf. Goth. *id-weitjian*, OHG. *ita-uuízón* (Tatian). Cf. E. *twit*.
edy; see **eadiȝ**.
ee; see **eȝe**[2].
eek, *conj.* also, C2, C3; **æc**, S; **ec**, S; **ek**, S, S2, P; **eik**, S3; **eke**, S, S2, S3, P; **eeke**, G.—AS. *éac*: Goth. *auk*.
eelde; see **elde**[1].
eem, *sb.* uncle, Prompt., CM; **eom**, S; **æm**, MD; **em**, MD; **eme**, S3, Voc., HD; **eyme**, S3; **eam**, HD.—AS. *éam*; cf. OHG. *óheim*.
eese; see **ese**[2].
eest, *adj. and sb.* east, W (Mt. 8. 11), MD; **est**, S, S2, C2, C3, Prompt.; **æst**, Prompt.—AS. *éast*: Icel. *austr*; cf. OHG. *óst (óstana*, Otfrid).
efenn; see **even**[1].
effecte, *sb.* effect, MD; **affecte**, H.—Lat. *effectus*.
effer, **effeir**; see **afere**.
effnenn, *v.* to make equal or even, S; see **evenen**.
effray, *sb.* terror, S3; **fray**, S3. Cf. **affray**.
efning; see **evenynge**.
eft, *adv.* again, afterwards, S, S2, S3, C2, W; **æft**, MD; **efte**, S3.—AS. *eft*.
efter, *prep.* after, S, S2; see **after**.

eft-sone, *adv.* again, soon after, S, S2, C3; **eftsoone**, W; **efsone**, S2.—AS. *eft-sóna.*

eft-sones, *adv.* soon after, S.

egal, *adj.* equal, CM; **egalle**, S3, CM.—OF. *egal*; Lat. *aequalem.*

egalite, *sb.* equality, CM.—OF. *egalite*; Lat. *aequalitatem.*

egen; see **eȝe**².

egge, *sb.* edge, W; **eg**, Voc., CM; **egges**, *pl.*, MD; **eggez**, S2.—AS. *ecg*: OS. *eggia*, see Sievers, 258; cf. Lat. *acies.*

eggement, *sb.* instigation, C3.

eggen, *v.* to sharpen, to incite, provoke, MD, H, CM; **eggede**, *pt. s.*, S2; **egged**, S3, P; **y-egged**, *pp.*, MD; **i-egged**, MD.—Icel. *eggja.*

eggyyng, *sb.* instigation, S2, CM; **eggyngis**, *pl.*, H.

eghe; see **eȝe**².

egle, *sb.* eagle, C2, PP.—AF. *egle*, OF. *aigle*; Lat. *aquila.*

egleche, *adj. pl.* war-like, S.—AS. *agléca*, *aglécea*, a warrior, *vexator* (Grein). See **eȝe**¹.

egre, *adj.* eager, sharp, fierce, C2, PP.—AF. *egre*, OF. *aigre*; Lat. *acrem.*

egremoin, *sb.* agrimony, C3; see **agrimony**.

ehe; see **eȝe**².

ehte, *sb.* property, S; **echte**, S; see **auhte**¹.

eie; see **eȝe**¹.

eighte¹, *num.* eight, C3; **eiȝte**, MD; **eihte**, PP; **eyhte**, PP; **aȝte**, S2; **aȝt**, S2; **æhte**, MD.—AS. *eahta* (*ahta*); cf. OHG. *ahto*, Lat. *octo.*

eighte², *ord.* eighth, G, PP.—AS. *eahtoðe.* Cf. **achtande**.

eightene, *num.* eighteen, MD; **æhtene**, S; **auchtene**, 83.—AS. *eahta-téne.*

eightetethe, *ord.* eighteenth, C2.—AS. *eahta-téoða.*

eihte, *sb.* property, S; **eyhte**, S; see **auhte**¹.

eild; see **elde**¹.

eire, *sb.* journey, circuit, SkD. *Phr.*: **ane ayr**, on circuit, S3.—AF. and OF. *eire, eyre, oire, oirre*, from *errer, edrer*, to make one's way, from Lat. *iter*, journey; see Constans.

eiren, *sb. pl.* eggs, PP; **eirun**, W2; see **ey**.

eise; see **ese**¹, **ese**².

eisel, eisil, *sb.* vinegar; see **aisille**.

eisful, *adj.* terrible, MD.—AS. *egesful.*

eislich, *adj.* terrible, MD; **eiseliche**, S.—AS. *egeslic*: OS. *egislik*; from AS. *egesa*: OS. *egiso*, horror; cf. OHG. *egiso* (Otfrid).

eisliche, *adv.* terribly, S; **aisliche**, timorously, S3.—AS. *egeslice.*

eiðer, *adj.* either, S, S2; **æiðer**, MD; **ayþer**, S2; **aiþer**, S; **eyðer**, S, S2; **ethir**, W; **er**, S.—AS. *á-g-hwæðer*; Sievers, 347.

eken, *v.* to ache, MD; see **aken**.

elch; see **eche**¹.

elde¹, *sb.* an age (of the world), age, time of a man's life, maturity, full age, old age, length of time, PP, S, S2, S3, G; **eelde**, W; **ealde**, S; **helde**, S; **ulde**, MD; **eld**, MD, S2; **held**, S2; **eild**, S2.—AS. *eldu, yldu.* See **old**.

elde², *v.* to grow old, H; **elded**, *pp.*, S2; **eldid**, H.—AS. *ealdian.*

elder, *comp.* older, S, C2; see **old**.

elderne, *sb. pl.* ancestors, S2; see **alder**¹.

eldryn, *adj.* old, H. *Comb.*: **eldryn-man**, old man, elder, H.

ele, *sb.* oil, MD, S; **eoli**, S; **eolie**, S. *Comb.*: **ele-sæw**, oil, S.—AS. *ele*; Late Lat. *olium* (cf. It. *olio*); Lat. *oleum*; Gr. ἔλαιον, from ἐλαία, an olive-tree; cf. OHG. *oli* (Tatian).

eleccioun, *sb.* election, choice, S2.—OF. *election*; Lat. *electionem.*

ele-lendisch, *adj.* foreign; **elelendis**, MD.—AS. *ele-lendisc*, of a foreign land.

elendisch, *adj.* foreign; **helendis**, MD.— From AS. *ellende* (Voc.).

elenge, *adj.* protracted, tedious, wearisome, dreary, lonely; also (by confusion with AS. *ellende*) strange, foreign, PP, HD; **elynge**, PP; **elyng**, PP; **alenge**, NED, HD; **alange**, NED, Prompt.—AS. *á-lenge*, lengthy, tedious; *é*, ever + *lenge*, long, from *lang.*

elengelich, *adv.* sadly, PP; **elyngliche**, PP.

elf, *sb.* elf, genius, *nympha, incubus*, MD, C3, Sh.; **alfe**, MD.—AS. *ælf.* Cf. **aulf**.

elf-lock, *sb.* hair matted together as if by the elves, Sh.

elf-queen, *sb.* fairy-queen, C2.

eliche, *adv.* alike, S3; see **iliche**¹.

elixir, *sb.* elixir, C3, SkD.—OF. *elixir* (Cotg.), Sp. *elixir*; Arab. *el iksír*, the philosopher's stone; Gr. ξηρόν, dry.

elldernemannes, *sb. gen.* alderman's, chief officer's, S; see **aldermon**.

elleft, *ord.* eleventh, S2.—AS. *endleofta.*

ellerne, *sb.* elder-tree, *sambucus*, S2, PP; **ellaern**, Voc.; **ellarne**, Voc.; **eller**, PP; **eldir**, PP.—AS. *ellarn.*

elles, *adv.* otherwise, else, S, S2, C2; **ellis**, S3, W.—AS. *elles*; cf. OHG. *alles*, otherwise (Otfrid): Goth. *aljis.*

elles-hware, *adv.* elsewhere, S; **elles-wher**, S, C3.—AS. *elles-hwǽr.*

elles-hwider, *adv.* else-whither, S.

elmesse, *sb.* alms, MD, NED; see **almesse**.

elmes-ȝeorn, *adj.* charitable, S.

eluish, *adj.* elvish, foolish, C2, C3. See **elf**.

eluish-marked, *pp.* disfigured by the elves, Sh.

elynge; see **elenge**.

embassade, *sb.* embassy, S3; see **ambassade**.

embassadour, *sb.* ambassador, C3.

embassadrie, *sb.* ambassadorship, S2, C3.

embatel, *sb.* battlement, S3 (19 a. 581).

embattail, *v.* to array for battle, Sh.

embrave, *v.* to adorn, S3.

em-cristen, *sb.* fellow-christian, S, S2. See **even**[2].

eme; see **eem**.

emeraude, *sb.* emerald, C2, CM.—OF. *emeraude*, *esmeraude* (*esmeralde*); Lat. *smaragdum* (acc.); Gr. σμάραγδος.

emete, emote, *sb.* ant; see **amete**.

em-forth, *prep.* according to, PP. See **even**[2].

empaled, *pp.* enclosed, S3.

emperere, *sb.* emperor, MD.—OF. *emperere* (*emperees*); Lat. *imperator*.

emperice, *sb.* empress, S, CM; **emperesse**, PP.—AF. *emperice*; Lat. *imperatricem*.

emperour, *sb.* emperor, PP, S2 (12. 212), C2, C3.—AF. *emperur*, OF. *emperëor*, *emperedor*; Lat. *imperatorem*.

empoisoner, *sb.* poisoner, C3. See **enpoisonen**.

empoisoning, *sb.* poisoning, C3.

emportured, *pp.* pourtrayed, S3.

emprise, *sb.* undertaking, S2, C2, C3; **enprise**, MD.—AF. *emprise*, *enprise*; Late Lat. *in-prensam*, *pp.* of *in-prendere*.

emtien, *v.* to empty, MD; **empte**, C3.—AS. *æmetgian*, to be at leisure, Ps. 45. 11 (VP).

emty, *adj.* empty, MD, Prompt.; **empti**, MD.—AS. *emtig* (*æmtig*) empty, idle.

emyspery, *sb.* hemisphere, S3.—Late Lat. *emisperia* (Voc.); Lat. *hemispherium*; Gr. ἡμισφαίριον.

enamelen, *v.* to enamel, MD; **enamelled**, *pp.* Sh.; **annamyllit**, S3. See **amellen**.

enbibing, *sb.* absorption, C3.

enbrouden, *v.* to embroider, MD; **enbroud**, *pp.* S3; **enbroudin**, S3; **enbrouded**, CM; **embrowded**, C.—AF. *enbroyder*. See **brayden**.

encens, *sb.* incense, MD, Voc., C.—AF. *encens*; Lat. *incensum*.

encense, *v.* to offer incense, C3; to perfume with incense, MD.—OF. *encenser* (Cotg.).

enchauntement, *sb.* enchantment, CM; **enchaunmens**, *pl.*, S2.—AF. *enchantement*.

enchesoun, *sb.* occasion, H, CM, JD; **encheison**, PP; **encheson**, C2, H.—AF. *enchesoun*. See **achesoun**.

encombren, *v.* to hinder, encumber, MD, S3 (3 b. 1098); **encombred**, *pp.* tired, troubled, C, CM.—AF. *encombrer*.

encorporing, *sb.* incorporation, C3.

encorsife, *adj.* fattened, H.—From OF. *encorser*, to get fat, to make flesh (Godefroy).

encrees, *sb.* increase, S2, C, C3, PP; **encres**, Prompt.

encressen, *v.* to increase, C2, C3; **encresen**, C2.—AF. *encresc-*, stem of *encrescerai*, fut. of *encrestre*; Lat. *increscere*.

ende, *sb.* end, district, territory, end of life, S, C3, PP; **ende**, PP; **ænde**, S; **hende**, S. *Comb.*: **on ende**, lastly, S.—AS. *ende* for *endi* = *andio* (Sievers, 130); cf. OHG. *enti* (Tatian): Goth. *andeis*, connected with *and*, *prep.* towards, through, see SkD.

ende-dai, *sb.* day of death, MD; **endedei**, S.—AS. *ende-dæg*.

endeles, *adj.* endless, C3; **endelese**, S.—AS. *endeléas*.

enden, *v.* to end, S.—AS. *endian*.

endenten, *v.* to write an indenture, PP.—AF. *endenter*, to indent, notch; Late Lat. *indentare*.

endentur, *sb.* notch, S2.—AF. *endenture*.

ender, *adj. comp.* latter, last past, S3; see **hindir**.

enditen, *v.* to compose, write, indict, accuse, G, PP; **endyte**, C2, C3.—AF. *enditer*; Late Lat. *indictare*.

end-lang, *adv.* and *prep.* along, S2, S3; **endelong**, S, C2; **alonge**, NED; **anlong**, MD; **andelong**, MD.—AS. *and-lang*; cf. Icel. *endlang*. See **alang**.

enduren, *v.* to harden, endure, remain, survive, W, PP.—OF. *endurer*; Lat. *indurare*, to harden.

ene[1], *adv.* once, S2.—AS. *ǽne*.

ene[2]; see **eʒe**[2].

enentysch, *v.* to bring to nought, H; **enentist**, *pp.*, H; see **anientise**.

enerite, *v.* to inherit, W2; **inherit**, to take possession, Sh.—AF. *enheriter*.

enes, *adv.* once, S. See **oones**.

eneuch, enough, S3; see **ynow**.

enfecte, *pp.* tainted, infected, C, HD.—OF. *infect*; Lat. *infectum*.

enfermer, *sb.* superintendent of the infirmary in a monastery, S2.—OF. *enfermier*; Church Lat. *infirmarium* (Ducange).

enfermerere, *sb.* infirmary officer, Cath. (p. 127 n). Cf. **fermerere**.

enflaumen, *v.* to inflame, MD, W; **enflawmed**, *pp.*, S2, W.—OF. *enflamer*, *enflammer*; Lat. *inflammare*.

enforce, *v.* to endeavour, strive, W; **enforse**, W2.

enforme, *v.* to establish, teach, PP; **enfourmeth**, *pr. s.*, P.—AF. *enfourmer*; Lat. *informare*.

Engel[1], *adj.* English, S. See **Angles**.

engel[2], *sb.* angel, MD, S; **engeles**, *pl.*, S; **enngless**, S; **englene**, *gen.*, S; **englen**, *dat.*, S. *Comb.*: **enngle þeod**, the angelic host, S.—AS. *engel*: OS. *engil*: Goth. *aggilus*: Gr. ἄγγελος. Cf. **angel**.

Engle-land, *sb.* England, S; **Engelond**, S2.—AS. *Engla land.*

Englene-lond, *sb.* the land of the English, England, S.—AS. *Englena land.*

engleymen, *v.* to bind together as with glue or viscous matter, MD, PP; **yngleymyn**, Prompt.; **engleymed**, *pp.*, MD; **engleymede**, H; **englymede**, H.

Englisch, *adj.* English, S2, PP; **Engliss**, S2; **Ænglisc**, S; **Englisse**, *dat.*, S; *pl.*, S2.— AS. *englisc.*

engreynen, *v.* to dye in grain, PP.

engyn, *sb.* understanding, craft, device, engine, MD, C2, C3; **engyne**, S3; **engine**, Sh.—AF. *engin*; Lat. *ingenium.*

engyned, *pp.* tortured, C.

enhached, *pp.* marked, S3, HD.

enhastyng, *pr. p.* hasting, S3; **enhasted**, *pp.*, HD.

enhaunsen, *v.* to raise, C, W, W2; **anhaunse**, NED; **enhansed**, *pp.*, PP.— AF. *enhauncer, enhancer.*

enhorten, *v.* to encourage, MD, C.—OF. *enhorter*; Lat. *inhortari.*

enke, *sb.* ink, MD, W; **ynke**, Voc.; **inke**, Cath.—OF. *enque* (Bartsch); Lat. *encaustum*; Gr. ἔγκαυστον.

enker, *adj.* special, particular. *Phr.*: **enker grene**, wholly green, MD, HD.

enkerly, *adv.* particularly, entirely, B, MD, JD; **enkrely**, B; **ynkirly**, B; **ynkurly**, S2, B.—Icel. *einkarliga*, variant of *einkanliga*, especially, particularly; see *einka-* in CV.

enleuene, *num.* eleven, PP, W; **enleuen**, W; **enleue**, PP; **elleuene**, PP; **elleue**, PP; **eleuene**, PP; **aleuin**, JD; **alewin**, S3; **allevin**, S3, NED.—AS. *endleofan, endlufan* (*ellefan*); Goth. *ain-lif*; see Douse, p. 80.

enluminen, *v.* to illumine, MD, C2; **enlumynyng**, *pr. p.*, S3.—AF. *enluminer.*

enluting, *sb.* daubing with clay, C3.—Cf. Late Lat. *lutare*, from Lat. *lutum*, clay.

ennewen, *v.* to renew, MD; **ennewed**, *pp.*, S3.

enoumbre; see **enumbren**.

ennuyed, *pp.* annoyed, P; see **anoyen**.

enoynt, *pp.* anointed, NED, C, H; **anoynt**, C.—AF. *enoint*; Lat. *inunctum*, pp. of *inungere.*

enpoisone, *sb.* poison; **enpoysone**, HD.

enpoisonen, *v.* to poison, MD, C2; **enpoysened**, *pp.*, S2.—OF. *enpoisoner.*

enquere, *v.* to inquire, C2, C3, G, W2; **enqueri**, S2.—OF. *enquerir, enquerre*; Lat. *inquirere.*

enqueringe, *sb.* enquiry, C3.

ensamplarie, *sb.* pattern, PP.

ensample, *sb.* example, S, S2, PP, C2, C3; **ensaumple**, S3, P.—AF. *ensample, essample*, OF. *example*; Lat. *exemplum.*

ensaumplid, *pp.* exemplified, S3.

ensele, *v.* to seal, PP. Cf. **aselen.**

enserchen, *v.* to search into, W, W2.

enstore, *v.* to restore, W; **instorid**, *pp.*, W.—Lat. *instaurare.* Cf. **astore.**

entailen, *v.* to cut, carve, MD; **entayled**, *pp.* S3.—OF. *entaillier, entallier.*

entencion, *sb.* intention, C2; **entencioun**, C3.—AF. *entenciun.*

entendement, *sb.* understanding, intelligence, S3.—OF. *entendement.*

entenden, *v.* to give attention to, MD, C2.—OF. *entendre*; Lat. *intendere.*

entente, *sb.* heed, attention, purpose, intention, S2, PP, C2, C3; **entent**, S2, S3, PP.— OF. *entente.*

ententif, *adj.* attentive, W2.—OF. *ententif.*

enteren, *v.* to inter, bury, MD; **enteryd**, *pt. s.*, S3.—OF. *enterrer*, It. *interrare*; from Lat. *in terra.*

enterment, *sb.* interment, MD.—AF. *enterrement.*

entraille, *sb.* entrails, C2; **entraile**, MD; **entraylys**, *pl.*, Voc.—AF. *entraille*; cf. Prov. *intralias*, pl.; Sp. *entrañas*, from Lat. *interanea*, the inward parts.

enumbren, *v.* to enshadow, obscure, hide, MD; **enoumbre**, S2.—OF. *enombrer*; Church Lat. *in-umbrare.*

enuenymen, *v.* to envenom, PP; **envenimed**, *pp.*, C2.—AF. *envenimer.*

envenymes, *sb. pl.* poisons, P.

envined, *pp.* provided with wine, C.—OF. *enviné* (Cotg.).

environ, *adv.* in a circuit, around, MD; **environ**, S3; **envyroun**, S3. *Comb.*: **in enuyrown**, S2; **bi enuyroun**, MD.—OF. *environ.*

envirouen, *v.* to surround, to move round, to go about, MD; **envyrone**, S2.—OF. *environner.*

envolupen, *v.* to wrap up, C3.—AF. *envoluper.*

enuye, *sb.* annoyance, S; see **anoy.**

eny, *adj.* any, PP, S, S2, G; **eni**, S, PP; **eani**, MD, S; **æi**, MD, S; **eie**, S; **ei**, MD, S; **aniȝ**, MD; **ani**, MD, S, S2; **oni**, MD; **ony**, S2, C, W. *Comb.*: **eanis weis**, in any way, any ways, S; **eisweis**, S; **eyweis**, NED (s.v. *anywise*); **any ways**, NED; **aniȝe wise**, in any wise, NED; **aniwise**, S.—AS. *ænig.*

eode, *pt. s.*, went, S; **iæde**, S; **eoden**, *pl.*, S2; **ieden**, S.—AS. *éode*; Goth. *iddja*; see Douse, pp. 185, 188, and Brugmann, § 61. Cf. **ȝeode.**

eoli; see **ele.**

eom[1], *1 pr. s.*, am, MD; see **am.**

eom[2]; see **eem.**

eornen, *v.* to run, S, S2; see **rennen.**

69

eorre

eorre, *sb.* anger, MD, S; **urre**, S, MD; **oerre**, S; **irre**, MD.—AS. *irre*, angry, anger: OS. *irri*, angry, OHG. *irri*, out of the right way (Otfrid): Goth. *airzeis*, astray; cf. Lat. *errare* for **ersare*. Cf. **erren**.

eorðe; see **erþe**².

eoten; see **eten**.

eouwer, *pron.* your, S; see **ʒoure**.

eppel, *sb.* apple, MD; see **appel**.

er¹, *pr. pl.* are, H; **ere**, S2; see **aren**².

er², *adv., conj.* and *prep.* ere, before, S, S2, C2, PP; **ear**, S, S3; **ayr**, S3; **yer**, S3; **her**, S; **ar**, S, S2, G, H, P; **or**, S, S2, S3, C3; **ore**, S2; **are**, S, S2, H, PP; **here**, S. *Comb.*: **or ere**, before, WW, Sh.; **ere euer**, WW. **erur**, *comp.* formerly, S; **erest**, *superl.* soonest, first, S, PP; **erst**, S, S2, S3, C2, C3; **earst**, S; **arst**, G, P; **orest**, S; **ærest**, S.—AS. *ér*, comp. *éror*, superl. *érest*.

erayn, *sb.* spider, H; see **aranye**.

erche-bissop, *sb.* archbishop; see **archebiscop**.

erche-dekene, *sb.* archdeacon, S2; see **archideken**.

erd, *sb.* native land, home, S; **ærd**, S; **erde**, *dat.*, P: **herdes**, *pl.*, S (15. 2410).—AS. *eard*; OS. *ard*.

erden, *v.* to dwell, MD; **erthe**, S, MD; **earden**, MD.—AS. *eardian*; cf. OHG. *artón* (Tatian).

erding-stouwe, *sb.* dwelling-place, MD; **eardingstowe**, S.

ere¹, *sb.* ear, S, C2, PP; **eere**, W2; **ære**, S; **earen**, *pl.*, S, S2; **eren**, S; **eeris**, W2, PP. *Comb.*: **eerering**, ear-ring, W2.—AS. *éare*: Goth. *auso*; cf. Lat. *auris*.

ere², *pr. pl.*, are, S2; **er**, H; see **aren**².

erende, *sb.* errand, message, business, PP, S; **ernde**, S2, PP; **earende**, MD; **arende**, MD; **ærnde**, MD; **herdne**, S.—AS. *érende*; cf. OS. *árundi*, Icel. *eyrindi*; OHG. *árunti* (Otfrid); connected with AS. *ár*, messenger.

erewe, *adj.* timid, S; **ergh**, JD; **ery**, eerie, JD; see **arwe**².

erfe, *sb.* cattle, MD; **errfe**, S; **erue**, S.—OMerc. *erfe*, *erbe*, inheritance (OET. P. 539): OS. *erbi*, OHG. *erbi* (Tatian, Otfrid): Goth. *arbi*; cf. OIr. *orbe* (Windisch); see **orf**.

erfeð, *adj.* difficult, MD; see **arfeþ**.

erien, *v.* to plough, MD, PP; **eren**, PP, W, C; **ear**, WW; **erynge**, *pr. p.*, W; **eriden**, *pt. pl.*, W2.—AS. *erian*: Goth. *arjan*; cf. Lat. *arare*; see Douse, p. 114 (*e*).

eringe, *sb.* ploughing, S2, PP; **earing**, S3.—AS. *erung*.

eritage, *sb.* heritage, S2, PP.—AF. *heritage*.

erl, *sb.* a man of noble birth, earl, MD, S, C2; **æorl**, S; **erle**, S3 (15 a. 1); **yerle**, S3;

eorles, *pl.*, S; **ʒierles**, S; **ærlen**, *dat.*, S.—AS. *eorl*: OS. *erl*; cf. Icel. *jarl*.

erl-dom, *sb.* earldom, PP; **erldome**, P.

erly, *adv.* early, C, C2; **erlyche**, S2; **arly**, H; **yerly**, S3; **arely**, H; **erliche**, S2.—AS. *érlice*.

erme¹, *adj. dat.* poor, S; see **arm**².

erme², *v.* to feel sad, grieve, C3, CM.—AS. *earmian*; see Ten Brink, Chaucer, 48, 4. See **arm**².

erming, *adj.* wretched, S; *sb.* a wretched being, S; **earmynges**, *pl.*, S.—AS. *earming*.

ermite, *sb.* hermit, PP; **eremite**, PP, S2; **heremyte**, S2; **ermytes**, *pl.*, S2, PP; **heremites**, P; **hermites**, S.—AF. *ermite* (*heremite, hermite*); Church Lat. *eremita* (*heremita*); Gr. ἐρημίτης from ἐρημία, a desert.

ern, *sb.* eagle, MD, JD, S; **erne**, S2; **aryn**, H; **arn**, HD; **ærn**, MD; **ernes**, *pl.*, CM; **hernez**, S2.—AS. *earn*, ONorth. *arn*; from Goth. *ara*; cf. OHG. *áro*, also *arn*, pl. *erni* (Tatian).

ernde; see **erende**.

ernen¹, *v.* to earn, MD; **arnen**, MD.—AS. *earnian*: OHG. *arnón*, to reap a harvest (Otfrid), from *arno*, harvest: Goth. *asans*.

ernen², *v.* to run, S; see **rennen**.

ernes, *sb.* a pledge, earnest, MD, W; **ernest**, S2; **ernesse**, *dat.*, S.—OF. *erres*, L *arra*; *ernesse* seems to represent an analysis into **er**² + **-nesse**. Cf. **arles**.

ernest, *sb.* eagerness, seriousness, earnest, C, MD; **eornest**, MD.—AS. *eornest*, earnestness: OHG. *ernust*, sorrow (Tatian).

ernestful, *adj.* earnest, MD, C2.

ernestly, *adv.* eagerly, quickly, S2, MD.

ernung, *sb.* earning, desert, MD; **earnynge**, S. See **ernen**¹.

erraunt, *adj.* vagabond, arrant, PP, MD.—OF. *errant*, wandering, vagabond (Cotg.). See **erren**.

erre, *sb.* a scar, wound, Voc. (680. 1); **arre**, NEI; **ar**, HD; **arr**, JD; **erres**, *pl.*, H, NED. Cf. Dan. *ar*, Icel. *ör, örr*.

erren, *v.* to wander, W, MD; **erriden**, *pt. pl.*, W.—OF. *errer*; Lat. *errare*. Cf. **eorre**.

ert, *2 pr. s.* art, S, S2, H, PP; **ertou**, art thou, S2.—AS. *eart*.

erthe¹, *v.* to dwell, S; see **erden**.

erthe², *sb.* earth, S, C2, C; **eorðe**, S; **yerthe**, S3; **vrþe**, S2; **erd**, S3. *Comb.*: **anerþe**, on earth, S2.—AS. *eorðe*; OS. *erða*; cf. OHG. *erda* (Otfrid).

ertheli, *adj.* earthly, S2; **erðliche**, S; **earðlich**, S.—AS. *eorthlice*.

erthe-mouyng, *sb.* earthquake, W.

erthe-schakyng, *sb.* earthquake, W.

erthe-tiliere, *sb.* tiller of land, W; **erthetileris**, *pl.*, W2.—Cf. AS. *eorþ-tilia*.

70

erthe-tiliynge, *sb.* husbandry, W.

erue; see **erfe**.

es[1], *conj.* as, PP; see **also**.

es[2], *pr. s.*, is, S, S2, H; **esse**, S2; see **is**.

escape, *sb.* transgression, HD, ND, Sh.; **escapes**, *pl.*, S3.

eschame, *v.* to be ashamed; **eschamyt**, *pp.*, S3; see NED (s.v. *ashame*).

eschapen, *v.* to escape, S2; **escapen**, MD; **ascapen**, W2, P; **chapyt**, *pp.*, S3.—AF. *eschaper*, *escaper*. Cf. **achape**.

eschaping, *sb.* escape, S2.

eschaunge, *sb.* exchange, C, PP.—AF. *eschaunge*.

escheker, *sb.* chess-board, treasury, exchequer, MD; **esscheker**, PP; **cheker**, P; **checker**, S3; **chekyr**, PP; **chesquier**, PP.—AF. *escheker*, OF. *eschequier*.

eschen, *v.* to ask, MD; see **asken**.

eschetes, *sb. pl.* escheats, PP; **escheytes**, forfeitures, PP; **chetes**, P.—AF. *eschete* (pl. *eschaetes*); *es* = *ex* + *chaet*, pp. of *chaoir*; Lat. *cadere*; see Bartsch, p. 511.

eschewen, *v.* to eschew, avoid, S3, PP; **eschuwen**, PP; **eschue**, C3, C, PP.—AF. *eschuer*, OF. *eschever*, *eschiver*; OHG. *sciuhan*, *sciuhen*, to be afraid of (Otfrid). See **schey**.

escrien, *v.* to cry out, MD; see **ascrien**.

ese[1], *sb.* ease, C2, C3, P; **eise**, S, PP; **eyse**, PP.—AF. *eise*, OF. *aise*, pleasure; cf. It. *agio*, ease, convenience (Florio).

ese[2], *adj.* easy, at leisure; **eese**, S2; **eise**, S.—OF. *aise*, glad.

eseliche, *adv.* easily, S2; **esily**, C2, C.

esement, *sb.* solace, S3.—AF. *esement*, *aisement*.

esen, *v.* to entertain, MD, C; **esed**, *pp.*, C.—OF. *aiser*, *aisier*.

esmayed, *pp.* dismayed, frightened, S3, HD.—OF. *esmaier*, to frighten; Lat. *ex* + Low Lat. **magare*, from Teutonic source; OHG. *mag-*, stem of *mugan*, to be able; cf. It. *smagare*, to vex out of his wits (Florio). Cf. **dismayen**.

esperance, *sb.* hope, S3; **espirance**, S3; **esperaunce**, CM.—OF. *esperance*.

espye, *v.* to see, discover, C, C3.—OF. *espier*, It. *spiare*; OHG. *spihan*, see Diez. See **aspien**.

est, *adj.* east, S, S2, C2, C3, Prompt. *Comb.*: **est del**, the east, S2; **estward**, eastward; C2; see **eest**.

estat, *sb.* state, C, MD; **estaat**, C3; **astate**, S3, NED; **estate**, PP; **astates**, *pl.*, ranks, S3.—OF. *estat*; Lat. *statum*. Cf. **stat**.

estatlich, *adj.* dignified, C.

este[1], *sb.* favour, grace, delicacy, dainty, S; **esten**, *pl.*, S; **estene**, *gen.*, S.—AS. *ést*: OS. *anst*, OHG. *anst* (Otfrid): Goth. *ansts* (stem *ansti-*).

este[2], *adj.* pleasant, kind, S2, MD.—AS. *éste*.

Ester, *sb.* Easter, S, S2; **Estren**, *dat.*, S. *Comb.*: **Estrene dae**, Easter-day, S.—AS. *éastro*, *sb. pl.* the passover, easter-tide, *eastrena* (gen. pl.), from *Eastre*, the AS. form of the name of a German goddess of light and spring sunshine; see Grimm, Teut. M., p. 289.

estre, *sb.* being, nature, quality, also, the place where one is, dwelling, quarters, chambers, or inner part of a house, HD, MD; **estres**, *pl.*, C, HD, CM; **esters**, CM.—OF. *estre*, a *sb.* from an infin. (Bartsch); Late Lat. *essere*, to be; see Brachet (s.v. *être*). See also *estre* in Cotg.

Estrin-land, *sb.* Eastern land, S2. See **est**.

esy, *adj.* easy, gentle, MD, C, PP, Prompt.; **eesy**, MD.—OF. *aisie*. See **ese**[2].

et, *prep.* at, S. *Comb.*: **et-foren**, before, S.—AS. *æt*.

eten, *v.* to eat, S, C2, PP; **æten**, S; **eoten**, S; **eet**, PP; **hete**, S; **ett**, *pr. s.*, S; **eet**, PP; **et**, PP; **et**, *pt. s.*, S; **ete**, S2; **eet**, C2, C3, PP; **æten**, *pl.*, S; **eten**, S, C2, PP; **eoten**, S; **eeten**, G; **eten**, *pp.*, S, PP; **iȝeten**, S, S2; **iȝete**, S2; **y-ete**, S2; **eyt**, S3.—AS. *etan*, pt. *s. ét* (pl. *éton*), pp. *eten*, see Sievers, 391, 3; Goth. *itan*, see Douse, p. 44.

eterne, *adj.* eternal, C, HD.—OF. *eterne*; Lat. *aeternum*.

etforen, **ethalden**; see **atfore**, **atholden**.

eth-, *prefix*, easily.—Cf. AS. *éaþ-*, *éþ-*, *ýþ-*; cf. Icel. *auð-*.

eth, *adj.* easy, H; **eað**, S, MD.—AS. *éaðe*, *éðe*: OS. *óði*; cf. Goth. *auþs*, desert, waste; Weigand (s.v. *öde*).

eðe, *adv.* easily, S, HD; **eaðe**, S.

eð-lich, *adj.* slight, light, S.

ethelyng, *sb.* a noble, S; see **aþeling**.

eðem, *sb.* breath, S.—AS. *éðm*, *éðm*; OHG. *átum* (G. *athem*), see Sievers, 45. 6.

eðe-moded, *adj.* gentle, well-disposed, S, MD.—Cf. AS. *éaðmódian*, to obey. See **eadmodien**.

eðen, *adv.* hence; see **heþen**[1].

eð-lete, *adj.* lightly esteemed, MD; **eðlate**, S. See **eþ-**, **eþ**.

eð-sene, *adj.* easily seen, S; **eðcene**, S; **etscene**, S.

etlunge, *sb.* purpose, conjecture, S; see **atlinge**.

etteleden, *pt. pl.* directed their way, went straight, S2; see **atlien**.

eu, you, S; see **ȝou**.

eu-bruche, *sb.* adultery, MD, S; **eaubruche**, MD; **æwbræche**, Voc.—AS. *æwbryce*. See **æ**.

eure, *pron.* your, S; see **ȝoure**.

euangelie, *sb.* gospel, PP, W; **euangile**, S2; **ewangelye**, S2, PP; **euangyles**, *pl.*, C3.—OF. *evangile*; Lat. *evangelium* (Vulg.); Gr. εὐαγγέλιον.

euangeliste, *sb.* evangelist, PP; **euangelist**, C2; **ewanigeliste**, S.—OF. *evangeliste* (AF. *ewangelist*); Lat. *evangelista* (Vulg.); Gr. εὐαγγελιστής.

euangelize, *v.* to preach, W.

euel, *adj.* and *adv.* evil, S, W2, S2, PP; see **yvel**.

euel-les, *adj.* guiltless, S3.

euen[1], *sb.* even, S, P; **efenn**, S; **eue**, S, C2, C3, PP. *Comb.*: **euene-sterre**, evening star, W2; **eue-song**, even-song, S2; **euynsonge**, S3; **euensonge**, P.—AS. *æfen (éfen)*: OHG. *áband* (Otfrid), see Sievers, 45.

euen[2], *adj.* even, equal, fellow, MD, S2, W; **euene**, C2, PP; *adv.*, PP; **efne**, S; **æfne**, S; **ewin**, S3. *Comb.*: **efen-ald**, of the same age, MD; **euen-cristene**, fellow-christian, S, PP, HD; **em-cristen**, S, S2; **euenforth**, according to, to the extent of, PP; **em-forth**, C, PP; **euen-forth**, directly forward, S3; **euen-forward**, directly forward, HD; **euene-long**, of proper height, S; **euene-worth**, of like value, W2.—AS. *efen*: OS. *eban*, OHG. *eban* (Otfrid).

euenen, *v.* to make equal, to be equal, MD, S; **effnenn**, S.—AS. *efnan*.

euenhed, *sb.* equality, equity, H (Ps, 108. 2); **euynhede**, Prompt.

euenli, *adv.* evenly, W2; **euenliche**, MD; **euelyche**, S.—AS. *efenlice*.

euennesse, *sb.* equity, W2.

euenynge, *sb.* an equal, S; **efning**, S.—Cf. Icel. *jafningi.*

euerich, *adj.* every, S, S2, C2; **averelc**, MD; **æverelch**, MD; **everech**, MD, S; **evrech**, MD, S; **afric**, S; **efrec**, MD; **evrec**, MD; **everilk**, MD, S3; **everilc**, MD, S; **euerich**, S, S2, C2; **eavrich**, MD; **æueric**, S; **ævric**, MD; **efrich**, MD; **eurich**, S, S2; **æueralche**, S; **auerich**, S; **afri**, S; **eaueriche**, S; **evereuch**, S; **eauereuch**, S. *Comb.*: **euerich on**, every one, S2, C2, C3; **everych one**, S2; **euerilk an**, S2.—AS. *æfre + ǽlc*; see **evre** and **eche**[1].

euese, *sb.* border, brink, edge (of a roof, mountain, forest), Prompt., MD; **heuese**, MD; **eueses**, *pl.*, PP.—AS. *efese*: OHG. *obisa, opasa*; see Sievers, 93. Cf. E. *eaves.*

euesien, *v.* to clip round, to shear, MD; **euesed**, *pp.*, S3; **i-eveset**, S.—AS. *efesian.*

euesunge, *sb.* a clipping, what is clipped off, MD; eaves, MD; **evesing**, Manip.;

aisings, *pl.*, PP (*n*). *Comb.*: **house-euysynge** (= *domicilium*), H.—AS. *efesung* (Voc.).

euete, *sb.* eft, newt, W2; **newte**, Voc. (642. 27); **eueten**, *pl.*, S; **ewtes**, MD.—AS. *efeta* (Voc.).

euorye, *sb.* ivory, HD; **yvory**, Prompt.; **everey**, Voc.—Prov. *evori (avori)*; Lat. *eboreum*, made of ivory; cf. F. *ivoire*, It. *avorio* (Florio); see Diez.

euour, *sb.* ivory, S3, HD; **euor**, H; **evir**, S3; **ivor**, Prompt.; **yuer**, W, W2.—Of French origin, from Lat. *ebur.*

eure, *adv.* ever, S, S2, PP; **euere**, S, S2, PP; **efre**, S, MD; **afre**, S; **efer**, S, MD; **eauer**, S, MD; **æfer**, MD; **auer**, S; **æuere**, S; **auere**, S; **æuere**, S; **ær**, MD; **er**, MD. *Comb.*: **euer among**, continually, S3; **euer eiþer**, each, S3; **efreni**, ever any, S; **euermo**, evermore, S, S2, C2, C3; **æfremo**, S; **euermor**, S; **æuer te**, ever as yet, S.—AS. *æfre*, from *áwa (á)*; see SkD, and Sievers, 192. 4.

ew, *sb.* yew, C, Voc.; **ewe**, Cath.—AS. *iw*; cf. OHG. *iwa.*

ewage, *sb.* beryl, PP.—OF. *ewage*, connected with water (Roquefort); Lat. *aquaticum.* The green beryl is called by jewellers *aqua marina.* See **ewe ardaunt.**

ewe ardaunt, *sb.* burning water, S2.—AF. *ewe, eue, aigue*; Lat. *aquam*, see Academy, No. 459, p. 139; cf. Goth. *alva.*

ewen, *v.* to show.—AS. *ȳwan*: Goth. *augjan*; cf. OHG. *ougen* (Otfrid). See **atewen**, **eȝe**[2].

ewer, *sb.* a water-carrier, also, vessel for water, Palsg.; **euwere**, MD; **eware**, *aquarius*, Prompt.—AF. *ewer*, SkD (p. 803); OF. *euwier, aiguier.*

ewilch, *adj.* every, MD (s.v. *ælc* **ewilche**; MD; **iwilch**, MD; **uwilc**, MD, S; **uwilch**, MD, S; **ewiche**, S.—AS. *é-g-hwilc*: OHG. *io-gi-welih* (Tatian), *eo-gi-hwelíh*; see Sievers, 347. 1.

ewin; see **even**[2].

exerce, *v.* to exercise, S3.—OF. *exercer*; Lat. *exercere.*

exhibition, *sb.* payment, S3, Sh.—AF. *exhibicioun*; Late Lat. *exhibitionem* (Ducange).

expert[1], *adj.* experienced, C3. See **apert**[1].

expert[2], *v.* to experience, S3.

expounen, *v.* to expound, PP, C2, C3; **expowne**, S2, S3; **expounde**, C2.—Lat. *exponere.*

expownyng, *sb.* interpretation, W.

ey, *sb.* egg, C, C3, Prompt.; **eye**, S3, W; **ay**, G, HD; **eyren**, *pl.*, PP; **eiren**, PP; **eirun**, W2; **ayren**, MD; **egges**, PP.—AS. *æg* (pl. *ægru*); cf. Icel. *egg*, whence E. *egg.*

eyle, *adj.* loathsome, troublesome, NED; AS. *egle*: OTeut. **agljo*; cf. Goth. *aglus*; see Sievers, 303.

eylen, *v.* to trouble, afflict, NED; **eilin**, S; **eileþ**, *pr. s.*, S2, PP; **eyleth**, C2, C3, C, PP.—AS. *eglan*: Goth. *agljan.*

eyre[1], *sb.* air, C3, P; **eire**, W; **eyr**, C; **eir**, W2, PP; **aier**, PP; **ayer**, S3; **air**, S2 (20. 167); **aire**, NED.—OF. *air*; Lat. *aerem.*

eyre[2], *sb.* heir, S2, PP; **eire**, W, PP; **ayre**, HD; **aire**, S2; **eir**, S, S2; **eyr**, G; **eyer**, S2; **heir**, S, C2; **heyr**, C3.—OF. *eir, heirs*; Lat. *heres.*

eyren, *sb. pl.*; see **ey.**

eyt; see **eten.**

eythes, *sb. pl.* harrows, PP.—AS. *egeðe*, harrow: OHG. *egida.*

eʒe[1], *sb.* awe, MD; **eie**, S; **eye**, S, G; **ʒeie**, S; **aʒeie**, S, NED; **aye**, HD; **eyʒe**, G.—AS. *ege*: Goth. *agis*; see Sievers, 263. 4. Cf. **awe.**

eʒe[2], *sb.* eye, S, S2, PP; **ehe**, S; **eghe**, S; **eie**, S2; **yë**, S2, C2, C3, G; **iʒe**, S3, W, W2;

yʒe, W2; **e**, S2, S3; **ee**, S3; **eʒen**, *pl.*, S, S2; **egen**, S; **eien**, S; **eyen**, S, S2, P; **eyn**, S3; **eghen**, S2, C; **eiʒen**, S2, PP; **eiʒyen**, S2; **eyne**, Sh.; **ehne**, S; **ene**, S3; **eye**, S2; **iʒen**, W, W2, S3; **yʒen**, S2; **iyen**, S3; **yën**, C2, C3; **eyghen**, P; **eighen**; **ine**, S2; **eyghes**, PP; **eyghe**, PP.—AS. *éage*: Goth. *augo*; cf. OHG. *ouga* (Otfrid).

eʒe-lid, *sb.* eye-lid, MD; **ehelid**, S.

eʒe-put, *sb.* the socket of the eye; **eʒe-puttes**, *pl.*, MD.

eʒe-þurl, *sb.* window; **ehþurl**, MD.—*éagþyrl*; cf. Goth. *auga-dauro*, window (eye-door).

eʒhe-sihðe, *sb.* the sight of the eye, presence, MD; **ehsihðe**, S; **iʒe-siʒt**, S3.

eʒ-sen, *sb.* presence; **eighesene**, *dat.*, MD; **æhseone**, MD; **ecsene**, MD; **exsene**, MD.—Cf. Icel. *aug-sýn*, OHG. *oug-siuni* (Tatian).

73

F

For some words of Teutonic origin beginning with **f-**, *see* **V** *below; see also in some cases* **W** *below.*

fa[1], *adj.* few, H; see **fewe**.
fa[2], **faa**, *sb.* foe, S, S2; see **foo**.
face, *sb.* face, PP; a term in astrology, C2.—OF. *face*; Lat. *faciem*.
facion, *sb.* fashion, S3; see **fasoun**.
facound, *sb.* eloquence, fluency, CM; **facunde**, H, Prompt.—OF. *faconde*; Lat. *facundia*.
facound, *adj.* eloquent, CM.—OF. *faconde*; Lat. *facundum*.
fade, *adj.* weak, faint (of colour), MD; **vad**, MD.—OF. *fade*.
faden, *v.* to fade, lose colour, wither, to cause to wither, MD, Cath., Prompt.; **vade**, MD, Sh., HD.
fader, *sb.* father, S, S2, C3; **feader**, S; **feder**, S; **vader**, S, S2; **veder**, S; **fadre**, S2; **faderes**, *gen. s.*, S; **fadres**, C2; **fader**, S2, C2, C3; **faderes**, *pl.*, S2; **fadres**, C2; **fadris**, W.—AS. *fæder*.
fadme, *sb.* fathom, *ulna*, MD, Prompt., C; **fadome**, CM; **fedme**, MD; **fadmen**, *pl.*, G.—AS. *fæðm*.
fadmen, *v.* to embrace, MD, Prompt.; **faðmen**, MD; **fadmede**, *pt. s.*, MD; **faþmed**, *pp.*, MD, S2.—AS. *fæðmian*.
fæc, *sb.* space, interval, portion of time; **fece**, *dat.*, S.—AS. *fæc*; cf. OHG. *fah* (MHG. *vach*), a wall, a compartment.
fæie, *adj. pl.* dead, S; see **feye**.
færd, *sb.* army, S; see **ferd**[1].
færen, *v.* to fare, S; see **faren**.
fæu, *adj.* few, S; see **fewe**.
fagen, *adj.* fain, S; see **fayn**[2].
fai, *sb.* faith, S2; **fay**, G; see **feiþ**.
faie, *sb.* fay, fairy, S2; see **fay**.
fail, *sb.* greensward, JD; **faill**, S3; **fail**, grassy clod cut from the sward, JD.—Gael. *fál*, wall, hedge, sod; OIr. *fál*, wall, hedge (Windisch).
fail-dyke, *sb.* dike built of sods, JD.
faille[1], *v.* to fail, S, C2; **fayle**, S2; **failede**, *pt. s.*, S.—AF. *faillir*; Late Lat. *fallire* for Lat. *fallere*.
faille[2], *sb.* fail, doubt, MD; **feale**, S3.
fainen, *v.* to rejoice, S2; see **faynen**[1].
faire, *sb.* fair, P; see **feyre**.
fairye, *sb.* fairy power, fairy land, C2; see **fayerye**.
fait, *sb.* deed, S2, PP; **faite**, PP; see **fet**[1].
faiten, *v.* to beg under false pretences, PP; **fayten**, PP.

faiterie, *sb.* deceit, PP; **fayterye**, Prompt., HD.
faitour, *sb.* pretender, impostor, vagabond, MD, PP; **faytowre**, *fictor*, Prompt.; **faytoures**, *pl.*, S3; **faitors**, H.—OF. *faitour*, *faiteör* (Godefroy); Late Lat. **factitorem*.
falding, *sb.* a kind of coarse cloth, C, HD; **faldynge**, *amphibalus*, *birrus*, Cath., Prompt.
fallace, *sb.* deceitfulness, W; **fallas**, W, HD.—OF. *fallace*; Lat. *fallacia* (Vulg.).
fallen, *v.* to fall, S, C2; **uallen**, S; **feol**, *pt. s.*, S; **fel**, S; **fil**, C2; **ful**, S; **fyl**, S2; **i-uel**, S; **fille**, S3; **vul**, S2; **feolle**, *subj.*, S; **fellen**, *pl.*, S; **felle**, S; **fille**, C2; **felden**, S2, W, W2; **y-fallen**, *pp.*, C2; **i-falle**, S; **falle**, S2, C2; **fallyng** (*Scotch form*), S3; **feld**, W.—AS. (*ge)feallan*, *pt. feoll*, *pp.* ge-*feallen*.
fallow[1], *sb.* fellow, S2, S3; see **felawe**.
fallow[2], *v.* to be fellow to, S3; see **felawen**.
fallynge, *sb.* a falling; **fallyngis**, *pl.*, ruins, W2, H.
fallynge-ax, *sb.* felling-axe, W2; see **fellen**.
fallynge-euylle, *sb.* the falling-sickness, epilepsy, S2.
fals, *adj.* false, MD, C2; **false**, MD, C2.—AF. *fals*; Lat. *falsum*.
fals-hede, *sb.* falsehood, S3, C3; **falset**, S3.
falsien, *v.* to make false, MD; **falsyn**, Prompt.; **falsed**, *pp.*, C2.—OF. *falser* (mod. *fausser*); Late Lat. *falsare*.
falsnessis, *sb. pl.* frauds, W2.
falten, *v.* to fail, to be wanting in, to stammer; **fauten**, *pl.*, PP.—OF. **falter* (whence F. *faute*); cf. It. *faltare*, freq. form of Lat. *fallere*.
faltren, *v.* to totter, SkD, C3, CM; to stammer, falter, Prompt.; **foltred**, *pp.*, S3.
falwe, *adj.* fallow, pale, yellow, MD.—AS. *fealu* (stem *fealwa*).
falwen, *v.* to become yellow, pallid, to fade, MD; **faluwen**, MD; **valuwen**, S.—AS. *fealuwian*.
familier, *adj.* familiar, Manip.; **famulier**, C; **famuler**, MD.—AF. *familier*; Lat. *familiarem*.
fand, *pt. s.* found, S, S2, S3; see **finden**.
fandien, *v.* to try, seek, strive, to prove, MD, S; **fande**, S2, H; **fonde**, S, S2, S3, C2; **uonden**, S; **faynd**, B; **i-fonded**, *pp.*, S.—AS. *fandian*; deriv. of **finden**.
fanding, *sb.* tempting, temptation, S2; **fandynge**, H; **fondunge**, S; **fondyng**, S2, G; **uondynge**, S.—AS. *fandung*.
fane, *sb.* banner, streamer, S3, MD; **fayn**, weather-vane, S3; **fan**, C3; **vane**, C2; **fanys**, *pl.*, streamers, S3.—AS. *fana*, a

74

fantasie

standard, Goth. *fana*, a bit of cloth; cf. Lat. *pannus (pānus)*, see Curtius, 362.

fantasie, *sb.* fancy, PP; **fantasy**, S3; **fantasies**, *pl.*, P; **fantasyes**, S2, C2.—OF. *fantasie*; Lat. *phantasia*; Gr. φαντασία.

fantome, *sb.* deceptive appearance, false-hood, apparition, MD, C3; **fantoum**, MD; **fantum**, S2, W; **fantom**, H; **fantesme**, MD; **fanteme**, MD.—OF. *fantosme* (Ps. 78. 4); Low Lat. **fantasuma* (cf. Prov. *fantauma*); Lat. *phantasma*; Gr. φάντασμα.

fare, *sb.* journey, S; doing, business, S2, C3, C; behaviour, G.

faren, *v.* to go, to fare, to behave, S, S2, C2; **uaren**, S; **færen**, S; **far**, S3; **vare**, S; **fair**, S3; **farst**, *2 pr. s.*, S; **feareð**, *pr. s.*, S; **fars**, S2; **varþ**, *pl.*, S2; **for**, *pt. s.*, S, S2; **i-faren**, *pp.*, S; **faren**, MD, S2; **fare**, S, S2, C2; **i-fare**, S, S2. *Comb.*: **far wel**, farewell, C2; *pl.* **fareth wel**, C3; **farewel**, it is all over!, C3.—AS. *faran*, pt. *fōr*, pp. *faren*.

farme, *sb.* a feast, meal, CM, MD; see **ferme**[1].

farsen, *v.* to stuff, HD; **farsed**, *pp.*, C; **farsid**, H.—OF. *farcir*; Lat. *farcire*.

fasoun, *sb.* fashion, make, shape, MD, CM; **fassoun**, S3; **faccion**, S3; **facions**, *pl.*, S3.—OF. *fason, fasson, façon*; Lat. *factionem*.

fast, *adj.* firm, fixed, SkD; **fest**, S; **faste**, *adv.* fast, firmly, quickly, soon, PP, S, C2; securely, S; **feste**, S; **fast**, soon, PP; close, S2; **ueste**, S; **uaste**, S2. *Phr.*: **fast aboute**, very eager, G.—AS. *fæst*, firm.

fasten[1], *v.* to make fast, *also* to fast (from food), *jejunare*, MD, W (Mt. 6. 16); **fest**, S2; **fæston**, *pt. pl.*, confirmed, S; **fested**, *pp.*, S2.—AS. *fæstan*; cf. Goth. *fastan*, 'jejunare'.

fasten[2], *sb.* fasting, S; **festen**, S.

fasting, *sb.* abstinence from food, MD; **fasttinng**, S.

fast-lice, *adv.* continuously, S.

fastnesse, *sb.* stronghold, MD; **festnes**, S2.

fast-rede, *adj.* firm in counsel, S.

fat[1], *sb.* vessel, S, Voc.; **fet**, MD; **uet**, MD; **feat**, MD; **ueat**, S; **faten**, *pl.*, S.—AS. *fæt*: OS. *fat*; cf. OHG. *faz* (Tatian).

fat[2], *adj.* fat, MD; **fet**, S; **fette**, *pl.*, S.—AS. *fæt*; cf. Icel. *feitr*.

faþmen, *v.* to embrace, S2; see **fadmen**.

faucon, *sb.* falcon, C2; **faucoun**, PP; **faukyn**, PP; **faucones**, *pl.*, P.—AF. *faucon*, *falcun*; Lat. *falconem*.

faunt, *sb.* child, infant, MD; **faunte**, HD; **fauntes**, *pl.*, P; **fauntis**, P.—OF. *fant*, It. *fante*; Lat. *infantem*.

fauntee, *sb.* childishness, PP.

fauntekyn, *sb.* little child, PP; **fawntkyne**, HD; **fantekyne**, HD.

fayrehed

fauntelet, *sb.* infancy, properly a little infant, PP.

fauntelte, *sb.* childishness, PP.

faur, *num.* four, MD; **faure**, S2; see **foure**.

faur-tend, *ord.* fourteenth, S2.

faute, *sb.* fault, MD; **faut**, S2.—OF. *faute*, *falte*. See **falten**.

fauel, *sb.* impersonification of Flattery, PP; **fauuel**, S2; **fauell**, flattery, S3.—OF. *favele*, talk; Lat. *fabella*, 'sermo brevis' (Ducange).

fawch, *sb.* fallow, S3; **fauch**, JD; **faugh**, HD; **fauf**, HD. *Comb.*: **fawch-ʒallow**, fallow-yellow, S3.

fawe, *adj.* few, S; see **fewe**.

fawely, *adv.* few, S3.

fawn, *sb.* fawn, the young of an animal, MD; *enulus* = *hinnulus*, a young mule, Voc.; **fawne**, *hinulus*, Voc.; **fowne**, *hinnilus*, Voc. [these Voc. words occur close to names for deer]; **fawne**, *hinnulus*, Cath.; **fownys**, *pl.*, S3.—OF. *faön, feön, foïn*; perhaps a derivative of Lat. *foetus*, see Diez, p. 580.

fay, *sb.* fay, fairy, a person endued with supernatural powers, HD; **faie**, S2; **faies**, *pl.*, RD.—OF. *faë (fee)*; Late Lat. *fata*, from Lat. *fatum*, a decree of destiny; cf. It. *fata*, Sp. *hada*.

fayerye, *sb.* magic, fairy world, a fairy, MD; **fayreye**, PP; **feyrye**, fairy origin, S2; **feyrie**, S2, PP; **fairye**, C2; **fairy**, P.—OF. *faerie*, enchantment, also *feerie*, (Cotg.).

faym, *sb.* foam, S3; see **foom**.

fayn[1], *sb.* streamer, weather-vane, S3; see **fane**.

fayn[2], *adj.* fain, glad, willing, S2, C2, MD; **fagen**, S; **fain**, MD; **uæin**, S; **fein**, MD; **uein**, MD; **feyn**, S2: **fawen**, MD; **fawe**, *adv.*, gladly, MD; **fainest**, *superl.*, CM.—AS. *fægen*.

faynen[1], *v.* to rejoice, PP; **fainen**, S2; **faunen**, to fawn, PP; **fawnyn**, Prompt.—AS. *fagenian, fægnian*.

faynen[2], *v.* to feign, S3; see **feynen**.

faynnes, *sb.* gladness, H (Ps. 67. 3); **faynes**, H. See **fayn**[2].

fayntise, *sb.* pretence, S3; **fayntis**, H; see **feyntise**.

fayre[1], *adj.* fair, C2, PP; **faʒʒerr**, MD; **fæiʒer**, MD; **faiger**, MD; **feiʒer**, MD; **feier**, S; **uair**, S2; **feir**, MD, S; **uayr**, S2; **fayr**, S; **vaire**, S; **faire**, *pl.*, S, **feyre**, S, S2; **veyrer**, *comp.*, S2; **fæirest**, *superl.*, S; **færeste**, *pl.*, S; **faireste**, S.—AS. *fæger*.

fayre[2], *adv.* courteously, kindly, PP; **fæire**, S; **faʒʒre**, S; **faire**, S, P; **feyre**, S, S2, CM; **feire**, S, S2; **uaire**, S2.

fayrehed, *sb.* beauty, fairness; **fairehed**, S2; **fairhede**, S; **uayrhede**, S2.

75

fayrnes, *sb.* beauty, MD; **fairnesse**, S, C2.
fayten, *v.* to tame, mortify, PP, S2; **faiten**, PP. See **afaiten**.
faȝe, *pl.* spotted, S; see **foh**.
feale, *sb.* fail, failure, S3; see **faille**².
fearen, *v.* to fare, S; see **faren**.
feawe, *adj.* few, S; see **fewe**.
feble, *adj.* feeble, S, S2, PP; **fieble**, C2, P; **feblore**, *comp.*, S2; **febelore**, PP; **fibler**, PP.—OF. *feble, floible*; Lat. *flebilem*.
feble-like, *adv.* in sorry fashion, S.
feblen, *v.* to become weak, to make weak, PP; **febli**, S2; **febly**, S2; **feblid**, *pp.*, MD.
fecchen, *v.* to fetch, S, S2, C2, P; **vecche**, S; **fechen**, S; **fache**, S3.—From AS. *fecce*, pr. s. of *feccan* (= *fetian*). See **fetten**.
fecht, *v.* to fight, B; see **fighten**.
fechtaris, *sb. pl.* fighters, S3, B.
fechting-sted, *sb.*, battle-ground, B.
fede, *sb.* enmity, S3; **feide**, MD.—AS. *fǽhð*. See **foo**.
feden, *v.* to feed, S, PP; **ueden**, S; **fet**, *pr. s.*, S; **fett**, S; **vedde**, *pt. s.*, S2; **fedde**, PP; **foded**, S2; **i-ued**, *pp.*, S; **i-uædde**, *pl.*, S.—AS. *fédan*: OS. *fódian*. See **fode**¹.
feder¹, *sb.* father, S; see **fader**.
feder², *sb.* feather, MD; see **feþer**.
fedramme, *sb.* plumage, S3; see **feþer-home**.
fee, *sb.* cattle, property, money, PP, S2; **feo**, MD; **fe**, S, S2, PP; **feh**, MD.—AS. *feoh*: OS. *fehu*; cf. Lat. *pecus*.
feend, *sb.* enemy, fiend, C2, C3; **fend**, S, S2; **feende**, PP; **feont**, S; **ueond**, S; **fond**, MD; **fynd**, MD; **fende**, S2, S3; **feondes**, *pl.*, S; **fendes**, S, S2; **fiendes**, S; **vyendes**, S2; **feendis**, W.—AS. *féond*, pr. p. of *féon*, to hate; cf. Goth. *fiands, fijands*, enemy, pr. p. of *fijan*, to hate.
feendli, *adj.* fierce, devilish (= Lat. *diabolica*), W; **feondliche**, *adv.* fiercely, S; **feendly**, C3.—AS. *féondlic, féondlice*.
feer, *sb.* companion, S3; see **fere**².
fees, *sb. pl.* landed possessions, cities, S2; **feys**, HD; **feus**, PP.—OF. *feu, fiu*, in pl. *feus, fieus, fius, fiez*, all found in Roland; also OF. *fie* (Bartsch), F. *fief*; probably of Teutonic origin, cf. OHG. *fihu*, property; see Braune, in ZRP. x. 262. See **fee**.
feet, *sb.* deed, C2, PP; see **fet**¹.
feffement, *sb.* possession, Manip., PP.
feffen, *v.* to put into possession, MD, PP; **feffede**, *pt. s.*, S2.—OF. *feffer*; cf. Low Lat. *feoffare*. See **fees**.
feht; see **fighten**.
fei, *sb.* faith, S2; **fey**, C2, C3; see **feiþ**.
feier, *adj.* fair, S; see **fayre**¹.
feierlec, *sb.* beauty, S.

feild, *sb.* field, MD. *Comb.*: **feild-going**, a walking out of doors, S3. See **feld**.
feir¹, *sb.* companion, S3; see **fere**².
feir², *adj.* fair, S, PP; see **fayre**¹.
feire, *adv.* kindly, PP, S, S2.
feiren, *v.* to make fair, S.
feið, *sb.* faith, S, PP; **feyth**, PP; **feth**, S3; **feiȝþ**, S2; **fei**, S2; **fey**, C2, C3; **fai**, S2; **fay**, G, PP. *Phr.*: **ye-feth**, in faith, S3.—OF. *fei, feit, feid*: Lat. *fidem*.
feið-ful, *adj.* faithful, MD; **faithfol**, PP; **feiȝtful**, S2.
feiðliche, *adv.* faithfully, MD; **feiȝliche**, S2; **feiȝþely**, S2; **feþli**, S2; **faithly**, PP.
fel¹, *sb.* a fell, mountain, S2; **fell**, MD; **felle**, MD, S2.—Icel. *fjall*.
fel², *adj.* base, cruel, treacherous, S2, PP, C2, G, W; **fell**, S3; **felle**, S2, S3, W2; *pl.*, PP, C2.—AF. *fel*, wicked, cruel.
felawe, *sb.* partner, companion, fellow, S, S2, C3, PP; **felaw**, S2, PP; **felow**, S3, PP; **felaȝe**, S; **fallow**, S2, S3; **felaus**, *pl.*, S2; **feolahes**, S; **uelaȝes**, S2.—Icel. *félagi*, partner in common property (*fé*). See **fee**.
felawen, *v.* to associate, to be fellow to; **fallow**, S3; **uelaȝen**, MD; **felaghid**, *pp.*, H.
felawrede, *sb.* fellowship, MD; **uelaȝrede**, S2.
felawschipe, *sb.* fellowship, society, crew, PP; **felaȝschipe**, S2; **feolahscipe**, S.
felawship, *v.* to associate, MD; **felouschipid**, *pp.*, W2.
felaȝliche, *adv.* intimately; **feolohlukest**, *superl.*, S.
feld, *sb.* field, S, PP; **feeld** (heraldic), C2; **ueld**, S2; **fild**, MD; **felde**, *dat.*, S, S2; **uelde**, S, S2; **ualde**, S; **feldes**, *pl.*, S, S3.—AS. *feld*.
feld-fare, *sb.* fieldfare, lit. 'field-farer', S2; *campester*, Voc.; *ruruscus*, Voc.
feldi, *adj.* champain (= Lat. *campestris*), MD; **feeldi**, W.
feldishe, *adj.* belonging to the country, S3.
fele, *adj.* many, S, S2, S3, C2, PP; **vele**, S, S2; **feole**, S, PP; **ueole**, S; **veale**, S; **vale**, S, HD; **felle**, S3.—AS. *fela*; cf. Goth. *filu*.
felefalden, *v.* to multiply, MD; **felefalded**, *pt. s.*, S2.
fele-folde, *adj.* manifold, S; many times, PP.
felen, *v.* to feel, S; **uele**, MD; **fel me**, *1 pr. s.*, S2; **felde**, *pt. s.*, S; **feld**, S2; **felte**, C2; **feelede**, C3.—AS. *félan*: OS. *fólian* (in *gifólian*), OHG. *fóljan*; cf. *fualen* (Otfrid).
fell, *sb.* skin, S3; **fel**, MD, S2, G, P; **felle**, S2; **felles**, *pl.*, S; **uelles**, S; **fellys**, S2.—AS. *fell*; cf. Goth. *fill*.
fellen, *v.* to fell, S, PP; **falle**, S2; **falleð**, *pr. pl.*, S; **felde**, *pt. s.*, G, PP.—AS. *fellan*,

OHG. *fallian*; OS. *fellian*, OHG. *fellen*
(Otfrid).

felnesse, *sb.* astuteness (= Lat. *astutia*), W2.

felon, *sb.* villain, traitor, PP; **feloun**, PP; **felloun**, S3; **felloune**, S3.—AF. *feloun*, *felon*, acc. of *fel*. See **fel**².

felonie, *sb.* base wickedness, MD; **felony**, S; **felonye**, S2, S3, C3, W2.

felonliche, *adv.* cruelly, PP; **felunlyche**, S2; **felounelich**, PP; **felunly**, S2.

fen¹, *sb.* a section of Avicenna's book on medicine called the Canon, C3, CM.— Arabic *fan*, a branch, division, category; cf. Ducange (s.v. *fen*).

fen², *sb.* mud, mire, marsh, dung, S2, S2, G, H; **fenne**, Voc., Prompt., W; **uenne**, S.— AS. *fenn*: Goth. *fani*, mud, clay.

fenden, *v.* to defend, PP; **fend**, *imp. s.*, S3.— From OF. *defendre*; Lat. *defendere*.

fenestre, *sb.* window, PP; **fenystaris**, *pl.*, S3.—OF. *fenestre*; Lat. *fenestra*.

feng; see **fon**¹, *v.*

fenkel, *sb.* fennel, MD, PP; **fenecel**, Voc.; **fenkil**, PP; **fynkel**, PP; **fynkyl**, Voc.; **fenel**, PP; **fenyl**, S2. *Comb.*: **fenel seed**, PP.—Lat. *feniculum, foeniculum*; cf. AS. *fenol* (Voc.).

feole; see **fele**.

feond, *sb.* enemy, PP; **feont**, S; **feondes**, *pl.*, S; see **feend**.

feord, *sb.* army, S; see **ferd**¹.

feorden, *pt. pl.*, fared, S; see **feren**.

fer¹, *sb.* fire, S; **fere**, *dat.*, S2; **uere**, S2; **ueree**, S; see **fur**¹.

fer², *adj., adv.* far, PP, S, S2, C2; **ferr**, S, S2, PP; **uer**, S2; **feor**, S; **ueor**, S; **for**, S; **ferre**, *comp.*, C; **ferrer**, S3, C, PP; **ferrest**, *superl.*, PP. *Comb.*: **ferforth**, far away, completely, S2, S3, C2, C3; **farforth**, S3; **feoruoþ**, S.—AS. *feorr*: OS. *fer*; cf. Goth. *fairra*. Cf. **aferre**.

ferd¹, *sb.* an expedition, army, MD; **færd**, S; **feord**, S; **uerd**, MD; **ferde**, MD; **furde**, *dat.*, MD; **ferde**, *pl.*, S; **ferdes**, MD; **verden**, *dat.*, S; **uerdes**, MD.—AS. *fird*, *fyrd, ferd*. See **faren**.

ferd², *sb.* fear, PP, G; **feerd**, MD; **ferde**, *dat.*, MD, CM, S2.

ferdful, *adj.* causing terror, timid, MD, W, W2; **feerdful**, W2.

ferdlayk, *sb.* fear, MD.

ferdnes, *sb.* fear, MD, S2.

fere¹, *v.* to frighten, terrify, PP, S2, W; **feare**, S3; **feere**, CM; **fered**, *pp.*, S2, C3; **ferd**, S2; **ferde**, S3; **feared**, S3.—AS. *féran*, to frighten.

fere², *sb.* companion, S, S2, S3, G; **uere**, S; **feer**, S3; **feir**, S3; **feren**, *pl.*, S; **ferin**, S;

feiren, S; **feres**, S, S2; **feeres**, S2. See **ifere**.

fere³, *adj.* well, sound, MD, S2; **fer**, S, B; **feir**, B. *Phr.*: **hoi and fer**, MD, S; **haill and feir**, safe and sound, B.—Icel. *færr*, able, strong (for travelling).

fere⁴, *sb.* power, ability, S, MD.—Icel. *færi*, opportunity, ability.

fere⁵, *sb.* fear, PP, S, C2, MD; **feer**, MD; **fer**, MD, PP; **feere**, PP; **feris**, *pl.*, MD; **feeris**, MD.—AS. *fér*, sudden danger; cf. Icel. *fár*, harm.

fere-full, *adj.* fear-causing, also timid, MD; **feerful**, MD; **ferful**, MD; **ferfullest**, *superl.*, CM.

feren, *v.* to fare, to go, to behave, MD; **ferde**, *pt. s.*, G, S, S2, C2; **ferden**, *pl.*, S3; **feorden**, S; **uerden**, S; **furde**, MD; **ferd**, S2.—AS. *féran* pt. *férde*; deriv. of **faren**.

ferien, *v.* to bring, MD; **fareð**, *pr. pl.*, S.— AS. *ferian*, Icel. *ferja*: Goth. *farjan*. Deriv. of **faren**.

ferlac, *sb.* fear, MD; **fearlac**, S; **farlac**, S. See **fere**⁵.

ferlien, *v.* to wonder, PP; **ferly**, JD; **ferleis**, *pr. pl.*, S3 (13. 80); **ferliede**, *pt. s.*, PP.

ferly¹, *adj.* dangerous, dreadful, sudden, strange, S2, PP, CM; **ferlich**, MD, S; **ferli**, S2; **ferliche**, *adv.*, S; **ferly**, S2.—AS. *færlic, férlice*.

ferly², *sb.* a wonder, S2, P; **farly**, MD; **ferlikes**, *pl.*, S2; **ferlyes**, S2; **ferleis**, S3; **ferlis**, P.

ferlyly, *adv.* wondrously, S2; **ferlilic**, S2.

fermacye, *sb.* pharmacy, medicine, C.—OF. *farmacie*; Late Lat. *pharmacia*; Gr. φαρμα-κεία.

fermance, *sb.* enclosure, S3; **fermance**, JD.—OF. *fermance*, from *fermer*, to shut; Lat. *firmare*, to strengthen.

ferme¹, *sb.* food, an entertainment, feast, meal, MD; **farme**; MD, CM; **ueorme**, MD.—AS. *feorm*; cf. Low Lat. *firma*, a feast (Ducange).

ferme², *adj.* firm, MD, C2.—AF. *ferme*; Lat. *firmum*.

ferme³, *sb.* rent, revenue, MD, S2, C; **fermes**, *pl.* farms, S3.—AF. *ferme*; Late Lat. *firma*.

fermen¹, *v.* to strengthen, PP.—OF. *fermer*, to strengthen, also to shut; Lat. *firmare*.

fermen², *v.* to hold land at a fixed rent, Prompt. See **ferme**³.

fermerer, *sb.* infirmary officer, Cath.; see **enfermerere**.

fermery, *sb.* infirmary, S3, Voc.; **fermorie**, PP; **fermory**, Cath.; **fermarye**, Cath. (*n*); **fermerye**, Prompt. Cath. (*n*).—OF.

enfermerie, infirmarie, infirmerie; Church Lat. *infirmaria*, a place for the infirm (Ducange).

fermour, *sb.* farmer, steward, CM, MD; **fermer**, Cath. See **ferme**[3].

fern[1], *sb.* fern, C2; **ferene**, *dat.*, S2. *Phr.*: **aisschen of ferne**, fern ashes, MD. *Comb.*: **fern-asshen**, fern ashes, C2.—AS. *fearn* (Voc.): OHG. *farn*.

fern[2], *adj.* and *adv.* old, long ago, C2, PP; **ferne**, CM; **furn**, MD. *Comb.*: **fern-ȝeres**, past years; **fern yere**, formerly, PP.—AS. *fyrn* (see Sievers); cf. OS. *furn, forn, fern*, Goth. *fairnis*.

ferreden, *sb.* company, S; **uerade**, S. See **ȝefered**.

ferren, *adj.* and *adv.* far, distant, MD; **feren**, S; **verrenne**, *pl.*, S; **ferne**, C.—AS. *feorran*, from afar. See **fer**[2].

ferret-silke, *sb.* coarse silk, S3, Florio.—It. *fioretti*, from *fióre*, flower. Cf. **floret-silk**.

fers, *adj.* fierce, brave, Prompt., C, PP; **fiers**, S2, C2, C3; **fierse**, PP.—OF. *fers, fiers* (Roland); Lat. *ferus*.

fersly, *adv.* fiercely, PP, B.

fersnesse, *sb.* fierceness, W2, PP; **feers-nesse**, W, W2.

ferst, *adj.* and *adv.* *superl.* first, S, S2, PP; **uerst**, S2; **furst**, S, S2, P; **forst**, S.—AS. *fyrst*: OHG. *furisto*. Superlative of **fore**.

fertre, *sb.* litter, bier, shrine, MD; **feertyr**, *feretrum*, Prompt.—OF. *fertere, fiertre*; Lat. *feretrum*; Gr. φέρετρον.

fertren, *v.* to place in a shrine; **fertered**, *pt. s.*, S2.

ferthe, *ord.* fourth, C3, PP; **fierthe**, PP, S; **feorthe**, PP, S; **feurthe**, S2; **ferth**, S2; **fierth**, S2; **ueorð**, S.—AS. *féorða*. See **foure**.

ferthyng, *sb.* farthing, S2, PP; **ferthing**, PP. *Comb.*: **ferþinges nok**, a farthing piece, S2 (p. 301); **ferþyng noke**, S2.—AS. *féorðung*.

fesaunt, *sb.* pheasant, S3; **fesant**, Voc.; **fes-auntes**, *pl.*, PP; **fesauns**, S2.—OF. *faisan*; Lat. *phasianum* (acc.); Gr. φασιανός.

fesien, *v.* to drive away, MD; **fesyn**, Prompt., HD; **veize**, DG; **pheeze**, ND, Sh.; **feazed**, *pp.*, ND.—AS. *fésian*, for *fýsian*, to drive away, see Sievers, 154. See **fusen**.

fest[1], *adj.* and *v.*; see **fast, fasten**[1].

fest[2], *sb.* fist, C3; see **fust**.

feste, *sb.* feast, S, PP, C2, C3; **fest**, S3; **festes**, *pl.*, S2.—AF. *feste*; Lat. *festa*.

festeien, *v.* to feast, to entertain, MD; **festeyinge**, *pr. p.*, C2.—OF. *festeier, festoier*; Late Lat. **festicare*; cf. Prov. *festegar*.

festen, *sb.* fasting, S; see **fasten**[2].

festlich, *adj.* festive, fond of feasts, C2. See **feste**.

festnen, *v.* to fasten, S; **festnin**, S; **fæstned**, *pp.*, S; **i-uestned**, S; **festnyd**, PP.—AS. *fæstnian*.

fet[1], *sb.* deed, PP; **feet**, C2, PP; **fait**, S2; **faite**, PP.—OF. *fet, fait*; Lat. *factum*.

fet[2], *adj.* fat, S; see **fat**[2].

fet[3], *sb. pl.*, feet, S; see **foot**.

fetel, *sb.* vessel, S2; **vetles**, MD; **fetles**, MD; *pl.*, S.—AS. *fætels*, pl. *fætelsas* (Voc.). See **fat**[2].

feter, *sb.* fetter, MD; **fetyr**, *compes*, Prompt.; **feteres**, *pl.*, G.—AS. *fetor*.

feteren, *v.* to fetter, MD, G; **fettren**, P; **y-fetered**, *pp.*, G; **fettred**, C2; **ifetered**, G.—AS. *(ge)feterian*.

fetis, *adj.* well-made, neat, handsome, MD, S2; **fetys**, S2, C3, C; **fetyce**, Prompt.—OF. *faitis* (f. *-ice*); Lat. *factitium*. See **fet**[1].

fetisliche, *adv.* neatly, S2, PP; **fetysly**, C.

fetten, *v.* to fetch, MD, S2, S3; **fete**, MD, S; **fetteth**, *imp. pl.*, G; **fette**, *pt. s.* S, C2, C3; **uette**, MD; **fatte**, MD; **uatte**, MD; **fet**, S3; **fetten**, *pl.*, S2, P; **y-fet**, *pp.*, C2; **fet**, MD, S2, C2; **fette**, *pl.*, MD.—AS. *fetian* (Grein). Cf. **fecchen**.

fettle[1], *sb.* order, condition. *Phr.*: **in good fettle**, JD, HD.

fettle[2], *sb.* girdle, belt, horse-girth, JD. Cf. Icel. *fetill*, OHG. *fezil*.

fettlen, *v.* to bind, fit, make ready, set in order, MD; **fettle**, to tie up, put in order, JD; **fetyl**, JD; **fettled**, *pp.*, S2.

feth, *sb.* faith, S3: **feðli**, *adv.* faithfully, S2; see **feiþ, feiþliche**.

fether, *sb.* feather, C2; **fyþer**, S2; **fedyr**, Prompt.; **feðres**, *pl.*, S; **fetheris**, wings, W2; **fedres**, MD.—AS. *feðer*.

feðer-foted, *adj.* four-footed, S.—Cf. AS. *fiðer-fóte*. With AS. *fiðer* cf. Goth. *fidwor*. See **foure**.

feðer-home, *sb.* plumage, MD; **fedr-amme**, S3.—AS. *feðer-hama*; cf. OS. *feðer-hamo*, Icel. *fjaðrhamr*, see Grimm, Teut. M., p. 327. See **feþer**.

feute, *sb.* track, scent, S2, MD; **fewte**, *vestigium*, Prompt.; **fute**, odour, Prompt.; **foute**, S. *Comb.*: **foote-saunte**, scent, DG.

feuer, *sb.* fever, PP; **feuere**, PP; **feure**, PP; **fyueris**, *pl.*, W.—AF. *fevre*; Lat. *febrem*.

Feuerere, *sb.* February, HD; **Feuerel**, HD; **Feuirȝer**, S3; **Feuerȝere**, HD (s.v. *fraiste*).—OF. *fevrier*; Late Lat. **febrarium*; Lat. *februarium (mensem)*.

fewe, *adj. pl.* few, S, PP; **feaw**, S2; **veaw**, S2; **fawe**, S; **feawe**, S; **vewe**, S2; **fæu**, S; **fo**, S; **fon**, S2; **fa**, H (Ps. 101. 25); **foner**, *comp.*, S2.—AS. *féawe*; cf. Goth. *faws*.

fewnyng, *sb.* thrusting, S3. See **foynen**.

78

fewte, *sb.* fealty, S3, Prompt., HD; **feute**, MD.—AF. *feaute*, *fealte*; Lat. *fidelitatem*.

fey; see **feiþ**.

feydom, *sb.* the state of being near death, or that conduct which is supposed to indicate it, JD. See **feye**.

feye, *adj.* dead, doomed to death, feeble, S, S2, MD; **fey**, JD, HD; **fay**, MD; **fæie**, *pl.* dead, S, MD; **fæiȝe**, MD.—AS. *fége*; cf. Icel. *feigr*; see CV.

feyn, *adj.* fain, S2; see **fayn**[2].

feynen, *v.* to feign, C2, C3, PP; **feine**, Prompt., MD; **feyneden**, *pt. pl.*, S2; **fayneden**, S3; **y-feyned**, *pp.*, C2.—AF. *feindre* (pr. p. *feignant*); Lat. *fingere*.

feynt, *adj.* feigned, false, also weak, faint, MD, Prompt.; **faint**, MD; **feynte**, *pl.*, PP.—OF. *feint*, pp. of *feindre*.

feynten, *v.* to be weak, MD, Prompt.

feynting, *sb.* fainting, failing, C2.

feyntise, *sb.* deceit, hypocrisy, also weakness, cowardice, MD, S2, P; **fayntis**, H; **fayntise**, S3.

feyre, *sb.* fair, PP; **faire**, P; **fayre**, PP; **feyres**, *pl.*, P. *Phr.*: **this feire is i-doon**, this fair is done, everything is sold, there is no more business to be done, G.—OF. *feire* (mod. *foire*); Late Lat. *feria*, a fair; from Lat. *feriae*, holidays.

feyrie, *sb.* fairy origin, S2; see **fayerye**.

feȝen, *v.* to join, MD; **veien**, MD; **i-ueied**, *pp.*, S.—AS. *fégan*; cf. OHG. *fuagen* (Otfrid). See **foȝ**.

ficchen, *v.* to fix, MD; **fitchid**, *pp.*, W, W2; **fichyt**, B.—OF. *ficher* (Ps. 31. 4); Late Lat. **figicare*, from Lat. *figere*, to fix, see Diez (s.v. *ficcare*).

fieble, *adj.* feeble, C2, P; see **feble**.

field, *sb.* field, S2; see **feld**.

field-wode, *sb.* name of a plant, S2.

field-wort, *sb.* gentian, HD; **feldwort**, *herba luminaria*, Alph.

fiers, *adj.* fierce, S2, C2, C3; **fierse**, PP; see **fers**.

fierðe, *ord.* fourth, S, P; see **ferþe**.

fife, *num.* five, S; **fyf**, PP, C2; **fiff**, B; **fiffe**, B; **uiue**, S; **fyue**, S2, PP; **fif**, PP.—AS. *fíf*: Goth. *fimf*, see Sievers, 185.

fifetende, *ord.* fifteenth, S2.

fif-fald, five-fold, MD; **fif-folde**, S.

fiff-sum, *adj.* five in all, B.

fifte, *ord.* fifth, S; **fifþe**, S; **fyfte**, PP.—AS. *fífta*.

fifte-siðe, *adv.* fifthly, S.

fighten, *v.* to fight, PP; **fiȝte**, S; **vyȝte**, S2; **fihten**, PP, S2; **feȝtande**, *pr. p.*, S2; **feaht**, *pt. s.*, MD; **faht**, MD; **feht**, MD; **fauht**, PP; **faught**, MD, C2; **fuhten**, *pl.*, S; **fuȝten**, S; **fouhten**, PP; **fouȝten**, PP; **i-fouhte**, *pp.*,

PP; **y-fouȝte**, PP; **foughten**, C; **fouȝten**, PP.—AS. *feohtan*, pr. s. *fiht*, pt. *feaht* (pl. *fuhton*), pp. *fohten*; cf. OHG. *fehtan* (Otfrid).

figure, *sb.* figure, MD, C2; **figour**, MD; **uigour**, MD; **figures** (of speech), C2.—AF. *figure*; Lat. *figura*.

figurie, *sb.* figured work, S3.

fihten, *v.* to fight, S2, PP; see **fighten**.

fiht-lac, *sb.* fighting, S.—AS. *feoht-lác*.

fikel, *adj.* fickle, treacherous, MD; **fikil**, H (Ps. 39. 21); **fykil**, G; **fickle**, fidgety, S3.—AS. *ficol*, inconstant.

fiken, *v.* to be fidgety, to go about idly, MD, HD; to flatter, play the hypocrite, deceive, MD.—Cf. AS. *be-fician*, to deceive, to go round.

fil, *pt. s.* fell, C2, PP; **fyl**, S2; see **fallen**.

file, *sb.* concubine, P; **fyle**, HD.—OF. *fille*, *filie*, daughter, wench; Lat. *filia*.

fille, *sb.* wild thyme, S2, MD; *serpillum*, Voc.; **fill**, rest-harrow, HD. *Phr.*: **not worth a fille**, MD.—AS. *fille*.

filstnien, *v.* to help; **filstnede**, *pt. s.*, S.—AS. See **fulst**.

filtz, *sb.* son, PP; **fitz**, PP; **fiz**, PP.—AF. *fiz* (*fitz*); OF. *filz*, *fils*; Lat. *filius*.

filthe, *sb.* filth, foulness, MD; **fuðle**, S.—AS. *fýlðu*. See **foul**[2].

filthehed, *sb.* dirtiness, W.

finden, *v.* to find, S; **fynden**, S; **vinden**, S; **vynde**, S; **fynt**, *pr. s.*, C3; **fint**, *pl.*, S; **fand**, *pt. s.*, S, S2, S3; **fant**, S; **fond**, S, S2, G, C2; **fonde**, S2; **font**, S2; **vond**, S2; **foond**, C2, W; **funden**, *pl.*, S; **funde**, S; **fonden**, S; **fand**, S2; **fonde**, C2; **founden**, S2; **i-funde**, *pp.*, S; **ifounde**, S; **hi-funde**, S; **founde**, C2; **funden**, S2; **funding**, S3.—AS. *findan*, *pt. fand* (pl. *fundon*), pp. *funden*.

findiȝ, *adj.* heavy, firm, compact, weighty, S, MD; **findy**, JD; **fundie**, MD.—AS. *findig*, heavy.

fine, *sb.* end, S3; **fyn**, S2, S3, C2, G.—OF. *fin*; Lat. *finem*.

finen, *v.* to end, S, MD; **fynde**, *1 pr. s.*, S3; **fon**, *pt. s.*, MD, S2; **fan**, MD; **fyned**, S2.—OF. *finer* for *finir*; Lat. *finire*.

firmentie, *sb.* frumenty, furmety, S3; see **frumentee**.

firsin, *v.* to put far away, S; **firsen**, S; **fersien**, MD; **fursen**, MD.—AS. *fyrsian*. See **fer**[2].

first, *sb.*; see **frest**.

fisch, *sb.* fish, S, W2; **fiss**, S; **fis**, S; **fisses**, *pl.*, S; **fysses**, S; **fissches**, S2; **fises**, S2; **fischis**, W2. *Comb.*: **fis-cynn**, fish-kind, S.—AS. *fisc*; cf. Lat. *piscis*; OIr. *iasc*.

fischen, *v.* to fish, W; **fissen**, S.

fischere, *sb.* fisher, W; **fissere**, S.

fischinge, *sb.* fishing, MD; **fissing**, S.

flex-hoppe

fisike, *sb.* natural science, art of healing, MD; **phisique**, MD; **phisik**, MD; **phesyk**, MD; **fisyk**, S2.—OF. *fisique*; Lat. *physica* (*ars*); from Gr. φυσικός.

fitz; see **filtz**.

fiðele, *sb.* fiddle, MD, C, PP; **fidylle**, *vidula*, *vidella*, *viella*, Cath.; **fythele**, *vitula*, Voc.; **fydyll**, *viella*, Prompt.; **vythule**, Voc.; **fydelys**, *pl.*, MD.—Etym. doubtful, probably connected with Low Lat. *vidula*, 'a vythule' (Voc.); cf. OF. *vïele*, a viol.

fiðelen, *v.* to play on the fiddle, PP; **vydele**, Voc.—Cf. Low Lat. *vidulare* (Voc.).

fitheler, *sb.* fiddler, PP; **vythulare**, Voc.—Cf. Low Lat. *vidularius* (Voc.).

fiz; see **filtz**.

flake, *sb.* thin slice, piece torn off. SkD; **flackes**, *pl.*, S3 (12. 2); **flockes**, S3.—Cf. Norw. *flak*, an ice-floe.

flan, *sb.* arrow, S, MD; **flon**, MD; **flone**, MD; **flonne**, *pl.*, HD; **flone**, HD; **flonez**, MD.—AS. *flán*; cf. Icel. *fleinn*. Cf. **flo**.

flanckring, *adj.* sparkling, HD.

flanke, *sb.* spark, MD; see **flaunke**.

flanker, *v.* to sparkle, HD.

flappe, *sb.* a blow, Prompt., Palsg.—Cf. Du. *flap*, a blow.

flappen, *v.* to flap, slap, clap, MD; **flapten**, *pt. pl.*, P.—Cf. Du. *flappen*, to flap.

flat, *v.* to flatter, S3.—OF. *flater*.

flateren, *v.* to flatter, PP.

flatlyngis, *adv.* flat, B.

flatour, *sb.* flatterer, C, MD; **ulatours**, *pl.*, MD.—OF. *flateör*; Prov. *flatador*.

flatten, *v.* to dash, cast quickly (water); **flatte**, pt. s., P; **flattide**, PP.—OF. *flatir*, to dash, throw down.

flaucht, *sb.* flake, flash, S3 (s.v. *fyre*); **flaghte**, flake, piece of turf, Cath. *Phr.*: **flaghte of snawe**, flake of snow, Cath.; **flyghte of snawe**, Cath.; **flaught of fire**, flash of lightning, JD. See **flawe**.

flaumbe, *sb.* flame, PP; **flambe**, CM; **flamme**, PP; **flawme**, Prompt.; **flaume**, PP; **flambes**, *pl.* C2, C3.—AF. *flambe*, OF. *flamme*; Lat. *flamma*.

flaun, *sb.* a kind of custard, HD; **flawn**, ND, SkD (p. 805); **flaunes**, *pl.*, S.—OF. *flaon* (mod. *flan*): Low Lat. *fladonem* (*flatonem*); cf. OHG. *flado*; see Ducange (Supplement).

flaunke, *sb.* spark of fire, S2; **flonke**, PP; **flunke**, MD; **flaunkes**, *pl.*, S2.—Cf. G. *flunkern*, to sparkle, Du. *flonkeren*.

flaunt-a-flaunt, *adv.* displayed in a showy manner, S3, SkD.

flawe, *sb.* flake; *in phr.*: **flawes of fyre**, flakes of fire, SkD.—Icel. *flaga*, a slab of stone. Cf. **flaucht**.

flay, *v.* to put to flight, to scare, S2; see **fleyen**.

flayle, *sb.* flail, PP; **fle33l**, S; **flaill**, B; **flayles**, *pl.*, PP; **fleiles**, PP.—OF. *flaël* Lat. *flagellum*; hence OHG. *flegil*.

fleck, *sb.* spot, blot, stain, RD.—Icel. *flekkr*; cf. OHG. *fleccho*.

flecked, *adj.* speckled, spotted, PP; **flekked**, C3, PP, Cath., MD.

flee, *sb.* flea, Prompt.; **fle**, MD; **fleen**, *pl.*, C3; **flen**, MD; **flees**, MD.—AS. *fléo* (Voc.).

fleen, *v.* to fly, flee, C2, PP; **fleon**, S; **fleo**, S, S2; **flen**, C; **fle**, S, S2, G; **vle**, S2; **fligh- and**, *pr. p.*, S2; **fli3st**, 2 *pr. s.*, S; **flegeð**, *pr. s.*, S; **fleð**, S; **flyþ**, S2; **fli3t**, S; **fleoð**, *pl.*, S; **fleen**, C2; **flen**, PP; **fleh**, *pt. s.*, S; **flegh**, S2, PP; **fleih**, S2, PP; **flaw**, S3; **fley**, C2, G, W; **flei3**, P, W; **fleigh**, C; **flugen**, *pl.*, S; **flowen**, S2, C, P; **flowe**, S2; **flowen**, *pp.*, MD; **flowe**, G. Weak forms: **fledde**, *pt. s.*, C2, PP; **fled**, *pp.*, MD.—AS. *fléogan*, *fléon*, pt. *fléah* (pl. *flugon*), pp. *flogen*.

flees, *sb.* fleece, S2, PP; **flus**, PP; **fleis**, PP; **fleose**, *dat.*, MD; **fleyce**, S3.—AS. *fléos* (*flýs*); cf. G. *vlies*.

fleich, *v.* to flatter, JD; **flechand**, *pr. p.*, B; **fleeching**, B; **fleichit**, *pp.*, S3.—OF. *flechir*, to bend, to move any one.

flem, *sb.* flight, MD; **ulem**, MD; **fleam**, Voc.; **fleme**, *dat.*, MD.—AS. *fléam*; cf. Icel. *flaumr* a flowing, OHG. *floum* (Otfrid).

fleme, *sb.* fugitive, S, S2.—AS. *fléma*, and *flýma* (Voc.).

flemen, *v.* to put to flight, MD, S2; **flemed**, *pt. s.*, S3; **flemden**, *pl.*, S; **flemed**, *pp.*, C3; **flemit**, S3.—AS. *fléman*, *flýman*.

flemer, *sb.* banisher, S2, C3.

flen, *v.* to flay, S; **fle**, S; **flo**, S; **flouh**, *pt. s.*, S; **ulo3en**, *pl.*, MD; **flayn**, *pp.*, MD; **flean**, HD.—AS. *flean*, pt. *flóh*, pp. *flagen*.

flesch, *sb.* flesh, PP; **flesc**, S; **fleis**, S, S2; **fleys**, PP; **fles**, S; **fleisch**, W; **fleysh**, S2; **fleissh**, S2; **flessh**, S, PP; **flesce**, *dat.*, S, W2.—AS. *flǽsc*; cf. OHG. *fleisc* (Otfrid).

flesche-flye, *sb.* flesh-fly, Prompt.; **fleisch-flie**, MD, W2 (Ps. 77. 45 and 104. 31).

fleschlich, *adj.* fleshly, S, PP; **flesliche**, *adv.* materially, S.

fleten, *v.* to float, swim, PP, B, S, S3, C, W; to flow, W2; **fleit**, S3; **fleyt**, S3; **fletes**, *pr. s.*, S2; **fleet**, S2, C3; **fleteth**, C3; **flet**, PP; **fleet**, *pt. s.*, MD; **fluten**, *pl.*, MD; **floten**, MD; **flote**, S2; **flette**, S2; **fletiden**, W2.—AS. *fléotan*, pt. *fléat* (pl. *fluton*), pp. *floten*.

flex, *sb.* flax, C, P, Voc.; **flax**, Prompt., PP.—AS. *fleax*.

flex-hoppe, *sb. linodium*, Voc.

fleyen, *v.* to put to flight, to scare away, frighten; **fley**, JD, S3; **flaien**, MD; **flay**, S2; **flayed**, *pp.*, S2; **fleyit**, B.—Cf. Icel. *fleyja*, to cause to fly, throw.

flicht, *sb.* flight, PP, B; **fliht**, MD; **fliȝt**, S; **fluht**, S.—AS. *flyht*: OHG. *fluht* (Tatian). See **fleen**.

flit, *sb.* strife, MD; **flyt**, S2.

fliten, *v.* to strive, contend, quarrel, PP, HD, H; **flytin**, Prompt.; **flitis**, *pr. s.*, scolds, H; **flytande**, *pr. p.*, S2; **flote**, *pt. s.*, MD; **fliten**, *pp.*, MD.—AS. *flītan*, pt. *flát* (pl. *fliton*), pp. *fliten*.

fliting, *sb.* quarrelling, scolding, PP; **flytynge**, H.

flo, *sb.* arrow, CM, MD; **fla**, MD; **flon**, *pl.*, MD, S2; **floon**, G; **flan**, MD; **flo**, MD.—AS. *flá* (Voc.). Cf. **flan**.

floc, *sb.* a gathering of men, beasts, birds, MD; **flocke** (of swine), W (Mt. 8. 30); **flockes**, *pl.*, S.—AS. *flocc.*

flocke, *v. tr.* and *intr.* to collect, gather, MD, S3.

floc-mele, *adv.* in crowds, MD; **flokmele**, C2.—AS. *flocmélum.*

flod, *sb.* flood, sea, S, S2, PP; **flood**, C2, W; **flode**, PP; **flodes**, *pl.*, PP; **fludis**, S3.—AS. *flód.*

flor, *sb.* floor, MD, S2; **flore**, *dat.*, S, PP.—AS. *flór.*

floret-silk, *sb.* coarse silk, Cotg.; **flurt-silk**, figured silk, HD.—OF. *fleuret* (Cotg.); cf. G. *florett.*—Cf. **ferret-silke**.

florin, *sb.* florin, originally the name of a coin stamped with the emblem of a lily, MD, C3; **floreines**, *pl.*, P.—OF. *florin* (Cotg.).

florischen, *v.* to flourish, also to cause to flourish, to make to prosper, to brandish, flourish a weapon, MD; **floryschyn**, to make flourishes in illuminating books, Prompt.; **fluricheþ**, *pr. s.*, adorns, decorates, S3.—OF. *floriss-* base of pr. p. of *florir*; Lat. *florere*; see Constans.

flot, *sb.* fat, scum, S2, JD.—Icel. *flot.*

flote[1], *sb.* a fleet, B; **flot**, B.—Icel. *floti.* See **fleten**.

flote[2], *sb.* company, multitude, S, MD.—OF. *flote* (*flotte* in Cotg.); Lat. *fluctum.*

flote[3], **floten**; see **fleten**.

floteren, *v.* to fluctuate, flutter, PP.—OF. *floter* (+ suffix -*er*); Lat. *fluctuare*; see Constans.

flotering, *sb.* restless motion, W2.

flour, *sb.* flower, C2, C3; **flur**, S; **floures**, *pl.*, youthful powers, S2.—AF. *flur*; Lat. *florem.*

flour-dammes, *sb.* ladies' flower, perhaps Dame's violet or Dame-wort, *Hesperis matronalis* (Britten's Plant-names; Mr Small suggests 'damask rose', S3.

floure-de-lice, *sb.* fleur-de-lis, S2; **flourde-lyss**, S3; **flour-de-lycis**, *pl.*, S3.—OF. *flor de lis* (Bartsch, 193. 2).

flouren, *v.* to flower, flourish, PP, C2, W2.—OF. *florir.*—Cf. **florischen**.

flowe, **flowen**; see **fleen**.

flowen, *v.* to flow, S, PP; **flowe**, to abound, W2; **flohþ**, *pr. s.*, S; **floȝed**, *pt. s.*, S2.—AS. *flówan*, pt. *fléow*, pp. *flówen.*

flowing, *sb.* flood, W2.

flowte, *sb.* pipe, *cambucus*, Prompt.; **floyte**, MD.—OF. *flaute*, It. *flauto.*

flowten, *v.* to blow on a wind instrument, MD; **flowtyn**, *calamiso*, *flo*, Prompt.; **floytynge**, *pr. p.*, C.—OF. *flaüter*; Late Lat. **flatuare* from Lat. *flatus*; see Constans.

flowtour, *sb.*, fluter, piper, CM.

flum, *sb.* river, MD; flow, flood, JD. Comb.: **Flum Jurdan**, river Jordan, MD; **flum iurdon**, S; **flom Jordan**, MD, W; **fleme Jordon**, MD.—OF. *flum*; Lat. *flumen* (cf. Vulg., Mk. 1. 5).

flye, *sb.* fly, C3, PP; **fliȝe**, MD; **fleȝe**, MD; **fle**, S3.—AS. *fléoge* (*flýge*). See **fleen**.

flytten, *v. tr.* and *intr.* to remove, to depart, MD, S3, PP; **flutten**, MD; **flitten**, MD, PP; **flute**, *imp. s.*, S; **vlutten**, to subsist, support oneself, S.—Icel. *flytja*, to carry, remove, support, *flytjask* (reflex.), to remove oneself, to flit, also, to support oneself.

fnast, *sb.* breath, S.—AS. *fnæst.*

fnasten, *v.* to breathe, to breathe hard, MD, S, HD.—Cf. OHG. *fnastón*, 'anhelare'.

fnesen, *v.* to breathe hard, to sneeze; **fneseth**, *pr. s.*, puffs, snorts, C3.—AS. *fnéosan.*

fnesynge, *sb.* snorting, Voc.; **fnesynge** (= Lat. *sternutatio*), W2 (Job 41. 9).—AS. *fnéosung* (Voc.).

fo, *adj.* few, S; see **fewe**.

foaȝe, *adj.* spotted, S; see **foh**.

fodder, *sb.* food for cattle, MD; **foddre**, *dat.*, S.—AS. *fódor*, *foddor.*

fode[1], *sb.* food, S, S2, MD; **uode**, S; **food**, MD; **fude**, MD.—AS. *fóda.*

fode[2], *sb.* child, lad, person, *alumnus*, S, S2, PP, HD, MD.

foh, *adj.* spotted, S, S2; **fou**, S; **faȝe**, *pl.*, S; **foaȝe**, S.—AS. *fáh*; cf. Goth. *faihus*, Gr. ποικίλος.

foine, *sb.* beech-marten, Cotg. (s.v. *fouïnne*); **foyne**, PP; **foynȝee**, S3; **fooyne**, the fur of the marten, Prompt.; **foyns**, *pl.*, fur, MD, HD.—OF. *foine*, *faine*, *faine*, the beech-marten, also *faine*, the fruit of the beech tree; Late Lat. *fagina*, 'mustela', also 'glans fagi' (Ducange); from Lat. *faginus*, from *fagus.*

foison, *sb.* abundance, plenty, might, MD, Sh., HD; **foyson**, S2, C3; **foysyn**, S2; **foy-**

soun, B; **fusioune**, B.—OF. *foison, fuison*; Lat. *fusionem*.

folc, *sb.* folk, people, S, S2, W2, PP; **uolk**, MD; **folk**, PP; **uolkes**, *gen.*, S; **folkene**, *gen. pl.*, S; **folken**, S2.—AS. *folc*.

folc-king, *sb.* the king of the people, MD; **folc-kinge**, *dat.*, S.

folde[1], *sb.* earth, ground, the world, S2, MD, HD, P.—AS. *folde*, OS. *folda*.

folde[2], *sb.* a fold, plait, MD, PP. *Phr.*: **in monie volde**, in manifold (ways), S.

folden, *v.* to fold, shut, embrace, PP; **falt**, *pr. s.*, S; **falde**, MD; **folde**, *pt. s.*, S3; **folden**, *pp.*, S2, PP.—AS. *fealdan*, pt. *féold*, pp. *fealden*. {The words *falt mi tunge* mean 'my tongue gives way'. For the various meanings of this verb **folden**, see MD (ii. 68).}

fole[1], *sb.* foal, S, PP; **foles**, *pl.*, PP; **folus**, P.—AS. *fola*: Goth. *fula*; cf. Lat. *pullus*; see Brugmann, § 208.

fole[2], *adj.* and *sb.* foolish, lustful, a fool, MD, S2; **foole**, S3; **foule**, H; **fule**, S2; **fool**, C2; **foles**, *pl.*, S2, S3, P.—AF. *fol*.

folgen; see **folwen**.

folie, *sb.* folly, S2, PP; **folye**, S, C2, PP; **folies**, *pl.*, S.—AF. *folie*.

folily, *adv.* foolishly, C3; **folili**, W.

follich, *adj.* foolish, MD; **foly**, S2; **folliche**, *adv.*, S.

fol-marde, *sb.* polecat, S2; see **fulmard**.

folte, *adj.* foolish, Prompt., Cath.; **folett**, Prompt.—OF. *folet* (Bartsch). See **fole**[2].

folten, *v.* to behave foolishly, MD, Prompt.; **folted**, *pp.* crazed, S2.

foltheed, *sb.* folly, PP.

foltische, *adj.* foolish, W; **foltish**, HD.

foltren, *v.* to totter, S3; see **faltren**.

foltrye, *sb.* foolishness, Prompt.

folwen, *v.* to follow, C2, C3, PP; **folȝen**, MD, S; **folewe**, S2, PP; **folgen**, S; **follȝhenn**, S; **folhin**, S; **fallow**, S2; **filghe**, S2; **foluand**, *pr. p.*, S2; **folheð**, *pr. s.*, S; **folhes**, S; **foleweð**, S; **feleweð**, S; **fulwes**, S2; **folgede**, *pt. s.*, MD; **folwede**, PP; **folgeden**, *pl.*, S; **folecheden**, S; **folud**, S2; **ȝe-folged**, *pp.*, S; **i-folewed**, PP; **y-folowed**, PP.—AS. *folgian* (*fylgean*); cf. OHG. *folgên* (Otfrid).

fon[1], *v.* to seize, grasp, take, receive, S, S2; **fo on**, *1 pr. pl. subj.*, begin, S; **feng**, *pt. s.* began, MD; **feng on**, S; **veng**, S2; **feng**, *pl.*, S2.—AS. *fôn*, 1 pr. s. *fô*, pt. *feng*, pp. *fongen*.

fon[2], *adj.* few, S2; **foner**, *comp.* fewer, S2; see **fewe**.

fond; see **fonnen**.

fongen, *v.* to take, receive, PP, S, S2, S3; **fangen**, PP; **fang**, S2; see **fon**[1].

fonger, *sb.* receiver, S2.

fo-man, *sb.* foeman, PP; **fomon**, S2; **famen**, *pl.*, S, S2; **vamen**, S. See **foo**.

fonne, *adj.* and *sb.* foolish, a fool, MD; **fone**, HD; **fon**, MD, H, HD.—Cf. Swed. *fåne*, a fool.

fonnen, *v.* to act foolishly, MD; **fonned**, *pp.* as *adj.* foolish, fond, W, HD; **fond**, S3, HD. See **fonne**.

font, *sb.* font, PP; **fount**, S2, PP; **founȝt**, S2. *Comb.*: **funt-fat**, font-vessel, S; **fant-ston**, font-stone, S; **fontstoon**, C3; **fun-ston**, HD.—Church Lat. *fontem*.

foo, *adj.* and *sb.*, hostile, guilty, a foe, PP, C2; **fo**, PP, S2; **uo**, S2; **fa**, S; **faa**, S2; **foon**, *pl.*, S3, C2, G, PP; **fon**, PP, S2; **fan**, S; **uan**, S; **foin**, HD; **foyn**, MD; **fo**, S; **foos**, PP, C2; **faas**, S2; **faes**, S2; **fais**, S2; **fays**, S3; **fayis**, S2.—AS. *fáh*, pl. *fá*; cf. Goth. *fihan*, to hate; see Brugmann, § 458. Cf. **feend**.

foole, *sb.* fool, S3; **fool**, PP. *Comb.*: **fool sage**, licensed jester, PP; **foole large**, foolishly liberal, S3; **foole largely**, S3; see **fole**[2].

foom, *sb.* foam, C3, MD; **fame**, HD; **fom**, S2, MD; **fome**, MD, C3; **faym**, S3.—AS. *fám*; cf. MHG. *feim*.

foot, *sb.* foot, also, a measure, S2, C3, HD; **fot**, S, S2; **fut**, B; **foote**, PP; **fote**, PP; **vote**, *dat.*, S; **fute**, B; **fet**, *pl.*, S; **fett**, S; **vet**, S. *Comb.*: **foothot**, instantly, S2, C3; **fote hote**, HD; **futhate**, **futhat**, B.—AS. *fôt*: Goth. *fôtus*.

foot-man, *sb.* foot-soldier, MD, HD; **fotman**, MD; **votmen**, *pl.*, S2.

foot-stappe, *sb.* footstep, Prompt.; **fetsteppes**, *pl.*, S.

for-[1], *prefix*, having generally the sense of 'loss' or 'destruction'. Often it is merely intensive, though generally in a bad sense.—AS. *for-*, Icel. *for-, fyrir-*, OHG. *for-* (Tatian), *fir-* (Otfrid), G. *ver-*, Goth. *fra-, fair-*.

for-[2], *prefix*, for, in the place of; see **for**[1] (*prep.*).

for-[3], *prefix*, standing for AS. *fore*, before; see **fore**.

for-[4], *prefix*, standing for OF. *for-*; Lat. *foris*, outside; cf. F. *hors*, from Lat. *foras*.

for[1], *prep.* for, by, for fear of, in spite of, in the place of, for the sake of, S, S2, PP; **forr**, S; **fore**, S, PP; **uor**, S.

for[2], *conj.* because, in order that, whether, S, S3, PP. *Comb.*: **for outen**, without, besides, S2, B; **for owtyn**, JD; **for out**, B; **for te**, for to, in order to, S, PP; **vor te**, S, S2; **for to**, PP; **vor to**, S2; **for þan þe**, because that, S; **for-þon**, S; **vorþan**, therefore, S; **for þat þe**, because that, S; **for þet**, for that reason, S; **for þi** for that cause, S, S2, PP; **uorði**, S; **for-þe**, S; **for-þy**, S2, PP;

forr-þi, because, S; **for till**, for to, S3; **for-whi**, wherefore, S2, PP; because, S3; **for-quhy**, S3; **for-why**, C3, PP.

for[3], *adv.* far, S; see **fer**[2].

for[4], *pt. s.* fared, S, S2; see **faren**.

forage, *sb.* forage, food, C2.—OF. *forrage*, from *forre*; Low Lat. *fodrum*, from a Teutonic source, cf. AS. *fôdor*. See **fodder**.

forager, *sb.* forager, messenger, PP. Cf. **forrayour**.

for-arnen, *v.* to cause to run about, to ride about; **uorarnd**, *pt. s.*, S2.—Cf. AS. *ærnan* (v. tr.), pt. *ærnde*, pp. *ærned*. (**for-**[1].)

for-bathde, *pp. pl.* bathed deep, S3. (**for-**[1].)

for-beden, *v.* to forbid, S, Prompt., S2, PP; **forbeode**, PP; **forbet**, *pr. s.*, S; **forbed**, S; **forbadde**, *pt. s.*, PP; **forbad**, MD; **uorbed**, S2; **fforbode**, *pl.*, MD; **forbude**, *subj.*, S; **forboden**, *pp.*, H, S3, P; **forbode**, S, PP; **forbedun**, W.—AS. *for-béodan*, pt. *-béad* (pl. *-budon*), pp. *-boden*. (**for-**[1].)

for-beren, *v.* to forbear, S, C, PP; **uorberen**, S; **forbar**, *pt. s.*, PP; **forbare**, P; **forbaren**, *pl.*, S; **forbore**, *pp.*, MD.—AS. *for-beran*, pt. *-bær* (pl. *-béron*), pp. *-boren*. (**for-**[1].)

for-bernen, *v. intr.* to burn up, to be destroyed by fire, S; **forbrenne**, MD; **uorbarnde**, *pt. s.*, MD; **forbrende**, MD; **for-bernen**, *v. tr.* to burn up, MD; **for-bærnen**, S; **forbearne**, S; **forbrenne**, PP; **forbrende**, *pt. s.*, PP, MD; **vorbarnd**, *pp.*, S2; **uorbernd**, S2, MD.—AS. *for-byrnan* (v. intr.), pt. *-barn* (pl. *-burnon*), pp. *-burnen*, also, *for-bærnan* (v. tr.), pt. *-bærnde*, pp. *-bærned*. (**for-**[1].)

for-bisne, *sb.* example, S; **uorbysne**, parable, S2; **forbusne**, PP.—AS. *fore-bysn*. (**for-**[3].)

for-blak, *adj.* very black, C. (**for-**[1].)

for-bode, *sb.* forbidding, S, P; **forbod**, S; **forbot**, S. *Phr.*: **Lordes forbode**, it is the Lord's forbidding, PP; **Goddes forbode**, PP; **Godys forbode**, S3.—AS. *forbod*. (**for-**[1].)

force, *sb.* force; **forss**, B; **fors**, B; **forse**, matter, consequence, PP. *Phr.*: **no forse**, it matters not, PP; **no fors**, S2, C2; **no force**, ND, HD, S3 (20b, 87); **to give no force**, not to care, HD, Palsg.; **make no fors**, C3.—AF. *force*: Late Lat. *fortia*. Cf. Cotg. (s.v.) *je ne fais point force de cela*, I care not for, I force not of, that thing.

forcere, *sb.* casket, strong-box, PP; **forcer**, HD; **focer**, HD; **fosar**, HD.—OF. *forsier*; Low Lat. *forsarium* (acc.), see Ducange.

for-cursæd, *pp.* utterly accursed, S. (**for-**[1].)

for-cwiddare, *sb.* foreteller, S. (**for-**[3].)

ford, *sb.* a ford, passage, course, MD; **forde**, PP; **forth**, PP, S2; **vorþ**, S2; **furth**, MD.—AS. *ford* (OET.).

for-dede, *sb.* previous deed, S2. (**for-**[3].)

for-demen, *v.* to condemn, MD; **fordemde**, *pt. s.*, S; **fordemed**, *pp.*, MD; **fordemet**, S; **fordempte**, *pl.*, MD.—AS. *for-déman*. (**for-**[1].)

for-don, *v.* to destroy, S, MD, S2, C, P; **fordoon**, S2; **fordoð**, *pr. s.*, S, PP; **uordonne**, *ger.*, S; **fordude**, *pt. s.*, PP; **fordede**, S; **fordeden**, *pl.*, S3; **fordo**, *pp.*, PP; **fordon**, S; **fordone**, S3.—AS. *for-dón*, pt. *-dyde*, pp. *-dón*. (**for-**[1].)

for-dreden, *v.* to frighten, MD; **fordred**, *pp.*, S. (**for-**[1].)

for-drenche, *v.* to make drunk, S. (**for-**[1].)

for-dronken, *pp.* drunken, C3; **uordrunken** S.

for-druȝe, *v.* to dry up, S; **fordruye**, *pp.*, MD, CM; **fordrye**, C2. (**for-**[1].)

for-dynnand, *pr. p.*, filling with loud din, S3; **foredinning**, S3. (**for-**[1].)

fore, *prep.* before, S; for, JD. *Comb.*: **for by**, past, by, B, C2, C3; **for gane**, opposite to, S3, B; **for outh**, before, in front of, B; **forowth**, B; **forrouth**, S2, B; **forrow**, S2, B.—AS. *for*, *fore*, in the sight of, before, Goth. *faura*.

forest, *sb.* forest, MD; **forestes**, *pl.*, PP.—OF. *forest*.

forester, *sb.* forester, MD; **forster**, C, PP, HD; **foster**, HD.

foreyn, *adj.* strange, MD; **foreynes**, *pl.* strangers, PP.—OF. *forain*; Late Lat. *foraneum*.

for-faren, *v.* to perish, to fare ill, PP, S2, G; **forfayr**, B; **forfarn**, *pp.* destroyed, S2.—AS. *for-faran*. (**for-**[1].)

for-fered, *pp.* exceedingly afraid, C2, MD. (**for-**[1].)

for-feren, *v.* to perish, MD; **forferden**, *pt. pl.*, MD; **forferde**, S2.—AS. *for-fêran*. (**for-**[1].)

forfet, *sb.* crime, forfeit, PP, MD.—OF. *forfet*, *forfait*; Late Lat. *forisfactum*, *forefacttum* (Ducange). (**for-**[4].)

forfeten, *v.* to do wrong, to fail, to forfeit, MD, PP; **forfaiten**, PP. (**for-**[4].)

for-feynted, *pp.* enfeebled, PP; **forfaynt**, S3. (**for-**[1].)

for-freten, *v.* to eat away, PP; **forfret**, *pr. s.*, PP. (**for-**[1].)

forgaf; see **forȝiven**.

for-gar, *v.* to lose; **forgart**, *pt. pl.*, S2.—Cf. Icel. *fyrir-göra*, to forfeit. **for-**[1].)

forgen, *v.* to make, construct, forge (of smith's work), MD; **forgeden**, *pt. pl.*, W2 (Ps. 128. 3); **forgit**, *pp.*, S3; **forgid**, PP.—

for-geten | for-stallen

OF. *forger, forgier* (Ps. 128. 3); Lat. *fabricare* (Vulg.).

for-geten, *v.* to forget, MD, S, S2; see **for-3eten.**

forgetil, *adj.* forgetful, H.—AS. *forgitol.*

forgetilnes, *sb.* forgetfulness, H.—AS. *forgitolnes.*

for-gilten, *v.* to forfeit, to make guilty, MD; **forgulten**, MD; to harm, PP; **forgilt**, *pt. s.*, MD; **forgulten**, *pl.*, MD; **forgult**, *pp.*, S, MD; **forrgilltedd**, S. (**for-**¹.)

for-gon, *v.* to forgo, S2, C3; **forga**, S2; **forgoon**, C2; **forgoð**, *pr. s.*, S; **forgan**, *pp.*, MD; **forgone**, MD, S3.—AS. *for-gán.* (**for-**¹.)

for-heden, *v.* to neglect, pay no heed to, S2.—From AS. *hédan.* (**for-**¹.)

for-heed, *sb.* forehead, C; **foreheued**, MD. (**for-**³.)

for-helen, *v.* to conceal, HD; **forholen**, *pp.*, S, HD; **forhole**, S, HD.—AS. *for-helan*, pt. *-hæl* (pl. *-hélon*), pp. *-holen.* (**for-**¹.)

for-hewed, *pp.*, hewn about, S3. (**for-**¹.)

for-hilen, *v.* to protect, MD. (**for-**¹.)

for-hiler, *sb.* protector, S2, HD.

for-hiling, *sb.* protection, S2.

for-hoght, *sb.* contempt, MD. (**for-**¹.)

for-ho3ien, *v.* to neglect, despise, S; **forhohien**, MD.—AS. *for-hogian.* (**for-**¹.)

for-langen, *v.* to long for; **forrlangedd**, *pp.*, S. (**for-**¹.)

for-lesen, *v.* to lose wholly, MD, HD; **forleosen**, MD; **forleost**, *2 pr. s.*, S; **vorleost**, *pr. s.*, S; **forleseþ**, S; **forles**, *pt. s.*, S; **forlesed**, *2 pt. s.*, destroyedst, S2; **forrlurenn**, *pl.*, S; **forloren**, *pp.*, S; **forrlorenn**, S; **vorloren**, S; **forlorne**, S3; **forlorn**, S2; **forlore**, S2, S3; **uorlore**, S2.—AS. *for-léosan*, pt. *léas* (pl. *luron*), pp. *loren.* (**for-**¹.)

for-leten, *v.* to leave off, forsake, yield up, S, S2, C2; **uorlete**, to forgive, S2; **forlet**, *pt. s.*, S; **forleten**, *pp.*, S.—AS. *for-létan*, pt. *-lét*, pp. *-léten.* (**for-**¹.)

for-leuen, *v.* to abandon, MD; **forleaf**, *imp. s.*, S. (**for-**¹.)

forloren; see **forlesen.**

forloynen, *v.* to go far astray, MD, HD; **forloyned**, *pp.*, S2.—OF. *forlonger*, to go far before (Cotg.). (**for-**⁴.)

formaylle, *sb.* the female hawk, MD, HD.—Cf. OF. *forme*, a kind of hawk (Cotg.).

forme¹, *adj. superl.* first, S, PP; **forrme**, S; **furme**, MD. *Comb.*: **forme-fader**, ancestor, S, S2, S3, H, PP; **forme-foster**, progenitor, S2; **forme-mete**, first meat, morning-meal, S.—AS. *forma*, superl. of *fore*, before.

forme², *sb.* form, figure, shape, MD; *scabellum*, Voc.; **furme**, MD; **fourme**,

MD, W; **fourm**, MD; **foorme**, form of a hare, Prompt. (see F. *forme*, Cotg.).—AF. *forme*; Lat. *forma.*

formel egle, *sb.* female eagle, MD, CM. Cf. **formaylle.**

formen, *v.* to form, Prompt.—OF. *former*; Lat. *formare.*

former, *sb.* former, creator, MD, PP.

formere, *adj. comp.* former, MD.—*Comb.*: **formere fader**, ancestor, S2.

formest, *adj. superl.* first, S, PP; **furmest**, S2.—AS. *fyrmest (formest).*

formour, *sb.* former, creator, MD, PP; **formeour**, PP; **formyour**, MD, S2.—OF. *formeör*; Lat. *formatorem.*

forn, *prep.* and *adv.* before, MD, HD; **foren**, S. *Comb.*: **forn a3ens**, over against, W.—AS. *foran*; cf. OHG. *forn*, 'olim' (Tatian).

forn-cast, *pp.* forecast, C, CM.

forneys, *sb.* furnace, C; **fornays**, MD; **furneise**, S; **fornes**, S2; **fourneys**, C2, C3; **fornesse**, HD.—OF. *fornaise*; Lat. *fornacem.*

for-nimen, *v.* to take away, MD; **fornumen**, *pp.*, S.—AS. *for-niman.* (**for-**¹.)

for-old, *adj.* very old, C. (**for-**¹.)

for-pinen, *v.* to torment, MD; **forpinede**, *pt. s.*, MD; **forpined**, *pp.*, HD; **forpyned**, CM, P; famished, wretched, PP. (**for-**¹.)

for-priken, *v.* to spur violently; **vor-priked**, *pt. s.*, S2. (**for-**¹.)

forray¹, *sb.* foray, B.

forray², *v.* to forage, B.

forrayour, *sb.* forayer, forager, B; **foreyours**, *pl.*, PP; **foreioures**, PP. Cf. **forager.**

forred, *pp.* furred, S2, PP; see **furren.**

for-reden, *v.* to betray, hurt, wrong, S; **forreaden**, S; **forradden**, *pt. pl.*, MD; **forrad**, *pp.*, MD; **forred**, S.—AS. *for-rédan.* (**for-**¹.)

for-saken, *v.* to forsake, to deny, refuse, PP, S, S2; **uorsake**, S; **forsoc**, *pt. s.*, S2; **for-sok**, PP; **uorsoc**, S; **forsake**, *2 pt. s.*, S; **forsoken**, *pl.*, PP; **forsake**, W2, PP.—AS. *for-sacan*, to renounce, pt. *-sóc*, pp. *-sacen.* (**for-**¹.)

for-seon, *v.* to despise, MD; **for-se**, HD; **forsest**, *2 pr. s.*, S; **forrse**, *subj.*, S.—AS. *for-séon.* (**for-**¹.)

for-slouthe, *v.* to lose through sloth, C; **forsleuthed**, *pp.*, wasted idly, P. (**for-**¹.)

for-sonke, *pp.* sunk deep, S3. (**for-**¹.)

for-spent, *pp.* exhausted, Sh.; **forespent**, S3. (**for-**¹.)

for-spreak, *sb.* an advocate, HD. (**for-**².)

for-stallen, *v.* to forestall, obstruct, PP. See SkD (p. 805). (**for-**³.)

84

for-standen, _v._ to stand for, avail; **forstod**, _pt. s._, S.—AS. _for-standan._ (**for-**².)

for-suneȝen, _v._ to be sinful, MD; **forsunegede**, _pp. pl._, sinful, MD; **forsinegede**, S.—AS. _for-syngian_, pp. _forsyngad._ (**for-**¹.)

for-swelten, _v._ to die, S, MD; _v. tr._, to kill, S, MD; **forswelte**, _pp._, MD.—AS. _for-sweltan_, 'mori, perire'. (**for-**¹.)

for-swelȝen, _v._ to swallow up, MD; **uorzwelȝe**, S2. (**for-**¹.)

for-swerien, _v._ to forswear, MD; **forsuore**, _pt. s._, MD; **forsworen**, _pp._, S, G, PP; **forswore**, PP; **uorsuore**, S2; **forsworene**, _pl._, S.—AS. _for-swerian_ pt. _swór_, pp. _-sworen._ (**for-**¹.)

for-swering, _sb._ perjury, C3.

for-sweten, _v._ to cover with sweat, MD; **forswat**, _pp._, S2, HD, B. (**for-**¹.)

for-swinken, _v._ to exhaust with toil; **forswonke**, _pp._, S3 (p. 364, l. 24).

for-trauailled, _pp._, wearied with toil, MD; **fortravalit**, S2, B. (**for-**¹.)

for-tuhting, _sb._ seduction, S; **fortihting**, S.—From AS. _for-tyhtan_, to lead astray. (**for-**¹.)

fortune¹, _sb._ fortune, chance, MD, Prompt.; **fortoun**, B.—OF. _fortune_; Lat. _fortuna._

fortune², _v._ to make fortunate, to happen, S3, HD, C.

fortunous, _adj._ fortunate, HD.

forth, _adv._ forth, henceforth, throughout, PP, S; **uorth**, S, S2; **furð**, S, S2; **forth**, _prep._, along, S2; **furth**, S3. _Comb._: **forth daies**, far advanced in the day, W; **fore days**, HD; **furth of**, forth from, S3; **forð riht**, straightway, MD; **forð rihtes**, S; **forð to**, until, S; **for to**, S2; **forte**, S, S2; **fort**, S; **uort**, S; **forthward**, forward, S, S2, O3; **forðwyth**, right before, S2; **forthwit**, S; **forwit**, S2.

forð-clepien, _v._ to call forth, S.

forðen¹, _adv._ even, also, MD; **forrþenn**, S.—AS. _forðum (furðum)._

forðen², _v._ to promote, perform, S.—AS. _forðian._

forther¹, _adv._ further, S2, PP; **ferther**, C2; **furder**, S3; **furðer**, MD. _Comb._: **forthermore**, furthermore, C2, C3; **forthermo**, C3; **forthirmar**, S3; **forther ouer**, more over, C3.—AS. _furðor_ (= _fore_ + suffix _-ðor_).

forther², _v._ to further, aid, S2; **forthren**, C; **furðren**, S; **firthren**, S.—AS. _fyrðrian._

forð-faren, _v._ to go forth, S, S2; **uorð-farinde**, _pr. p. pl._, S.

forð-feren, _v._ to depart, die; **forðfeorde**, _pt. s._, S.—AS. _forð-féran._

for-þresten, _v._ to destroy, MD; **forþrast**, _pp._, S2. (**for-**¹.)

forð-teon, _v._ to draw forth, bring up, MD; **forðteh**, _pt. s._, S.—AS. _forð-téon._

for-þunchen, _v._ to repent, S; **forthynketh**, _pr. s._ _impers._, MD; **forthenkith**, W; **forþynkez**, 82; **forthinke**, _imp. pl._, S2; **forthouȝte**, _pt. s._, W. (**for-**¹.)

for-waked, _pp._ tired out with watching, S2, C3; **forwake**, S2. (**for-**¹.)

for-wandred, _pp._ wearied out with wandering, P. (**for-**¹.)

for-wanyen, _v._ to spoil by indulgence, PP; **forweny**, PP; **forwene**, PP. (**for-**¹.)

for-ward, _sb._ agreement, PP, S, C, C2; **foreward**, S, S2, PP; **voreward**, S; **forwarde**, PP, S2; **vorewarde**, S2.—AS. _foreweard._ (**for-**³.)

for-waste, _pp._ utterly wasted, wasted with misery, S3. (**for-**¹.)

forwe, _sb._ furrow, PP; see **fur**².

for-werien, _v._ to wear out, MD; **forwerd**, _pp._, S3. (**for-**¹.)

for-werien, _v._ to cast aside, renounce, MD; **forrwerrpenn**, S; **forrwarrp**, _pt. s._, MD; **forrwurrpenn**, _pl._, S; **forrworrpenn**, _pp._, S.—AS. _for-weorpan_, pt. _-wearp_ (pl. _-wurpon_), pp. _-worpen._ (**for-**¹.)

for-wetyng, _sb._ foreknowledge, C. (**for-**³.)

for-wit, _sb._ forethought, foreknowledge, P. (**for-**³.)

for-witen, _v._ to foreknow, MD; **forwot**, _pr. s._, C; **forwoot**, MD.—AS. _fore-witan_, pt. pr. _-wát._ (**for-**³.)

for-withered, _pp._ utterly withered, S3. (**for-**¹.)

for-wounded, _pp._ desperately wounded, S3; **uorwounded**, _pt. s._, S2. (**for-**¹.)

for-wrapped, _pp._ wrapped up, C3. (**for-**¹.)

for-wreien, _v._ to accuse, S; **forwreye**, S; **forwreiȝet**, _pp._, MD.—AS. _for-wrégan_, (**for-**¹.)

for-wurðen, _v._ to perish, S; **furwurðen**, S; **uorwurðen**, S; **forworthes**, _pr. pl._, S2.—AS. _for-weorðan_, pt. _-wearð_ (pl. _-wurdon_), pp. _-worden._ (**for-**¹.)

for-ȝelden, _v._ to reward, S, MD, S2; **forȝelde**, C2; **for-yhelde**, to render, S2; **for-yheld**, _pt. s._, S2.—AS. _for-geldan._ (**for-**¹.)

for-ȝeldinge, _sb._ retribution, S2; **for-yheldinges**, _pl._, S2. (**for-**¹.)

for-ȝemen, _v._ to neglect, MD; **foryemen**, S.—AS. _for-géman._ (**for-**¹.)

for-ȝerd, _sb._ court, W. (**for-**³.)

for-ȝeten, _v._ to forget, S, PP; **forȝuten**, PP; **foryeten**, S; **forgeten**, S, S2; **vorȝete**, S; **forgetith**, _imp. pl._, G; **forȝieteð**, _pr. s._, S; **forȝiet**, S; **forȝet**, S; **foryet**, S; **forgat**, _pt. s._, W; **forgeten**, _pp._, S, C2; **forȝieten**, S; **foryete**, S2, PP; **forȝete**, P,

W2; **forgen**, H.—AS. *for-gitan*, pt. *-geat* (pl. *-géaton*), pp. *-giten*. (**for-**[1].)

for-ȝetful, *adj.* forgetful, W (Jas. 1. 25); **foryetful**, C2.

for-ȝiuen, *v.* to forgive, PP; **foryeue**, C3; **forȝeuen**, PP; **forȝieue**, S; **forrȝifenn**, S; **foryiue**, C2; **uorȝiuen**, S; **forgifen** S; **forȝef**, *imp. s.*, S; **forgaf**, *pt. s.*, S; **forȝaf**, G, W, PP; **forȝouen**, *pp.*, S2; **forȝeuen**, PP; **forȝouun**, W; **forȝoue**, W2.—AS. *forgifan*. (**for-**[1].)

for-ȝiuenesse, *sb.* forgiveness, MD; **forrȝifenesse**, S; **foryeuenesse**, S, PP; **forȝieuenesse**, S.

foster, *sb.* nourishment, MD, HD; one nurtured, a child, MD; **fostyr**, nurturer, fosterer, S3.—AS. *fóstor* (= *fód-stor*), nourishment. See **fode**[1].

fostren, *v.* to foster, support, cherish, PP; **fosstrenn**, S; **fostred**, *pt. s.*, C2, C3; **y-fostred**, *pp.*, C2.—AS. *fóstrian*.

fother, *sb.* a carriage-load, a load, MD, C; **fothyr**, B; **fudder**, JD; **fudyr**, B; **uoðere**, *pl.*, MD.—AS. *fóðer*; cf. OHG. *fuodar* (mod. *fuder*), whence F. *foudre*.

fou, *adj.* spotted, S; see **foh**.

foul[1], *sb.* fowl, bird, S2, C, PP; **foȝel**, S; **fowel**, C, PP; **foghill**, H; **fuhel**, S; **foull**, S3; **fugeles**, *pl.*, S; **fuȝeles**, S; **fughils**, H; **fueles**, S; **fuweles**, S; **fogheles**, S2; **foghles**, S2.—AS. *fugol*.

foul[2], *adj.* foul, PP, MD; **uoul**, MD, S2; **ful**, S; **fule**, *adv.*, S; **foule**, G; **fuluste**, *superl.*, MD. *Comb.*: **ful-itowen**, badly disciplined, wanton, MD; **ful-itohen**, S; **fulitohe**, S.—AS. *fúl*, Goth. *fuls*.

foule, *sb.* fool, H; see **fole**[2].

foulen, *v.* to make foul, defile, revile, destroy, S2, PP; **fowlen**, S2; **fulen**, S; **filen**, S2; **fild**, *pp.*, S2.—AS. *fúlian*, to become foul, *fýlan*, 'inquinare'. See **foul**[2].

foulere, *sb.* a taker of birds, W2. See **foul**[1].

foul-hed, *sb.* folly, H. See **foule**.

foundement, *sb.* foundation, S3, W.

founden, *v.* to found, PP; **fundit**, *pp.*, S3; **y-founde**, S3; **foundun**, W.—OF. *fonder*, Lat. *fundare*.

foundour, *sb.* founder, PP.—OF. *fondeur*, Lat. *fundatorem*.

foundren, *v.* to founder, also to cause to sink, MD; **foundre**, C; **foundered**, *pp.*, S2; **fowndryd** (as horse), PP.—OF. *fondrer*, an extended form of *fonder*, to fall (Bartsch); see also Diez, p. 144.

founs, *sb.* bottom, S2; **founce**, MD, WA.—OF. *fons* (Bartsch); Lat. *fundus*; cf. Prov. *founs*, deep (Diez, p. 143).

foure, *num.* four, C3, PP; **fower**, S; **uour**, S; **fuwer**, MD; **faur**, MD; **faure**, S2; **fawre**,

S2; **fowre**, S2.—AS. *féower*, OS. *fiuwar*: Goth. *fidwor*; cf. OWel. *petguar*, Lat. *quatuor*.

foute, *sb.* scent, trace of a beast of chase, S2; see **feute**.

fownys, *sb. pl.* fawns, S3; see **fawn**.

foyne, *sb.* a foin, thrust, S3; prick, *punctus*, Manip.; **foines**, *pl.*, ND.

foynen, *v.* to thrust or lunge with a sword, MD, C; **feyne**, MD; **foignen**, MD; **foin**, ND, Sh.; **foygnede**, *pt. s.*, MD; **foyneden**, *pl.*, MD; **fwnȝeit**, B.

foȝ, *sb.* mutual consent, *junctura*, MD; **foȝe**, *dat.*, S.—AS. *fóg, gefóg.*

fra, **fra-**; see **fro**.

fraisten, *v.* to try, prove, MD, JD, HD; **fraisted**, *pp.*, MD, S2, HD.—Icel. *freista*; cf. Goth. *fraisan*, AS. *frásian.*

frake, *sb.* a man, HD; see **freke**.

frakly, *adv.* keenly, greedily, hastily, S2, B, JD. See **frek**.

frakne, *sb.* freckle, *lentigo*, Prompt.; **frakyn**, *lenticula*, Voc.; **freken**, *neuus*, Manip., HD; **frecken**, Palsg., Manip.; **fraknes**, *pl.*, HD, C; **freknes**, MD.—Icel. *frekna.*

fraknede, *pp.* freckled, HD.

frakny, *adj.* freckled, Prompt.

fram, *prep.* from, S, S2, PP; **vram**, S2; **urom**, S. *Comb.*: **fram-ward**, *prep.* away from, MD, HD; **frommard**, S; **urommard**, S.—AS. *fram* (*from*) and *fromweard*, 'aversus'. Cf. **fro**.

frame, *sb.* benefit, advantage, S, S2; **freme**, MD; **ureme**, MD.—AS. *fremu*; Icel. *frami*, advancement. *Fremu* is from AS. *fram* (*from*), excellent.

framien, *v.* to serve, benefit, refresh, accomplish, MD; **fremmen**, MD; **freme**, S, HD; **frame**, JD.—AS. *fremian.*

franke, *adj.* free, Manip.—AF. *franc*, cf. *franke homme*, freeman.

frankeleyn, *sb.* freedman, *libertinus*, MD; also a freeholder, C, HD, G; **frankeleyne**, Prompt., PP; **frankelayn**, Voc., PP; **frankelin**, C2; **francoleyn**, MD; **frankeleyns**, *pl.*, C (A. 216).—AF. *fraunkelayn*, *fraunclein*; Low Lat. *franchilanus*. The suffix *-lanus* is of Teutonic origin; cf. AS. *-ling*; see SkD. (s.v. *chamberlain*).

fraught, *pp.* freighted, laden with cargo, MD, C3; **fraughted**, S3.

fraunchise, *sb.* freedom, prerogative, liberality, MD, PP; **fraunchyse**, C2; **franchis**, H; **franchiss**, B.—AF. *franchise* (*fraunchise*); formed with suffix *-itia*; see Apfelstedt, Introd. 67. See **franke**.

fray, *sb.* terror, S3, B; see **effray**.

frayd, *pp.* frightened, S3; **fraid**, scared, S3; see **afrayen**.

frayel, *sb.* basket, PP; **freyel**, PP; **frayle**, Prompt.; **fraile**, HD.—OF. *frayel, frael*; whence Low Lat. *fraellum* (Ducange).

fraynen, *v.* to ask, S2, S3, C2, PP; **frainen**, PP; **fraʒʒnenn**, MD; **freinede**, *pt. pt. s.*, S; **freinde**, S; **fraind**, S2; **freyned**, *pp.*, C3.—Icel. *fregna*, AS. *frignan*.

fre, *adj.* free, free-born, generous, S, S2, C, C2, PP; **free**, C2, PP; **fry**, HD; **freo**, PP, S2.—AS. *fréo*.

freden, *v.* to feel, experience, MD, HD; **fredde**, *pt. s.*, MD.—AS. *(ge)frédan*, from AS. *fród*, wise, sensible, experienced, aged; cf. OHG. *fruali*, experienced (Otfrid).

fredom, *sb.* freedom, liberality, S, S2, C2, C3; **fredome**, S2, B.—AS. *fréodóm*.

freitour, *sb.* refectory, hall for meals, S3, MD, PP; **fratour**, HD; **fraytour**, S3; **freitur**, MD; **fraitur**, S3; **fratery**, HD; **froyter**, HD (p. 379).—OF. *refretoir* Late Lat. *refectorium*.

frek, *adj.* eager, greedy, bold, S2; **frak**, JD; **frike**, MD; **fryke**, HD.—AS. *frec*; cf. Goth. *friks*, greedy (in *faihufriks*); Icel. *frekr*.

freke, *sb.* a bold man, a warrior, a man, MD, S2, P; **freek**, PP; **frek**, S2, PP; **freyke**, S3; **fraik**, PP; **frayk**, PP; **freik**, PP; **frake**, HD; **freckys**, *pl.*, S3; **frekis**, P.—AS. *freca*, a bold man, warrior.

frekel, *sb.* freckle; **freklys**, *pl.*, S3; **freckles**, *variolae*, Manip. See **frakne**.

frele, *adj.* frail, S2, P; **freyle**, MD; **freel**, PP.—OF. *frele, fraile*; Lat. *fragilem*.

freletee, *sb.* frailty, C2; **frelete**, P.

frely, *adj.* noble, gracious, S2, C2, B; **freolich**, S; **freyliche**, S2; **freliche**, *adv.* freely, PP, S2.—AS. *fréolic*, adv. *fréolice*. See **fre**.

fre-man, *sb.* freeman, S.—AS. *fréomon*.

fremde, *adj.* and *sb.* strange, foreign, stranger, S, C2, PP; **fremmde**, S; **fremede**, S; **fremmed**, PP.—AS. *fremede, fremde*, strange.

fremen, *v.* to accomplish, S, HD; see **framien**.

frend, *sb.* friend, S, C; **freonde**, PP; **freondes**, *pl.*, PP; **freond**, S, S2; **ureondes**, S; **frendes**, C3, PP; **frenden**, *dat.*, S.—AS. *fréond*.

frenden, *v. reflex.* to gain friends; **ureonden**, S.

frendesse, *sb.* female friend, W2.

frendrede, *sb.* friendship, HD.—AS. *fréondréden*.

frendschipe, *sb.* friendship, S, C; **freontschipe**, S.—AS. *fréondscipe*.

freoien, *v.* to free, MD; **vri**, *imp. s.*, S2; **freode**, *pt. s.*, MD; **fried**, *pp.*, S.—AS. *fréogan (fréon)*, pt. *fréode*, pp. *fréod*. See **fre**.

freolsen, *v.* to free, to celebrate, MD; **frelsen**, MD.—AS. *fréolsian*, 'diem festum celebrare'; cf. Icel. *frjálsa*, to free. From AS. *fréols* freedom, festival: Goth. *freihals*, 'collum liberum', freedom.

frere, *sb.* brother, friar, MD, C, G, P; **freir**, S3; **frer**, B; **freres**, *pl.*, C2, P.—OF. *frere*, *fredre*; Lat. *fratrem*.

fresch, *adj.* fresh, new, MD, C; **fersch**, S2; **fresche**, W2, PP; **freis**, S2; **freissh**, S2.—AS. *fersc*.

freschly, *adv.* freshly, B.

fresen, *v.* to freeze, PP; **freost**, *pr. s.*, S; **frese**, *pt. s.*, MD; **froren**, *pp.*, MD.—AS. *fréosan*, pt. *fréas* (pl. *fruron*), pp. *froren*.

frest, *sb.* delay, MD, S2, B; **ferst**, MD; **first**, MD; **furst**, S; **virst**, S.—Icel. *frest*, AS. *fierst, fyrst, first*, an interval.

fresten, *v.* to delay, to lend, MD, Prompt.

freten, *v.* to devour, S, S2, C2, P; **freate**, to fret, feel vexed, S3; **fret**, *pt. s.*, MD, S2, PP; **freten**, *pp.*, S, S2; **frete**, S2, C3.—AS. *fretan*, pt. *frét* (pl. *fréton*), pp. *freten*, a compound of *etan*, to eat; cf. Goth. *fra-itan* = *fra* + *itan*, to eat.

fretten, *v.* to adorn, furnish, MD, S2; **fret**, *pp.*, MD, S3; **fretted**, P.—AS. *frætwian*, 'ornare'; cf. OS. *fratahón*.

freuren, *v.* to comfort, S.—AS. *fréfrian*. See **frofren**.

Fri-dæi, *sb.* Friday, the week-day sacred to Freya, the AS. name of a Teutonic goddess having attributes similar to those of the Roman Venus, S; **Fridai**, MD.—AS. *Frígedæg*.

Frie, *sb.* Freya, the wife of Woden, MD; **Fre**, S; **Frye**, S.—AS. *Fríg* (attested only in *Frígedæg*; see Grimm, Teut. M., p. 299.

frien, *v.* to fry, MD; **i-friʒet**, *pp.*, S2; **fryed**, PP; **yfryed**, PP.—OF. *frire*; Lat. *frigere*.

frigt, *sb.* fright, MD; **friʒt**, MD.—AS. *fyrhto*.

frigten, *v.* to fear, also to alarm, MD; **fricht**, *pp.*, S3.—AS. *forhtian*, pp. *forht*.

frigti, *adj.* timid, S.—*Comb.*: **frigti luue**, reverence, S.

frigtihed, *sb.* alarm, S.

frigtilike, *adv.* timidly, S.

frið, *sb.* peace, security, deer-park, forest, wood, S, S2, PP, HD; **fryth**, S2, PP.—AS. *frið*; cf. OHG. *fridu* (Otfrid).

friðien, *v.* to free, protect, spare, MD; **friðie**, S; **frithed**, *pp.*, enclosed, P.—AS. *(ge)friðian*, to protect.

fro, *prep.* from, S, S2, C2, PP; **froo**, PP; **fra**, S, S2, S3. *Comb.*: **frathine**, from thence, S3, B; **fraward**, away from, forward, S2, MD; **frawart**, S3.—AS. *fram*, Icel. *frá*. Cf. **fram**.

frofre, *sb.* comfort, MD; **frouer**, S; **froure**, S, MD.—AS. *frófor*.

frofren, *v.* to comfort, S; **frouren**, S; **frefrien**, MD; **freureð**, *pr. s.*, S.—AS. *frófrian, fréfrian*.

frogge, *sb.* frog, S, Voc.; **frock**, HD; **froggen**, *pl.*, S; **frogges**, MD.—AS. *frocga*.

froit; see **frut**.

frokke, *sb.* frock, PP, MD; **frogge**, PP; **froggis**, *pl.*, B.—OF. *froc* (Cotg.); cf. Low Lat. *frocus, flocus*, see Ducange. For interchange of *fr* and *fl*, cf. **frounce**.

frosche, *sb.* frog, Voc.; **froske**, MD, H; **froskes**, *pl.*, MD; **froskis**, H; **frosses**, MD.—AS. *frox*; cf. Icel. *froskr*.

froten, *v.* to rub, MD, H; **frotynge**, *pr. p.*, W; **frotyng**, grating, S2; **yfroted**, *pp.*, S2.—OF. *froter*: It. *frettare*: Lat. *frictum*, from *fricare*; see Constans.

froðe, *sb.* froth, foam, MD, Prompt.; **forþe**, S2.—Icel. *froða, frauð*; cf. Dan. *fråde*, Sw. *fradga*.

frothen, *v.* to froth, C, MD.

frounce, *sb.* a fold, plait, ND; **frounces**, *pl.*, PP; **flounce**, SkD.—OF. *fronce*, wrinkle (Bartsch). For interchange of *fr* and *fl* cf. **frokke**.

frouncen, *v.* to knit the brow, wrinkle, fold, MD, ND, HD; **frounsen**, HD; **frounced**, *pp.*, S3; **fronst**, HD.—OF. *froncer*; Late Lat. *frontiare*.

frount, *sb.* front, forehead, S2, MD, B.—AF. *frount, frunt*; Lat. *frontem*.

frude, *sb.* frog, MD; **fruden**, *pl.*, S.—Icel. *frauðr*; cf. Dan. *frø*.

frume, *sb.* beginning, MD; **frome**, MD.—AS. *fruma*; cf. Goth. *frums*.

frumentee, *sb.* frumenty, furmety, wheat boiled in milk, MD, HD; **frumenty**, MD, HD; **furmente**, MD; **firmentie**, S3.—OF. *frumentee, fromentee*; Late Lat. *frumentata*; from Lat. *frumentum*, corn (OF. *froment, forment*, wheat, corn).

frumðe, *sb.* beginning, S; **urumðe**, MD.—AS. *frymða (frumð)*.

frustir, *adj.* frustrated, useless, JD, S3.—Cf. OF. *frustrer*; Lat. *frustrare*.

frut, *sb.* fruit, S, S2; **fruit**, S; **fruyt**, C3; **froit**, MD; **froyt**, H (Ps. 125. 6); **fryt**, S2; **frutis**, *pl.*, B; **froytis**, B.—OF. *frut (fruit)*; Lat. *fructum*.

fruytesteres, *sb. pl. f.*, women fruit-sellers, C3.

fugel, fuhel; see **foul**[1].

ful[1], *adj.* foul, S; **fule**, *adv.*, S. *Comb.*; **ful-itohen**, S. See **foul**[2].

ful[2], *pt. s.*, fell, S, PP. See **fallen**.

ful[3], *adj.* full, S. *Comb.*: **ful iwis**, full assuredly, S; **fol iwis**, S; **ful out**, completely, W2; **to ful**, completely, S2. See **full**.

ful[4], *sb.* a goblet full of drink, a toast at a heathen feast; **uul**, S.—AS. *ful*; cf. Icel. *full*; see Grimm, Teut. M., p. 60.

ful-bringen, *v.* to complete, MD; **full-brohht**, *pp.*, MD.

fulcning, *sb.* baptism, S; **folcninge**, *dat.*, S. See **fulhtnen**.

ful-don, *v.* to accomplish, S.

ful-endin, *v.* to bring to an end, S; **fulendy**, S.

ful-forðien, *v.* to perform, S.

ful-fremien, *v.* to perfect, MD; **full-fremedd**, *pp.*, S.

ful-fullen, *v.* to fulfil, perfect, to fill full, MD; **folvellet**, *imp. pl.*, S; **fulfellþ**, *pr. s.*, S; **uul-uelden**, *pt. pl.*, S; **folfult**, *pp.*, S2; **fulfild**, S2.

ful-hed, *sb.* fulness, S2; **folhed**, MD.

fulhtnen, *v.* to baptize, MD; **fullhtnenn**, S. See **fulluht**.

full, *adj.* full, MD; **ful**, S; **fol**, S2; **vol**, S2; **fulle**, *dat.*, S, PP; *adv.*, S; **follest**, *superl.*, S2.

fulle, *sb.* fill, S; **fylle**, S2.—AS. *fyllo*: OHG. *fulli*.

fullen, *v.* to fill, complete, S; **felle**, S; **fulde**, *pt. s.*, S; **felde**, S2; **vulde**, S2; **fylden**, *pl.*, S; **i-fullet**, *pp.*, S; **i-uulled**, S; **hi-fulled**, S; **ifuld**, S2; **filt**, S; **fulde**, *pl.*, S.—AS. *fyllan*: OS. *fullian*: Goth. *fulljan*.

fulliche, *adv.* fully, S; **folliche**, S; **volliche**, S2.

fulluht, *sb.* baptism, S; **fullouht**, MD; **fullouȝt**, MD; **fulloȝt**, MD.—AS. *fulwiht* (OET.). See **full**.

ful-mard, *sb.* polecat, MD, Voc.; **fulmarde**, Palsg.; **fulmerde**, Voc.; **fulmare**, Manip.; **fulmere**, Voc., Prompt. (p. 407); **fol-marde**, S2.—AS. *fúl + mearð*, marten. See **foul**[1].

fulnesse, *sb.* fulness, MD; **uolnesse**, S2.

fulst, *sb.* help, S.—AS. *fylst (ful + læst)*; cf. OS. *ful-lésti*. See **full**.

fulsten, *v.* to help, S.—AS. *fylstan*: OS. *ful-léstian*.

ful-sum, *adj.* plenteous, S. See **full**.

fulsumhed, *sb.* abundance, S.

fulsumnesse, *sb.* satiety, MD; **fulsomnesse**, C2.

fultum, *sb.* help, MD; **fultume**, *dat.*, MD; *pl.*, S.—AS. *fultum (= ful + téam)*. See **full**.

fulðe, *sb.* fulness, MD. See **full**.

fulwes; see **folwen**.

fulȝeis, *sb. pl.*, leaves, S3.—OF. *fuille, foille*; Lat. *folium*.

fume, *sb.* fume, smoke, MD; confusion in the brain produced by drunkenness, C.—OF. *fum*; Lat. *fumum*.

fumetere, *sb.* the herb fumitory, *fumus terrae*, earth-smoke, Alph., Voc., C; **fumytere**, Voc.; **fumeter**, Prompt.—OF. *fumeterre*; Late Lat. *fumus terrae* (Alph.).

fumosite, *sb.* indigestibility, MD; **fumositee**, the quality of getting into the head (of wines), C2, C3; **fumositie**, smoakiness, Manip.

fumouse, *adj.* angry, Palsg. (p. 774).

funden[1], *v.* to hasten, go, to strive, S, MD; **fonde**, S, S3; **foonde**, S2; **founde**, S2, B.—AS. *fundian*, to hasten. See **finden**.

funden[2], *pt. pl.*, found, S; see **finden**.

fundie, *adj.* heavy, MD; see **findi3**.

fundles, *sb.* a finding, S; **fundless**, HD.

fundling, *sb.* foundling, S.

fundy, *v.* to become stiff with cold, JD.

fundying, *sb.* benumbment with cold, B.

funt, *sb.* font, S; **funte**, Voc. *Comb.*: **funt-fat**, font, S. See **font**.

fur[1], *sb.* fire, S, S2, PP; **fir**, S; **fer**, S; **feer**, S2; **fyr**, PP, C2; **fuyr**, PP; **fuir**, S2, PP; **fyre**, MD; **fere**, *dat.*, S2; **uere**, S2.—AS. *fyr*: OHG. *fiur* (Otfrid).

fur[2], *sb.* furrow, S3; **furgh**, MD; **furch**, MD; **forwe**, PP; **forwes**, *pl.*, P. *Comb.*: **furbreid**, furrow's breadth, S3; **furlong**, furrow's length, C2, C3, PP; **fourlonge**, P; **forlang**, PP.—AS. *furh*.

fureur, *sb.* fury, S3.—OF. *fureur*; Lat. *furorem*.

furial, *adj.* raging, C2.—Lat. *furialis*.

furre, *sb.* fur, Prompt., Palsg.; **furris**, *pl.*, PP.—OF. *fuerre*, a sheath (Bartsch); cf. Sp. *forro*, lining: It. *fódero*, lining, a furred garment, a sheath, scabbard: Goth. *fodr*, sheath; cf. Icel. *fóðr*, lining, OHG. *fuatar*, see Kluge and Weigand (s.v. *futter*).

furren, *v.* to line with fur, MD; **furryn**, Prompt.; **furred**, *pp.*, MD; **forred**, S2, PP.—OF. *forrer* (Bartsch), also *fourrer* (Cotg.).

furst, *sb.* delay, S; see **frest**.

fus, *adj.* eager, prompt, MD; **fous**, MD; **vous**, MD.—Icel. *fúss*: OHG. *funs* (Otfrid).

fusen, *v.* to hurry, MD; **fusede**, *pt. s.*, MD.—AS. *fýsan*: OS. *fúsian*.

fust, *sb.* fist, S2, PP; **fyste**, Voc.; **fist**, MD; **fest**, MD, C3; **feste**, *dat.*, C3.—AS. *fýst*: OHG. *fúst* (G. *faust*).

fu3ten; see **fighten**.

fylyng, *sb.* defiling, S2. See **foulen**.

fyn, *sb.* end, S2, S3, C2, G; see **fine**.

fyr, *sb.* fire, PP, C2; **fyre**, MD. *Comb.*: **fyreflaucht**, lightning, S3; **fyr-reed**, red as fire, C. See **fur**[1].

fyrth, *sb.* a passage, inlet of the sea, S3; **firth**, JD.—Icel. *fjörðr*.

fyry, *adj.* fiery, C; **fery**, S3. See **fur**[1].

fy3te[1], *v.* to fight, PP; see **fighten**.

fy3te[2], *sb.* fight, PP; **fi3te**, S, S2; **uihte**, S; **feht**, MD; **fe3t**, S2; **fæht**, MD; **fæhte**, S.—AS. *feoht*: OS. *fehta*.

G

ga, *v.* to go; see **gan**[1].

gabben, *v.* to lie, mock, scoff, jest, prate, S, C, PP, Prompt., Cath., JD.—Icel. *gabba*, to mock.

gabbynge, *sb.* lying, deceit, PP, Prompt., HD.

gabbere, *sb.* liar, chatterer, CM, Prompt. (*n*).

gadeling, *sb.* comrade, fellow, vagabond; gadelyng, PP, G, CM; gadlyng, HD; gedelynge, PP, HD; gedelyng, S2.—AS. *gædeling* OS. *gaduling*, a kinsman; cf. Goth. *gadiliggs*, a sister's son.

gaderare, *sb.* gatherer, S.

gaderen, *v.* to gather, S, PP, C; gadery, S2; gadir, S2; gadire, W2; gedern, S; gedre, S2; gaddreð, *pr. s.*, S; gaderid, *pt. s.*, PP; gadred, S2; gederide, PP; 3e-gadered, *pp.*, S; y-gadered, S3; gedrid, S2.—AS. *gaderian, gædrian*.

gadering, *sb.* gathering, S.—AS. *gaderung*.

gæde, *pt. s.* went, S.—AS. *ge-éode* (OET. p. 622). Cf. 3eode.

gær, *sb.* year, S; see 3eer.

gærsume, *s. pl.* treasures; see gersum.

gæt, *sb. pl.* goats, S; see goot.

gagates, *sb.* jet, S2.—Lat. *gagates*, jet; Gr. γαγάτης. See jette[1].

gage, *v.* to measure the contents of a vessel, to gauge, S3, Sh.—AF. *gauger* (F. *jauger*); from OF. **gauge*; cf. Low Lat. *jalagium*, 'jus mensuræ' (Ducange).

gaignage, *sb.* crop, fruit of tilled or planted ground, HD; gaynage, S3.—OF. *gaignage*, produce, revenue, Cotg.; from OF. *gaigner*, to get, win.

gainges, *sb. pl.* goings, S2. See gan[1].

gair, *sb.* a gore; see gore[1].

gairding, *sb.* garden, S3; see gardin.

gait, *sb.* way, S3; see gate[1].

gal, *adj.* lascivious, S; gole, *pl.*, MD.—AS. *gál*; cf. OHG. *geil*.

galamelle, *sb.* a sweet and nourishing drink, S2.

gale, *sb.* sore, S3; see galle[2].

gale-gale, *sb.* a sing-song fellow, S.

galen, *v.* to sing, cry out, to caw (as crows or rooks), Prompt., S3, CM.—AS. *galan*. Cf. E. *nightingale*.

galeye, *sb.* galley, ship, Prompt.; galeie, S; galey, Voc.; galay, S2; gaylayes, *pl.*, S2.—AF. *galeye, galie*; cf. Low Lat. *galea*.

galianes, *sb. pl.* drinks named after *Galen* (called *Galien* in ME.), C3.

galiard, *adj.* gay, sprightly, HD; gal3art, S3; galyarde, HD.—OF. *gaillard*, vigorous (Roland).

galingale, *sb.* a plant from the root of which a spice was prepared, Cath. (s.v. *galynga*), ND, HD; galyngale, Alph., C3, Prompt.; galangale, ND.—OF. *galingal*, the root of the rush called cypress (cf. Low Lat. *gallingar*), from *galangue*; cf. Low Lat. *galanga* (Alph.).

galiote, *sb.* large galley, S2.—It. *galeótta*, a good handsome big galley (Florio). See galeye.

galle[1], *sb.* the gall, bitterness, anger, S, Prompt., Voc., C2, C3, PP; bitter drink, S2.—AS. *gealla* (Voc.).

galle[2], *sb.* sore in man or beast, Prompt.; gale, S3.—OF. *galle*, scab, itch; cf. Low Lat. *galla* (Ducange).

galnesse, *sb.* lasciviousness, MD; golnesse, S; galnes, S. See gal.

galoche, *sb.* a kind of patten, C2, Prompt.; galoches, *pl.*, PP; galage, 'sandalium', Manip.; gallage, Manip. (*n*).—AF. *galoche*; Low Lat. *calopodia*, clogs; Gr. καλοπόδιον, dimin. of καλόπους, i.e. wood-foot, a last.

galoun, *sb.* gallon, W, C3, P; galun, S.—AF. *galoun*.

galpen, *v.* to yawn, PP, Voc., C2.—OS. *galpôn*, 'clamare'.

galwe, *sb.* cross, gibbet; galowe, Prompt.; galwes, *pl.*, gallows, Voc., C2; galues, S.—AS. *gealga*, also *galga* (Voc.)

galwe-tre, *sb.* gallows-tree, S, Prompt.—AS. *gealg-tréow*.

gal3art, *adj.* gay; see galiard.

game-gobelyn, *sb.* a demon who plays with men, Voc.

gamen[1], *sb.* play, sport, CM, S, S2, G, PP, H; gammyn, S2; gomen, S; game, S, G, Prompt., Voc., C2, C3; gome, S.—AS. *gamen*.

gamen[2], *v.* to be pleasant; him gamede, *pt. s.*, it was pleasant to him, C.

gan[1], *v.* to go, S; gon, S, S2, C2; goon, C2; go, S; ga, S2; gonde, *pr. p.*, S; ga, *imp. s.*, S; gais, S2; goð, *pl.*, S, S2, C2; gooth, C2; gest, *2 pr. s.*, S, S2; gaas, S2; goost, C2; gaþ, *pr. s.*, S; geð, S, S2; goð, S, C2; gas, S2; god, *pl.*, S; gon, S2; goon, C2; gan, *pp.*, S2; goon, C2; goo, S3; ygon, C2, C3; igon, G; igoon, G; ygo, S2; igo, G.—AS. *gán*.

gan[2], *pt. s.* began, did; see ginnen.

90

gane, *v.* to fit, avail, JD; **ganyde**, *pt. pl.*, S3;
ganand, *pr. p.* as *adj.*, suitable, becoming,
S3; see **geꝫnen**.
gang, *sb.* going, S2.
gangen, *v.* to go, S, PP; **gang**, S3; **gang-
ande**, *pr. p.*, PP; **gangand**, S2; **gonge**, *2
pr. s. subj.*, S.—AS. *gangan*.
ganien, *v.* to yawn, gape, SkD; **gane**,
Manip., Palsg., S3, C3; **gone**, S2; **ꝫanin**,
Prompt.—AS. *gánian* (Voc.).
gar, *v.* to cause, make, S3; **gare**, H; **gart**, *pt.
s.*, S2, PP; see **ger**[2].
gardin, *sb.* garden, SkD, C2; **gardyn**, PP;
gardyne, PP; **gardayne**, Manip.;
gairding, S3.—AF. *gardin* (F. *jardin*).
garget, *sb.* throat, CM; see **gorget**.
garite, *sb.* a watch-tower, look-out on the
roof of a house or castle-wall, S3; **garytte**, a
high 'solere', Prompt.; **garett**, HD; **garret**,
Cotg. (s.v. *tourelle*); **garettes**, *pl.*, Prompt.
(*n*); **garrettes**, *projecta*, Manip.—OF. *garite*;
cf. Span. *garita*.
garlek, *sb.* garlick, PP; **garleke**, Alph.; **gar-
leek**, C; **garlekke**, Prompt.; **garlike**, P;
garlik, PP.—AS. *gárléac* (Voc.).
garnet, *sb.* a kind of precious stone; **gar-
nettes**, *pl.*, SkD; **granat**, Cotg. (s.v. *grenat*);
granate-stone (Florio). Cf. It. *granáta*,
pomegranate, garnet. See **greyn**[2].
garnet-appille, *sb.* pomegranate, HD. See
apple-garnade.
garth, *sb.* an enclosure, HD, S3, H; orchard,
Manip.; **garthe**, *sepes*, Cath.; **garthis**, *pl.*,
H.—Icel. *garð*. See **ꝫerd**.
gas, *pr. s.* goes; see **gan**[1].
gast, *sb.* spirit, S, S2; see **gost**.
gastlike, *adj.* spiritual, S; see **gostliche**.
gat, *sb.* goat, S; **gayte**, S3; *pl.*, H; **gate**, S,
S3; see **goot**.
gate[1], *sb.* way, path, street, PP, CM, S2,
Prompt., HD, S3, H; **gat**, S2; **gait**, S3.—
Icel. *gata*; Goth. *gatwo*, street.
gate[2], *sb.* gate, PP, Prompt.; **ꝫate**, S2, G, H,
Prompt.; **yate**, C2, CM, S3, Prompt.; **gat**,
S; **ꝫat**, PP; **yat**, G; **yatt**, H; **ꝫett**, S3; **ꝫiate**,
dat., S; **ꝫeate**, S.—AS. *geat*, Icel. *gat*.
gate-ward, *sb.* gate-keeper, S, PP; **ꝫate-
ward**, PP; **gatwarde**, PP.
gatte, *pt. s.* granted, S; see **ꝫeten**[2].
gat-tothed, *adj.* lascivious, C, CM.
gaude[1], *sb.* weld, *Reseda luteola*, dyer's green-
weed, producing a green dye (distinct from
woad, Florio being here wrong). *Comb.*:
gaude grene, a light green colour, C, HD;
gawdy grene, 'subviridis', Prompt.—OF.
gaude (Cotg.): Sp. *gualda*, a herb to dye
yellow with (Minsheu); cf. It. *gualdo*, woad to
dye blue with (Florio), Low Lat. *gualda*,
gualdum, 'glastum' (Ducange).

gaude[2], *sb.* a toy, piece of finery, also a jest,
trick, CM; **gawde**, a jape, *nuga*, Prompt.;
gaud, HD, ND; ornament, CM; trick,
C3.—Late Lat. *gaudium*, a large bead; Lat.
gaudium, joy.
gaude[3], *v.* to sport, jest, keep festival, ND; to
scoff, Manip.
gaudiouse, *adj.* festal, *solennis*, Manip.
gaudying, *sb.* toying, S3; **gauding**, scoffing,
Manip.
gauren, *v.* to gaze, CM, C2, C3; **gawren**,
CM.
gaurish, *adj.* garish, S3.
gayn, *adj.* convenient, S2; **gaynliche**, *adv.*
readily, S2; see **geyn**.
gaynage, *sb.* crop, S3; see **gaignage**.
gaynen, *v.* to avail, CM, S2; see **geꝫnen**.
gayn-ras, *sb.* return (= Lat. *occursus*), H;
gaynrase, *dat.* meeting, H; see **ꝫeyn**.
gayn-stand, *v.* to withstand, S3.
gaytre-beryis, *sb. pl.* berries of the gayter-
tree, C (C. 145), CM, MD.—Cf. Scot. *gait-
berry*, bramble-berry, JD; *gaiter-tree*, the
bramble, JD.
ge-, *prefix*; see **ꝫe-**.
ge, ye, S; see **ꝫe**.
geaunt, *sb.* giant, S, C2; **giaunt**, W2;
gyaunt, PP; **ieaunt**, PP; **geauntes**, *pl.*,
PP; **ieauntez**, S2.—AF. *geant*; Lat. *gigantem*.
gede, *pt. s.* went, S.—AS. *ge-éode*, Cf. **gæde**.
gedelynge, *sb.* vagabond, PP; see **gadeling**.
gederen **gedre**; see **gaderen**.
gees, *sb. pl.* geese; see **gos**.
geet[1], *sb.* jet, C; **geete**, Prompt.; see **jette**[1].
geet[2], *sb. pl.* goats, W2; **geete**, W2; see **goot**.
geet-buckis, *sb. pl.* he-goats, W2.
geinen, *v.* to avail, profit, S, S2; see **geꝫnen**.
geld, *pt. s.* paid, requited, S; see **ꝫelden**.
gelden, *v.* to geld, *castrare*, Prompt., Manip.;
geldid, *pp.*, W (Mt. 19. 12).—Icel. *gelda*.
gelding, *sb.* eunuch, W (Acts 8. 34); **ꝫeld-
ing**, W (Acts 8. 27); **geldingis**, *pl.*, W.
gelty, *adj.* guilty; see **gulty**.
gemme, *sb.* gem; **gemmes**, *pl.*, PP, G2;
jemis, S3.—OF. *gemme*; Lat. *gemma*, gem,
bud. See **ꝫimmes**.
gemmyt, *adj.* covered with buds, S3.
gendre, *sb.* gender, kind, PP; **gendrez**, *pl.*,
S2.—OF. *genre*; Lat. *genere*, abl. of *genus*.
gendre, *v.* to beget; **gendrith**, *pr. s.*, W2;
gendrid, *pp.*, W2.
gendrer, *sb.* progenitor, PP.
gendrure, *sb.* engendering, W2.
gendrynge, *sb.* begetting, PP.
genette, *sb.* a small Spanish horse, a jennet,
SkD; **iennet**, S3, Sh.—OF. *genette* (Cotg.);
Sp. *ginete*, a light horseman (Minsheu): from
Ẕenāta, the name of a tribe in Barbary, see
Dozy.

genge, *sb.* a going, expedition, army, S; *pl.* nations, S2, H.

gent, *adj.* noble, nobly-born, PP, C2; sprucc, gay, SkD (p. 813), S3; **gente**, S.—OF. *gent*; Lat. *genitum*, born, well-born.

gentil, *adj.* worthy, excellent, gentle, compassionate, C2; noble, PP; **gentils**, *sb. pl.*, people well born, C2, C3.—AF. *gentil*, noble, beautiful; Lat. *gentilem*.

gentillesse, *sb.* nobleness, gracefulness, C2, C3.—OF. *gentillesse*.

gentrise, *sb.* noble nature, PP; **gentrice**, PP.—AF. *genterise*.

gentrye, *sb.* gentleness, PP.

gepoun, *sb.* a short cassock, CM; see **gipoun**.

ger¹, *pl.* years, S; see **ȝeer**.

ger², *v.* to cause, make, S2, JD; **gere**, to make, H; **gar**, JD, S3; **gare**, H; **geren**, to prepare, S; **gare**, *imp.*, H; **gers**, *pr. s.*, H; *2 pr. s.*, H; **gerte**, *pt. s.*, PP; **gert**, S2, PP, S3, H; **garte**, PP; **gart**, S2, PP; **garde**, *pl.*, S3; **gert**, *pp.*, PP, H.—Icel. *göra* (for *görva*). See **ȝare²**.

geraflour; see **gerraflour**.

gere, *sb.* gear, apparel, property, material, business, CM, PP, C, C2, C3, S2; **geare**, S3; **ger**, C, S3; **geeres**, *pl.*, habits, manners, C.—Cf. OS. *garuwi*, gear.

ger-fawcon, *sb.* a kind of falcon, HD; **ger-faucun**, Prompt.; **gerfawcune**, Voc.; **gerfawkyn**, Voc., Prompt.; **gerfaukun**, W2; **gerfawcun**, W2.—Lat. *gyrofalconem*.

ger-ful, *adj.* changeable, C, CM. See **gery**.

gerken, *v.* to prepare, S; see **ȝarken**.

gerland, *sb.* garland, C3, C; **gerelande**, PP; **garlaunde**, PP.—AF. *gerlaunde*.

gerles, *sb. pl.* children; see **gurles**.

gern, *adv.* eagerly, S2; see **ȝerne²**.

gerner, *sb.* garner, C, PP.—AF. *gerner*, OF. *gernier*, *grenier*; Late Lat. *granarium*.

gerraflour, *sb.* gilly-flower, S3; **geraflour**, HD; **gylofre**, MD, S2 (s.v. *clowe*); **gyllofre**, *gariophilus*, *galiofolus*, Prompt.; **gillofer**, ND, Palsg.; **gyllofyr**, clove, Prompt.; **gillyvor**, Sh.; **ielofer**, S3; **gelofer**, ND, MD.—Cf. OF. *girofle*, the clove (Bartsch); Low Lat. *gariophilus*, (Alph.), also *caryophyllum*; Gr. καρυόφυλλον, lit. nut-leaf.

gerss-pilis, *sb. pl.* blades of grass, S3. See **gras**.

gersum, *sb.* treasure; **gersom**, HD; **gær-sume**, *pl.*, S; **garisome**, S; **gersoms**, HD.—AS. *gærsum*; cf. Icel. *gersemi*, a costly thing, jewel.

gert¹, *pp.* made, S2; see **ger²**.

gert², *pp.* girt, S2; see **girden¹**.

gerte, *pt. s.* struck, G; see **girden²**.

gerth, *sb.* girth, SkD; **gerthis**, *pl.*, PP.—Icel. *gerð*.

gery, *adj.* changeful, PP, C. See **gerful**.

gessen, *v.* to suppose, imagine, CM, S2, C2, C3, W, W2; **gessist**, *2 pr. s.*, S2; **gessiden**, *pt. pl.*, S2.—Cf. Du. *gissen*.

gesserant, *sb.* a coat of mail, S3; **gesseron**, S3; see **jesseraunt**.

gessynge, *sb.* guessing (i.e. doubt), S2.

gest¹, *2 pr. s.* goest, S, S2; **geð**, *pr. s.*, S. S2; see **gan¹**.

gest², *sb.* guest, Prompt., S2, C2; **geste**, PP; **gestes**, *pl.*, S, PP, S2, C2; **geste**, S; **gistes**, PP; **gustes**, PP.—AS. *gæst*: Goth. *gasts*; cf. Lat. *hostis*.

geste¹, *sb.* story, romance, PP, C2; **gest**, S3, Manip.; **jest**, fun, Sh.; **gestes**, *pl.*, PP, C2, C3; **ieestes**, PP; **gestis**, deeds, W2, H.—AF. *geste*, an exploit, history of exploits, romance; Lat. *(res) gesta*, a thing performed.

geste², *v.* to tell romances, Prompt., MD; **jest**, to act in sport, Sh.

gesten, *pp.* lodged (?), S2.

gesting, *sb.* lodgings, S2.

gestinge, *sb.* jesting, S3; **gestynge**, romancing, Prompt. See **geste¹**.

gesten, *v.* to feast, entertain; **gestened**, *pt. s.*, HD; **igistned**, *pp.*, S2.

gestninge, *sb.* feast, banquet, S; **gestening**, S2; **gistninge**, S; **gystninge**, S.

gestour, *sb.* a reciter of tales, C2; **gestowre**, Prompt.; **gestiours**, *pl.*, CM. See **geste¹**.

get, *sb.* fashion, behaviour, CM, C, C3, Prompt.; see **jette²**.

geten, *v.* to gain, get, beget, PP; **get**, *pr. s.*, S2, PP; **gat**, *pt. s.*, S, PP; **geten**, *pl.*, PP; **geten**, *pp.*, PP, G; **gete**, PP.—AS. *gitan*, pt. *geat* (pl. *géaton*), pp. *giten*.

gett¹, *sb.* jet, Prompt.; see **jette¹**.

gett², *pp.* granted, S2; see **ȝeten²**.

geð, *pr. s.* goes; see **gan¹**.

geue-like, *adj.* equal. *Phr.*: **o geuelike**, on equal terms, S.—AS. *ge-efenlic*. See **even²**.

geyn, *adj.* near, convenient, ready, direct, S3; **geyne**, Prompt.; **gayn**, S2; **gain**, HD; **gane**, JD; **geynest**, *superl.*, fairest, S2.—Icel. *gegn*.

geȝnen, *v.* to meet, suit, avail; **geȝȝnenn**, S; **geinen**, to avail, profit, S, S2; **gayne**, CM; **ȝene**, to reply, S; **gane**, to fit, JD; **gayned**, *pt. s.*, S2; **ganyde**, *pl.*, S3; **ganand**, *pr. p.*, becoming, suitable, S3.—Icel. *gegna*, to go against, to answer, to suit. See **ȝeyn**.

giarkien, *v.* to prepare, S; see **ȝarken**.

giaunt, *sb.* giant, W2; see **geaunt**.

giet, *conj.* yet, S; see **ȝet**.

gif, gief, if, S2; see **ȝif**.

gigelot, *sb.* a strumpet, MD, H; **gygelot**, wench, *agagula*, Prompt.; **giglot**, ND, Sh.; **gigglet**, ND.

giggyng, *sb.* clattering, C.

gigour, *sb.* musician, S.—OF. *gigüeor* (Low Lat. *gigatorem*), from OF. *gigue* (Low Lat. *giga*), a musical instrument; cf. G. *geige*, violin.

gildir, *v.* to deceive; **gildirs**, *pr. s.*, H; **gildird**, *pp.*, H.—Icel. *gildra*, to trap.

gildire, *sb.* deceit, snare, H; **gildirs**, *pl.*, H.—Icel. *gildra*, a trap.

gile, *sb.* guile, deceit, fraud, PP, C.—AF. *gile*, OF. *guile*: AS. *wíle* (Chron. ann. 1128).

gilen, *v.* to beguile, PP; **gylen**, S2; **giled**, *pp.*, S.

gilery, *sb.* deceit, H; **gilrys**, *pl.*, H.—OF. *gillerie*.

gill, *sb.* a familiar term for a woman, S3, ND, Sh.; **jill**, Sh.—Short for *Gillian*, a woman's name, Sh., ND; Lat. *Juliana*.

gill-burnt-tayle, *sb.* the ignis-fatuus, ND (s.v. *gyl*).

gille, *sb.* a gill (measure), PP; **gylle**, PP, Prompt.; **iille**, P.—OF. *gelle*.

gill-flurt, *sb.* a flirt, ND.

gillofer, **gillyvor**; see **gerraflour**.

gilour, *sb.* deceiver, PP; **gyloure**, H.—AF. *gilour*.

gilt, *sb.* guilt, S, PP; see **gult**.

giltlese, *adj.* guiltless, S; **gilteles**, C; **giltlees**, C3.

gin, *sb.* engine, contrivance, artifice, C2, C3, S3; **gyn**, PP, S2; **ginne**, S, S2; **gynne**, PP.—OF. *engin*, *engien*, craft, deceit, contrivance.

ginful, *adj.* guileful, deceitful, PP.

gingebreed, *sb.* gingerbread, C2; **gyngebred**, *gingium*, Voc. Cf. Low Lat. *gingibretum* (Ducange), also OF. *gigimbrait*, a preparation of ginger, *gingenbret*, ginger (Bartsch).

gingiuere, *sb.* ginger, SkD, Cath. (*n*); **gingiuer**, HD; **gyngyre**, *zinzibrum*, Voc.; **ginger**, *zinziber*, **zinzebrum**, Cath.; **gyngere**, Prompt.—OF. *gingenbre*, *gengibre*; Lat. *zingibrum*, acc. of *zingiber*; Gr. ζιγγίβερις.

ginnen, *v.* to begin, S; **gynne**, S, PP, S3; **gan**, *pt. s.*, began, S, S2; **gon**, PP; **gonne**, *pl.*, S2; **gan**, *pt. s.* (used as an auxiliary), did, S, S2, S3; **gon**, S, PP, S2; **gun**, S2; **gunnen**, *pl.*, S; **gunne**, S, PP; **gonne**, S, PP, S2, C2, G.—AS. *-ginnan*, pt. *-gan* (pl. *-gunnon*), pp. *-gunnen*.

gipe, *sb.* cassock, CM; **jub**, Florio.—OF. *juppe* (Cotg.) It. *giuppa*, *giubba* (Florio), Sp. *al-juba* (Minsheu); Arab. *al-jubbah*, a woollen undergarment; cf. MHG. *schube*, G. *schaube* (Weigand).

gipoun, *sb.* a short cassock, CM; **gypoun**, C; **gepoun**, C; **jupon**, HD; **joupone**, HD.—OF. *gippon*, *jupon* (Cotg.), It. *giubbone*, a doublet (Florio.). See **gipe**.

gipser, *sb.* pouch, purse, C; **gypcer**, Prompt.; **gypsere**, Prompt.; **gypcyere**, Prompt.—OF. *gibbeciere* (Cotg.), from *gibier*, game.

girdel, *sb.* girdle, C, C2; **gurdel**, S.—AS. *gyrdel*.

girden[1], *v.* to gird, *cingere*, MD; **gurden**, MD; **girde**, *2 pt. s.*, S2; **gyrte**, *pt. s.*, S; **i-gurd**, *pp.*, S, S2; **gird**, C, W2; **gert**, S2.—AS. *gyrdan*.

girden[2], *v.* to strike, CM, HD, C2, G; **gurdeþ**, *imp. pl.*, S2; **girt**, *pt. s.*, cast, PP; **gerte**, G; **gorde**, *pt. pl.*, rushed, S2; **girt**, *pp.*, SkD (s.v. *gride*), C. See **ӡerde**.

gisel, *sb.* hostage, MD; **gysles**, *pl.*, S; **ӡisles**, MD; **ӡislen**, *dat.*, MD.—AS. *gísel*; cf. Icel. *gísl*.

gist, *sb.* guest; see **gest**[2].

giste, *sb.* a beam, balk, joist, MD; **gyyste**, Prompt.; **gyst**, Palsg.; **gistes**, *pl.*, MD; **joystes**, SkD.—OF. *giste*, joist, something to lie on. See **joist**.

gistninge, *sb.* banquet, S; see **gestninge**.

giterne, *sb.* guitar, C3, PP, MD, CM; **gyterne**, PP, Prompt.; **geterne**, MD; **getyrne**, Voc.—OF. *guiterne*; cf. It. *chitarra*; Lat. *cithara*. See **citole**.

giuenesse, *sb.* forgiveness, S.—AS. *gifnes*, grace.

glad[1], *pt. s.* glided, MD; **glade**, S2; **glaid**, S3; see **gliden**.

glad[2], *adj.* glad, S, S2; **gled**, S; **glaid**, S3; **gladur**, *comp.*, S; **gladdore**, S2.—AS. *glæd*.

gladien, *v.* to make glad, make merry, S; **gladen**, S, C2; **glade**, S3; **glaid**, S3; **gleadien**, S; **gledien**, S, S2; **gladed**, *pt. s.*, S2.—AS. *gladian*.

gladliche, *adv.* gladly, PP; **gledliche**, S.

gladnesse, *sb.* gladness, MD; **glednesse**, S.

gladschipe, *sb.* gladness, MD; **gledschipe**, S; **gledscipe**, S; **gleadschipes**, *pl.*, S.

gladsom, *adj.* pleasant, C2.

gladynge, *sb.* gladness, MD; **gleadunge**, S.

glam, *sb.* word, message, S2; loud talk, noise, MD.—Icel. *glam*, a tinkling sound.

glaren, *v.* to shine brightly, S, SkD.

glas, *sb.* glass, S, C2.—AS. *glæs*.

glasen[1], *adj.* made of glass, PP.

glasen[2], *v.* to furnish with glass, PP.

glað, *adj.* glad, MD; **glaðe**, S.—Icel. *glaðr*.

glaue, *sb.* sword, S3; see **gleyve**.

glayre, *sb.* the white of an egg, Cath.; **gleyre**.

gle, *sb.* joy, glee, music, singing, S, S2, PP; **glee**, C2; **glie**, S; **gleu**, C2 (*n*). MD; **glew**,

MD, S3; **glu**, Prompt.; **gleo**, S; **glewis**, *pl.*, freaks, S3.—AS. *gléo*, stem *gliwo-*, see Sievers, 250.

gleaw, *adj.* wise, S; **gleu**, S.—AS. *gliaw*.

gled, *adj.* glad; see **glad**[2].

glede[1], *sb.* a kite, *milvus*, H (Ps. 62. 8), ND, WW, Voc.—AS. *glida* (Voc.).

glede[2], *sb.* glowing coal, S, PP, S3, C2; **gleede**, C; **gleden**, *pl.*, S; **gledess**, S.— AS. *gléd*: OS. *glód* (stem *glódi*); cf. OHG. *gluot* (dat. *gluoti*). See **glowen**.

gledien, *v.* to make merry, S, S2; see **gladien**.

gledliche, *v.* gladly, S.

glednesse, *sb.* gladness, S.

gledschipe, *sb.* gladness, S.

gle-man, *sb.*; see **gleoman**.

glenten, *v.* to glance, to move swiftly, MD; **glente**, *pt. s.*, MD; **glent**, S3, HD; shone, SkD (p. 808).—Swed. *glinta*, to glance aside (Rietz).

gleo, *sb.* music, S; see **gle**.

gleo-beames, *sb. pl.* harps, S.

gleo-dreames, *sb. pl.* joys of music, S.

gleo-man, *sb.* minstrel, PP; **glewman**, PP; **gleman**, PP.

gleowien, *v.* to make music, to make merry, MD.

gleowinge, *sb.* music, S.

glette, *sb.* phlegm, slimy matter in the throat, *viscositas*, filth, Cath. (*n*), S2; **glett**, Cath.; **glet**, H, Cath. (*n*).—OF. *glette*, 'flegm, filth, which a hawk throws out at her beak after her casting', Cotg.; cf. North. E. *glit*, tough phlegm, JD.

gleu, *adj.* wise, S; see **gleaw**.

glew[1], *sb.* joy, glee, S3; see **gle**.

glew[2], *sb.* glue, MD; see **glu**.

gleyme, *sb.* slime, *limus, gluten*, Prompt.; **gleym**, subtlety, S3; **gleme**, *viscus*, Prompt. (*n*).

gleymows, *adj.* slimy, *viscosus*, Prompt.; **glaymous**, HD.

gleyre, *sb.* the white of an egg, C3, Prompt., Cath. (*n*); **glayre**, Cath.; **glarye**, Manip.— OF. *glaire*, the white of an egg (Cotg.); Low Lat. *glara* (Voc.); Late Lat. *clara ovi* (Ducange); cf. Sp. *clara de huevo*, also It. *chiára* (Florio).

gleyue, *sb.* sword, CM; **glayue**, SkD; **glave**, S3, ND; **gleiue**, SkD; **gleave**, Cotg., ND.—OF., *glaive*; Lat. *gladium* (acc.)—for the *v* in *glaive*, see Brachet (s.v. *corvée*).

gliden, *v.* to glide, S; **glyde**, C2, C3; **glydande**, *pr. p.*, walking, S2; **glit**, *pr. s.*, MD; **glad**, *pt. s.*, MD; **glade**, S2; **glaid**, S3; **glod**, MD, S2; **glood**, C2; **glode**, MD; **gliden**, *pl.*, MD; **gliden**, *pp.*, MD.—AS. *glídan*, pt. *glád* (*glidon*), pp. *gliden*.

glie, *sb.* music, S; see **gle**.

gliffen, *v.* to glance, *spectare*; **gliffe**, to look back, Manip.; **gliff**, to be scared, JD; **glyfte**, *pt. s.*, MD.

gliffni, *v.* to glance; **gliffnyt**, *pt. s.*, S2.

glod, *pt. s.* glided, S2, MD; **glode**, MD; **glood**, C2; see **gliden**.

glommen, *v.* to look glum, to frown, MD; **glomben**, MD; **glowmbe**, CM; **glum**, S3; **gloom**, ND; **gloume**, Manip.; **glom-mede**, *pt. s.*, HD.—Swed. *glomma*, to stare (Rietz).

glopen, *v.* to look askance, MD; **glop**, to stare, HD; **gloppen**, to be startled, HD. Cf. Du. *gluipen*, to peep, sneak.

glopnen, *v.* to look downcast, MD; **glop-nid**, *pp.*, frightened, S2.—Icel. *glúpna*.

glorie, *sb.* glory, PP; **glore**, S3.—AF. *glorie*; Lat. *gloria*.

glose, *sb.* a gloss, comment, explanation, PP, Prompt., C2; **glosis**, *pl.*, S3.—OF. *glose*; Lat. *glossa*, a gloss; Gr. γλῶσσα.

glosen, *v.* to explain, flatter, deceive, PP, Prompt., S3, C2, C3; **glosed**, *pt. s.*, spoke smoothly, S2; **y-glosed**, *pp.*, C3.—OF. *gloser*, to gloss, expound; Late Lat. *glosare*. See **glose**.

glosynge, *sb.* an expounding, Prompt.; flattering, Prompt.; **glosing**, flattery, W.

glotonie, *sb.* gluttony, S2, Prompt.; **glot-onyes**, *pl.*, C3.—OF. *glotonie*.

glotori, *sb.* gluttony, H; **glutiry**, H; **glutrie**, MD.

glotoun, *sb.* glutton, S, PP, W2; **gluton**, S.—AF. *glutun*; Lat. *glutonem*.

gloume, *v.*, see **glommen**.

glowen, *v.* to glow, PP, Prompt., C; **glouand**, *pr. p.*, S2; **glowennde**, S.—Cf. OHG. *gluojan*.

glu, *sb.* glue, Prompt.; **glew**, MD.—OF. *glu*; Lat. *gluten*.

gluen, *v.* to glue, MD; **y-glewed**, *pp.*, C2.

glum, *v.* to look gloomy, S3; see **glommen**.

glutenerie, *sb.* gluttony, S.—AF. *glutunerie*.

gluton, *sb.* glutton, S; see **glotoun**.

glutrie, *sb.* gluttony, MD; see **glotori**.

gnar, *v.* to snarl, S3; **gnarre**, ND. Cf. *gnarl*, to snarl, Sh.

gnasten, *v.* to gnash the teeth, Prompt., Palsg., W2, H; **gnayste**, H; **gnashe**, Manip.; **gnastiden**, *pt. pl.*, W, W2; **gnaistid**, H.—Cf. Icel. *gnastan*, a gnashing.

gnawen, *v.* to gnaw, PP; **gnaghe**, H; **gneʒeð**, *pr. pl.*, S; **gnow**, *pt. s.*, C2; **gnew**, SkD; **gnawiden**, *pt. pl.*, W2; **knawen**, *pp.*, S3.—AS. *gnagan*, pt. *gnóh* (pl. *gnógon*), pp. *gnagen*.

gniden, *v.* to rub, SD, S2; **gnyde**, S; **gniden**, *pt. pl.*, MD.—AS. *gnídan* (Voc.).

gobelin, *sb.* goblin, demon; **gobelyn**, W2, MD; **goblin**, Sh.—OF. *gobelin*; cf. Low Lat. *gobelinum* (acc.).

gobet, *sb.* a small piece, Prompt., C, W; **gobbet**, Manip.; **gobetis**, *pl.*, S2, W.—Norm.F. *gobet*, see Diez, p. 599; cf. OF. *gobeau*, a bit, gobbet (Cotg.).

god[1], *adj.* good, S, S2. *Phr.*: **to goder hele**, to the good health of, S2, MD; **goderhele**, MD; **godder-hele**, HD. See **good**[1].

god[2], **God**, *sb.* god, God, S; **godd**, S; **gode**, *dat.*, S; **godes**, *gen.*, S; *pl.*, S; **goden**, S.—AS. *god*.

god-child, *sb.* godchild, S.

godcund, *adj.* divine, godly, MD.

godcundhede, *sb.* piety, MD.

godcundnesse, *sb.* divinity, S; **godcunnesse**, S.

goddcundleȝȝc, *sb.* divinity, S.

Goddot, God knows, S; **Goddoth**, S.—AS. *God wát*.

godhede, *sb.* deity, C.

godien, *v.* to endow; **goded**, *pt. s.*, S; **i-goded**, *pp.*, benefited, S.—AS. *gódian*.

godlec, *sb.* goodness, S, MD.—Cf. Icel. *góðleiki*.

godles, *adj.* without good, needy, S2, MD; **godelease**, S.—AS. *gódléas*.

godly, *adv.* kindly, S2; **goddeli**, S2; **gudely**, S3.—AS. *gódlice*.

godnesse, *sb.* goodness, S; **godnisse**, S, S2; **godenesse**, S2.

god-spel, *sb.* gospel, S; **god-spell**, S3; **gospel**, MD.—AS. *godspel*.

godspelboc, *sb.* gospel-book, S.

Gog, *sb.* A corrupt form of **God** employed in oaths; *phr.*: **Gog's arms**, S3.

gogelen, *v.* to goggle, MD.

gogil-iȝed, *adj.* squint-eyed, W; **gogyl-eyid**, Prompt.; **goggle-eyed**, *louche* (Palsg.).

gold, *sb.* gold, S; **gol**, S; **gulde**, *dat.*, S.—AS. *gold*; cf. Icel. *gull*.

gold-beten, *pp.* adorned with beaten gold, S3.

golde, *sb.* marigold, *souci*, Palsg.; **goolde**, *solsequium*, Prompt.; **guldes**, *pl.*, C.—Cf. OF. *goude* (Cotg.)

gold-spynk, *sb.* goldfinch, S3.

gole, *sb.* throat, SD, HD; **golle**, HD.—OF. *gole, goule, gule*; Lat. *gula*.

golet, *sb.* gullet, C3, Prompt., HD.—OF. *goulet*.

goliardeys, *sb.* buffoon, MD, PP; **golyardeys**, C.—OF. *goliardeis (goliardois)*; Low Lat. *goliardensis*.

golnesse, *sb.* lasciviousness, S; see **galnesse**.

gome[1], *sb.* a man, PP, S, S2; **gomes**, *gen.*, S2; **gumen**, *pl.*, S.—AS. *guma* (stem *guman-*); cf. Lat. *homo* (stem *homin-*).

gome[2], *sb.* care, PP; **gom**, MD.—OS. *góma*, care; cf. OHG. *gouma*, provision, supper (Tatian).

gomen, *sb.* play, S; **gome**, S; see **gamen**[1].

gomme, *sb.* gum, CM; **gumme**, Cath.; **gommes**, *pl.*, P.—OF. *gomme*; Lat. *gummi*; Gr. κόμμι.

gon, *v.* to go, S, S2, C2; **gonde**, *pr. p.*, S; **goon**, *pp.*, C2; see **gan**[1].

gone, *v.* to gape, S2; see **ganien**.

gonge, *2 pr. s. subj.* go, S; see **gangen**.

gonne, *sb.* gun, PP, CM; **gunne**, Cath., Prompt.; **gon**, S3.—Cf. Low Lat. *gunna*.

good[1], *adj.* good, MD; **god**, S, S2; **godd**, S2; **goud**, MD; **guod**, MD; **gud**, MD.—AS. *gód*.

good[2], *sb.* good, MD; **goud**, S2; **gud**, S3; **god**, S, S2; **godes**, *pl.*, S, S2; **guodes**, S2.—AS. *gód*.

goodman, *sb.* master of the house, C3.

goot, *sb.* goat, Prompt., C3; **gayte**, S3; **gat**, S; **gæt**, *pl.*, S; **gate**, S, S3; **geet**, W2; **geete**, W2; **gaite**, H; **gaytes**, H; **gayte**, H.—AS. *gát*.

gorde, *pt. pl.* rushed, S2; see **girden**[2].

gore[1], *sb.* a triangular piece of cloth inserted, HD; **gremiale**, apron, Manip.; **goore**, Prompt.; **gair**, JD. *Phr.*: **under gore**, under clothing, S2, HD.—Cf. AS. *gára*, an angular point of land.

gore[2], *sb.* mire, Prompt., HD; filth, S2.—AS. *gor* (Voc.).

gorge, *sb.* throat, Manip., PP.—OF. *gorge*; Lat. *gurgitem* (acc.); see Ducange.

gorget, *sb.* throat, piece of armour to protect the throat, SkD; 'torques', Manip.; **garget**, C; **gargate**, HD.—OF. *gorgette*, throat, also *gargaite*, (Roland, 1654).

gorst, *sb.* gorse, furze, Voc., MD; **gorstez**, *pl.*, S2; **gorstys tre**, Prompt.—AS. *gorst*.

gos, *sb.* goose, S3; **goos**, MD; **gees**, *pl.*, S; **gysse**, S3.—AS. *gós*.

gos-hawke, *sb.* goshawk, Prompt., Voc.; **gos-hauk**, C2.—AS. *gós-hafuc* (Voc.).

gosse, *sb.* in *phr.*: **by gosse** (a profane oath), S3.

gossib, *sb.* sponsor, PP, CM; **godsyb**, friend, PP.—AS. *god-sibb*.

gossomer, *sb.* gossamer, Prompt., C2; **gossummer**, Voc.; **gosesomere**, Voc.

gost, *sb.* spirit, mind, soul, life, ghost, PP, S, S2, C3; **goost**, C2, PP; **gast**, S, S2; **gostes**, *pl.*, S2; **gostus**, PP; **gastes**, S2.—AS. *gást*.

gostliche, *adj.* spiritual, S; **gostly**, S3, C3; **goostliche**, PP; **gastlike**, S; **gastelich**, S; **gasteli**, *adv.*, S2.

gote, *sb.* water-channel, Prompt., HD; **goote**, Prompt.; **gotez**, *pl.*, S2.—Cf. Low G. *gote*, Du. *goot*.

gotere, *sb.* gutter, water-channel, Prompt.; **goteris**, *pl.*, drops, *stillicidia*, rain falling drop by drop, W2; **goters**, HD.—OF. *goutiere*, gutter, from *gote*, a drop; Lat. *gutta*.

goulen, *v.* to howl, cry, S, S2; **gowland**, *pr. p.*, S3; see **ʒoulen**.

goules, *sb. pl.* the heraldic name for red, gules, SkD; **gowlis**, HD; **gowlys**, S3, HD.—AF. *goules*; Late Lat. *gulas* acc. pl. of *gula*, 'pellis rubricata' (Ducange).

goune, *sb.* gown, PP, C; **gowne**, PP; **gunes**, *pl.*, MD.—AF. *goune*, OF. *gone*.

goune-cloth, *sb.* cloth enough to make a gown, CM.

gourde, *sb.* gourd, C3, H; **goord**, Prompt.; **gowrdes**, *pl.*, S2.—OF. *gourde, gouhourde, cougourde*; Lat. *cucurbita*.

gouernaille, *sb.* management, C2; **gouernaile**, rudder, W; **gouernails**, *pl.*, W2.— OF. *gouvernail*, rudder; Lat. *gubernaculum*.

gouernance, *sb.* government, behaviour, PP, C2, C3; **gouernaunce**, C, C2, C3; **gouernauncis**, *pl.*, rules for conduct, customs, S3.

gouerne, *v.* to govern, PP, C2.—AF. *governer*; Lat. *gubernare*.

gouernour, *sb.* governor, C2; steersman, W, W2.—OF. *gouverneur*; Lat. *gubernatorem* (acc.).

gradde, *pt. s.*, S, S2, PP; see **greden**.

gradi, *adj.* greedy, S; see **gredy**.

graffe, *sb.* a slip, young shoot, PP, Prompt.; **graff**, Cotg.—Late Lat. *graphium*, a stile (Gr. γραφεῖον); hence Low Lat. *graffiolum*, a graft, sucker; cf. OF. *greffe*.

graffen, *v.* to graft, PP; **graffid**, *pp.*, W.

graith[1], *adj.* exact, direct, S2, PP; see **greiþ**.

graith[2], *sb.* preparation, PP.

graithen, *v.* to prepare, H; **grathis**, *pr. s.*, dresses, S3. See **greiþen**.

graithly, *adv.* readily, PP; **gratheli**, S2; see **greiðliche**.

gramcund, *adj.* angry, S.

grame, *sb.* vexation, anger, S, HD, C3; **grome**, S; **gram**, S2; **greme**, S2.—AS. *grama*; cf. Icel. *gramr*, wrath.

gramercy; see **graunt**.

gramien, *v.* to vex, to be angry, MD; **grame**, PP, S; **gromien**, MD.—AS. *gramian*; cf. Goth. *gramjan*. See **gremien**.

granand, *pr. p.* groaning, S2; see **gronen**.

granat, *sb.* a garnet; see **garnet**.

granyt, *pp.* dyed in grain, S3; **grained**, Sh. See **greyne**.

grape, *v.* to handle, *palpare*, H; see **gropien**.

grapers, *sb. pl.* grappling-irons, S3.

gras, *sb.* grass, S, PP, C2; **gres**, S, Prompt.; **gresse**, Prompt., S2; **grases**, *pl.*, 82; **greses**, S2; **gyrss**, S3.—AS. *græs*: Goth. *gras*.

grathis, *pr. s.* dresses, S3; see **graiþen**.

graunt, *adj.* great, PP. *Phr.*: **graunt-mercy**, many thanks, C2, C3, PP; **gramercy**, PP, Sh.; **gramercies**, *pl.*, S3.—AF. *grant*, OF. *grand*; Lat. *grandem*.

grauntye, *v.* to grant, give, agree, allow, PP; **grawntyn**, Prompt., C2; **graunte**, PP; **granti**, S, S2; **graunti**, *1 pr. s.*, S; **grante**, *imp. s.*, S; **y-graunted**, *pp.*, C3, P; **i-granted**, S2.—AF. *gräanter* (*graunter, granter*); OF. *crëanter*; Late Lat. *credentare*, from Lat. *credentem*, pr. p. of *credere*.

grauen, *v.* to bury, S, PP, C2, H; to engrave, PP; **grof**, *pt. s.*, H; **grauen**, *pp.*, buried, S, PP, G, H; **i-grauen**, engraved, S; **i-graue**, S, G; **graue**, PP.—AS. *grafan*, to dig, pt. *gróf*, pp. *grafen*.

grauynge, *sb.* engraving, S2, P; burying, H.

gravys, *pl.* groves, S3; see **grove**.

gray; see **grey**.

gre, *sb.* step, degree, S3, PP, MD; worthiness, *gradus*, Prompt.; **gree**, HD; **grees**, *pl.*, W, MD, HD; **greis**, H.—OF. *gre*; Lat. *gradum* (acc.).

grece, *sb.* stair, MD, Prompt., Cath., Palsg.; **greece**, Manip.; **grese**, MD, HD; **greese**, Cotg. (s.v. *degré*), HD; **grize**, Sh.; **greces**, *pl.*, W2; **grises**, Prompt. (*n*).—From *grees*, steps, a flight of steps, *pl.* of **gre** (above).

greden, *v.* to cry aloud, S, PP, S2; **gradde**, *pt. s.*, S, PP, 82; **gredde**, PP.—AS. *grédan*, pt. *grédde*.

gredinge, *sb.* crying, MD; **gredynges**, *pl.*, S2.

gredy, *adj.* greedy, PP; **gradi**, S; **gredi**, S.—AS. *grédig*; cf. Icel. *gráðugr*.

gree[1], *sb.* favour, S2, C2, C3; prize, PP, C. *Phr.*: **take in gre**, agree to, S3.—OF. *gre, gred, gret*, pleasure, recompense; Lat. *gratum*, pleasing.

gree[2], *v.* to agree, HD; **greeing**, *pr. p.*, S3.— OF. *gréer*, to agree, to accept; Late Lat. *gratare* (for Lat. *gratari*).

greesings, *sb. pl.* steps, HD. See **grece**.

gref, *sb.* grief, MD; **greeue**, *dat.*, G.—OF. *gref*, from Lat. *gravem*, heavy.

gre-hounde; see **greyhownd**.

greit, *sb.* grit, S3; see **greot**.

greith, *adj.* ready, PP; **graith**, exact, direct, PP, S2; **grayþ**, PP; **grayþest**, *superl.*, PP, S2; **graith**, *adv.*, S3.—Icel. *greiðr*, ready: Goth. *ga-raids*, exact.

greiðen, *v.* to prepare, SD; **graithe**, H, HD; **grathis**, *pr. s.*, dresses, S3; **graithed**, *pt. s.*, S2; **greythede**, S; **greithide**, S2;

greithede, *pl.*, S2; **greythed**, *pp.*, S; **greȝȝþedd**, S; **grepþed**, S; **graythed**, HD, S2; **i-greiðet**, S; **y-greiðed**, S3; **graid**, H.—Icel. *greiða*.

greiðliche, *adv.* readily, PP; **graithly**, PP, HD; **graythely**, S2; **gratheli**, S2.

gremien, *v.* to vex, to be angry, MD, S; **greme**, S; **ȝe-gremed**, *pp.*, S.—AS. *gremian*. See **gramien**.

grene[1], *sb.* snare; see **grin**.

grene[2], *adj.* and *sb.* green, S, PP, S2, C2, C3; **greyne**, B.—AS. *gréne*: OS. *gróni*; cf. OHG. *gruoni* (Tatian).

grenehede, *sb.* greenness, wantonness, S2, C3.

grennen, *v.* to grin, show the teeth (as a dog), S, W; **grennyn**, Prompt.—AS. *grennian*.

grennunge, *sb.* grinning, S; **grennynge**, Prompt.

greot, *sb.* gravel, grit, PP; **greit**, S3; **greete**, Manip.; **grith**, PP.—AS. *gréot*.

gres, *sb.* grass, S, Prompt. See **gras**.

gresy, *adj.* grassy, S3.

gret, *adj.* great, S, S2, C2, PP; **greet**, C2; **grete**, Prompt., PP, S2, C2; **grette**, PP; **greate**, S; **grate**, S; **gretture**, *comp.* S; **grettoure**, PP; **grettour**, PP; **gretter**, C2; **grettere**, W2; **grettest**, *superl.*, PP; **grete**, *adv.*, S3.—AS. *gréat*.

greten[1], *v.* to salute, S, PP, S2; **gret**, *imp. s.*, S; **greteth**, *pl.*, G; **grette**, *pt. s.*, S, PP, S2, C2, C3, W; **grette**, *pl.*, G; **gretten**, W; **gret**, *pp.*, W.—AS. *grétan*, to approach (also *ge-grétan*), pt. *grétte*, pp. *gréted*: OS. *grótian*; cf. OHG. *gruazen* (Otfrid).

greten[2], *v.* to weep, S, PP, H; **greete**, S3; **gret**, S2; **groten**, S; **gretande**, *pr. p.*, HD; **gretand**, S2, S3, H; **gret**, *pr. s.*, S; **gret**, *pt. s.*, S, H; **grete**, HD; **grete**, *pp.*, HD, S2.—AS. *grétan* (*grǽtan*), pt. *grét* (pl. *gréton*), pp. *gréten*: Icel. *gráta*.

gretien, *v.* to magnify; **i-gret**, *pp.*, S.—AS. *gréatian*.

gretliche, *adv.* greatly, S, PP; **gretly**, S2; **gretluker**, *comp.*, S.

gret-wombede, *adj.* big-bellied, S3.

gretyng, *sb.* lamentation, S2; **gretynge**, H.

gretyngful, *adj.* sorrowful, H.

greuaunce, *sb.* grievance, hurt, C2; **grewance**, S3; **greuaunces**, *pl.*, PP.—OF. *grevance*.

greue, *sb.* thicket, grove, MD; **greues**, *pl.*, S2, CM, HD; **grevis**, S3.

greuen, *v.* to grieve, PP, S, C2.—AF. *grever*, to burden; Lat. *gravare*.

greuous, *adj.* grievous, PP; **greuousere**, *comp.*, W2.

grey, *adj.* grey, PP; **gray**, PP, MD; **greye**, *sb.* grey clothing, PP; **grai**, grey fur, S;

grey, S; badger, S3; **gray**, HD; badger's skin, HD.—AS. *grǽg*.

greyce, *adj.* grey, S3. See **grys**.

grey-hownd, *sb.* greyhound, *leporarius*, Voc.; **grayhund**, Voc.; **grayhownd**, Voc.; **grehunde**, Voc.; **grehownde**, Prompt.; **greahund**, SkD; **grehoundes**, *pl.*, S3; **greahondes**, S3; **greihoundes**, SkD.— Icel. *greyhundr*, greyhound; *grey*, a dog.

greyn[1], *sb.* handle, branch, MD; **grayn**, MD; **grayne**, WA.—Icel. *grein*.

greyn[2], *sb.* grain of corn, a kind of spice, MD, PP, CM; **greyne**, Prompt.; **greyn de Parys**, CM.—AF. *grein*, *grain*; Lat. *granum*.

greyne, *sb.* colour, dye, PP, MD; **greyn**, S3, C2; **grayn**, C2.—AF. *graine*; Late Lat. *grana*, cochineal dye (Ducange).

greyn-horne, *sb.* Greenhorn, the name of an ox in the Towneley Mysteries, HD.

griffoun, *sb.* griffin, C, S2; **gryffown**, Prompt.—OF. *griffon*, a gripe (Cotg.).

gril, *adj.* horrible, rough, fierce, MD; **gryl**, S2, Prompt.—Cf. MHG. *grel*, angry.

grillen, *v.* to vex, MD; **grulde**, *pt. s.*, twanged, S; **i-gruld**, *pp.*, provoked, SD.—AS. *grillan*.

grim, *adj.* fierce, S; **grym**, heavy, PP, S2, C; **grimme**, *pl.*, horrible, S.—AS. *grim*.

grimlich, *adj.* horrible, S; **grimlych**, S; **grimliche**, *adv.* terribly, S, PP; **grymly**, sharply, PP.

grin, *sb.* snare, noose, S, Voc.; **gryn**, W; **grene**, *laqueus*, MD, Voc.; **grune**, MD; **grone**, MD; **grane**, MD.—AS. *grin*.

grinden, *v.* to grind, MD; **y-grounde**, *pp.*, C2; **grundyn**, S3; **grounden**, C3.—AS. *grindan*, pt. *grand* (pl. *grundon*), pp. *grunden*.

grindere, *sb.* grinder; **grynderis**, *pl.*, W2.

grip, *sb.* vulture, S; **grype**, Voc., Prompt.— Icel. *gripr*.

gripen, *v.* to grip, S, PP, H; **grap**, *pt. s.*, MD; **grop**, MD; **gripen**, *pl.*, MD; **grepen**, MD; **gripen**, *pp.*, MD; **grypen**, PP; **griped**, PP.—AS. *grípan*, pt. *gráp* (pl. *gripon*), pp. *gripen*.

gris, *sb.* a young pig, PP; **grise**, Cath.; **gryse**, Voc.; **gryce**, Prompt.; **grys**, *pl.*, MD, S2, PP.—Icel. *gríss*.

grisen, *v.* to shudder, S2; **gryse**, to be frightened, HD; **him gros**, *pt. s. reflex.*, S.— AS. *grísan*, pt. *grós* (pl. *grison*), pp. *grisen*.

grislich, *adj.* horrible, S; **grislic**, S; **grysliche**, S, PP; **grisli**, S2; **grisly**, C2, C3; **grisliche** *adv.*, S; **grieslie**, S3.—AS. *grislic*.

grist, *sb.* ground corn, SkD.—AS. *grist*, from *grindan*; for loss of *n* before *s*, see Sievers, 185.

grist-batinge, *sb.* grinding of the teeth, MD; **grisbayting**, MD; **gris-bitting**, S2.

grith, *sb.* peace, S; **griðe**, *dat.*, S.—Icel. *grið*, domicile, place of safety, peace; hence *grið* in the Chron.

grið-bruche, *sb.* breach of the peace, S.

griðful, *adj.* peaceful, MD.

griðfulnesse, *sb.* peacefulness, S.

grocchen, *v.* to grudge, grumble, S2, S3. See **grucchen**.

grof[1], *pt. s.* dug, buried, H. See **graven**.

grof[2], *adv.* flat on one's face, CT (951); **gruf**, MD, C2, C. *Phr.* **a gruf**, MD; **on groufe**, MD; **one the groffe**, MD.—Cf. Icel. *liggja á grúfu*, to lie on one's face.

groflinges, *adv.* groveling, MD; **grouelings**, S2; **grouelynge**, *supinus*, Prompt.; **grufelynge**, Cath. See **grof**[2].

grom, *sb.* lad, servant, PP, **grome**, PP, S (*n*); **gromes**, *pl.*, S, PP.—Cf. ODu. *grom*, stripling.

grome, *sb.* vexation, anger, S. See **grame**.

gronen, *v.* to groan, PP, CM, Prompt.; **grony**, S2; **graninde**, *pr. p.*, S; **granand**, S2; **gronte**, *pt. s.*, C2.—AS. *gránian*.

grop, *pt. s.*; see **gripen**.

gropien, *v.* to seize, handle, MD; **gropyn**, Prompt.; **grope**, C, C3; **grape**, *palpare*, H, Manip.—AS. *grápian*, from *grípan*. See **gripen**.

gros, *pt. s. reflex.* was afraid, S. See **grisen**.

grot[1], *sb.* weeping, S, MD. See **greten**[2].

grot[2], *sb.* atom, MD; **grotes**, *pl.*, S.—AS. *grot*, particle.

grote, *sb.* groat, C3, PP; **grotte**, S3.—OLG. *grote*, a coin of Bremen; cf. Du. *groot*, great. Cf. **gret**.

groten, *v.* to weep, S, MD; see **greten**[2].

ground, *sb.* ground, foundation, bottom (of water, of a well), MD; **grund**, S; **grounde**, PP; **gronde**, *dat.*, S2; **groundes**, *pl.* foundations, S2. *Phr.*: **to grounde com**, came to the ground, i.e. was ruined, S2.—AS. *grund*.

grounden, *v.* to found; **grownden**, Prompt.; **groundes**, *2 pr. s.*, S2; **grounded**, *pp.*, S2.

groue, *sb.* a little wood, Prompt., MD; **gravys**, *pl.*, S3.—AS. *gráf*.

grouelings, *adv.* flat on one's face, S2; see **groflinges**.

groyn, *sb.* the snout of a pig, CM; **groyne**, Prompt.; **groon**, Manip.; **grune**, Cath.—OF. *groing, groin*.

groynen, *v.* to grunt, to murmur, W, **groignen**, MD.—OF. *groigner, grogner*.

groynyng, *sb.* murmuring, discontent, C2.

grucchen, *v.* to grudge, grumble, PP, S2, C, C2; **grocching**, *pr. p.*, S2; **grocched**, *pt. s.*, S3; **grutchiden**, *pt. pl.*, W, W2.—OF. *groucher, groucer, grocer*.

grucching, *sb.* grumbling, S; **grucchyng**, G; **grutchyng**, W.

gruf, *adv.* flat on one's face; see **grof**[2].

grulde, *pt. s.*, twanged, S; see **grillen**.

grund, *sb.*; see **ground**.

grundlike, *adv.* thoroughly, heartily, MD, S. See **ground**.

grunten, *v.* to grunt, MD; **gryntiden**, *pt. pl.*, MD. Cf. OHG. *grunzen*.

gruntyng, *sb.* grunting, gnashing, W; **grynting**, W; **grentyng**, W.

grure, *sb.* horror, MD.—AS. *gryre*; OS. *gruri*.

grure-ful, *adj.* horrible, S.

gruselien, *v.* to munch, S.

grusen, *v.* to munch, MD; **gryze**, HD; **gruse**, JD.

grys, *sb.* a costly fur, the fur of the grey squirrel, C, S2, PP, HD; grey, C3; **gryce**, Prompt.; **greys**, PP; **greyce**, S3.—OF. *gris*, gray.

gu, you, S; see **3ou**.

guerdon, *sb.* reward, S3, CM; **guerdone**, S3, CM.—AF. *guerdon*: It. *guidardone*; Low Lat. *widerdonum* (Ducange).

guerdonen, *v.* to reward, CM.—OF. *guerredoner* (Bartsch).

guerdonlesse, *adj.* without reward, CM.

guerdonyng, *sb.* reward, CM.

gukgo, *sb.* cuckoo, S3; see **cukkow**.

gulche-cuppe, *sb.* a toss-cup, S.

gulchen, *v.* to gulp, swallow greedily, MD.

gulde[1], *sb. dat.* gold, S; see **gold**.

gulde[2], *sb.* marigold, C; see **golde**.

gulden, *adj.* golden. S, MD; **gilden**, S2, MD.—AS. *gylden*.

gult, *sb.* guilt, S, S2, C, PP; **gylt**, C; **gilt**, S, PP; **gylte**, PP; **gilte**, PP; **gultes**, *pl.* faults, S, PP; **gultus**, S2.—AS. *gylt*.

gulten, *v.* to sin, S; **gilte**, *pt. s.*, S; **gulte**, *pl.*, PP; **i-gult**, *pp.*, S.—AS. *gyltan*.

gulty, *adj.* guilty, C, PP; **gylty**, PP; **gilty**, PP; **gelty**, S.—AS. *gyltig*.

gultyf, *adj.* guilty, G; **giltyf**, G, HD.

gumen, *pl.* men, S; see **gome**[1].

gumme, *sb.* gum; see **gomme**.

gunge, *adj.* young, S; **gungest**, *superl.*, youngest, S; **gunkeste**, S; see **3ong**.

gunnen, *pt. pl.* began, did; see **ginnen**.

gur, your, S; see **3e**.

gurdel, *sb.* girdle, S; see **girdel**.

gurden, *v.* to strike, MD; **gurdeþ**, *imp. pl.*, S2; see **girden**[2].

gurles, *sb. pl.* children (of either sex), C, PP; **gerles**, PP. *Phr.*: **knave gerlys**, boys, HD. Cf. **gyrle**.

guðhede, *sb.* youth, S; see **3ouþede**.

gyde[1], *sb.* clothing, C3, MD; **gide**, MD, JD.

gyde[2], *sb.* guide, C3.

gyden, *v.* to guide, C2, C3, Palsg.—OF. *guider*.

gyen, *v.* to guide, direct, PP, Prompt.; **gye**, S3, C2, C3; **gie**, PP; **gyede**, *pt. s.*, PP, S2.—OF. *guïer, guider.*

gylofre, *sb.* gillyflower, S2 (s.v. *clowe*); see **gerraflour.**

gylt[1], *adj.* gilt, PP; **gulte**, PP; **gilte**, PP, C2.

gylt[2], *v.* to gild, S3.

gymp, *adj.* slim, delicate, short, scanty, S3; **gimp**, JD; neat, HD; **jimp**, HD, DG; **gym**, trim, spruce, S3; **gim**, DG; **jim**, DG; **jemmy**, DG.

gyrle, *sb.* a child, generally a girl, but also used of a boy, MD; **gerles**, *pl.*, MD; **girles**, MD. Cf. **gurles.**

gryrss, *sb.* grass; see **gras.**

gyse, *sb.* guise, manner, C, PP, Prompt.; **gise**, C, S3; **gyss**, S3.—AF. *guise.* See **wyse.**

gysse, *sb. pl.* geese, S3; see **gos.**

99

H

ha, *pron.* he, S, S2. See **he**.
habben, **habe**; see **haven**.
haberdasher, *sb.* a seller of small wares, C, SkD (p. 809).
haberdashrie, *sb.* haberdashery, SkD.
haberioun, *sb.* habergeon, a piece of armour to defend the neck and breast, PP; **haburioun**, W, W2; **hawbyrgon**, Voc.; **haburjon**, S2; **habergeoun**, C2; **haber-ion**, PP.—OF. *hauberjon* from *hauberc*. See **hauberk**.
habide, *v.* to abide, resist, S2; see **abiden**.
habilitie, *sb.* ability, S3. See **abilite**.
hable, *adj.* able, S3, MD. See **abil**.
haboundanle, *adv.* abundantly, S3. See **habundantly**.
habounde, *v.* to abound, NED, S3, C2; see **habunde**.
habundance, *sb.* abundance, C2.
habundant, *adj.* abundant, C2.
habundantly, *adv.* abundantly, C3.
habunde, *v.* to abound, NED.—OF. *habonder*, *abunder*; Lat. *abundare*.
hac, *conj.* but, S; see **ac**.
hacche, *sb.* hatch, PP; **hach**, hatch of a ship, S2.—Cf. Dan. *hække*.
had, *sb.* state, order, rank, person (of Christ), S; *pl.* ranks (of angels), S.—AS. *hád*; cf. OHG. *heit*.
hæ-; see also words beginning in **he-**.
hæhst, highest; see **heighest**.
hæleð, *sb.* warrior; see **heleþ**.
hæne, *adj. pl.* poor, S. See **heyne**.
hærre, *sb.* lord, S. See **herre**[2].
hæʒe, *adv.* highly, S; see **heighe**.
haf, hafst, hafð; see **haven**.
hafed, *sb.* head, S. See **heved**.
hafed-men, *sb. pl.* prelates, S.
hage-faderen, *sb.* heh-fader.
hagge, *sb.* a hag, P; **hegge**, MD.
hagt, *sb.* (?), S. {Dr F. Holthausen suggests that this word means 'danger, peril', comparing this ME. *hagt* with Icel. *hætta* which has the same meaning. Kluge connects this *hætta* with Gothic *hāhan*, to hang, so that it may mean radically 'a state of being in suspense'. The word must have come into England in the form **haht*, before the assimilation of *ht* to *tt*.}
hah, *adj.* high, S; see **heigh**.
hail[1], *sb.* hail, PP; **heal**, S3; **haille**, PP; **hayle**, PP.—AS. *hagol*.
hail[2], *adj.* hale, whole, sound, S; **hæil**, S; **heil**, S. Cf. **hool**.
haile, *adv.* wholly, S3; **haill**, S3.

hailen, *v.* to greet, Cath., MD; **heilen**, MD, S2.
hailsen, *v.* to greet, to say 'hail', MD, Cath., P, S3; **haylsen**, S3; **halsen**, S2, S3.—Icel. *heilsa*; cf. AS. *hálsian*, to greet, see Sievers, 411.
hailsinge, *sb.* salutation, Cath.; **halsing**, S2.
hailsum, *adj.* wholesome, S3.
hakeney, *sb.* horse, nag, C3, PP; *equillus*, Voc.; *mannus*, Voc.—AF. *hakenai, hakeney*.
hakeney-man, *sb.* one who lets out horses, P; *equiferus*, Voc.; **hakneyman**, Voc.
hal[1], *sb.* a secret place, MD; **hale**, *dat.*, S.
hal[2], *adj.* all, S2; see **al**[1].
halde, *pt. s.* inclined, S. See **helden**.
halely, *adv.* wholly, S2; **haly**, S2. See **hail**[2].
halen, *v.* to hale, drag, S, S2, S3, Prompt.; **halie**, PP.—OS. *halón*; cf. OFris. *halia*; from Teutonic comes OF. *haler*.
Halende, *sb.* the Saviour, S; see **Helende**.
halewen, *v.* to hallow, consecrate, S2, W2, PP; **halwen**, S2, S3, PP, C3; **haliʒen**, S; **halʒed**, *pt. s.*, S2; **y-halʒed**, S2.—AS. *hálgian*. See **holi**.
halewis, *sb. pl.* saints, W; **halechen**, S; see **halwes**.
half, *sb.* side, S, S2; **hælf**, S; **halue**, *dat.*, S; *pl.*, S; **halues**, G. *Phr.*: **o Godess hallfe**, on God's behalf, S.—AS. *healf*.
halflingis, *adv.* half, S3.
halfpeny, *sb.* halfpeny, MD; **halpens**, *pl.*, W.
hali, *adj.* holy, S, S2. See **holi**.
halidom, *sb.* a holy thing, holy relics, S, P; **halydom**, S2; **haliʒdomess**, *pl.*, S.—AS. *háligdóm*.
hali-write, *sb.* holy writ, S.
haliʒen, *v.* to hallow, S; see **halewen**.
halke, *sb.* corner, recess, S, Prompt., MD; **halkes**, *pl.*, C3; **halkeʒ**, S2.
halle, *sb.* hall, Cath., S, C2; **hallen**, *dat.*, S.—AS. *heall*.
halp, *pt. s.*; see **helpen**.
hals, *sb.* neck, S, S2, C2, C3.—AS. *heals*; cf. Icel. *háls*.
halsien, *v.* to embrace, MD; **halsen**, Cath., Prompt.; **hals**, H.—AS. *healsian*; cf. Icel. *hálsa*.
halsien, *v.* to beseech, conjure, MD; **halsen**, S2, C2.
hals-man, *sb.* executioner, HD.
halsynge, *sb.* embrace, Cath.
halt, *adj.* lame, MD.

halten, *v.* to walk as lame, MD; **halted**, *pt. pl.*, S2.—AS. *healtian.*

haluen-del, *sb.* the half, S, G; **haluendele**, PP.

halwes, *sb. pl.* saints, C3; **halewis**, W; **halhes**, S; **halechen**, S; **hale3en**, *dat.*, S; **hal3en**, S2; **halhen**, S; **halege**, *sb.*, saint, S; **halgh**, S2. See **holi.**

hal3ed, *pt. s.*; see **halewen.**

ham[1], them, S, S2; see **hem.**

ham[2], *sb.* home, S. See **hoom.**

ham[3], *1 pr. s.* am, S; see **am.**

hamer, *sb.* hammer, C, C3.—AS. *hamor.*

hamly, *adv.* familiarly, heartily, H. See **homliche.**

hamlynes, *sb.* intimacy, H. See **homlinesse.**

hand, *sb.* hand, MD; **hond**, S, S2, C2; **hoond**, W, W2; **honde**, *dat.*, S, S2, C3; **hand**, *pl.*, S; **bend**, S, S2; **hende**, S2; **honde**, S; **honden**, S, S2; **handes**, S; **hondes**, S, S3, C2, C3, P.—AS. *hand* (*hond*).

hand-ful, *sb.* sheaf, S, MD.

handidandi, *sb.* forfeit, P; **handiedandie**, HD.

handlen, *v.* to handle, S, C2.

hangen[1], *v.* (*strong*), to hang; (1) *tr.*, MD; **heng**, *pt. s.*; C2; **hengen**, *pl.*, S; **heengen**, S2; **hongen**, *pp.*, MD; (2) *intr.* **heng**, *pt. s.*, C3, MD; **hyng**, S2, MD; **hing**, MD; **hong**, S3, MD; **hynge**, C.—AS. *hange*, 1 pr. s., *héng*, pt. s., *hangen*, pp.

hangen[2], *v.* (*weak*) to hang; (1) *intr.*, MD; **hengen**, S, MD; **hongen**, S, S2, S3; **hongien**, MD; **hingen**, S2; **hing**, MD; **hyng**, S2, S3, H; **henged**, *pt. s.*, MD, S; **honged**, *pl.*, S3, G; **hangiden**, W; **henged**, *pp.*, S; (2) *tr.* **hongede**, *pt. s.*, S2; **hongide**, W; **hangede**, MD; **hanged**, *pp.*, P; **y-honged**, S2.—AS. *hangian.*

hanselle, *sb.* handsel, earnest-money on a purchase, a gift, PP, Cath.; **hansale**, *strena*, Prompt.; **haunsel**, MD; **hansel**, P, HD.—Icel. *handsal*, the confirming of a bargain by shaking hands.

hansellen, *v.* to handsel, to betroth, MD, Cath., Palsg.; **i-hondsald**, *pp.*, S.—Icel. *handsala.*

hap, *sb.* chance, fortune, C2, C3, PP; **happe**, S2, W; **happes**, *pl.*, P.—Icel. *happ.*

happen, *v.* to hap, chance, P, S2, C2, C3; **hapte**, *pt. s.*, MD.

happiliche, *adv.* perchance, P; **happily**, P.

happy, *adj.* lucky, S3.

happyn, *v.* to wrap up, Prompt., MD; **hap**, JD; **happis**, *pr. s.*, S3; **happid**, *pt. s.*, HD; **happid**, *pp.*, H.

happynge, *sb.* wrapping, H.

harborowe, *v.* to harbour; see **herberwe**[2].

harde, *adj.* hard, severe, disastrous, parsimonious, PP, C2; **hard**, S; **harde**, **herdure**, *adj. comp.*, S; **harde**, *adv.*, severely, S, S2; **hard**, with difficulty, W. *Comb.*: **harde clodes**, sackcloth, S. *Phr.*: **of hard**, with difficulty, W, W2.—AS. *heard.*

hardeliche, *adv.* bravely, S, S2; **hardely**, S3.

harden, *v.* to make hard; **y-harded**, *pp.*, C2.

hardenen, *v.* to harden; **harrdenesst**, *2 pr. s.*, S.

hardi, *adj.* hardy, S, W2; bold, daring, S2; **hardy**, C2, PP.—OF. *hardi.*

hardiliche, *adv.* boldly, P; **hardilike**, S; **hardily**, C2; **hardiloker**, *comp.*, PP.

hardiment, *sb.* boldness, MD; **hardyment**, S2.

hardinesse, *sb.* boldness, C2; **hardynesse**, W, PP.

harding, *sb.* a hardening, C2.

hares, *pl.* hairs, S2; **haris**, S3. See **here**[1].

harlot, *sb.* beggar, vagabond, ribald, buffoon, rascal, C, PP; **herlot**, acrobat, H; **harlotte**, MD; **harlotes**, *pl.*, P; **herlotis**, H; *adj.* scoundrelly, S3.—OF. *harlot, herlot, arlot.*

harlotrie, *sb.* tale-telling, jesting talk, ribaldry, buffoonery, P; **harlatrye**, jesting = Lat. *scurrilitas* (εὐτραπελία), W; **harlotries**, *pl.*, C.

harm, *sb.* harm, S; **hærm**, S; **hearm**, S; **harem**, S; **hærme**, *dat.*, S; **harme**, S, C2; **hermes**, *pl.*, damages, S; **harmes**, PP.—AS. *hearm.*

harmen, *v.* to harm, S; **hearmed**, *pr. s.*, S; **hermie**, *subj.*, S.—AS. *hearmian.*

harne-panne, *sb.* the cranium, skull, Cath.; **harnpanne**, Voc.; **harnpane**, Voc.; **hernepanne**, HD.

harnes, *sb. pl.* brains, Voc., Cath., HD; **hærnes**, S; **hernes**, S2.—Icel. *hjarni*, the brain; cf. Goth. *hvairnei.*

harneys, *sb.* armour, C, PP, S3; **herneys**, C, PP.—OF. *harneis.*

harneysed, *pp.* equipped, C.

haro! *interj.*, a cry for assistance raised in Normandy by any one wronged, HD; **harow**, PP; **harrow**, an exclamation of distress, C, C3, PP.—AF. *harro!* OF. *haro, harol*, Cotg., Palsg., p. 501, Bartsch.

harre, *sb.* hinge, C, CM. See **herre**[1].

harryng, *sb.* growling like a dog, S2.

harwen, *v.* to harrow, harry, ravage, PP, MD, CM; **herwen**, MD; **herien**, S2; **harowen**, PP, MD; **hær3ien**; **her3ien**, MD.—AS. *hergian.*

hary, *v.* to drag violently, CM; **harry**, to drag, to vex, HD; **haried**, *pp.*, C.—OF. *harier*, to harry, hurry, vex (Cotg.).

has   **hawe-þorne**

has, *sb.* command, S; see **heste**.
hasard, *sb.* the game of hazard played with dice, C3, Voc.—OF. *hasard, hasart.*
hasardour, *sb.* a dice-player, C3, Voc.; **haserder**, Voc.—AF. *hasardour*, OF. *hasardeur.*
hasardrye, *sb.* gaming, playing at hazard, C3.
hase, *adj.* hoarse, H. See **hoos**.
haske, *sb.* a wicker fish-basket, ND, S3.
haspe, *sb.* a hasp, fastening of a door, Manip.; **hespe**, Prompt., Cath.—AS. *hæpse* (Voc.).
haspen, *v.* to hasp, *obserare*, Manip.; **hasped**, *pp.*, S2; **y-hasped**, P; **i-haspet**, S2.
hast, *sb.* haste, PP.—Cf. OSwed. *hast.*
hasten, *v.* to haste; **hasteth**, *imp. pl.*, C3.
hastif, *adj.* hasty, C2; **hastyfe**, S3.—OF. *hastif.*
hastiliche, *adv.* quickly, S2; **hasteliche**, S; **hastily**, C2; **hastly**, S2: **hestely**, S3.
hat, *adj.* hot, S; **hatere**, *comp.*, S. See **hoot**.
hate, *sb.* heat, S; see **hete**[1].
haten[1], *v.* to bid, promise, call; **hete**, *1 pr. s.*, S2, C3; **hote**, S2; **hicht**, S2; **hight**, S3; **hateð**, *pr. s.*, bids, S; **hat**, S; **hot**, S; **hoot**, S; **hat**, *pl.*, S2; **hæhte**, *pt. s.*, called, S; **hehte**, ordered, called, S; **hihte**, S2; **hiht**, S2; **hi3t**, S2; **het**, ordered, promised, S, S2; **hæhten**, *pl.*, S; **hight**, S2; **hyghte**, C2; **hoteð**, *imp. pl.*, promise, S; **heete**, *pr. s. subj.*, C; **gehaten**, *pp.*, S; **i-haten**, S; **i-hate**, S; **i-hote**, S; **y-oten**, S; **hoten**, called, S, P; **hotene**, promised, S; **hote**, P; **hette**, S2; **hight**, S2; **hyht**, S2; **hecht**, S3; **y-hy3t**, S2; **y-hoten**, PP; **y-hote**, PP; **i-hote**, S2.—AS. *hátan*, pt. *héht*, pp. *háten.*
haten[2], *v.* to be called; **hoten**, S, MD; **hote**, C; **hatte**, MD; **het**, MD; **hight**, MD; **hi3t**, *1 pr. s.*, S2; **hy3t**, *pr. s.*, S2; **hat**, P; **hattest**, *2 pr. s.*, S; **hatte**, *1 pr. s.*, am called, S; *pr. s.*, S2; **hatte**, *pt. s.*, was called, S, MD; **hette**, MD; **hete**, MD; **highte**, C2; **hæhte**, S; **hehte**, S; **hecht**, S3; **hyghte**, S2; **hiht**, S2; **hy3t**, S2; **het**, S, S2; **hat**, S2.—AS. *hátan*, pr. and pt. *hátte*; cf. Goth. *haitada*, I am called, see Sievers, 367. The forms of AS. *hátan*[1] are often used by confusion in the place of the old passive forms.
hatere, *sb.* clothing, HD, PP, Prompt.; **hater**, PP; **heater**, S; **hatren**, *pl.*, clothes, S2.—AS. *hæteru*, pl. garments, see Sievers, 290.
haterynge, *sb.* dress, PP.
hatien[1], *v.* to become hot; **hatte**, *pt. s.*, S; **yhat**, *pp.*, S2.—AS. *hátian*. See **hoot**.
hatien[2], *v.* to hate, MD, S, S2; **hatede**, *pt. s.*, C2.—AS. *hatian.*
hatreden, *sb.* hatred, MD; **hateredyn**, H; **hatredyn**, H; **hatrede**, *dat.*, S.

hatterliche, *adv.* savagely, S; see **heterly**.
hathel, *sb.* noble one, S2; see **aþel**.
hauberk, *sb.* a coat of ringed mail, S2, C, C2.—OF. *hauberc*; OHG. *halsberc*, lit. neck-defence.
hauk, *sb.* hawk, C2, PP, S2; **hauec**, S; **havekes**, *gen.*, S; *pl.*, S2; **heauekes**, S.
hauke, *v.* to hawk, C2; **hawkyd**, *pt. s.*, PP.
haukynge, *sb.* hawking, P; **an haukyng**, on hawking, a-hawking, C2.
haunt, *sb.* abode, C2; skill from practice, C; use, custom, PP.
haunten, *v.* to frequent, practise, make use of, PP, C3, S3, S2, W, H; **hant**, S3, HD.—OF. *hanter*, to frequent.
hauteyn, *adj.* loud, MD, C3; **havteyn**, haughty, H; **howteyne**, H (*n*).—OF. *hautain*, high.
hauekes, *gen.* of **hauk**.
hauen, *v.* to have, S; **habben**, S, S2; **abbe**, S2; **haben**, S; **habe**, S; **han**, S2, C2; **haue**, C2, PP; **haf**, S2; **aue**, *1 pr. s.*, S; **ha**, *pr. s. subj.*, S3; **hafst**, *2 pr. s.*, S; **hafesst**, S; **hæfuest**, S; **hauest**, S2; **hest**, S; **hafð**, *pr. s.*, S; **hafeð**, S; **haueð**, S; **haues**, S2; **hat3**, S2; **heþ**, S2; **hes**, S3; **aueð**, S; **aþ**, S2; **habbet**, *2 pl.*, S; **habbeð**, *pl.*, S, S2; **abbeð**, S2; **habeð**, S; **habbe3**, S2; **han**, S2, S3; **hafd**, *1 pt. s.*, S2; **haued**, S2; **hauid**, S2; **hafdes**, *2 pt. s.*, S; **hafde**, *pt. s.*, S; **haffde**, S; **hefde**, S; **hefede**, S; **hedde**, S; **heude**, S; **hadde**, S2, C2; **adde**, S; **hæfden**, *pl.*, S; **hafden**, S; **haffdenn**, S; **hefden**, S; **hedden**, S; **hadden**, S, C2; **hadde**, S; **hade**, S; **heuede**, S2; **hafd**, *pp.*, S2; **y-hadde**, S2; **haiffeing**, *pr. p.*, S3; **haze = hae + us**, have us, S3.—AS. *habban*, pr. s. *hæfde*, pp. *gehæfd.*
hauene[1], *sb.* haven, S, S2, CM; **haunes**, *pl.*, 2.—AS. *hæfene.*
hauene[2], *v.* to take harbour; **hauenyden**, *pt. pl.*, W.
hauer, *sb.* oats, P; **havyr**, Cath.; **hafyr**, Voc.—Cf. Du. *haver*, G. *hafer.*
hauer-cake, *sb.* oat-cake, Cath. (*n*); **havyre-cake**, HD.
hauer-grasse, *sb.* wild oats, Cath. (*n*), HD.
havyng, *sb.* behaviour, S2; **hawyng**, S2.
haw, *adj.* azure, S3, JD; **hawe**, grey, MD; **haa**, MD.—Cf. AS. *héwen*, sea-blue.
hawbart, *sb.* halberd, S3.—OF. *halebarde.*
hawe[1], *sb.* hedge, enclosure, C3, MD; **ha3e**, MD; **hahe**, MD; **hagh**, HD.—AS. *haga*, hedge (Voc.).
hawe[2], *sb.* hawthorn-berry, MD, C2, PP, Cath.—AS. *haga* (Voc.).
hawe-thorne, *sb.* hawthorn, PP, Prompt.; **ha3þorn**, MD.—ONorth. *hagaþorn* (Mat. 7. 16).

102

haxede, *pt. s.* asked, S; see **asken**.
haye, *sb.* a hedge, a kind of springe to catch rabbits, S3; **hay**, ND.—OF. *haie* (*haye*), a hedge.
hay-warde, *sb.* hedge-warden, PP; **haiwarde**, PP; **hayward**, Voc.; **heiward**, S.—From AS. *hege*, hedge, and *weard*.
haȝheliȝ, *adv.* becomingly, S; **haȝhelike**, S.—Icel. *hagliga*, skilfully, suitably, from *hagr*.
haȝher, *adj.* skilful, MD; **hawur**, MD; **haver**, MD; **haȝherrlike**, *adv.*, becomingly, S. See **haȝheliȝ**.
he, *pron.* he, S; used indefinitely, = one of you, P; **heo**, S; **hi**, S; **hie**, S; **ha**, S, S2; **a**, S2; **ȝe**, S2; **e**, S; **has** = **he** + **hes**, he them, S; **has** = **he** + **hes**, he her, S.
hea-; see also words beginning in **he-**.
heal, *sb.* hail, S3; see **hail**[1].
healden, *v.* to pour, S; see **helden**.
healen, *sb. pl. dat.* heels, S; see **heele**.
heanen, *v.* to oppress, afflict, S; **heande**, *pt. s.*, S; **heaned**, *pp.*, afflicted, S.—Cf. AS. *hýnan*, to humble, from *héan*, despised. See **heyne**.
heas, *sb.* command; **hease**, *dat.*, S. See **heste**.
heascen, *v.* to insult, MD; **heascede**, *pt. s.*, S.—Cf. AS. *hyscan*.
heater, *sb.* clothing, S; see **hatere**.
heaued, *sb.* head, S; see **heved**.
heaued-sunne, *sb.* capital sin, deadly sin, S.
hecht; see **haten**[1], **haten**[2].
hecseities, *pl.* a term in logic, S3.
hedde, **hedden**, had; see **haven**.
hede, *sb.* heed, care, C2, PP.
heden, *v.* to heed, S; **hedde**, *pt. s.*, SkD; **hedd**, MD.—AS. *hédan*: OS. *hódian*, cf. OHG. *huaten* (Otfrid).
hee-; see also words beginning in **he-**.
hee, *adj.* high; see **heigh**.
heed, *sb.* head, C2, C3, G, W; see **heved**.
heedlyng, *adv.* headlong, W.
heele, *sb.* heel, PP; **helis**, *pl.*, PP; **helen**, *dat.*, S; **healen**, S.—AS. *héla*.
heep, *sb.* heap, crowd, number, PP, W2; **hep**, PP; **hepe**, Cath., G, PP.—AS. *héap*; cf. OHG. *houf* (Otfrid).
heer[1], *sb.* hair, S3, C3; **heere**, W, PP; see **here**[1].
heer[2], *adv.* here, C2, PP; **her**, S, S2, C; **hær**, S; **hier**, S2; **hire**, G. *Comb.*: **her-afterward**, hereafter, C3; **her-biuore**, heretofore, S2; **herbiforn**, C3; **her-inne**, herein, C3; **her-onont**, as regards this, S; **her-to**, hereto, C3; for this cause, W; **heer-vpon**, hereupon, C2.
heete; see **haten**[1].
hefden; see **haven**.

hegge, *sb.* hedge, S, C, W2; **hegges**, *pl.*, P; **heggis**, W2.—AS. *hegge* (*dat.*) in Chron. ann. 547.
hegh, *sb.* haste, H; see **hye**.
heh, *adj.* high, S, S2, PP; see **heigh**.
heh-dai, *sb.* high day, festival, MD; **hæȝedæie**, *dat.*, S.
hehe, *adv.* highly, S; see **heighe**.
heh-engel, *sb.* archangel, S.—AS. *héahengel*.
heh-fader, *sb.* patriarch, SD; **hagefaderen**, *pl. dat.*, S.—AS. *héahfader*.
hehlich, *adj.* noble, proud, perfect, MD; **hely**, S3.—AS. *héahlic*.
hehliche, *adv.* highly, splendidly, loudly, MD; **heihliche**, S2; **heȝlyche**; **hæhliche**, S; **hehlice**, S; **heglice**, S.—AS. *héahlice*.
hehne, *adj.* contemptible, S; see **heyne**.
hehnesse, *sb.* highness, MD; **heynesse**, S3; **heghnes**, S2; **hiȝnesse**, W.—AS. *héahness*.
heh-seotel, *sb.* high-seat, throne, S; **hegsettle**, *dat.*, S.—AS. *héahsetl*.
hei[1], *sb.* hay, grass, Voc., W; see **hey**[2].
hei[2], *adj.* high, S, S2; see **heigh**.
heien, *v.* to extol, S; see **hiȝen**[1].
heigh, *adj.* high, chief, principal, noble, PP, CM, C2, S2; **heiȝ**, PP, S2; **heyȝ**, S3; **heih**, S; **heh**, S, S2, PP; **hegh**, S2, S3; **hey**, PP, C2, S, S2; **hei**, S, S2; **heg**, S; **heȝe**, S, S2; **hiȝ**, W, S; **hyȝe**, S2; **hihe**, C; **hi**, PP; **hy**, C2; **hæh**, S; **hah**, S; **hee**, S2.—AS. *héah*, *héh*.
heighe, *adv.* highly, PP; **heiȝe**, PP, S2; **heye**, S, S2, PP; **hehȝe**, S; **hehe**, S; **heie**, S, S2; **hye**, C2; **he**, S2; **hæȝe**, S.—AS. *héage*, *héah*.
heigher, *adj. comp.* higher, C, CM; **heyer**, S2, C3; **hyer**, S3; **herre**, S, P.—AS. *hérra*.
heighest, *adj. superl.* highest, PP; **heghest**, S2; **hehȝhesst**, S; **hegest**, S; **hest**, S2; **hæhst**, S.—AS. *héhst*.
heih, *adj.* high; see **heigh**.
heind, *adj.*; see **hende**[2].
heir, *sb.* heir, S, C2; see **eyre**[2].
hei-uol, *adj.* haughty, S2. See **heigh**.
hei-ward, *sb.* hedge-warden, hayward, S; see **hay-warde**.
hekele, *sb.* hatchel, *mataxa*, Prompt.; **hechele**, hatchel for flax, HD; **hekylle**, *mataxa*, Voc., Cath.; **heckle**, comb, Manip.; **hekkill**, heckle, cock's comb, S3; **heckle**, HD.—Cf. Du. *hekel*, hatchel.
helde[1], *sb.* age, S; see **elde**[1].
helde[2], *sb.* a slope, S; **heldes**, *pl.*, MD.
helden, *v.* to tilt, to incline, S, S2, W; **healden**, to pour, S; **helde**, *pt. s.*, W; **halde**, S; **helded**, S2; **heldid**, H; **held**, *pp.*, S2.—AS. *heldan* cf. Icel. *halla*, to incline; E. *heel* (*over*). See **hell**.
heldynge, *sb.* an inclining aside, H.

hele, *sb.* health, soundness, S, S2, S3, C; **hale**, S; **heale**, S, S3; **hel**, S2; **heles**, *pl.*, S2.—AS. *hǽlu*.

helen[1], *v.* to cover, conceal, CM, P, S, S2; **heolen**, S; **halen**, *pp.*, S; **heled**, S2; **hole**, MD.—AS. *helan*, pt. *hæl*, pp. *holen*; cf. OHG. *helan* (Otfrid).

helen[2], *v.* to heal, PP, S2, C2; **halyd**, *pp.*, H.—AS. *hélan*; cf. OHG. *heilen* (Otfrid).

Helende, *sb.* the Saviour, the Healer, S; **Halende**, S; **Healent**, S.—AS. *hǽlend*; cf. OHG. *heilant* (Otfrid).

heleth, *sb.* armed man, warrior, MD; **hæleð**, MD; **heleðes**, *pl.*, S.—AS. *heleð*; cf. G. *held.*

helfter, *sb.* noose, snare, S.—AS. *hælftre* (Voc.); see SkD. (s.v. *halter*).

heling, *sb.* salvation, S2.

hell, *v.* to pour out, H; **hel**, *1 pr. s.*, H; **hell**, *imp. s.*, H; **helles**, *pl.*, H; **helland**, *pr. p.*, H; **helt**, *pt. s.*, H; *pp.*, H.—Icel. *hella*, to pour. See **helden**.

helle, *sb.* hell, C2, MD, PP; = *infernum*, W.—AS. *hell*: OHG. *hella*: Goth. *halja*.

helle-fur, *sb.* hell-fire, S.—AS. *helle-fýr*.

helle-hound, *sb.* hell-hound, MD.

helle-muð, *sb.* mouth of hell, S.

helme, *sb.* a helm, covering for the head, PP, CM; **helm**, MD.—AS. *helm*; cf. Goth. *hilms*.

helmed, *adj.* provided with a helm, C2, CM.

help, *sb.* help, C2, PP.

helpen, *v.* to help, S2; **halp**, *pt. s.*, C2, PP; **halpe**, PP, S2; *pl.*, P; **holpyn**, P; **hulpen**, P; **holpen**, *pp.*, C, C2, PP; **holpe**, P; **hulpe**, P.—AS. *helpan*; pt. *healp*; pp. *holpen*; cf. Goth. *hilpan*.

helplees, *adj.* helpless, C3; **helples**, PP.

helthe, *sb.* health, salvation, S2; **heelthe**, W.—AS. *hǽlð*.

hem, *pron. pl. dat.* and *acc.* them, S, S2, S3, C2, W, PP; **hom**, S, S2; **ham**, S, S2; **him**, C2; **heom**, S.—AS. *him, heom*, dat. pl.

hem-self, *pron.* themselves, S, C3, PP; **hemseluen**, PP; **hemsilf**, W, W2; **hemsilue**, PP.

hende[1], *adv.* at hand, S2.

hende[2], *adj.* near at hand, handy, courteous, S, S2, G, P; **heind**, S2; **hinde**; S3; **hendest**, *superl.*, S; **hændest**, S.—AS. *(ge)hende.*

hendeliche, *adv.* courteously, S, S2, P; **hændeliche**, S; **hendely**, S2; **hendliche**, S3.

hendi, *adj.* gracious, courteous, S2; **hendy**, S2, MD.—AS. *hendig* (in compounds): Goth. *handugs*, clever.

heng, *pt. s.* hung; see **hangen**[1] (*strong*).

henge, *sb.* hinge, MD; **hengis**, *pl.*, W2. See **hangen**[2] (*weak*).

henne, *adv.* hence, S, C3, PP; **heonne**, S; **hennen**, S.—AS. *heonan.*

hennes, *adv.* hence, S, S2, P, W; **hennus**, W; **heonnes**, PP.

hennes-forth, *adv.* henceforth, C2.

henten, *v.* to seize, Prompt., S3, C3, P; **hente**, *pt. s.*, PP, S2, C2, C3, HD; **hynt**, S3; **hent**, S2, PP, S3; *pp.*, S3, C2, C3; y-hent, C3.—AS. *hentan.*

henter, *sb.* a thief, HD.

heo-; see also words beginning in **he-**.

heo[1], *pron.* she, S, S2, P; **hi**, S; **hye**, S; **hie**, MD; **he**, S, S2, P; **hue**, S2; **ha**, S; **ho**, S2, S3; **ʒeo**, S; **ʒho**, S; **ʒhe**, S2; **ʒe**, S (s.v. *ge*); **heo**, *acc.*, her, S.—AS. *héo.*

heo[2], *pron.* he, S; see **he.**

heom, *pron.* them, S; see **hem**.

heo-seolf, she herself, S.

hep, *sb.* heap; see **heep**.

hepe, *sb.* hip, the fruit of the dog-rose, SkD, MD; **heepe**, CM.—AS. *heope.*

hepe-tre, *sb.* *cornus*, Voc., Cath.

heraud, *sb.* herald, S3, C; **heraudes**, *pl.*, C, PP.—OF. *heraud, herault, heralt.*

herbe, *sb.* herb, Voc.; **eerbe**, W2; **hairbis**, *pl.*, S3; **herbes**, C2; **erbez**, S2; **eerbis**, W2.—OF. *herbe*; Lat. *herba.*

herbere, *sb.* garden of herbs, S3; **herber**, PP, CM; **erber**, PP; **erberes**, *pl.*, S3.

herbergage, *sb.* lodging, S2, C2, C3.—AF. *herbergage*, from OF. *herberge*, encampment (Roland).

herbergeour, *sb.* provider of lodging, C3.—OF. *herbergeour.*

herbergeri, *sb.* lodging, S2.—OF. *herbergerie.*

herberwe[1], *sb.* lodging, shelter, harbour, place of refuge, camp, S, PP; **herborewe**, W; **herbergh**, C, PP; **herborʒ**, PP; **herbore**, W.—Icel. *herbergi* lit. army-shelter. See **here**[3].

herberwe[2], *v.* to harbour, lodge, S3, PP; **herborowe**, PP; **harborowe**, S3; **herborwe**, PP; **herborwed**, *pp.*, S; **herborid**, W. See **herberwe**[1].

herbore-les, *adj.* homeless, W.

herce, *sb.* triangular form, S3; **herse**, a framework whereon lighted candles were placed at funerals, HD; burden of a song, S3.—OF. *herce*, a harrow; Lat. *hirpicem.*

herd, *adj.* haired, C.

herde[1], *adj. pl.* hard, S; see **harde.**

herde[2], *sb.* herd, *grex*, PP.—AS. *heord.*

herde[3], *sb.* shepherd, CM; **hirde**, S, H; **hird**, S3, H; **hurde**, keeper, guardian, S; **hirdis**, *pl.*, W, H.—AS. *hierde* (*heorde*), herdsman; cf. OHG. *hirti* (Otfrid).

herde-man, *sb.* herdsman, S3; **heorde-monne**, *gen. pl.*, S.

herdes[1], *sb. pl.* the refuse of flax, MD; **hardes**, Voc., Cath.; **heerdis**, CM; **hyrdys**, Prompt.; **heorden**, *dat.*, S.—AS. *heordan*.

herdes[2], *pl.* lands, S; see **erd**.

here[1], *sb.* hair, S, CM, S3; **her**, S2; **heer**, S3, C3; **heere**, W, PP; **heare**, S3; **hore**, MD; **hares**, *pl.*, S2; **haris**, S3; **heres**, C2; **heeris**, W; **heiris**, W2.—AS. *hǽr*; cf. OHG. *hár* (Otfrid).

here[2], *sb.* hair-cloth, S, S2; **haire**, Cath.; **hayre**, Voc.; **heare**, S; **heire**, W2, PP; **heyre**, C3, P, W; **haigre**, *dat.*, S.—AS. *hǽre*.

here[3], *sb.* host, army, S, S2.—AS. *here*: Goth. *harjis*.

here[4], *pron.* of them, their, S, S2, C, PP; **her**, S, S3, C2, C3, PP; **heore**, S; **huere**, S2; **hore**, S; **hor**, S2; **hare**, S, S2; **hir**, C2; **hire**, S; **hern**, **herne**, *gen.* theirs, W, W2.—AS. *hira (heora)*.

here[5], *pron. and poss. pron.* her, C3, PP; see **hire**[1].

here[6], *adv.* before, S; see **er**[2].

hered-men, *sb. pl.* retainers, S; see **hired-men**.

heremyte, *sb.* hermit, S2; **heremites**, *pl.*, P; see **ermite**.

heren, *v.* to hear, S, C2; **hiren**, to obey, S, MD; **huren**, MD; **hæren**, S; **hieren**, MD, S2; **heir**, S3; **heoreð**, *1 pr. pl.*, S; **herde**, *pt. s.*, S, S2, C2; **herd**, S2; **hurde**, S2; **hard**, S3; **herden**, *pl.*, G; **hard**, *pp.*, S3; **herd**, C2; **y-hyerd**, S2; **ihurd**, S2.—AS. *héran*: OS. *hórian*.

here-toȝe, *sb.* leader of an army, MD; **heretoche**, S.—AS. *heretoga*; cf. G. *herzog*.

here-word, *sb.* praise, S.

here-wurðe, *adj.* worthy of praise, S.

herield, *adj.* given as a heriot, S3.—Low Lat. *heregeldum*, see Ducange (s.v. *heriotum*). See **heriet**.

herien[1], *v.* to praise, S, C2, C3; **herie**, W; **herye**, S3, S2; **i-heret**, *pp.*, S.—AS. *herian*: Goth. *hazjan*.

herien[2], *v.* to harry, S2; see **harwen**.

heriet, *sb.* a heriot, equipment falling to the lord of the manor on decease of a tenant, MD.—AS. *heregeatu*, military equipment. See **here**[3], **herield**.

hering, *sb.* herring, MD; **herynge**, S2 (8 b. 46); **elringe**, S2 (probably an error). Cf. AF. *harang*.

heriynge, *sb.* praise, W; **heryinge**, S2.

herken, *v.* to hark, MD; **herk**, S2.

herknen, *v.* to hearken, S, C2; **hercnen**, **hercni**, S.—AS. *hearcnian*.

herknere, *sb.* listener, S3.

herlot, *sb.* acrobat, H; see **harlot**.

hermes, *sb. pl.* harms, damages, S; see **harm**.

hermyne, *sb.* ermine, S; **ermine**, S.—OF. *hermine*.

herne[1], *sb.* a corner, S2, C3, P; **hirne**, S, PP, H, S3; **hyrne**, H; **hurne**, S, S2; **huirnes**, *pl.*, S2, PP.—AS. *hyrne*.

herne[2], *sb.* heron, Prompt.; see **heron**.

herne-panne, *sb.* skull, HD; see **harne-panne**.

hernes, *sb. pl.* brains, S2; see **harnes**.

herneys, *sb.* armour, C; see **harneys**.

hernez, *sb. pl.* eagles, S2; see **ern**.

heron, *sb.* heron, MD; **heiroun**, MD; **heyrone**, MD; **heroun**, MD; **herne**, Prompt.; **heern**, Prompt.; **heryn**, Prompt.—OF. *hairon*: It. *aghirone*: OHG. *heigero*.

heronsewe, *sb.* a heron, a young heron, C2, Cath.; **herunsew**, HD; **hearnesew**, HD; **hernshaw**, HD, SkD.—AF. *herouncel* (OF. *heronceau*).

herre[1], *sb.* a hinge, Prompt., MD; **harre**, Cath., C; **har**, JD, Voc.; **herris**, *pl.*, W2; **herrys**, H.—AS. *heorr*; cf. Icel. *hjarri*.

herre[2], *sb.* lord, master, MD; **hærre**, S.—AS. *hearra*; cf. OS. *hérro*.

herse, *sb.* burden of a song, S3; see **herce**.

hert, *sb.* hart, S2, C, C2, W2; **hertes**, *pl.*, S2; **hertis**, W2, PP.—AS. *heort, heorot, heorut*; see Brugmann, § 67. 5.

herte, *sb.* heart, S, PP, S2, C2; **hairt**, S3; **hurte**, S2; **huerte**, S2; **hierte**, S; **heorte**, S, PP; **hert**, S2; **hertes**, *pl.*, S, C2, C3; **hertis**, P.—AS. *heorte*; cf. Goth. *hairto*.

herte-blood, *sb.* heart's blood, C3.

herteles, *adj.* without courage, C; **hart-lesse**, S3; **hertles**, foolish, W2.

hertely[1], *adj.* hearty, MD; **hertly**, C2; joyous, W2.

hertely[2], *adv.* heartily, S3, C2; **herteliche**, S.

herten, *v.* to cheer, HD, S3, S; **hertid**, *pp.*, wise, W2.

herte-spon, *sb.* brisket-bone, C.

herting, *sb.* cheering, S.

heruest, *sb.* harvest, S, S2, P.—AS. *hærfest*.

heruest-trees, *sb. pl.* autumnal trees = *arbores autumnales*, W.

hes, he, her; see **he**.

hesmel, *sb.* collar (?), S.

hesn, *sb.* command, MD; **hesne**, *pl.*, S.— Formed from AS. *hǽs*. See **heste**.

hespe, *sb.* hasp; see **haspe**.

heste, *sb.* command, S, S2, C2, C3, PP; **has**, S; **hes**, S; **hest**, S; **hease**, *dat.* S; **hese**, *pl.*,

S; **hestes**, S, S2, S3, C2; **heestis**, W; **hestene**, *gen.*, S.—AS. *hés.*

hete[1], *sb.* heat, S, C3, PP; **hæte**, S; **heat**, S; **hit**, S; **hate**, *dat.*, S.—AS. *hǽtu.*

hete[2], *v.* to heat, Cath., S2.—AS. *hǽtan.*

hete[3], *sb.* hate, S.—AS. *hete*: OS. *heti.*

hetel, *adj.* hateful, cruel, horrible, MD.

hetelifaste, *adv.* cruelly, S.

heten, *v.* to promise, MD, S2, C3, H; see **haten**[1].

heter, *adj.* rough, MD.

heterly, *adv.* fiercely, violently, S2; **hetterly**, S2; **heterliche**, MD; **hatterliche**, S; **heatterliche**, S.

hette; see **haten**[1], **haten**[2].

hetyng, *sb.* promising, H. See **heten**.

heth, *sb.* heath, PP, CM; **heethe**, *dat.*, C.—AS. *hǽð*; cf. Icel. *heiðr.*

heðen[1], *adv.* hence, S, S2, S3, H; **eðen**, S.—Icel. *héðan.*

hethen[2], *adj.* heathen, S, S2, C3, PP; **hathene**, S; **heaðene**, S; **hæðene**, S.—AS. *hǽðen.*

hethenesse, *sb.* heathendom, S, C3, PP.—AS. *hǽðennis.*

hethenlich, *adv.* in heathen manner. W.

heðing, *sb.* scoffing, scorn, S2, HD, CM; **hethyngis**, *pl.*, H.—Icel. *hǽðing.*

heued, *sb.* head, S, S2, PP; **heaued**, S; **heauet**, S; **hafed**, S; **hæfedd**, S; **hæued**, S; **hefed**, S; **heeued**, S2; **heuet**, S; **heed**, C2, C3, G, W; **heuede**, *dat.*, S2; **hæfden**, *pl.*, S; **heuedes**, C2; **heuiddes**, S2; **hedes**, C3; **heedes**, C2, G; **heedis**, W.—AS. *héafod.*

heued-cloð, *sb.* head-cloth, S.

heued-sunne, *sb.* a capital sin, deadly sin, S; **hefed-sunne**, S; **heaued-sunne**, S.

heuegeð, *pr. s.* bears heavy on, S.—AS. *hefigian.*

heuen, *v.* to heave, raise, S, S2, C; **houe**, *pt. s.*, S, MD; **houen**, *pp.*, S2, MD.—AS. *hebban*, pt. *hóf*, pp. *hafen.*

heuene, *sb.* heaven, PP; **heouene**, S; **heuen**, C2; **heoffness**, *gen.*, S; **hewynnis**, S3; **heofene**, *dat.*, S; **heouene**, S; **heoffne**, S; **hefene**, S; **heuene**, S, C2; **hefenen**, *pl.*, S.—AS. *heofon.*

heuenen, *v.* to raise, MD, S2. See **heuen**.

heuene-riche, *sb.* kingdom of heaven, S, S2, P; **heoueneriche**, S; **heoueriche**, S; **heueriche**, S; **heofeneriche**, S.—AS. *heofonríce.*

heuen-king, *sb.* King of Heaven, S.

heuenliche, *adj.* heavenly, S, C; **heouen-lich**, S.

heuy, *adj.* heavy, mournful, PP; *molestus*, W; **heuie**, S; **hefiȝ**, S; **heuy**, *adv.*, W.—AS. *hefig.*

heuyed, *pp.* made heavy, W.

heuynesse, *sb.* heaviness, grief, PP, C2.

hew, *sb.* colour, S, S2, S3; **heou**, S; **heu**, S2; **huȝ**, S2; **hu**, S2; **hiu**, S; **heowe**, *dat.*, S; **hewe**, S2, C2; **hewes**, *pl.*, colours for painting, C.—AS. *hiw.*

hewe, *sb.* servant, P, MD; **hewen**, *pl.*, P, MD.—AS. *híwan*, pl. domestics, from *híw*, family. See **hyne**, **hired**.

hewed, *adj.* hued, S3, C; **hwed**, S2.

hewen, *v.* to hew, knock, C, PP; **hiewh**, *pt. s.*, S2.—AS. *héawan.*

hey[1], *adj.* high; see **heigh**.

hey[2], *sb.* hay, S2, C2, C3, W; **hei**, W; **hai**, S2; **heye**, W.—AS. *hég* (OET).

heyda, *interj.* ho there!, SkD; **hoighdagh**, S3.—Cf. G. *heida.*

heyne, *adj.* as *sb.* despised, worthless person, C3, CM, MD; **hehne**, *adj. dat.*, contemptible, S; **hæne**, *pl.*, poor, S.—AS. *héan*; cf. Goth. *hauns.*

heyre, *sb.* hair-cloth, C3, P, W; see **here**[2].

heythe, *sb.* height, Prompt.; **heȝthe**, S2; **heyt**, S2; **hycht**, S3. *Phr.*: **on highte**, aloud, C.—AS. *héhðu.* See **heigh**.

heȝe, *adj.* high; see **heigh**.

hi-, *prefix*; see also words beginning with **ȝe-**.

hi[1], *pron. nom.* and *acc.* they, S, S2; **hy**, S, S2; **i**, S; **hie**, S; **hii**, S, S2; **hij**, P; **hei**, S; **heo**, S, S2; **ho**, S; **he**, S, S3; **ha**, S; **hue**, S2; **a**, S2.—AS. *hí* (*hig*), *híe*, *héo.*

hi[2], *pron.* he, S; **hie**, S; see **he**.

hid, *sb.* privity = *absconditum*, H (p. 96).

hidel, *sb.* secrecy, secret, MD; **hidils**, H, W, HD. *Phr.*: **in hiddlis** = (*in occulto*), W, W2.—AS. *hýdels.*

hiden, *v.* to hide, PP; see **huden**.

hider, *adv.* hither, S, S2, C2, G, PP; **hyder**, PP; **huder**, PP; **hidur**, HD.—AS. *hider*, *hiðer.*

hider-to, *adv.* hitherto, S.

hider-ward, *adv.* hitherward, S, S2, C2, P.

hidous, *adj.* hideous, C; **hydus**, S2; **hydows**, *immanis*, Prompt.—OF. *hidus* (F. *hideux*).

hidousnesse, *sb.* horror, W2.

hierte, *sb.* heart, S; see **herte**.

hight; see **haten**[1], **haten**[2].

hihe; see **heigh**.

hi-heren, *v.* to hear, S.—AS. *ge-héran.* See **ȝe-**.

hiht; see **haten**[1], **haten**[2].

hihten; see **hiȝten**[2].

hil, *sb.* hill, S; see **hul**.

hilen, *v.* to cover, protect, S, S2, W, H; **hulen**, S, S2; PP; **hiled**, *pp.*, C, P, H; **hilid**, W, H; **hild**, H; **y-hyled**, S3.—Icel. *hylja.*

hilere, *sb.* protector, H; **heyler**, H.

hiling, *sb.* covering, 82, W, W2; **hilynge**, H.

him, *pron. dat. s.* him, C2.

him-seluen, *pron.* himself, C2, PP.

hindir, *adj. comp.* hinder, latter, S3; **hinder**, JD; **ender**, 83. *Phr.*: **this hyndyr nycht**, this night last past, 83; **this ender daie**, S3.—Icel. *hindri*, hinder, latter.

hine[1], *pron. acc.* him, S; **hyne**, S, S2; **hin**, S.—AS. *hine*.

hine[2], *sb.* servant, MD; used of the Virgin Mary, MD; *pl.*, S, S2; **hinen**, S; see **hyne**.

hine-hede, *sb.* service, S2.

hirde, *sb.* shepherd, S, H; see **herde**[3].

hirdnesse, *sb.* flocks under a shepherd's care, S. See **herde**[2].

hire[1], *pron. and poss. pron.* her, S, S2, C; **hure**, PP, S; **here**, C3, PP; **hir**, C3, PP; **ire**, S2; **hires**, hers, S2, C3; **hire-selue**, herself, S2; **hir-selue**, AS. *hire (hyre)*.

hire[2], *adv.* here, G; see **heer**[2].

hired, *sb.* body of retainers, S, MD; **hird**, household, company, courtiers, S, MD.—AS. *híred*, household = *híw + réd*. See **hewe**.

hired-men, *sb. pl.* retainers, S; **heredmen**, S.

hiren, *v.* to obey, S; see **heren**.

hirne, *sb.* corner, S, S3, PP, H; see **herne**[1].

hirten, *v.* to hurt, dash against, W, W2; see **hurten**.

hirtyng, *sb.* stumbling, W, W2; *dat.*, hurting, H (p. 96).

his[1], *pron. f. acc.* her, MD (p. 446), S; **hies**, S; **hes**, S; **ys**, MD; **is**, 82; **hyse**, MD.

his[2], *pron. pl. acc.* them, S, S2; **hise**, S2; **hes**, S; **is**, S, S2: **es**, MD; **ys**, MD.

his[3], *pron. poss.* his, S, S2; **hisse**, S2; **es**, S; **is**, S, S2; **hise**, *pl.*, S, W, PP; **hyse**, S, PP.

hit[1], *pron.* it, S, S2; **hyt**, S2; **it**, S, S2; **hiȝt**, S2; **hit** (used as *gen.*), S2.—AS. *hit*.

hit[2], *sb.* heat, S; see **hete**[1].

hitten, *v.* to hit, Cath., PP, S2; **hutten**, MD; **hitte**, *pt. s.*, cast down hastily, P; **hutte**, PP; **y-hyt**, *pp.*, S2. Icel. *hitta*: Goth. *hinþan*, to catch.

hiȝ, *adj.* high, W, S; see **heigh**.

hiȝen[1], *v.* to heighten, extol, W; **heien**, S; **hieth**, *pr. s.*, W; **i-heied**, *pp.*, S (p. 123); **i-hæȝed**, S; **heghid**, H.

hiȝen[2], *v.* to hie, hasten, MD, W; **hyȝen**, S2; **hyen**, S3, PP; **hye**, *reflex.*, S2, C3; **hiȝede**, *pt. s.*, S, S2, S3, PP; **hiȝed**, *pp.*, W; **hied**, PP.—AS. *higan, higian*.

hiȝingli, *adv.* hastily, W.

hiȝt; see **haten**[1], **haten**[2].

hiȝte, *sb.* delight, joy, S.—AS. *hyht*, joy; cf. *hihting*, joy, exultation (Voc.).

hiȝten[1], *v.* to rejoice, be glad, S.—AS. *hyhtan*; cf. *ge-hihtan* (Voc.).

hiȝten[2], *v.* to adorn, Trevisa, (1. 41, 235 and 2. 363); **hight**, HD; **hihten**, *pt. pl.*, S.

hiȝter, *sb.* embellisher, Trevisa, (1. 7).

hoball, *sb.* an idiot, S3; **hobbil**, HD.—Cf. Du. *hobbelen*, to toss, stammer, stutter.

ho-bestez, *sb. pl.* she-beasts, S2. See **heo**[1].

hobie, *sb.* a kind of hawk, Manip.; **hoby**, Voc., Cath.; **hobby**, HD; **hobies**, *pl.*, S3.—Cf. OF. *hobreau* (Cotg.).

hod, *sb.* hood, S2, S3, PP; **hode**, C2, P; see **hood**.

hoddy-peke, *sb.* a hood-pick, HD; see **huddy-peke**.

hohful, *adj.* anxious, MD; **hohfulle**, S.—AS. *hohful*, from *hogu*, care.

hoise, *v.* to hoist, lift up, WW; **hoyse**, S3; **hyce**, Palsg.; **hyse**, Palsg.; **highced**, *pp.*, WW.—Cf. ODu. *hyssen*, G. *hissen*, Du. *hijschen*, also F. *hisser*.

hok, *sb.* hook, MD; **hoc**, S2; **hokes**, *pl.*, P.—AS. *hóc*.

hoked, *adj.* provided with a hook, P; **i-hoked**, hooked, S.

hoker, *sb.* mockery, scorn, MD; **hokere**, *dat.*, S; **hokeres**, *pl.*, S.—AS. *hócor*.

hoker-lahter, *sb.* the laughter of scorn, S.

hokerliche, *adv.* scornfully, S.

hokerunge, *sb.* scorn, MD; **hokerringe**, *dat.*, S.

hokkerye; see **hukkerye**.

hold[1], *sb.* a stronghold, C3.

hold[2], *adj.* inclined to any one, gracious, friendly, S; **holde**, *pl.*, S2.—AS. *hold*: Goth. *hulps*.

holdelike, *adv.* graciously, S.

holden, *v.* to hold, observe, keep, consider, S, S2, PP; **healden**, S; **halden**, S, S2, PP; **hælden**, also F; **helde**, S; **halst**, *2 pr. s.*, S; **halt**, *pr. s.*, S, S2, S3, C2; **hallt**, S; **hauld**, *pl.*, S3; **haldes, haldis**, *imp. pl.*, S; **heold**, *pt. s.*, S; **heeld**, C2; **hield**, S2; **huld**, S2; **heoldon**, *pl.*, S; **heolden**, S; **heolde**, S; **helde**, C2, PP; **hielden**, S; **hulde**, S2; **i-halden**, *pp.*, S; **halden**, S2; **i-holde**, S, S2; **holden**, S, C2; **holde**, beholden, S2; kept, C2; **y-holde**, S2, C3; **y-holden**, P; **i-hialde**, S.—AS. *healdan*.

hole[1], *pp.* covered; see **helen**[1].

hole[2], *adj.* whole, C3; *pl.*, entire, i.e. neatly mended up, P; see **hool**.

hole-foted, *adj.* whole-footed (i.e. web-footed), S2.

hole-ly, *adv.* wholly, P; **holly**, S2, C; **hollyche**, S3; **holliche**, PP; **holiche**, PP.

holi, *adj.* holy, S, PP; **holy**, PP; **hali**, S, S2; **heali**, S; **ali**, S; **haliȝ**, S; **hallȝhe**, S; **haliche**, *adv.*, S.—AS. *hálig*.

Holi-cherche, *sb.* Holy Church, P; **Holi-kirke**, P.

holi-dai, *sb.* holiday, PP; **haliday**, P.

Holi-gost, *sb.* Holy Ghost, PP; **Hali-gast**, S.

holle

holle, *sb.* hull of a ship, SKD (p. 811), MD, Voc., Prompt.—AS. *holh.* Cf. **holwe**.

holly, *sb.* holly, MD; **holie**, S; **holy**, Prompt. See **holyn**.

holpen, *pp.*; see **helpen**.

holsumliche, *adv.* wholesomely, S. See **hool**.

holt, *sb.* a wood, wooded hill, grove, MD; **holte**, C, PP; **holtes**, *pl.*, S3, PP.—AS. *holt* (OET.).

holwe, *adj.* hollow, C3, PP; **howe**, *pl.*, S3, JD.—Cf. AS. *holh*, a hollow.

holyn, *sb.* holly, S (p. 116), Voc., MD, Cath.; **holin**, S (p. 116); **hollen**, MD.—AS. *holen, holegn.*

holyn-bery, *sb.* holly-berry, Cath.

homage, *sb.* men, retainers, vassalage, S.—OF. *homage.*

homicyde[1], *sb.* assassin, C2.—AF. *homicide*; Lat. *homicida* (Vulg.).

homicyde[2], *sb.* manslaughter, murder, C3.—OF. *homicide*; Lat. *homicidium* (Vulg.).

homliche, *adj.* meek, *domesticus*, W; **homeli**, W; **hamly**, *adv.* familiarly, heartily, H. See **hoom**.

homlinesse, *sb.* domesticity, C2; **hamlynes**, intimacy, H.

homward, *adv.* homeward, S, C2.

hon-; see also words beginning in **hun-**.

hond, *sb.* hand, S, S2, C2. See **hand**.

hond-fast, *pp.* fastened by the hands, G.

honest, *adj.* honourable, worthy, C2, C3, PP; **onest**, W; **oneste** W.—OF. *honeste*; Lat. *honestum.*

honestetee, *sb.* honourableness, C2.

honestly, *adv.* honourably, C3.

hong, *pt. s.* hung; see **hangen**[1].

hongede, *pt. s.* hanged; see **hangen**[2].

honour, *sb.* honour, MD; **honur**, S2.—OF. *honur*; Lat. *honorem.*

honoure, *v.* to honour, PP, C2; **onuri**, S; **honur**, S2; **anuri**, S; **onourynge**, *pr. p.*, W; **anuret**, *imp. pl.*, S; **anurede**, *pt. pl.*, S; **anured**, *pp.*, S; **onourid**, W2.—OF. *honorer (onurer)*; Lat. *honarare.*

hony, *sb.* honey, PP, W.—AS. *hunig.*

hony-socle, *sb.* honeysuckle, Prompt.; *locusta*, Prompt.

hony-souke, *sb.* chervil, *cerifolium*, Voc.; *serpillum*, pellitory, Voc.; *locusta*, Voc.; **honysoukis**, *pl.* (= *locustae*), W.—AS. *hunigsúge*, privet, also *hunisuce* (Voc.).

hood, *sb.* hood, PP, MD; **hud**, MD; **hod**, S2, S3, PP; **hode**, C2, MD, P; **hoode**, C2; **hude**, Cath.—AS. *hód.*

hool, *adj.* whole, C2, W, PP; **hoi**, S, S2, PP; **hoole**, S2, S3; **hole**, C3; **hal**, S.—AS. *hál*; cf. Icel. *heill.* Cf. **hail**[2].

hostellere

hoolsum, *adj.* wholesome, W; **hoisome**, S3; **holsum**, S.—Cf. Icel. *heilsamr.*

hoom, *sb.* home, CM; **horn**, S, S2; **om**, S; **ham**, S; **hom**, *adv.*, S2, C2; **hoom**, C2; **haym**, S3; **heame**, S3; **whome**, S3.—AS. *ham*, nom. and dat. loc., see Sievers, 237.

hoor, *adj.* hoar, gray, C3; **hor**, PP; **hore**, *pl.*, S3, G, P.—AS. *hár.*

hoornesse, *sb.* hoariness, W2.

hoos, *adj.* hoarse, PP; **hos**, PP; **hoose**, W2; **hors**, PP; **horse**, CM; **hase**, H.—AS. *hás*; cf. G. *heiser.*

hoot, *adj.* hot, C3; **hat**, S; **hate**, S; **hot**, PP; **hote**, *adv.*, S2; **hatere**, *comp.*, S; **hatture**, S.—AS. *hát*; cf. G. *heiss.*

hope, *sb.* hope, MD; **hoip**, S3.—AS. *hopa.*

hopen, *v.* to hope, MD; **hope**, to think, expect, H.

hopper, *sb.* a seed-basket, HD; **hoper**, P; **hopyr**, corn-basket, Voc.; **hoppyr**, *farricapsa molendini*, Cath.

hoppesteres, *sb. pl.* dancers (viz. the ships), MD, C.—AS. *hoppestre.*

hord, *sb.* hoard, S2, C3; **horde**, S, PP.—AS. *hord*: Goth. *huzd*; cf. Lat. *custos*, see Brugmann, § 469.

horde-hows, *sb.* treasury, HD.

hordere, *sb.* treasurer, SD.—AS. *hordere* (Voc.)

horder-wice, *sb.* the office of treasurer; **horderwycan**, S.

hore, *sb.* whore, PP; **hoore**, W, W2; **horis**, *pl.*, W; **hooris**, W.—Icel. *hóra.*

horedom, *sb.* whoredom, PP; **hordom**, S, S2.—Icel. *hórdómr.*

horeling, *sb.* fornicator, MD; **horlinges**, S.

hori, *adj.* dirty, MD; **hoory**, MD.—AS. *horig.*

horlege, *sb.* time-teller, clock, Cath. See **orologe.**

horlege-loker, *sb.* a diviner, *haruspex*, Cath.

horowe, *adj.* foul, unclean, CM.—From AS. *horh*, filth (gen. *horwes*).

horwed, *pp.* as *adj.* unclean, S2.

hors, *sb.* horse, S; *pl.*, S, C2, PP; **horse**, PP; **horsus**, PP.—AS. *hors.*

horse-corser, *sb.* horse-dealer, S3.

horsly, *adj.* horselike, C2.

horte, *sb.* hurt, S3. See **hurte.**

horten, *v.* to hurt, MD; see **hurten.**

hortynge, *sb.* hurting, H (p. 96); see **hirtyng.**

hosel, *sb.* the Eucharist, MD; see **husel.**

hoseli, *v.* to housel, S2; see **huslen.**

hosen, *sb. pl.* stockings, S, C2, G; **hoosis**, W.—AS. *hosan*, pl.

hoskins, *sb. pl.* gaiters, S3; **hokshynes**, S3.

hoste, *sb.* host, entertainer, MD; see **ooste.**

hostel, *sb.* lodging, MD; see **ostel.**

hostellere, *sb.* inn-keeper, P; see **ostelere.**

hostelrie, *sb.* inn, C; see **ostelrie**.

hostery, *sb.* inn, MD; see **ostery**.

hoten, *v.* to bid, promise, MD; see **haten**[1].

hou, *adv.* how, S2, PP; **hw**, S; **hwu**, S; **wu**, S, S2; **hu**, S, S2; **whou**, S3; **whouȝ**, S3; **wouȝ**, S3.—AS. *hú.* Cf. **whi**.

houch-senous, *sb. pl.* hock-sinews, S3; see **houȝ-senue**.

houge, *adj.* huge, WW; see **huge**.

hound, *sb.* hound, dog, MD, C2; **hund**, S; **hunde**, *dat.*, S.—AS. *hund.*

hound-fleȝe, *sb.* dog-fly, *cinomia*, MD; **hund-fleghe**, H; **hundeflee**, Cath.; **hundfle**, H.—AS. *hundesfléoge* (Voc.).

houre, *sb.* hour, MD; **our**, S2, S3; **oware**, S3; **houres**, *pl.*, hours, devotions at certain hours (see *Horae* in Ducange), S2, P; **oures**, P; **houris**, orisons, songs of praise, S3; **vres**, S.—AF. *houre*, OF. *hore* (*eure*, *ure*); Lat. *hora.*

hous, *sb.* house, also a term in astrology, PP, S2, C2; **hus**, S.—AS. *hús.*

housbond, *sb.* the master of a house, husband, C2, C3, G; **housebond**, PP; **hose-bonde**, farmer, PP; **husband**, S, S2, S3; **husbonde**, S; **husebonde**, S.—Icel. *hús-bondi.*

housbonderye, *sb.* economy, P; **hous-bondry**, C; **hosboundrie**, PP; **hus-bandry**, Sh.

hous-coppis, *sb. pl.* house-tops, W2.

housel, *sb.* the Eucharist, CM; see **husel**.

houselen, *v.* to housel, CM; see **huslen**.

house-wif, *sb.* house-wife, PP; **hosewyues**, *pl.*, W.

houten, *v.* to hoot, PP; **howten**, Prompt.; **huten**, MD; **y-howted**, *pp.*, PP.—Cf. OSwed. *huta*, with which is related OF. *huter* (*huer*).

houȝ-senue, *sb.* hock-sinew, MD; **houch-senous**, *pl.*, S3.—AS. *hóh-sinu*; cf. Icel. *há-sin.*

houe, *sb.* hoof, *ungula*, MD; **hufe**, Cath., MD; **houys**, *pl.*, MD; **hoeues**, S3.—AS. *hóf.*

houe-daunce, *sb.* a court-dance, HD, MD, Caxton (Reynard, p. 54). Cf. ODu. *hofdans.*

houen, *v.* to wait about, remain, S, S2, S3, P; **hufe**, S3.

howe, *sb.* high hill, tumulus; **how**, H (p. 374), JD; **howis**, *pl.*, H.—Icel. *haugr.*

howfe, *sb.* hood, coif, *tena*, Cath.; **howue**, P, CM, C2 (p. 178); **houue**, PP; **houues**, *pl.*, S2, P.—AS. *húfe.*

hoxterye, *sb.* retail-dealing, S2, PP; see **huksterie**.

huche, *sb.* hutch, clothes-box, a chest, the ark of Israel, Prompt., H, MD; **hucche**, P, HD; **hutche**, Prompt.—OF. *huche.*

hud, *sb.* hood, MD; see **hood**.

huddy-peke, *sb.* a hood-pick, one who thieves out of a man's hood, simpleton, S3; **hudpik**, S3 (p. 422); **hoddypeke**, S3 (p. 421), HD.

hude, *sb.* hide, S; **hide**, MD; **hiden**, *pl.*, S2.—AS. *hýd*: OS. *húd*; cf. Lat. *cutis.*

huden, *v.* to hide, S, PP; **hiden**, S, PP; **huyden**, PP; **hyde**, C2; **huide**, S; **hud**, *imp. s.*, S; **hit**, *pr. s.*, C2; **hut**, MD; **hudde**, *pt. s.*, PP; **hidde**, C2, PP; **y-hid**, *pp.*, C3; **i-hud**, S; **hidd**, S; **hudde**, S.—AS. *hýdan.*

hudinge, *sb.* concealment, S2.

hue, *sb.* a loud cry, SkD, Sh.—AF. *hu.* See **houten**.

huerte, *sb.* heart, S2; see **herte**.

hufe[1], *sb.* hoof, Cath., MD; see **hove**.

hufe[2], *v.* to hover about, S3; see **hoven**.

huge, *adj.* huge, MD; **hoge**, MD; **hugie**, S3; **houge**, WW; **hogge**, HD, MD.

hugely, *adv.*, hugely, greatly, Cath.

huide, *v.* to hide, S; see **huden**.

huirnes, *sb. pl.* corners, S2, PP; see **herne**[1].

hukken, *v.* to hawk, to retail, Voc.; **hucke**, Palsg.—Cf. ODu. *huken*, to stoop down (Du. *heuken*, to retail).

hukker, *sb.* a hawker, retailer of small articles, Voc.—Cf. Du. *heuker.*

hukkerye, *sb.* retail dealing, PP; **hokkerye**, PP.

hukster, *sb.* huckster, Voc., MD, Cath.; **hukkester**, Voc.; **hokester**, MD.

huksterie, *sb.* retail dealing; **huckustrye**, PP; **hoxterye**, S2, PP.

hul, *sb.* hill, S2, PP, Voc.; **hil**, S; **hille**, *dat.*, S; **hulle**, S; *pl.*, S; **hulles**, S2, P; **hilles**, MD.—AS. *hyll.*

hulden, *v.* to flay, MD, S2; **hild**, HD; **helden**, MD; **hylt**, *pp.*, HD.—AS. *(be)hyldan*, to flay, skin; cf. Icel. *hylda.*

hule, *sb.* a hull, husk, covering of grain or nuts, PP; **hole**, Prompt.; **hoole**, Prompt., SkD (p. 811).

hulpen; see **helpen**.

huly[1], *adj.* slow, moderate, JD; **hoolie**, JD.—Icel. *hógligr*, adj.

huly[2], *adv.* slowly, H; **holy**, H.—Icel. *hógliga.*

hulynes, *sb.* slowness, H; **huliness**, JD.

humble, *adj.* humble, MD; **humyll**, S3.—OF. *humble*, *humile*; Lat. *humilem.*

humblesse, *sb.* humility, S2, C2, C3.

humilitee, *sb.* humility, C2.

hund, *sb.* hound, S; see **hound**.

hund-fle, *sb.* dog-fly, H; see **hound-fleȝe**.

hundred, *num.* hundred, S, P, Cath.; **hundret**, S; **hondreð**, P; **hondred**, S2; **hundereth**, S2; **hundreth**, WW.—Icel. *hundrað.*

hundred-feald, hundredfold, S.

hunger, *sb.* hunger, famine, S; **hungær**, S; **honger**, S2; **hungre**, *dat.*, S.—AS. *hungor*.

hunger-bitten, *adj.* famished, WW.

hungren, *v.* to hunger, S; **hungrede**, *pt. s.*, was hungry, S.—AS. *hyngran*.

hungri, *adj.* hungry, S.—AS. *hungrig*.

hunte, *sb.* hunter, S, C; **honte**, C.—AS. *hunta* (Voc.).

hunten, *v.* to hunt, S, C2.—AS. *huntian*.

hunteresse, *sb.* huntress, C.

hunteð, *sb.* a hunting, MD; **honteð**, S2, MD.—AS. *huntoð*.

hunting, *sb.*; **an huntinge**, on hunting, a-hunting, S, C2; **on hontyng**, C.

hupe, *sb.* hip, MD; **hepe**, MD; **hupes**, *pl.*, CM, MD; **hipes**, C; **hipis**, W.—AS. *hype*.

huppen, *v.* to leap, dance, jump, MD; **hupte**, *pt. s.*, S, S2.—Cf. G. *hüpfen*.

hurde[1], *sb.* keeper, S; see **herde**[3].

hurde[2], *pt. s.* heard, S2; see **heren**.

hure[1], *adv.* at least; **hure and hure**, at intervals, S, MD; **hur and hur**, frequently, S.—AS. *huru*, at least. Cf. **la hwure** at **la**.

hure[2], *sb.* hire, S, S2, G, PP; **huire**, S, S2, P; **huyre**, P.—AS. *hýr*.

huren, *v.* to hire, MD; **huyre**, *ger.*, G; **hyre**, G; **hurede**, *pt. s.*, S; **hyred**, *pp.*, C2; **huyred**, P; **ihuret**, S2.—AS. *hýrian*.

hurkelen, *v.* to stoop down, crouch, rest, MD; **hurkle**, HD; **hurkled**, *pt. s.*, S2.

hurlen, *v.* to rush, dash against, hurl, S2, C3, W2; **hurlle**, PP; **hurliden**, *pt. pl.*, threw down, W.

hurne, *sb.* corner, S, S2; see **herne**[1].

hurrok, *sb.* oar (?), S2, MD.—Cf. *orruck-holes*, oar-drawing holes (?), in the Norfolk dialect, cited in MD.

hurte, *sb.* hurt, *collisio*, Cath.; **hurt**, PP, C2; **hortis**, *pl.*, S3.

hurten, *v.* to dash against, push, injure, MD; Prompt., PP; **horten**, MD; **hirten**, W, W2; **y-hurt**, *pp.*, S2, S3.—OF. *hurter*.

hurtlen, *v.* to dash against, rattle, dash down, C, W, W2.

huschen, *v.* to hush, MD; **hussen**, MD; **hussht**, *pp.*, MD; **hoscht**, MD; **hust**, *pp.*, C.

husel, *sb.* the sacrifice of the Eucharist, S; **housel**, CM; **hosel**, MD.—AS. *húsel*.

huslen, *v.* to administer the Eucharist, MD; **hoseli**, S2; **hoslen**, S; **houselen**, CM; **huseled**, *pp.*, **houseled**, S; **hosled**, S; **y-housled**, S2.

hus-lewe, *sb.* house-shelter, S; see **hous**.

huyre, *sb.*; see **hure**[2].

hy, *adj.* high; see **heigh**.

hye, *sb.* haste, S2, S3, CM, C3; **hie**, MD; **heye**, MD; **hegh**, H.

hyen, *v.* to hasten, S3, PP; see **hiȝen**[2].

hyne, *sb.* domestic, servant, hind, S2, P, C3, W; **hine** (used of the Virgin Mary), MD; **hind**, Sh.; **hine**, *pl.*, S, S2; **hinen**, S.—Cf. AS. *hína man*, a man of the domestics. *Hína*, also written *hiwna*, gen. pl. of *hiwan*, domestics. See **hewe**.

I

*For words in which initial **i-** has the sound of **j-**, see under **J** below.*

i-, *prefix;* see also words beginning in **ʒe-**.
iæde, *pt. s.* went, S; **ieden**, *pl.*, S; see **eode**.
i-bede, *sb.* prayer, S; **ibeden**, *pl.*, S.—AS. *gebed.* See **bede**.
i-bere, *sb.* noise, S.—AS. *gebére*, gesture, cry: OS. *gi-bári.*
i-beten, *v.* to amend, S.—AS. *ge-bétan.*
i-biden, *v.* to have to do with, S.—AS. *ge-bídan.*
i-biten, *v.* to bite, eat, taste, S.—AS. *ge-bítan.*
i-blissien, *v. reflex.* to rejoice, S.—AS. *ge-blissian.*
i-bod, *sb.* command, S.—AS. *ge-bod.*
i-bon, *pp.* prepared, adorned, S.—AS. *ge-bún*, pp. of *ge-búan.* See **boun**.
i-borhen, *pp.* saved, S; **iboreʒe**, S; **iboruwen**, S; see **berʒen**.
i-brucen, *v.* to enjoy, S.—AS. *ge-brúcan.*
i-brusted, *pp.* made bristly, S.
i-bureð, *pr. s.* (it) behoveth, S.—AS. *ge-byrian.*
i-bureʒen, *v.* to deliver, S.—AS. *ge + borgian.* See **borwen**.
ich[1], *pron.* I, S, S2, S3, C2; **icc**, S; **ik**, P; **hic**, S; **hy**, S2; **ic**, S; **ih**, S: **ihc**, S; **y**, S, W, W2. *Comb.*: **ichabbe**, I have, S2; **icham**, I am, S2; **ichaue**, I have, S2; **icholle**, I will, S2; **ichcholle**, S2; **ichulle**, S2, S; **ichim**, I + him, S; **ichot**, I wot, S2; **ychabbe**, I have, S2; **ycham**, I am, S2.—AS. *ic*; cf. OHG. *ih* (Otfrid).
ich[2], *adj.* each, S, S2; see **eche**[1].
i-chaped, *pp.* furnished with a chape, C. See **chape**.
i-cnowen, *v.* to know, S.—AS. *ge-cnáwan.* See **knowen**.
i-coren, *pp.* chosen, S; see **chesen**.
i-cundur, *adj. com.* more natural, S; see **ʒe-cende**.
i-cwede, *pp.* spoken, S; see **queþen**.
i-cweme, *adj.* pleasing, S.—AS. *ge-cwéme.*
i-cwemen, *v.* to please, S; **i-queme**, S; **i-quemde**, *pt. s.*, S.—AS. *ge-cwéman.*
idel, *adj.* idle, empty, useless, S; **ydel**, S, C2, P; **idul**, W. *Phr.*: **an ydel**, in vain, P; **on idel**, S.—AS. *ídel*; cf. OHG. *ítal* (Tatian).
idelliche, *adj.* idly, SD; **ydelly**, C3.
idelnesse, *sb.* idleness, S; **idelnisse**, S2.—AS. *idelnis.*
idiote, *sb.* unlearned person, a man not holding public office, TG, PP; **ydiot**, W; **ideot**, Cotg.; **ydiote**, PP.—OF. *idiot*, one that hath no charge in a commonwealth, an

unprofitable person, a ninny, a natural fool (Cotg.); Lat. *idiota* (Vulg.); Gr. ἰδιώτης, ignorant (NT), lit. one occupied with τὰ ἴδια his private affairs, from ἴδιος, one's own.
i-dreaued, *pp.* troubled, S; see **drovy**.
ieden, *pt. pl.* went, S; see **eode**.
i-fæied, *pp.* hated, SD; **i-uaid**, S; **i-væid**, SD.—AS. *ge-féoged*, pp. of *ge-féogan*, to hate.
i-fellen, *v.* to fell, SD; **i-uælþ**, *pr. pl.*, S; **yfelde**, *pt. s.*, S; **ifulde**, S.—AS. *ge-fellan.*
i-fere, *sb.* a fellow-farer, companion, *comes*, S; **ʒe-feren**, *pl.*, S; **i-feren**, S; **i-ueren**, S; **y-fere**, S; **i-uere**, S.—AS. *ge-féra.*
i-feren, *adv.* together, S; see **in**[1], *prep.*
i-finden, *v.* to find, S; **i-uinden**, S; **i-uynde**, S; **y-fynde**, C2.—AS. *ge-fíndan.*
i-fon, *v.* to take; **i-uo**, S; **ifoð**, *pr. pl.*, S.—AS. *ge-fón.* See **fon**[1].
i-fulde, *pt. s.* felled, S; see **ifellen**.
igain, *prep.* and *adv.* against, again, S2; see **aʒein**.
igain-sawe, *sb.* contradiction, S2. Cf. **ogain-saghe**.
i-gistned, *pp.* lodged, S2; see **gestnen**.
i-gon, *v.* to go, S.—AS. *ge-gán.*
i-grætten, *pt. pl.* saluted, S; **igret**, *pp.*, S (7. 105).—AS. *gegrétton*, pt. pl. of *grétan.* See **greten**[1].
i-grede, *sb.* shouting, clamour, S. See **greden**.
i-healden, *v.* to hold, keep, S; **iholde**, S.—AS. *ge-healdan.* See **holden**.
i-hende, *adv.* near, S.—AS. *ge-hende*; see **hende**[2].
i-heorted, *adj. in phr.*; **heie iheorted**, proud-hearted, S.
i-heren, *v.* to hear, S; **ihure**, S, S2; **hi-heren**, S; **yhyren**, S2; **ihærde**, *pt. s.*, S; **ihorde**, S.—AS. *ge-héran.*
i-hold, *sb.* fortress, hold, S.—AS. *ge-heald.* See **hold**[1].
i-holde; see **ihealden**.
i-hudeket, *pp.* hooded, S. See **hood**.
i-hure; see **iheren**.
i-hwulen, *v.* to be at leisure, S. See **while**.
ik, *pron.* I, P. See **ich**[1].
i-latet, *adj.* visaged, S. See **late**[1].
-ild, *suffix.* As in **beggild**, MD; **cheapild**, S; **fostrild**, MD.
ile, *sb.* isle, S, S2, C3; **yle**, C2, PP, S3.—OF. *ile, isle*; Lat. *insula.*
i-leaded, *pp.* fitted with lead, S.
i-leaue, *sb.* leave, S2.—AS. *ge-léaf.*
i-ledene, *sb. pl.* of one's people, compatriots, S.—AS. *ge-léod.* See **leode**.

111

i-leoten, *v.* to fall to one's lot, SD; **iloten**, *pp.*, befallen, S.—AS. *ge-hléotan*, to share, get; pp. *ge-hloten*. See **lot**.

iles-piles, *sb. pl.* hedgehogs, S; **ilspiles**, S (*n*). Properly 'the quills of the hedgehog'; AS. *íl, ígel*, hedgehog (OET) + *píl*, a dart (Grein); Lat. *pilum*.

i-lete, *sb.* face, demeanour, S. Cf. ODu. *ge-lát*. See **leten**[1].

i-lethered, *adj.* made of leather, S.

i-leue, *sb.* belief; **i-læfe**, SD; **i-leave**, SD; **i-leuen**, *pl.*, S.—AS. *ge-léafa*; cf. OHG. *giloubo* (Otfrid).

i-leuen, *v.* to believe, S, S2; **ilef**, *imp. s.*, S.—AS. *ge-léfan, ge-líefan*: Goth. *ga-laubjan*; cf. OHG. *gi-louben* (Otfrid). Cf. **yleven**.

ilich, *adj.* like, S; **iliche**, S; **ylyche**, S2; **ylike**, S3; **ilik**, S; **ilikest**, *superl.*, S.—AS. *ge-líc*.

iliche[1], *adv.* alike, S; **ilyche**, S; **yliche**, C2; **ylyke**, C2; **eliche**, S3; **elyk**, S3; **ȝelice**, S.—AS. *ge-líce*. Cf. **aliche**.

iliche[2], *sb.* an equal, likeness, S; **ilike**, S.

ilke, *adj.* the same, S, G, C3, S2, S3, C2, H; **ilk**, H; **ilce**, S; **ulke**, S; **yche**, S2.—AS. *ilca* (*ylca*) = *i-lic*; with *i-* cf. Goth. *ei*, Lat. *i-* in *i-dem*, see Grimm, German Grammar, 3. 50, Fick, 3. 728.

ille[1], *adj., sb.* bad, ill, S; **ylle**, S2; **þe ille**, the evil one, i.e. the devil, S. *Comb.*: **il torned**, perverse, S2.—Icel. *íllr* (*illr*).

ille[2], *adv.* badly, S, HD.

ille[3], *v.* to make wicked; **illid**, *pt. pl.*, H.—Icel. *illa*, to harm.

illuster, *adj.* illustrious, JD; **illustare**, S3.—OF. *illustre*; Lat. *illustrem*.

i-lokien, *v.* to observe, S; **iloken**, S.—AS. *ge-lócian*.

i-lome, *adv.* frequently, S, S2; **ylome**, S2.—AS. *ge-lóme*. Cf. **lome**[2].

i-lomp, *pt. s.* happened, S; see **ȝelimpen**.

i-long, *adv.* S, NED (p. 250); **longe**, S2. *Phr.*: **al ilong of**, entirely belonging to, dependent on, owing to, S; **long on**, C3, S2; **all long of**, long of, Sh.—AS. *gelang*, belong-ing, depending, *gelang on, gelang æt*, because of, owing to. Cf. **along on**. (**a-**[6].)

i-loten, *pp.* befallen, S.—AS. *ge-hloten*, pp. of *ge-hléotan*, to share. See **ileoten**.

i-melen, *v.* to speak, S.—AS. *ge-mǽlan*.

i-membred, *pp.* parti-coloured, S.—Cf. OF. *membre* (Cotg.), and see Ducange (s.v. *membrare*). See **membre**.

i-mene, *adj.* common, S.—AS. *ge-mǽne*.

i-mid, in the midst, S2; **i-middes**, S.

i-mong, *prep.* among, S, SD; **imange**, S2.—AS. *ge-mang*; see NED (s.v. *among*).

impayable, *adj.* implacable, H. (**in-**[3].)

impne, *sb.* hymn, Prompt.; **imne**, Prompt.; **ympne**, W, CM; **ympnes**, *pl.*, W2;

ympnys, HD.—OF. *ymne* (Ps. 64. 1); Lat. *hymnus* (Vulg.); Gr. ὕμνος.

importable, *adj.* intolerable, C2.—Lat. *importabilis*. (**in-**[3].)

in-[1], *prefix*, representing the Eng. prep. *in*. See **in**[1].

in-[2], *prefix*, standing for the Latin prefix *in-*, which is the prep. *in* in composition.

in-[3], *prefix*, the negative Latin prefix *in-*, equivalent to Eng. *un-*. See **un-**[1].

in[1], *prep.* in, into, on, S, S2, PP; **hin**, S; **I**, S, SD. *Comb.*: **in-fere**, together, MD (p. 104), C3, S2, S3; **yfere**, S2, S3, C2; **in feere**, G; **iuere**, S; **iferen**, S; **i-whils**, while, H; **ywhils**, H; **ewhils**, H; **in-like**, in like manner, H; **in-lich**, inly, SD; **i-mid**, in the midst, S2; **imiddes**, S; **ymydis**, H; **in-mongez**, among, S2; **itwix**, betwixt, meanwhile, H; **in-with**, within, S, C2, B.

in[2], *sb.* dwelling, lodging, abode, S, S3, C2, C3; **hin**, S; **ynne**, S3; **inne**, *dat.*, S.—AS. *inn*.

inche, *sb.* inch, Prompt., Cath.; **enches**, *pl.*, S3.—AS. *ynce* (SkD); Lat. *uncia*, ounce, inch. Cf. **ounce**.

incontinent, *adj.* incontinent; *adv.* immediately, S3, Sh. (**in-**[3].)

influence, *sb.* influence of the planets, SkD.—OF. *influence* (Cotg.); Late Lat. *influentia*. (**in-**[2].)

influent, *adj.* possessing influence (astro-logy), S3.—Lat. *influentem*, pr. p. of *influere*, to flow into. (**in-**[2].)

inforce, *v. reflex.* to strive, S3. (**in-**[2].)

infortunat, *adj.* unlucky, S2, C3. (**in-**[3].)

infortune, *sb.* misfortune, C2. (**in-**[3].)

ingot, *sb.* mould for pouring metals into, C3, SkD. (**in-**[1].)

in-hinen, *sb. pl.* indoor-members of a household, S. See **hine**[2].

in-like, in like manner, H.

inne[1], *prep., adv.* into, in, S, S2, PP, C2; **ine**, S, S2; **ynne**, S2; **inre**, *adj. comp.*, inner, S; **inerere**, *pl.*, H; **innresst**, *superl.*, S; **inne-mest**, SkD; **ynneste**, W2.—AS. *inne*, comp. *innera*, superl. *innemest*, see Sievers, 314.

inne[2], *dat.* of **in**[2], *sb.*

innen[1], *prep.* within, into, SD, S.—AS. *innan*.

innen[2], *v.* to lodge, C; **ynnen**, C.—AS. *innian*.

innoð, *sb.* womb, S.—AS. *innoð*.

inobedience, *sb.* disobedience, S, W.—Late Lat. *inobedientia* (Vulg.). (**in-**[3].)

inobedient, *adj.* disobedient, S2.—Late Lat. *inobedientem* (Vulg.). (**in-**[3].)

inoh, enough, S; **innoh**, S; **inow**, S; **inouh**, S; **inou**, S2; **inoȝe**, S; **inoȝh**, S; **inough**, C; **innoghe**, S2; **inouwe**, *pl.*, S2; see **ynow**.

inpassyble, *adj.* incapable of suffering, H. (**in-**³.)

inpossible, *adj.* impossible, S2, PP.—Late Lat. *impossibilis (in-)*. (**in-**³.)

in-ras, *sb.* inroad, H. (**in-**¹.)

inunctment, *sb.* ointment, S3.—From Lat. *inunctus*, pp. of *in-ungere*, to anoint. (**in-**².)

in-with, within, S, C2, B.

in-wyt, *sb.* conscience, consciousness, S2; **inwit**, PP; **ynwitt**, PP.—AS. *inwit*, craft. (**in-**¹.)

i-orne, *pp.* run, S; see **rennen**.

ipotaynes, *sb. pl.* hippopotamuses, S2.

i-queme, *v.* to please, S; see **icwemen**.

irchon, *sb.* hedgehog, S2; **urchon**, Prompt.; **urchone**, Palsg.; **urchin**, Sh.; **vrchuns**, *pl.*, H; **irchouns**, W2.—OF. *ireçon, ereçon*; Late Lat. **ericionem*, from Lat. *ericius*, from *hēr*; cf. Gr. χήρ, hedgehog, see SkD (s.v. *formidable*).

iren¹, *sb.* iron, S, Cath.; **yren**, C3, PP; **irun**, W2; **yrun**, W, W2; **yre**, S2; **yrens**, *pl.*, P; **yrnes**, P.—OMerc. *īren* (OET): WS. *īsern*: OHG. *īsarn*; cf. OIr. *iarn*: Gaulish *īsarnos*.

iren², *adj.* iron, *ferreus*, SD, Cath.; **irnene**, *pl.*, S.—OMerc. *īren*: WS. *īsern*, see OET.

i-reste, *sb.* rest, S.—AS. *ge-rest*.

Irisse, *adj.* Irish, S; **Yrisse**, S; **Irish**, S; **Ersche**, S3.—AS. *īrisc*.

is, *pr. s.* is, S; **his**, S, S2; **es**, S, S2, H; **esse**, S2.—AS. *is*.

ische, *v.* to issue, cause to issue, JD; **isch**, B; **ischit**, *pt. s.*, S3, B.—OF. *issir*; Lat. *ex-ire*.

i-secgan, *v.* to confess; **isecgð**, *pr. s.*, S.—AS. *ge-secgan*.

i-sechen, *v.* to seek; **isoȝte**, *pt. pl.*, S.—AS. *ge-sécan*.

i-selðe, *sb.* happiness, S.—AS. *ge-sǽlð*. See **selþe**.

i-sene, *adj.* evident, seen, S; **y-sene**, S3, C.—AS. *gesýne*. Cf. **sene**¹.

i-seon, *v.* to see, S; **i-seo**, S2; **i-sien**, S; **y-se**, S2; **i-si**, S; **y-zi**, S2; **i-se**, S2; **y-zy**, S2; **i-seonne**, *ger.*, S; **i-seo**, *1 pr. s.*, S; **i-seoð**, *pr. s.*, S; **i-seȝð**, S; **i-sið**, S; **i-sist**, *2 pr. s.*, S; **i-sæh**, *pt. s.*, S; **i-seh**, S; **i-seih**, S; **i-seyh**, S; **i-sey**, S2; **i-seȝ**, S; **i-sei**, S2; **y-sey**, S2; **i-zeȝ**, *1 pt. s.*, S2; **i-seȝe þe**, *2 pt. s.*, S2; **i-seien**, *pl.*, S; **i-seyen**, S; **i-seȝe**, S, S2; **i-saye**, S2; **y-zeȝen**, S2; **i-sehen**, *pp.*, S; **i-seien**, S; **y-seye**, S2; **y-soȝe**, S2; **y-zoȝe**, S2.—AS. *ge-séon*.

i-set, *pp.* said, S (3a. 93); see **seggen**¹.

i-sihðe, *sb.* sight, S; **ȝesecðe**, S.—AS. *ge-sihð*.

isle, *sb.* glowing ashes, *favilla*, HD; **isyl**, Prompt.; **iselle**, Cath.; **easle**, HD; **ysels**, *pl.*, HD; **useles**, Trevisa, 4. 431; **usellez**, S2; **iselen**, *dat.*, SD, Cath. (*n*).—Icel. *usli*;

cf. MHG. *üsele* (G. *üssel*). The same stem *us-* is found in Lat. *us-ere* (*urere*), to burn.

i-some, *adj.* agreed, peaceable, S.—AS. *gesóm*.

i-soȝte, *pt. s.*, sought; see **isechen**.

isturbed, *pp.* disturbed, S.—OF. *estorber*; Lat. *ex- + turbare*.

i-swink, *sb.* toil, S.—AS. *ge-swinc*.

i-tiden, *v.* to betide, S; **itit**, *pr. s.*, S; **ityt**, S.—AS. *ge-tídan*.

i-timien, *v.* to happen, S.—AS. *ge-tímian*; cf. Icel. *tíma*.

i-twix, meanwhile, H.

i-þank, *sb.* thought, intention, S.

i-þenchen, *v.* to think, S; **i-þohten**, *pt. pl.*, S.—AS. *ge-þencan*.

i-þeȝ, *pt. s.* thrived, S2; see **þeen**.

i-þolien, *v.* to endure, S.—AS. *ge-þolian*.

i-þoncked, *adj.* minded, S.

i-uaid, *pp.* hated, S; see **ifæied**.

i-ueied, *pp.* joined, S; see **feȝen**.

i-ueiþed, *pp.* treated with enmity, S. See **fede**.

iuel, *adj.* evil, S, W2, S2. See **yvel**.

i-uelen, *v.* to feel, S.—AS. *ge-félan*.

iuen, *sb.* ivy, Cath.; **yven**, Cath. (*n*); **ivin**, HD, EDS (C. vi).—AS. *ífegn* (Voc.).

i-uere, *sb.* companion, S; see **ifere**.

iui, *sb.* ivy, S; **ive**, S3.—AS. *ífig*.

i-uo, *v.* to take, S; see **ifon**.

i-ureden, *v.* to hurt, injure, S.—ME. *i-ureden* = *i-wreden* = *i-werden*; AS. *ge-werdan, ge-wyrdan* (BT). See **werd**¹. {More likely AS (*ge*)*wierdan* to injure, but see also **freden** from AS (*ge*)*frédan* to feel.}

i-war, *adj.* aware, wary, S, PP; **ywar**, PP.—AS. *ge-wær*. See **war**¹.

i-whilc, *adj.* every, S.—AS. *ge-hwilc*.

i-whils, *adv.* while, H.

i-wil, *sb.* will, S.—AS. *ge-will*.

i-wis, *adv.* truly, certainly, S, PP, S2; **iwiss**, S; **iwys**, G; **ywis**, S, S2, C2; **ywys**, S2, PP; **ywisse**, PP; **iwisse**, S3. *Comb.*: **wel ywisse**, S; **mid iwisse**, S.—AS. *ge-wiss*, certain, formed from *wisse*, pt. of *witan*, see Sievers, 232 d.

i-witen¹, *v.* to know, S; **i-wyten**, S; **y-witen**, S2; **i-wiste**, *pt. s.*, S.—AS. *ge-witan*.

i-witen², *v.* to protect, S. See **witen**².

i-woned, *pp.* accustomed, S2; **y-woned**, S2; **i-wuned**, S; **woned**, S, S3; **wont**, S3; **wunt**, S2; **woonted**, S3.—AS. *ge-wunod*, pp. of *ge-wunian*, to dwell, to be accustomed. See **wonen**¹.

i-wune, *sb.* custom, S.—AS. *ge-wuna*. Cf. **wone**².

i-wurðen, *v.* to become, to happen, S; **i-worðe**, S; **y-worðe**, P, S2; **i-worðe**, *pp.*, S.—AS. *ge-weorðan*.

J

*For words in which initial **i-** is a vowel, see under **I** above.*

iacynte, *sb.* jacinth, SkD; **iacynct**, SkD; **jacint**, Cotg.; **iacinctus**, W (Rev. 21. 20); **jagounce**, HD; **iacynctis**, *pl.*, W2 (= Heb. tarshish).—OF. *jacinthe* (Cotg.); Lat. *hyacinthus* (Vulg.); Gr. ὑάκινθος (NT); cf. OF. *jagonce*.

iagge[1], *v.* to jag, notch, Prompt., Palsg.; **jag**, HD; **jaggede**, *pt. s.*, HD; **jaggde**, *pp. pl.*, S3; **jaggede**, HD.

iagge[2], *sb.* a jag of cloth, Prompt.

ialous, *adj.* jealous, C2, C3.—OF. *jalous*; Late Lat. *zelōsum*, from Lat. *zelus*; Gr. ζῆλος, zeal.

ialousye, *sb.* jealousy, PP, C2, C3; **ielesye**, PP.—OF. *jalousie*.

iambeux, *sb. pl.* armour for the legs, C2, HD; **giambeux**, ND.—Cf. OF. *jambiere*, armour for a leg (Cotg.), from *jambe*, leg: It. *gamba* (Florio).

iane, *sb.* a small coin of Genoa, ND, C2, HD.—See Ducange (s.v. *januini*).

iangle, *v.* to jangle, chatter, murmur, argue, quarrel, S2, PP, Sh., S3, C2, C3; **gangle**, SkD; **iangland**, *pr. p.*, S2, H.—OF. *jangler*, to jest, mock (Bartsch).

ianglere, *sb.* brawler, wrangler, W2; prater, chatterer, H; **iangeler**, story-teller, S2, PP; **iangelere**, Prompt.

iape, *sb.* joke, jest, mockery, PP, S3, C2, C3, Prompt.; **iapes**, *pl.*, S2.

iapen, *v.* to jest, mock, play tricks, act the buffoon, PP, C2, C3; **iapede**, *pt. s.*, S2.—OF. *japper*, to yapp (of dogs), Cotg.

iaper, *sb.* jester, buffoon, PP, Prompt.; **iapers**, *pl.*, S2.

iargoun, *sb.* jargon, S2; **jergon**, SkD.—OF. *jargon*.

iaunys, *sb.* the yellow disease, jaundice, S2, SkD, HD; **iawnes**, Cath., HD, Voc.; **jaundys**, Cath. (*n*); **jandis**, Voc.—OF. *jaunisse*, from *jaune*, *gaune*, yellow; Lat. *galbinum*, from *galbus*.

ieaunt, *sb.* giant, PP, S2; see **geaunt**.

ielesye, *sb.* jealousy, PP; see **jalousye**.

ielofer, *sb.* gillyflower, S3; see **gerraflour**.

iemis, *sb. pl.* gems, S3; see **gemme**.

iennet, *sb.* a small Spanish horse, S3; see **genette**.

ient-man, *sb.* gentleman, S3. See **gent**.

ieoperdie, *sb.* jeopardy, S3; see **jupartie**.

ierkin, *sb.* jerkin, jacket, S3.—Cf. Du. *jurk*, a frock.

iesseraunt, *sb.* a coat or cuirass of fine mail, HD; **gesserant**, S3; **gesseron**, S3.—OF. *jazerant* (Ducange), *jazeran*, *iaseran* (Cotg.), *jazerenc* (Roland); cf. It. *ghiazzerino* (Florio).

iette[1], *sb.* jet, SkD; **jet**, SkD; **geet**, C; **geete**, Prompt.; **gett**, Prompt.—OF. *jet, jaet*; Lat. *gagatem*. See **gagates**.

iette[2], *sb.* fashion, custom, PP, Palsg.; **gette**, Palsg.; **iutte**, rude slight, S3; **jet**, a device, HD; **get**, Prompt., SkD (**jet**), C, C3.

ietten, *v.* to throw out, to fling about the body, to strut about, SkD, Prompt., Palsg.; **getten**, Prompt.; **ietting**, *pr. p.*, S3.—OF. *jetter* (*getter*), *jecter* (*gecter*); Lat. *iactare*, freq. of *iacēre*, to throw.

Iewe, *sb.* Jew, PP; **Iewes**, *pl.*, PP; **Geus**, S; **Gius**, S; **Gyus**, S.—AF. *Geu*, OF. *Jueu*, *Judeu*; Lat. *Iudæum*.

iewise, *sb.*; see **juwise**.

iogelen, *v.* to juggle, play false, PP, Prompt.; **iuglen**, S3, SkD.

iogelour, *sb.* buffoon, juggler, CM, C2, PP; **ioguloure**, Prompt., **iogulor**, deceiver, H; **iuguler**, Cath.; **iuglur**, S.—AF. *jugleör*; Lat. *ioculatorem*.

ioie, *sb.* joy, S, C2; **joye**, S, S2, C2, PP.—AF. *joie*, OF. *goie*; Lat. *gaudia*, pl. of *gaudium*, rejoicing.

ioien, *v.* to rejoice, W2, PP.

ioist, *v.* to put out cattle to graze at a fixed rate, to agist cattle, HD, EDS (C. vi); **jyst**, EDS (C. xxvi); **ioyst**, *pp.*, lodged (of cattle), S2.—OF. *gister*, to lodge, from *giste*, a place to lie in, a pp. form of *gesir*; Lat. *iacēre*, to lie; see NED (s.v. *agist*).

iolif, *adj.* gay, merry, C, H, PP; **iolef**, S2; **ioli**, W2, PP; **joly**, C2.—AF. *jolyf, jolif*.

iolifte, *sb.* amusement, enjoyment, joviality, H; **iolitee**, C2, C3.—OF. *jolivete*.

iolily, *adv.* merrily, G.

iolynesse, *sb.* festivity, C, C2.

iorne, *sb.* journey, S2; **jornay**, S2; see **journe**.

iouisaunce, *sb.* enjoyment, S3.—OF. *jouissance* (Cotg.), from OF. *joïr*: Prov. *gaudir*; Lat. *gaudere*.

iourne, *sb.* a day's work or travel, PP; **iornay**, S2; **jurneie**, SkD; **iourney**, S3, C2; **iornes**, *pl.*, S2; **iournes**, H (Ps. 22. 9).—OF. *jornee*, *journée*, a day, a day's journey, a fixed day (cf. AF. *jorneie*, day on which a court is held); Low Lat. *jornata*, *diurnata*, from Lat. *diurnus*.

iousten, *v.* to approach, encounter, to joust, tilt, PP, CM; **iusten**, C3.—OF. *jouster*

114

(*joster*), *juster*; Late Lat. *juxtare*, to approach, from Lat. *iuxta*.

iouster, *sb*. champion, PP.

ioustes, *sb. pl.* tournaments, CM.—AF. *joustes*.

ioutes, *sb. pl.* a food made from herbs, broth, P, HD, Prompt. (*n*); **iowtes**, *lap-pates*, Cath., Prompt. (*n*); **iowtys**, potage, Prompt.; **jutes**, Voc.; **eowtus**, Prompt. (*n*).—OF. *ioute*, 'olera' (Ps. 36. 2); Low Lat. *jūta*, 'awilled meolc' (Voc.); *jutta* (Ducange); prob. of Celtic origin, cf. Breton *iot*, porridge, Wel. *uwd*, OIr. *ith*, see Rhys, Lectures on Welsh Philology, p. 7. {For other cognates of this wide-spread word, see Kluge (s.v. *jauche*). See also s.v. *käse*, where Kluge remarks that Icel. *ostr*, cheese, and Finnish *juusto*, cheese, are etymologically connected with G. *jauche*, and Latin *jus*.}

ioynen, *v.* to join, PP, C3; **joyneaunt**, *pr. p.*, joining, S3.—OF. *joindre* (pr. p. *joignant*); Lat. *iungere*.

ioynturis, *sb. pl.* joinings, W; **ioyntours**, W.—OF. *jointure*; Lat. *iunctura* (Vulg.).

iuge, *sb.* judge, S2, Voc., C2, C3; **jugge**, C; **jugges**, *pl.*, P; **juges**, S3.—AF. *juge*; Lat. *iudicem*.

iugement, *sb.* judgement, S2, C2, C3; **juggement**, C.—AF. *jugement*.

iugen, *v.* to judge, decide, PP; **iugge**, PP, CM.—OF. *juger*; Lat. *iudicare*.

iugge-man, *sb.* judge, G.

iuglen, *v.* to juggle, S3; see **jogelen**.

iuguler, *sb.* buffoon, Cath.; see **jogelour**.

iugulynge, *sb.* juggling, S3.

iumpred, *sb.* mourning, S2.—AS. *géomer* + *réden*. See **ʒemer**.

iunglenges, *sb. pl.*, disciples, S; see **ʒonglyng**.

iupartie, *sb.* jeopardy, CM, C3; **ieoperdie**, S3; **jeobertie**, HD.—OF. *jeu parti*, a divided game, a poetical discussion (Bartsch); Late Lat. *jocus partitus* (Ducange).

ius, *sb.* juice, S2, HD.—OF. *jus*; Lat. *ius*, broth.

iusten, *v.* to joust, C3; see **jousten**.

iustlen, *v.* to jostle, push, S3.

iutes, broth; see **joutes**.

iutte, *sb.* a piece of scornful behaviour, S3; see **jette**[2].

iuuente, *sb.* youth, S2, PP.—OF. *jovente* (Bartsch); Lat. *iuventa*.

iuwise, *sb.* judgement, PP; **iuwyse**, CM, C; **iewise**, HD; **iewis**, PP; **iuyse**, C3; **iuise**, HD.—AF. *juise*; Lat. *iudicium*.

K

*For other words with the sound of initial **k-**, see under* **C** *above and* **Q** *below.*

kacherel, *sb.* bailiff, S2; see **cacherel**.

kærf, *pt. s.* cut, carved, S; see **kerven**.

kairen, *v.* to go, P; see **kayren**.

kaiser, *sb.* Cæsar, emperor; **cayser**, MD; **caysere**, MD; **caisere**, MD; **kaysere**, S; **kayser**, S2; **keiser**, S; **keysar**, S3.—Cf. Goth. *kaisar*; Lat. *Caesar*.

kale, *sb.* cabbage, cale, H; see **cole**[1].

karf, *pt. s.* cut, S; see **kerven**.

kateyl, *sb.* property, S2; see **catel**.

kayren, *v.* to go, move oneself, S2, MD; **kairen**, P; **cair**, to drive backward and forwards, JD.—Icel. *keyra*, to impel, drive.

kechyn, *sb.* kitchen, S2; see **kuchene**.

kedde, *pt.* made known, S; see **kyþen**.

kele, *v.* to cool, W, S2, H, PP.—AS. *célan*.

keling, *sb.* a large kind of cod, MD, HD, S2 (s.v. *lobbe*); **kelynge**, MD; **keeling**, JD.— Cf. Icel. *keila*, 'gadus'.

kemben, *v.* to comb, S, C2, PP; **kemyn**, Prompt.; **kempt**, *pp.*, MD.—AS. *cemban*. See **combe**.

kemelyn, *sb.* tub, CM.

kempe[1], *sb.* warrior, S, MD, Cath.—AS. *cempa*, Icel. *kempa*: OHG. *chemphio*, also *kempho* (Tatian); Late Lat. *campio*, from Lat. *campus*. See **camp**.

kempe[2], *adj.* shaggy, rough, C, CM; **campe**, C (p. 155), EETS (1).

kempster, *sb. f.* flax-comber, Palsg.; **kemster**, Voc. See **kemben**.

ken, *sb. pl.* cows, S2; see **cow**.

kende[1], *adj.* natural, kind, S2; see **kynde**[1].

kende[2], *sb.* race, kind, S2; see **kynde**[2].

kendeliche, *adv.* naturally, S2; see **kyndely**[2].

kendlen, *v.*; see **kindlen**[1].

kene, *adj.* bold, keen, sharp, S, C, C2; **keyn**, MD; **kenre**, *comp.*, MD; **kennest**, *superl.*, MD.—AS. *céne*; OTeut. **kōni*; cf. OHG. *kuani* (Otfrid), *chuoni*.

kenne, *sb. dat.* kin, S, S2; see **kyn**[2].

kennen[1], *v.* to beget, engender, to bring forth, to be born, MD, PP; **y-kend**, *pp.*, S2; **kenned**, MD.—AS. *cennan*, to beget, conceive, bring forth; OS. *kennian*, to beget, causal from OTeut. root **kan-*, to generate, see Kluge (s.v. *kina*).

kennen[2], *v.* to show, declare, teach, S2, PP, SkD (s.v. *ken*), Prompt., H; **kende**, *pt. s.*, S2.—AS. *cennan*, to make to know: Goth. *kannjan* = **kannian*, causal of OTeut. **kann-*, base of **konnan*, to know.

kennen[3], *v.* to know, SkD. (s.v. *ken*); **ken**, S3, JD; **kend**, *pt. pl.*, S3; **kend**, *pp.*, S3.—Icel. *kenna*, to know. See **kennen**[2].

keoruen, *v.* to carve, S; see **kerven**.

kepe, *sb.* heed, S2, S3, C2; **kep**, S3.

kepen, *v.* to keep, mark, observe, regard, S, S2, S3, C2; **keped**, *pt. s.*, S2; **kipte**, S2.— AS. *cépan*, later form of *cýpan* (= *céapian*), see Sievers, 97. {AS. *cépan*, to keep, should be kept quite distinct from AS. *cýpan*, to sell. AS. *cýpan* is the phonetic representative of OTeut. **kaupjan*, whereas *cépan* represents an OTeut. **kōpjan*. Cf. E. *keen*, the representative of AS. *céne*, OTeut. **kōni* (G. *kühn*). See Kluge's note in P. & B. Beiträge, viii. 538.}

keppen, *sb. pl.* caps, S; see **cappe**.

kernel, *sb.* a loophole in a fortress, a battlement, PP; **crenelle**, HD; **kyrnellis**, *pl.*, S3; **kirnelis**, PP.—OF. *crenel*, from *cren* (*cran*), a notch; Lat. *crena*.

kerneled, *adj.* furnished with battlements, P.

kertel, *sb.*; see **kirtel**.

keruen, *v.* to carve, MD, Prompt., S, C2; **keoruen**, MD, S; **cærf**, *pt. s.*, MD; **kærf**, S; **kerf**, MD; **karf**, MD, S; **carf**, C2; **curuen**, *pl.*, MD; **coruen**, *pp.*, MD, S3, C; **icoruen**, S3; **y-coruen**, S3, C3; **y-koruen**, C2; **i-koruen**, S; **kerued**, S3.— AS. *ceorfan*, *pt.* *cearf* (pl. *curfon*), pp. *corfen*.

kesse, *v.* to kiss, S2; see **cussen**.

keste, *v.* to cast, S2; see **casten**.

kete, *adj.* bold, lively, gay, powerful, MD, S2, PP; **ket**, irascible, JD.—Cf. Icel. *kátr*, merry, Dan. *kåd*.

kete-lokes, *sb. pl.* trefoil, H; see **cat-cluke**.

keuel, *sb.* a bit for a horse, a gag, a small piece of wood used in casting lots, MD, H, S; **kevyl**, Prompt.; **cavel**, JD; **kevelles**, *pl.*, MD; **caflis**, MD, JD.—Icel. *kefli*.

keueren, *v.* to recover one's health, MD, PP; **keuord**, *pt. s.*, H; see **coveren**[2].

keueringe, *sb.* recovery, S2.

keye, *sb.* key; **kay**, MD; **cays**, *pl.*, MD; **keis**, S; **keiȝes**, S2.—AS. *cæg*.

kidde, *pt. s.* made known, S, P; *pp.*, S; **kid**, S; see **kyþen**.

kidnere, *sb.* kidney, SkD; **kydney**, Voc.— Icel. *kviðr*, belly + *nýra*, kidney. See **nere**[1].

kien, *sb. pl.* cows, W2; see **cow**.

kiken, *v.* to kick, MD, W; **kycke**, Palsg.— Cf. *kiken*, *kiksen* in G. dialects.

kime, *sb.* coming, S.—AS. *cyme*. See **come**.

kindle, *sb.* offspring, brood, MD; **kundel**, MD; **kyndlis**, *pl.*, MD.

116

kindlen[1], *v.* to bear young, S; **kyndlyn**, Prompt.; **kendlen**, MD; **kundlen**, MD; **i-kindled**, *pp.*, S. See **kynde**[2].

kindlen[2], *v.* to set fire to, MD; **kyndlen**, C; **kinlen**, MD.

kine- (used in compounds), royal; see below.—AS. *cyne*.

kine-boren, *adj.* of royal birth, MD; **kineborne**, S.—AS. *cyne-boren*.

kine-dom, *sb.* kingdom, MD, S, S2.—AS. *cyne-dóm*.

kine-helm, *sb.* royal helmet, crown, MD.—AS. *cyne-helm*.

kine-lond, *sb.* kingdom, S, MD.

kine-merk, *sb.* royal mark; **kynemerk**, S.

kine-riche, *sb.* kingdom, rule, MD; **cyne-rice**, S.—AS. *cyne-ríce*.

kine-scrud, *sb.* royal robes, S.

kine-stol, *sb.* throne, S.—AS. *cynestól*.

kine-þeod, *sb.* subjects of a king, MD.

kine-wurðe, *adj.* royal, S, MD.

kine-ȝerde, *sb.* sceptre, MD.—AS. *cyne-gerd* (Voc.).

king, *sb.* king, MD, S; **kyng**, S; **kyngene**, *pl. gen.*, S2, PP.—AS. *cyning*: OS. *kuning*.

kingdom, *sb.* kingdom, MD.

kinghed, *sb.* Kingship, PP.

king-riche, *sb.* kingdom, S, MD; **kingrike**, S2; **kyngrike**, H; **kyngriche**, P.

kipte, *pt. s.* received, S2; see **kepen**.

kirke, *sb.* church, S, S2, P; see **chirche**.

kirnel, *sb.* loop-hole, PP; see **kernel**.

kirtel, *sb.* kirtle, a short gown or petticoat, tunic, S3, P, CM; **kurtel**, S; **cortel**, MD; **kirrtell**, MD; **kirtil**, H; **kyrtyl**, S2; **kertel**, MD; **kirtel**, S3, P; **curtel**, MD.

kist, *sb.* chest, coffin, MD; **cyst**, MD.; **kyst**, S2; **kiste**, S2; **kyste**, S2, PP; **cyste**, *munificentia*, Voc.; **chist**, MD.—AS. *cist*; Lat. *cista*; Gr. κίστη.—Cf. **chest**[2].

kitlen, *v.* to tickle; **kittle**, HD, JD; **kytlys**, *pr. s.*, S3. See **kitlynge**.

kitlynge, *sb.* tickling, H; **kitellynge**, MD, HD.—AS. *kitelung*, 'titillatio' (Voc.).

kitoun, *sb.* kitten, P; **kyton**, PP.

kitte, *pt. s.* cut, S2, C2, C3; **kittide**, W; see **kutten**.

kitte-pors, *sb.* thief, PP; see **cut-purs**.

kittingis, *sb. pl.* cuttings, W.

kith, *sb.* one's country, PP; see **kyþ**.

kithen, *v.* to make known, S, S2; see **kyþen**.

kithing, *sb.* telling, S2.

kleþing, *sb.* clothing, S2. See **cloþ**.

knack, *sb.* a snap, crack, a jester's trick, a trifle, toy, SkD, MD; **knakkes**, *pl.*, CM; **knackes**, S3.

knaing, *sb.* knowing, acquaintance, S2; see **knowen**.

knap, *v.* to snap, break with a noise, SkD; *imp. s.*, strike (the bell), S3.—Cf. G. *knappen*, to crack.

knappes, *sb. pl.* knobs, S2, P; see **knoppe**.

knarre, *sb.* a knot in wood, SkD (s.v. *gnarled*), C, CM.—Cf. MDu. *cnorre*, Du. *knor*, a knurl.

knarry, *adj.* full of knots, C.

knaue, *sb.* a boy-baby, boy, servant, knave, S, S2, C2; **cnafe**, MD; **cnaue**, MD.—AS. *cnafa*; cf. OHG. *chnabe* (G. *knabe*).

knaue-child, *sb.* a male child, W.

knawe, *v.* to know, S2; see **knowen**.

knawen, *pp.* gnawed, S3; see **gnawen**.

kne, *sb.* knee, S, S2; **cneowe**, *dat.*, S; **cnouwe**, S; **knes**, *pl.*, S; **kneon**, S; **knowes**, C2, P.—AS. *cnéow* (*cnéo*).

kneden, *v.* to knead, Voc., Palsg.; **cneden**, S, MD; **knodyn**, *pp.*, MD; **knodon**, Prompt.; **kned**, CM; **knodden**, HD.—AS. *cnedan*, pp. *cnoden* (*cneden*), see SkD.

knelen, *v.* to kneel, S; **knely**, S2; **kneolen**, PP; **knewlen**, *pr. pl.*, PP.—Cf. Low G. *knélen*.

knelyng, *sb.* kneeling, PP; **cnelinng**, S; **knewelyng**, S.

kneon, *sb. pl.* knees, S; see **kne**.

knippen, *v.* to nip, break off the edge; **nippen**, SkD; **nyppen**, PP; **knyp**, *pp.*, S3.—Cf. Du. *knippen*, to crack, snap.

kniȝt, *sb.* knight, soldier, armed retainer, S, S2; **knict**, S; **knyht**, S; **knyght**, C3; **cnihtes**, *pl.*, S; **knictes**, S; **knyhtes**, S; **knyȝtis**, W, W2; **kniȝtes**, S; **cnihten**, S.—AS. *cniht*; cf. OHG. *kneht*, 'puer' (Tatian), 'miles, discipulus' (Otfrid).

kniȝten, *v.* to knight, S.

kniȝthod, *sb.* knighthood, S; **knyghthode**, *dat.*, C2; **knighthede**, C; **knyȝthod**, army, warfare, W, W2.

knoppe, *sb.* knob, buckle, bud, MD, Prompt., Cath., Palsg., S3; **knobbe**, C; **knappes**, *pl.*, S2, P; **knoppes**, CM, PP.—Cf. Dan. *knop*.

knopped, *adj.* full of knobs, S3.

knotte, *sb.* knot, C2, PP, Prompt., S3.—AS. *cnotta*.

knowen, *v.* to know, MD; **knawe**, S2; **cnawen**, S; **knaa**, HD; **cnoweð**, *pr. s.*, S; **kneuȝ**, *pt. s.*, S2; **knewen**, *pl.*, S; **i-cnawen**, *pp.*, S; **ȝe-cnowe**, S; **y-cnowen**, S3; **y-knowe**, S2; **knowun**, W; **cnowen**, S2; **knawen**, S2; **knawin**, S3.—AS. *cnáwan*, pt. *cnéow*, pp. *cnáwen*.

knowes, *sb. pl.* knees, C2, P; see **kne**.

knowleche, *sb.* knowledge, MD; **knouleche**, acquaintance (= Lat. *notos*), W; **knawlache**, MD; **knawlage**, MD; **knowlych**, S2. See **-leȝȝc**.

knowlechen, *v.* to acknowledge, S2, W2, P; **cnawlechen**, MD; **knouleche**, W; **knoulechide**, *pt. s.*, W; **knowlechiden**, *pl.*, W.

knowleching, *sb.* the acknowledging, C3; **cnawlechunge**, S; **knaulechynge**, S2; **knowleching**, C3; **knoulechyng**, W2.

knucche, *sb.* small bundle, MD, Cath. (*n*); **knyche**, Cath.; **knitch**, JD; **knytchis**, *pl.*, W.—Cf. G. *knocke* (Kluge).

knytten, *v.* to knit, bind, Prompt., S2, C3, PP; **knutte**, *pt. s.*, MD; **knette**, MD; **knitte**, C3; **knyt**, *pp.*, MD; **knit**, C2.—AS. *cnyttan.* See **knotte**.

ko, *pt. s.* quoth, S3; see **koþ**.

kokewolde, *sb.* cuckold, P; see **cokewold**.

kole-plantes, *sb. pl.* cabbages, P; see **cole**[1].

kollen, *v.* to embrace, S2; see **collen**.

kon, *pt. pr.* can, S; see **kunnen**.

konning, *sb.* skill, C2; see **conning**[1].

konyng, *sb.* cony, rabbit, S; see **conyng**.

koth, *pt. s.* quoth, S3; **cothe**, MD; see **queþen**.

koude, *pt. s.* knew, W2; see **kunnen**.

kouren, *v.* to cower, S2; **couren**, MD.—Icel. *kúra*, to sit quiet; cf. G. *kauern*, see Weigand.

kourte-by, *sb.* short coat, P; see **courte-py**.

kouthe, *pt. s.* could, S; *pp.* S2; see **kunnen**.

kraghan, *sb.* burnt grass = *cremium*, dry firewood, H; **crakan**, Cath.—Cf. North.E. *crack*, to make a noise (JD).

krake, *sb.* crow, H; **crake**, Cath.; **krakis**, *pl.*, H.—Icel. *krákr*.

kremelen, *v.* to anoint with oil or fat; **kremelyd**, *pp.*, MD; see **cremelen**.

krike, *sb.* creek, S; see **crike**.

krune, *sb.* crown, S; see **corone**.

ku, *sb.* cow, S; see **cow**.

kuchene, *sb.* kitchen, S; **kychene**, MD; **kechyn**, S2; **kychens**, *pl.*, S3.—AS. *cycene.*

kud, *pp.* made known, S2; **i-kud**, S; see **kunnen**.

kudde, *pt. s.* made known, S2; **kude**, *pl.*, S; see **kunnen**.

kude, *pt. pl.* could, S; see **kunnen**.

kueade, *adj. dat.* bad, S2; see **quad**[1].

kulle, *v.* to strike, to kill, P, MD; **kylle**, Cath.; **kyllyn**, Prompt.; **colen**, MD; **culle**, P.—The word means properly to knock on the head; cf. Norweg. *kylla*, to poll, to cut the shoots off trees, from *koll*, the top, head; Icel. *kollr*, head, crown.

kumen, *v.* to come, S; see **comen**.

kun[1], *v.* to get to know, to learn, H; see **conne**[1].

kun[2], *sb.* kin, S2; **kunnes**, *gen.*, S2; **kunne**, *dat.*, S, S2; see **kyn**[2].

kunde[1], *adj.* natural, kind, S2; see **kynde**[1].

kunde[2], *sb.* kind, race, nature, S2; see **kynde**[2].

kundel, *sb.* offspring, MD.

kundite, *sb.* a conduit, S3; see **conduit**.

kunes-men, *sb. pl.* kinsmen, S, S2; see **kynes-man**.

kunnen, *v.* to know, to know how, to be able, S, S3, W2, CM; **cunnen**, S, S2; **conne**, S, S3, P; **cun**, H; **con**, *pt. pr.*, S; **kon**, S; **can**, S, S2; **kan**, S, S2; **con**, **can**, *used as auxil.*, S2; **canstu**, 2 *pr. s.*, with *pron.*, S; **canstow**, S2; **cuðe**, *pt. s.*, S; **kuðe**, S; **couthe**, S, S2, S3; **cowthe**, G; **couȝðe**, S2; **cuth**, S2; **coude**, S2; **cowde**, G; **koude**, W2; **couȝde**, S2; **kouthen**, *pl.*, S; **kude**, S; **cuð**, *pp.*, S (17 b. 161); **kuð**, S; **couth**, C2; **couðe**, S2; **kouthe**, S2.—AS. *cunnan*, pt. *cúðe*, pp. *cúð* (used as adj.).

kun-rede, *sb.* kindred, S; see **kynrede**.

kuppe, *sb.* cup, S; see **cuppe**.

kussen, *v.* to kiss, S; see **cussen**.

kut, *sb.* lot, a cut twig, H; see **cut**.

kutten, *v.* to cut, MD, CM; **kitt**, MD; **kut**, *pt. s.*, MD; **kitte**, S2, C2, C3; **kittide**, W, MD; **ketten**, *pl.*, P; **kyt**, *pp.*, W; **kit**, W.

kuth, *sb.* kith, friends, PP.

kuðe, *pt. s.*, could, knew, S; see **kunnen**.

kutthe (i.e. **kuþþe**), country, PP; see **kyþ**.

kuþþes, *sb. pl.* manners, S2, HD, MD; see **kyþ**.

kuueren, *v.* to recover one's health, S2; see **coveren**[2].

kuynde, *adj.* natural, S2, PP; see **kynde**[1].

kwene, *sb.* queen, S; see **quene**.

ky, *sb. pl.* cows, S3; see **cow**.

kychen, *sb.* kitchen, S3; see **kuchene**.

kyn[1], *sb. pl.* cows, S2, C; see **cow**.

kyn[2], *sb.* kin, kind, generation, S, W, MD; **kun**, S2; **kin**, S, S2, C2; **cun**, MD, S; **kunnes**, *gen.*, S2; **cunne**, *dat.*, S; **kunne**, S, S2; **kenne**, S, S2; **kynne**, P.—AS. *cynn:* OS. *kunni*, OHG. *kunni* (Otfrid): Goth. *kuni:* from Teut. base **konya*, from root **kan-*.

kynde[1], *adj.* natural, kind, S2, S3, P; **kunde**, S2, MD; **cunde**, MD; **kinde**, S; **kende**, S2, PP; **kuynde**, S2, PP.—AS. *cynde.*

kynde[2], *sb.* kind, nature, race, children, natural disposition, PP, S2, S3, C2, C3, W; **kunde**, S2; **cunde**, S; **kinde**, S. S2; **kende**, S2; **kynd**, S3.—AS. (*ge*)*cynd.*

kyndely[1], *adj.* natural, kindly, MD; **kyndli**, W; **kyndly**, Cath.; **kundeliche**, MD.—AS. *cyndelic.*

kyndely[2], *adv.* naturally, kindly, S2; **kyndli**, W; **kindely**, S2; **kindelike**, S; **kende-liche**, S2; **kyndeliche**, S2, PP; **cunde-liche**, S.—AS. *cyndelice.*

kyndlyn, *v.* to bear young, Prompt.; see **kindlen**[1].

kyndlyngis, *sb. pl.* brood, litter of beasts, W.

kynes-man, *sb.* kinsman, MD; **cunesmon**, S; **kunesmen**, *pl.*, S, S2.

kynrede, *sb.* kindred, S3, W2, C; **kunrede**, S; **kynredyn**, H; **kinredis**, *pl.*, W; **cunreadnes**, *pl.*, S.—AS. *cynn* + *rǽden*, condition.

kysse, *sb.* kiss, Palsg.—From AS. *cysan*. See **cussen**.

kyth, *sb.* one's country, native land, relatives, kith, friends, PP, S2; **kith**, PP; **kuth**, PP; **cuth**, PP; **kutthe**, PP; **kitthe**, PP; **cuððe**, S, PP; **couthe**, PP; **kythez**, *pl.*, S2; **ceðen**, S; **cheðen**, S; **kuþþes**, manners, S2.—AS. *cýððu* (*cýð*): OHG. *cundida*, race, kinship; see Sievers, 255.

kythen, *v.* to make known, MD, C2, C3, PP, S3; **kiðen**, S, S2; **cuðen**, S; **couthe**, MD, PP; **couth**, *pr. s.*, P; **kydde**, *pt. s.*, PP; **kidde**, PP, S; **kudde**, S2; **cudde**, S; **kedde**, S, MD; **kyd**, S2; **kid**, MD; **kydst**, *2 pt. s.*, S3; **i-kud**, *pp.*, S; **kud**, S2; **kyd**, S2; **kid**, S; **kidde** (as *adj.*), S.—AS. *(ge)cýðan*: OS. *kúðian*; OHG. *kundjan*, also *kunden* (Otfrid).

L

la, *interj.* lo!, S; **lo**, W2 (Ps. 67. 34).—AS. *lá*.
Comb.: **la hwure**, at least, S.
laas, *sb.* snare, C, C3; see **las**.
labbe, *sb.* he that can keep no counsel, Prompt., CM; **lab**, a blab, tittle-tattle, HD.
labben, *v.* to blab, babble, PP; **labbing**, *pr. p.*, C2.—Cf. Du. *labben*, to blab.
labbyng, *adj.* blabbing, CM.
-lac, *suffix*, used in forming abstract nouns; see **-leȝȝc**.
lacchen, *v.* to catch, seize, snatch, PP; **lauhte**, *pt. s.* seized, practised, PP; **lauȝte**, PP, S2; **laȝte**, S; **laucte**, S; **lacchide**, *pl.*, PP; **lauht**, *pp.*, PP; **lagt**, S; **latchyd**, Prompt.—AS. *læccan, ge-læccan.*
lacching, *sb.* taking, S2.
lacert, *sb.* a fleshy muscle, C, CM.—OF. *lacerte* (Cotg.); Lat. *lacertum* (acc.), a muscle, strength, usually, the muscular part of the arm.
lad, ladde; see **leden**[1].
ladel, *sb.* ladle, PP, C3; **ladylle**, *coclear*, Prompt.; *hausorium*, Voc.
laden, *v.* to burden, to charge with burdens, Prompt., WW; to draw water to lade, Prompt.; **laden**, *pp.* *oneratus*, Prompt., SkD.—AS. *hladan* (pt. *hlód*, pp. *hladen*): Icel. *hlaða*, Goth. *hlaþan* (in comp.).
læfdi, *sb.* lady, S; see **levedy**.
læfe, lafe, *sb.* belief, S; see **leve**[2].
læn, *sb.* a grant, loan, S.—AS. *lén* (OET).
laf, *sb.* loaf, S; see **loof**[1].
lage, lahe, *sb.* law, S; see **lawe**.
lah, *adj.* low, S; see **louh**.
lahfulnesse, *sb.* lawfulness, S.
lahhen, *v.* to laugh, S; **lauhen**, PP; **laughe**, PP, C2 **lauȝen**, PP, S3; **lauȝwe**, S3; **lauȝwhen**, PP; **lawghe**, PP, C; **leiȝen**, W; **lauhwen**, S, PP, S2; **lahynde**, *pr. p.*, S2; **laȝinge**, S2; **louh**, *pt. s.*, PP; **lough**, C2, C3; **lowh**, PP; **lowȝ**, PP; **loh**, S2; **lewch**, S3; **loȝen**, *pl.*, S2; **lough**, S3; **louȝe**, *subj.*, S.—AS. *hlehhan* (pt. *hlóh*): Goth. *hlahjan.*
lahter, *sb.* laughter, S; **leiȝtir**, W2; **leihtre**, *dat.*, S.—AS. *hleahtor.*
laif, *sb.* the remainder, B, S3; **laiff**, B; **layff**, B, S2, S3; **lafe**, B; **lave**, B, JD, HD.—AS. *láf*, what is left, heritage (Voc.), from *-lífan* (Grein), only found in compounds, e.g. *be-lífan*, to remain; cf. OHG. *bi-líban*, to remain (Tatian) G. *bleiben.*
laire, *sb.* clay, mud, mire, WA, H, HD; **layre**, H; **lare**, H; quagmire, HD.—Icel. *leir*, clay, mire.

lairy, *adj.* miry, H; **layry**, H; **layri**, H; **layery**, HD.
laiten, *v.* to seek, SD, HD, S2, WA; **leȝten**, SD.—Icel. *leita*: Goth. *wlaiton*, to look about.
laitis, *sb. pl.* gestures, S3; see **late**[1].
laith, *adj.* loathsome, H; see **loþ**.
lake[1], *sb.* a kind of fine linen, C2, HD, CM.—Cf. Du. *laken*, cloth, a sheet, OHG. *lahhan*, also *lachan* (Otfrid).
lake[2], *sb.* standing-water, Prompt.; *rivulus*, Voc.; **llak**, *pl.*, S2. *Comb.*: **lake-ryftes**, chines worn by water, S2.—AF. *lake*, OF. *lac*; Lat. *lacum.*
lake[3], *sb. dat.* a gift, offering, S; see **lok**[1].
laken, *v.* to offer to God, S.—AS. *(ge)lácian*, to give.
lakke, *sb.* defect, a failing, C2; **lak**, Prompt., C; **lac**, SkD; **lake**, blame, WA, S3; **lakke**, C2; **lakkes**, *pl.* faults, PP.—Cf. Du. *lak*, blemish.
lakken[1], *v.* to lack, PP, C; **him lakked**, *pt. s.* there lacked to him, C2.
lakken[2], *v.* to blame, G, PP, Prompt.; **lak**, JD; **lakes**, *pr. s.*, S2; **lackand**, *pr. p.*, H; **y-lakked**, *pp.*, P.—Cf. Du. *laken*, to blame.
Lammasse, *sb.* Lammas, the first of August, PP, S2; **Lammesse**, Prompt.—AS. *hlam-mæsse, hláfmæsse*, loaf-mass, named from the Blessing of Bread. The Feast is called in the Sarum Manual *Benedictio novorum fructuum.*
lampe[1], *sb.* lamp, Cath., PP; **laumpe**, S2, PP; **lawmpe**, Voc., Prompt.; **lampes**, *pl.*, C3.—AF. *lampe*; Lat. *lampadem.*
lampe[2], *sb.* a thin plate, C3; **lamm**, HD, ND.—OF. *lame*; Lat. *lamina.*
laner, *sb.* a kind of hawk, *basterdus*, Voc.; **lanner**, Cotg.; **lannard**, HD.—OF. *lanier* (Cotg.); Lat. *laniarium*, that which tears, from *laniare*, to tear.
lanere, *sb.* a thong, Prompt.; see **laynere**.
lang, *adj.* long, tall, S; **long**, S, PP; **lengre**, *comp.*, S; **lenger**, S2, C2, PP; **lengore**, S2; **lange**, *adv.* long, S; **longe**, S, S2; **lang**, S2; **leng**, *comp.*, S; **lenger**, S3; **lengere**, S, S2; **langar**, S3; **lengest**, *superl.*, S, S2.—AS. *lang.*
langage, *sb.* language, C, C2, PP.—AF. *langage.*
langes, *pr. pl.* belong, S2; see **longen**.
Lang-Fridai, *sb.* Long-Friday, i.e. Good-Friday, S; **Lange-Fridai**, S.—Icel. *langi-frjádagr.*
langmode, *adj.* long-suffering, S2.—AS. *lang-mód.*

120

langour, *sb.* languishment, slow starvation, C2, PP; **langours**, *pl.* sicknesses, W.—AF. *langour, illness*; Lat. *languorem.*

languor, *sb.* disease, sickness, W; **languores**, *pl.*, W.—Lat. *languor* (Vulg.).

lan3er, *sb.* a thong, Cath.; see **laynere.**

lappe, *sb.* lap, bosom, PP, C2, C3; **a lappet**, skirt, PP, S; the lobe of the ear, Cath.—AS. *lappa* (OET).

lappen, *v.* to wrap, W, H, Cath., SkD, HD: see **wlappen.**

lare[1], *sb.* lore, S, S2, H; see **lore.**

lare[2], *sb.* clay; see **laire.**

lare-fadir, *sb.* teacher, doctor, H; **larfadir**, H; **larefather**, HD; **lorefadyr**, HD.

large, *adj.* liberal, generous, S, G, PP, C; plentiful, S2; *sb.* size, S2.—AF. *large.*

largeliche, *adv.* bountifully, PP, S2; **largely**, G.

largesse, *sb.* largess, bounty, PP, S3.—AF. *largesce.*

lar-þawes, *sb. pl.* teachers, S; see **lorþeaw.**

las, *sb.* snare, lace, HD, SkD, C; **laz**, S; **laas**, C3, C; **lase**, Voc.—OF. *las, laqs*; Lat. *laqueus*; cf. AF. *laz.*

lase, *v.* to fasten, C; **lasynge**, *pr. p.*, C; **lacede**, *pt. s.*, S; **i-laced**, *pp.*, S.—OF. *lacier.*

laser, *sb.* leisure, S2, S3; see **leyser.**

lasnen, *v.* to lessen; **lasned**, *pt. s.*, S2.

lasse, *adj. and adv. comp.* less, S, S2, S3, C3, PP; **lesse**, S. *Phr.*: **lasse and more**, smaller and greater, i.e. all, C2; **on les that**, on a less supposition than that, unless, SkD; **onlesse that**, Palsg.; **onlesse**, SkD; **þi les þe**, lest, SD; **leste**, S, PP; **les when**, lest at some time, H.—AS. *lǽssa, adj.*; and *lǽs, adv.*; *þý lǽs þe*, lest.

last[1], *sb.* weight, burden, ship's cargo, C2.—AS. *hlǽst*; see Sievers, 232. See **laden.**

last[2], *sb.* fault, SD; **lest**, SD; **laste**, *dat.*, S.—Icel. *löstr* (stem *lasta*); cf. OHG. *lastar*, abuse, blame (Otfrid).

lasten[1], *v.* to find fault, blame, SD.

lasten[2], *v.* to follow out, last, endure, S, PP; **lesten**, S, S2; **last**, *pr. s.*, S, C2; **lest**, S; **laste**, *pt. s.*, S, C2; **lastede**, S; **lestyt**, *pp.*, S3.—AS. *léstan*, to perform, to last: Goth. *laistjan*, from *laists* (AS. *lást*), a foot-track.

lastingly, *adv.* constantly, W.

lat[1], *pr. s.* leads, S; see **leden**[1].

lat[2]; see **leten**[1].

late[1], *sb.* behaviour, look, gesture, S, S2; **lete**, S; **lote**, S; **lates**, *pl.*, S; **laitis**, S3; **loten**, S.—Icel. *lát.* See **leten**[1].

late[2], *adj. and adv.* slow, late, S, PP; **later**, *comp.*, S, PP; **latere**, *adv.*, S2; **latst**, *superl.*, S.—AS. *lǽt*: Goth. *lats*, slothful.

lateful, *adj.* late, W.

laten; see **leten**[1], **leten**[2].

latimer, *sb.* interpreter, S; **latymer**, HD; **latineres**, *pl.*, SD, HD.—AF. *latymer*, OF. *latinier*, interpreter, lit. one knowing Latin; Late Lat. *latinarium* (Ducange).

latis, *sb.* lattice; **latijs**, W2; **latisis**, *pl.*, W2.—Cf. F. *lattis.*

latly, *adv.* late, scarcely, H; **latlier**, *comp.*, H.—AS. *lǽtlice*; cf. Icel. *latlíga.* See **late**[2].

laton, *sb.* auricalcum, Prompt., C2; **latoun**, C3, C, W, WA; **latten**, Sh., ND, HD.—OF. *laton.*

latrede, *adj.* tardy, CM.—AS. *lǽtrǽde.* See **late**[2].

latsum, *adj.* backward, SD.—AS. *lǽtsum.*

latsumnes, *sb.* backwardness, H.

laδ[1], *adj.* hateful, loath, S, S2; see **loþ.**

laδ[2], *sb.* hatred, S.—AS. *láδ.*

laδe, *sb.* barn, *horreum, granarium*, Cath., Voc., HD; **laδes**, *pl.*, S.—Icel. *hlaδa.*

laδful, *adj.* hateful, S.

laδien, *v.* to invite, summon to a feast, SD.—AS. *laδian*; cf. OHG. *ladón* (Otfrid).

laδiere, *sb.* inviter, S.

laude, *sb.* praise, C2.—Lat. *laudem.*

lauhen, *v.* to laugh, PP; **laughe**, PP, C2; see **lahhen.**

lauhte, *pt. s.* seized, PP; **lau3te**, PP, S2; **laucte**, S; **la3te**, S; see **lacchen.**

laumpe, *sb.* lamp, S2; see **lampe**[1].

launce, *sb.* lance, PP, WA; **lance**, Cath.—AF. *launce, lance*; Lat. *lancea.*

launcegay, *sb.* a kind of spear, C2; **lancegaye**, ND; **lawncegay**, Prompt.—AF. *launcegay* (Godefroy).

launcen, *v.* to hurl, fling, dart, to leap, hurry, to spring up, S3, PP; **lanse**, S2; **launchen**, to skip over a dike with a long pole; **lawnchyn**, Prompt.—OF. *lancer, lancier, lanchier.*

launde, *sb.* a wild, untilled, shrubby, bushy plain, PP, CM, C, HD; **laund**, Sh., ND, Cotg.; **lawnd**, *saltus*, Voc.; **land**, Cotg.; **lawnde**, Cath.—AF. *launde*, forest, plain, OF. *lande* (Cotg.).

laurer, *sb.* laurel, C; **lory3er**, Prompt.; **loryel**, **lorel**, Prompt.—OF. *laurier, lorier*, Late Lat. **laurarium*; from Lat. *laurus.*

lau3en, *v.* to laugh, S3, PP; **laughe**, C2, PP; **lauhwen**, S, S2, PP; see **lahhen.**

laue, *sb.* the remainder, B, JD, HD; see **laif.**

lauen, *v.* to lave, wash, PP; **lauande**, *pr. p.*, S2.—OF. *laver*; Lat. *lavare.*

lauerd, *sb.* lord, S, S2; see **loverd.**

lauerding, *sb.* nobleman, S2. Cf. **loverdinges.**

lauerdschipe, *sb.* lordship, S; **lordschipe**, W2.

laueroc, *sb.* lark, *alauda*, SD; **lauerok**, SD, JD; **lauerokke**, CM; **lauerock**, S2;

larke, PP, Prompt., Voc.—AS. *láwerce* (Voc.).

lauour, *sb.* laver, cistern, S3, CM, WW; **laver**, WW.

law, *adj.* low, S3; see **louh**.

lawe, *sb.* law, S, PP; **laȝe**, S; **laghe**, S, H; **lahe**, S; **lage**, S; **lages**, *pl.*, S; **lahen**, S; **lawes**, S; **laȝe**, S; **laȝen**, S; **laȝhess**, S. *Phr.*: **of the beste lawe**, in the best order, G.—Icel. *lög* (stem *lagu*), statute, decree.

laweful, *adj.* lawful, SD; **lawfulle**, Cath.

lawelese, *adj.* lawless, S; **laȝelease**, S.

lawelyche, *adj.* lawful, S; **lagelice**, *adv.*, S.

lay, *sb.* law, CM; religion, fidelity, S2; creed, C2, C3; **laies**, *pl.*, PP.—OF. *lai, ley, lei*; Lat. *legem.*

layes, *sb. pl.* leas, meadows, S3; see **leye**[2].

layke, *sb.* game, sport, trial of strength, PP, S2; **laike**, WA; **laik**, PP.—Icel. *leikr.* Cf. **lok**[1].

layken, *v.* to play, sport, S2, PP, Prompt., Manip.; **laike**, PP, WA; **leyke**, S.—Icel. *leika*; cf. AS. *lácan*, to spring, leap for joy, dance, contend: Goth. *laikan*, to leap for joy.

layking, *sb.* play-thing; **laykyn'**, Prompt.; **lakan**, Prompt. (*n*); **leikin**, a sweet-heart, Prompt. (*n*).

laynere, *sb.* a thong, C, CM; **layner**, SkD (p. 814); **lanȝer**, Cath.; **lanyer**, Palsg.; **lanyr**, Voc.; **lanere**, Prompt.—OF. *laniere* (Cotg.), *lasniere* (Palsg.), *lasnier* (Bartsch); Late Lat. **laniaria (linea)*, the thong for a *lanner*. See **laner**.

laȝe, *sb.* law, S; see **lawe**.

laȝte, *pt. s.* took, S; see **lacchen**.

lazar, *sb.* leper, PP; **lazer**, C; **lazars**, *pl.*, PP, C.—Church Lat. *lazari*, lepers (Ducange); from *Lazarus*; Gr. Λάζαρος (Lu. 16. 20); Heb. *Eleazar*, God helpeth.

leahtor, *sb.* vice; **leahtrum**, *pl. dat.*, S.—AS. *leahtor*, from *leahan* (*léan*), to blame: OS. *lahan.*

lean, *sb.* reward, S.—AS. *léan*: Icel. *laun*, OHG. *lón* (Tatian).

leasing, *sb.* falsehood, WW; see **leesinge**.

lebard, *sb.* leopard, S2; see **leopart**.

leccherye, *sb.* lewdness, PP; **lecherie**, S, S2, PP.—AF. *lecherie.*

leche, *sb.* physician, S, S2, S3, C3, H; **leeche**, W; **lache**, S; **leches**, *pl.*, S3; **lechis**, W.—AS. *léce*: Goth. *lēkeis.*

leche-craft, *sb.* knowledge of medicine, S2, C, PP.

lechen, *v.* to heal, S2, HD, PP.

lechnien, *v.* to heal, SD.—AS. *lácnian.*

lechnunge, *sb.* healing, S.—AS. *lácnung.*

lechour, *sb.* a dissolute person, PP; **letchour**, W; **lechur**, S; **lechours**, *pl.*, PP; **lechouris**, W; **letchours**, W.—AF.

lecheur, glutton, from OF. *lecher*, to lick; cf. OHG. *gi-lechon* (Otfrid). See **licken**.

lede, *sb.* man, PP; **ledes**, *pl.*, tenements, PP; see **leod**.

leden[1], *v.* to lead, carry, S, S2, Prompt.; **laden**, S; **leaden**, S; **leide**, S3; **lat**, *pr. s.*, S, PP; **ledys**, *pr. pl.*, S3; **ledde**, *pt. s.*, S2; **ladde**, S, S2, S3; **læd**, S; **lad**, S2, **lædden**, *pl.*, S; **ladde**, C2, PP; **i-led**, *pp.*, S; **i-lad**, S, G; **lad**, S2, S3; **lede**, S2; **ladde**, PP.—AS. *lédan*, to lead, carry, lift (pt. *lédde*, pp. *léded*), from *lád*, a way. See **lode**.

leden[2], *adj.* leaden, C3. See **leed**[1].

leden[3], *sb.* language, S2; **leoden**, SD; **lede**, WA; **ludene**, voice, PP; **ledene**, *dat.*, C2 (*n*); PP; **ledenes**, *pl.*, S.—AS. *lyden*, language, also *leden*, Latin (*on leden gereorde*, Latina lingua, Voc.); Lat. *latinus*; cf. OF. *latin*, speech (the warbling of birds), Bartsch, 385. 29, It. *latino*, language.

lee-; see also words beginning in **le-, leo-**.

leed[1], *sb.* lead, S2, S3, C3, Voc., Prompt.; **led**, PP; **lede**, S3, P.—AS. *léad* (OET); cf. OLG. *lód*; see Weigand (s.v. *lód*).

leed[2], *sb.* a kitchen copper, CM (2. 7); **leede**, *dat.*, C.—Cf. **lead** (in dialects), HD, EDS. 21 (Tusser).

leef[1], *sb.* leaf, a piece, PP, C; **lef**, PP; **lyf**, S2, PP; **leues**, *pl.*, PP; **levis**, S3; **leyvis**, S3.—AS. *léaf*: Goth. *laufs, laubs.*

leef[2], *adj.* dear, S3, C; see **leof**.

leel, *adj.* leal, S3; see **lel**.

leendis, *sb. pl.* loins, S2; see **lende**[1].

leep, *sb.* basket, W; see **lepe**.

lees[1], *sb.* leash, snare, C3, CM, Prompt.; **leese**, CM; see **lese**.

lees[2], *adj. and sb.* false, a lie, S2, PP; **les**, S; **less**, S2, S3; **lease**, S; **lese**, S; **lessere**, *comp.*, S.—AS. *léas*; cf. Icel. *laus*, loose, dissolute.

leesinge, *sb.* falsehood, S3; **leasung**, **lesing**, S, S2, C3, W2; **leasing**, WW; **leesing**, W.—AS. *léasung.*

lefdi, *sb.* lady, S, S2; see **levedy**.

lef-ful, *adj.* believing, S. See **leve**[2].

lefsum, *adj.* allowable, PP; see **leifsum**.

lege, *adj.* liege, S3; see **lige**.

leggen, *v.* to lay, S, S2, W; **leyn**, S, S3; **leie to**, to add, W2; **leist**, *2 pr. s.*, S; **leȝȝesst**, S; **leið**, *pr. s.*, S; **leyð**, S; **legeð**, *pl.*, S; **leide**, *pt. s.*, S, S2; **leyde**, S; **leȝȝde**, S; **læide**, S; **læiden**, *pl.*, S; **leyden**, S2; **leid**, *pp.*, S; **leyd**, S, S2; **i-leid**, S; **i-leyd**, S; **y-leid**, S3; **y-leyd**, C2.—AS. *lecgan*: Goth. *lagian.*

legistre, *sb.* a legist, man skilled in the law; **legister**, Prompt.; **legistres**, *pl.*, P.—AF. *legistre*; Late Lat. *legista.*

leif, *sb.* leave, licence, B; see **leve**[1].

leifsum, *adj.* allowable, S3; **lefsum**, PP.

leir, *sb.* a couch, bed; **leire**, *dat.*, S.—AS. *leger*, lying, illness.
leiren, *v.* to lay low, *sternere*; **leirede**, *pp.*, SD; laid on a sick bed, S.—AS. *legerian* (Leo).
leir-stowe, *sb.* sepulchre, SD.
leit, *sb.* lightning, S, W, W2; **leyt**, W2; **leitis**, *pl.*, W, W2.—AS. *léget*, *liget*, Mt. 24. 27, *líeget*; see Sievers, 247.
leiten, *v.* to flame, SD; to lighten, W2; **leitinde**, *pr. p.*, S. See **leit**.
leityngis, *sb. pl.* lightnings, W.
leiȝen, *v.* to laugh, W; see **lahhen**.
leiȝtir, *sb.* laughter, W2; see **lahter**.
leiȝyng, *sb.* laughing, W.
lel, *adj.* leal, loyal, true, S2, S3; **leel**, PP, S3; **lele**, S2.—AF. *lëal*, OF. *leial*; Lat. *legalem*.
lelliche, *adv.* truly, S2, S3, PP; **lelly**, S2, S3, PP; **leelly**, S2, PP; **lelye**, S2; **lely**, H; **lelest**, *superl.*, PP.
leme, *sb.* gleam, light, S, S2, PP, CM; **leom**, PP; **leome**, S; **lemes**, *pl.*, CM; **leemes**, C; **leames**, S3; **lemys**, S3; **leomene**, *pl. gen.*, S; **lemene**, S.—AS. *léoma*.
lemen, *v.* to shine, SD; **leomen**, SD; **lemand**, *pr. p.*, S3, WA; **leomede**, *pt. s.*, SD; **lemede**, SD; **lemed**, PP.—AS. *lýman*.
lemman, *sb.* sweetheart, lover (of both sexes), mistress, concubine, S, C2, C3, PP; **lemmans**, *pl.*, WA; see **leofmon**.
lende[1], *sb.* loin, *lumbus*, Voc., S2; **lendes**, *pl.*, HD, G; **leendis**, S2, W, W2; **lendis**, H; **lendys**, PP.—AS. *lendenu*, pl. (Voc.); cf. OHG. *lendi* (G. *lende*), *lentîn* (Tatian).
lende[2], *v.* to land, arrive, to remain, dwell, to cause to land, S, PP; **lend**, *pt. pl.*, S2; **lended**, *pp.*, S2; **ylent**, S2.—Icel. *lenda*, to land; cf. AS. *(ge)lændian*, to cause to land. See **lond**.
lene, *adj.* lean, S, PP, C2, Prompt., Cath.—AS. *hlǽne*.
lenen[1], *v.* to lean, PP; **len**, H; **lenede**, *pt. s.*, PP; **leonede**, PP, S2; **lent**, *pp.*, S3.—AS. *hlionian*; cf. Lat. *clinare* (in *inclinare*).
lenen[2], *v.* to lend, grant, S, PP, S2, S3, C3; **leenen**, W; **lennen**, Cath.; **leendyn**, Prompt.; **len**, *imp. s.*, S2; **lenys**, *pr. s.*, H; **lennys**, H; **lenð**, S (1. 51); **lantez**, *2 pt. s.*, S2; **i-lenet**, *pp.*, S; **y-lent**, C3; **i-leaned**, S; **land**, S2; **lend**, S2; **lent**, S2.—AS. *lǽnan*. See **læn**, **lone**[2].
lener, *sb.* lender, usurer, W; **leyner**, Cath.
leng, **lenger**, **lengre**; see **lang**.
lenge, *v.* to linger, remain, dwell, PP, S2; **lenged**, *pt. s.*, PP.—AS. *lengan*. See **lang**.
lengðe, *sb.* length, S, PP; **lenðe**, S2.—AS. *lengð*.
lennen, *v.* to lend, Cath.; see **lenen**[2].
lennynge, *sb.* a lending, H; **lendynge**, Prompt.
lenten, *sb.* spring, lent, S2, PP; **lente**, PP, C2.—AS. *lengten*.
leo-; see also words beginning in **le-**.
leod, *sb.* a man, also, a tenement, possession, PP, S2; **leode**, PP; **lede**, PP, WA; **lud**, S2; **leodes**, *pl.*, PP; **leodis**, PP; **ledes**, S2, PP; **ledis**, PP, WA; **leedes**, PP, G; **ludes**, S2.—AS. *léod*, a prince (Grein).
leode, *sb.* country-men, people, S; **leede**, G; **leoden**, *dat.*, S; **lede**, HD, S2, WA; **leode**, S2. *Phr.*: **land and lede**, HD.—AS. *léod*, sb. f. a people, pl. *léode*, men (Grein); cf. OHG. *liut* (Otfrid).
leof, *adj.* dear, beloved, glad, S, PP, S2; **lief**, S, S3, C2, PP; **lef**, S, S3, HD; **leef**, S3, C, PP; **lif**, S; **lefe**, S2; **leue**, PP, S, S2, S3, C2; **lieue**, S; **luef**, S2; **luf**, S2; **leoue**, S; **leofue**, S; **leuer**, *comp.*, S3, C2; **leof**, *adv.* PP; **luf**, PP; **leuere**, *comp.*, S, S2; **leouere**, S; **leuer**, H; **leouest**, *superl.*, S, S2; **louest**, S; **leueste**, S2.—AS. *léof.*
leofliche, *adj.* dear, precious, S; *adv.*, S; **leuelike**, S; **leoflukest**, *adj. superl.*, S.—AS. *léoflic*, adj.; *léoflice*, adv.
leof-mon, *sb.* dear one, beloved one, lover (used of both sexes), S; **lefmon**, S, HD; **lemman**, S, PP, C2, C3; **leouemon**, S; **lemmanes**, *pl.* sweethearts, PP; **lemmons**, concubines, PP.
leofsum, *adj.* precious, S; **lefsum**, SD.
leoften, *v.* to flatter, caress; **leoftede**, *pt. s.*, S.
leome[1], *sb.* limb, S2; see **lim**.
leome[2], **leomen**; see **leme**, **lemen**.
leon, *sb.* lion, S2, C2, WA; **leun**, S; **leoun**, S, S2, C2; **lyoun**, S2; **liuns**, *pl.*, S; **leuns**, S.—AF. *liun*, OF. *leon*; Lat. *leonem*.
leonyn, *adj.* lion-like, C2.—OF. *leonin* Lat. *leoninum*.
leopart, *sb.* leopard, PP; **leparde**, Voc.; **lepart**, C; **lebard**, Voc.; **leberde**, Voc.; **lyberde**, Cath.; **libard**, B; **labbarde**, Prompt.; **lebbard**, Prompt.; **leoperdes**, *pl.*, PP; **lepardes**, C2; **lebardez**, S2; **libardes**, S2; **liberdes**, S3.—AF. *leopard*, *leopart*, *lepart*, pl. *leoparz*.
leor, *sb.* cheek, face, S, PP, S2; **lere**, PP, S2, S3, WA; **lire**, PP; **lure**, SD.—AS. *hléor*, the cheek, face, look.
leornen, *v.* to learn, S, S2; see **lernen**.
leorning-cniht, *sb.* disciple, SD, S.
leoðre, *adj.* bad, S; see **luþer**.
lepe, *sb.* basket, Voc., HD, H (s.v. *ber*), Palsg.; **leep**, W, W2, Prompt.; **leap**, Cotg. (s.v. *nasse*); **lepis**, *pl.*, W; **lepes**, S (s.v. *bread*).—AS. *léap*; cf. Icel. *laupr*.
lepen, *v.* to leap, run, PP, G; **lope**, Cath., HD; **leop**, *pt. s.*, PP, S2; **lep**, PP; **leep**, PP; **lap**, S2, S3; **lepe**, PP; **loupe**, P; **lope**, S2,

PP; **lep**, *pl.*, S2; **lopen**, P; **lope**, P; **lopen**, *pp.*, PP, S2, HD; **lepte**, *pt. s.* (weak), S2; **lippide**, W; **lepten**, *pl.*, PP.—AS. *hléapan*, pt. *hléop* (pl. *hléopon*), pp. *hléapen*: Goth. *hlaupan*; cf. Icel. *hlaupa*.

leper, *sb.* leaper, Cath.; **loper**, Cath.; **leperes**, *pl.* runners, wanderers, PP.

lepe-ȝere, *sb.* leap-year, Voc., Cath.

lepre, *sb.* leprosy, S2; **leprye**, Manip.—AF. *lepre*; Lat. *lepra* (Vulg.); Gr. λέπρα.

lere[1], *sb.* flesh, muscle, C2; see **lyre**.

lere[2], *sb.* cheek, face, S2, S3; see **leor**.

lered, *pp.* used as *adj.*; **læredd**, the learned, clergy, S; **lerud**, instructed, W, W2.—AS. *léred*.

lered-men, *sb. pl.* the learned, the clergy, S.

leren, *v.* (1) to teach, S, S2, S3, H; **learen**, S; **leoren**, S; **ler**, *imp. s.*, S; **lerede**, *pt. s.*, S; **leorde**, S; **lerde**, S2; **y-lered**, *pp.*, S2. (2) **leren**, *v.* to learn, S, S2, S3, C2, H.—AS. *léran*: Goth. *laisjan*, to make to find out, to teach.

lerned, *adj.* learned, C2, PP.

lernen, *v.* to learn, teach, S, S2, S3, PP, W2; **lurnen**, S2; **leornen**, S, S2; **leornin**, S.—AS. *leornian*.

les, **lese**, *adj.* false, S; see **lees**[2].

lese, *sb.* a leash, *laxa*, Cath., PP; **lees**, Prompt., C3; **leece**, Prompt.; **lease**, Cotg. (s.v. *laisse*); **lesshe**, Palsg.; **leesshe**, HD; **leysche**, S2.—OF. *laisse*; Lat. *laxa*, a loose rope.

lesen[1], *v.* to lose, S2, S3, C2, PP, W; **liese**, S; **leese**, PP, S3; to destroy, W; **leosen**, S, S2, PP; **leest**, *2 pr. s.*, PP; **lest**, *pr. s.*, S2; **lees**, *pt. s.*, PP; **les**, PP; **lese**, PP; **loren**, *pl.*, PP; **lorn**, *pp.*, PP, S2; **lorne**, S3; **lore**, PP, G, S2; **ilore**, G; **y-lore**, S2; **loste**, *pt. s.* (weak), W; **losten**, *pl.*, PP, C3, C, W2; **loste**, *pp.*, PP; **lost**, PP; **y-lost**, C3.—AS. *léosan*, pt. *léas* (pl. *luron*), pp. *loren*.

lesen[2], *v.* to set free, redeem, S, HD, H; **les**, *imp. s.*, S2; **lese**, G; **lesde**, *pt. s.*, S; **lesed**, *pp.*, S; **i-lesed**, S.—AS. *lésan*: OS. *lósian*.

leser, *sb.* releaser, SD, HD, S2.

lesewe, *sb.* pasture, W2; **leesewe**, W2; **lese**, SD, S2; **lewse**, *dat.*, S; **lesewis**, *pl.*, W; **lyssouris**, S3.—AS. *lesu*, *læsu*.

lesewin, *v.* to feed; **lesewynge**, *pr. p.*, W, S2; **lesewid**, *pp.*, W2.—AS. *læswian*.

lesing, *sb.* a lie, S, S2, C3, W; **lesyng**, PP; see **leesinge**.

lesing-monger, *sb.* liar, W.

lesnesse, *sb.* remission), S2. See **lesen**[2].

lesse, *adj. comp.* less, S.

lessin, *v.* to diminish, Prompt.; **lessi**, S2.

lessinge, *sb.* diminution, S2.

lest[1], *sb.* desire, C2; see **lust**[2].

lest[2], *sb.* fault, SD; see **last**[2].

lest[3], *pr. s.* it pleases, PP; *pt. s.*, PP; see **lusten**[2].

lest[4], *pr. s.* loses, S2; see **lesen**[1].

leste[1], *adj. superl.* least, S2, C2, G, PP; **lest**, S, PP; **last**, S.—AS. *læst*.

leste[2], *imp. s.* listen, S; see **lusten**[1].

lesten, *v.* to last, S, S2; see **lasten**[2].

lestinde, *adj.* lasting, S; **leastinde**, S.

lesty, *adj.* cunning, skilful, S3. See **liste**[3].

les-when, *conj.* lest at some time, H. See **lasse**.

lesynge, *sb.* loss, PP; **lesyng**, S3, C2, PP; **losyng**, S2. See **lesen**[1].

leten[1], *v.* (1) to let, cause, permit, (2) to let go, (3) to leave, forsake, neglect, desist, (4) to behave, pretend, (5) to esteem, S, S2, C3, H; **laten**, S; **leoten**, S; **læte**, S; **late**, *imp. s.*, S2; **lat**, C2; **lest**, *2 pr. s.*, S; **letiþ**, *pr. s.*, S2; **lates**, C2; **lattis**, H; **læt**, *pt. s.*, S; **let**, S2, S3; **leet**, S2, C2; **i-leten**, *pp.*, S; **latun**, W; **laten**, H.—AS. *létan*, *létan*, pt. *lét*, *léot*, pp. *laten*; cf. Icel. *láta*.

leten[2], *v.* to delay, S; **laten**, S.—AS. *latian*. Cf. **letten**.

lette, *sb.* delay, S, S3, C2; **let**, S2.

letten, *v.* to hinder, to make late, PP, S2, S3, C2; **let**, *pr. s.*, S, PP; **lette**, *pt. s.*, S, C2; **letted**, S3; **lettid**, H.—AS. *lettan*: Icel. *letja*: Goth. *latjan*, to be late.

lettere, *sb.* hinderer, S2, PP.

lettre, *sb.* writing, C2, PP; **lettres**, *pl.*, C3, PP.—AF. *lettre*; Lat. *littera*.

lettrure, *sb.* writing, scripture, learning, PP, W2; **letterure**, C2, PP, C3; **lettyreure**, H.—AF. *lettrure*, OF. *letreüre*; Lat. *litteratura*.

letuarie, *sb.* electuary, C3; **lettwary**, Cath.; **letuaries**, *pl.*, Cath. (*n*), C.—OF. *laituaire*, *leiture*, *letuaire*, *electuaire*; Lat. *electuarium*, a medicine dissolving in the mouth (Ducange).

letherien, *v.* to be in a lather, SkD; **liðeri**, *pr. s. subj.*, S.—ONorth. *leðrian*, to anoint (John 11. 2), from AS. *léaðor*, lather (Voc.); cf. Icel. *lauðr*, froth.

leude, *adj.* ignorant, H; see **lewed**.

leun, *sb.* lion, S; see **leon**.

leute, *sb.* loyalty, PP; see **lewte**.

leue[1], *sb.* permission, Prompt., S, S2, C2, PP; **leaue**, S; **leif**, B. *Phr.*: **nom læue**, took leave, took permission to go, S; **nam lefue**, S; **tok his leue**, S, C2; **tuk his leyff**, S3; **be ȝoure leue**, by your leave, WA.—AS. *léaf*.

leue[2], *sb.* belief, S; **leeue**, S3; **læfe**, S; **lafe**, S.—AS. *(ge)léafa*.

leue[3], *adj.* dear, S, S2, S3, C2; see **leof**.

leue[4], *v.* to live, S2, S3; see **livien**.

leued, *adj.* covered with leaves, PP, S2.

leuedy, *sb.* lady, S2, H; **leuedi**, S2, S; **lefdye**, S2; **lefdi**, S, S2; **leafdi**, S; **lauedi**, S; **læuedi**, S; **læfdi**, S.—AS. *hlǽfdige*.

leueful, *adj.* allowable, PP; **leeueful**, S2, C3, W; **leefful**, S2; **leeful**, S2, S3.—AS. *léafful.*

leuen[1], *v.* to permit, S, S2, S3, C2, PP; **lef**, *imp. s.*, S.—AS. *lýfan*, to allow.

leuen[2], *v.* to believe, S, S2, S3, C2, PP; **leauen**, S; **leeuen**, S2; **leyue**, PP; **lefenn**, S; **lyue**, PP; **lef**, *imp. s.*, S, PP; **leef**, PP, S2; **leues**, *pl.*, S2; **leueden**, *pt. pl.*, W; **leeued**, *pp.*, S3.—AS. (*ge*)*lýfan*: Goth. (*ga*)*laubjan.*

leuen[3], *v.* to leave, to dismiss, to remain, *relinquere, relinqui*, PP, S, S2, S3; **leauen**, S; **lef**, S2; **leaf**, *imp. s.*, S; **lef**, S; **leeue**, S2; **leues**, *pr. pl.*, S2; **lefde**, *pt. s.*, S; **leafde**, S; **lefte**, S2, S3; **leuede**, *pl.*, S2; **lafte**, C2; **laft**, *pp.*, S2, C2; **lewyt**, S3; **y-left**, S2.— AS. *léfan*, to leave, from *láf*, remains, heritage. See **laif.**

leuene, *sb.* lightning, Cath. (*n*), Prompt.; **levin**, JD, SD, ND; **levyn**, Prompt.—Cf. Goth. *lauhmuni*, also Dan. *lyn*; see Douse, p. 103.

leuenen, *v.* to smite with lightning, to shine; **levyn**, Cath.; **leuenand**, *pr. p.*, Cath. (*n*), H.

leuenynge, *sb.* lightning, Cath., H; **leuening**, S2; **leyfnyng**, Voc.; **leuenyngis**, *pl.*, H.

leuere, *adj. comp.* dearer, preferable, PP, S, S2; *adv.* more dearly, sooner, rather, PP, S2; **leuer**, PP, S2, S3; see **leof.**

levy[1], *sb.* a raising, esp. of money, SkD (p. 815).—OF. *levée*, a levy (Cotg.).

levy[2], *v.* to raise (money), SkD; **leueyed**, *pp.*, S3.—OF. *lever*; Lat. *leuare.*

lewch, *pt. s.* laughed, S3; see **lahhen.**

lewde, *adj.* ignorant, S3; see **lewed.**

-lewe, *suffix.* Cf. **chekelew** suffocating, **costlewe** costly, **drunkelewe** given to drinking, **siklewe** sickly, **þurstlewe** thirsty.—Icel. suffix *-ligr*, passing into *-liw*, and then into *-lew* by influence of *w* on *i*; cf. Icel. *kostligr*, ME. *costlewe*, costly (W.W.S.).

lewe[1], *sb.* shelter, S; **lew**, HD.—AS. *hleow, hléo.*

lewe[2], *adj.* warm, tepid, S; **lew**, HD, W.

lewed, *adj.* unlearned, ignorant, worthless, S2, C, C2, PP, H; **læwedd**, S; **lewde**, S3, Prompt.; **lewid**, W; **lawd**, H; **lawde**, H; **leude**, H; **lewedeste**, *superl.*, PP.—AS. *léwed*, lay, 'laicus' (Voc.), (*ge*)*léwed*, pp. of *léwan*, to weaken.

lewedly, *adv.* ignorantly, C2, C3.

lewednesse, *sb.* ignorance, PP, S2, C2; **lewdnesse**, PP; **lewdnes**, S3; **lewdenesse**, Prompt.

lewke, *adj.* tepid, Cath.; **luke**, Cath. (*n*).

lewse, *sb.* pasture, S; see **lesewe.**

lewte, *sb.* loyalty, fidelity, G, Prompt., PP; **leute**, PP.—AF. *lealte*, OF. *léalted*; Lat. *legalitatem.*

lewth, *sb.* shelter, HD.—AS. *hleowð, hléoð.*

leye[1], *sb.* flame, PP, S; **leie**, S; **lei**, SD.—AS. *lég*: Icel. *logi.* Cf. **lowe**[2].

leye[2], *sb.* untilled land, PP; **lay**, Prompt.; **laye**, *dat.*, S3; **laye**, *adj.*, G; **layes**, *pl.* meadows, S3; **leys**, S3; **leyes**, PP; **ley3es**, PP; **leas**, S3 (p. 228).—AS. *léah.*

leye-lond, *sb.* lea-land, PP; **laylande**, 'terre nouvellement labourée', Palsg.

leyen, *pt. pl.* lay, S, S3; **leyn**, *pp.*, lain, S3; see **liggen.**

leyn, *v.* to lay, S, S3; **leyde**, *pt. s.*, S; **leyd**, *pp.*, S, S2; see **leggen.**

leyser, *sb.* leisure, C, C2; **laser**, S2, S3: **laysure**, Manip.—AF. *leisir*; Lat. *licere.*

-le33c, *suffix*, used in forming abstract nouns, found in Ormulum, S.—Icel. *-leikr*, or *-leiki.* Cf. **-lac.** {The suffix *-lac* occurs in words such as **ferlac**, **fihtlac**, **reflac**.}

li-; see also words beginning in **ly-**.

libben, *v.* to live, S, S2, S3; see **livien.**

lich, *sb.* body, form, PP, SkD; **liche**, S, PP, WA; **like**, WA; **lyche**, dead body, Prompt. *Comb.*: **lichewake**, the watch held over the body of the dead, C, SD; **lyke-waik**, JD, Prompt. (*n*).—AS. *líc*, the body, generally the living body; cf. Goth. *leik*, the body, also a corpse. Cf. **liche.**

lic-hame, *sb.* body, S; **licham**, S; **lykhame**, PP; **licame**, S, PP; **licam**, PP, S2; **likame**, PP; **likam**, PP; **lykame**, S2; **lycome**, S; **liham**, PP; **lichames**, *gen.*, S; **licames**, PP.—AS. *líc-hama*, a body, properly 'body-covering'; cf. Icel. *líkami.*

lichamliche, *adj.* bodily, carnal, S; **lichomliche**, S.—AS. *líchamlic.*

-liche, *suffix*, found in adjectives and adverbs.—AS. *-lic*, adj. suffix, *-lice*, adv. suffix.

liche, *adj.* like, resembling, PP, S3; **lyche**, PP, S2; **lich**, S2; **lijk**, W2; **lyik**, W2; **lykkest**, *superl.*, S2.—AS. *líc*, found usually in the form *ge-líc.* Cf. **lich**, **ilich.**

licht[1], *adj.* not heavy, easy, S2, B; see **liht.**

licht[2], *pr. s.* lights, S; see **li3ten**[1].

lichtlines, *sb.* levity, jesting; **lychtlynes**, S3.

licken, *v.* to lick, SkD; **lickiden**, *pt. pl.*, W (Lu. 16. 21). *Comb.*: **lyck-peny**, a name for London from its licking up the penny, swallowing money, S3; **lick-penny**, S3 (*n*).—AS. *liccian*; cf. OHG. *lechón* in *gi-lechón* (Otfrid) see Brugmann, § 214. Cf. **lechour.**

125

licour, *sb.* liquor, juice, S2, C3; **lycour**, PP; **liquoure**, Manip.; **licur**, SkD.—OF. *licur*; Lat. *liquorem*.

lic-wurðe, *adj.* pleasing, S.

lid, *sb.* a cover, lid, SD; **lydde**, Cath.; book-cover, HD; **lides**, *pl.*, lids of the eyes, S.—AS. *hlid*.

liden, *v.* to cover, SD.—AS. *hlídan*, to cover (in *be-hlídan*), pp. *hliden*.

lieftenant, *sb.* lieutenant, deputy, S3; **lief-tenants**, *pl.*, S3.—AF. *lieutenant*; Lat. *locumtenentem*.

liese, *v.* to lose, S; see **lesen**¹.

lifes, *pr. s.* lives, S2; see **livien**.

lift, *adj.* left, S, S2, PP; see **lyft**¹.

lige, *adj.* liege, free, PP, C2, C3; **lyge**, PP; **liege**, PP; **lege**, S3, PP, SkD; **leege**, PP; **lyche**, Prompt.; **lige**, *sb. pl.*, liege servants, PP, C2; **lyges**, PP; **lieges**, S2, C3; **liegis**, PP; **leges**, PP.—OF. *lige* (Bartsch), *lige seignur*, liege lord (Roland, 2421); cf. AF. *seignour lige*, and *homes liges*; cf. Low Lat. *ligius*.

ligeaunce, *sb.* allegiance, C3.—OF. *ligeance*, see NED (s.v. *allegiance*).

ligen, *v.* to tell a lie, S; see **lyȝen**.

liggen, *v.* to lie, S, S2, H, C2, W; **ligen**, H; **liȝen**, S2; **lien**, S; **leȝe**, S; **list**, *2 pr. s.*, S; **lið**, *pr. s.*, S, S2; **lyð**, S; **ligeð**, *pl.*, S; **ligges**, continue, S2; **lygge**, *pr. pl. subj.*, S2; **lai**, *pt. s.*, S; **lay to**, suited, S2; **leigen**, *pl.*, S; **leyen**, S, S3; **y-leye**, *pp.*, P; **i-leie**, S; **leie**, W; **leyn**, S3; **y-layne**, S3; **i-leiȝen**, S2.—AS. *licgan*, pt. *læg*, pl. *lǽgon* (*lágon*), pp. *gelegen*.

liggyng, *sb.* lying down, W.

lighte, *v.* to make less heavy, to relieve a horse of his burden by descending, to alight, CM; **lyghte**, S3, C3, Cath.; **light**, S2, S3; **liȝten**, S, S2; **ligten**, S; **lihten**, S; **lyȝt**, S2; **liȝte**, *pt. s.*, PP; **lyȝte**, PP; **lyȝt**, S2; **lychtyt**, *pl.*, S3; **liht**, *pp.*, S2; **ligt**, S.—AS. *líhtan*. See **liht**.

lihen, *v.* to deceive, S; see **lyȝen**.

liht, *adj.* light, not heavy, easy, S; **lyht**, S; **licht**, S2; **liȝt**, W2; **liȝte**, active, S; *adv.*, S2; **liȝtere**, *comp.*, S2, W.—AS. *leoht*: OHG. *líhti*; cf. Goth. *leihts*; see Sievers, 83.

lihtlich, *adj.* easy, light, S; **lihtliche**, *adv.*, S; **liȝtliche**, S, S2.—AS. *leohtlic*, *leohtlice*.

lihtschipe, *sb.* swiftness, S.

liken, *v.* to please, SkD, PP, WW, S3; **liki**, S; **lykyen**, S; **like**, to rejoice, S2; **likeð**, *pr. s. impers.*, PP, S2; **lykeð**, PP, S2, C2; **lykede**, *pt. s.*, S2.—AS. *lícian* (also *lícan*), to please, literally, to be *like* or suitable for. See **liche**.

likerous, *adj.* dainty, lecherous, S2, PP, C3; **lykerous**, PP; **lycorouse**, dainty-mouthed, Palsg.; **licorous**, Cotg. (s.v. *lecheresse*). See **lechour**.

likful, *adj.* pleasing, SD.

likinge¹, *sb.* pleasure, S, W; **liking**, PP, W2; **lykyng**, S2, C2.

likinge², *adj.* favourable; **lykynge**, S2.

likli, *adj.* likely, SD.

liklihed, *sb.* likelihood, SkD; **lyklihede**, C2.

liklinesse, *sb.* probability; **lyklinesse**, C2.

liknen, *v.* to liken, to compare, PP; **lykne**, PP; **lickne**, PP; **lykned**, *pp.*, C2; **licned**, W; **iliknet**, S2.

liknesse, *sb.* likeness, appearance, PP, W; **liccness**, S; **liknes**, S2; **lyknes**, S3.—AS. *gelícnes*.

lilburne, *sb.* a heavy stupid fellow, S3.

lilie, *sb.* lily, *argentea*, S, S2. *Comb.*: **lylie-whyt**, lily-white, S2.—AS. *lilie* (Voc.); Lat. *lilia*, pl. of *lilium*; cf. OHG. *lilia* (Otfrid).

lim, *sb.* limb, S; **lym**, S2; **lyme**, PP; **leome**, PP, S2; **limen**, *pl.*, S; **lemes**, PP; **limes**, S; **lymes**, limbs, W2, S2, PP, C2; creatures, PP; **lyms**, S3; **limmes**, C2. *Phr.*: **feondes lymes**, limbs of the fiend, PP (cf. Icel. *limir Fjándans*); **the deuyl and his lymmes**, H (Ps. 108. 30). *Comb.*: **lim-mele**, limb-meal, SD; **limel**, S.—AS. *lim*, *lim-mélum*, 'membratim'.

limpen, *v.* to happen, to belong to, S; **lomp**, *pt. s.*, SD; **lymppede** (*weak*), HD; **lumpen**, *pp.*, S2.—AS. *limpan*, pt. *lamp* (pl. *lumpon*), pp. *gelumpen*.

-ling, *suffix.* See SkD (s.v. *darkling*).

linnen, *v.* to cease, S; **lynne**, S; **lin**, HD; **lyn**, S3; **lan**, *pt. s.*, SD.—AS. *linnan*, pt. *lann* (pl. *lunnon*), pp. *lunnen*; cf. Icel. *linna*.

linnunge, *sb.* ceasing, S.

lipnen, *v.* to trust; **lippin**, JD.

lipning, *sb.* trust; **lypnyng**, B.

lire, *sb.* cheek, face, PP; see **leor**.

lispen, *v.* to lisp, SkD; **lyspe**, Cath.; **lipsede**, *pt. s.*, C.—AS. *wlispian*.

lisse, *sb.* ease, rest, joy, happiness, S, PP; **lysse**, S, PP.—AS. *liss* (for *lið-s*); see Sievers, 258. See **liþe**².

lissien, *v.* to ease, SD; **lisse**, HD; **lyss**, S3.—AS. *lissian*.

list, *pr. s. impers.* it pleases him, S2, S3, C2; see **lusten**².

liste¹, *v.* to desire, PP; see **lusten**².

liste², *sb.* list or edge of cloth, PP, Manip.; **lyste**, PP, S2, Palsg., Cath.; **lyyste**, Prompt.; **lyyst**, Prompt. *Comb.*: **lyste of the ear**, *mol de l'oraylle*, Palsg.—OF. *liste*; Icel. *lista*.

liste³, *sb.* craft, astuteness, S, S2.—AS. *list*; cf. Icel. *list*, OHG. *list*, from Teut. base LIS. Cf. **lore**.

listely, *adv.* slily, S2.—AS. *listlice*.

listes, *sb. pl.* the lists, the ground enclosed for a tournament, C2; **lystes**, C.—AF. *listes*,

pl.; OF. *lisse,* (also *lice*), a tilt-yard; see Ducange (s.v. *licia*).

listre, *sb.* a lector, preaching friar, PP; **listyr,** Prompt.; reader, Trevisa, 6. 257; **listres,** *pl.,* PP.—OF. *listre* for *litre*; Church Lat. *lector* (Ducange).

lit¹, *adj.* little, S; see **lyte.**

lit², *sb.* stain, dye, colour, S, SD; **littis,** *pl.,* WA.—Icel. *litr,* colour, complexion, countenance, dye. See **wliten.**

litarge, *sb.* litharge, protoxyde of lead, C, C3.—OF. *litharge*; Lat. *lithargyrus*; Gr. λιθάργυρος.

liteled, *pt. s. 2 p.* didst esteem lower, S2; see **lutlin.**

litte, *v.* to dye, H, Cath., HD; **liten,** Prompt.—Icel. *lita,* to dye. See **lit².**

littester, *sb.* dyer, *tinctor, tinctrix,* Cath.; **lytster,** *tinctor,* Voc.; **lyster,** Cath.; **lystare,** Prompt.; **litsters,** *pl.,* HD. See **lit².**

lith, *sb.* joint, limb, member, PP, S, S2, C; **lyth,** HD; **lythe,** Prompt.—AS. *lið*; cf. Icel. *liðr,* Goth. *lipus.*

liðe¹, *v.* to go, pass through, S; **liðen,** S.— AS. *líðan*; cf. Icel. *líða,* OHG. *líðan,* to go through, suffer (Otfrid), Goth. *leiþan.*

liðe², *adj.* gentle, mild, soft, calm, sweet, S; **lythe,** Prompt.; **lythe,** *adv.,* HD.—AS. *líðe* (for *linth-j-a*); cf. OHG. *lindi, lind,* Icel. *linr.* Cf. **linnen.**

liðeliche, *adv.* gently, S.—AS. *líðelíce.*

liðer, *adj.* bad, S2; see **luþer.**

liðien, *v.* to relax, S, SD; **liðe,** PP, WA; **lethe,** to alleviate, S2; to grow calm, S2.—AS. *líðian.*

liðnien, *v.* to ease; **liðnid,** *pp.,* PP.

liue, liues; see **lyf¹.**

liuelod, *sb.* sustenance, S3; see **lyflode.**

liuenoðe, *sb.* sustenance, S.—Icel. *lífnaðr,* conduct of life.

liuien, *v.* to live, S; **liue,** S; **leiffe,** S3; **lefien,** S; **leue,** S2, S3; **leeuen,** S3; **libben,** S, S2, S3; **lybbe,** S2, S3; **liuiende,** *pr. p.,* S; **libbinde,** S; **leuand,** S3; **leowinde,** S; **lyfand,** S2; **liffand,** S2; **lifes, lyfes,** *pr. pl.,* S2; **lifd,** *pt. s.,* S2; **i-leued,** *pp.,* S; **i-luued,** S; **leyffyt,** S3.—AS. *lifian, libban,* to remain, to be left, to live; cf. AS. *lífan,* to leave, and OHG. *be-líban,* to remain (Tatian).

liuing, *sb.* means of livelihood, S3.

lixt, *2 pr. s.* liest, G; see **ly3en.**

li3t¹, *sb.* light, S; **lyht,** S, S2; **licht,** S; **lict,** S; **liht,** S, PP; **ly3t,** S2; **loht,** S; **li3t,** *pl.,* S2.— AS. *léoht*: Goth. *liuhaþ*; cf. OHG. *lioht* (Otfrid).

li3t², *adj.* light, bright, WA; **lyht,** S2.—AS. *léoht*; cf. OHG. *lioht* (Otfrid).

li3ten¹, *v.* to light, enlighten, to become bright, S; **lihten,** S; **lict,** *imp.,* S; **licht,** *pr.*

s., S; **lihtede,** *pt. s.,* S; **i-li3t,** *pp.,* S2; **liht,** S; **lyht,** S2.—AS. *lýhtan, líhtan.*

li3ten², *v.* to alight, S, S2; see **lighte.**

li3ti, *adj.* bright, shining, W.

li3tinge, *sb.* lightning, S2.

li3tne, *v.* to enlighten, shine, dawn, W, W2; **li3tnede,** *pt. s.,* W.

li3tnere, *sb.* enlightener, W2.

li3tnyng, *sb.* illumination, W, W2.

lob, *sb.* a clown, a clumsy fellow, HD; a lout, lubber, Sh.

lobbe-keling, *sb.* a large cod, S2.

lob-cocke, *sb.* lubber, S3, Cotg. (s.v. *baligaut*), HD. See **lob.**

lobres, *sb. pl.* lubbers, PP, S2.

loby, *sb.* looby, PP; **lobyes,** *pl.,* PP.

lode, *sb.* a way, path, SD; **loode,** something carried, a load, *vectura,* Prompt.; **lade,** SD.—AS. *(ge)lád,* a way, path, from *líðan,* to go. See **liþe¹.**

lode-menage, *sb.* pilotage, C.

lodesman, *sb.* pilot, Palsg.; **lodezmon,** S2; **lodysmanne,** 'vector, vehicularius', Prompt.

lode-star, *sb.* load-star, S3; **lode-sterre,** CM.

lode-stone, *sb.* loadstone, SkD.

lof¹, *sb.* praise, S, S2; **lofe,** S, WA; **loft,** S.— AS. *lof*; Icel. *lof,* praise, permission, OS. *lof*; cf. OHG. *lob* (Otfrid).

lof², *sb.* loaf, S; see **loof¹.**

lofen, *v.* to praise, S, S2; **loue,** SD, S2, S3, H; **lovand,** *pr. p.,* HD, S2, H.—AS. *lofian,* to praise; cf. Icel. *lofa,* to praise, to permit.

lof-song, *sb.* song of praise, S; **loftsong,** S; **loftsonges,** *pl.,* S.—AS. *lof-sang.*

loft, *sb.* an upper room, height, PP, G, SkD. *Phr.:* **on lofte,** aloft, literally, in the air, PP, S2, C3; **on þe lofte,** S.—Icel. *lopt,* air, sky, an upper room, balcony; *á lopt,* aloft, in the air. Cf. **lyft².**

logge, *sb.* a lodge, hut, small cottage, B, CM; **loge,** WA; **lodge,** WW; **luge,** HD.—AF. *loge.*

loggen, *v.* to lodge, dwell, PP; **lodge,** WW; **logeth,** *pr. s.,* PP; **logged,** *pt. s.,* S3, CM; **lugede,** *pp.,* HD; **lugit,** S3.—AF. *loger.*

loggyng, *sb.* lodging, CM; **luging,** S3; **logyng,** B.

loghe, *sb.* water, lake, S2; **lo3,** PP; **lo3e,** WA; **lowis,** *pl.* S3. Cf. AS. *lagu-flod,* 'obscura unda' (Voc.); also Icel. *lögr* (gen. *lagar*).

loh, *pt. s.* laughed, S2; see **lahhen.**

lok¹, *sb.* an offering, gift, S; **loc,** S; **lac,** S; **loke,** sport, PP; **lake,** *dat.,* S; **lac,** *pl.,* S; **lakes,** S.—AS. *lác,* a leaping for joy, sport,

contest, also, a sacrifice, gift: Goth. *laiks.*
sport, dance. Cf. **layken, laken.**
lok[2], *sb.* lock, fastening, S2, PP; **lokkes**, *pl.*,
PP. See **louken.**
loken[1], *v.* to look, observe, S, S2, PP; **lokin**,
S; **lokien**, S; **loki**, to protect, S; **loky**, to
guard, S2; **luke**, S3; **locan on**, to observe,
S; **loc**, *imp.*, S; **lokede**, *pt. s.*, S.—AS. *lócian.*
loken[2], *pp.* locked, S; see **louken.**
loking, *sb.* looking, PP; **lokyng**, custody, S;
appearance, W; **lokinge**, decision, S2;
lokynge, PP; protection, S2; **lokunge**, S.
lokken, *v.* to lock, SkD; **lok**, Cath.;
ylokked, *pp.*, S2. See **lok**[2].
lokrand, *pr. p.* as *adj.* curling S3; **lokke-
rand**, Cath. (*n*).
lokyrynge, *sb.* curliness, *crispitudo*, Cath.
lollen, *v.* to loll, limp about, lounge, rest,
also, to flap, wag, PP; **lollede**, *pt. s.*, S3;
lullede, S2.
lollere, *sb.* loller, idle vagabond, PP; **loller**,
C2, CM.
lomb, *sb.* lamb, C3, W2, PP; **lombe**, Voc.,
PP, W; **lambren**, *pl.*, PP, W, W2; **lambre**,
W2; **lombe**, S2.—AS. *lamb, lomb.*
lome[1], *sb.* tool, instrument, S2, WA; a vessel
(the ark in the deluge), S2; **lomes**, *pl.*, S2,
PP; **lomen**, S2.—AS. *gelóma*, 'utensile'
(Voc.).
lome[2], *adv.* frequently, S, PP; *phr.*: **oft and
lome**, HD; **i-lome**, S, S2; **ylome**, S2;
lomer, *comp.*, PP; **lommere**, PP.—AS.
gelóme.
lomp, *pt. s.* happened; see **limpen.**
lond, *sb.* land, S, S2, PP; **lont**, S; **lon**, S;
londe, *dat.*, S2; **londes**, *pl.*, S.—AS. *land.*
londe, *v.* to land, S.
lond-folk, *sb.* countryfolk, S.
londisse, *adj.* native, S.
lone[1], *sb.* lane, PP; **lones**, *pl.*, S2, PP.—AS.
lonu, see Sievers, 279.
lone[2], *sb.* loan, S, S2, PP, Prompt.—AS. *lán*;
cf. Icel. *lán.*
longe[1], *sb.* lung; **longen**, *pl.*, PP; **lunges**,
SkD, Cath.; **longes**, C, PP.—AS. *lunge*, pl.
lungan.
longe[2], *adv.* See **ilong.**
longen, *v.* to become long, to long for, to
belong to, S, S2, S3, C2, PP, SkD; **langen**,
S2, H.—AS. *langian.* See **lang.**
longinge, *sb.* longing, S2; **longynge**, PP;
longenge, S.
loof[1], *sb.* loaf, W2, PP; **lof**, S, PP; **laf**, S; **lofe**,
Cath.; **loues**, *pl.*, C3; **loouys**, S2; **looues**,
W2.—AS. *hláf.*
loof[2], *sb.* a kind of rudder or apparatus for
steering, SkD; **loues**, *pl.*, SkD.—Cf. OF.
lof, the windward side of a vessel (Rabelais).

loop, *v.* to melt and run together in a mass,
HD.—Icel. *hlaupa*, to curdle; cf. *blóð-hlaup*,
curdled blood. Cf. **lepen.**
loos[1], *sb.* loss, PP; **los**, PP, C2.—ONorth. *los*
(Matt. 7. 13). See **lesen**[1].
loos[2], *sb.* fame, report, Prompt., PP, CM,
C3; **lose**, H (67. 33).—AF. *loos*, OF. *los*;
Lat. *laus* or *laudes*, see Constans.
lopen, *pp.* run away, S2; see **lepen.**
lopir, *v.* to curdle, clot, coagulate; **lopper**,
JD; **lopird**, *pp.*, H, HD; **lappered**, JD;
lopyrde (as milk), Cath. See **loop.**
lopirynge, *sb.* curdling, H.
lord, *sb.* husband, S; see **loverd.**
lorde, *v.* to idle about, S3. See **lourde.**
lordinges, *sb. pl.* sirs, masters, S, S2, G; see
loverdinges.
lordschipe, *sb.* lordship, W2; see **laverd-
schipe.**
lordschiping, *sb.* domination, W.
lordshipen, *v.* to rule over, S2.
lore, *sb.* learning, lore, S, S2, S3, C3, PP;
lare, S, S2, H; **lores**, *pl.*, S2.—AS. *lár* (for
*laisa), from OTeut. base **lis-*, to find out.
lorel[1], *sb.* an abandoned fellow, *perditissimus*,
P, CM, PP, S3; **lozel**, ND; **losel**, PP,
Prompt.; **lorels**, *pl.*, S3; **losells**, S3;
loseles, P. See **lesen**[1].
lorel[2], *sb.* laurel, Prompt.; see **laurer.**
lorn, *pp.* lost, S2; see **lesen**[1].
lor-þeaw, *sb.* a teacher, S; **lareaw**, SD; **lor-
þeawe**, *dat.*, S; **lorþeawes**, *pl.*, S; **lar-
þawes**, S; **larewes**, SD.—AS. *lárþéow*
(*láréow*). See **lore.**
lorзer, *sb.* laurel, Prompt.; see **laurer.**
lose[1], *v.* to set free, G; **louse**, *imp. s.*, G;
loside, *pt. s.*, W2. Cf. **lesen**[2].
lose[2], *sb.* praise, H; see **loos**[2].
losel; see **lorel**[1].
losen, *v.* to praise, PP; **losed**, *pp.*, WA.
losenge, *sb.* a kind of quadrilateral figure;
losynges, *pl.*, CM.—OF. *losenge*, praise,
flattery, encomium, then grave-stone,
square slab, lozenge in heraldry.
losengere, *sb.* flatterer, deceiver, WA;
losanger, sluggard, S3; **losengour**, C;
losenjour, HD.—OF. *losengier* (Cotg.), also
(with different suffix) *losengëor, losengetour*,
flatterer.
losengerye, *sb.* flattery, lying, PP.
lossom, *adj.* loveable, pleasant, S2; see
lufsum.
lot, *sb.* lot, S; **loten**, *pl.*, S; **lotes**, S.—AS.
hlot; cf. Goth. *hlauts.*
loteby, *sb.* concubine, HD, PP (*n*); **ludby**,
HD; **lutby**, H; **lotebyes**, *pl.*, PP.—
Literally, 'a secret lier with', cf. *Lyerby*, HD.
See **lotyen.**

lotyen, *v.* to lurk; **lotyeth**, *pr. pl.*, PP; **lotinge**, *pr. p.*, C3.—AS. *lutian* (Grein).

loth, *adj.* hostile, hateful, grievous, unpleasant, unwilling, S, S2, PP, C; **looth**, C2; **laõ**, S, S2; **layth**, S2; **laith**, H, PP; **loõere**, *comp.*, S; **lother**, PP; **lathere**, *adv.*, H; **loõest**, *superl.*, S.—AS. *láõ*; cf. Icel. *leiõr*.

lothe, *v.* to loathe, PP; **laõin**, S.—AS. *láõian*.

lothelich, *adj.* hateful, P; **loõlich**, S; **loõli**, S2; **lodlich**, S, S2; **ladlic**, S.—AS. *láõlic*.

loõlesnesse, *sb.* innocence, S; **lodlesnesse**, S.

loud, *adj.* loud; **lowd**, PP; **lud**, S; **lude**, *adv.* S; **lowde**, PP, C; **loude**, PP.—AS. *hlúd*; cf. Gr. κλυτός, renowned.

lough, *pt. s.* laughed, C2, C3; **louh**, PP; see **lahhen**.

louh, *adj.* low, S, S2, PP; **law**, S3; **loge**, S; **lowe**, S; **laghe**, H; **lah**, S; **lahe**, *adv.*, S; **loʒe**, S; **lowe**, PP; **louwe**, S; **law**, S3; **lauer**, *comp.*, S2.—Icel. *lágr*.

louhnesse, *sb.* lowliness, PP.

louken, *v.* to close, H, PP; **luken**, S; **lowke**, PP, H; **lowkande**, *pr. p.*, S2; **leac**, *pt. s.*, SD; **lec**, SD; **læc**, SD; **luken**, *pl.*, SD; **loken**, *pp.*, S, SD; **lokenn**, S; **lowkyt** (*weak*), S3.—AS. *lúcan*, pt. *léac* (pl. *lucon*), pp. *locen*; cf. Icel. *lúka*.

lourde, *adj.* lazy, sluggish, HD; **loord**, *sb.*, ND.—OF. *lourd*; Lat. *luridum*, dirty, lazy, heavy; see Diez.

lourdeine, *sb.* a lazy rascal, PP; **lordein**, PP; **lurdeyn**, PP; **lurden**, HD; **lourdeines**, *pl.* vagabonds, PP.—OF. *lourdein*. See **lourde**.

loure, *v.* to lower, S2, S3; see **luren**.

louten, *v.* to stoop, bow down, worship, H, PP, S2, C2; to treat as a lout, S3; **lutende**, *pr. p.*, S; **loutede**, *pt. s.*, PP, S2; **luted**, *pl.*, S2; **lutten**, *pl.*, S.—Cf. AS. *lútan*, to bow down, also *lútian*, to hide (OET.).

louabil, *adj.* worthy to be praised, H. See **lof¹**.

loue¹, *sb.* love; see **lufe**.

loue², *v.* to praise, S2, S3, H; see **lofen**.

louely, *adj.* worthy to be praised, H.

louen, *v.* to praise, S2, S3, H; see **lofen**.

louerd, *sb.* lord, S, S2, S3, PP; **laford**, S; **laferrd**, S; **lauerd**, S, S2; **lowerd**, S; **lord**, husband, S; **lauerõ**, S.—AS. *hláford*.

louerdinges, *sb. pl.* sirs, masters, S; **lordinges**, S, S2, G; **lordynges**, PP. Cf. **laverding**.

louyen, *v.* to love, PP; **luuen**, S; **luuien**, S; **lufenn**, S; **luf**, H; **louien**, S; **loue**, S2; **lofuieõ**, *pr. pl.*, S; **luuede**, *pt. s.*, S; **louede**, S.—AS. *lufian*.

louyere, *sb.* lover, C; **luffaris**, *pl.*, S3.

lowable, *adj.* praiseworthy, PP.

lowe¹, *v.* to approve of, praise, S3.—OF. *louer*, *loër*, *loder*, *laudar*; Lat. *laudare*. Cf. **laude**.

lowe², *sb.* flame, Prompt., Cath., PP, WA.—Icel. *log*. Cf. **leye¹**.

lowe³, *adj.* low, lowly, humble, S, PP; see **louh**.

lowe⁴, *v. refl.* to humble oneself, PP, W; **lowed**, *pt. s.* stooped, PP.

lowe⁵, *2 pt. s.* toldest lies, PP; **lowen vpon**, *pp.* lied against, PP; see **lyʒen**.

lowen, *v.* to low, bellow, W2 (Job 6. 5); **loowes**, *pr. s.*, S3.—AS. *hlówan*.

lowne, *adj.* serene, calm, S3, JD; sheltered, HD; **loun**, JD.—Icel. *logn*, a calm.

lownyt, *pp.* sheltered, B.

loʒ, *sb.* sea, lake, S2; see **loghe**.

lozel; see **lorel¹**.

luce, *sb.* a fish, a pike, C, CM, Voc., Prompt., ND.—OF. *luz* (Bartsch).

lud¹, *adj.* loud, S; **lude**, *adv.* S; see **loud**.

lud², *sb.* sound, voice, S2; **lude**, *dat.*, SD; **luden**, *pl.*, SD.—AS. *hlýd*, *ge-hlýd*; cf. OHG. *lútí* (Otfrid).

lud³, *sb.* person, S2; **ludes**, *pl.*, tenements, S2; see **leod**.

ludene, *sb.* voice, PP; see **leden³**.

luf, *adj.* dear, S2; see **leof**.

lufe, *sb.* love, S, WA; **luf**, H; **luue**, S, loue, PP. *Comb.*: **loue-day**, a day for the settlement of disputes by arbitration, S2, PP; **loue-drury**, affection, C2; **luue-eie**, reverence, S; **loue-longinge**, desire, fond affection, C2, S2; **luf-reden**, good-will, S2; **lufredyn**, H (AS. *lufréden*); **luue-wurõe**, loveworthy, S.—AS. *lufu*.

lufli, *adj.* lovely, H; **luuelich**, loving, lovely, S; **louelokest**, *superl.*, S2; **luueliche**, *adv.*, S.—AS. *luflic*, adv. *luflice*.

lufsum, *adj.* loveable, pleasant, SD; **lossom**, S2.—AS. *lufsum*.

lufsumliche, *adv.* pleasantly, S.—AS. *lufsumlice*.

luft¹, *adj.* left, S, S2, PP; see **lyft¹**.

luft², *sb.* a weak creature, worthless fellow, PP; **lift**, HD. See **lyft¹**.

lugen, *v.* to drift about (on the waves), S2; **luggid**, *pp.*, pulled about, PP.

lugit, *pp.* lodged, S3; see **loggen**.

luke, *v.* to look, S3; see **loken¹**.

lumpen, *pp.* befallen, S2; see **limpen**.

lunarie, *sb.* moon-wort, C3; **lunary**, HD.—OF. *lunarie*; Late Lat. *lunaria*.

lure¹, *sb.* a bait, enticement, C3, HD.—OF. *loerre*, (now *leurre*); MHG. *luoder*, a bait (now *luder*).

lure², *sb.* loss, S; **lere**, SD; **lire**, SD.—AS. *lyre*. See **lesen¹**.

lure³, *sb.* face, SD; see **leor**.

luren, *v.* to lower, to look sullen, S; **loure**, S2, S3, PP; **lowren**, PP.

luring, *sb.* a looking sullen, S.

lurken, *v.* to lurk, PP; **lorken**, PP; **lurkand**, *pr. p.*, S2; **lorked**, *pt. s.*, S2.

lurking, *sb.* hiding-place, S2.

lust[1], *sb.* the sense of hearing, S.—AS. *hlyst*: Icel. *hlust*, the ear.

lust[2], *sb.* desire, inclination, pleasure, PP, S, S2, S3, H; **lest**, C2; **hleste**, S; **lostes**, *pl.*, S2; **lustis**, W.—AS. *lust*.

lusten[1], *v.* to give ear, to list, S, PP; **listen**, S; **hlesten**, S; **lhesten**, S2; **letsen**, S2, S.—AS. *hlystan*; cf. Icel. *hlusta*.

lusten[2], *v.* to desire, S, S3; **lyst**, *1 pr. s.*, S3; **lust**, *pr. s. impers.*, it pleases him, S, PP; **list**, S2, S3, C2, PP; **lest**, PP; **liste**, *pr. s. subj.*, it may please, S; **leste**, S, S3, C2, PP; **luste**, *pt. s. impers.*, S, S2; **liste**, S2, S3, C2; **leste**, C2.—AS. *lystan*.

lustiheed, *sb.* pleasure, C2.

lustinesse, *sb.* pleasantness, S3.

lustnen, *v.* to listen, S; **lestenen**, G; **listnede**, *pt. s.*, S; **lestned**, S2.

lusty, *adj.* pleasant, S3, C2, C3, PP; **lusti**, joyful, S.

lutby, *sb.* paramour, H; see **loteby**.

lute, *adj.* little, S; see **lyte**.

lutel, *adj.* little, S, S2; see **lytel**.

luten, *v.* to stoop; see **louten**.

lutlin, *v.* to diminish, S; **lutlen**, S; **liteled**, *pt. s.*, S2.—AS. *lytlian*. See **lytel**.

luðer, *adj.* bad, false, treacherous, S, PP, S2; **lyðer**, PP, H; **liðer**, PP, S2; **liðere**, S, H; **leoðre**, S.—AS. *lyðre*.

luðerliche, *adv.* vilely, S.

luue, *sb.* love; see **lufe**.

lycorys, *sb.* liquorice, C2; **lycoresse**, Cath.—AF. *lycorys*; Late Lat. *liquiritia, glycyrrhiza*; Gr. γλυκύρριζα, lit. 'sweet root'.

lyf[1], *sb.* life, S, S2; **lifue**, S; **liues**, *gen.* as *adv.*, alive, S; **lyues**, S, C2; **liue**, *dat.*, S, S2; **lyue**, S. *Phr.*: **bring o liue**, to kill, S2 (7. 198); **on lyue**, alive, S, C2; **his lyf**, during his life, C2.—AS. *lif*.

lyf[2], *sb.* a living person, a man, PP; **lif**, S2; **lyfe**, WA.

lyf-day, *sb.* life-time, PP; **lif-daȝe**, *dat.*, S; **lyfe-days**, *pl.*, WA.—AS. *lif-dæg*.

lyflode, *sb.* way of life, mode of life, S2, PP; **liflode**, S, W; means of living, PP; **lijflode**, W2; **lyuelade**, *victus*, Cath.; **liuelod**, S3; **lyuelode**, W.—AS. *lif* + *lád*, a course, provisions.

lyfly, *adv.* in a lively manner, S3.

lyft[1], *adj.* left, PP, S2; **luft**, S, PP, S2; **lift**, S, PP, S2; **left**, SkD. *Comb.*: **lift-half**, left side, W2; **luft-hond**, left hand, PP.—AS. *lyft*, weak; cf. ODu. *luft*, 'laevus'.

lyft[2], *sb.* air, sky, PP, S3; **lift**, HD, S2, H; **lyfte**, S2; **lufte**, *dat.*, S; **lifte**, S2; **lyfte**, S2.—AS. *lyft*; cf. OS. *luft*, OHG. *luft*, Goth. *luftus*. Cf. **loft**.

lyften, *v.* to lift, shift, raise, PP; **lyftande**, *pr. p.*, S2; **lyft**, *pt. s.*, PP.—Icel. *lypta*. See **loft**.

lyik, *adj.* like, W2; see **liche**.

lyke-waik; see **lich**.

lykhame, *sb.* body, PP; see **lichame**.

lym, *sb.* lime, *calx*, S2, C3; **lyme**, Voc. *Comb.*: **lym-rod**, a limed rod, C2; **lym-ȝerde**, a limed twig, S3.—AS. *lim*.

lymaille, *sb.* file-dust, C3; **lymail**, C3.—OF. *limaille*, from *limer*, to file; Lat. *limare*.

lymit, *sb.* limit, WA.—OF. *limite*; Lat. *limitem* (acc.).

lymytour, *sb.* a friar licensed to ask alms within a certain limit, PP, C, CM; *limitator*, Cath.; **limitour**, PP.—OF. *limiteur* (Cotg.); Church Lat. *limitatorem* (Cath.).

lynage, *sb.* lineage, descent, parentage, PP, S3, C2, W; **linage**, C2, C3; **lynages**, *pl.*, tribes, S2; **lynagis**, W2.—AF. *linage*.

lynde, *sb.* linden-tree, HD, Voc., C2, C; **linde**, S.—AS. *lind*, 'tilia' (Voc.).

lyne, *sb.* cord, net, PP, S; **line**, S; **lynes**, *pl.*, snares for birds, PP; **lines**, PP.—AF. *line*; Lat. *linea*.

lynt-quhite, *sb.* linnet, S3, JD; **lint-white**, lark, HD.—Cf. AS. *linet-wige*, 'carduelis' (Voc.), 'fronulus' (Voc.), *linet-uigle*, 'fronulus' (Voc.).

lyp, *sb.* lip, Voc.; **lyppe**, Voc., Cath.; **lippe**, *pl.*, S; **lippes**, PP. *Comb.*: **lyp-labour**, lip-labour, recitation of prayers, S3.—OFris. *lippa* (= *lip-j-a*); cf. Lat. *labium*; see Brugmann, § 337.

lype, *sb.* leap, S2.—AS. *hlýp* (Voc.). See **lepen**.

lypp, *sb.* rennet, runnet, Voc. (666. 17); **lepe**, Voc. (703. 44); **leb**, Voc. (591. 15). See **loop**.

lyre, *sb.* the muscle of the thigh, Cath.; **lere**, C2; **leer**, the flank, HD.—AS. *lira*, 'pulpa, viscum, caro' (Voc.); cf. Icel. *lær*.

lysure, *sb.* list, edge of cloth, Prompt.; **lisure**, PP; **lysour**, PP; **lyser**, PP.—OF. *lisiere* (for *listiere*). See **liste**[2].

lyte, *adj.* little, PP, S2, S3; **lute**, S; **lite**, S2, C2; **lut**, S; **lyt**, C3; **lit**, S; **luyte**, S2; **lyte**, *adv.*, PP, C2, C3; **lite**, PP; **lute**, S2.—AS. *lyt*: OS. *lut*.

lytel, *adj.* little, PP; **lutel**, S, S2; **litel**, S2, C2; **luitel**, PP; **luytel**, PP; **lutel**, *adv.*, S, S2; **litel**, S; **litl**, S.—AS. *lytel*; cf. OS. *luttil*, OHG. *luzil* (Otfrid).

lyth, *sb.* property; **lythe**, *dat.*, HD. *Phr.*: **loud and lith**, PP. Notes (p. 326); **lond ne lith**, HD.—Cf. Icel. *lýðr*, the common people;

lýð-skylda, the homage of a liegeman to his lord. Cf. **leod**.

lyðen, *v.* to listen, S, PP, HD; **lithen**, PP; **liðe**, S; **liðeð**, *imp. pl.*, S, G; **lytheth**, G.— Icel. *hlýða*, from *hljóð*, hearing, what is heard, a sound. See **loud**.

lyðer, *adj.* bad, H, PP; **liðer**, S2, PP; see **luþer**.

lyverè, *sb.* something delivered to a dependent, livery, C; **lyverey** (of cloth or other gifts), *liberata*, Prompt., G; **lyveray**, *corrodium*, Cath.; **levere**, B.—AF. *liveree*, delivery, livery; Late Lat. *liberata* (Cath.).

lyȝen, *v.* to lie, tell lies, S2, PP; **liȝen**, S; **lihen**, to deceive, S; **lye**, S; **lyte**, PP; **ligen**, S; **lixt**, *2 pr. s.*, PP, G; **lixte**, PP; **leȝheþþ**, *pr. s.* S; **lihð**, PP, S2; **lith**, PP; **lyȝeð**, S2; **lowe**, *2 pt. s.*, PP; **lyȝede**, *pt. s.* (*weak*), PP; **lighed**, *pl.* (*weak*), S2; **luȝen**, *pl.*, S; **lowen**, *pp.*, concealed by lying, S; **lowen vpon**, lied against, PP; **i-loȝe**, lied, S.— AS. *léogan*, pt. *léag* (pl. *lugon*), pp. *logen*.

lyȝere, *sb.* liar, S2, PP; **leghere**, H; **liȝere**, PP, S; **lyȝers**, *pl.*, S2.—AS. *léogere*.

lyȝte, *pt. s.* alighted, PP; **lyȝt**, *pp.*, S2; see **lighte**.

M

m, the first letter of *master* or *mastership*, S3.

ma[1], *v.* to make, S2; see **make**.

ma[2], *adv.* more, S, S2; see **mo**.

mace, *sb.* mace, club, PP, Cath., Voc.; *sceptrum*, ND, Manip.; **mas**, *pl.*, B; **masis**, B; **macyss**, B.—AF. *mace* (F. *masse*); cf. Low Lat. *massa* (Ducange); It. *mazza*; Late Lat. *matia*; Lat. **matea* (found in *mateola*); see Diez.

macer, *sb.* mace-bearer (in court of justice); maceres, *pl.*, PP.

macull, *sb.* stain, S3. Lat. *macula*.

mad[1], *adj.* mad, foolish, PP; **maad**, SD; **made**, Cath.; **mad**, *sb.*, a mad person, S2; **madde**, *pl.*, PP.

mad[2], *pp.* made, S, C, G; see **maken**.

madden, *v.* to be mad, PP; **maddith**, *pr. s.*, W; **maddist** 2 *pr. s.*, W; **maddid**, *pt. s.*, maddened, PP; *pp.* W.

mæi[1], *pr. s.* may, can, S; **mai**, S; **may**, S2; **maig**, S; **maiȝ**, S; **mei**, S; **mey**, S2; **maȝie, maȝȝ**, S; **maht**, 2 *pr. s.*, S; **mahht**, S; **miȝt**, S; **miht**, S, S2; **mihht**, S; **myht**, S, S2; **maȝen**, *pl.*, S; **mahen**, S; **mahe**, S; **mawe**, S; **mowen**, S; **mo**, S; **mowe**, S, S3, C; **muge**, S; **muhe**, S; **muee**, S; **mwue**, S; **muwen**, S; **muȝen**, S; **muȝhenn**, S; **muȝe**, S; **moun**, S, W; **mouwen**, S; **mown**, S2; **moȝe**, S2; **mow**, P; **y-may**, S3. *Comb.*: **maistow**, mayest thou, S3.—AS. *mæg*, I can, 2 *pr. s.*, *meaht*, *miht*, pl. *magon*, opt. *mæge*, *mage*, *muge*, pl. *mahan*, *mugon*. See Sievers, 424.

mæi[2], *sb.* kinsman, S; **mai**, S; **mey**, S; **may**, a person, S2.—AS. *mæg* (pl. *mágas*): Goth. *mēgs*; see Sievers, 17. Cf. **may**[2].

mæsse-dæi, *sb.* mass-day, S; see **messe**.

Mahoun, *sb.* Muhammad, S2; **Mahounde**, HD.—OF. *Mahom*, *Mahoms*, also *Mahum*, *Mahumet* (Roland); Arab. *Muhammed*, 'the praised' Cf. **maumet**.

maht; see **mæi**[1].

mahte, *pt. s.* might, S; **mihte**, S; **michte**, S; **migte**, S; **micte**, S; **myhte**, S; **moucte**, S; **muhte**, S; **miȝte**, S2; **mught**, S2, H; **myȝte**, S2; **mought**, S3, H; **mocht**, *pl.*, S2; **moght**, S2. *Comb.*: **mihti** (for *mihte hi*), might they, S; **mihti** (for *miht I*), might I, S2; **maihtou**, mightest thou, PP.—AS. *meahte*, *mihte*, pt. s. of *mæg*, I can. See **mæi**[1].

maille, *sb.* mail-armour, C2; **maylle**, Cath.; **male**, S3, Cath.; **mayles**, *pl.*, SkD.—OF. *maille* Lat. *macula*. See **macull**.

make, *sb.* mate, spouse, S, S2, S3, C, C2, P, Prompt.; **makes**, *pl.*, S2; **makez**, S2; **makys**, S3.—AS. *(ge)maca*.

maken, *v.* to make, cause, build, compose, write, PP, S; **makien**, S; **macien**, S; **makye**, S2; **mak**, S2; **ma**, S2, B; **mais**, *pr. s.*, B, S2; **mas**, S2; **mais**, *pl.*, B; **makede**, *pt. s.*, S; **machede**, S; **makked**, *pl.*, S2; **maden**, S, PP; **maked**, *pp.*, PP, S, C; **maad**, C, PP; **mad**, S, C, G; **y-maked**, S2, C2; **y-maad**, S2, C2; **y-mad**, S2; **i-maked**, S; **i-maket**, S2; **i-made**, P; **i-mad**, G; **hi-makede**, S.—AS. *macian*; cf. OHG. *machón* (Otfrid).

maker, *sb.* maker, writer, author, SkD, Cath., ND; **makyere**, S2.

male, *sb.* bag, portmanteau, mail, C, C3, Prompt., Cath.; **males**, *pl.*, P.—OF. *male* (Cotg.); cf. Low Lat. *mala* (Ducange).

malencolye, *sb.* melancholy, PP; **malencolie**, C, Prompt.; **malicoly**, WA.—OF. *melancolie*.

malencolyk, *adj.* melancholy, C.—OF. *melancolique*.

malengine, *sb.* wicked artifice, HD; **malengyne**, malice, evil disposition, S3.—AF. *malengin*, fraud, ill-meaning; *engin*, deceit, treachery (Bartsch).

malese, *sb.* sickness, PP; **male ese**, W; **male ess**, B.—OF. *malaise* (Cotg.).

malice, *sb.* evil, W.—AF. *malice*; Lat. *malitia*.

malisun, *sb.* malediction, S, H, ND; **malisoun**, C3.—OF. *malison*, *maleiceon*, *maldeceon*, *maldisson* (Ps. 108. 17); Lat. *maledictionem*.

malliable, *adj.* malleable, C3.—OF. *malleable*, pliant to the hammer, hammerable (Cotg.).

mamelek, *sb.* a mameluke, S3.—Arab. *mamlûk*, a slave, a possession, from *malaka*, he possessed; cf. It. *mamalúcco* (Florio).

mamely, *v.* to mumble, P; see **momelen**.

man[1], *1 pr. s.* I must, SD; *2 pr. pl.*, S2, B; see **mon**[1].

man[2], *sb.* man, any one, S; husband, W; **mann**, S; **men**, S2; **mon**, S, S2; **manne**, *dat.*, S; **me**, S, S2, S3, W; **mæn**, *pl.*, S; **mænn**, S; **mannen**, *gen.*, S; **manne**, S2; **mannen**, manne; *dat.*, S; **menne**, S. *Comb.*: **manhed(e)**, manhood, S2, C; **manheid**, S2; **mankin**, mankind, S; **mon-kin**, S; **moncun**, S; **man-ken**, S; **man-kunne**, S; **mon-kunne**, S; **man-qualm**, pestilence, H; **man-quellere**, murderer, executioner, S2, S3, W, W2; **mon-quellere**, S; **man-red(e)**, homage, S; **man-scipe**, homage, honour, S; **mon-slaȝe**, man-slayer, S; **man-slecht**, man-slaughter, S;

132

man-sleiht, S; **man-sleere**, murderer, W2; **mon-þewes**, the morality of a grown up man, S.—AS. *man.*

manace, *sb.* threat, C, SkD; **manas**, S2, WA, SkD; **manauce**, B; **manassis**, **manaasis**, *pl.*, W.—OF. *manace*; Lat. *minacia*; see Constans.

manacen, *v.* to threaten, C2, PP; **manasside**, *pt. s.*, S2, W; **manaasside**, W2; **manausyt**, B.—OF. *menacer.*

manasyng, *sb.* threatening, C, B.

man-að, *sb.* perjury, SD; **manaðas**, *pl.*, S.—AS. *mán-áð*; cf. Icel. *mein-eiðr.* AS. *mán*, wicked, wickedness; cf. Icel. *meinn*, base, *mein*, harm.

manciple, *sb.* purveyor, S; see **maunciple.**

manden, *v.* to send forth, to command, S2.—OF. *mander*; Lat. *mandare.*

mandragora, *sb.* mandrake, ND; **mandrogoris**, *pl.*, W2.—OF. *mandragore* (Cotg.); Lat. *mandragora* (Vulg.).

mandrak, *sb.* mandrake, Voc.; **mandragge**, Prompt.; **mandrage**, Cath.

mane, *sb.* complaint, S2; see **mone**[2].

maner, *sb.* manor, PP; **manere**, P, Voc.; **manoir**, PP; **maners**, *pl.*, farms, possessions, W; **maneres**, P.—AF. *manere, maner, manoir*; Late Lat. *manerium* (Ducange).

manere, *sb.* a kind, sort, also manner, custom, S, S2, C, P; **maneir**, S2; **maner**, S3, C, P; measure, moderation, W; **maners**, *pl.*, S2. *Phr.*: **of manere**, in his behaviour, C2; **maner doctrine**, kind of doctrine, C2; **maner thing, maner sergeant, maner wyse, maner wyght**, C2.—AF. *manere*; Late Lat. *maneria*, a kind, species (Ducange).

mangen, mangerie; see **maungen, maungerye.**

manicle, *sb.* manacle, Cotg.; **manycle**, Prompt.; **manakelle**, Cath.; **manykils**, *pl.*, H.—AF. *manicle*; Lat. *manicula*, dimin. of *manica*, glove, handcuff.

maniple, *sb.* a scarf-like ornament worn about the left wrist of a sacrificing priest (Cotg.).—OF. *manople* (Cotg.).

manke, *sb.* mancus, a piece of money, S; Low Lat. *mancus* (Ducange).

manliche, *adj.* humane, P; **manly**, *adv.*, boldly, S2, G; **monluker**, *comp.*, S.

mansed, *pp.* excommunicated, cursed, P; **mousede**, PP.—For *amansed*; AS. *amánsed.* See **amansien.**

mansion, *sb.* mansion (a term in astrology), C2.—AF. *mansion*; Late Lat. *mansionem.*

mantel, *sb.* mantle, S; **mentil**, W2.—AF. *mantel.*

mantelet, *sb.* a little mantle, C.—OF. *mantelet* (Cotg.).

mantled, *pp.* covered, adorned with flowers, S3; **i-mantlet**, mantled, S.

manye, *adj.* many, PP; **manige**, S; **maniʒe**, S; **manie, mani**, S; **moni**, S, S2; **mony**, S. *Comb.*: **manifeald**, manifold, S; **manifald**, S; **manigefold**, S; **monifald**, **moniuold**, S; **manifældlice**, manifold, S; **monyvolde**, S2; **monimon**, S2; **monion**, S2; **maniʒ-whatt**, many a subject, S; **manywhat**, S2.—AS. *manig.*

marchaundise, *sb.* merchandise, traffic, PP; **marchaundye**, S2.—AF. *marchaundise.*

marchaunt, *sb.* merchant, PP; **marchantz**, *pl.*, S2; **marchans**, PP.—AF. *marchant, merchaunt*, OF. *marchëant, marcëant* (Bartsch); Late Lat. *mercatantem*, see Brachet.

Marche[1], *sb.* the month of March, Prompt.; **Mershe**, S2.—Late Lat. *marcius* (Prompt.); Lat. *martius*, the month of Mars.

marche[2], *sb.* a border of a territory, district, province, PP, Cath. *Comb.*: **march-parti**, border-country, S3.—AF. *marche.*

marchen[1], *v.* to border, SD; **marcheth to**, borders on, S2.

marchen[2], *v.* to march, go, PP.—OF. *marcher* (Cotg.).

mare, *adj. comp.* greater, S; see **more**[3].

marewe, *sb.* morning, S2; see **morwe.**

margarite, *sb.* pearl, Cath., W, W2; **margrite**, WA; **margery**, Prompt.; **margaritis**, *pl.*, W. *Comb.*: **margery(e)-perles**, pearls, S2, PP, Palsg.—Lat. *margarita* (Vulg.); Gr. μαργαρίτης.

marie[1], *v.* to give in marriage, PP; **marieden**, *pt. pl.*, were married, PP; **maried**, PP; **y-maried**, PP.—OF. *marier*; Lat. *maritare.*

marie[2], *interj.* marry! (i.e. the Virgin Mary), C3; **mari**, PP.

mark, *sb.* a coin, Prompt., C3, PP; **marke**, PP; **mark**, *pl.*, C3; **marc**, S3.—AF. *marc*; cf. Low Lat. *marca* (Ducange).

markis, *sb.* marquis, C2.—AF. *marchis*; Low Lat. *marchensis*, the governor of the marches or frontiers. See **marche**[2].

markisesse, *sb.* marchioness, C2.

marle, *sb.* marl, *creta*, Cath., Voc.; **marle**, *marga*, Manip.; **marl**, chalk, Prompt.—OF. *marle* (mod. *marne*); Late Lat. *margila*; dimin. of *marga* (Pliny).

marl-pytte, *sb.* chalk-pit, Prompt.

marlyd, *adj. cretatus*, Prompt.; **y-marled**, S2.

marschal, *sb.* marshal, steward, C, PP; **marchal**, PP; **marschall**, B; **marschalle**, Cath.; **mareschal**, PP.—AF. *mareschal* (*marchal*); Low Lat. *mariscalcus*; OHG. *maraschalh*, a horse-servant; OHG. *marah* + OHG. *schalh*: Goth. *skalks.* See **mere**[2].

martre, *sb.* marten, a kind of weasel. SkD.—
OF. *martre.*—AS. *meard.* {Cf. **ful-mard** and
methes-chele.}

martrik, *sb.* marten, S3; **mertrik**, JD.

martryn, *sb.* marten's fur, HD; **marterns**,
pl., HD; **marterons**, HD; **matrons**, HD.

martyr[1], *sb.* martyr, Cath.—AF. *martir*;
Church Lat. *martyr* (Vulg.); Gr. μάρτυρ.

martyr[2], *v.* to torment, Cath.; **martyre**,
C.—AF. *martirer.*

martyrdome, *sb.* torment, martyrdom,
Cath.; **martirdam**, C.

mary, *sb.* marrow, C, C3, Prompt., Cath. (*n*);
marghe, Cath.; **mergh**, H; 144 **merghe**,
Cath. (*n*), H; **marȝ**, Cath. (*n*); **merowȝ**,
W2; **merowis**, *pl.*, W2.—AS. *mearh.*

maschen, *v.* to mash, beat into a confused
mass; **maschyn** (in brewing), Prompt.;
meshe, S.—Cf. MHG. *meisch*; see Kluge.

mase, *sb.* maze, confusion, a wild fancy, confused throng, P, S2, C.

mased, *pp.* confused, bewildered, WA, PP,
S2, C3.

masednesse, *sb.* amaze, C2.

maseliche, *adv.* confusedly, SkD (s.v. *maze*).

maselin, *sb.* a kind of drinking-cup, sometimes made of *maslin*, HD; **maselyn**, C2.
See **mestling**[1].

massage, *sb.* message, S3; see **message**.

masse, *sb.* mass, P; see **messe**.

mast, most, S2; see **most**.

mastilȝon, *sb. mixtilio*, a mixture of wheat and
rye, Cath.; **mastlyone**, HD (s.v. *maslin*);
mastline, ND; **mestlyone**, *mixtilio*,
Prompt.—Late Lat. *mestillionem, mistilionem,
mestilonem*, see Ducange (s.v. *mixtum*), also
mixtilionem (Voc.); cf. OF. *mesteil* (*meteil* in
Cotg.). Cf. **mestling**[2].

mat, *pt. s.* measured, W; see **meten**[4].

mate[1], *adj.* defeated utterly, confounded,
exhausted, dispirited, B, SkD; **mat**, C3;
maat, C, S3.—OF. *mat*; Arab. *mât*, dead
(used in chess).

mate[2], *sb.* checkmate, S3.

maten, *v.* to checkmate, defeat, confound,
S3, HD; **matyn**, Prompt.—OF. *mater.*

matere, *sb.* material, stuff, matter, subject,
S2, C, C2, C3, PP; **mater**, PP; **mateere**,
C, PP; **matiere**, S2; **materie**, S2.—OF.
matere; Lat. *materia.*

matrimoyne, *sb.* matrimony, C; **mater-
moyn**, H.—AF. *matrimonie*; Lat. *matrimon-
ium.*

maðelen, *v.* to talk, S.—AS. *maðelian*, to
harangue, from *mæðel*, council, meeting; cf.
Goth. *mapljan*, to speak, from *mapl*, a
meeting-place, market, also Icel. *mæla*, from
mál; herewith is connected Low Lat. *mallum*,
parliament.

maðem, *sb.* treasure, SD; **madmes**, *pl.*,
S.—AS. *máðum* (*mádm*).

maugre[1], *prep.* in spite of, S2, S3, C, C2;
maugree, S2; **mawgre**, C; **mawgreith**,
PP.—OF. *maugre* (F. *malgré*); Lat. *malum +
gratum.*

maugre[2], *sb.* illwill, PP; **mawgre**, S2, P;
mawgry, Cath.; **magger**, S3. *Phr.*: **in the
magger of**, in spite of, S3; **addylle
mawgry**, *demeritare*, Cath.

maumet, *sb.* idol, puppet, doll, ND, S2, PP;
mawmet, W, H; **mawment**, Prompt.,
Cath.; **mawmez**, **mawmex**, *pl.*, S;.
maumettis, W; **maumetys**, **mawmetis**,
pl., H; **mammets**, Sh.—OF. *mahumet* idol,
also Muhammad. See **Mahoun.**

maumettrie, *sb.* idolatry, Islam, the Muslim
religion, S2; **maumettrye**, C3; **mawme-
try**, H; **mawmetrye**, PP; **mawmentrye**,
Prompt.; **maumentry**, WA.

maunciple, *sb.* purveyor, C, C3; **manciple**, S.—OF. *mancipe*: OIt. *mancipio*, slave,
vassal, bailiff, manciple; Lat. *mancipium*,
slave, properly possession, property. For the
intrusive *l*, see **cronicle.**

maundee, *sb.* maundy, the washing of the
disciples' feet, PP.—OF. *mandé*; Church Lat.
mandatum, the foot-washing (Ducange); Lat.
mandatum, something commanded. See
manden.

maundement, *sb.* commandment, W, PP;
maundemens, *pl.*, S2.—OF. *mandement*
(Cotg.).

maungen, *v.* to eat, PP; **maunged**, *pp.*, P;
i-maunget, S2; **manged**, PP.—OF.
mangier; Lat. *manducare.*

maungerye, *sb.* a feast, PP; **mangerie**, PP;
mangerye, G.—AF. *mangerie.*

mavis, *sb.* the thrush, Cotg.; **mavice**,
Prompt.; **mavys**, Palsg.; **mavyss**, S3.—
OF. *mauvis* (Cotg.); cf. It. *maluíccio* (Florio).

mawe[1], *sb.* maw, stomach, C2, C3, W2, PP;
maw, PP; **maghe** (= *vulva*), H.—AS. *maga*
(Voc.).

mawe[2], **mayct**; see **mæi**[1].

May[1], *sb.* the month of May, PP; **Mey**, S2.—
OF. *mai*; Lat. *maius.*

may[2], *sb.* a virgin, S2, S3, C, C3, PP, JD.—AS.
mǽg, '(cognata) femina, virgo'; see Grein.
Cf. **mæi**[2].

may[3], *pr. s.* may, can, S2; see **mæi**[1].

may[4], *adj. comp. pl.* more in number, B; see
mo.

mayde, *sb.* maid, PP, SkD; **maide**, PP, S;
meide, S; **mede**, S.

mayden, *sb.* maiden, PP; **maydene**, PP;
meiden, S, SkD; **mæiden**, S; **mayd-
enes**, *pl.*, bachelors and spinsters, PP;

maidenes, S; **maydnes**, S.—AS. *mæden* (Voc.), *mægden* (Grein).

maydenhod(e), *sb.* virginity, PP, C; **maydenhede**, C3; **meidenhed**, SkD.

mayn, *sb.* strength, S3, G, PP, B; **main**, S: **mane**, B.—AS. *mægen*; cf. Icel. *megin*.

mayne, *sb.* a company, S2; **mayny**, S2; see **meynè**.

maynful, *adj.* powerful, SD; **meinfule**, S.

mayre, *sb.* mayor, PP; **maire**, PP; **meyr**, Prompt.; **maires**, *pl.*, P; **meires**, S2, PP; **meyris**, chief justices, W.—AF. *meyre*, *metre*, *meir*, *maire*; Lat. *maiorem*, greater.

mayster[1], *sb.* master, S, C, S2; **maystyr**, Prompt.; **maister**, S, C, C2, S2; **maistre**, P; **meister**, S; **mistres**, *pl.*, S2, G, P; **maistris**, W2.—OF. *maistre*; Lat. *magistrum*.

mayster[2], *adj.* chief; **maister**, C, C2; **leister**, S.—OF. *maistre*.

maysterful, *adj.* powerful; **maistirful**, W.

maystresse, *sb.* mistress, Prompt.; **maistresse**, S2, C2.—OF. *maistresse* (Cotg.).

maystrye, *sb.* mastery, Prompt., PP, S2; **maistri(e)**, S2, W2; **maistry**, S3; **maistre**, C; meystry, S2; **mastry**, B.—OF. *maistrie*.

me[1], *conj.* but, S, SD.—Cf. OLG. *men*.

me[2], *pron. indef.* a man, one, people, PP, G, S2, S3, W; see **men**.

mearren, *v.* to mar, S; see **merren**.

mebles, *sb. pl.* moveable property, PP; see **mobyle**.

mede[1], *sb.* mead (the drink), C2, Prompt.; **methe**, SkD; **meth**, CM.—AS. *meodu* (see Sievers, 106); cf. μέθυ.

mede[2], *sb.* mead, meadow, S, C, PP; **medewe**, Prompt. *Comb.*: **medwe-grene**, green as a meadow, S2.—AS. *mæd* (pl. *mædwa*); see Sievers, 259.

mede[3], *sb.* reward, bribery, S, S2, S3, W2, P; **meede**, S2, G; **meed**, S3; **meede**, C, W. *Comb.*: med-ȝierne, yearning for reward, S; **medyorne**, S.—AS. *méd*: OMerc. *meord* (OET): Goth. *mizdo*; see Sievers, 181.

meden, *v.* to reward, PP, Prompt.

medlee, *adj.* mixed in colour, C; **medle**, Prompt.—OF. *medle, mesle*. Cf. **mellè**.

medlen, *v.* to mix, Prompt., C3, W2, W; **mell**, S3; **melland**,*pr. p.*, B; **melles**,*pr. s.*, H; **mellede**,*pt. s.*, S2; **mellid**, PP; **mellit**, *pp.*, S3; **y-melled**, S2; **y-medled**, S3.—OF. *medler, mesler*; Late Lat. *misculare*, from *miscere*.

medlynge, *sb.* mixture, joining; **meddlynge**, W, W2; **mellyng**, mingling, fighting, S2.

medwe-grene, *adj.* green as a meadow, S2; see **mede**[2].

meel, *sb.* a stated time, meal, C, C3; **mel**, S; **mele**, *pl.*, meal-times, S; **meeles**, S2, PP; **meles**, PP.—AS. *mæl*: Goth. *mēl*; see Sievers, 17.

meiden, *sb.* maiden, S; see **mayden**.

meined, *pp.* mixed, S2; **meint**, S3; see **mengen**[2].

meinfule, *adj.* powerful, S; see **maynful**.

meire, *sb.* mayor, S2; see **mayre**.

meister[1], *sb.* master, S; see **mayster**[1].

meister[2], *adj.* chief, S; see **mayster**[2].

meistre, *sb.* mistress, S.

meistren, *v.* to be master of, S.

meið-had, *sb.* virginity; **meiðhades**, *gen.*, S.—AS. *mægðhád*, from *mægð*, virgin, woman: Goth. *magaþs*; see Sievers, 49.

meke, *adj.* meek, C, C2, Prompt.; **meoc**, S.—Icel. *mjúkr*, soft.

mekely, *adv.* meekly, Prompt.; **mekly**, S2; **meocliȝ**, S.

meken, *v.* to render meek, to humble, S2, S3, W, W2, P, Prompt.

mekenesse, *sb.* softness, clemency, Prompt.; **meknes**, S2; **meocnesse** S.

mekil, *adj.* much, S3; see **muchel**.

mel, *sb.* a meal, S; see **meel**.

melden, *v.* to show, SD; **meld**, to accuse, S2.—AS. *meldian* (Voc.); cf. OHG. *meldôn* (Otfrid).

mele, *sb.* meal, ground corn, S, PP.—AS. *meolu* (Sievers, 249); cf. OHG. *melo* (Tatian).

melen, *v.* to speak, to converse, PP, S2, WA; **melleth**, *pr. s.*, P; **mellud**, *pt. s.*, P.—AS. *(ge)mélan*.

mell, *v.* to mix, mingle, meddle, fight with, B, S3, H, WA; see **medlen**.

mellè, *sb.* an affray, contest, medley, B.—OF. *mellee, meslee*. Cf. **medlee**.

mellere, *sb.* miller, C; see **mylnere**.

mel-stan, *sb.* mill-stone, S; see **mylle**.

melten, *v.* to melt, PP; **molte**, *pt. s.*, S3.—AS. *meltan*, pt. s. *mealt* (*mált*), pl. *multon*, pp. *molten*.

membre, *sb.* member, limb, PP.—AF. *membre*; Lat. *membrum*.

men, *pron. indef.* a man, one, people, PP, S2; **me**, S. See **man**[2].

mene[1], *adj.* common, poor, mean, PP, S3; **meane**, S.—AS. *(ge)máne*, common.

mene[2], *adj.* mean, middle, C, C3; **meyne**, Cath. *Comb.*: **menewhile**, meanwhile, S2; **menewhiles**, S2.—AF. *mene*; OF. *meiain* (F. *moyen*); Lat. *medianum*.

mene[3], *sb.* a mean, mediator, PP, HD; **meane**, S3; **menes**, *pl.*, means, C2, C3, P. See **mene**[2].

menen[1], *v.* to mean, signify, to intend, PP, S, CM, S2, WA.

menen[2], *v.* to remember, H, HD; **meyne**, B.

menen[3], *v.* to complain, lament, bemoan, S2, PP, WA; **meyne**, B; **menys**, *pr. s.*, S3; **menyt**, *pt. s.*, S2; **ment** S2.—AS. *ménan*, to make moan, complain. See **mone**[2].

mengen[1], *v.* to commemorate, mention, remember, PP, WA; **munge**, PP; **min-egen**, S; **mengen here**, *v. refl.* to remember herself, reflect, PP.—AS. *(ge)mynegian*, to remember, remind.

mengen[2], *v.* to mix, PP, H, S2; **mingen**, S3; **myngen**, W; **myngide**, *pt. s.*, W; **meynde**, S; **mæingde**, S; **i-mengd**, *pp.*, S; **meynd**, S, S2, W; **meined**, S2; **meint**, S3; **meynt**, S3; **ment**, S3; **y-mengd**, S2; **y-meynd**, C; **i-meind**, S.—AS. *(ge)mengan*.

mennesse, *sb.* communion, fellowship, S2. See **mene**[1].

mennisc, *adj. humanus*, SD; **mannish**, man-like, C3.—AS. *mennisc*, mannish, human; cf. Icel. *mennskr*.

mennisscle33c, *sb.* humanity, S.

mennisscnesse, *sb.* humanity, S.

menske, *sb.* honour, dignity among men, S, S2, HD; **mensk**, S2, B; **mensc**, favour, S2.—Icel. *mennska*, humanity.

menskelye, *adv.* worthily, reverently, S2; **menskly**, B.

mensken, *v.* to honour, S, HD, S2, P.

menskful, *adj.* worshipful, noble, S2.

menskfully, *adv.* honourably, B.

menstralcye, *sb.* minstrelsy, C; see **myn-stralcie**.

ment; see **menen**[3] and **mengen**[2].

mentil, *sb.* mantle, W2; see **mantel**.

menusen, *v.* to minish, make less, SkD, WW, CM; **minyshe**, S3.—AF. *menuser*, OF. *menuisier*; Late Lat. *minutiare*, from *minutus*, lessened.

menyng(e)[1], *sb.* remembrance, mention, H.

menyng(e)[2], *sb.* complaining, PP.

menynge[3], *sb.* meaning, signification, intention, PP.

men3e, a company, S2; **men3he**, S2; see **meyne**.

meobles, *sb. pl.*, moveable property, PP; see **mobyle**.

meoc, *adj.* meek, S; see **meke**.

meocle33c, *sb.* meekness, S.—Icel. *mjúkleikr*, nimbleness.

meocnesse, *sb.* meekness, S; see **meke-nesse**.

mercy, *sb.* mercy, Prompt., **merci**, S, mercy, (your) pardon, P.—AF. *merci*, OF. *mercid*; Late Lat. *mercedem*, a gratuity, pity, mercy; in Lat. pay, reward.

mercyable, *adj.* merciful, C2, PP.

mercyen, *v.* to thank, PP, S2; **mercien**, to amerce, fine, PP.—OF. *mercier*, to thank.

mercyment, *sb.* amercement, fine, P, Prompt., Cath.—Late Lat. *merciamentum*.

mere[1], *adj.* famous, S; **mare**, S.—AS. *mére* (*mére*): Goth. *mêrs*; see Fick (7. 233), and Sievers, 17.

mere[2], *sb.* a mare, S2, C, Cath.; **meere**, Prompt.—AS. *mere*, f. of *mearh*, horse; cf. OIr. *marc*.

mere[3], *sb.* limit, boundary, S2; **meer**, Prompt. *Comb.*: **mere-stane**, boundary stone, Cath.—AS. *(ge)mére*.

mere[4], *sb.* sea, a mere, Prompt., WA. *Comb.*: **mere-mayd**, mermaid, siren, CM; **mer-mayde**, C; **mere-swin**, porpoise, SD; **mersuine**, *pl.*, S2.—AS. *mere*, sea, lake: OHG. *mari*; cf. Goth. *marei*.

merels, *sb. pl.* merelles, or nine men's morris, S3.—OF. *merelles* (Cotg.); *merel* (Ducange); cf. Low Lat. *merellus, merallus*, a counter, token, a piece in draughts (Ducange); see Brachet.

merghe, *sb.* marrow, H, Cath. (*n*); see **mary**.

merghid, *pp.* full of marrow, H.

meridional, *adj.* southern, C2.—OF. *meridional* (Cotg.). From Lat. *meridies*, midday.

merke[1], *adj.* dark, mirk, murky, PP, CM, S2, H; **mirke**, S, S2, H; **myrk**, S2, H; **merk**, PP; **meerk**, PP.—AS. *myrce, mirce, murc*; cf. Icel. *myrkr*, Dan. *mørk*.

merke[2], *sb.* darkness, PP.

merkenesse, *sb.* darkness, PP; **mirkenes**, S2, H; **myrknes**, S2, H.

merle, *sb.* blackbird, S3, ND.—OF. *merle* (Cotg.); Lat. *merula*.

merling, *sb.* the whiting, S2, Manip., Cotg.; **merlynge**, Prompt.—OF. *merlan* (Cotg.), from Lat. *merula* (cf. Late Lat. *merula* in Voc. 642. 13).

merlion, *sb.* merlin, a small hawk, CM; **merlyone**, Prompt.; **marlin**, Cotg.—OF. *esmerillon* (Cotg.), dimin. of **esmerle*; cf. It. *smerlo* (Florio), G. *schmerl*.

mermayde, *sb.* mermaid, C; see **mere**[4], *sb.*

merren, *v.* to mar, S; **mearren**, S; **marre**, PP; **merrið**, *pr. pl.*, S.—AS. *merran* (in compounds): OS. *merrian*, to hinder: OHG. *marrjan*: Goth. *marzjan*.

mersche, *sb.* marsh, SkD; **mershe**, *dat.*, S.—AS. *mersc*.

Mershe, *sb.* March, S2; see **Marche**[1].

mersuine, *sb. pl.* porpoises, S2; see **mere**[4], *sb.*

merthe, *sb.* mirth, PP; see **murþe**.

merueile, *sb.* marvel, wonder, PP; **mer-ueyle**, S2; **meruaille**, C2; **mervaylle**, C.—OF. *merveille*; Lat. *mirabilia* (n. *pl.*).

merueillous(e), *adj.* marvellous, C2, PP.—OF. *merveillos*.

mery, *adj.* merry, cheerful, pleasant, PP; **merie**, S, C, C2; **merye**, W2; **miri**, S; **mirye**, CM; **myry**, Prompt.; **myrie**, W2; **muri(e)**, S, C; **merie**, *adv.*, S2, C2; **muryer**, *comp.*, P; **myriest**, *superl.*, S2, Comb.: **merimake**, merrymaking, S3; **merie men**, followers, C2; **myry tottyr**, a merry totter, swing, Prompt.; **myry weder**, pleasant weather, Prompt.; **mery weder**, Prompt. (*n*), Bardsley (p. 473).— AS. *merg* (Grein).

mes-, *prefix*; **mis-**; **mys-**.—OF. *mes-*; Lat. *minus*, see Constans.

mesauentur, *sb.* misadventure, S; **mesaunture**, S2; **misauenture**, C2, C3.

meschaunce, *sb.* mischance, S2, C, C2, P; **myschaunce**, S2.

mescheuen, *v.* to come to mischief, SD; **mischeefe**, *destruere*, Manip.

meschief, *sb.* ill-fortune, C; **myschief**, S2, P; **mischiefe**, *flagitium*, Manip.

meseise, *sb.* discomfort, PP, S2; **miseise**, PP; **myseise**, PP, S2, W; **myseese**, W; **myseyse**, *adj.*, uneasy, P; **mesaise**, *sb.*, S. **meseiste**, *sb.* poverty; **myseiste**, W2.

mesel, *sb.* leper, CM, PP, W.—AF. *mesel*; Late Lat. *misellus*, leper (Ducange), dimin. of Lat. *miser*, wretched.

meselrye, *sb.* leprosy, Cath. (*n*); **mesylery**, Voc.—OF. *mesellerie*, leprosy (Ducange). See **mesel**.

meson-deu, *sb.* hospital, PP; **maison-dewe**, Cath. (*n*), HD; **masyndewe**, Cath.; **mesondieux**, *pl.*, P.—OF. *maison Dieu*, hospital (Cotg.).

message, *sb.* mission, message, messenger, S2, C3; **massage**, S3.—AF. *message*; Late Lat. *missaticum* (Brachet).

messager, *sb.* messenger, S2, C, C2, C3, G, PP; **masager**, PP; **messanger**, PP.— AF. *messager*.

messe, *sb.* mass, S, P; **mess**, S3; **masse**, P; **messes**, *pl.*, P. *Comb.*: **messe-bok**, mass-book, S; **messe-cos**, mass-kiss, S; **mæsse-dæi**, mass-day, S; **messe-gere**, mass-gear, S; **masse-peny**, mass-fee, S3; **masse-pans**, *pl.*, P.—AS. *mæsse*; Church Lat. *missa*.

meste, *adj. superl.* greatest, chief, S, S2; **meste**, C2; see **most**.

mester[1], *sb.* art, trade, occupation, PP, C, CM; **mestier**, PP, HD; **meister**, S; **meoster**, S; **myster**, PP, B; **mister**, B; **misteir**, B. *Phr.*: **mester men**, sort of men, C.—OF. and AF. *mester, mestier*, occupation, business, need; Lat. *ministerium*, see Brachet (s.v. *métier*).

mester[2], *sb.* need, want; **mister**, S2, B, HD, Cath.; **myster**, C, B; **mysteir**, S2; **mystur**, HD; **mystir**, B; **mystere**, HD,

H. The same word as above, see NQ (6. 4. 161).

mestling[1], *sb.* a kind of mixed metal, Cath. (*p.* 230, *n.* 3); **masalyne**, Cath.—AS. *mæstling* (*mæstlinc*, 'auricalcos', Voc.). Cf. **maselin**.

mestling[2], *sb.* mixed corn, Cath. (*p.* 230, *n.* 3); **mastlyn**, HD; **masslin**, Cotg. (s.v. *metail*); **maslin**, HD; **meslin**, Prompt. (*p.* 335 *n*) Cotg. (s.v. *tramois*); **messling**, Cotg. Cf. **mastilʒon**.

mesurable, *adj.* moderate, C, C2, C3, P; **mesurabul**, S2.

mesure, *sb.* measure, moderation, S2, C2, PP; **mesur**, S2, B; **meosure**, S.—AF. *mesure*; Lat. *mensura*.

met, *sb.* measure, moderation, S; **mete**, *dat.*, S; **meete**, S2.—AS. (*ge*)*met*. Cf. **meten**[4].

mete[1], *adj.* meet, fitting, close-fitting, S2, S3, Prompt.—AS. *méte*, tight-fitting; cf. (*ge*)*met*, meet, fit, see SkD.

mete[2], *sb.* food, a meal, feast, S, S2, C, W2, PP; **meten**, *pl.*, S; **meetis**, W2. *Comb.*: **mete-graces**, graces at meat, S; **mete-niðinges**, meat-niggards, S.—AS. *mete* (OET): Goth. *mats*, from *matjan*, to eat; see Sievers, 263.

metels, *sb.* dream, vision, PP; **meteles**, PP. See **meten**[1].

meten[1], *v.* to dream, CM, PP, S; **meeten**, S2, PP; **mette**, *pt. s.*, C2, P; **met**, *pp.*, C.—AS. *métan*.

meten[2], *v.* to paint, design, SD; **metedd**, *pp.*, S.

meten[3], *v.* to meet, PP; **mette**, *pt. s.*, S.—AS. *métan*: OS. *mótian*. From AS. *mót*. See **moot**.

meten[4], *v.* to mete, measure, S2; **meete**, W2; **mete**, S; **met**, S2; **meten**, *pr. pl.*, W; **mat**, *pt. s.*, W.—AS. (*ge*)*metan*; cf. Goth. *mitan*, see Sievers, 19.

mete-wand, *sb.* a measuring stick, WW.

mete-yarde, *sb.* measuring-rod, S3, WW.

metrete, *sb.* measure, W.—Lat. *metreta* (Vulg.).

metyng(e)[1], *sb.* dreaming, PP; **metinge**, S.—AS. *méting* (Grein).

metynge[2], *sb.* measuring, measure; **metinge**, S2.

meth[1], *adj.* mild, courteous, HD; **methe**, HD.

meth[2], *sb.* moderation, mildness, S, S2, WA; **meað**, S; **meþe**, S2.—AS. *mǽð*, measure.

methes-chele, *sb.* marten's skin, S.—AS. *mearð* (Voc.).

meað-ful, *adj.* moderate, S.

meað-les, *adj.* immoderate; **meþelez**, S2.

meuen, *v.* to move, suggest, PP; **meued**, *pp.*, S3; see **moven**.

mewe, *sb.* a coop for fowls, C, C2, Manip.; **mue**, SD.—OF. *mue*, a coop for fowls, the moulting of feathers (Cotg.). See **mewen**.

mewen, *v.* to mew, moult, SkD, Cotg.—OF. *muer* (Cotg.); Lat. *mutare*, to change. Cf. **moutin**.

Mey, *sb.* May, S2; see **May**[1].

meyn[1], *sb.* intent, S3; **mein**, JD. See **menen**[1].

meyn[2], *v.* to remember, be mindful of, B; **meyne**, B; see **menen**[2].

meyne, *v.* to moan, lament, B; see **menen**[3].

meynè, *sb.* household, retinue, train, company, S2, S3, C, W, PP; **meynee**, C2, W2; **meyny**, S2; **mayne**, S2; **mayny**, S2, S3; **meine**, S2; **menȝe**, S2, H, Cath.; **menȝhe**, S2; **meany**, S3; **meny**, Prompt.; **meynes**, *pl.*, W; **meynees**, W2; **menȝes**, **menȝis**, H.—OF. *meisnee, maisnee*; Low Lat. *maisnada, *mansionata*, from Lat. *mansio*.

meyneal, *adj.* homely, W; of one's household, W2; **menyall**, SkD; **meyneals**, *sb. pl.*, they of the household, W2. See **meynè**.

meynpernour, *sb.* a taker by the hand, bail, surety, P.—AF. *meynpernour*.

meynprise[1], *sb.* a taking by the hand, bail, security, P; **maynpris**, G.—AF. *meinprise*.

meynprise[2], *v.* to be surety for, PP.

meyntene, *v.* to support, abet (in an action at law), P, S2; **mayntene**, to maintain, C, P.—AF. *meyntener*.

meyntenour, *sb.* supporter, PP.—AF. *meintenour*.

miche, *adj.* much, S2; see **moche**.

mid[1], *prep.* with, S, S2; **myd**, S, S2, P; **mit**, S; **mide**, S, S2; **myde**, S2. *Comb.*: **mitte** (**mit þe**), with the, S2; **mitte** (**mit þe**), with thee, S; **mid-al**, withal, S; **midalle**, altogether, S; **mid-iwisse**, certainly, S; **mid-ywisse**, S; **myd-iwisse**, S.—AS. *mid*.

mid[2], *adj.* mid, SD. *Comb.*: **mid-morwen**, mid-morning, S; **mid-morwetide**, SD; **mid-ouernon**, middle of the afternoon; **hei midouernon**, fully the middle of the afternoon, S2; **Midewinter**, Christmas, S2; **Midwinterdæi**, *sb. dat.*, Christmas-day, S; **Midwinter-day**, S2; **mid-ward**, middle, S2.—AS. *mid-*.

middel, *adj. and sb.* middle, waist, SkD, S, S2, C; **myddel**, PP; **myddil**, W; **myddeleste**, *superl.*, G. *Comb.*: **middel-niȝte**, midnight, S.—AS. *middel*, sb.

middel-erd, *sb.* the middle abode, the world, S; **middeleard**, S; **myddelerd**, S, PP; **midelerd**, S; **mydlerd**, S2, PP; **mydelerd**, PP; **medlert**, JD.—Cf. OS. *middilgard*, OHG. *mittila gart* (Tatian). Cf. **middeneard**.

midden-eard, *sb.* the middle abode, the abode of men, S; **middenærd**, S; **middenard**, S; **midenarde**, *dat.*, S.—AS. *middan-eard* for *middan-geard*, 'middle enclosure' (OET), the earth situated between heaven and hell, see Sweet, and Sievers, 214, n. 5; cf. Goth. *midjungards*, Icel. *miðgarðr*. See CV., and Grimm, Teut. M, p. 794.

middes, *only in phr.*: **in middes**, in the midst, PP; **in þe myddes**, PP, S2; **in þe myddis, fro þe myddis**, PP, S3, W, W2; **in the mydis**, W2.—From *mid*, adj. The *-es* gives the phrase an adverbial force. The older forms (in Layamon) are *a midde*, *a midden*; AS. *on middan*.

midwif, *sb.* midwife, SD, SkD; **mydwyf**, SkD; **mydwyfe**, Prompt.; **mydewyf**, SkD; **medwyfe**, Cath.; **medewife**, SkD; **medewyues**, *pl.*, S2. See **mid**[1].

mightand, *pr. p.*, as *adj.* having might, S2.

Mihel, *sb.* Michael, SD; **Myȝhele**, HD; **Mihil**, ND.—Church Lat. *Michael* (Vulg.), from the Heb.

Mihel-masse, *sb.* Michaelmas, SD; **Mihelmas**, ND; **Myhelmasse**, PP; **Misselmasse**, S2.

miht, *2 pr. s.* mayest, S; see **mæi**[1].

mihte, *pt. s.* might, S; **micte**, S; **michte**, S; **migte**, S; see **mahte**.

mikel, *adj. and adv.* great, much, S, S2; see **muchel**.

milce, *sb.* mercy, S, S2, HD; **mylce**, S; **milche**, S.—AS. *milts*, from *milde*, mild, gentle; see Sievers, 198, 4.

milcien, *v.* to show mercy, S; **milcenn**, S; **milsien**, S.—AS. *milsian, miltsian*.

milde, *adj.* mild, S, S2; **myld**, S. *Comb.*: **mild-heorte**, merciful in heart, SD; **mild-heorted**, S; **milde-herted**, S2; **mild-herrtleȝȝc**, mildheartedness, compassion, S; **mild-heortnesse**, clemency, S; **mild-hertnesse**, S.—AS. *milde*.

miles, *sb. pl.*, animals, S2.—Cf. W. *mil*, an animal, beast; *miled*, a wild animal (W.W.S.).

min[1], *pron. poss.* my, S, S2; **myn**, S, C2, PP; **mi**, S, S2; **mines**, *gen.*, S; **mine**, *dat.*, S; **mire**, *gen. and dat. f.*, S; **mynen**, *pl.*, W2. *Phr.*: **myn one**, by myself, alone, PP.—AS. *mín*.

min[2], *sb.* memory, S2; see **mynne**[1].

mines, *2 pr. s.* rememberest, S2; see **mynne**[2].

minion[1], *sb.* a favourite, a lover, Sh. TG, ND; *bellulus*, Manip.; **minyons**, *pl.*, S3.—OF. *mignon* (Cotg.); cf. It. *mignone* (Florio).

minion[2], *adj.* small, pretty; **mynyon**, ND; **mynionly**, *adv.* delicately, ND.

-mint, *suffix.*—AS. *mynt, -mynd*: Goth. *-mundiþa*, see Sievers, 255, 3. Cf. **wurþmint**.

mint, *pt. s.* purposed, S; see **munten**.

minute

minute, *sb.* a mite, moment of time, HD; **mynute**, Prompt.; **mynutis**, *pl.*, small pieces of money, W. *Comb.*: **mynutwhile**, PP; **myntwhile**, PP; **myntewhile**, PP.— Lat. *minutum* (Vulg.). Cf. **mite**.

minyshe, *v.* to minish, S3; see **menusen**.

mire[1], *sb.* ant, S; **mowre**, Cath.—Cf. Dan. *myre*, Icel. *maurr*.

mire[2], my, *gen.* and *dat. f.* of **min**.

mirky, *adj.* dark, H. See **merke**[1].

mirre, *sb.* myrrh, S, PP; **mir**, S2; **murre**, PP; **myrre**, PP.—AS. *myrre*; Lat. *myrrha* (Vulg.); Gr. μύῤῥα.

mirye, *adj.* merry, CM; see **mery**.

mis-[1], *prefix*; **mys-**, PP; **mysse-**, PP.—AS. *mis-*; Goth. *missa-*. *Comb.*: **misbileue**, suspicion, C3; **misboden**, injured, C, CM; **misdede**, misdeed, S, PP; **misdeparten**, to divide amiss, C2; **misdo**, to do amiss, PP, S, S2, C2; **misfaren**, to behave amiss, S; **mysfare**, to miscarry, PP; **misgouern-aunce**, misconduct, C2; **misgyed**, misguided, C2; **mys-happen**, to meet with misfortune, PP; **myshopand**, despairing, H; **misleuen**, to believe wrongly, S; **misliken**, to displease, to be displeased, S, S2; **misliking**, displeasure, S2; **myspay**, to displease, H; **misrede**, to advise ill, S; **misrempe**, to go wide of the mark, S; **mysreule**, to misgovern, S3, PP; **mys-sayde**, abused, rebuked, slandered, PP; **misseid**, S2; **missemand**, **misemand**, unseemly, H; **misteoðien**, to mistithe (**mis-iteoðeget**, S); **mistriste**, to mistrust, C3; **mysturne**, to pervert, W, W2.

mis-[2], *prefix (of F. origin)*; see **mes-**.

mis, *adv.* amiss, S, C3; **mys**, PP; **mysse**, S2.

miselle; see **mizzle**.

mislich, *adj.* various, S; **misliche**, *adv.*, S; **mistlice**, S.—AS. *mislic (mistlic)*, various, adv. *mislice (mistlice*, Grein). For the insertion of *t*, see Sievers, 196, 1.

misliche, *adv.* badly, miserably, S; **missely**, wrongly, S2.

misse, *sb.* want, lack, fault, S; **mysse**, S, PP.

missen, *v.* to miss, SD; **mis**, S2; **mysseþ**, *pr. s.*, is without, PP.

mister; see **mester**[1], **mester**[2].

mistiloker, *adj. comp.* more mystic, PP; **mystiloker**, PP.

misty[1], *adj.* mystic, mysterious; **mysty**, *misticus*, Prompt.; **mistier**, *comp.*, PP.

misty[2], *adj.* misty, *nebulosus*, Cath., Prompt.

mite, *sb.* a mite, small coin, thing of no value, C3, Cotg. (s.v. *minute*); **myte**, PP; *minutum*, Cath., Prompt., WW. *Comb.*: **mytewhile**, a little while, PP. Cf. **minute**.

miteyn, *sb.* mitten, glove, C3; see **myteyne**.

mole

mithen, *v.* to conceal, S, SD.—AS. *míðan*; cf. OHG. *(bi)mídan* (Tatian, p. 493).

mix, *sb.* dung, S; a vile wretch, S2.—AS. *mix*, *meox*, *meohx*, Goth. *maihstus*; cf. OHG. *mist* (Tatian).

mizzle, *v.* to rain slightly, S3, HD; **miselle**, **mysylle**, *pluuitare*, Cath.

mo, *adj.* and *adv.* more, besides, others, S, S2, S3, C; **moo**, S3; **ma**, S, S2; **may**, *pl.*, S3.— AS. *má*. (*Mo* properly means more in number; *more* means greater in magnitude.)

mobyle, *adj.* moveable, S3; **moebles**, *sb. pl.*, moveables, property, PP, C3; **meobles**, PP; **mebles**, PP.—OF. *moble*, also *meuble* (Cotg.); Lat. *mobilem*.

moche, *adj.* and *adv.* great, much, S, S2, C2; see **muche**.

mochel; see **muchel**.

mod; see **mood**.

modder, *sb.* a young girl, Manip.; **moder**, Prompt.

moder, *sb.* mother, S, S2, C, C3, PP; **moderr**, S; **modir**, W; **modur**, PP; **mooder**, S2, C2, C3; **muddir**, S3; **moder**, *gen.*, S2, PP; **modres**, C3, PP. *Comb.*: **moder-burh**, metropolis, SD; **moder-child**, mother's child, S; **modirles**, motherless, W2.—AS. *módor*: Lat. *máter*; see Douse, p. 51.

modiȝleȝȝc, *sb.* pride, S.

modiȝnesse, *sb.* pride, S.

mody, *adj.* spirited, *animosus*, proud, PP, S2.

moeued, *pt. s.* moved, disturbed, C3; see **moven**.

moght, *pt. s.* might, S2; see **mahte**.

moich, *adj.* close, muggy, S3, JD.

moile, *v.* to toil, to drudge, to defile, pollute, daub with dirt, SkD; **moillen**, to wet, SkD; **moylynge**, *pr. p.*, S3.—AF. *moiler*, *moiller*, to wet; Late Lat. **molliare*, from *mollis*, soft.

moillier, *sb.* woman, wife, PP; **muliere**, PP; **moylere**, P.—OF. *moillier*, *muiller*; Lat. *mulierem*; cf. AF. *muiler*, *muller*.

mok, *sb.* muck, filthy lucre, PP; **muk**, PP; **mukke**, Prompt.

moky, *adj.* misty, HD. Cf. **moich**.

molde, *sb.* crumbling ground, earth, mould, S, S2, P, G; **moolde**, PP; **mulde**, WA; **moldez**, *pl.*, dry pieces of mould, S2. *Phr.*: **on molde**, on the earth, in the world, S2, PP. *Comb.*: **molde-ale**, a funeral ale or banquet, Prompt.; **mulde-mete**, a funeral banquet, JD; **moldwerp**, mole, mouldcaster, SkD; **moldwarp**, Sh.; **moldewarpe**, Cath.—AS. *molde*. Cf. **mull**.

mole, *sb.* the moldwarp, *talpa*, Sh.; **mowle**, S3; **molle**, Prompt.—This word is short for *molde-warp*. See **molde**.

molte

molte (*for* molt), *pt. s.* melted, S3; see melten.

mom, *sb.* the least sound that can be made with closed lips, PP, S2; mum, S3.

momelen, *v.* to mumble, PP; mamely, P.

mon[1], *1 pr. s.* I must, B; *pr. s.*, B; *2 pr. s.*, S3; mone, mayest, S2; *pr. s.*, shall, S2; man, *1 pr. s.*, SD; *2 pr. pl.*, S2, B; mun, *pr. s.*, S2, H.—Icel. *munu*, 'debere', pr. s. *man* (pl. *munu*).

mon[2], *sb.* man, S; see man[2].

monchen, *v.* to munch, Cath. (*n*), Palsg., SkD; mounch, Sh.; munche, CM (4. 145); maunche, Palsg. (s.v. *briffault*); manche, Palsg.; mounchynge, *pr. p.*, S3. *Comb.*: mounch-present, HD; maunche-present, Palsg., HD (s.v. *munch*); mawnche-presande, sycophant, Cath.; manch-present, *dorophagus*, Cath. (*n*).—Probably a variety of ME. *maungen*; OF. *manger*. For *che* = *ge* cf. ME. *charche*; OF. *charche* = *charge* (see MD), also F. *revancher* = OF. *revenger* (SkD).

mone[1], *sb.* share, companion, S.—AS. (*ge*)*mána*, 'societas' (Voc.). See ymone.

mone[2], *sb.* moan, complaint, PP, S, S2; moone, PP, C; moon, S2; mayn, B; mayne, B, S3; mane, S2.

mone[3], *sb.* moon, S, S2, S3, P; a lunation, P; moyne, Cath., B; moyn, B. *Comb.*: Monedæi, *dies lunae*, Monday, S; Moneday, S; mone-licht, moonlight, S.—AS. *móna*.

monè, *sb.* money, S2; see moneye.

monek, *sb.* monk, S2; see monk.

monesten, *v.* to teach, admonish, W, W2, CM; moneishen, Cath. (*n*); monysche, Cath.; monest, *pt. pl.*, B. See amoneste.

monestyng, *sb.* an admonition, W. W2, B; monyschynge, Cath.

moneth, *sb.* month, S3, C, PP, B, WW, ND, Cath.; mooneþ, S2, PP; monythe, Prompt.; monyth, S2; monethe, W; monthe, PP; monthe, *pl.*, C2; monethis, W. *Comb.*: moneth-minde, a service in memory of the dead a month after decease, ND; month-mind, HD; months minde, ND; months mind, a strong inclination, ND, Sh.—AS. *mónað*, from *móna*, moon.

moneye, *sb.* money, C3, PP; monè, S2, PP.—AF. *moneie*, *moneye*, *monee*; Lat. *moneta*.

moneyeles, *adj.* moneyless, PP; monelees, PP.

mong-corn(e), *sb.* mixed corn, S3, Prompt.; moncorne, HD. See mengen[2]

moni, *adj.* many, S, S2; mony, S; see manye.

monk, *sb.* monk, PP; monek, S2; munec, S; muneces, *pl.*, S; munekes, S; monekes, S, S2; monkes, S.—AS. *munec*; Lat. *monachus*; Gr. μοναχός, solitary.

morris

monkrye, *sb.* monkery, the race of monks, S3.

monsede, *pp.* cursed, PP; see mansed.

moo-; see also words beginning in mo-.

mood, *sb.* anger, pride, mind, C; mod, S, S2; mode, *dat.*, S, S2.—AS. *mód*; cf. OHG. *muot* (Tatian).

moode, *sb.* mud, S3; see mud.

mool-bery, *sb.* mulberry, SkD; mulbery, Cath.—Cf. MHG. *mülber* (G. *maulbeere*); OHG. *mürberi*, *mörberi* (the *l* in the later forms being due to dissimilation); see Kluge; AS. *mór*; OHG. *mōr*; Lat. *morus*. See more[1].

moot, *sb.* assembly, G, PP; mot, PP. *Comb.*: moot-halle, hall of assembly, court, P, G, W; mote-halle, G, PP.—AS. *mót*. Cf. mote[2].

moralitee, *sb.* morality, i.e. a moral tale, C3.—OF. *moralite* (Cotg.).

mordre, *sb.* murder, C; see morþer[1].

more[1], *sb.* mulberry-tree; mours, *pl.*, H. *Comb.*: more-tre, mulberry-tree, W; moore-trees, *pl.*, W2; mur-berien, *pl.* mulberries, Voc.—Lat. *morus*, mulberry-tree (Vulg.); cf. Gr. μόρον, mulberry. Cf. moolbery.

more[2], *sb.* moor, Prompt., H, PP; mor, S2; mwr, B; mwre, S2, B.—AS. *mór*.

more[3], *adj.* and *adv. comp.* more, greater, elder, S, S2, W, W2, PP, WW; mor, S, PP; moare, S; mayr, S3, B; mair, B; mære, S; mare, S, S2; mar, S, B; marere, H.—AS. *mára*. See mo.

more[4], *sb.* root, S2, PP, HD; moore, CM.—AS. *mora* (Voc. 135. 28, 29, 32); cf. MHG. *morâ*, *more*, see Weigand (s.v. *möhre*).

moreyne, *sb.* murrain, PP; moreyn, S2, Prompt.; morrein, WW; moryn, H; murrins, *pl.*, WW.—AF. *morine*; cf. Low Lat. *morina*, a pestilence among animals (Ducange).

morkin, *sb.* a beast that dies by disease or accident, RD, HD, ND.—Cf. Late Lat. *morticinium* (Ducange), whence Ir. *muirtchenn*, Wel. *burgyn*.

morknen, *v.* to rot, SD; mourkne, S2.—Icel. *morkna*.

mormal, *sb.* cancer or gangrene, CM, C, Prompt., RD, SD, ND, HD; mormall, Palsg.; mortmal, ND; morimal, RD; marmole, RD.—Cf. Late Lat. *malum mortuum*, a disease of the teet and shins (Ducange).

morris, *adj.* Moorish, *sb.* morris-dance, Sh., ND; morisco, SkD; a morris-dancer, SkD. *Comb.*: morris-dance, Moorish dance, Sh.; morrys-daunce, HD; morres-dauncers, morris-dancers, HD; morrice-

140

bells, bells for a morris-dance, S3;
morris-pike, a large pike (weapon), HD,
Sh.—Late Lat. *moriscus*, Moorish.
morsel, *sb.* morsel, PP, B; **mossel**, SkD;
mussel, W, W2, PP; **musselle**, Voc.—
AF. *morsel*; Lat. *morsellum*, a little bit; dimin.
of *morsus*. Cf. **mosel**.
mortifie, *v.* to mortify, to produce change by
chemical action, C3.—OF. *mortifier*; Lat.
mortificare.
mortreux, *sb.* messes of pounded meat, C;
mortrewes, CM, PP; **mortrwys**, Prompt.;
mortrws, Cath.; **mortesse**, Palsg.; **mor-
trels**, PP; **mortreuus**, (mortrews), PP,
Prompt. (*n*) Voc.; **mortrus**, Voc.—OF.
mortreux, see Ducange (s.v. *mortea*), connected with Lat. *mortarium*, a morter.
morther[1], *sb.* murder; **morthir**, PP;
morthre, C; **morder**, PP; **mordre**, C.—
AS. *morðor*; cf. Low Lat. *murdrum*.
morther[2], *v.* to murder, PP, S2; **morthre**,
C; **mordre**, C, C2; **murther**, C.
mortherer, *sb.* murderer, PP; **mordrer**, C,
C2.
morwe, *sb.* morrow, the morning, PP, S2,
C2, C3; **marewe**, S2; **morow**, S3. *Phr.*: **to
morwe**, *cras*, Voc. *Comb.*: **morȝe-mete**,
morning meal, S; **morewtid**, morrow, W;
morowtid, W; **morutid**, W2; **morȝeue**,
dos nuptialis, SD; **moryve**, Prompt.
morwen, *sb.* morn, morrow, S, PP;
morȝen, SD. *Phr.*: **to morwen**, S.—AS.
morgen, Goth. *maurgins*.
morwenynge, *sb.* morning, PP, C2;
morwnynge, S2; **moreȝening**, S.
mose, *sb.* titmouse, S.—AS. *máse*, see SkD.
(s.v. *titmouse*).
mosel, *sb.* muzzle, nose of an animal, C,
CM.—OF. *musel* (now *museau*): Prov. *mursel*:
OF. **morsel*. See **morsel**, and cf. **musen**.
mosell, *v.* to muzzle, SkD; **moosel**, Manip.
moskles, *sb. pl.* mussels (shell fish), S2; see
muskylle.
most, *adj. superl.* greatest, chief, PP, S2;
moste, S, PP; **mooste**, W2; **mast**, S2;
maste, S2; **maist**, B; **mayst**, B; **mest**, S,
S2; **meste**, C2; **meast**, S. *Comb.*: **meste
del**, the greatest part, S2.—AS. *mǽst*.
mot, *1 pr. s.* may, must, S, C2, C3, PP;
mote, S, PP; **most**, *2 pr. s.*, must, S, S2;
mot, *2 pr. s. subj.*, S3; **mot**, *pr. s.*, can, must,
S, S2, S3; **moot**, S2, C; **moȝt**, S2; **moten**,
pl., S, PP; **mote**, S2, PP; **moste**, *pt. s.*, was
obliged, S, S2, C3, PP; *pl.*, S, S2; **most**, S2,
PP; **moist**, *pt. s.*, S3.—AS. *mót*, 2 pr. s.,
móst, pl. *móton*, pt. s. *móste*.
mote[1], *sb.* moat, *agger, fossa*, P; a pond,
Manip.; castle, palace, WA; **moote**,

Prompt.; **mot**, PP.—OF. *mote*, embank-
ment, also *motte* (Cotg.).
mote[2], *v.* to summon before a *mot* (court), to
plead, dispute, discuss a law case, PP, S2;
mootyn, Prompt.; **motien**, S.—AS. *mótian*
(Leo). See **moot**.
mote[3], *sb.* note on the huntsman's horn,
CM; **moot**, HD; **mot**, S3 (7. 16).—OF.
mot, 'the note winded by an huntsman on
his horn' (Cotg.).
motlè, *sb.* motley, a dress of many colours,
Prompt.; **motley**, Sh., ND; **motteleye**, C;
mottelay, Cath.—OF. *mattele*, clotted,
curdled (Cotg.).
motoun, *sb.* a gold coin called a 'mutton' or
sheep, P; **mutoun**, S2, PP; **moton**, PP.—
OF. *mouton*; Late Lat. *multonem* (Ducange).
motyf, *sb.* motive, incitement, S2, C3; **motif**,
motion, argument, question, subject, PP.—
OF. *motif* (Cotg.); Late Lat. *motivum*
(Ducange).
moucte, *pt. s.* might, S; **mought**, S3; see
mahte.
moun, *1 pr. pl.* may, S; see **mæi**[1].
mountance, *sb.* amount, space, duration,
C3, CM; **mountouns**, S2, HD.—AF.
mountance, OF. *montance*; see Ducange (s.v.
montare).
mounte, *sb.* mount, PP; **mont**, S2; **munt**,
S; **munte**, *dat.*, S.—AS. *munt*; Lat. *montem*;
cf. AF. *munt*, *mont*, *mount*.
mountein, *sb.* mountain, PP; **montaine**,
S2; **montain**, S2; **montaigne**, C2;
mountaigne, PP.—AF. *mountaygne*; Late
Lat. *montanea*, 'locus montanus' (Ducange).
mounten, *v.* to mount, PP.—OF. *monter*;
Late Lat. *montare*.
mountenaunce, *sb.* amount; **mownten-
awnce**, Prompt.; **mountenance**, S3, ND.
See **mountance**.
mour, *sb.* mulberry-tree, H; see **more**[1].
mournen, *v.* to mourn, S2, PP; **mornen**,
PP, S; **murnen**, S; **morenen**, *pr. pl.*, W2;
morenyden, *pt. pl.*, W2.—AS. *murnan*.
mournyng, *pr. p.* and *adj.* mourning, PP;
moorning, C, C3; **mornyng**, S2.
mous, *sb.* mouse, C, PP; **mus**, S; **muse**, *dat.*,
S; **mys**, *pl.*, P; **mees**, PP; *Comb.*: **mows-
falle**, mousetrap, Prompt.; **muse-stoch**,
mousetrap, S.—AS. *mús*.
moutin, *v.* to mew, moult, cast feathers,
Prompt., mowtyn, Prompt., HD; moult,
Sh.; **moutes**, *pr. s.*, S2, SkD.—Lat. *mutare*.
Cf. **mewen**.
mouth, *sb.* mouth, face, PP, W2; **muð**, S;
mudh, S. *Comb.*: **muð-freo**, mouth-free,
S.—AS. *múð*: Goth. *munþs*; cf. OHG. *mund*
(Otfrid); see Sievers, 30.

mouthen, *v.* to talk about, P; **mouthed**, *pt. s.*, P.

mouȝt, *sb.* moth, W; **mouȝte**, W2, SkD; **moghte**, Cath.—ONorth. and AS. *mohðe* (Mt. 6. 20).

mouen, *v.* to move, suggest, S; **moeue**, PP; **meuen**, PP; **meuez**, *pr. s.*, S2; **moeued**, *pt. s.*, C3; **moeuyng**, *pr. p.*, S2, C3; **meued**, *pp.*, S3.—AF. *mover*, OF. *muveir*, *movoir*, *moveir*; Lat. *mouēre*.

mow, *v.* to be able, H; **mown**, Prompt.; **mugen**, S.—AS. **mugan* (not found), see Sievers, 424. See **mæi**[1].

mowe[1], *sb.* kinswoman, S; **mow**, sister-in-law, Prompt.; **moȝe**, S; **maȝe**, SD.—AS. *máge*.

mowe[2], *sb.* a grimace, CM, Prompt.; **moe**, Cotg., WW (p. 407); **mow**, WW.—OF. *mouë* (Cotg.).

mowen[1], *v.* to make a grimace, Cath.; **mowyn**, Prompt. *Der.*: **mowing**, grimacing, S3; **mowyng**, W2; *cachinnatus*, Cath.; **mouwyng**, W2.

mowen[2], *v.* to mow, reap, S, PP.—AS. *máwan*.

mowtard, *sb.* moulting bird, Prompt. See **moutin**.

mowtynge, *sb.* moulting-season, PP, Prompt.

moyste, *adj.* fresh, new, C2, C3, SkD; **moyst**, *humidus*, Prompt.; **moste**, moist, Cath.—OF. *moiste*, damp, moist; Late Lat. **mustius*, **musteus* (see BH, § 74, also Roland, p. 420); from Lat. *mustum*. See **must**.

moystin, *v.* to make moist, W, Prompt.; **moyste**, Voc.; **moysted**, *pp.*, S2, Cath. (*n*).

moystnesse, *sb.* moistness, *humor*, Voc.

moysture, *sb.* moisture, Prompt.; **mostour**, *maditas*, Cath.

moȝe, *sb.* kinswoman, S; see **mowe**[1].

muche, *adj.* and *adv.* great, much, S, S2, PP; **moche**, S, S2, C2, PP; **miche**, S2; **myche**, S, W, W2. *Comb.*: **muchedel**, a great part, S2; **mychefold**, manifold, W.

muchel, *adj.* and *adv.* great, much, numerous, S, C2, PP; **mochel**, S2, C2, C3, PP; **mochele**, S; **michel**, S; **micel**, S; **mikel**, S, S2; **mycel**, S; **mykel**, S2, P; **mukel**, S, S2; **mucele**, S; **mikle**, S2; **mekill**, S3. *Der.*: **muchelhede**, greatness, SD; **mykelhede**, S2; **mychilnesse**, greatness, W2.—AS. *micel* (*mycel*): Goth. *mikils*.

muchelin, *v.* to magnify, S; **muclien**, S; **mucli**, S; **mikeland**, *pr. p.*, S2; **milkeled**, *pp.*, S2.—AS. *myclian*: Goth. *mikiljan*.

mud, *sb.* mud, Prompt.; **moode**, S3; **mudde**, S2 (13. 407), Cath., Manip.—Cf. OLG. *mudde*, see SkD.

mudly, *adj.* muddy, H.

mugen, *v.* to be able, S; see **mæi**[1].

mught, *pt. s.* might, S2, H; **muhte**, S; see **mahte**.

muk, *sb.* muck, filthy lucre, PP; see **mok**.

mukel, *adj.* great, S, S2; see **muchel**.

mull, *sb.* mould, rubbish, S2, Cath. (*n*); **molle**, Cath.; **mol**, Cath. (*n*); **mul**, Cath. (*n*).—Cf. Du. *mul*. See **molde**.

mullok, *sb.* rubbish, C3; **mollocke**, Cath. (*n*).

multiplicacioun, *sb.* multiplying, i.e. the art of alchemy, C3.

multiplye, *v.* to make gold and silver by the arts of alchemy, C3; **multeplie**, to increase, PP.—OF. *multiplier*; Lat. *multiplicare*.

mum; see **mom**.

mun, *pr. s.* must, S2, H; see **mon**[1].

munec, *sb.* monk, S; see **monk**.

munen, *v.* to remind, to be mindful, S; see **mynne**[2].

muneȝing, *sb.* commemoration, S.

mungen, *v.* to remember, PP; see **mengen**[1].

mungunge, *sb.* remembrance, reminding, S; **munegunge**, S; **muneȝing**, S.—AS. *mynegung*.

munne, *v.* to relate, mention, remind, S: see **mynne**[2].

munstral, *sb.* minstrel, S2; see **mynstral**.

munt, *sb.* mount, S; see **mounte**.

munten, *v.* to think, to purpose, S2; **myntis**, *pr. s.* points, WA; **munte**, *pt. s.*, S3; **mint**, S; **i-munt**, *pp.*, S; **i-mint**, S; **i-ment**, S.—AS. *(ge)myntan*. See **mynde**.

murcnen, *v.* to murmur; **murrcnesst**, *2 pr. s.*, S.—AS. *murcnian* (Leo).

murne, *adj.* sad, S, HD.—Cf. AS. *murnan*, to mourn.

murnen, *v.* to mourn, S, WA; see **mournen**.

murnyn, *sb.* mourning, B.

murrin, *sb.* murrain, WW; see **moreyne**.

murthe, *sb.* mirth, joy, PP, S; **murth**, PP; **murhðe**, S; **murȝþe**, S; **myrthe**, PP; **mirthe**, C; **merthe**, PP; **muirth**, PP; **murþhes**, *pl.*, merrymakings, amusements, PP, S2; **merthes**, G.—AS. *myrð*, *mirhð*, from *merg*. See **mery**.

mury(e), *adj.* merry, S, C; see **mery**.

murȝen, *v.* to make merry, SD; **murgeþ**, *pr. pl.*, S2.

mus, *sb.* mouse, S; see **mous**.

musard, *sb.* a dreamy fellow, HD, Bardsley; **musarde**, CM.—OF. *musart*.

muse, *sb.* dreaming vacancy, Spenser.

musen, *v.* to ponder, wonder, PP, C3, WA, ND.—OF. *muser*, to muse, study, linger about a matter, to sniff as a hound, from **muse*, a muzzle, nose of an animal (whence F. *museau*); Lat. *morsus*. For F. *-u-* from an orig. Lat. *-or-* cf. OF. *jus* from Late Lat.

jūsum, Lat. *deorsum*, and F. *sus* from Lat. *sūsum*, *seorsum*, see Apfelstedt, § 43, and Constans (glossary). Cf. **mosel**.

muskylle, *sb.* mussel, a shell-fish, Cath.; **muscles**, *pl.*, PP; **moskles**, S2.—AF. *muskeles*, pl., OF. *muscle*; Lat. *musculum* (acc.), dimin. of *mus*, mouse; cf. AS. *musclan scel* (Voc.).

mussel, *sb.* morsel, W, W2; see **morsel**.

must, *sb.* new wine, W, W2.—Lat. *mustum* (Vulg.). Cf. **moyste**.

mustour, *sb.* dial, clock, WA.—Cf. F. *montre* (Brachet).

mute, *v.* to dung (used of birds), SkD, WW, ND; **meuted**, *pp.*, WW.—OF. *mutir* (Cotg.), *esmeutir* (Cotg.), *esmeltir*, (Littré); of Teutonic origin, cf. ODu. *smelten*, to smelt, liquefy; cf. It. *smaltare*, to mute as a hawk (Florio). Cf. **amellen**.

mutoun; see **motoun**.

muwen, *pr. pl.* may, S; **mu3en**, S; see **mæi**[1].

mwre, *sb.* moor, S2; see **more**[2].

mydge, *sb.* midge, H (Ps. 104. 29); **midge**, Manip.; **myge**, gnat, *culex*, Voc., Cath.; **myghe**, S3.—AS. *mycg* (Voc.).

myghte[1], *pt. s.* could, PP; **my3te**, S2; see **mahte**.

myghte[2], *sb.* might, power, PP; **mi3t**, PP, S; **miht**, S, S2, PP; **my3t**, S2; **myhte**, S; **mi3te**, S; **mightes**, *pl.*, powers, virtues, S2; **myhte**, S.—AS. *miht*.

myghtful, *adj.* powerful, PP; **mihtful**, PP; **mi3tful**, PP; **my3tful**, PP; **my3tuolle**, S2.

myghtfulnes, *sb.* strength, S2.

myghty, *adj.* mighty, SD; **ma3ty**, S2; **mæhti**, S; **magti**, S; **mihti**, S; **michti**, S; **mi3thi**, S2; **myghtely**, *adv.*, CM.—AS. *meahtig*.

myht, *2 pr. s.* mayest; see **mæi**[1].

myke, *sb.* the crutches of a boat, which sustain the main-boom or mast when lowered, S2.—Cf. Swed. *mick*, a crutch (sea-term).

mylle, *sb.* mill, Prompt. *Comb.*: **mylle-stone**, mill-stone, Prompt.; **myl-ston**, Voc.; **melstan**, S; **myln-stoon**, W; **mulle-stones**, *pl.*, PP.—AS. *myln* (Voc.); Lat. *molina*.

mylnere, *sb.* miller, PP; **mylner**, PP; **mulnere**, PP; **melner**, PP; **mellere**, PP, C.

mynde, *sb.* memory, remembrance, mention, PP, S2, S3, W, W2, CM, C2, Cath.;

mende, Prompt.; **mind**, memory, mind, Sh.—AS. *(ge)mynd*; cf. OHG. *gimunt*, memory (Tatian). See **mynne**[1].

mynen, *v.* to mine, S2, W, W2.—OF. *miner* cf. Late Lat. *minare* (Ducange).

myne-ye-ple, *sb.* (?), S3 (7. 62, *note*).

mynne[1], *sb.* memory, SD; **min**, S2.—Icel. *minni*, memory; cf. AS. *myne*, mind. Cf. **mynde**.

mynne[2], *v.* to remember, mention, PP, S2, HD; **munne**, S; **munyen**, S; **munen**, S; **mynand**, *pr. p.*, H; **mines**, *2 pr. s.*, S2; **mined**, *pp.*, S2.—AS. *(ge)mynnan (gemynian)*, to remember; also *(ge)munan*.

mynnyng-day, *sb.* the day of memory of the dead, HD.

mynour, *sb.* miner, C, SkD, PP; **minour**, PP.—AF. *minour*; Late Lat. *minatorem* (Ducange). See **mynen**.

mynstral, *sb.* minstrel, PP, Prompt.; **minstral**, PP; **munstral**, PP, S2; **minstrales**, *pl.*, C2; **menestrales**, PP.—AF. *menestral*; Late Lat. *ministralem*, a servant (Brachet).

mynstralcie, *sb.* music, minstrelsy, PP, C; **minstralcye**, C2; **menstralcye**, C; **mynstracie**, PP; **minstracie**, PP; **mynstrasye**, Prompt., S2.—AF. *mynstralcye*.

mynstre, *sb.* minster, monastery, S, PP; **minstre**, S; **ministre**, S2; **minnstre**, the Jewish temple, S.—AS. *mynster*; Church Lat. *monasterium*; Gr. μοναστήριον.

myrie, *adj.* pleasant, W2; see **mery**.

myrk[1], *adj.* dark, S2, H; see **merke**[1].

myrk[2], *v.* to darken, H.

mys-, *prefix*; *see both* **mis-** *and* **mes-**.

mysteir, *v.* to be necessary, B; **mysters**, *pr. s.* is needful, WA.

myster[1], *sb.* trade, occupation, PP; see **mester**[1].

myster[2], *sb.* need, want, C, WA, B; see **mester**[2].

mystir, *adj.* lacking, needful, B.

mystyrit, *pp.* injured by loss (of blood), S3.

mysylle; see **mizzle**.

myteyne, *sb.* cuff, glove, Prompt., S3; **miteyn**, C3; **mytane**, Cath.; **myttan**, Voc.—OF. *mitaine* (Cotg.); cf. Low Lat. *mitana* (Ducange).

my3t, *sb.* power, S2; see **myghte**[2].

my3te, *pt. s.* might, S2; see **mahte**.

N

na[1], *adv.* not, S; see **no**.

na[2], *adj.* no, S; see **nan**.

nabben, *v.* not to have; **naue**, *1 pr. s.*, PP; **nauest**, *2 pr. s.*, S; **nauestu**, thou hast not, S; **nastu**, S; **naueþ**, *pr. s.*, S; **naðd**, S, PP, S2; **neþ**, S2; **nabbeþ**, *pl.*, S2; **naue**, S2; **nadde**, *pt. s.*, S; **nad**, PP; **nedde**, PP, S2; **nauedes**, *2 pt. s.*, S; **næueden**, *pl.*, S.—AS. *nabban* (= *ne habban*).

nabod, *for* **ne abod**, abode not, S. See **abiden**.

nacioun, *sb.* nation, C; **nacion**, Cath., WA.—AF. *nacioun, naciun*; Lat. *nationem*.

naddren, *pl.* adders, S; **nadres**, S; see **nedder**.

nadrinke, *for* **ne adrinke**, let (it) not drown, S.

naht[1], *sb.* night, SD; see **nyght**.

naht[2], *adv.* not, S; see **nought**[1].

nahte, *pt. s.* had not, S; see **owen**[1].

naked, *adj.* naked, bare, undefended by body-armour, PP, C3; **naket**, PP, S; **nakid**, S2; **nakit**, S2. *Phr.*: **in naked bedde**, *au lict couché tout nud*, Palsg., HD, ND.—AS. *nacod*; cf. OHG. *nakot* (Otfrid), Icel. *naktr*.

naken, *v.* to lay bare, SkD (s.v. *naked*).—ONorth. *(ge)nacian* (Mk. 2. 4).

naker, *sb.* kettle-drum, S2, C, HD.—OF. *nacre*, also *nagaire, nacaire, naquaire, anacaire* (cf. Byzantine Gr. ἀνάκαρον); a word borrowed from the Turks; cf. Kurdish *nakára*, see Ducange, Diez.

naknen, *v.* to strip; **nacnes**, *pr. s.*, S; **nakned**, *pp.*, HD.

nale; *in phr.* **atte nale** for **at ten ale** (**at þen ale**), at the ale, P. See **ale**.

nam[1], *1 pr. s.* am not, S, S2, P, C; **næm**, S; **nart**, *2 pr. s.*, S, S2; **nis**, *pr. s.*, is not, S, C, C2; **nys**, S; **nas**, *pt. s.*, S, S2, HD, PP; **nes**, S, S2; **nere**, *pl.*, S, S2, C; **neoren** S; **nare**, S.—ONorth. *nam* (= *ne am*).

nam[2], *pt. s.* took, S; see **nimen**.

nameliche, *adv.* especially, S2, C; see **nomeliche**.

nan, *adj.* none, no, S; see **non**.

nap, *sb.* cup, S; **neppe**, *dat.*, S.—AS. *hnæp* (Voc.); cf. OHG. *hnapf*, OF. *hanap* (Bartsch), Low Lat. *nappus* (Ducange).

nappen, *v.* to nap, slumber, nod, PP, C3, W. *Der.*: **napping**, slumber, W2; **nappy**, sleep-inducing, S3, ND.—AS. *hnæppian*.

napron, *sb.* apron, SkD; **naprun**, Prompt.—OF. *naperon*, from *nape*, a cloth; Low Lat. *napa*; Lat. *mappa* (Punic word).

narde, *sb.* nard, an unguent, W.—Lat. *nardus* (Vulg.); Gr. ναρδός (Persian word).

narwe, *adj.* narrow, C; **narewe**, S; **nareu**, S; **narwȝ**, W; **nearowe**, S; **neruwe**, S; **narwe**, *adv.*, closely, PP.—AS. *nearu*, adv. *nearwe*.

nas, *pt. s.* was not, S, S2; see **nam**[1].

nat, *for* **ne at**, nor at, S2.

natiuite, *sb.* nativity, S2, C2.—OF. *nativité* (Cotg.); Lat. *natiuitatem*.

natte, *sb.* mat, *scorium, buda*, Voc., Cath.; **natt**, HD, Voc.; **nat**, Palsg.—OF. *natte* (Cotg.); Late Lat. *natta*; Lat. *matta* (probably a variant of *mappa*). See **napron**.

naðd, *pr. s.* has not, S, PP, S2; see **nabben**.

nauȝty, *adj.* having nothing, very poor, P. See **nought**[2].

naue, nauest; see **nabben**.

nauele, *sb.* navel, PP; **nawle**, W2; **naule**, PP; **navyle**, Voc.; **nawelle**, Voc.; **nawylle**, Voc.—AS. *nafela*.

nay, *adv.* nay, PP, S3, WA; **nai**, S, S2. *Phr.*: **nay whan**, nay when? i.e. not so, when (will you do it), S3; **withoute nay**, without denial, G; **it is no nay**, there is no denying it, G, C2.—Cf. Icel. *nei*.

nayl, *sb.* nail, finger-nail, S, C2; **nayle**, Voc.; **neil**, S; **nayles**, *pl.*, PP.—AS. *nægel* cf. Icel. *nagl*.

naylen, *v.* to nail, Cath.; **naȝlen**, S; **nailen**, PP, C2.

nayten, *v.* employ, use, S2, WA.—Icel. *neyta*; cf. AS. *notian*; weak verb, from Icel. *njóta*; cf. AS. *néotan*. Cf. **noten**.

naytly, *adv.* neatly, fit for use, S2.—From Icel. *neytr*, fit for use.

naytyn, *v.* to deny, Prompt., SD, HD.—Icel. *neita*. Cf. **niten**[1].

ne, *adv.* and *conj.* not, nor, S, S2, S3.—AS. *ne*, not, nor.

neb, *sb.* face, S, HD. *Der.*: **nebsseft**, face, appearance, presence, S2; **nebscheft**, SD.—AS. *nebb*, beak, face (OET).

nece, *sb.* niece; PP; **neipce**, granddaughter, S3; **neece**, WW (p. 417).—AF. *nece, niece*; Late Lat. *neptia*; in the place of Lat. *neptis*, a granddaughter, a niece; see BH, § 32.

nedde, *pt. s.* had not, S; see **nabben**.

nedder, *sb.* adder, snake, H; **neddyr**, Cath., Prompt.; **neddere**, Cath. (*n*); **neddre**, S; **nedyr**, Voc.; **nedyre**, Voc.; **naddren**, *pl.*, S; **nadres**, S; **nedris**, HD; **neddren**, S. *Comb.*: **nedyrcopp**, spider, Voc.—AS. *nædre*: Goth. *nadrs*; cf. OHG. *natrá* (Tatian).

144

nede, *sb.* need, peril, business, also as *pred.*
adj. necessary, needful, C2, W, PP; **neode**,
PP, S; **niede**, S; **neod**, S, S2, PP; **ned**, S;
need, C2; **neid**, B; **nedes**, *pl.*, S2, PP;
nede, *adv.*, necessarily, S, C2, PP; **nedes**,
needs, of necessity, S2, C, PP; **nedis**, W;
neodes, S2, PP; **needely**, C; **nedelich**,
W. *Der.*: **nedful**, needy, necessary, S;
nedfol, S2, PP; **neodful**, S, PP; **needles**,
needlessly, C2; **neidwais**, of necessity, S2,
B.—OMerc. *néd* (VP), AS. *nýd*: Goth. *nauþs*;
cf. OS. *nód*, OHG. *nót* (Tatian).
neden, *v.* to force, compel, to need, S; **neid**,
B; **nedeþ**, *pr. s.*, there is need, it is necessary, PP, C; **neodeþ**, S, PP.—AS. *nédan*
(OET).
nedle, *sb.* needle, C3, P; **nedele**, PP; **nedel**,
PP; **nelde**, PP; **neelde**, PP.—*Der.*: **nedel-
ere**, needle-seller, PP; **neldere**, PP.—AS.
nédl: OHG. *nádela*, also *náldá* (Tatian).
neer, *adj. comp.* nearer, C2; see **nerre**.
neet, *sb.* ox, cattle, PP, S, S2, C; **net**, S;
niatt, S; **nowt**, S; **nete**, H, PP. *Comb.*:
neet-hirde, *sb.* neat-herd, Prompt.—AS.
néat, ox, cattle: Icel. *naut*; cf. OHG. *nóz*,
'jumentum' (Tatian).
nefen, *v.* to name, S2; see **nevenen**.
ne-for-thi, *adv.* nevertheless, S2.—AS. *ne for
ðý*.
neghen, *num.* nine, S2; see **nyne**.
nehlechen, *v.* to approach, S; **neolechin**,
S.—AS. *néalécan* from *néah*. See **neih**.
neih, *adv.* nigh, nearly, almost, PP, S; **neyh**,
G; **neh**, S, S2; **ney**, PP, S; **neȝ**, S, PP; **negh**,
PP; **ny**, PP, Prompt.; **niȝ**, W; **nyȝ**, W, W2;
neigh, S2; **neiȝe**, P; **neighe**, PP; **nyȝe**, PP.
Comb.: **neyhebour**, neighbour, G; **neighe-
bor**, C2; **neighburgh**, S2; **nehgebur**, S;
neihhond, close at hand, S.—AS. *néah*; cf.
OHG. *náh* (Tatian).
neihen, *v.* to be nigh to, to approach, PP;
neighen, PP; **neghen**, PP, H, S2; **neiȝen**,
PP, W; **neȝen**, S2; **neȝh**, S2; **neyȝhen**,
S2.—AS. *néhwan*: Goth. *nehjan*, from *nehva*,
nigh. See **neih**.
neipce, *sb.* granddaughter, S3; see **nece**.
neither, *neg. pron.* and *conj.* neither, SD;
neyþer, S; **noither**, P; **neithyr**, Prompt.;
nethir, not, W.—AS. *ne + ǽghwæðer*. See
eiþer.
neiȝ, *in phr.* **no neiȝ** *for* **non eiȝ**, i.e. no eggs,
S2. See **ey**.
nekke, *sb.* neck, S, C, PP. *Comb.*; **nekke-
boon**, neck-bone, S2, C2; **nekke-bon**,
PP.—AS. *hnecca* (OET.).
nelle, *1* and *3 pr. s.* will not, PP, S; **nell**, S;
nel, S; **nele**, S; **nulle**, S, PP; **nule**, S; **nul**,
PP, S2; **nile**, S, PP; **nil**, PP, C2; **nullich**, I
will not, S; **nulich**, S; **nuly**, S2; **nult**, *2 pr.*

s., wilt not, S; **neltu**, thou wilt not, S;
neltow, P; **nultu**, S; **nelleð**, *pl.*, S;
nolleþ, S2; **nollen**, PP; **nulleþ**, S; **nulen**,
S; **nolde**, *pt. s.*, would not, S, PP; **nalde**,
S.—AS. *nyllan*. See **wille**[1].
nemnen, *v.* to name, mention, call, S, S2,
S3; **nempnen**, PP, S2.—AS. *nemnan*: Goth.
namnjan. Cf. **nevenen**.
neod, neodes; see **nede**.
neodeþ, *pr. s.* is needful, S; see **neden**.
neomen, *v.* to take, receive, S; see **nimen**.
neomenye, *sb.* feast of the new moon, W.—
Lat. *neomenia* (Vulg.); Gr. νουμηνία, νεο-
μηνία.
neowcin, *sb.* harm, injury, S.—Icel. *nauðsyn*,
need, impediment, see SkD (s.v. *essoin*, p.
802).
neowe, *adj.* new, S; see **newe**.
neowel, *adj.* deep; **niwel**, SD; **nuel**, SD.
Der.: **neowelnesse**, the deep, abyss, S.—
AS. *neowol, néol, niwol*, prone, deep (GET,
Grein).
neoȝe, *num.* nine, S2; see **nyne**.
neppe, *sb.* turnip, *rapa*, Voc.; **nepe**, Alph.—
AS. *nép*; Lat. *nápus*.
nercotyk, *sb.* narcotic, C.—Late Lat. *narco-
ticum* [*medicamen*], (SB); Gr. ναρκωτικός,
benumbing.
nere[1], *sb.* kidney, Voc.; **neere**, Prompt.;
neres, *pl.*, reins, H; **nerys**, *ren*, Voc. *Comb.*:
kidnere, kidney, SkD; **kydney**, Voc.—
Icel. *nýra*, pl. *nýru*: OHG. *niero*; cf. Gr.
νεφρός see Curtius, ii. 93.
nere[2], *pt. pl.* were not, S, S2, C; see **nam**[1].
nerre, *adj.* and *adv. comp.* nearer, H, PP;
narre, H; **nere**, PP; **ner**, PP, C2, C; **nier**,
S; **neer**, W, C2. *Comb.*: **nerhand**, nearly,
H.—AS. *néarra* (*néara*), adj.; *néar*, adv.
neruwe, *adj.* narrow, S; see **narwe**.
nes, *pt. s.* was not, S, S2; see **nam**[1].
nesche, *adj.* tender, soft, S; **nesshe**, S;
neshe, Voc.; **nesh**, ND; **nasche**, S2;
neische, W2; **nesse**, HD. *Der.*: **ness-
hede**, tenderness, S2.—AS. *hnesce*.
neschen, *v.* to soften, SD; **nesshen**, S;
nessen, H; **neyssen**, H.—AS. *hnescian*.
nese, *sb.* nose, S, S2, Prompt., PP, Voc.;
neose, PP; **nose**, Voc.; **noose**, WA. *Comb.*:
nosebleed, the plant yarrow, Alph.; **nose-
blede**, *millifolium*, Alph.; **nese-hende**,
purulus, Voc.; **nese-thirl**, nostril, H; **nes-
thyrylle**, Voc.; **nose-thirl**, W2; **nose-
thurl**, C; **noyss-thyrlys**, *pl.*, S3.—AS.
nosu; cf. OHG. *nasa*; see Kluge, and Sievers,
274.
nesen, *v.* to sneeze, Prompt.; **neese**, Prompt.;
WW.—Cf. Icel. *hnjósa*.
nest[1], *adj.* and *adv. superl.* next, nearest, PP, S,
S2; **neist**, S2; **nixte**, S; **nexte**, C, PP;

nexst, S, S2. *Comb.*: **nestfald**, nearest, S.—AS. *níehsta*, adj.; *néhst* adv.

nest[2], *sb.* nest, PP; **nestes**, *pl.*, PP. *Der.*: **nestlingis**, nestlings, PP.—AS. *nest*; cf. Lat. *nīdus* (for *nisdus*), OIr. *net*; see Brugmann, § 590.

nesten, *pt. pl.* knew not, S; see **not**.

nestlen, *v.* to build nests, S2.

nette, *sb.* net, Cath., Manip.; **nett**, Prompt., Voc., W (p. 234); **net**, W (p. 123); **nettes**, *pl.*, C2.—AS. *nett*: Goth. *nati*, see Sievers, 247.

neþ, *pr. s.* has not, S2; see **nabben**.

neðen, *adv.* from below, S.—AS. *neoðan*, beneath.

neðer, *adj. comp.* nether, S; see **niþer**.

neue, *sb.* nephew, S.—AS. *nefa*.

neuenen, *v.* to name, S2, C3, H, HD; **nefen**, S2. *Der.*: **neuening**, naming, S.— Icel. *nefna*, (from *nafn*, name): Goth. *namnjan*, from *namn-* stem of *namo*, name. Cf. **nemnen**.

neuere, *adv.* never, PP, S; **neure**, S, PP; **næuere**, S; **næure**, S; **neauer**, S; **nauere**, S; **nefre**, S; **nefer**, S; **nafre**, S; **neare**, S3; **nere**, W; **ner**, HD, S2. *Comb.*: **neuer a del**, not a bit, C3; **neuremore**, nevermore, S; **neuer the neer**, none the nearer, C3; **neuer the latter**, nevertheless, H.—AS. *néfre*.

neueu, *sb.* nephew, S2; **nevew**, C2; **nevo**, B.—AF. *nevu*, nephew, grandson; Lat. *nepótem*.

newe, *adj.* new, PP, C2; **neowe**, S; **nywe**, S; **niwe**, S2; **newe**, *adv.*, newly, anew, PP, C; **newly**, newly, again, PP; **nuly**, S3. *Comb.*: **newefangel**, catching at novelty, C2; **newefangelnes**, fondness for novelty, C2, S3.—AS. *neowe*, *niwe*.

newen, *v.* renew, S, S2, PP.—AS. *niwian*.

newte, *sb.* newt, Prompt.; **ewte**, Prompt. See **evete**.

ney, *adv.* nigh, nearly, S; **neȝ**, S; see **neih**.

neynd, *ord.* ninth, S2; see **nyne**.

neȝen, *v.* to neigh, SkD. *Der.*: **neiyng**, *sb.* a neighing, W2.—AS. *hnǽgan*; cf. Icel. *hneggja*.

niatt, *sb. pl.* cattle, S; see **neet**.

nich, *adv.* no, S.—AS. *ne + ic*, I; see Sievers, 332.

nieþe, *ord.* ninth, S; see **nyne**.

nif, *for* **ne if**, if not, except; **nyf**, S2.

nifle, *sb.* trifle, HD, ND; **nyfles**, *pl.*, CM, Palsg.; **nines**, Cotg. (o.v. *nigories*). OF. *nifles*, trifles (Palsg.). Cf. **nivelen**.

nigard, *sb.* a niggard, a miser, PP; **nygard**, C, CM, PP; **nygarde**, PP, Palsg.; **nygart**, CM. Cf. **nygun**.

nigardie, *sb.* stinginess, SkD, HD; **nigardye**, CM; **nygardye**, CM.

night, **nigt**, **niht**; see **nyght**.

nigromancye, *sb.* magic, sorcery, PP; **nigramauncy**, S2; **nigramansy**, B; **nigromance**, Cath.—OF. *nigromance* (Bartsch); cf. Low Lat. *nigromantia* (Ducange); Late Lat. *necromantia*, necromancy; Gr. νεκρομαντεία, divination by communion with the dead.

niker, *sb.* water-sprite, SD; **nykyr**, siren, Prompt.; **nyckers**, *pl.*, SPD; **nykeren**, SPD (p. 255).—AS. *nicor*, a water-demon (Grein); cf. Icel. *nykr*, hippopotamus: OHG. *nichus*, 'crocodilus', see Grimm, Teut. M. p. 488.

nil, *pr. s.* will not, C2; see **nelle**.

nimen, *v.* to take, S, S2; **nymen**, PP; **nemen**, PP; **neomen**, S; **nam**, *pt. s.*, PP, G, S; **nom**, S, S2; **nem**, S2; **nome**, *2 pt. s.*, S, PP; **nomen**, *pl.* S, PP; **neme**, S; **numen**, *pp.*, seized, gone, S; **nummun**, S2; **nome**, S2. *Der.*: **niminge**, a taking, capture, S.—AS. *niman*, pt. nam (pl. *námon*), pp. *numen*.

nin, *for* **ne in**, nor in, C2.

nis, *pr. s.* is not, S, C, C2; see **nam**[1].

niseien, *pt. pl. for* **ne iseien**, saw not, S.

niste, *pt. s.* knew not, S; see **not**.

niswicst, *2 pr. s. for* **ne iswicst**, ceasest not, S.

niten[1], *v.* to refuse, S2, JD; **nyte**, JD; **nite**, *pp.*, WA.—Icel. *níta*, to deny. Cf. **naytyn**.

niten[2], *pr. pl.* know not, S; see **not**.

nið, *sb.* envy, malice, S. *Der.*: **niðful**, envious, S; **nyþful**, S.—AS. *níð*; cf. Goth. *neiþ*.

niðen, *v.* to envy, SD.—Icel. *níða*, to revile.

niðer, *adv.* below, S; *adj. comp.*, lower, S; **neðer**, S; **nethir**, B; **neðement**, *superl.*, lowest, SD. *Der.*: **neðerward**, downwards, SD.—AS. *niðer*, *nioðor*, downward, *neoðera*, lower, nether, SkD.

niðer-wenden, *v.* to go down, S.

niðing, *sb.* a coward, a niggard, S; **nything**, PP.—AS. *níðing*, a coward, outlaw; cf. Icel. *níðingr*.

niuelen, *v.* to snivel, S; **nyuelen**, PP.—Cf. OF. *nifler* (Cotg.). See **nifle**.

niwe, *adj.* new, S2; see **newe**.

niȝen, *num.* nine, S; see **nyne**.

no, *adv.* and *conj.* not, nor, no, S, S2, SkD, B, HD; **na**, S, S2, B. *Comb.*: **no but**, except, unless, S2, W; **no þe les**, not the less, nevertheless, S; **na þe les**, S, S2; **neoþeles**, S; **ne the les**, W; **na þe mo**, none the more, S2; **na war**, were it not for, but for, S2, B.—AS. *ná* (= *ne + á*).

noble[1], *adj.* noble, WA; **nobylle**, Cath.; **nobliche**, *adv.*, nobly, S2; **nobilly**, Cath.—AF. *noble*; Lat. *nobilem*.

noble², *sb.* noble, a coin so called worth 6*s.* 8*d.*, S3, C3, P, WA.—Cf. Late Lat. *nobile* (Ducange).

noblen, *v.* to ennoble, C3.

noblesse, *sb.* nobility, worthy behaviour, S2, C3; magnificence, honour, C2.—F. *noblesse*; OF. *noblesce*; Late Lat. *nobilitia*.

noblete, *sb.* nobleness, richness, S2.—OF. *noblete* (Bartsch); Lat. *nobilitatem*.

nobley, *sb.* splendour, grandeur, dignity, nobility, assembly of nobles, C3, HD; **nobleye**, S2, C2; **noblay**, H, B, WA; **nobelay**, HD; **nobillay**, B.—AF. *noblei*; Late Lat. *nobletum*; cf. OF. *noblet* (Bartsch).

nodle, *sb.* noddle, head, Prompt.; **nodyl**, Prompt.; **noddle**, Sh.

noff, *for* **ne off**, nor of, S.

nok, *sb.* nook, corner, piece, SD; **nuk**, B; **nwk**, B; **noke**, WA, HD. *Comb.*: **ferþyng noke**, a piece of a farthing, S2; **nookshotten**, spawned in a corner, Sh.

noke, *in phr.*: **atte noke** = atten oke, at the oak, S2. See **ook**.

nokke, *sb.* nock, notch, Prompt. *Comb.*: **nocke of a bow**, *oche de l'arc*, Palsg.

nol, *sb.* the head, the neck, W, W2; **noll**, WA; **nolle**, PP.—AS. *hnoll*, the top of the head.

nolde, *pt. s.* would not, S; see **nelle**.

nolleþ, *1 pr. pl.* we desire not, S2; see **nelle**.

nombre, *sb.* number, C; **nowmber**, Cath.; **nummer**, S3.—AF. *numbre, noumbre*; Lat. *numerum* (acc.).

nombren, *v.* to number, PP; **noumbren**, W2; **y-noumbred**, *pp.*, S3.—AF. *numbrer, noumbrer*; Lat. *numerare*.

nome¹, *sb.* pledge, hostage, S.—AS. *nám*, pledge seized (Schmid). See **nimen**.

nome², *sb.* name, PP, S, S2; **nam**, S2; **name**, Voc.—AS. *nama* (*noma*): Goth. *namo*.

nomeliche, *adv.* especially, S; **nameiche**, S2, C; **namelich**, P, S3; **namely**, PP.

non, *adj.* no one, none, no, PP, S, S2; **noon**, C2; **nan**, S, S2; **no**, PP, S; **na**, S, S2, B; **nane**, B; **nenne**, *acc.*, S. *Comb.*: **na kyn**, of no kind, B; **nakin**, B; **na kyn thing**, in no degree, B, S2; **na kyn wiss**, no way, B; **nan more**, no more, S; **na more**, S, S2; **na mare**, S2; **na mo**, P; **nammo**, S2; **no mo**, C; **na þing**, nothing, not at all, S; **no þing**, S2; **no whar**, nowhere, S; **no war**, S; **no hwer**, S; **nour**, S2; **nou hwider**, no whither, S; **no hwider**, S; **no wider wardes**, in no direction, S; **nones kunnes**, of no kind, S; **nones weis**, in no way, S; **nanes weis**, S.—AS. *nán*.

none, *sb.* the hour of 'none', i.e. the ninth hour, 3 p.m., also noon, mid-day, S, PP; **nowne**, S3; **noyne**, B; **non**, S, S2, PP;

noon, PP; **nones**, *pl.*, the noon-tide meal, PP. *Comb.*: **nun-mete**, a noon meal, Prompt.; **none-chenche**, a noon-drinking, nunchion, SkD; **noone-steede**, place of noon, meridian, S3; **non-tid**, noon-tide, S.—AS. *nón*; Lat. *nōna* (*hora*).

nones, *in phr.* **for þe nones** (for **for þen ones**), i.e. for the once, for the nonce, for the occasion, S2, S3, C2; **with the nones**, on the condition, G. See **oones**.

nonne, *sb.* nun, S2, C, C2, P; **nunne**, PP.—OF. *nonne*; Late Lat. *nonna*; cf. AS. *nunne*, in the Laws (Schmid).

nonnerie, *sb.* nunnery, S2.—OF. *nonnerie*.

noot, *1* and *3 pr. s.* know not, knows not, C; see **not**.

noppe¹, *sb.* nap (of cloth), Prompt., Cath.

noppe², *v.* to take the nap off, Cath.—AS. *hnoppian*, see Voc.

norice, *sb.* nurse, C, C2, SkD; **nurice**, SkD; **nursche**, W.—AF. *norice*; Lat. *nutricem*.

norischen, *v.* to nourish, PP; **norischi**, S2; **norishen**, C2; **nurischen**, W, W2; **nurschen**, PP; **norsshen**, PP.—OF. *noriss-*, stem of *norissant*, pp. of *norir*; Lat. *nutrire*.

norture, *sb.* good breeding, nurture, SkD, G.—AF. *norture, noriture*; Late Lat. *nutritura* (Ducange).

noselen¹, *v.* to thrust the nose in, to nuzzle; **nosyll**, Palsg.; **nousle**, Sh. See **nese**.

noselen², *v.* to cause children to put their noses in, to nurse, to rear up, to fondle closely; **nosell**, S3; **nousle**, Sh.; **nusled**, *pp.*, HD (s.v. *nousle*).

nose-thirl, *sb.* nostril, W2; see **nese**.

not, *1* and *3 pr. s.* know not, knows not, PP, S, S2; **noot**, PP, C; **note**, S3; **niten**, *pl.*, S; **nuten**, S; **nuste**, *pt. s.*, S, S2, PP; **nyste**, S2; **niste**, C2; **neste**, PP; **nyst**, *pl.*, PP; **nesten**, S.—AS. *nytan* (= *ne witan*). See **witen**¹.

notable, *adj.* well-known, conspicuous, notorious, dazzling, WW.—OF. *notable*; Lat. *notabilem*.

note¹, *sb.* nut, S, S2, Voc.; **nute**, SkD. *Comb.*: **not-heed**, a head like a nut, C; **note-muge**, nutmeg, S2, C2; **note-migge**, Prompt.; **nut-shale**, nutshell, S3.—AS. *hnutu*. {A better explanation of *not-heed* is 'with the hair of the head closely cut'. The verb *not* means to cut the hair close. 'Tondre', to sheer, clip, cut, powle, *nott*'. Cotgrave.}

note², *sb.* business, attempt, employment, labour, S2, WA; **not**, B.—AS. *notu*, use, employment.

noteful, *adj.* useful, serviceable, H.

noten, *v.* to enjoy, S; **notye**, PP.—AS. *notian*, to enjoy; cf. Icel. *neyta*. Cf. **nayten**.

147

nother, *neg. pron. and conj.* neither, nor, PP, S, S2, SkD; **nothir**, B; **nouðer**, S, S2; **nouþur**, PP; **nowðer**, S; **nawþer**, S2; **naðer**, S; **nor**, SkD.—AS. *náhwæðer (náwþer, náþer)*. See **oþer**[1].

nou, *adv.* now, PP, S, S2; **nu**, S, S2. *Comb.*: **nou a dayes**, now-a-days, PP; **now and now**, occasionally, C2.—AS. *nú*.

nouche, *sb.* clasp, buckle, jewel, CM, WA; **nowche**, C2, Prompt., SkD; **ouche**, WW; **owche**, SkD; **ouches**, *pl.*, broaches, *monilles*, Cotg., WW; **owchis**, WW.—OF. *nouche, nosche*, also *nusche* (Roland); OHG. *nuscha*.

nought[1], *neg. pron. and adv.* nothing, not, C; **nouht**, S, PP; **nouct**, S; **nouȝt**, PP; **noht**, S; **nocht**, S; **noȝt**, S, S2; **noght**, S2; **nout**, S, S2; **nowt**, S; **nowiȝt**, S; **nowiht**, S; **nacht**, S; **naht**, S; **nawiht**, S; **nawt**, S; **naut**, S; **naȝt**, S2; **naght**, S2; **nauȝt**, PP, S2; **naught**, C2; **nat**, PP, S2, C; **not**, W; **nogth**, H (Ps. 108. 25); **nouth**, S (18. 442); **nouthe**, HD. *Comb.*: **nocht forthi**, notwithstanding, nevertheless, S2; **noght forthi**, H; **nat for thy**, S2.—AS. *náwiht* (= *ne + áwiht*). See **ought**.

nought[2], *adj.* worthless, bad, naught, naughty, WW; **naught**, S3; **nauht**, PP. *Der.*: **naughty**, bad, WW, Sh.; **nauȝty**, having nothing, PP.

noumbles, *sb. pl.* entrails of a deer or beast, Palsg.; **nombles**, *burbilia*, Cath. (*n*) HD, Voc.; **nownbils**, Cath.; **nowmyllis**, Cath. *Phr.*: **numbles of a stag**, *nombles d'un cerf* Cotg.—OF. *nombles*, pl.; cf. Late Lat. *numbulus* for Lat. *lumbulus*, dimin. of *lumbus*, loin.

noumbren, *v.* to number, W2; see **nombren**.

noumpere, *sb.* umpire, arbitrator, SkD, P; **nowmpere**, Prompt.; **nompeyr**, PP; **nounpere**, PP; **owmpere**, Prompt.; **umpere**, SkD.—OF. *non per*, odd, not even; Lat. *non parem*.

nouthe, *adv.* now, C, P; **now þe**, S2; **nuðe**, S.—AS. *nú ðá*, now then.

nouelrie, *sb.* novelty, C2; **nouellerie**, S2.—OF. *novelerie*, from *novel*, novel, new.

nouys, *sb.* novice, C2, Voc.; **nouyce**, WW.—OF. *novice* (Cotg.); Lat. *nouicium*.

Nowel, *sb.* Christmas, CM; **Nowelle**, HD.—OF. *noël*; Lat. *natalem*.

nowt, *sb.* cattle, S. See **neet**.

noye, *sb.* suffering, annoyance, PP; **nuy**, PP, S2; **nwy**, S2. See **anoy**.

noyen, *v.* to annoy, to grieve, to harm, S2, W, P, H; **nuyen**, 2; **nwyen**, S2. See **anoyen**.

noyful, *adj.* hurtful; **noiful**, W2.

noynement; **a noynement** (for **an oynement**), an ointment, S2. See **oynement**.

noyous, *adj.* hurtful, annoying, W, WW (p. 421).

nul, nule, nulle; see **nelle**.

nultu, wilt not, S; see **nelle**.

numen, *pp.* taken, seized, S; see **nimen**.

nummer, *sb.* number, S3; see **nombre**.

nunne, *sb.* nun, PP; see **nonne**.

nurhð, *sb.* murmuring, S.

nurnen, *v.* to murmur, SD.—AS. *gnornian*, to mourn.

nursche, *sb.* nurse, W; see **norice**.

nurschen, *v.* to nourish, PP; see **norischen**.

nuste, *pt. s.* knew not, S, S2, PP; see **not**.

nuy, *sb.* annoyance, S2; see **noye**.

nyce, *adj.* foolish, C2, C3, PP; **nic-** PP, C2; **nise**, PP; **nyse**, S2; **nyss**, S3.—OF. *nice* (Bartsch); Lat. *nēscium*, ignorant, see Brachet, § 60.

nycete, *sb.* folly, B, PP; **nycetee**, C3 **nysete**, PP; **nysste**, B.—AF. *nicet* timidity, also in OF. sloth, simplicity (Cotg.).

nyght, *sb.* night, Voc., PP; **niȝt**, S2, PP; **nicht**, S; **nyht**, S2; **niht**, S, PP; **naht**, SD; **naȝt**, S2; **nyth**, PP; **night**, *pl.*, C; **nigt**, S; **niht**, *adv.*, at night, by night, S; **nihtes**, S2; **niȝtes**, PP; **nyghtes** PP; **nyȝtes**, PP. *Adv. phr.*: **a nyghtes** PP; **bi nihtes**, S; **bi nihte**, S; **a niȝt**, S; **o nigt**, S. *Comb.*: **nyhtegale**, nightingale, S2; **niȝtegale**, S; **nyghtingale** C3; **niȝtingale**, S; **nycht-hyrd**, guardian of the night, S3; **niht-old**, a night old stale, not freshly gathered, S2; **nyȝt-old** PP; **nightertale**, the night-time, C; **nyȝtertale**, WA; **naghtertale**, S2.—AS. *niht, neht, neaht*: Goth. *nahts*; cf. Lat. *noctem*. With the deriv. *nightertale* cf. Icel. *náttartal* a number of nights.

nygun, *sb.* niggard, miser, S2; **nyggoun**, G, CM. Cf. **nigard**.

nykken, *v. in phr.*: **nykken with nay**, to deny, refuse, HD.

nymyl, *adj.* quick at seizing, nimble, active, Prompt.—AS. *numol* (in compounds). See **nimen**.

nyne, *num.* nine, PP; **niȝen**, S; **neghen**, S2; **neoȝe**, S2; **nihe**, S. *Der.*: **nynt**, ninth, S3; **neynd**, S2; **nieþe**, S.—AS. *nigon* (WS. *neogon*): Goth. *niun*; cf. Lat. *nouem*; see Brugmann, § 152.

nyrvyl, *sb.* a little man, Prompt.; **nuruyll**, a dwarf, Prompt.—Cf. Icel. *nyrfill*, a miser.

nyȝ, *adv.* nigh, nearly, W, W2; see **neih**.

O

o-, *prefix*; see **on-**[1].

o[1], *num.* one, a, S; see **oon**.

o[2], *adv.* ever, aye, always, S; **oo**, S2, NED; **a**, S; **aa**, S. *Comb.*: **a buten**, ever without, S, SkD (s.v. *aye*); **a bute**, S; **for ay and oo**, for ever and ever, NED.—AS. *a* (for *áwa*); cf. Goth. *aiw*, ever. Cf. **ay**[1].

obediencer, *sb.* an officer in a monastery, PP.—Church Lat. *obedientiarius* (Ducange).

obeisant, *adj.* obedient, C2; **obeysand**, B.—OF. *obeïssant*, pr. p. of *obeïr*.

obeisaunce, *sb.* obedience, C, C2; **obeisances**, *pl.*, submissive acts, C2.—AF. *obeïsaunce*.

obeiss, *v.* to obey, B; **obeischen**, S2, W; **obeschynge**, *pr. p.*, W.—From OF. *obeïss-* stem of *obeïssant*, pr. p. of *obeïr*.

obeley, *sb.* oblation, *oblata*, Voc.; see **oble**.

obeye, *v.* to obey, W, C2; **obeiede**, *pt. s.*, W.—OF. *obeier*, for *obeïr*; Lat. *obedire*.

oble, *sb.* oblation; **obles**, *pl.*, *oblationes*, H.— OF. *oble*, Lat. *oblatum*; cf. OF. *oblee* (now *oublie*); Church Lat. *oblata* (Ducange). Cf. **ovelete**.

oblischen, *v.* to bind, W2; **oblyse**, JD; **oblyste**, *pp.*, S3; **oblysched**, HD; **oblisched**, HD; **oblyshed**, HD.—AF. *obliger*; Lat. *obligare*.

obout, *adv.* about, S2; see **abouten**.

obout-ga, *v.* to go about, S2.

o-brode, *adv.* abroad, P; see **abrode**.

obseruance, *sb.* homage, C, S3; **obseruances**, *pl.*, attentions, C2.—OF. *observance* (Cotg.).

obserue, *v.* to favour, C2.—OF. *observer*; Lat. *obseruare*.

obumbrat, *pp.* overshadowed, S3.—Lat. *obumbratus*.

oc, *conj.* but, S, HD; **occ**, S; see **ac**.

occean, *sb.* ocean, S2; **occian**, SD, W2; **occyan**, WA, HD.—AF. *occyane*; Late Lat. *occeanus*; Lat. *oceanus*: Gr. ὠκεανός.

occident, *sb.* West, S2, S3, C3.—AF. *occident*; Lat. *occidentem*, pr. p. of *occidere*, to set (of the sun).

occupy, *v.* to make use of, employ, possess, S3, C2, PP, B.—OF. *occuper*; Lat. *occupare*, see SkD.

odde, *adj.* odd, single, S2, SD.—Cf. Icel. *oddi*, point of land, odd number. See **ord**.

oerre, *sb.* anger, S. See **eorre**.

of[1], *prep.* and *adv.* of, out of, from, by, off, S, S2, C2, C3, WW; **o**, S, S2, H; **off**, SkD; **a**, S2, PP, S3.—AS. *of*: Goth. *af*: OHG. *aba* (Tatian): Gr. ἀπό; see Sievers, 51, 130.

of[2], *conj.* though, H (Ps. 125. 1), WA.—For ME. *þof*. See **þoз**.

of-dreden, *v.* to frighten; *reflex.* to dread greatly, S; **of-drade**, S; **of-dradde**, *pt. s.*, S; **of-drad**, *pp.*, S; **of-dred**, S; **of-dret**, S2.—AS. *of-drǽdan*. Cf. **adrad** (**a-**[3].)

o-ferrum, *adv.* afar, S2; **oferrom**, WA; see **aferre**.

offensioun, *sb.* offence, damage, C; **offencioun**, W.—Lat. *offensionem*.

of-feren, *v.* to terrify, SD; **offearen**, S; **offerd**, *pp.*, S; **oferd**, S.

offertoire, *sb.* offertory, anthem sung before the oblation, C.—OF. *offertoire* (Cotg.); Church Lat. *offertorium*.

office, *sb.* office, C2; **offiz**, S; **offices**, *pl.*, church services, PP.—AF. *office* (*offyz*); Lat. *officium*.

offrende, *sb.* offering, S; **offrand**, H; **offerands**, *pl.*, S2.—OF. *offrande* (Bartsch); Lat. *offerenda*; see Constans.

offri, *v.* to offer, S; **offren**, S, PP; **offrand**, *pr. p.*, S2; **i-offred**, *pp.*, S.—AS. *offrian*; cf. OF. *offerre* (Bartsch); Lat. *offerre*.

offringe, *sb.* offering, S; **offrinke**, S; **offryng**, C.

of-fruht, *pp.* terrified, S; **ofrigt**, S; **offruhte**, *pl.*, S.—Cf. AS. *of-fyrhtan*, to terrify.

of-hungred, *pp.* an-hungered, famished, PP; **of-hongret**, PP; **of-hongred**, PP; **offingred**, SD; **afingred**, SD; **afingret**, NED, HD; **afyngred**, NED, P, HD.—AS. *of-hyngrod*. Cf. **ahungerd**.

ofne, *sb. dat.* oven, S; see **oven**.

of-newe, *adv.* anew, S3, C2, C3. Cf. **anewe**.

of-rechen, *v.* to obtain, overtake, attain, reach, S, PP (*n*); **ofrauзte**, *pt. pl.*, PP.

ofrigt, *pp.* terrified, S; see **offruht**.

of-saken, *v.* to deny, SD.—AS. *of-sacan*. Cf. **asaken**. (**a-**[3].)

of-scapie, *v.* to escape, S2. See **ascapie**.

of-sen, *v.* to perceive; **ofsaw**, *pt. s.*, S2; **ofseie**, S2.—AS. *of-séon*.

of-senden, *v.* to send for, S2; **of-sente**, *pt. s.*, S2, PP; **of-sent**, P.

of-seruen, *v.* to merit, deserve, SD, S.

of-slen, *v.* to slay; **of-sloh**, *pt. s.*, SD; **of-sloзen**, *pl.*, S; **of-slaзen**, *pp.*, S; **of-slæзen**, S; **of-slaзe**, S.—AS. *of-sléan*.

of-spring, *sb.* offspring, S; **ofspreng**, S; **ofsprung**, S; **ospryng**, HD; **ox-spring**, S2.—AS. *of-spring*.

of-taken, *pp.* taken away, C2.

ofte, *adv.* often, S, C2; **oft**, PP, WW; **oftere**, *comp.*, S; **ofter**, S, C2. *Comb.*: **oftesiðen**, oftentimes, SD; **ofte siðe**, SD; **ofte sithes**, C, S3 (s.v. *eft*); **oft siss**, S2, B; **ofte-time**, oftimes, SD; **oft tyme**, PP.—AS. *oft*: OHG. *ofto* (Otfrid): Goth. *ufta*; cf. Gr. ὕπατος, superl. of ὑπέρ; see Sievers, 25.

often, *adj.* frequent, WW.

of-teonen, *v.* to vex, irritate; **of-teoned**, *pp.*, S.

of-þunchen, *v.* to be sorry for, to repent, S; **of-þinche**, S; **of-þinke**, S; **of-ðuhte**, *pt. s.*, S.—AS. *of-þyncan.*

of-þurst, *pp.* athirst, S; **of-þerst**, PP; **afyrst**, PP; **afurst**, PP; **afrust**, PP.—AS. *of-þyrsted* (Grein).

of-wundred, *pp.* amazed; **of-uundred**, S.

og, *pr. s.* possesses, S; see **owen**[1].

ogain, *prep.*, *adv.* against, again, NED; see **aȝein**.

ogaines, *prep.* against, S2; **ogaynes**, S2; see **aȝeines**.

ogain-saghe, *sb.* contradiction, S2. Cf. **igainsawe**.

ogain-torne, *v.* to turn again, S2.

ogen, *adj.* own, S; see **owen**[2].

ogremoyne, *sb.* agrimony, Voc.; see **agrimony**.

oht[1], *sb.* aught, anything, S2; see **ought**.

oht[2], *adj.* valiant, doughty, S; see **auht**.

ohtliche, *adv.* valiantly, NED; see **ahtlice**.

oise[1], *sb.* use, H; **oyse**, H; **oys**, JD, HD; **oyss**, B.—AF. *us*; Lat. *usum*.

oise[2], *v.* to use, H; **oyse**, H, HD; **oysede**, *pp.*, HD; **oysit**, B.—OF. *user*.

oist, *sb.* an army, B; **oyst**, B; see **oost**.

ok, **oke**, *pt. s.* ached, MD; see **aken**.

oken, *adj.* oaken, G. See **ook**.

oker, *sb.* usury, SD; **okir**, S2; **okyr**, Cath.; **okur**, SD; **ocker**, H; **okere**, H.—Icel. *ókr*: AS. *wócor*, increase, growth, fruit; cf. OHG. *wuachar*, gain (Otfrid).

okerer, *sb.* usurer, S2, H, Cath.; **okerere**, S2; **okyrere**, H.

okering, *sb.* usury, S2; **okeringe**, H.

old, *adj.* old, Voc.; **eald**, MD; **ald**, MD, S, S2; **oold**, MD; **hold**, S, MD; **eld**, MD, W2; **eeld**, W2; **auld**, S3; **olt**, S2; **ealde**, S, MD; **alde**, MD, S2; **olde**, Voc.; **elde**, S, W; **yealde**, MD; **aulde**, MD; **alder**, *comp.*, MD; **ælder**, MD; **eldre**, S, W; **elder**, S, C2; **eldure**, S; **eldore**, S2; **heoldre**, S; **elþer**, S2; **aldeste**, *superl.*, S; **heldeste**, MD; **eldoste**, S2.—AS. *eald*, *alde*; cf. OHG. *alt* (Otfrid).

oldli, *adj.* old, W2.

oliuere, *sb.* olive-yard, C2.—Late Lat. *olivarium* (Ducange).

oluhnen, *v.* to flatter, S.

oluhnung, *sb.* blandishment, flattery; **olhnunge**, *dat.*, S.

olyfaunte, *sb.* elephant, Cath., Voc.; **olefawnt**, Voc.; **oliphant**, S3; **olifant**, WA; **ollivant**, HD; **olyfaunce**, *pl.*, HD.—OF. *olifant*, elephant, ivory, ivory horn, also *elefant*; Lat. *elephantem*; Gr. ἐλέφας (-αντα).

on-[1], *prefix*, standing for **on**, *prep.*

on-[2], *prefix*, standing for AS. *and-*, against, in return, toward.—AS. *on-*, *ond-*, *and-*, Goth. *and-*, *anda-*; cf. OHG. *ant-* (*ent-*).

on-[3], *prefix*, with negative force. (**un-**[1].)

on-[4], *prefix*, before verbs. (**un-**[2].)

on[1], *prep.* on, at, in, among, of, S, S2, S3, C2, WW; **one**, S; **onne**, S; **a**, S, S2, C2, PP; **o**, S, S2, H; **an**, S, S2, PP.—AS. *an*, *on*.

on[2], *num.* one, S, S2; see **oon**.

onan, *adv.* at once, S2; **onon**, S, S3; see **anon**.

on-bydraw, *v.* to withdraw; **on-bydrew**, *pt. s.*, S3. (**on-**[4].)

on-come, *sb.* attack, JD; **on-comys**, *pl.*, H. (**on-**[1].)

onde, *sb.* breath, emotion, hatred, envy S, S2, HD, CM; **aande**, WA; **ande**, MD H, WA, Cath.; **aynd**, JD, B; **hand**, S2.—AS. *anda*: OS. *ando*; cf. Icel. *andi*, breath, the spirit (in theology).

ondful, *adj.* envious, MD; **ontful**, S.

ond-swere, *sb.* answer, S; see **answere**.

ondswerien, *v.* to answer, S; see **answeren**.

ondyn, *v.* to breathe, Prompt.; **ande**, Cath.

ondyng, *sb.* smelling, PP; **aynding**, B.

ones, *adv.* once, S2, S3, C3, G, P; see **oones**.

one-sprute, *sb.* inspiration, S2.

on-ferrum, *adv.* afar, S2; see **aferre**. (**on-**[1].)

on-fon, *v.* to receive, endure; **onnfoð**, *pr. s.*, S; **onfanged**, *pt. s.*, S2.—AS. *on-fón* for *ond-fón*; see Sievers, 198, 5. 1. Cf. **afon**. (**on-**[2].)

ongel, *sb.* angel, S; see **angel**.

on-halsien, *v.* to adjure, entreat, S. (**on-**[1].)

onhede, *sb.* unity, Voc.; see **oonhed**.

oniȝt, *adv.* by night, S; see **anyghte**.

on-imete, *adj.* immeasurable, S; see **unimet**. (**on-**[3].)

on-lappyt, *pt. s.* unfolded, S3; see **unlappe**.

on-lepi, *adj.* only, S, S2; see **oonlepy**.

onlepiliche, *adv.* only, singly, S MD.

on-lesum, *adj.* not allowable, S3; see **unleuesum**. (**on-**[3].)

onlich, *adj.* only, S; see **oonli**[1].

on-lofte, *adv.* aloft, S2, C2; see **alofte**. (**on-**[1].)

on-losti, *adj.* idle, S2; see **unlusti**.

on-lyue, *adv.* alive, C2, G; **onliue**, S.—AS. *on lífe*. Cf. **alyve**. (**on-**[1].)

onoh, enough, S; see **ynow**.

onond, *prep.* as regards, respecting, S; **onont**, S; see **anent**.

on-rounde, *adv.* around, S2. (**on-**[1].)

on-sage, *sb.* affirmation, charge; **on-sagen**, *pl. dat.*, S.—AS. *on-sagu*, affirmation (Schmid), for *ond-sagu*, see Sievers, 198, 5. 1. (**on-²**.)
on-sene, *sb.* face, SD; **onsene**, *dat.*, S.—AS. *on-séon*, *on sýn*, *an-sýn* (Mt. 28. 3). (**on-¹**.)
on-side, *adv.* aside, NED. (**on-¹**.)
on-sides, *adv.* aside, NED.
on-sidis-hond, *adv.* aside, S2.
on-sihðe, *sb.* appearance, S. (**on-¹**.)
on-slepe, *adv.* asleep, S2. (**on-¹**.)
on-spekinde, *pr. p.* unspeaking, unspeakable, S2. (**on-³**.)
on-swere, *sb.* answer, S; see **answere**.
on-swerde, *pt. s.* answered, S; see **answeren**.
on-tenden, *v.* to set on fire; **ontent**, *pr. s.*, S; **ontende**, *pp.*, S.—AS. *on-tendan*. Cf. **a-tenden**. (**on-¹**.)
ontful, *adj.* envious, S; see **ondful**.
on-till, *prep.* until, to, B; see **until**.
on-todelinde, *pr. p.*, *adj.* undividing, indivisible, S2.—AS. *un-todélende*. (**on-³**.)
on-þolyinde, *pr. p.* not enduring, intolerable, S2. (**on-³**.)
on-uppe, *prep.* above, S; see **anuppe**.
on-vale, *v.* to unveil, S3. (**on-⁴**.)
on-uast, *prep.* fast by, S.
on-wald, *sb.* power; **anwalde**, *dat.*, S; **anwolde**, S; **onwalde**, S; **onwolde**, S.—AS. *anwald*. (**on-¹**.)
on-wurþi, *adj.* unworthy, Prompt.; see **unwurði**.
on-zyginde, *pr. p.* unseeing, used in sense of 'invisible', S2. (**on-³**.)
ook, *sb.* oak, C2, C3; **ak**, Voc.; **ok**, S2; **ake**, Voc.; **oke**, Voc., Cath., G; **akis**, *pl.*, S3.—AS. *ác*; cf. OHG. *eich* (*eih*). Cf. **noke**.
oon, *num.* and *indef. art.* one, S2, S3, C2, C3, G; **an**, one, an, S, S2, H; **ane**, MD, S3, H; **a**, MD, S2, H; **on**, S, S2, S3, C2, G; **one**, MD, S, S2; **o**, S, S2, S3, C3, G; **oo**, S3, C3; **æn**, S; **ann**, S; **ænne**, S; **enne**, S, S2; **ene**, S; **anæ**, S; **ane**, S; **onne**, S; **ore**, *dat. f.*, S. *Phr.*: **by him one**, by himself, MD; **be it ane**, by itself, H (Ps. 101. 7); **all himm ane**, all by himself, S; **hire ane**, by herself, S; **ower ones**, of you alone, S.—AS. *án*.
oone-fold, *adj.* onefold, single, simple, MD; **anfald**, S, HD.—AS. *án-feald*.
oones, *adv.* once, G; **ones**, MD, S2, S3, C3, G, P; **onis**, P; **onys**, W2; **enes**, S, S2; **æness**, S. *Phr.*: **at anes**, at once, MD; **et enes**, S; **at ones**, MD, S2, C3; **at ans**, S2; **at oones**, G.—AS. *ánes*, gen. m. of *án*, used in ME. adverbially. AS. *éne* is used to express 'once, at once'. Cf. **nones**.
oonhed, *sb.* unity, HD (p. 588); **one-heede**, HD; **onhede**, Voc.; **anhed**, H; **anhede**, H.

oonlepy, *adj.*, *adv.* only, sole, MD; **onlepi**, S, S2; **olepi**, S, S2; **anlepi**, S, H.—AS. *ánlepig*.
oonli¹, *adj.* only, sole, MD; **onlich**, MD, S; **anli**, **anly**, H. *Comb.*: **anly stede**, solitude, H.—AS. *án-lic*, *æn-lic*.
oonli², *adv.* only, W; **onliche**, PP; **onlych**, S2; **oneliche**, PP; **anli**, MD; **anly**, S2; **onli**, MD; **oneli**, W (John 5. 18).
oor, *sb.* ore, unrefined metal, S2; **ore**, Voc.; **oore**, Manip.—AS. *ór* (SkD).
oost, *sb.* an army, B, S3, W, W2; **oist**, B; **oyst**, B; **ost**, B, S2; **oostis**, *pl.*, W, W2.—AF. *ost*, *host*; Lat. *hostem*, enemy, stranger.
ooste, *sb.* host, inn-keeper, MD; **ost**, CM, MD; **host**, MD; **hoost**, C; **hoste**, *dat.*, MD.—OF. *oste*, *hoste*; Lat. *hospitem*.
open, *adj.* open, S2, SD; **ope**, S; **upon**, S2; **opyn**. W; open, *pl.*, S.—AS. *open*; cf. Icel. *opinn*, and OHG. *offan* (Otfrid).
open-heaued, *adj.* bare-headed, S.
openin, *v.* to open, explain, S; **oppenand**, *pr. p.*, S2.—AS. (*ge-*)*openian*.
open-lic, *adj.* open, S2; **openliche**, *adv.*, S; **opeliche**, S.—AS. *openlic*, adv. *openlice*.
opposen, *v.* to question, SkD; **oposyn**, Prompt.; **opposed**, *pt. s.*, PP.—OF. *opposer*; Lat. *ob* + *pausare*. Cf. **aposen**.
opye, *sb.* opium, C, CM.—OF. *opie*; Lat. *opium*; Gr. ὄπιον, poppy-juice, from ὀπός, sap.
or-, *prefix*, out, without, excessive.—AS. *or-*: OHG. *ur-* (Tatian): Goth. *us-*. (**a-¹**.)
or¹, *pron.* your, S2; **ore**, S2; see **ʒoure**.
or², *prep.*, *conj.*, *adv.* before. *Comb.*: **or ever**, WW. See **er²**.
or³, *conj.* or, S; see **oþer¹**.
oratorye, *sb.* a place for prayer, C.—OF. *oratoire*; Lat. *oratorium* (Vulg.).
orcheʒard, *sb.* orchard, S3; **orchærd**, SD; **orchard**, Voc.—AS. *orcerd* (Voc.), *ort-geard* (BT): Goth. *aurtigards*; see Fick, 7. 35.
ord, *sb.* point, beginning, S, HD, C2; **orde**, *dat.*, S.—AS. *ord* (Voc.); cf. OHG. *ort*, a point, limit, district, Icel. *oddr*, 'cuspis'; see Kluge.
ordal, *sb.* ordeal, a severe test before judge, CM, SkD.—AS. *or-dél*, OS. *ur-déli*; cf. OHG. *ur-deili*, 'judicium' (Otfrid). (**or-**.)
ordeynen, *v.* to ordain, appoint, S2, PP; **ordayny**, S2; **ordand**, *pt. s.*, S3; **ordeigned**, P; **ordaynt**, *pp.*, S2; **i-ordeyned**, S2.—AF. *ordeiner*, OF. *ordener* Lat. *ordinare*.
ordeynour, *sb.* arranger, S2.
ordinance, *sb.* provision, array, S2.—AF. *ordinance* (*ordenance*).
ordinatly, *adv.* in good order, S3.

ordre, *sb.* order, PP, C3; **ordres**, *pl.*, orders (of friars), PP; holy orders, PP.—AF. *ordre*; OF. *ordene, ordine*; Lat. *ordinem*.

ordren, *v.* to arrange, rank, SD; **i-ordret**, *pp.*, S.

ore[1], *sb.* oar, S; **are**, MD; **ayr**, B; **ores**, *pl.*, S.—AS. *ár*.

ore[2], *num. dat. fem.* one, S; see **oon**.

ore[3], *sb.* honour, grace, favour, clemency, happy augury, S, S2, G, CM; see **are**[1].

ore[4], *sb.* ore, Voc.; see **oor**.

ore-les, *adj.* merciless, S2; **oreleas**, S; see **areles**.

orest, *adj.* and *adv. superl.* first, S; see **er**[2].

orf, *sb.* an inheritance, hence, cattle, S, S2.—Icel. *arfr*. See **erfe**.

organ, *sb.* organ, PP; **organs**, *pl.*, *organum*, Voc.; **orguns**, harps (= *organa*), W2; **orgoyns**, H.—Lat. *organum*; Gr. ὄργανον.

orgeilus, *adj.* proud, S, SD; **orgillous**, Sh.—OF. *orgueilleus* (Bartsch).

orgel, *sb.* pride, SD; **orhel**, S; **orgul**, SD.—AS. *orgel*; cf. OF. *orguel* (Bartsch). Probably of Teut. origin; cf. OHG. *ur-gilo*, excessively, oppressively (Otfrid). (**or-**.)

orient, *sb.* the East, S3, C2.—AF. *orient* Lat. *orientem*, the rising (sun).

orientales, *sb. pl.* sapphires, P.

orisoun, *sb.* prayer, orison, C, S2; **ureisun**, S; **oreisouns**, *pl.*, S2; **orisons**, C3.—AF. *oreison*, (*ur-*), *oraisun*; Church Lat. *orationem*, prayer, from *orare*, to pray.

orlege, *sb.* time-teller, JD; see **orologe**.

orleger, *sb.* clock, dial, S3; **orlager**, JD. See **orlege** and **orologe**.

or-mete, *adj.* immense, S.—AS. *ormáte*.

orologe, *sb.* time-teller, dial, clock, S3; **orloge**, Cath. (*n*); **orlogge**, C, CM; **horologe**, Voc.; **orlege**, JD; **horlege**, Cath., Prompt. (p. 120); **orlage**, Voc.—Lat. *horologium*; Gr. ὡρολόγιον; cf. F. *horloge*, Sp. *relox* (Minsheu).

orped, *adj.* valiant, S2, HD, SD; **orpud**, Prompt.; **orpid**, HD; **orpit**, proud, also fretful, habitually chiding, JD; **horpid**, SD; **horpyd**, HD; **orpede**, HD; used as a descriptive personal name, Bardsley; **horpede**, Bardsley.

orpedliche, *adv.* boldly, SD; **orpedlich**, HD; **orpedli**, SD.

orpedschipe, *sb.* bravery, SD.

orpiment, *sb.* orpiment, C2.—AF. *orpiment*, Late Lat. *auripigmentum*; Lat. *aurum*, gold + *pigmentum*, colouring material.

orpine, *sb.* a kind of stone-crop, Cath., SkD; yellow arsenic, HD; **orpyne**, Voc.; **orpin**, *telepinum*, Manip.; **orpyn**, *crassula major*, Prompt.—OF. *orpin*, orpin; also orpine, orpiment, or arsenic (Cotg.).

orrible, *adj.* horrible, MD.—OF. *orrible*; Lat. *horribilem*.

orrour, *sb.* horror, dread, W2.—OF. *orreur* (Bartsch); Lat. *horrorem*.

orts, *sb. pl.* remnants, Sh.; **ortus**, Prompt.; **ortys**, Cath.—AS. **or-ét*, 'reliquiae pabuli'; cf. ODu. *oor-ete*, what is left after eating. (**or-**.)

osse[1], *sb.* omen, prophecy, ND.

osse[2], *v.* to prophesy, HD; **osses**, *pr. s.*, WA; **ossed**, *pp.*, WA.—OF. *oser*, to venture, to dare; Late Lat. *ausare* (It. *ausare*), from Lat. *audere* (pp. *aus-us*).

ossing, *sb.* attempt, WA. See **osse**[2].

ostage, *sb.* hostage, S2; **hostage**, B.—AF. *ostage* (*hostage*); Late Lat. **obsidaticum* (cf. It. *statico*.), from Lat. *obsidem*, hostage, one who remains behind, from *obsid-*, stem of *obsidere*.

oste, *sb.* host, MD; **ost**, CM, MD; see **ooste**.

ostel, *sb.* hostel, Prompt., MD; **hostel**, MD; **osteyl**, HD; **ostayle**, HD.—OF. *ostel*, *hostel*; Lat. *hospitale*, relating to a guest. See **ooste**.

ostelere, *sb.* inn-keeper, Prompt.; **ostiler**, W; **hostiler**, C; **hostellere**, P.

ostelrie, *sb.* hostelry, MD, CM; **hostelrie**, C.

ostery, *sb.* inn, HD, MD; **ostrie**, W; **hostery**, MD.

ostryche, *sb.* ostrich, Voc.; **ostridge**, Cotg.; **estridge**, HD; **ostrigis**, *pl.*, W2.—OF. *ostruce* (Cotg.), *austruce* (Brachet): Sp. *avestruz*; Late Lat. *avis-strucio*; *strucio* for *struthio*; Gr. στρουθίων an ostrich, from στρουθός, a bird.

otes, *sb. pl.* oats, C2, P; **otys**, Voc.—AS. *áte* (OET).

oter, *sb.* otter, S; **otyr**, Voc.; **otyre**, HD.—AS. *otor* (Voc.).

o-twinne, apart, in two, S; **otwyn**, H. Cf. **atwynne**. (**o-**.)

oth[1], *prep.* and *conj.* up to, until; **oð**, S; **a**, S, NED (p. 3 c). Comb.: **a-þet**, until that, S.—AS. *óð*: OS. and Goth. *und*. (**un-**[3].)

oth[2], *sb.* oath, MD; **oþ**, S, S2, C; **ot**, S; **athes**, *pl.*, S; **oþes**, S, C2, C3.—AS. *áð*: Goth. *aiþs*; cf. OHG. *eid* (Tatian).

oðer[1], *conj.* either … or, S, S2, S3, C3; **ouðer**, S2, H, G; **or**, S; *adv.* even, S2; **auþer**, HD.—AS. *á-hwæðer* (*óhwæðer, áwðer, ówðer, áuðer, áðer, áðor*). See Sievers, 346.

other[2], *adj.* second, relating to one of two, other, S, S2, G, Ph.; **day and other**, continually, G.—AS. *oðer*: OS. *óðar, andar*; cf. OHG. *ander* (Otfrid), Goth. *anþar*, Skt. *antara*. For the suffix *-þar* cf. **forþer**[1].

other-gatis, *adv.* otherwise, H.

oðer-luker, *adv. comp.* otherwise, S.—AS. *óðerlicor*.

oðer-weies, *adv.* in another way, otherwise, S; **otherweyes**, C2.

oþer-while, *adv.* occasionally, S2, P.

otherwyse, *adv.* on any other condition, C2.

ou, *pron.* you, S, S2, PP; see **ȝou**.

ought, *sb.* aught, anything, S2, C2; **awiht, eawiht**, MD; **oht**, MD, S2; **ohht**, S; **ouȝt**, W; **oȝt**, S; **ouct**, S; **out**, S; **ahct**, S; **ahte**, S.—AS. *á-wiht.* Cf. **auht.**

ouh, *pr. s.* possesses, S; **ouhte**, *pt. s.*, S; **oughten**, *pt. pl.*, C2; see **owen**[1].

oule[1], *sb.* owl, S2; **hule**, S; **oules**, *pl.*, C2.— AS. *úle* (Voc.).

oule[2], *v.* to howl, *ululare*, Manip.

ounce, *sb.* ounce, C2; **ouns**, Voc.; **unce**, SkD, C, Cath; **ounces**, *pl.*, C2.—AF. *unce*; Lat. *uncia.* See **inche.**

ouphe, *sb.* elf, Sh.; see **aulf.**

our-, *prefix.* For many words beginning in **our-**, see **over-** below.

our, *pron.* your, S; **oure**, S2, PP; see **ȝoure**.

oure, *pron. poss.* our, W; **ure**, S, S2; **ur**, S, S2; **hure**, S; **hur**, S; **oure**, ours, W; **ourun**, W; **ures**, *pl.*, S2.—AS. *úre, úser*, of us, our: Goth. *unsara.*

ournement, *sb.* ornament, W2.—OF. *ornement.*

ournen, *v.* to adorn, W2; **ournede**, *pt. s.*, W2; **ourned**, *pp.*, W, W2.—OF. *orner*; Lat. *ornare.*

ournyng, *sb.* an adorning, W.

ous, *pron. dat.* and *acc.* us, S2, PP; **ows**, PP; **vus**, S2; **us**, C2. *Comb.*: **us self**, ourselves, S, C2; **us selue**, P; **us silf**, W.—AS. *ús*: Goth. *uns.*

out[1], *adv.* out, WA; **ut**, S; **owt**, B; **oute**, WA; **out**, *interj.*, out! away! S2; **uttere**, *adj. comp.*, outer, S; **utter**, C3; **uttereste**, *superl.*, extreme, C2; **outemest**, SD. *Comb.*: **utmer**, outer, W; **uttermere**, W2; **utnume**, exceptionally, S; **out taken**, except, S2, C3; **out takun**, W, W2; **outtane**, S2; **outane**, B; **owtane**, B; **utward**, outward, S; **ute wit**, outside, S2; **outwith**, WA.

out[2], *sb.* aught, S; see **ought.**

out-beren, *v.* to bear out, S2.

out-blasten, *v.* to blow out; **out-blaste**, *pt. s.*, S2.

out-bray, *v.* to bray out, S3.

out-breiden, *v.* to awake; **oute-breyde**, *pt. s.*, S2.

out-bresten, *v.* to burst out; **owt-brastyng**, *pr. p.*, S3; **ute-brast**, *pt. s.*, S2; **out-brast**, S3.

outen[1], *adj.* strange, foreign, S2.

outen[2], *v.* to utter, C2, C3, SkD (s.v. *utter*).— AS. *útian.*

outerly, *adv.* utterly, C2, C3; **uterly**, S3 (s.v. *al*); **utrely**, S2.

outhees, *sb.* the hue and cry. C, HD; **utheste**, S.—Low Lat. *uthesium* (Schmid), for *hutesium* (*huesium*), from OF. *huter* (*huer*), see Ducange. (s.v. *huesium*). See **houten.**

out-ioiyng, *sb.* extreme joy, W2.

out-lawe, *sb.* outlaw, PP, Manip.; **ut-laȝe**, S.—AS. *útlaga* (Schmid); Icel. *útlaga*, outlawed, *útlagi*, outlaw.

out-leden, *v.* to produce, *educere*; **oute-leden**, S2.

out-let, *sb.* outlet; **utlete**, *dat.*, S.—Cf. Icel. *út-lát.*

outrage[1], *sb.* outrage, excessive insult, SD, H, B, *luxus*, Manip.; **owterage**, *excessus*, Prompt.—OF. *outrage, oltrage*; cf. It. *oltraggio* (Florio), Low Lat. *ultragium*; from OF. *oltre*; Lat. *ultra.*

outrage[2], *adj.* outrageous, S3; **wtrage**, S3; **owtrage**, S3.

outrage[3], *v.* to outrage, destroy, to lose temper, C2; **outrayed**, *pt. s.* S3.—OF. *oultrager* (Cotg.).

outragely, *adv.* superfluously, H.

outrageous, *adj.* excessive, C3, B.

outrageusly, *adv.* excessively, H.

outrance, *sb.* excess, extremity, S3, JD.— OF. *oultrance* (Cotg.).

outrayed, *pt. s.* destroyed, S3; see **outrage**[3].

outren, *v.* to utter, to put out and circulate, SkD.

out-ryde, *v.* to ride out, PP; to outride, overtake in riding, S.

out-senden, *v.* to send out, S2.

out-take, *v.* to take out, except, deliver, S2; **out toke**, *pt. s.*, S2; **out taken**, *pp.*, S2, C3; **out takun**, W, W2; **out tane**, S2; **outakun**, W2. See **out**[1].

ouðer, *conj.* either, or, SD, S2, H; see **oþer**[1].

ouȝt, *sb.* aught, W; see **ought.**

ouȝte, *pt. s.* possessed, W; see **owen**[1].

ouelete, *sb.* the oblation in the Eucharist, S.—AS. *ofléte* (Leo), *oflate* (OET); Church Lat. *oblata* (Ducange). Cf. **oble.**

ouen, *sb.* oven, S; **ofne**, dat., S.—AS. *ofen*, OHG. *ofan* (Tatian): Goth. *auhns*: OTeut. stem **uhwna-*, see Douse, p. 80.

ouer-, *prefix*, over-; **our-**, B; **or-**, S2.

ouer, *prep., adv.* over, above, beyond, S, C2, W; **uferr**, S; **our**, S2, S3, B; **oure**, S3; **ouer**, *adj.*, upper, C, SkD; **ouerer**, *comp.*, W2, H; **ouereste**, *superl.*, C, S2. *Comb.*: **oueral**, all over, everywhere, S, S2, C, C2, C3; **ouur al**, S2; **ouir litil**, too little, Prompt.; **or-litel**, S2; **ouer mykel**, over much, S2; **ouer þwert**, across, perverse, S2, W; **ouer thwart**, across, crossways, C; **our-thwort**, B.—AS. *ofer*: Goth. *ufar* (see Sievers, 25. 1); cf. OHG. *ubar* (Otfrid).

ouer-cummen, *v.* to overcome, S; **ouer-come**, S, S2, W2; **ofercom**, *pt. s.*, S; **ouer-com**, S2; **ouercumen**, *pp.*, S; **ouercome**, S2.—AS. *ofer-cuman.*

ouer-dede, *sb.* excess, S.

ouer-fare, *v.* to pass over, S2.—AS. *ofer-faran.*

our-fret, *pt. s.* fretted over, S3.

ouer-gan, *v.* to go over, *superare*, SD, S2; **ouergon**, S, W; **ourga**, B; **ouergon**, *pp.*, S2.—AS. *ofer-gán*: OHG. *ubar-gán* (Otfrid).

our-hailing, *pr. p.* overhauling, considering, S3.

our-heldand, *pr. p.* covering over, S3.

ouer-howen, *v.* to disregard, despise; **ofer-howeð**, *pr. s.*, S; **ofer-hoȝien**, SD.

ouer-lede, *v.* to domineer over. P.

ouer-leiyng, *sb.* pressure, W.

ouer-liggen, *v.* to lie upon, S.—AS. *ofer-licgan.*

ouer-lippe, *sb.* upper lip, S2, C.

ouer-lop, *sb.* omission, S2.

ouerlyng, *sb.* a superior, H, HD.

ouer-maistrien, *v.* to overmaster, P.

ouermastes, *sb. pl.* summits, S2.

ouer-non, *sb.* afternoon, S2 (1 a. 164).

ouer-sen, *v.* to observe, survey, look down upon, to despise, overlook, P; **ouersihð**, *pr. s.*, S; **ouerseȝ**, *pt. s.*, S (16. 30); **ouer-sene**, *pp.*, WW, S3; **ouer-seye (me)**, *pp.*, forgotten myself, P.—AS. *ofer-séon.*

ouer-sloppe, *sb.* upper garment, C3.

our-straught, *pp.* Streched across, S3.

ouer-take, *v.* to overtake, SD; **ouertan**, *pp.*, S2; **ourtane**, B.

ouer-tild, *pp.* covered over, S.—AS. *ofer-teldan* to cover over.

ouertlye, *adv.* openly, S2.—From AF. *overt*) pp. of *ovrir*, OF. *aövrir*, *aüvrir*, Prov. *adubrir*; Lat. *ad + de + operire.*

ouer-trowynge, *pr. p.* anxious, overconscious, W.

ouer-þogt, *adj.* anxious, S.

over-throwe, *v.* to fall down, G; **over-threw**, *pt. s.*, G.

ouer-walten, *v.* to overflow, S2.

ouer-wente, *pt. s.* overcame, S. See **over-gan**.

ouet, *sb.* fruit, S2.—AS. *ofet*; cf. OHG. *obaz* (G. *obst*), Du. *ooft*; see Kluge.

ow¹, *interj.* ow! alas! G.

ow², *pron.* you, S, S2; see **ȝou**.

owai, *adv.* away, S2. *Phr.*: **owai do þam**, do away with them; destroy them, S2. See **away**.

owel, *sb.* awl, S, Voc.; see **aul**.

owen¹, *v.* to have, possess, to have to do, to be obliged, to owe, MD, S, Cs, PP; **oȝen**, S; **aȝen**, S; **aȝhenn**, MD; **aghe**, H; **awen**, MD; **agen**, S; **ahen**, S; **owe**, *pr. s.*, P; **og**, S; **ouh**, S; **aȝh**, S2; **ah**, S; **au**, S2; **ouhte**, *pt. s.*, PP, S; **ouȝte**, PP, W; **auhte**, S; **aucte**, S; **ahte**, S; **aghte**, H; **agte**, S; **aȝte**, S2; **auȝt**, W; **aght**, S2; **aucht**, *pl.*, S2; **oughten**, C2.—AS. *ágan*, 1 and 3 *pr. s. áh* (pl. *ágon*), pt. *áhte*, pp. *ágen*.

owen², *adj.* own, S, S2, S3, C2, C3, PP; **oȝen**, S, S2; **ogen**, S; **aȝen**, S; **agen**, S; **aȝhenn**, S; **ahen**, S; **awin**, S3; **awyn**, S3; **awn**, S3; **owe**, S, S2; **oghe**, S; **oge**, S; **oune**, S, S2, PP; **oȝene**, S2; **oghne**, S2.—AS. *ágen*, own, possessed, pp. of *ágan*, to possess.

ower, *pron.* your, S; see **ȝoure**.

o-wher, *adv.* somewhere, anywhere, C, C3, SD (s.v. *âwhẽr*, p. 12); **owhar**, SD, S2 (7. 417); **ouer** (for **ouuer**?), S.—AS. *á-hwér.* See **o**² (*adv.*).

o-whider, *adv.* anywhither, SD (p. 12); **o-hwider**, S.—AS. *á-hwider.* See **o**² (*adv.*).

o-whils, *conj.* on whiles, during the time that, H.

oxe, *sb.* ox, S; **exen**, *pl.*, HD; **oxis**, W.—AS. *oxa*: OHG. *ohso* (Tatian): Goth. *auhsa*; cf. Skt. *ukśan*. The AS. pl. forms are *oxan*, *æxen*, *exen.*

oxe-stalle, *sb.* ox-stall, C2.

oxspring, *sb.* offspring, S2; see **ofspring**.

oyle, *sb.* oil, C3, MD; **oylle**, S2; **oyele**, S2; **oli**, MD; **oilles**, *pl.*, flattery, PP. *Phr.*: **bere up oile**, to flatter, PP (*n*); **hilde vp þe kynges oyl**, Trevisa, 3. 447, see NQ (6. 1. 75).—AF. *oile*, *olie*; Late Lat. *olium*; Lat. *oleum*. Cf. **ele**.

oynement, *sb.* ointment, W, C; **oyne-mentis**, *pl.*, S3, W.—AF. *oignement*, from *ongier*, to anoint; Lat. *ungere*. Cf. **noyne-ment**.

oyntynge, *sb.* anointing, H.

oynoun, *sb.* onion, CM; **oynon**, Voc.; **oingnum**, Voc.; **oynouns**, *pl.*, C; **oyneȝones**, HD.—AF. *oynoun* (F. *oignon*); Lat. *unionem.*

oȝein, *prep.* against, MD; see **aȝein**.

oȝeines, *prep.* in comparison with, S; see **aȝeines**.

oȝen¹, *v.* to owe, S; see **owen**¹, *v.*

oȝen², *adj.* own, S; see **owen**², *adj.*

oȝt, *sb.* aught, S; see **ought**.

P

pace[1], *sb.*; see **pas.**

pace[2], *v.*; see **passen.**

padde, *sb.* toad, SkD; **pades**, *pl.*, S; **paddis**, SkD. *Comb.*: **pad-stoole**, toadstool, Manip.—Icel. *padda.*

paddok, *sb.* toad, Prompt.; frog, W2; **paddoke**, *rana*, Voc. (*n*); **padockes**, *pl.*, *grenouilles*, Palsg. *Comb.*: **paddok-stole**, *fungus*, toad-stool, Cath.

paene, *adj.* pagan, S; see **payen**[2].

pagent[1], *sb.* a pageant, *pagina*, Prompt.; **pageant**, *scena, theatrum*, Manip.

pagent[2], *sb.* a page, writing; see **pagyne.**

pagyne, *sb.* page, writing, HD; **pagine**, SkD; **pagent**, SkD (s.v. *page*). *Phr.*: **perfeccioun of dyuyne pagyne**, H (p. 4).—Lat. *pagina*, a written page, that which is written, a paragraph or book.

pais, *sb.* peace, S; see **pees.**

pak, *sb.* a small bundle, PP; **pakke**, *sarcina*, Prompt.

pakken, *v.* to pack, PP, Prompt.

pak-nelde, *sb.* packing-needle, PP; **pakneelde**, S2; **paknedle**, PP.

pakok, *sb.* a peacock, PP; see **pecok.**

palesye, *sb.* paralysis, palsy, PP, S2; **perlesy**, HD; **palesye**, PP, S2; **palesie**, S2; **palasie**, S2; **palacye**, PP; **palesy**, W; **palsye**, P, Prompt.; **parlesy**, Cath., SkD.—OF. *paralysie*; Lat. *paralysin*; from Gr. παράλυσις.

paleys, *sb.* palace, C, C2, PP; **paleis**, PP; **palais**, S; **palys**, PP; **paleyses**, *pl.*, PP; **paleis**, PP.—AF. *paleis*, OF. *palais*; Lat. *palatium.*

palfrey, *sb.* palfrey, saddle-horse, S2, C, PP; **palfray**, PP; **palefrei**, S.—AF. *palefrei*, OF. *palefreid* (Roland); Low Lat. *paraveredum.*

palle, *sb.* the archbishop's pallium, funeral pall, a costly kind of texture, a canopy, Prompt., HD, Voc.; **pall**, HD, WA; **pal**, S; **pelle**, Prompt., S; **pell**, S2; **pelles**, *pl.*, S. *Comb.*: **pallen webis**, fabrics of pall or fine cloth, WA.—Late Lat. *pallium* and *palla*, see Ducange; cf. OF. *pale*, a kind of cloth (Ducange), and AS. *pæll*, a rich texture (Voc.).

pallen, *v.* to pall, to become vapid, Prompt., Palsg., SkD; **palled**, *pp.* enfeebled, C3.—OF. *pallir*, to grow pale; see Constans.

palme, *sb.* palm (tree), palm of victory, WA; **palm**, palm-branch, C3.—AF. *palme*; Lat. *palma.*

palmere, *sb.* palmer, S, PP; **palmers**, *pl.* S2.—AF. *palmer*; Church Lat. *palmarium* (acc.). See **palme.**

palmestrye, *sb.* palmistry, S3. See **paume.**

paltok, *sb.* jacket, PP, Prompt.; **paltocke**, HD, Palsg.; **paltoke**, Voc.—OF. *paletocque* (Prompt., *n*). For cognates, see SkD (s.v. *paltry*).

pament, *sb.* pavement, S3; see **pavement.**

pane, *sb.* a part or division of a thing, a skirt, Prompt., HD, SkD.—OF. *pan*, a piece (Bartsch); Lat. *pannum* (acc.). Cf. **peny.**

panel, *sb.* a division, compartment, jurylist, piece of cloth on horse's back, Cath. (*n*) PP, Sh.; **panell**, PP; **panelle**, *subsellium.* Cath.; **pannell**, HD, Palsg.—AF. *panel.* See **pane.**

paneter, *sb.* butler, PP; **pantere**, Voc.; **panter**, PP.—AF. *panneter*; Late Lat. *panetarium* (acc.). See **payn.**

panne, *sb.* pan, brain-pan, skull, PP, C3, Voc., Prompt.; **ponne**, PP; **pan**, C.—AS. *panne* (Voc.); cf. Low Lat. *panna* (Ducange), and G. *pfanne.*

pans, *sb. pl.* pence, W; see **peny.**

panter, *sb.* painter, *pictor*, Voc. See **peynten.**

panter, *sb.* a net, snare, CM, HD, Voc.; **pantere**, Prompt.; **panther**, Palsg., HD.—OF. *pantiere*; Late Lat. *panthēra*; Gr. πανθήρα; see Ducange.

pantere, *sb.* panther, S3, Voc.—OF. *pantere*; Lat. *panthēra*; from Gr. πάνθηρ.

panyer, *sb.* pannier, bread-basket, PP; **payneres**, *pl.*, PP.—AF. *panyer.* See **payn.**

papejay, *sb.* parrot, popinjay, C2; **popeiay**, PP; **papinjay**. Voc.; **popinjay**, Voc.; **popyngay**, S3, HD; **papyngay**, HD; **papingais**, *pl.*, S3; **popyngayes**, S3.—AF. *popejaye* parrot (mod. *papegai*); cf. OF. *papegaux* pl.; Low Lat. *pappagallus* by popular etymology from the Low Gr. παπαγάς, see Ducange.

pappe, *sb.* breast, S, Voc.; **pappes**, *pl.*, S (*n*), WW; **pappys**, HD.

par-; see also words beginning in **per-**.

par, *prep.* by, with. *Comb.*: **par amour**, by love, with love, C; **for paramour**, for love, C2; **paramour**, a lover (of either sex), C, WA; **paranioure**, Manip.; **par auenture**, peradventure, S2, C2, C3, PP; **perauntere**, H; **parauntre**, S2; **perauenture**, W; **par cas**, by chance, C3; **par de** (*par Dieu*), C, C3; **pardee**, C2 **par fay**, by my faith, C2, C3.

parage, *sb.* kindred, family; hence, birth, descent, HD, JD, CM; equality, DG.—AF. *parage*; Late Lat. **paraticum*, an equality, from Lat. *par*, equal. Cf. **disparage**.

parcel, *sb.* part, share, little bit, PP; **parcele**, WA.—AF. *parcele*, part; Late Lat. *particella*; cf. It. *particella*.

parcel-mele, *adv.* separately, bit by bit, PP; **percel-mel**, S2, PP.

parcenel, *sb.* partner, H.

parcenelynge, *sb.* partnership, H.

parcener, *sb.* sharer, HD, W2; **partener**, W; **partynere**, S3; **parceneris**, *pl.*, W, W2; **parteneris**, W; **partyneris**, W.— AF. *parcenere*, *parsenere*, pl. *parceners*, *perceners*; Late Lat. *partionarinm* (acc.).

parchementer, *sb.* preparer of parchment, Cath.; **parmenter**, Voc.

parchemyn, *sb.* parchment, W, PP; **perchemyn**, PP; **perchemen**, WA.—AF. *parchemin*, Gr. περγαμηνή from Πέργαμος (cf. Lat. *pergamena*).

parchment; see **passamen**.

parclos, *sb.* an enclosure, partition, screen, S3, Palsg.; **parcloos**, Prompt.; **perclos**, HD; **perclose**, HD.—OF. *parclos*, pp., closed completely; Lat. *per + clausum*.

pardon, *sb.* pardon, PP.—AF. *pardun*.

pardoner, *sb.* a seller of pardons, C, PP; **pardonere**, Prompt.

parement, *sb.* an adorning, C2, CM; **paramentz**, *pl.*, C. *Phr.*: **chambre of parementz**, the presence-chamber, C2.—OF. *parement*; also *chambre de parement*, the Chamber of Presence (Cotg.).

parfit, *adj.* perfect, S2, PP, GS, W; **parfyt**, PP; **perfyt**, C; **parfight**, C; **perfit**, C3, W; **perfight**, C.—OF. *parfit*, *parfeit*; Lat. *perfectum*.

parfitliche, *adv.* perfectly, PP; **perfitliche**, PP; **parfitly**, C2, CM; **parfitli**, W; **perfytliest**, *superl.*, H.

parfournen, *v.* to perform, PP, C2, CM, SPD (p. 280); **parforme**, PP; **perfourne**, PP; **performen**, PP.—AF. *parurnir*, *parfournir*, to perform, to furnish.

parische, *sb.* parish, PP; **parisch**, PP; **paresche**, PP; **parsche**, PP.—OF. *paroisse*; Church Lat. *paroecia* (also *parochia*); Gr. παροικία.

parischen, *sb.* parishioner, Cath., C; **parisschens**, *pl.*, PP, S2; **parshens**, PP.—OF. *paroission*. See **parische**.

paritorie, *sb.* pellitory, C3, SkD; **peritorie**, the wall-plant bartram, Manip.; **paratory**, *colitropium*, Voc.; **parietary**, HD.—OF. *paritoire*, pellitory (Cotg.) and *paritarie* (Alph.); Late Lat. *paritaria* (Alph.); Lat. *parietaria*, from *paries*, wall.

parlement, *sb.* parliament, conference, PP, S2.—AF. *parlement*, from OF. *parler*, to talk; Low Lat. *parabolare* (Brachet).

parlesy; see **palesye**.

parloure, *sb.* the conversation room in nunneries, PP; **parlowr**, 'colloquotorium', Cath.; **parlur**, S.—OF. *parloir*; Church Lat. *parlatorium* (Ducange).

parochien, *sb.* parishioner, PP; **perrochioun**, S3; **paroschienes**, *pl.*, PP.—OF. *parochien*; Church Lat. *parochianum*; from *parochia*. See **parische**.

partie, *sb.* part, portion, PP; **partye**, party (in a law suit), PP; **party**, side, S2; **parties**, *pl.*, parts, S2. *Phr.*: **a party**, partially, S2.— AF. *partie* (*partye*), person; Lat. *partita*, divided.

partly, *adv.* briskly; see **perk**.

partriche, *sb.* partridge, S3, PP; **partrich**, C; **pertryche**, Prompt.—AF. *perdrice*, *perdriz*; Lat. *perdicem*.

parvis, *sb.* the open space in front of St. Paul's cathedral, HD; **parvys**, C, CM; **parvyse**, HD; **parvyce**, Prompt.—OF. *parvis*, the porch of a church, the outer court of a palace (hence Low Lat. *parvisum*), *parevis*, *pareïs*, *paraïs*; Late Lat. *paradisum* (acc.), the portico of St. Peter's, Rome (Ducange), also paradise (Vulg.); Gr. παράδεισος. For the intercalation of *v* in OF. *parvis*, see Brachet (s.v. *corvée*).

pas, *sb.* a step, pace, pass, passage, canto, narrow path, C2, C3, PP, S2; **paas**, C3; **pass**, S2; **pace**, Prompt.; **pas**, *pl.*, S2; **pases**, S2.—AF. *pas*; Lat. *passum* (acc.).

paschen, *v.* to dash, to strike; **pash**, HD; **paschte**, *pt. s.*, PP; **passhed**, *pp.*, **passchet**, *pp.*, S2.

paske, *sb.* passover, W, PP, HD; **pask**, W.—AF. *pask*; Church Lat. *pascha*; Gr. πάσχα; Heb. *pesak*, a passing-over.

passamen, *sb.* a kind of lace, SPD (p. 272), HD; **passements**, *pl.*, SPD, DG. *Comb.*: **passamen lace**, NQ (5. 9. 231); **parchment lace**, SPD.—OF. *passement*, a lace (Cotg.): It. *passamáno* (Florio); cf. Sp. *passamáno*, Q. *posament* (Weigand). Cf. **perchmentier**.

passen, *v.* to pass, surpass, PP, C2, C3; **pace**, S2, C2, C3; to die, C2; **y-passed**, *pp.*, PP; **pasand**, *pr. p.*, S3.—AF. *passer*.

passyng, *pr. p.* as adv. surpassing, i.e. very, S3; *adj.*, C3.

passyngly, *adv.* in a surpassing degree, S3.

pas-tans, *sb.* pastime, S3; **pastance**, S3; **pastaunce**, HD.—OF. *passe-tans*, *passe-tens*, *passe-temps*.

patter, *v.* to repeat prayers, to say repeatedly, S3; **patred**, *pt.s.*, S3 (*n*), HD.—

From Church Lat. *pater*, the first word in
the *pater-noster* ('Our Father').

paume, *sb.* palm of the hand, PP; **pawme**,
PP, W, Prompt.; **pame**, Voc. *Comb.*:
palme-play, game of ball played with the
hand, S3.—OF. *paume*, palm of the hand;
Lat. *palma*; cf. F. *jeu de paume*, tennis.

pautener, *sb.* a vagabond, a libertine, HD;
adj., rascally, ribald, B.—OF. *pautonier*, *pal-
tunier*, a rascal (Bartsch); cf. Low Lat. *pal-
tonarius* (Ducange). For cognates see SkD
(s.v. *paltry*).

paue, *v.* to pave; **y-paued**, *pp.*, S3.—OF.
pauer.

pauement, *sb.* pavement, C2; **pauiment**,
SkD; **pament**, S3, Voc., Cath. (*n*), H; **paw-
ment**, Prompt.—AF. *pavement*; Lat.
pauimentum.

pauilon, *sb.* pavilion, tent, PP; **pauilyoune**,
S2; **pauiloun**, lawyer's coif, PP; **pauyloun**,
coif, PP; **pauylons**, *pl.*, tents, S2.—AF.
pavillon, tent; Lat. *papilionem*, a tent, a
butterfly.

pavyce, *sb.* a shield, defence, Prompt.;
pauice, SkD; **pauys**, Prompt. (*n*), SkD,
Voc., HD; **pavisse**, HD; **pauish**, Prompt.
(*n*), HD; **paluoise**, Florio (s.v. *testudine*);
palueise, Florio (s.v. *pauese*).—AF. *pavise*;
Low Lat. *pavisium* (acc.), also *pavesium*; cf.
OF. *pavois* (Cotg.); Low Lat. *pavensem*
(Ducange).

pavyser, *sb.* a soldier armed with a pavise,
HD.

pax-brede, *sb.* a tablet with a crucifix which
received from the worshippers the 'osculum
pacis', Voc., HD. See **bred**[2].

paye, *sb.* satisfaction, HD, S2, PP; **paie**, S2;
pay, S2.—AF. *paie*.

payen[1], *v.* to please, satisfy, pay, PP, S2, H;
payed, *pp.*, satisfied, PP; **paied**, W; **payd**,
S2; **paid**, S2; **y-payed**, C.—OF. *paier*, to
satisfy, pay: Prov. *pagar*; Lat. *pacare*.

payen[2], *adj.* and *sb.* pagan, heathen, C; *as a
personal name*, Bardsley; **payn**, S; **paene**, S;
payns, *pl.*, S; **paynes**, S; **pains**, S;
paens, S; **payens**, S2, C3, CM.—AF.
païen; Late Lat. *paganum*, heathen.

payn, *sb.* bread, PP; **payne**, PP. *Comb.*:
payn-demayn, bread made of the finest
flour, C2; **paynmayn**, Voc.; **paynemayn**,
C2 (*n*); **payman**, Voc., HD.—OF. *pain
demaine*, *demeine*; Church Lat. *panem
dominicum*, bread of our Lord.

payne, *sb.* penalty, S2; see **peyne**.

paynyme, *sb.* heathendom, S; **painime**, S;
paynym, a pagan, Saracen (an incorrect
use), PP, H; **payneme**, S2; **paynymes**,
pl., PP; **painems**, HD (s.v. *payen*).—AF.
paenime, heathen lands; paganism; OF.

paienisme; Late Lat. *paganismum* (acc.). See
payen[2].

paynymery, *sb.* paganism, Cath.

peak, *v.* to pry about narrowly, to peep, ND.
Comb.: **peak-goose**, a peaking goose, ND;
peek-goos, S3; **pea-goose**, 'a simple,
doltish fellow, a noddy peak, a ninny-
hammer, a coxe', Cotg. (s.v. *benet*).

peakish, *adj.* looking sneakingly, ND.

peas, *sb.* peace, S3; see **pees**.

pease, *v.* to become peaceable; **peaste**, *pt.
s.*, S3.

pece, *sb.* a bit, portion, a cup, S2, PP,
Prompt., Cath., Palsg., HD; **peyce**, S3.—
AF. *pece*, *piece*; cf. Low Lat. *pecia*, a piece
(Voc.), a cup (Ducange).

pecok, *sb.* peacock, PP; **pecoke**, Voc.;
pekok, PP; **pacoke**, Cath.; **pacok**, Voc.;
pakok, PP; **pocok**, PP, C; **pokok**, PP;
pocokk, Voc.; **pokoc**, Voc.; **pacokkis**,
pl., S3.—AS. *péa* (*páwo*); Lat. *pauo*; see
Sievers, 37. 2. Cf. **poun**.

peekgoose, *sb.* a silly fellow, S3; see **peak**.

peel, *sb.* skin, rind of fruit, Cotg. (s.v.
coupeau).—OF. *pel*; Lat. *pellem*.

pees, *sb.* peace, silence, S2, C2, W, PP; **pes**,
S, S2; **peas**, S3; **pays**, PP; **pais**, S.—AF.
pees, *pes*, OF. *pais*; Lat. *pacem*.

peesid, *pp.* appeased, W2.

peirement, *sb.* damage, detriment, W.

peiren, *v.* to injure, PP, CM; **peyren**, PP;
peired, *pp.*, S2.—OF. *peirier*; Late Lat.
peiorare; cf. OF. *empeirier*, to become worse,
to make worse, impair (Bartsch).

peiryng, *sb.* damage, destruction, W.

peis, *sb.* weight, PP; **peys**, S2, PP; **peyce**,
Prompt.; **peise**, S3, Prompt.; **poys**, S3.—
OF. *peis* (*pois*); Lat. *pensum*.

peisen, *v.* to weigh, W2; **peysede**, *pt. s.*, S2;
peised, PP; **poised**, PP.—AF. *peiser*
(*poiser*); Lat. *pensare*.

peitrel, *sb.* breast-plate of a horse in armour,
HD; **peytrel**, C3, Prompt.; **pewtrel**,
Manip.; **peytrelle**, CM; **paytrelle**, HD,
Voc.; **pettrylle**, Voc.—AF. *peitrel*; Lat.
pectorale.

pelet, *sb.* pellet, stone-ball, S2, PP, Cath.,
CM, Prompt.; **pelot**, Prompt.; **pylotes**,
pl., Cath. (*n*).—AF. *pelote*, ball, cf. It. *pillótta*
(Florio); dimin. of Lat. *pila*.

pelle, *sb.* a pall, Prompt.; see **palle**.

pelrimage, *sb.* pilgrimage, S; see **pylgrimage**.

pelte, *pt. s.* pushed, S; see **pulten**.

pelure, *sb.* fur-work, PP; **pellure**, S2,
Prompt., PP.—AF. *pelure*, OF. *peleüre* (from
OF. *pel*); Late Lat. *pellatura*, from Lat. *pellem*,
skin.

pen, *sb.* a pen, enclosure, crib, Sh., SkD; **penne**, *caula*, Manip.; **penez**, *pl.*, S2. See **pynnen**.

penaunce, *sb.* suffering, punishment, penance, penitence, W, C, PP.—OF. *penance, peneänce*; Lat. *poenitentia*.

penauncer, *sb.* one who imposes a penance, PP.

penaunt, *sb.* one undergoing penance, C2, PP; **penawnte**, Prompt.—OF. *penant, peneänt*; Lat. *poenitentem*.

pencell, *sb.* a little banner, pennon, S2; **pensel**, PP, CM; **pensell**, Palsg., Cath. (p. 280 *n*).—OF. *penoncel, pennoncel*, dimin. of *pennon*, a flag, streamer. See **penoun**.

penible, *adj.* careful to please, C2; see **peyneble**.

penid, *sb.* a pennet, little wreath of sugar taken in a cold, sugar-candy, Florio (s.v. *diapiéde*); **penet**, Florio; **pennet**, ND, Cotg., PP, Notes (p. 110); **penydes**, *pl.*, Alph.—OF. *penide* (Cotg.); Late Gr. πηνίδιον, a little twist of thread, from Gr. πήνη, thread. Cf. **dia-penidion**.

penne, *sb.* quill of a feather, Voc.; a pen, Cath.; **pennes**, *pl.*, S2, W2.—AF. *penne*; Lat. *penna*.

penoun, *sb.* a pennon, small banner, SkD; **pynoun**, C; **penounes**, *pl.*, S3.—AF. *penon*, feather of a cross-bow bolt, OF. *pennon*, feather of an arrow, flag, streamer; cf. It. *pennóne* (Florio).

peny, *sb.* penny, S2; **penye**, S; **peny**, S2; **peni**, S; **pens**, *pl.*, W, S2, S3, C3; **pons**, S2; **pans**, W. *Comb.*: **penny-breid**, penny's breadth, S3.—AS. *pening* (Mk. 12. 15), *penning* (Schmid), *pending*, a little pledge or token (SkD); cf. OHG. *phending* (Tatian), dimin. of *phand*; Lat. *pannus*, a piece of cloth; Late Lat. *pannum*, pledge, something pledged or pawned (Ducange). Cf. **pane**.

peosen, *sb. pl.* peas, S2; see **pese**.

per-; see also words beginning in **par-**.

perauntere, peradventure, H; see **par**.

percelmel, *adv.* bit by bit, S2; see **parcel-mele**.

percen, *v.* to pierce, S2, PP, C2; **persen**, W, PP; **perche**, Cath., HD; **pershaunt**, *pr. p.*, PP; **persand**, S3; **pearst**, *pp.*, S3; **persid**, W2.—AF. *percer*; OF. *percher*; Late Lat. **particare*, to part. For suffix *-icare*, cf. Late Lat. **coacticare* (whence F. *cacher*); see BH, § 97. Cf. also OF. *person = partitionem*, Ps. 15. 6 (Apfelstedt).

perchmentier, *sb.* dealer in 'parchment lace', S3.—Cf. It. *passamentiere* (Florio). See **passamen**.

percyl, *sb.* parsley, S2; **percil**, PP; **percyll**, Prompt.; **parcelle**, Cath.; **persylle**, Voc.;

percelle, Cath.; **persile**, Alph.—OF. *persil*; Late Lat. *petrocillum* (Voc.); from Gr. πετροσέλινον. For the effect of the Greek accent see Brachet, and cf. F. *encre* (**enke**).

pere[1], *adj.* and *sb.* equal, a peer, PP, C2; **per**, SkD; **peer**, PP, C2; **peare**, S3; **peres**, *pl.*, PP; **pieres**, S3.—AF. *per* (pl. *pers, peres*); Lat. *parem*.

pere[2], *sb.* pear, Voc., Cath.; **peere**, Prompt.; **perys**, *pl.*, CM. *Comb.*: **peere apple**, Prompt.; **pere-ionette**, an early ripe pear, PP; **perjonette**, CM.—AS. *pere, peru*; Lat. *pirum*. Cf. **pereye**.

peregrin[1], *adj.* foreign; **peregryn**, C2.—OF. *peregrin*; Lat. *peregrinum*. Cf. **pylgrim**.

peregrin[2], *sb.* a kind of falcon, HD.—Cf. Late Lat. *peregrina falco* (Ducange).

peren, *v.* to appear, P.—OF. *pareir* (*paroir*); Lat. *parēre*, to appear.

pereye, *sb.* perry, S2, Voc.; **perre**, Prompt.; **pirrey**, Cath.; **pirre**, Cath. *Comb.*: **piri-whit**, white perry, S2, PP.—OF. *perey, peré, peiré* (mod. *poiré*), from *peire* (mod. *poire*), pear; cf. Late Lat. *piretum* (Voc.), from *pirum*.

perfet, *adj.* perfect, C3, W; see **parfit**.

perk, *adj.* proud, pert, elated, HD; **perke**, ND; **pert**, SkD; **partly**, *adv.*, briskly, S3.

perken, *v.* to smarten, to trim, SkD (s.v. *pert*); **pyrkis**, *pr. s.*, S3.

Pernel, *sb.* Pernel, or Parnel, a common female name, S2, Bardsley; **purnele**, a concubine, PP.—OF. *Peronelle*; Late Lat. *Petronilla*, name of a saint.

perreye, *sb.* jewelry, precious stones, PP; **perreie**, S2; **perrye**, C, PP, HD; **perrey**, S2; **perree**, C2.—AF. *perrye*; OF. *pierrerie*, precious stones; from OF. *piere, pere*; Lat. *petra*, stone.

pers, *adj.* dark rich blue, sky-coloured, bluish grey, CM, C; **perss**, S3.—OF. *pers* (Bartsch); cf. It. *perso*, Low Lat. *persus, perseus* (Ducange).

perte, *adj.* manifest, obvious, S2, PP; *adv.* openly, PP. See **apert**[2].

pertelyche, *adv.* plainly, evidently, S2; **pertelich**, *adv.* pertly, truly, S2; openly, P; **pertely**, completely, S2.

pes, *sb.* peace, S, S2; see **pees**.

pese, *sb.* a pea, PP; **peose**, PP; **peese**, PP; **pesen**, *pl.*, PP; **peosen**, S2; **peses**, PP. *Comb.*: **pese-coddes**, pea-pods, S2, P; **pes-codes**, S3; **pese-lof**, loaf made with peas, P.—AS. *plôsē* (*pyse, pise*), pease; Lat. *pisa*, pl. of *pisum*.

pesibilte, *sb.* a calm, W. See **pees**.

pesible, *adj.* peaceful, W2.—OF. *paisible*; Late Lat. *pacibilem*.

pesiblenesse, *sb.* calm, S2, W; **pesibil-nesse**, W.

pettail, *sb.* rabble, B; see **pitaile**.

pettes, *sb. pl.* pits, S2; see **pyt**.

peyne, *sb.* pain, penalty, C2, W, PP; **peine**, S2; **payne**, S2.—AF. *payne, paine*, OF. *peine*; Late Lat. *pēna*; Lat. *poena*. Cf. **pyne**.

peyneble, *adj.* pains-taking, S2; **penyble**, HD; **penible**, C2.—OF. *penible*, laborious.

peynen, *v. reflex.* to take pains, PP, S2, C2; **peyned**, *pp.*, punished, W.

peynten, *v.* to paint, CM, PP; **peynt**, *pp.*, S3, CM; **peynted**, C2; **y-peynt**, S3.— From OF. *peint*, pp. of *peindre*; Lat. *pingere*, see Brachet.

peynture, *sb.* picture, CM.—OF. *peinture* (AF. *painture*).

phantasie, *sb.* fancy, S3.—Gr. φαντασία.

philautia, *sb.* explained 'philosophy', S3; **philautie**, self-love, ND.—Gr. φιλαυτία, self-love.

philosophre, *sb.* philosopher, C2, C3; **philosophres**, *pl.*, C3; **philosophers**, PP.— OF. *philosophe*; Lat. *philosophum* (acc.); Gr. φιλόσοφος, a lover of wisdom. For the *r* added in the English word, cf. *chorister* for F. *choriste*.

picchen, *v.* to pitch, to fix, to pick, divide with a sharp point, P; **pitchinge**, *pr. p.*, W; **piȝte**, *pt. s.*, SD; **pighte him**, pitched, fell, SkD; **piȝten**, *pl.*, W; **piht**, *pp.*, PP; **piȝt**, WA; **pight**, S3, PP, ND; **pyȝte**, PP. Cf. **pyken**.

pich, *sb.* pitch, S; see **pikke**.

pigge, *sb.* pig, *porcellus*, Manip.; **pygge**, Prompt. *Comb.*: **pigsnie**, 'pig's eye', a term of endearment, ND; **piggesneyghe**, CM; **pigsny**, ND, S3.

pike, *v.* to pitch, S; **pykke**, Cath.

pikke, *sb.* pitch, Cath.; **pyk**, Prompt.; **pyche**, Prompt.; **pych**, S; **pich**, S.—AS. *pic* (Voc.); Lat. *picem*.

piler, *sb.* pillar, S, PP, C2, C; **pyler**, PP; **pilere**, W; **pylere**, Prompt.—AF. *piler*; Low Lat. *pilare* (Ducange).

pillage, *sb.* plunder; **pyllage**, SkD; **pilage**, WA.

pillen[1], *v.* to peel, Prompt.; **pille**, Cath.; **pill**, Cotg., WW; **pilie**, PP; **pilled**, *pp.*, bald, WW, Prompt.; **piled**, C; **pilde**, peeled, bare, S3. *Phr.*: **pille garleke**, *vellicare*, Cath.—OF. *peler* (Cotg.), also *piller* (Palsg.); Lat. *pilare*, to deprive of hair, from *pilus*, hair.

pillen[2], *v.* to plunder, CM, ND; **pylle**, S3; **pilen**, PP; **pil**, H; **pylen**, PP; **pylled**, *pt. pl.*, S3.—OF. *piller* (Cotg.); Late Lat. *pilare* (Ducange).

pillery, *sb.* rapine, ND.

pilling, *sb.* robbery, S3.

pillour, *sb.* plunderer, PP; **piloure**, PP; **pyllars**, *pl.*, S3.

pilwe, *sb.* pillow, CM; **pilewe**, S2; **pilous**, *pl.*, CM.—AS. *pyle* (= **pulwi*); Lat. *pulvinus*; cf. OHG. *phuliwi* (Tatian).

pilwe-beer, *sb.* pillow-case, C; **pillowebere**, Cath.; **pyllo-berys**, *pl.*, HD.

pinchen, *v.* to find fault, C3; **pynche**, C; **i-pynched**, *pp.*, plaited, C. *Phr.*: **I pynche courtaysye**, *je fays le nyce*, Palsg.—OF. *pincer*; It. *picciare*, to pinch with a beak (Florio); from *piccio*, a beak, bill (Florio).

pirie, *sb.* pear-tree, S2, P.—AS. *pirige* (Voc.). See **pere**[2].

piri-whit, *sb.* white perry, S2; see **pereye**.

pirries, *sb. pl.* storms of wind, S3; see **pyrry**.

piscence, *sb.* might, S3; see **puyssaunce**.

pistle, *sb.* epistle, PP, W, S3; **pystyl**, Prompt.; **pistil**, PP, C2; **pistill**, WA; **pistlis**, *pl.*, W.—OF. *epistle (epistre*, Cotg.); Lat. *epistola*; Gr. ἐπιστολή, message.

pitaile, *sb.* footsoldiers, infantry, S2; **pettaill**, rabble, B; **pitaill**, B; **pitall**, B.— AF. *pitaille*, foot-soldiers, OF. *pietaille*, a troop of footmen (Cotg.); from OF. *piet*; Lat. *pedem*.

pitaunce, *sb.* provision, share, portion, dole, PP, C, CM; **pytaunce**, PP; **pytawnce**, Prompt.—OF. *pitance* (Bartsch); Low Lat. *pictancia* (Ducange).

plage[1], *sb.* plague (= Lat. *plaga*), W; **plague**, Sh.; **plagis**, *pl.*, W.—Lat. *plāga* (Vulg.); Gr. πληγή, a blow, stroke, plague (LXX); cf. OF. *plaie*.

plage[2], *sb.* a region, Cath.; **plages**, *pl.*, S2, C3, HD.—OF. *plage*, a region, land, seacoast (Cotg.); Lat. *plāga* (Vulg.).

plaid, *sb.* plea, dispute in a law-court, S; **plait**, S; **plee**, Prompt.; *placitum*, Voc.; **ple**, SkD, W; **play**, SkD; **place**, *pl.*, pleas, S3.—AF. *plait, play*, OF. *plaid, plait, plat*, proceedings in a law-court, a trial, lawcourt; Late Lat. *placitum*, literally, what is pleasing, hence a decision, law-court, pleading.

plaidi, *v.* to plead, bring a complaint, argue, S; **plede**, PP; *placitare*, Voc.; **plete**, PP, S3, Prompt.—AF. *plaider*, OF. *pleidier*.

plaiding, *sb.* pleading, S; **pledyng**, PP; **pletynge**, S3, Prompt.

plat, *adj.* flat, level, Prompt.; *adv.* completely, fully, JD, C2.—OF. *plat*.

platly, *adv.* fatly, fully, S3, HD, Prompt.

plate, *sb.* plate-armour, S2, C2; **plates**, *pl.*, PP.—AF. *plate*, a plate of metal, bullion, silver-plate, *f.* of *plat*, flat.

platte, *pt. s. reflex.* threw himself flat, PP, S2.

playn, *adv.* plainly, clearly, C2, C3; see **pleyn**[1].

playne, *v.* to complain, S2, PP; **playn**, S3; **pleyne**, PP, C2; **pleyn**, S3; **plane**, S3; **pleignen**, *pr. pl.*, S2; **pleynand**, *pr. p.*, S2; **plenand**, H.—OF. *plaign-*, stem of *plaignant*, pr. p. of *plaindre* (*pleindre*); Lat. *plangere*.

playnte, *sb.* complaint, lament, PP; **pleinte**, C2; **pleyntes**, *pl.*, C3.—OF. *pleinte*; Late Lat. *plancta*, from Lat. *plangere*.

playnyng, *sb.* complaint, S3.

playte, *sb.* a fold, *plica*, Prompt.; **pleytes**, *pl.*, plaits of a cord, HD.—OF. *pleit*, a fold; Lat. *plicitum*, folded. Cf. **plite**.

playten, *v.* to fold, Prompt.; **plettand**, *pr. p.*, S3; **pletede**, *pt. s.*, S2.

ple, *sb.* plea, W; see **plaid**.

pleinte, *sb.* complaint, C2; see **playnte**.

plenere, *adj.* full, PP; *adv.* in full numbers, PP; **plener**, PP, HD.—OF. *plenier*; Late Lat. *plenarium*.

plenerliche, *adv.* fully, HD; **plenerly**, S2.

plenissen, *v.* to fill; **plenyst**, *pp.*, S3.—From OF. *pleniss-*, stem of *plenissant*, pr. p. of *plenir*, from Lat. *plenum*.

plentee, *sb.* plenty, C2; **plente**, Prompt.—OF. *plenté*; Lat. *plenitatem*.

plenteuous, *adj.* plenteous, abundant, C, PP; **plenteuouse**, W; **plentiuous**, SkD; **plentefous**, H; **plentuos**, S2; **plenteus**, SkD.—OF. *plentivous*.

plenteuouslier, *adv. comp.* more plenteously, W.

plenteuousnesse, *sb.* plenteousness, HD.

plentuuste, *sb.* plentifulness, H.

plesaunce, *sb.* pleasure, kindness, PP; **plesance**, B, S2, Cath., C2.—OF. *plaisance*.

plete, *v.* to plead, S3, PP, HD, Prompt.; see **plaidi**.

pletede, *pt. s.* plaited, folded up, S2; see **playten**.

pley, *sb.* play, C2; **pleie**, S.—AS. *plega*, brisk motion, fight, play (OET).

pleyen, *v.* to play, amuse oneself, PP, C2; **pleien**, S, PP; **pleiden**, *pt. pl. refl.*, S2.—AS. *plegian* (OET), to play on an instrument (OET), to play, 'ludere', to move briskly (Grein), *plegan* (Sievers, 391): OS. *plegan*, to wager, to answer for; cf. OHG. *plegan* (Otfrid).

pleyn[1], *adj.* even, level, plain, clear, Prompt., C, C3; **playn**, B; *adv.* plainly, clearly, C3; **playn**, C3.—AF. *plain*; Lat. *planum*.

pleyn[2], *v.* to complain, S3; see **playne**.

pleyn[3], *adj.* full, C, C3, PP.—OF. *plein*; Lat. *plenum*.

pleynly, *adv.* fully, C.

pliht, *sb.* danger, S2; **pli3t**, WA.—AS. *pliht* (OET.).

plihten, *v.* to pledge, plight, PP, S2; **plyghte**, PP, Prompt.; **pli3te**, S; **plyghte**, *pt. s.*, PP; **ply3hten**, *pl.*, PP; **pliht**, *pp.*, PP,

S2; **plyht**, S2; **pli3t**, PP; **ply3t**, S3; **plight**, PP; **plyght**, C3; **i-pluht**, S; **y-pli3te**, PP; **i-pli3t**, S2.—AS. *plihtan*, to imperil, to venture (Schmid).

plihtful, *adj.* dangerous, S2.

plite, *sb.* state, condition, manner, SkD (p. 822), CM, WA; see **plyte**.

plouh, *sb.* plough, PP; **plow**, Prompt.; **plewch**, B; **plou3**, PP; **ploh**, S2; **plewys**, *pl.*, S3. *Comb.*: **plouh-fot**, plough-foot, PP; **plow-lond**, a measure of land, *carrucata*, S2; **plowelond**, Voc.; **plowlond**, Prompt.; **ploghe of lande**, Cath.; **plowes of lond**, G; **plow-man**, ploughman, C2, PP; **plou3man**, PP; **pluch-ox**, plough-ox, S3; **plowstert**, plough-tail or handle, Prompt.—Icel. *plógr*, plough; cf. AS. *ploh*, ploughland (SkD); OHG. *pluag*, plough (Otfrid).

plukken, *v.* to pluck, PP, Prompt.; **plokken**, PP; **plyghte**, *pt. s.*, CM, C2, PP; **plyght**, *pp.*, C2 (p. 290).—AS. *pluccian*.

plume, *sb.* feather; **plumes**, *pl.*, PP; **plomys**, S3.—OF. *plume*; Lat. *pluma*.

plye, *v.* to bend, C2.—AF. *plier*; Lat. *plicare*, to fold.

plyght, *pp.* plighted, pledged, C3; see **plihten**.

plyghte, *pt. s.* plucked, pulled, C2; see **plukken**.

plyte, *sb.* state, condition, Prompt., C3, WA; **plite**, CM, WA; **plit**, S2.—OF. *plite*, SkD (p. 822), *pliste*; Late Lat. **plicita*, from Lat. *plicare*, to fold. Cf. **playte**, **plye**.

poer, *sb.* power, S2; **poeir**, S2; **power**, Prompt.; **powere**, army, WA; **pouwer**, PP.—OF. *poër*, *poeir*; Late Lat. *potēre*, to be able.

poised, *pt. s.* weighed, PP; see **peisen**.

poke, *sb.* a bag, Cath., PP, S; **pooke**, Prompt.; **poc**, S2; **powke**, PP; **pouh3**, PP.—Cf. ODu. *poke*.

poket, *sb.* pocket, Prompt.; **pokets**, *pl.*, C3.

pokke, *sb.* pustule, Prompt.; **poke**, Voc.; **pokkes**, *pl.*, C3, Voc., PP.

pokok, *sb.* a peacock, PP; see **pecok**.

polcat, *sb.* polecat, C3; **pulkat**, Prompt., Voc.; **pulcatte**, SkD; **powlkat**, SkD.—ME. *pol-*; OF. *pole*, *polle*; Lat. *pulla*. Cf. **pulte**.

poletes, *sb. pl.* pullets, S2; see **pulte**.

polische, *v.* to polish, PP, **pulische**, Cath.; **puliche**, Cath.; **polsche**, PP; **pulsche**, PP; **pulched**, *pp.*, S3.—From OF. *poliss-*, stem of *polissant*, pr. p. of *polir*; Lat. *polire*.

poll[1], *sb.* poll, head, WW; head, person, WA; **pol**, PP; **polles**, *pl.*, PP. *Comb.*: **poll-ax**, pole-axe, C; **polax**, CM.

poll

poll[2], *v.* to cut off the hair, WW, Manip.; **powled**, *pt. pl.*, WW; **pollid**, *pp.*, W, W2; **powled**, WW. *Comb.*: **polled hen**, C (p. 125); **pulled hen**, bald, moulting hen, C.

polle, *v.* to get money unfairly, by extortion, Palsg.; **poll**, *spoliare*, Manip., S3, ND, Sh.— The same word as above.

poller, *sb.* an extortioner, ND.

polling, *sb.* unfair exaction, S3.

polyue, *sb.* pulley, C2, CM; **polyff**, ONE (l. 108).

pomade, *sb.* cider, PP.

pomage, *sb.* cider, HD.

pome, *sb.* pomade, S3. *Comb.*: **pome-water**, a kind of apple, HD; **pom-water**, the apple of the eye, HD.—OF. *pome*, apple; Lat. *pomum*.

pomel, *sb.* a knob, a boss, C, W2; **pomels**, *pl.*, S3; **pomelles**, HD.

pomely, *adj.* spotted like an apple, C, C3; **pomelee**, HD. *Comb.*: **pomely gris** (= *gris pommelé*), dapple grey, Cotg.—OF. *pommelé*.

ponne, *sb.* pan, PP; see **panne**.

pons, *sb. pl.* pence, S2; see **peny**.

pope, *sb.* the pope, PP; **pape**, S. *Der.*: **popetrie**, popery, S3.—AS. *pápa*; Church Lat. *papa*.

popet, *sb.* puppet, C2, SkD, CM.—OF. *poupette*.

popyngay, *sb.* parrot, popinjay, S3; see **papejay**.

poraille, *sb.* poor people, C; see **poveraill**.

porchas, *sb.* gain, winnings, S2; see **purchas**.

pore, *adj.* poor, S2; see **povre**.

poret, *sb.* a kind of leek, PP, Prompt.; **porettes**, *pl.*, S2, P.—OF. *porrette* (Cotg.).

pors, *sb.* purse, S2; see **purse**.

portatyf, *adj.* portable, light, P.—OF. *portatif*, lively of body (Cotg.).

porte, *sb.* gate, WW; **port**, Sh.; **portis**, *pl.*, S3.—AF. *porte*; Lat. *porta*.

portrey, *v.* to pourtray, FP; **purtreye**, PP; **purtraye**, PP; **purtreied**, *pp.*, S3; **portred**, S3; **porturat**, S3.—OF. *portray-*, stem of *portrayant*, pr. p. of *portraire*; Late Lat. *protrahere*.

porueid, *pp.* provided, S2; see **purveyen**.

pose, *sb.* cold in the head, S2, Prompt., Cath., Palsg., Voc., C3.—Wel. *pas*, a cough; for cognates see SkD (s.v. *wheeze*), and Brugmann, § 441.

possen, *v.* to push, S, PP, CM, Prompt.; **posshen**, PP.—OF. *pousser, poulser*; Lat. *pulsare*, frequent. of *pellere*.

pot, *sb.* a vessel for cooking or drinking from, SkD. *Comb.*: **pot-parlament**, a talk over one's cups, S3; **pot-sherd**, pot-sherd, S3;

poynt

pot-styk, pot-stick, *motarium*, Voc.; **pot-stykke**, *motarium*, Voc.; **pot-stick**, S3.

potte, *pt. s.* put, S2; see **putten**.

pouderen, *v.* to powder, SkD; **poulderen**, S3; **pulderit**, *pp.*, S3.—OF. *poudrer, poldrer*; Lat. *puluerare*.

poudre, *sb.* powder, C3, W; **pouder**, PP; **poudir**, W; **poulder**, HD; **pulder**, S3. *Comb.*: **poudre marchaunt**, flavouring powder, C.—AF. *poudre, puldre*, OF. **pulre*; Lat. *puluerem*, dust.

povn, *sb.* peacock, S3.—OF. *poun, paon*; Lat. *pauonem*; see BH (Introd., 27). Cf. **pecok**.

pound[1], *sb.* pound, PP; **punde**, *dat.*, S; **pownd**, *pl.*, S2. *Comb.*: **pound-mele**, by pounds at a time, PP, S2; **pound-mel**, P.—AS. *pund*; Lat. *pondus*, a weight.

pound[2], *sb.* an enclosure, pound, pond, S2; **pond**, SkD; **ponde**, Prompt.; **poonde**, Cath. *Comb.*: **pondfolde**, a pound, pinfold, PP; **poundfalde**, PP; **ponfolde**, PP.—AS. *pund*, an enclosure (Schmid).

pouren, *v.* to pore, gaze steadily, C3; **pore**, CM; **powre**, C; **pure**, S; **pirith**, *pr. s.*, PP.

pous, *sb.* pulse, PP, CM; **pouce**, S2; **powce**, Prompt.—OF. *pouls, polz*; Lat. *pulsum* (acc.).

poustè, *sb.* power, P, B, HD, H (77. 65); **poste**, HD; **potestat**, W; **poustees**, *pl.*, violent attacks, PP; **potestatis**, powers, W.—AF. *pouste, poëste*, OF. *podeste*; Lat. *potestatem*.

pout, *v.* to poke, to stir with a long instrument, JD. *Comb.*: **pout-staff**, a net fastened to two poles, used for poking the banks of rivers, JD, S3.

poueraill (**poveraill**), *sb.* the poor people, B; **purraile**, PP; **poraille**, PP, C; **porails**, *pl.*, W2.—AF. *poverail*.

pouertè (**povertè**), *sb.* poverty, meanness, shabbiness, PP, C2, WA; **powerte**, B; **pouert**, WA, PP, S2, S3, C3, W, W2.—OF. *povertè*; Late Lat. *paupertam*; see Constans (Supplément, p. 32).

poure (**povre**), *adj.* poor, S, PP, S2, C2; **pouere**, PP, S2; **pouer**, S2; **pore**, S, S2; **pure**, S2, S3; **pouerore**, *comp.*, S2; **pourest**, *superl.*, C2; **poure**, *adv.*, C2.—OF. *povre*; Lat. *pauperem*.

poureliche (**povreliche**), *adv.* poorly, C2; **pourely**, C.

poynt, *sb.* point, a small portion, a bit, S2; **poynte**, Prompt. *Phr.*: **at the poynt**, conveniently placed, S2; **in point**, at the point, about to, S2.—OF. *point*; Lat. *punctum*. *Comb.*: **point-deuys**, **at point-deuys**, with the greatest exactness, in detail, minutely, CM, C2; **point-device**, HD.—OF. *point*; Lat. *punctum*.

161

poyntil, *sb.* a style to write with, W, W2; **poyntyle**, Voc.—OF. *pointille*.

poys, *sb.* weight, S3; see **peis**.

prane, *sb.* prawn, Prompt., Manip., Palsg., ND; **praune**, SkD; **pranys**, *pl.*, S3.—OF. **parne, *perne*; Lat. *perna*, a ham; cf. It. *perna*, a nakre fish (Florio). For the changes in meaning, cf. It. *gambarelli*, prawns (Florio), from *gamba*, a leg.

pranglen, *v.* to press; **prangled**, S.—Cf. Du. *prangen*; Goth. *praggan*, to press.

prank, *adj.* full of sensational tricks; **pranker**, *comp.*, ND.

pranken, *v.* to arrange the folds of a dress, SkD, Prompt., Palsg., HD; **prancke**, ND; **pranke**, to frisk about, Manip.

pranker, *sb.* one who dresses gaily, ND.

prankie, *adj.* fine, gorgeous, S3.

praty, *adj.* pretty, *elegantulus*, Prompt.; *prestans*, Cath.; **pretie**, *scitus, facetus*, Manip.; **prately**, *adv.*, CM.—Cf. Late Lat. *practicus*, 'peritus' (Ducange).

prayabill, *adj.* to be entreated, H.

prayen, *v.* to pray, PP; see **preyen**.

prechen, *v.* to preach, C2.—OF. *precher* (*prescher*); Lat. *praedicare*.

prechour, *sb.* preachers, PP; **prechoures**, *pl.*, PP, S3.—OF. *precheör*; Lat. *praedicatorem*.

predicament, *sb.* in logic, one of the most general classes into which things can be distributed; **predicamentes**, *pl.*, S3.—Schol. Lat. *praedicamentum*.

prees, *sb.*; see **presse**.

preie, *sb.* prey, S; **pray**, Prompt., PP; **prayes**, *pl.*, spoils, S2.—OF. *preie* (mod. *proie*); Late Lat. *prēda*; Lat. *praeda*); cf. AF. *praie*.

prente, *sb.* print, impression, SkD; **prent**, S3; **preynt**, Prompt.; **prynte**, PP, W.—OF. *preint*, pp. of *preindre*; Lat. *premere*, to press.

prenten, *v.* to print, impress, CM; **preentyn**, Prompt.

prentis, *sb.* apprentice, S2, P; **prentyce**, Prompt.; **prentys**, PP; *pl.*, PP; **prentises**, PP. See **aprentis**.

prentishode, *sb.* apprenticeship, PP.

presse, *sb.* a press, throng, SkD, PP; **pres**, CM, C2; **prees**, CM, S2, C2, C3; **prease**, Cotg., S3; **preace**, S3.—AF. *presse*, a throng.

pressour, *sb.* press for cloth, S2, PP; wine-press, W; **pressoure**, *pressorium*, Cath.; **pressour**, W; **pressoure**, *pl.*, W2. OF. *pressoir*; Lat. *pressorium*.

prest¹, *adj.* ready, quick, G, S2, S3; *adv.*, PP, S3; **presteste**, *superl.*, S2; **prestest**, P; **prestliche**, *adv.*, readily, PP; **prestly**, PP; **prestely**, S2.—AF. *prest*; Late Lat. *praestum* (Ducange).

prest², *sb.* priest, S, PP, S2, C2; **preest**, PP; **preeste**, Prompt.; **preostes**, *pl.*, S2; **prestes**, S2; **prustes**, S2.—AS. *préost*; Church Lat. *presbyter* (Vulg.); Gr. πρεσβύτερος, elder (LXX).

preste, *adj. superl.* (for *pret-ste*), proudest, highest, S2; see **proud**.

presthod, *sb.* presthood, PP; **preesthood**, Prompt.

preuen, *v.* to prove, try, test, abide a test, C2, C3; see **proven**.

prevy, *adj.* privy, secret, S3; see **pryve**.

preyen, *v.* to pray, C2, PP, Prompt.; **preien**, PP, S, S2; **preith**, *pr. s.*, S2; **preiȝede**, *pt. s.*, PP; **preide**, S, PP; **preyd**, S2; **y-prayed**, *pp.*, S2, C2.—AF. *preier* (*praier*); Late Lat. *precare*. (Lat. *precari*).

preyere, *sb.* prayer, Prompt., S2, C2; **preiere**, PP.—AF. *preiere*: It. *pregaria*; Church Lat. *precaria*.

pricasour, *sb.* a hard rider, C, CM.

price, *sb.* high esteem, S2; see **prys¹**.

pricket, *sb.* a buck; see **pryket**.

primate, *sb.* the first place, H.—Lat. *primatus* (Vulg.).

primordyall, *sb.* origin, S3.—OF. *primordial*; Church Lat. *primordialem* (Ducange).

prim-seȝnen, *v.* to give the *prima signatio*, to sign with the cross, an act preliminary to christening; **primm-seȝȝnesst**, *2 pr. s.*, S; **y-primisined**, *pp.*, S2.—OF. *primseigner* (Ducange); cf. Icel. *primsigna*.

principatus, *sb. pl.* powers, dominions, rulers, W.—Lat. *principatus* (Vulg.).

prisun¹, *sb.* prison, S.—AF. *prisun*; Lat. *prensionem, prehensionem*, a taking, a capture. Cf. **pryson**.

prisun², *sb.* a prisoner; **prisunes**, *pl.*, S; **prysouns**, PP; **prysuns**, H; **prisons**, S2; **prisounes**, *pl.*, *presons*, WA.—AF. *prisoun*, OF. *prison*; see Constans.

prisuner, *sb.* gaoler, keeper of a prison, S.

proces, *sb.* narrative, history, C2, HD, WA.—OF. *procès*; Lat. *processum*.

proche, *v.* to approach; **prochinge**, *pr.p.*, S3.—OF. *procher* (in *approcher*); Late Lat. *propiare*.

procuratour, *sb.* proctor, agent, PP; **procuratoure**, steward, W; **proketowre**, Prompt.—AF. *procuratour*; Lat. *procuratorem* (Vulg.).

profyte, *sb.* profit, Prompt.; **prophete**, PP. AF. *profit*; Lat. *profectum*.

profyten, *v.* to profit, Prompt.; **profitide**, *pt. s.*, grew, W; **prophitide**, *pl.*, S2.

proheme, *sb.* a proem, prologue, C2.—OF. *proëme*; Lat. *proemium*; Gr. προοίμιον.

proinen, *v.* to prune, preen, trim, adorn, SkD, HD, ND; **proigne**, HD; **prune**, H;

CM, SkD; **proynd**, *pp.*, S3.—OF. *progner,*
also *provigner,* to propagate by taking
cuttings (Cotg.); from OF. *provin,* a sucker
(Cotg.), also *provain*; Lat. *propaginem.*

proiner, *sb.* pruner, ND.

prollen, *v.* to search about, prowl, C3,
Prompt., Palsg.; **proule**, Manip.

promissioun, *sb.* promise. *Phr.*: **the lond
of promyssioim (or of beheste)**, the
Holy Land, S2.—Lat. *promissionem*; cf. *terra
repromissionis* (Heb. II.9, Vulg.).

promyt, *v.* to promise, S3, JD.—Lat.
promittere; cf. OF. *prometre.*

propre, *adj.* separate, distinct, PP, C2; **fine,
goodly**, PP, C3; **proper**, S2.—AF. *propre,*
fit; Lat. *proprium.*

propreliche, *adv.* properly, suitably, PP.

proprete, *sb.* property, peculiarity, SkD;
propirte, PP; **propertes**, *pl.*, S2, WA;
propurtes, PP.—OF. *proprieté,* a property
(Cotg.); Lat. *proprietatem.*

prospectyues, *sb. pl.* perspective glasses,
C2. *Comb.*: **prospective glass**, telescope,
C2 (*n*).—OF. *prospective,* 'the prospective,
perspective or Optick art' (Cotg.).

proud, *adj.* proud, PP, WA; **prowd**, PP;
prout, PP, S2; **prud**, S; **prut**, S; **prute**,
pl., S; **prude**, S; **preste (pretste)**, *superl.*,
S2.—AS. *prút*; cf. Icel. *prúðr.*

proue, *sb.* proof, S3; **preue**, CM, C2;
preef, C3; **prief**, S3.—OF. *preuve*; Late
Lat. *proba*; from Lat. *probare.*

prouen, *v.* to prove, try, test, PP, S; **preouen**,
S2, PP; **preuen**, PP, C2, C3; **pruf**, *imp. pl.*,
1, S2; **preuede**, *pt. s.*, S2; **proued**, *pl.*, S2;
preued, *pp.*, S3.—OF. *prover (prouver)*; Lat.
probare.

prouende, *sb.* food, Manip.; **prouendre**,
food, PP; a prebend, ecclesiastical benefice,
PP, CM.—OF. *provende (provendre)*; Church
Lat. *praebenda,* a ration, allowance, see BH
(Introd. § 40).

prouendre, *sb.* a prebendary, SkD.—OF.
provendier.

prouendren, *v.* to provide with prebends, P.

prouendreres, *sb. pl.* men who hold
prebends, S2, PP.

prouisours, *sb. pl.* men named by the pope
to a living not vacant, S2, PP.—Church
Lat. *provisores* (Ducange).

prow, *sb.* profit, advantage, C, C3, G, H, PP,
HD; **prou**, H.—OF. *prou, pru,* advantage
(Bartsch).

prowesse, *sb.* prowess, S2; **pruesse**, S.—
AF. *pruesse,* OF. *proece.*

prustes, *sb. pl.* priests, S2; see **prest**[2].

prut, *adj.* proud, S; see **proud**.

pryde, *sb.* pride, PP; **prute**, S2; **prude**, PP,
S, S2; **pruyde**, P; **pruide**, PP, S2; **pride**,
S2 (p. 74).—AS. *prýte.* See **proud**.

prydeles, *adj.* void of pride, C2.

pryen, *v.* to pry, PP, C3; **prien**, PP; **pry**,
Cath.; **prie**, *1 pr. s.*, Palsg.

pryk, *sb.* a sting, Prompt.; **prik**, point, WA.

pryket, *sb.* a young buck, *capriolus,* Prompt.;
pricket, a buck in his second year (named
from his *pricking* horns), S3, HD, Cotg. (s.v.
dagard).

prykie, *v.* to prick, goad, spur, ride fast, PP;
prikken, C2, Prompt.; **pryghte**, *pt. s.*, C2.

prykiere, *sb.* rider, horseman, PP.

prykke, *sb.* a broach, Prompt.; **prikke**,
puncture, sting, C, C2.

pryklyng, *pr. p.* urging, S3.

pryme, *sb.* the period from six o'clock to 9
a.m., also 9 a.m., Prompt., S, PP, C2, C3;
prime, S, S3, WA. *Phr.*: **heiȝ prime**, high
prime, 9 a.m., PP. *Comb.*: **prime-tide**,
prime, S.—Church Lat. *prima.*

prymer, *sb.* primer, C2.

pryns, *sb.* prince, PP; **prynce**, Prompt.—
AF. *prince*; Lat. *principem.*

prynshode, *sb.* princely dignity, W; **prins-
hod**, W.

prynte, *sb.* print, W; see **prente**.

prys[1], *sb.* price, prize, value, excellence, high
esteem, C, C2, PP; **pris**, S, S2, PP; **price**,
WA, S2; **pryce**, Prompt.—AF. *pris*; Lat.
prĕtium, see BH, § 32.

prys[2], *adj.* prize, chief, PP; **pris**, S2; **prijs**,
S3.

prysen, *v.* to set a price, Prompt.; **priss**, to
prize, S2.

pryson, *v.* to put in prison, Prompt.;
y-prisoned, *pp.*, G. See **prisun**[1].

prysonere, *sb.* prisoner, captive, Prompt.;
prisonere, PP.—OF. *prisonier,* AF. *prisuner.*

pryue, *adj.* secret, intimate, PP, S2; **priuee**,
C2, C3; **priuei**, S2; **prevy**, S3; **priuee**,
adv., C2; **priues**, *pl.*, secret friends, P;
priueliche, *adv.*, secretly, S2, PP; **priuely**,
C2; **pryuely**, C2.—AF. *prive*; Lat. *priuatum.*

pryuen, *v.* to deprive, Prompt.; **prife**, H;
pryuyd, *pt. s.*, H.—OF. *priver*; Lat. *priuare.*

pryuete, *sb.* privity, secret counsel, PP;
priuitee, S2, C2, C; **pryuyte**, S2.—AF.
privete.

psalme, *sb.* psalm, H, PP; see **salm**.

psautere, *sb.* psalter, H (p. 3); see **sauter**.

publisshen, *v.* to make public, PP, C2;
puplische, W (Mt. 1. 19); **pupplische**,
S2; **publice**, *imp. s.*, PP.—A form due to
analogy from OF. *publier*; Lat. *publicare.*

pucelle, *sb.* a girl, maiden; **pucell**, S3.—
OF. *pucelle, pulcelle*; dimin. from Lat. *pullus,*

the young of any animal; cf. OF. *polle,*
maiden (Bartsch). Cf. **pulte, polcat.**
pukken, *v.* to poke, push, incite, P; **pukked,**
pt. s., P.
pulched, *pp.* polished, S3; see **polische.**
pulte, *sb.* pullet, Prompt.; **poletes,** *pl.,* S2,
PP.—OF. *polete;* dim. of *pole, polle;* Lat. *pulla.*
Cf. **pucelle, polcat.**
pulten, *v.* to push, beat, strike, put, PP, S2;
pelte, PP; **pilte,** PP, SkD (s.v. *pelt*); **pulte,**
pt. s., PP; **pult,** PP, S2; **pelte,** S; **pelt,** PP;
i-pilt, *pp.,* G; **pilt,** S, SkD.
pulter, *sb.* poulterer, Cath.—AF. *poleter,*
pulleter.
pultrie, *sb.* poultry, S3, C, Prompt.;
pultery, name of a London street, the
Poultry, S3.—AF. *pultrie, poletrie.*
punde, *sb. dat.* pound; see **pound**[1].
puple, *sb.* people, PP, Prompt., W2; **pupel,**
S2; **poeple,** PP; **puplis,** *pl.,* W2.—OF.
peuple, poeple (AF. *people*); Lat. *populum.*
pur, *adj.* pure, thorough, complete, S2, PP;
pure, PP, S3, C; **puir,** PP; **puire,** PP;
pur, *adv.,* completely, S2; **pure,** merely,
very, S3; **purlyche,** *adv.,* purely, completely, S3.—OF. *pur;* Lat. *purum.*
purchacen, *v.* to acquire, purchase, PP;
purchasen, C3.—AF. *purchacer,* to pursue,
to acquire; OF. *porchacier.*
purchas, *sb.* gain, winnings, C, G; **porchas,** S2.—AF. *purchas.*
purchasour, *sb.* prosecutor, C.—AF. *pure-
chasour.*
purchasyng, *sb.* prosecution, C.
purfil, *sb.* the furred trimming of a dress, P;
purfyle, P; **purfle,** a hem, Manip.
purfilen, *v.* to embroider on an edge, to
purl, C, P; **purfle,** Cotg.—OF. *pourfiler,*
from *filer,* to twist threads, from *fil,* thread;
Lat. *filum.*
purpre, *sb.* purple garments, S, PP;
purpire, H (44. 11); **purpour,** *adj.,* S3;
purpur, W; **purpres,** *pl.,* purple cover-
ings, S.—AF. *purpre;* Lat. *purpura.*
purpurat, *adj.* of a purple colour, S3.—Lat.
purpuratus, clad in purple.
purpuresse, *sb.* a seller of purple (=
purpuraria), W.
purse, *sb.* purse, bag, PP, S, C3; **purs,** PP,
C2, C; **porse,** PP; **pors,** S2.—AS. *purs*
(Engl. Studien, xi. 65, 1.36); Late Lat. *bursa;*
Gr. βύρση, a skin.
purtenaunce, *sb.* appurtenance, belong-
ings, PP; **purtenance,** the intestines of an
animal, WW; **portenaunce,** Palsg.;
purtenancis, *pl.,* S3.—OF. *appartenance*
(Cotg.).
purtreied, *pp.* pourtrayed, S3; see **portrey.**

purveour, *sb.* purveyor, PP, SkD.—AF.
purveour.
purveyaunce, *sb.* providence, provision,
plan, means of getting, equipment, W; **pur-
veiance,** S2, C3; **pureance,** S2.—AF.
purveaunce, OF.*pörveänce;* Lat. *providentia.*
purueyen, *v.* to provide, W2, C2, PP;
puruay, S2, H; **poruayen,** H; **por-
ueynde,** *pr. p.,* S2; **purueid,** *pp.,* S3;
pourveid, S2; **porueid,** S2.—AF. *purveier,*
purvëer, for OF. *porvëoir;* Lat. *prouidëre.*
putten, *v.* to put, push, PP, W; **puten,** S;
puiten, PP; **puttide,** *pt. s.,* S2; **potte,** S2;
pot, *pl.,* S2; **putten to,** added, assented,
W; **put,** *pp.,* H; **y-put,** C3; **i-put,** G.
puttynge, *sb.* pushing, instigation, H.
puðeren, *v.* to poke about, S (9. 96).
puyssant, *adj.* powerful, SkD; **puissant,**
S3.—OF. *puissant, poissant;* Late Lat. **poc-
sentem, *possentem* (cf. It. *possente*), from Lat.
posse, to be able; see Constans (Notes, p. 23).
puyssaunce, *sb.* might, power, HD; **puys-
aunce,** S3; **piscence,** S3.—OF. *puissance,*
poissance.
pykare, *sb.* a little thief, Prompt.; **pykers,**
pl., PP.
pyke, *sb.* a pike, pointed pole, staff furnished
with a spike, Prompt.; **pyk,** S2; **pykis,** *pl.,*
thorns, prickles, S3. *Comb.:* **pyk-staf,** pike-
staff, PP.
pyken, *v.* to pick, to steal, PP, Prompt.;
picke, WW; **pykkand,** *pr. p.,* S3; **pikid,**
pt. s., PP. *Comb.:* **pyke-herneis,** plunderers
of armour, PP; **pyke-hernois,** PP; **pyke-
porse,** one who steals a purse, PP; **picke-
purse,** S3; **pick-purse,** a maker for Paris,
S3 (p. 374); **pike-purs,** C. Cf. **picchen.**
pykeys, *sb.* a mattock, tool for digging,
Prompt.; **pykoys,** P; **pycows,** Voc.—OF.
picois (Ducange).
pylche, *sb.* a furred garment, Voc., HD,
Prompt.; **pilche,** S3, HD, ND. *Comb.:*
pilche-clut, a pilch-clout, rag of a pilch,
S.—AS. *pylce;* Lat. *pellicia,* made of fur
(Voc.).
pylgrim, *sb.* pilgrim, PP; **pilegrym,** S; **pele-
grim,** SkD; **pylgrymes,** *pl.,* PP.—Prov.
pellegrins; Lat. *peregrinus;* cf. OF. *pelerin.* See
peregrin[1].
pylgrimage, *sb.* pilgrimage, PP; **pelrimage,** S.—AF. *pilrymage;* OF. *pelerinage.*
pyment, *sb.* spiced wine and honey, CM,
Voc.; **pirment,** *nectar,* Voc., HD; **py-
mente,** Prompt.—OF. *piment, pigment*
(Bartsch); Late Lat. *pigmentum* (Ducange).
pynden, *v.* to shut in the pound, Cath.;
punt, *pr. s.,* S.—AS. *pyndan* (in *for-pyndan*);
cf. Icel. *pynda.* See **pound**[2].

pynder, *sb.* a pindar, pinner, one who impounds stray cattle, Cath., Bardsley; **pyndare**, Prompt.; **pinder**, ND; **pynner**, Manip., Bardsley; **pinner**, Bardsley.

pyne, *sb.* anguish, torment, S, S3, C2, C3; **pyn**, S2; **pines**, *pl.*, S, S2; **pynes**, S2; **pine**, S; **pinen**, S; **pynen**, S2.—AS. *pín*; Late Lat. *pēna*, see Sievers, 69. Cf. **peyne**. **pynen**, *v.* to torment, S2; **pinen**, S; **pyns**, *pr. s.*, S2; **pinede**, *pt.*, S., suffered, PP; **pynede**, S2; **pined**, *pp.*, S; tormented, S2; **y-pyned**, S2; **i-pined**, S.—AS. *pínian* (BT).

pyning, *sb.* torture; **pining**, S. *Comb.*: **pynyng-stoles**, stools of punishment, cucking-stools, PP, S2.—AS. *pínung.*

pynne, *sb.* pin, peg, bolt, bar, PP; **pyn**, G.—AS. *pinn*, pin, peg (BT).

pynnen, *v.* to shut up, enclose, pen, PP; **pinnen**, PP, S2; **pennen**, SkD.—AS. *pennan* (in *on-pennan*).

pynoun, *sb.* a pennon, C; see **penoun**.

pyony, *sb.* peony, Prompt.; **pyon**, Cath.; **pyany**, Prompt.; **piones**, *pl.*, seeds of the peony, P; **pyonies**, PP.—OF. *pione, pion* (Cotg.); Lat. *p(a)eonia*; Gr. παιωνία, the peony.

pyry, *sb.* storm of wind, gust, Prompt.; **pyrie**, S3 (p. 437); **pirie**, HD, Prompt. (*n*); **pyrry**, Palsg., ND: **pirrie**, S3, ND; **perrie**, Prompt. (*n*), ND; **berrie**, Cotg. (s.v. *tourbillor*); **berry**, Florio (s.v. *cróscia d'ácque*), HD.

pyt, *sb.* pit, pool, Prompt.; **put**, S. PP; **pit**, S; **pytte**, Prompt.; **putte**, S, PP, S2; **pette**, S2.—AS. *pytt*; Late Lat. **putius*; Lat. *puteus*.

Q

For other words with the sound of initial **kw-**, *see under* **C** *and* **K** *above.*

quad[1], *adj.* and *sb.* evil, bad, the Evil One, MD, C2; **qued**, MD, PP; **cwed**, MD; **quet**, MD; **kueade**, *dat.*, S2; **queade**, S2; **quede**, S2.—AS. *cwead;* cf. Du. *kwaad.*

quad[2], *pt. s.* quoth, S; see **queþen.**

quaile, *v.* to wither, to die, S3 (28a. 91), SkD, ND. Sh.; to overpower, intimidate, ND, SkD, Sh.

quain, *sb.* trouble, mourning, S2.—AS. **hwán.* See **quainen.**

quainen, *v.* to lament, MD (s.v. *hwenen*); **whene**, MD.—AS. *hwánan* (in *á-hwǽnan*, BT).

quair, *sb.* quire, book, S3; **quayre**, Manip., CM; **quayer**, Voc.—OF. *quayer* (F. *cahier*), Prov. *cazern* for *cadern*; It. *quaderno*; Lat. *quaternum;* cf. Late Lat. *quaternio* a sheet folded in four (Voc.). See **quartern.**

quaken, *v.* to quake, tremble, S2; **cwakien**, S; **quakede**, *pt. s.*, PP, MD; **quok** (*strong form*), PP; **quook**, C2, SkD; **quoke**, S2, H.—AS. *cwacian.*

quakynge, *sb.* trembling, Prompt., MD; **quakyng**, W.—AS. *cwacung.*

qual, *sb.* whale, MD, Cath. (*n*); **qwal**, Prompt.; **qwaylle**, Cath.; **quale**, S2; **whal**, W2; **hwel**, MD; **qualle**, *pl.*, S2, Cath. (*n*); **quhalis**, S3, Cath. (*n*).—AS. *hwæl.*

qualm, *sb.* death, pestilence, S2, H; **cwalm**, MD; **qualme**, *dat.*, C.—AS. *cwealm.* See **quelen.**

quarel, *sb.* a square-headed cross-bow bolt, quarrel, WA, SkD; **quarelle**, S2; **quarrel**, WA, ND.—AF. *quarel*, cross-bow bolt; Late Lat. *quadrellum* (acc.), a quarrel, a square tile, dimin. of Lat. *quadrus*, square.

quarere, *sb.* quarry, Prompt.; **quareres**, *pl.*, S2.—OF. *quarriere* (Cotg.); Late Lat. *quadraria*, quarry, deriv. from *quadrus*. See **quarel.**

quartern, *sb.* prison; **cwarterne**, *dat.*, MD; **quarterne**, S, MD.—AS. *cweartern*, prison, perhaps for AS. *quatern*, 'quaternio' (OET). Cf. Fr. *caserne* (Sp. *caserna*), barracks; Lat. *quaterna* (see Brachet); an ętym. illustrated by the Fr. sea-term *casernet*, log-book, a deriv. of Lat. *quaternum*, see Diez, p. 755 (s.v. *cahier*).—See **quair.**

quarteroun, *sb.* a quarter, P, HD; **quartrun**, PP.

quat, *pt. s.* quoth, S; see **queþen.**

quatriuials, *sb. pl.* the quadrivials, the quadrivium, the four higher sciences: astrology, geometry, arithmetic, music, S3 (14. 511).—From Late Lat. *quadrivium*, the four mathematical sciences; in Lat. a place where four ways meet.

quað, *pt. s.* quoth, S; see **queþen.**

quave-mire, *sb.* quagmire, HD; **quamier**, DG.

quauen, *v.* to shake, S2, PP, Prompt.; **quave**, HD, JD, DG.

quauynge, *sb.* shaking, MD.

quayle, *v.* to curdle, to coagulate, Palsg., Prompt., Manip.—OF. *coailler* Lat. *coagulare.*

quaynt, *adj.* prudent, wise, H; **quaynte**, quaint, curious, WA; see **coint.**

quayntis, *sb.* wisdom, prudence, H; see **cointise.**

quayre, *sb.* quire, book, CM see **quair.**

queade, *sb.* evil, iniquity, S2; see **quad**[1].

queale, *sb.* a blister, pimple, *pupula*, Manip.; see **whele**[2].

quecchen, *v.* to shake, MD; **qvycchyn**, Prompt.; **quytche**, Palsg.; **quitch**, Cotg. (s.v. *oeil*); **cwehte**, *pt. s.*, MD; **quehte**, MD.—AS. *cweccan.*

qued, *adj.* bad, S2, PP; see **quad**[1].

quedschipe, *sb.* wickedness, MD; **queadschipe**, S; **cweadschipe**, S.

queere, *sb.* quire, choir, Prompt.; **queer**, W2; **quere**, W2; **queir**, S3.—OF. *choeur* (Cotg.); Lat. *chorum* (acc.); Gr. χορός.

quek, *adj.* living, S2; see **quik.**

quelen, *v.* to die, MD; **cwelen**, MD.—AS. *cwelan*, pt. *cwæl* (pl. *cwǽlon*), pp. *cwolen.* Cf. OHG. *quelan*, 'cruciari' (Tatian).

quellen, *v.* to kill, S, S2, C3, C; **quelde**, *pt. s.*, S; **cwelled**, *pp.*, S.—AS. *cwellan;* cf. OHG. *quelen* 'cruciare' (Tatian), *quellen* (Otfrid).

quellere, *sb.* executioner, MD.—AS. *cwellere.*

queme, *adj.* pleasing, S, MD; **qweme**, convenient, WA; **cweme**, S; **wheme**, MD.—AS. (*ge*)*cwéme*, from *c(w)óm*, pt. of *cuman;* cf. OHG. (*bi*)*queman*, to come to, to suit, fit (Otfrid); see Kluge (s.v. *bequem*). See **comen.**

quemeful, *adj.* placable, W2.

quemen, *v.* to please, S, H, PP; **cwernen**, S; **cwemde**, *pt. s.*, S; **i-quemd**, *pp.*, S; **i-cwemet**, S.—AS. *cwéman.*

quenchen, *v.* to quench, S, Prompt., S3, SkD; **cwennkenn**, S; **queynte**, *pt. s.*, MD,

166

S2; **queynt**, *pp.*, MD, C; **y-kuenct**, S2;
quenchid, W2.—AS. *cwencan*.
quene, *sb.* queen, wife, woman, quean, S,
C2, C3, WA; **quen**, S, C; **cuen**, S; **kuen**,
MD; **kwene**, S; **cwene**, MD.—AS. *cwén*;
cf. OHG. *quena*, wife (Otfrid); for root see
Brugmann, § 467, 3. {It should be noted
that E. *queen* is not precisely the same word
as E. *quean*. For *queen* is the phonetic
equivalent of AS. *cwén*, Goth. *qēns*, whereas
quean represents AS. *cwĕne*, Goth. *qinō*.}
querel, *sb.* a complaint, dispute, quarrel, S2,
W2; **querele**, SkD.—AF. *querele*; Late Lat.
*querella, for Lat. *querēla*.
querne, *sb.* hand-mill, C2, Prompt., Palsg.,
MD; **queerne**, W.—AS. *cweorn*; cf. Goth.
qairnus; see Brugmann, § 442.
querrour, *sb.* quarry-man, CM. See **quarere**.
quest, *sb.* an inquiry, jury, verdict, G.—OF.
queste, a quest (Cotg.). *Quest* is used for the
proper legal term *enquest*; OF. *enqueste*.
queste, *sb.* will, bequest, G; **quiste**, S. A
corrupt form of **quide** (q.v.), influenced by
the above word.
queðen, *v.* to speak, MD; **cweðen**, S, MD;
cwað, *pt. s.*, S; **cweð**, S; **queð**, S; **quað**, S,
S2; **quoð**, S; **quat**, S; **quad**, S; **quod**, S,
S2, C2; **koth**, S3; **couth**, MD; **cothe**,
MD; **hwat**, MD; **wat**, S; **ko**, S3; **i-cwede**,
pp., S.—AS. *cweðan*, pt. *cwæð* (pl. *cwǽdon*), pp.
ge-cweden.
queynt, *adj.* prudent, fine, quaint, MD;
queynte, S3, C2, MD; see **coint**.
queynte, *pt. s.* was extinguished, S2; see
quenchen.
queyntelich, *adv.* skilfully, neatly, MD;
queynteli, S3; see **cointeliche**.
queyntise, *sb.* skill, S3; see **cointise**.
quide, *sb.* speech, bequest, MD; **cwide**, S,
MD.—AS. *cwide*; cf. OHG. *quiti*, 'testimonium' (Tatian). See **queþen**.
quidities, *sb. pl.*, S3.—From Late Lat.
quiditas, a term of the Schoolmen; that
which relates to the essence of a thing,
having reference to the question *quid est*,
what is it? Cf. OF. *quidditatif*, 'quidditative,

doubtful, full of quirks, contentions,
wrangling' (Cotg.).
quik, *adj.* and *adv.* living, quick, flowing (of
water), S, S2, W; **quic**, S, S2; **quek**, S2;
quyk, S3, W, W2; **cwic**, S; **cwike**, S;
cwuce, S; **quicke**, S; **quike**, *pl.*, S, S2;
quyke, S, C; **quycke**, S3.—AS. *cwic (cuc)*;
cf. OHG. *quek* (Otfrid).
quikie, *v.* to cause to revive, also, to be
kindled, PP; **quike**, C3; **quyke**, C;
cwikien, MD.—AS. *cwician*.
quikliche, *adv.* quickly, PP; **quicliche**, S2.
quiknen, *v.* to give life, to receive life, SkD;
quykene, W, W2.
quiste, *sb.* will, bequest, S; see **queste**.
quiten, *v.* to repay, PP; see **quyten**.
quitter, *sb.* filth that runs from a wound,
HD: **quytur**, rottenness, HD; **quytere**,
W2; **quitture**, DG.
quod, *pt. s.* quoth, S, S2, C2; see **queþen**.
quok, *pt. s.* quaked, C2; see **quaken**.
quoynte, *adj.* skilful, MD, HD; see **coint**.
quoynteliche, *adv.* skilfully, MD; see
cointeliche.
quoyntyse, *sb.* quaintness of dress, PP;
quointise, stratagem, S2; see **cointise**.
quyk, *adj.* living, moving, S3, W, W2; see
quik.
quyk-myre, *sb.* quagmire, S3.
quyknar, *sb.* giver of life, S3.
quyr-boilly, *sb.* boiled leather, used for
making defensive armour, C2.—OF. *cuir
bouilli* (Cotg.).
quyrry, *sb.* the quarry, the dog's share in the
slaughtered game, S3; **quyrre**, SkD (s.v.
quarry, p. 824); **guerre**, SkD.—OF. *cuiree*;
Late Lat. *coriata*, from Lat. *corium*, hide, skin
(OF. *cuir*).
quyten, *v.* to requite, repay, settle, satisfy,
S2, C2, C3, PP, W, H; **quiten**, S2, PP;
quitte, *pt. s.* G; **qwit**, H; **quyt**, *pp.*, PP; **y-quit**, C2.—OF. *quiter*; Late Lat. *quietare*.
quytly, *adj.* quite, H; **whitely**, H.
quytter, *v.* to twitter, S3.
quytur, *sb.* rotteinness, HD (p. 660); see
quitter.

R

ra, *sb.* roe, deer, CM; see **roo**[1].
rabete, *sb.* a war-horse; **rabett**, HD; **rabyghte**, HD; **rabetis**, *pl.*, WA.—Icel. *rábítr*, an Arabian steed; cf. Icel. *rábitar*, Arabs, see CV; cf. OF. *arrabi* (BH).
rac, *sb.* driven vapour, S2; see **wrak**.
rachenteges, *pl.* chains, S; see **rakenteie**.
racke, *v.* to stretch rent to its full value, S3. Cf. ODu. *racken*, to rack, *recken*, to stretch, reach out.
rad[1], *adj.* afraid, S2, SD, H, JD, B; **redd**, WA; **rade**, S2, H; **radde**, S2.—Icel. *hræddr*.
rad[2], *pt. s.* rode, S2; see **riden**.
rad[3], *adj.* quick, S; **rade**, ready, S; see **raþe**[1].
radde, *pt. s.* advised, S2; see **reden**[1].
raddour, *sb.* violence, WA; see **reddour**.
rade, *sb.* road, S2; see **rode**[1].
radnesse, *sb.* terror, SD; **radnes**, B.
radyous, *adj.* radiant, shining, S3; **radious**, S3; **radius**, S3.—Lat. *radiosus*; cf. F. *radieux*. See **ray**.
ræd, *sb.* advice, counsel, S; see **rede**[3].
ræh, *adj.* fierce, cruel, SD, S; **reh**, SD.—AS. *hréoh*.
ræueden, *pt. pl.* spoiled, S; see **reven**.
ræueres, *sb. pl.* robbers, S; see **revere**.
rafte, *pt. s.* reft, robbed, C2; see **reven**.
rage[1], *sb.* madness, S2.—AF. *rage*; Lat. *rabiem*.
rage[2], *v.* to toy wantonly, C; **ragid**, *pp.*, been wanton, WA.
ragerie, *sb.* wantonness, CM.
raght, *pp.* reached, S2; see **rechen**[3].
ragman, *sb.* a craven, the devil; **rageman**, PP; **raggeman**, PP.—Icel. *ragr* (for *argr*), craven, cowardly.
ragman-roll, *sb.* the craven's roll, a term in Scottish history, JD, ND; a game, HD; **ragman's rewe**, a long jest, DG; **ragmanrew**, *series*, Manip. Hence **ragman**, a deed sealed, a papal bull, PP; **ragemon**, S2; **rageman**, a list, S3; **ragman**, a tedious story, JD; **ragment**, JD.—Cf. E. *rigmarole*.
rair, *v.* to roar, S3; see **roren**.
raiss, *pt. s.* rose, S2; see **rysen**.
rake[1], *sb.* only in compounds, as in **erendrake**, messenger, SD.—AS. *ǽrend-raca*; cf. Icel. *eyrend-reki*, so *land-reki*, a king, see CV (s.v. *reki*). See **ærnd-race**.
rake[2], *v.* to run, wander, go, S, S3, HD, PP, JD, B; **rayke**, H, S2; **raik**, WA, JD; **reyke**, JD; **reke**, HD; **raykande**, *pr. p.*, S2.—Icel. *reika*, to wander, cf. Swed. *raka*, to run hastily (Rietz).
rake[3], *sb.* course, way, WA; **rakke**, WA.

rakel, *adj.* hasty, rash, CM, SkD (s.v. *rake*); **rakle**, CM; **racle**, CM; **rackel**, JD; **rakyl**, Manip.; **rakehell**, a bad fellow, Manip., ND.—Icel. *reikull*, wandering, unsettled. See **rake**[2].
raken, *v.* to scrape, diminish, to rake, S, Prompt.; **raked**, *pp.*, C2.—Icel. *raka*, to scrape, to rake away.
raken-teie, *sb.* chain; **raketeie**, S; **raketeye**, S; **rachenteges**, *pl.*, S; **rakenteis**, HD.—AS. *racentéah* (Voc.); *racente*, a chain + *téah*, a tye. With *racente*, cf. Icel. *rekendr*, OHG. *rahhinza*. See **rekenthis**.
ram, *sb.* a ram, Prompt.—AS. *ram* (Voc.).
ramage, *adj.* wild, CM, HD.—OF. *ramage*, wild (of a hawk), living in the branches (Cotg.); Late Lat. **ramaticum*, from *ramus*, a branch.
rammish, *adj.* strong-scented, C3, CM.
ramne, *sb.* bramble, W2; **ramyn**, H; **rammyn**, H.—Lat. *rhamnus* (Vulg.); Gr. ῥάμνος (LXX).
rampe, *sb.* an ill-conditioned woman, C2 (*n*), HD.
rampen, *v.* to ramp, to seize or scratch with the paws, to rage, C2; **raumpe**, S2; **rawmpide**, *pt. s.*, HD.—AF. *raumper*, OF. *ramper*, to clamber.
rande, *sb.* a strip or slice of meat, S3, HD; **rand**, Cotg. (s.v. *giste*), ND.—AS. *rand*, a rim, edge; cf. Swed. *rand*, a strip, stripe, Icel. *rönd* (pl. *randir*).
randoun, *sb.* force, impetuosity, SkD. Phr.: **in a randoun**, in a furious course, B; **at randon**, left to one's own force, SkD.—OF. *randon*, 'the swiftness and force of a strong and violent stream' (Cotg.); from OTeut. **randa*, a rim; cf. AS. *rand*. See **rande**.
ranke, *adj.* strong, luxuriant, rebellious, WA, Prompt.; **rank**, S3; **ronk**, S2; **rang**, HD.—AS. *ranc*; cf. Icel. *rakkr* (for *rankr*), straight, upright, bold.
ransaken, *v.* to search, S, PP, C, H.—Icel. *rannsaka*, to search a house; Icel. *rann*: Goth. *razn*; cf. AS. *ræsn* a plank, a beam, see Sievers, 179.
rap[1], *sb.* rope, S; see **rop**.
rap[2], *pt. s.* reaped, W, see **repen**.
rape[1], *sb.* haste, S, PP, Prompt.; **rap**, S2.—Icel. *hrap*, a falling down.
rape[2], *adj.* hasty, G; **rapest**, *superl.*, PP.
rapeliche, *adv.* hastily, PP; **rapely**, G; **rapelike**, S; **rapli**, S2, G; **rapelier**, *comp.*, PP.

rapen, *v.* to hasten, S, PP, Prompt.; **rappe**, PP; **rappe adoune**, to hurry along, PP. *Phr.*: **rape and renne**, to seize and plunder, C3; **rapen and rinen**, C3 (*n*); **rap and rend**, HD; **rap or rende**, Palsg.; **rap and run**, HD; **rap and ran**, C3 (*n*); **rap and reeve**, C3 (*n*); **rap and ree**, C3 (*n*).—Icel. *hrapa*, to fall, rush headlong, hurry.

rascall, *sb.* scrapings, refuse; **rascaile**, PP; **rascayle**, an animal not a beast of the chase, a hart not six years old, Prompt. (*n*); the common people, Prompt.; **raskaille**, the common herd, SkD; **rascall**, refuse beast, Palsg., ND; **rascalles**, *pl.*, common sort of men, low fellows, villains, S3.—AF. *rascaille* (*raskaylle, raskayle*), a rabble; cf. F. *racaille*; from OF. *rasquer*, to scrape (Ducange); cf. OIt. *rascare* (Florio).

rascall, *adj.* common, low, HD; *Comb.*: **rascall wine**, *tortivum vinum*, Prompt. (*n*).

rase[1], *v.* to run, to race, SD, S2; **rese**, S2; **reysed**, *pp.* ridden, C.—AS. *rásan*.

rase[2], *sb.* a race, rush, SkD; **ras**, SkD, S2; **rese**, S2; **res**, SD, G (*n*); **rees**, attack, fit of passion, G.—AS. *rǽs*.

rasen, *v.* to scrape, Prompt.—OF. *raser*; Late Lat. *rasare*, freq. of Lat. *radere*.

rasour, *sb.* razor, C2, C, W2; **rasure**, H (Ps. 51. 2).—OF. *rasoir*; Late Lat. *rasorium*.

raspen, *v.* to rasp, scrape, SkD; **rospen**, S.—OF. *rasper*; OHG. *raspón*, see Weigand.

rasse, *sb.* a raised mound or eminence, a cairn of stones, S2; **raise**, HD. See **reysen**.

rat, *pr. s.* reads, PP; see **reden**[2].

raton, *sb.* rat, PP, Cath.; **ratoun**, PP; **ratones**, *pl.*, PP.

ratoner, *sb.* rat-catcher, PP, Voc.; **ratonere**, PP.

ratte, *sb.* rat, PP; **rotte**, Voc.; **rattis**, *pl.*, PP.—AS. *rǽt* (Voc.).

ratten, *v.* to tear, SD.—Cf. MHG. *ratzen*, see Weigand (s.v. *ratsche*).

rattes, *sb. pl.* rags, S; **rats**, pieces, shreds, HD.

raþ, *sb.* advice, S, SD.—Icel. *ráð*.

raðe[1], *adj.* quick, swift, SD; **rad**, quick, S; **rade**, *pl.*, S; **raddere**, *comp. pl.*, S.—AS. *hræð, hreð*, also *hræd, hred*, quick, also *rad*. Cf. Chron. ann. 755 (Parker) with the Laud MS.

rathe[2], *v.* to advise, HD.—Icel. *ráð*.

rathe[3], *adv.* early, PP, S2, S3; quickly, S, S2; **reaðe**, S; **rath**, B; **raðer**, *comp.*, sooner, rather, PP, S, S2, C2; **redþer**, S; **raðest**, *superl.*, PP; **raðeste**, S.

rathly, *adv.* quickly, S2; **reaðliche**, S; **readliche**, S; **radeliche**, HD; **radely**, S2; **redliche**, S.—AS. *hræðlice*.

raughte, *pt. s.* reached, C2; see **rechen**[3].

raunson, *v.* to ransom, redeem, PP.

raunsoun, *sb.* ransom, S2, C; **raunson**, S2; **raunsun**, S2; **raunceoun**, PP; **ransoune**, B.—AF. *raunson, ranson*, OF. *raënson, reänçon*; Lat. *redemptionem*.

raueyn, *sb.* rapine, prey, W, PP; **ravyne**, S3; **ravyn**, Cath.; **raueyns**, *pl.*, W2.—AF. *ravine*; Lat. *rapina* see BH, § 150.

raueynour, *sb.* robber; **raueinour**, W; **rauynour**, W2.

ravin[1], *adj.* ravenous, S3, Sh.

ravin[2], *v.* to seize and devour greedily, Sh., WW.

ravined, *adj.* ravenous, Sh.

rauischen, *v.* to seize with violence, PP; **ravish**, WW; **raueische**, *imp. pl.*, W2; **rauyschiden**, *pt. pl.*, W2.—AF. *ravir* (pr. p. *ravissant*); Late Lat. **rapīre*; Lat. *rapere*.

rawe, *sb.* row, Cath.; **raw**, B, JD, SkD, S3, S2; **rowe**, SkD; **rewe**, C, G, W; **rewis**, *pl.*, S3.—AS. *ráwe, réwe*.

ray, *sb.* striped cloth, *rella, pannus*, Voc.; *stragulum*, Voc., Cath., HD; **raye**, S3; **rayes**, *pl.*, S2, PP. *Comb.*: **ray-cloth**, striped cloth, W2, Prompt.—AF. *drap de raye*, cloth of ray, pl. *reies*, OF. *rai, raid*; Lat. *radium* (acc.).

rayeres, *sb. pl.* sellers of *ray*, PP.

rayid, *adj.* striped, Prompt.

raykez, *pr. s.* roams, S2; **raykande**, *pr. pt.*, advancing, S2. See **rake**[2].

rayl, *sb.* rail, Prompt.; **raylle**, Cath.—Cf. Low G. *regel*, G. *riegel*, a bolt; see Kluge.

rayle[1], *v.* to rail, arrange in a row, S2; **railed**, *pp.*, S2.

rayle[2], *sb.* a kerchief, Palsg.; see **reȝel**.

raylle, *v.* to flow, S3; **raile**, ND; **reilen**, SD.

raymen, *v.* to roam about, S2; see **romen**.

raynes, *sb.* fine linen of Rheims, WA.—So named from Rheims; see SkD (p. 815); cf. It. *renso*, fine flax (Diez, p. 393).

read, *sb.* advice, S; see **rede**[3].

reade, *adj.* red, S; see **reed**[3].

readen, *v.* to advise, care for, S; see **reden**[1].

readi, *adj.* ready, S; see **redi**.

real[1], *adj.* real, a term in medieval philosophy; **reall**, S3.—OF. *real*; Schol. Lat. *realem*, from *res*.

real[2], *adj.* royal, CM; **riall**, S3, PP, CM; **ryall**, S3, CM; **ryell**, S3; **roial**, CM; **roialler**, *comp.*, S2, C3.—OF. *real*, AF. *roial, reial*; Lat. *regalem*.

realte, *sb.* royalty, royal state, PP; **reaulte**, PP; **reaute**, PP; **roialtee**, C3.—AF. *realte*; Late Lat. *regalitatem*.

realyche, *adv.* royally, S2; **realy**, S2; **rially**, CM.

reame, *sb.* kingdom, S2; see **rewme**.

rearde, *sb.* voice, cry, S2; see **rerd**.

reaðe, *adv.* quickly, S; see **raþe**[1].

reaðliche, *adv.* quickly, S; see **raþly**.

reaume, *sb.* realm, kingdom, C2, S2; see **rewme**.

rebekke, *sb.* a kind of fiddle, SkD; see **rybybe**.

rebounden, *v.* to re-echo; **rebownden**, to sound again, *reboare*, Prompt.; **rebounde**, *pt. s.*, S2.—AF. *rebundir*, to re-echo, cf. OF. *bundir*, to resound (Roland, 3119); inchoative verb, from Late Lat. *bombitare*.

receyt, *sb.* receipt, recipe, retreat, Prompt., Manip.; **receit**, C3, WW, Manip., S3; **receite**, WW; **reset**, place of refuge, B.— AF. *receite*; Late Lat. *recepta* (Ducange).

reche, *sb.* smoke, S3; see **reke**.

recheles, *adj.* careless, S, PP; **reccheles**, PP; **retcheles**, S3; **rekkeles**, S3; **recchelees**, S2, C2; **rechlesse**, S3.—AS. *réceléas*, also *recceléas*.

rechelesnesse, *sb.* carelessness, PP; **recchelesnes**, PP.

rechen[1], *v.* to care, reck, S, HD; **reke**, H; **recche**, S, HD, S2, C2; **rekke**, HD, C2; **rekþ**, *pr. s.*, S; **reches**, S2; **roȝte**, *pt. s.*, S; **roughte**, C2; **roght**, H; **rohten**, *pl.*, S; **roucht**, *pt. s., subj.*, S2.—AS. *récan*: OS. *rókian*; also, AS. **reccan*.

rechen[2], *v.* to explain, S; **ræcchen**, to relate, S; **rechede**, *pt. s.*, S.—AS. *reccan*: OS. *rekkian*: OHG. *rachjan*, in Otfrid *rachón*.

rechen[3], *v.* to reach, attain, S3, PP; **rauhte**, *pt. s.*, PP, S2; **rauȝte**, PP; **raghte**, PP; **raughte**, C2; **raught**, S3; **raght**, *pp.*, S2.—AS. *récan* (BT), also *récean*, to get into one's power, pt. s. *réhte*, see Sievers, 407.

reclayme, *v.* to bring a hawk to the wrist by a call, C3; **recleymyn**, to make tame, Prompt.; **recleymyd**, *pp. redomitus* (used of hawks), Prompt.—OF. *reclaimer*, *recleimer*, *reclamer*; cf. AF. *reclame*, pp., reclaimed (as a falcon).

recles, *sb.* incense, S; see **rekels**.

recluse[1], *sb.* a female anchorite, SkD; 'ankyr, anachorita' Prompt.—AF. *reclus*; *recluse*, a f. pp. from OF. *reclure*, to shut up; Late Lat. *recludere*.

recluse[2], *sb.* convent, monastery, S3.—OF. *recluse*.

reclused, *pp.* shut up, withdrawn from the world, PP.

recognisance, *sb.* an obligation binding one over to do some particular act, S3, SkD.— AF. *reconisance*, OF. *recoignisance*.

recomand, *v.* to commend, S2, C3; **recomaundiþ**, PP.—OF. *recommander*, *recumander*.

reconforte, *v.* to comfort, C; **reconforted**, *pp.*, P.—OF. *reconforter*; cf. AF. *recunforter*.

reconsyle, *v.* to recover, regain the possession of; **reconsyled**, *pp.*, S2; **recounselid**, W.—AF. *reconciler*; Lat. *reconciliare*, to reconcile, re-establish, restore.

record, *sb.* witness, S3, WW; **recorde**, PP.—AF. *record*, OF. *recort*, mention (Bartsch).

recorde, *v.* to call to mind, C, PP; **recorded**, *pt. pl.* declared, PP.—OF. *recorder*; Late Lat. *recordare*; Lat. *recordari*.

recoure, *v.* to recover, PP; **recour**, HD; **recure**, HD; **recured**, *pp.*, S3.—AF. *recoverer*; OF. *recourer*, *recouvrer*; Lat. *recuperare*.

recours, *sb.* recourse, C2.—AF. *recours*, soleill *recours*, sunset.

recouerer, *sb.* restorer, saviour, S2.

recrayed, *pp.* defeated, PP. See **recreaunt**.

recreaunt, *adj.* recreant, defeated, CM, PP; **recreant**, PP.—AF. *recreaunt*, OF. *recreänt*; giving up the contest; Late Lat. *recredentem*.

recueil, *sb.* a collection, compilation, DG; **recuyell**, S3; **recule**, HD.—OF. *recueil* (Cotg.).

recule, *v.* to recoil, S3, Palsg., SkD, ND.— OF. *reculer*.

reculyng, *sb.* recoiling, S3.

recure[1], *sb.* recovery, S3.

recure[2], *v.* to recover, HD; see **recoure**.

reddour, *sb.* violence, rigour, HD, Trevisa (3. 313); **raddour**, WA.—OF. *rador*, later *roideur* (Cotg.); from *rade*, *roide*; Lat. *rigidum*.

rede[1], *adj.* red, C2; see **reed**[3].

rede[2], *adj.* ready, WA; **redeliche**, *adv.*, PP; **redeli**, S2.—AS. *(ge)réde*: Goth. *(ga)raids*.

rede[3], *sb.* advice, S, S2, S3, B; **read**, S; **red**, S, S2, B; **reed**, C2; **reid**, B; **ræde**, S; **reade**, S; **rade**, S; **reades**, *pl.* S.—AS. *réd*.

redels, *sb.* riddle, SkD; **redeles**, PP; **rydels**, Cath.; **rydel**, Prompt.; **riddle**, Manip.

-reden, *suffix* (used to form abstracts).— AS. *-réden*. See **hatreden**, SkD; **cunreden**, kindred, SkD; **ferreden**, S; **ȝefered**, S; **uelaȝrede**, S2.

reden[1], *v.* to give advice, to take counsel, S, S2, S3, C2, B; **readen**, S; **raden**, to succour, S; **raddest**, *2 pt. s.*, S; **radde**, *pt. s.*, HD, S2, P; **redden**, *pl.*, B, **rad**, *pp.*, S2.—AS. *(ge)rǽdan*, pt. *rǽdde*, pp. *geréd*.

reden[2], *v.* to read, S, C2, C3; **raden**, S; **rat**, *pr. s.*, PP; **reed**, *pt. s.*, PP; **radden**, *pl.*, W; **redden**, W; **radde**, *pt. s.*, S2; **rad**, *pp.*, S, C3; **red**, S3, W. *Der.*: **redunge**, passage read, S.—AS. *(ge)rǽdan*.

redgownd, *sb.* a sickness of young children, *scrophulus*, Prompt.; **reed gounde**, Palsg.; **radegoundes**, *pl.*, sores, PP.—ME. *rede*, red + *gownde*, a sore; AS. *gund*. Cf. E. *red-gum*.

redi, *adj.* ready, S, W, PP; **redy**, C2; **reddy**, B; **readi**, S; **rædiȝ**, SD; **rediliche**, *adv.*, PP, S2; **redily**, C3.

redliche, *adv.* quickly, S; see **raþly**.

redoutable, *adj.* to be feared, redoubtable, SkD.

redouten, *v.* to fear; **redoubt**, Cotg.—AF. *reduter*, OF. *redouter*; Lat. *re* + *dubitare*.

redoutyng, *sb.* reverence, C.

reduce, *v.* to bring back, S3, ND.—Lat. *reducere*.

redymyte, *pp.* wreathed, crowned, S3.— Lat. *redimitus*, pp. of *redimire*.

reed[1], *sb.* advice, C2; see **rede**[3].

reed[2], *sb.* reed, PP, Prompt.; **reod**, PP; **rehed**, W, W2; **reheed**, W2; **reodes**, *pl.*, PP; **redes**, PP. *Comb.*: **red-ȝerde**, a reed-sceptre, S.—AS. *hréod*.

reed[3], *adj.* red, C2, C3, S2, W2, PP; **rede**, C2, C3, S2, PP, B; **reid**, S3; **reade**, S.— AS. *réad*.

reednesse, *sb.* redness, C3.

rees, *sb.* fit of passion, G; see **rase**[2].

reest, *adj.* rancid (as flesh), Prompt.; **reste**, Cath.

reestyn, *v.* to be rancid, Prompt.

reeuell, *sb.* joy, revelry, PP; **reuel**, C, C2; **rule**, SPD; **reueles**, *pl.*, revels, C2.—OF. *revel*, joy (Bartsch).

refen, *v.* to roof in, S.—AS. *(ge)hréfan*. See **roof**.

reflac, *sb.* robbery, S; see **reven**.

refreissche, *v.* to refresh, C; **refreschyn**, Prompt.—AF. *refreschir*.

refreyne, *sb.* the burden of a song, literally, a repetition, CM; **refraine**, SkD.—OF. *refrain*, from *refraindre*, to repeat, to sing a song (see Constans); Lat. *re* + *frangere*.

refreynen, *v.* to bridle, *refrenare*, W, Prompt.; **refrayne**, Manip.; **refrain**, WW.—OF. *refrener*, to bridle; Lat. *refrenare* (Vulg.).

refute, *sb.* refuge, Prompt., W2; **refuit**, W2; **refuyt**, CM, HD, W2; **refut**, S2, C3; **refutt**, W2.—AF. *refute*; OF. *refuite*, *re* + *fuite*; Lat. *fugita*, pp. f. of *fugere*.

regal, *adj.* as *sb.* kingly (power), S2.—AF. *regal* Lat. *regalem*. Cf. **real**[2].

regne, *sb.* rule, a kingdom, S2, C2, C3; **rengne**, S; **ryngis**, pl., S3.—AF. *regne*; Lat. *regnum*.

regnen, *v.* to reign, C2, PP; **ring**, S3; **ryngis**, *pr. pl.*, S3; **reygned**, *pp.*, S2; **rengned**, S2.—AF. *regner*; Lat. *regnare*.

regrate, *v.* to retail wares, HD.—OF. *regrater*, to mend, scour, trick up an old thing

for sale (F. *regratter*, to bargain): It. *rigattáre*, to strive for the victory, to regrate, to sell by retail (Florio); Sp. *regateár*, 'to huck in buying or selling' (Minsheu). Cf. E. *regatta*; It. *rigátta*, a struggling for the mastery (Florio).

regratere, *sb.* retail dealer, PP.—OF. *regratier*; cf. Low Lat. *regratarium* (Ducange).

regratorie, *sb.* selling by retail, PP, S2; **regraterye**, PP.—OF. *regraterie*.

regratour, *sb.* retail dealer, S2, PP.—AF. *regratour*.

reguerdon, *sb.* reward, ND; **reguerdoun**, S2.—Cf. OF. *reguerdonner*, to guerdon abundantly (Cotg.).

reguerdonment, *sb.* requital, DG.

rehed, *sb.* reed, W, W2; see **reed**[2].

rehersaille, *sb.* rehearsal, C3.

rehersen, *v.* to rehearse, enumerate, C2, S2, PP; **rehercen**, PP, C2; **rehearse**, WW, Sh.—AF. *reherser*, *rehercer*. See **herce**.

rehersyng, *sb.* rehearsal, C.

reheten, *v.* to refresh, to cheer, H, CM, WA, HD, JD; **reheyit**, H; **rehetid**, *pp.*, H.— OF. *rehaitier* (Bartsch), cf. OF. *haitier*, to make joyful, see BH, Diez, p. 609.

rehetynge, *sb.* comfort, refreshing, H.

reioysen, *v.* to rejoice, PP, C2; **reioisshen**, PP; **reiosyng**, *pr. p.*, S3.—OF. *resjoïss-*, stem of *resjoïssant*, pr. p. of *resjoïr*, from *re* + *esjoïr*; Lat. *ex* + *gaudēre* (Late Lat. **gaudīre*); see Constans, glossaire (prefix *res-*).

reke, *sb.* vapour, smoke, S2, H (Ps. 67. 2), Cath.; **reyk**, B; **reik**, B; **reche**, S2.—AS. *réc*; cf. Icel. *reykr*. OTeut. **rauki-*; see Kluge (s.v. *rauch*).

rekels, *sb.* incense, Cath.; **recles**, S, S2. *Comb.*: **recle-fat**, incense-vessel, censer, S, SD.—AS. *récels*.

reken, *v.* to smoke, Cath.—AS. *récan*.

rekenen, *v.* to reckon up, to give account, C2, W, PP; **rekne**, S2, PP; **rikenen**, S, PP; **rikynyd**, *pp.*, W2; **y-rekened**, C2. Cf. Du. *rekenen*.

rekeninge, *sb.* reckoning, C3.

rekenthis, *sb. pl.* chains, WA; **rekanthes**, WA.—AS. *racente*; cf. Icel. *rekendr*.

rakenteie

rekkeles, *adj.* careless, S3; see **recheles**.

rekken, *v.* to reck, care, C2; see **rechen**[1].

relenten, *v.* to melt, C3, Palsg.; Prompt.; SkD.—OF. *ralentir* (Cotg.).

reles, *sb.* relaxation, forgiveness, also taste, odour, Prompt.; **relees**, Prompt. (*n*); **relece**, Prompt. *Phr.*: **out of relees**, without ceasing, C3.—AF. *reles*, *relees*, *relais*. See **releschen**.

releschen, *v.* to relax, release; **relecen**, Prompt.; **relesse**, C3; **releschand**, *pr. p.*, S3; **relessed**, *pt. s.*, forgave, C2; **relesed**, *pp.*, forgiven, PP; **relessed**, PP.—AF. *relascher, relesser, releisser* Lat. *relaxare.*

releuen, *v.* to raise up again, to rise, PP, C3; **relyue**, S3; **relieve**, *imp.*, take up again, S3.—AF. *relever;* Lat. *releuare.*

relif, *sb.* what remains, a fragment taken up from the table; **releef**, Prompt.; **relefe**, Cath., SkD; **reliefe**, Cath. (*n*); **relifs**, *pl.*, W, W2; **relifes**, W; **relifis**, W2; **relyues**, S2.—OF. *relief*, remainder (Bartsch), from *reliev-*, accented stem of *relever*, to raise up; Lat. *releuāre.*

relikes, *sb. pl.* remains, H; **relikis**, W2.—AF. *relikes;* Lat. *reliquias.*

relyen, *v.* to rally, call back, re-assemble, to take courage again, PP; **rely**, B; **releyt**, *pt. s.*, B, S2; **releit**, *pp.*, S2, B.—AF. *relier*, to rally (OF. *ralier*, in Bartsch); Lat. *re + ligare*, to bind.

relyue, *v.* to rise, S3; **relyued**, *pt. s.*, raised, S3; see **releven**.

rem[1], *sb.* a kingdom, S2; **reme**, C; see **rewme**.

rem[2], *sb.* a cry, S; **reames**, *pl.*, S.—AS. *hréam*, OS. *hróm*, Icel. *rómr.*

reme, *v.* to cry, roar, S, PP; **raum**, HD; **romy**, H; **romiand**, *pr. p.*, S2; **rumyand**, H; **romyd**, *pt. s.*, H; **remden**, *pl.*, S.—AS. *hréman*: OS. *hrómian.*

remedie, *sb.* remedy, C2; **remede**, S3.—OF. *remede*, AF. *remedie*; Lat. *remedium.*

remen, *v.* to give place, to quit, S, SD; **roume**, PP; **rumen**, SD; **rimen**, SD.—AS. *rýman*: OS. *rúmian;* cf. OFris. *rêma*, G. *räumen*, see Weigand. See **rowm.**

remenant, *sb.* remnant, C2, C3, S3; **remenaunt**, C, Prompt.; **remanand**, B; **remelawnt**, Prompt.; **remlawnt**, HD; **remlin**, Prompt. (*n*).—AF. *remenant*, OF. *remanant*, *pr. p.* of *remanoir* (Bartsch); Lat. *remanēre.*

remlet, *sb.* remnant, HD, Prompt. (*n*). See **remenant.**

remouyn, *v.* to remove, Prompt.; **remeuen**, S3, C3, Palsg., SkD.—AF. *remoever* (with change of conjugation) from OF. *removoir*; Lat. *re + mouēre.*

remuen, *v.* to remove, CM, ND, SkD; **remown**, Prompt.; **remwe**, to depart, S3; **remewed**, *pp.*, C2.—OF. *remuёr*; Lat. *re + mutare.*

renable, *adj.* eloquent, PP; see **resunable.**

renably, *adv.* reasonably, CM; **runnably**, HD. See **renable.**

rend, *v.* to make to run into a shape, to cast metal, melt, H; **rind**, **rynde**, to melt, as lard, etc., JD.—Icel. *renna*, to make to run, to pour (of a melted substance), causal of *renna* (*rinna*), to run. See **rennen.**

renden, *v.* to tear, PP; **reendyn**, Prompt.; **rente**, *pt. s.*, S; **rended**, *pp.*, S2; **y-rent**, C3.—ONorth. *rendan*, to cut or tear down (BT).

renegat, *sb.* renegade, C3; **runagate**, WW.—OF. *renegat*; Late Lat. *renegatum.*

renewlen, *v.* to renew, W; **renule**, W2; **renewlid**, *pp.*, W; **renulid**, W2.—AF. *renoveler*; Late Lat. *renovellare.*

reneye, *v.* to deny, reject, abandon, S2, PP, C2, CM.—OF. *reneier*; Late Lat. *renegare.*

reng, *sb.* rank, SD; **renges**, *pl.*, C; **rengis**, HD.—OF. *reng, renc;* cf. AF. *renc*, ring of people, *rencs*, ranks; OHG. *hring*, ring. See **ring.**

renk, *sb.* a man, PP; **renke**, PP; **renkes**, *pl.*, men, creatures, PP, HD; **renkkes**, S2; **reynkes**, PP.—Icel. *rekkr* (for *renkr*), a man, used in poetry, also in law. Cf. AS. *rinc*, a warrior, a man (Grein). See **ranke.**

renne, *v.* See **rapen.**

rennen, *v.* to run, SD, S, S2, S3, C2, W, PP; **rin**, S3; **rynne**, S3; **ryn**, S2; **eornen**, S, S2; **ernen**, S; **urnen**, S; **ʒerne**, S; **ærneð**, *pr. pl.*, S; **rynnys**, S3; **ron**, *pt. s.*, S2, PP; **urnen**, *pl.*, S; **eorn**, S; **iorne**, *pp.*, S; **ronnen**, PP; **ronne**, PP, C2; **y-ronne**, C2; **y-ronnen**, C; **arnde**, *pt. s.* (weak), S, SD; **ernde**, SD; **ærnden**, *pl.*, SD.—AS. *rinnan*, *pt. s.* *ran*, pp. *gerunnen*, also *irnan*, *yrnan*, *pt. s.* *arn*, pl. *urnon*, pp. *urnen.*

rennyng, *sb.* running, S3; **rennyngis**, *pl.*, currents, streams, W2.

renome, *sb.* renown, WW, S3; **renoume**, WW; **renowme**, WW. See **renomee.**

renomee, *sb.* renown, WW; **renoume**, B.—OF. *renomee*; Late Lat. **renominatam.*

renoumed, *adj.* renowned, WW; **renowmed**, WW.—Cf. OF. *renommé;* see Constans.

renoun, *sb.* renown, SkD; **renowne**, B.—AF. *renoun, renun*, OF. *renon, renom;* Lat. *re + nomen;* cf. Sp. *renombre*, renown (Minsheu).

rente, *sb.* revenue, pay, reward, S, C2; **rent**, Prompt.; **rentes**, *pl.*, S, PP, S2; **rentis**, PP.—AF. *rente;* Late Lat. **rendita;* Lat. *reddita;* from OF. *rendre;* Lat. *reddere.*

renten, *v.* to endow, PP.

renule, *v.* to renew, W2; see **renewlen.**

reod, *sb.* a reed, PP; see **reed**[2].

reousien, *v.* to grieve, SD.—AS. *hréowsian*, see Sievers, 411. See **rewen.**

reowen, *v.* to grieve, vex, S; see **rewen.**

reowsunge, *sb.* repentance, SD.—AS. *hréowsung.*

reowðe, *sb.* ruth, pity, S; see **rewþe.**

repair, *sb.* a place of resort, ND; **repeir**, return, S3.—OF. *repaire.*

repairen, *v.* to go to, C2, C3; **repeiring**, *pr. p.*, C2; **raparyt**, *pt. pl.*, S3; **reparit**, *pp.*,

S2.—AF. *repeirer*, OF. *repairier*; Lat. *repatriare*, to return to one's country.

reparailen, *v.* to repair; **reparaild**, *pp.*, H.—OF. *repareiller*; cf. *apareillier*, to prepare; from *pareil*, like; Late Lat. *pariculum* (Ducange).

reparaylynge, *sb.* restoration, H.

repe, *sb.* sheaf, *manipulus*, Voc., SD; **reepe**, SD; **repis**, *pl.*, H.

repen, *v.* to cut grain, PP, W, W2; **ripen**, S; **rap**, *pt. s.*, W; **repen**, *pl.*, S; **ropen**, PP; **ropun**, W; **rope**, W2.—OMerc. *rēpan* (*rȳpan, rípan*) Goth. *raupjan*, to pluck; see Sievers, 159.

repples, *sb. pl.* staves, cudgels (?), S.

repreuable, *adj.* reprehensible, C3, W.

repreue[1], *v.* to reprove, PP, Prompt., C3; **repreued**, *pp.*, S2.—OF. *repruever, reprover*; Lat. *reprŏbare*.

repreue[2], *sb.* reproof, C3; **repreef**, W.

repreuynges, *sb. pl.* reproofs, S2.

repromyssioun, *sb.* promise, W.—Lat. *repromissionem* (Vulg.).

repugnen, *v.* to fight against, W2; to deny, PP.—Lat. *repugnare*.

repylle-stok, *sb.* an implement for cleaning flax, Voc. See **ripple**.

rerage, *sb.* arrears, PP, HD; **rerages**, *pl.*, PP. Cf. **arerage**.

rerd, *sb.* voice, sound, SD; **rerid**, WA; **reorde**, S; **rorde**, SD: **rearde**, S2; **rurd**, S2; **rerde**, *dat.*, SD, HD.—AS. *reord* for *reard*, cf. OHG. *rarta*: Goth. *razda*; cf. Icel. *rödd* (gen. *raddar*).

rerden, *v.* to speak, to sound; **reordien**, SD; **rerdit**, *pt. pl.*, S3.—AS. *reordian*.

reren, *v.* to make to rise, to rear, S2, B; **rerde**, *pt. s.*, S, S2; **rerid**, *pp.*, S2; **rered**, S2.—AS. *rēran*: Goth. *raisjan*. See **rysen**.

resalgar, *sb.* realgar, red orpiment, C3, HD.—Sp. *rejalgar*, arsenic (Minsheu).

rescouen, *v.* to rescue, SkD; **rescowe**, CM; **reskew**, B.—OF. *rescou-*, stem of *rescouant*, *rescoant*, pr. p. of *rescorre*. See **rescous**.

rescous, *sb.* rescue, S3, C, SkD, CM.—OF. *rescous (rescos)* pp. of *rescorre*, to help, repair a damage, also *resqueure* (BH); Lat. *re + excutere*, to shake off.

rese, *sb.* and *v.*; see **rase**[1], **rase**[2].

resen, *v.* to shake, C; see **rusien**.

reset, *sb.* place of refuge, B; see **receyt**.

resownen, *v.* to resound; **resowne**, C; **resouned**, *pt. s.*, C2.—OF. *resoner*; Lat. *resonare*.

respyt, *sb.* respite, delay, leisure, C3, C; **respyte**, Prompt., Cath.; **respit**, B.—AF. *respit*; Late Lat. *respectum* (acc.), respite, prorogation (Ducange); a technical sense of Lat. *respectus*, consideration.

rest, *sb.* rest; **reste**, S.—AS. *rest*; cf. OHG. *resti* (Tatian).

resten, *v.* to rest, S.—AS. *restan*; cf. OHG. *resten* (Tatian).

resun, *sb.* reason, talk, S2, PP, Prompt.; **resoun**, C2, S2, PP; **reson**, C2, PP, HD; **reison**, PP.—AF. *resoun (reison, reasoun)*, also *raisoun*, reason, language; Lat. *rationem*.

resunable, *adj.* reasonable, talkative, eloquent, Prompt.; **resonable**, PP; **resnabyl**, HD; **renable**, PP; **runnable**, PP. Notes (p. 23).—AF. *resonable*, OF. *resnable*, *raisnable*; Lat. *rationabilem*.

retenaunce, *sb.* retinue, company, PP, HD.—AF. *retenaunce*; Late Lat. *retinentia* (Ducange).

retenue, *sb.* retinue, suite, C2.—OF. *retenuë*, a retinue (Cotg.); Late Lat. *retenuta* (Ducange). In F. *retenue* means 'reserve, modesty', and has become obsolete in the English sense of a 'suite', a body of attendants.

rethor, *sb.* orator, C, C2, Manip.—Late Lat. *rhethor*; Lat. *rhetor*; Gr. ῥήτωρ.

rethoryke, *sb.* rhetoric, C2; **retoryke**, PP; **retoryk**, PP.—Lat. *rhetorica*.

retten, *v.* to account, impute, C, H, Prompt., W; **rectyn**, Prompt.—AF. *retter, reter*, to accuse (pp. *rette, rete*); Lat. *reputare* see BH, § 153; by popular etymology Low Lat. *rectare*, 'in jus vocare', *rectatus*, accused (Schmid). Cf. **aretten**.

reuful, *adj.* compassionate, S2; see **rewful**.

reule, *sb.* rule, PP, C; **rewle**, PP, S3; **riwle**, S; **reuel**, S2; **reul**, S2; **riulen**, *pl.*, S.—AF. *reule*; Lat. *regula*; also OF. *riule, rigle*; Late Lat. *rigula* (for *regula*).

reulen, *v.* to rule, PP, C; **rewled**, *pt. s.*, S2.—AF. *reuler*; Lat. *regulare*.

reuliche, *adv.* ruefully, S2; see **rewliche**.

reume, *sb.* kingdom; see **rewme**.

reue[1], *sb.* reeve, prefect, minister of state, steward, S, PP, Prompt.; **reeve**, C; **reuen**, *pl.*, S. Comb., **ref-schipe**, reeveship, prefecture, S.—AS. *(ge)réfa*.

reue[2], *sb.* clothing, spoil, plunder, SD; **ræf**, SD. Comb.: **ref-lac**, robbery, S, SD.—AS. *réaf* clothing, spoil; cf. Icel. *rauf*, spoil. Cf. **robe**.

reuel, *sb.* revel, C; see **reevel**.

reuen, *v.* to rob, plunder, S, S2, S3; **reaue**, S2; **rieue**, S3; **refand**, *pr. p.*, H; **reuede**, *pt. s.*, S; **rafte**, C2; **ræueden**, *pl.*, S: **y-raft**, *pp.*, C.—AS. *réafian*, to despoil.

reuere, *sb.* robber, SD; **reuer**, S3; **ræueres**, *pl.*, S.—AS. *réafere*.

reuing, *sb.* robbery, S; **rauing**, S.

rewe, *sb.* row, C; **rewis**, *pl.*, S3; see **rawe**.

rewel (?). Comb.; **rewel boon**, C2; **rowel boon**, CM; **reuylle bone**, C2 (*n*); **ruelle**

rewen

bones, *pl.*, HD, C2 (*n*); **rewle stone**, HD (p. 698).

rewen, *v.* to rue, grieve, S, PP, S2, S3, C2; **reowen**, S; **ruwyn**, Prompt.; **rewing**, *pr. p.*, S3; **reouð**, *pr. s.*, S; **rwez**, S2; **rewede**, *pt. s.*, S.—AS. *hréowan*; cf. OS. *hrewan*.

rewere, *sb.* one who pities; **reewere**, S2.

rewful, *adj.* piteous, S, S2, C3; **reuful**, S2; **reowfule**, *pl.*, S.

rewle, *sb.* rule, S2; see **reule**.

rewliche, *adj.* pitiable, PP; **rewli**, piteous, S; **reweli**, S; **ruly**, HD.—AS. *hréowlic*.

rewliche, *adv.* piteously, S; **reowliche**, S; **reuliche**, S2; **rewli**, S; **rwly**, S2.—AS. *hréowlice*.

rewlyngis, *sb. pl.* rough shoes, S3; see **riveling**.

rewme, *sb.* kingdom, S2, W, H, PP; **realme**, CM; **reaume**, C2, S2; **reume**, PP, S2; **reame**, S2, PP; **reme**, C, PP, Cath.; **rem**, S2; **reum**, H.—OF. *reaume*, AF. *realme*; Late Lat. **regalimen*.

rewðe, *sb.* ruth, pity, S, C2, C3, G; **reowðe**, S; **rouðe**, S2, G; **reoðe**, S; **routh**, S3; **ruþe**, S, S3; **rawðe**, S2; **rewþes**, *pl.*, S2. See **rewen**.

rewðelese, *adj.* ruthless, C3; **rewðles**, PP.

reyn, *sb.* rain, W2, PP, C2; **rien**, S; **rein**, S; **reyne**, PP; **reane**, S3; **ran**, S3.—AS. *regn* (*rén*).

reynen, *v.* to rain, PP; **reinen**, S; **ranyt**, *pt. s.*, B.—AS. *regnian* (also *rignan*, *rínan*), see Sievers, 92.

reysed, *pp.* ridden, C; see **rase**[1].

reysen, *v.* to raise, G, CM; **reisen**, W2, S; **reas**, S3.—Icel. *reisa*; cf. Goth. *raisjan*. See **rysen**, **reren**.

reȝel, *sb.* a garment, rail, SkD; **rail**, JD; **raile**, HD; **rayle**, a kerchief, Palsg., Voc.; **rayles**, *pl.*, ND.—AS. *hrægl* (Voc.). Cf. **yrayled**.

riall, *adj.* royal, CM, S3, PP; see **real**[2].

rially, *adv.* royally, CM; see **realyche**.

ribaud, *sb.* villain, worthless creature, ribald, PP; **rybaud**, PP; **ribaude**, the Evil One, PP; **ribalde**, PP; **ribaut**, S3; **ribaudes**, *pl.*, sinners, PP; **ribauz**, S.—AF. *ribald* (pl. *ribaus*, *ribaldes*), OF. *ribaud*.

ribaudie, *sb.* sin, S2, PP; ribald jesting, C3.—OF. *ribaudie*.

ribaudour, *sb.* profligate fellow, PP; **rybaudour**, PP.

ribaudrie, *sb.* ribaldry, PP; **rybaudrie**, PP, S3.

riche[1], *adj.* powerful, rich, S; **ryche**, PP; **ryke**, PP; **rice**, S.—OF. *riche*.

riche[2], *sb.* kingdom, S2; **ryche**, PP; **rice**, S; **rike**, H, S2.—AS. *ríce*.

richelike, *adv.* richly, S; **richeliche**, S2.

ripe

richen, *v.* to grow rich, PP; **recheð**, *pr. pl.*, PP.

richesse, *sb.* wealth, PP, S2, S3, C2; **ritchesse**, W; **richeise**, S; **riches**, WW; **richesses**, *pl.*, costly articles, S2; **ricchessis**, WW; **riȝtchessis**, W.—OF. *richese*, AF. *richesce*.

rict, *adj.* right, S; see **ryght**[2].

riden, *v.* to ride, S, S2; **ridend**, *pr. p.*, S; **rydinge**, C3; **ryd**, *imp.*, S; **rit**, *pr. s.*, PP, C3; **ritt**, PP; **ryt**, PP, C; **rad**, *pt. s.*, S2, B; **rod**, S, S2; **rood**, C2; **riden**, *pl.*, S, C3, C; **rade**, S2; **raid**, B; **riden**, *pp.*, C2; **rad**, B. *Comb.*: **redyng-kyng**, a kind of feudal retainer, PP; **redyng-kynges**, *pl.*, PP.—AS. *rídan*, pt. s. *rád*, pl. *ridon*.

ridere, *sb.* rider, S; **rideres**, *pl.*, S; **rideren**, S.

ridil, *sb.* a sieve, Prompt.; **rydelle**, Cath.; **ryddel**, ruddle, Cath. (*n*). Cf. **rydder**.

ridilen, *v.* to sift; **rydelyn**, Prompt.; **ridile**, W; **ridlande**, *pr. p.*, S2. *Phr.*: **riddlide watris** = Lat. *cribrans aquas* (Vulg.), Cath. (*n*).

rif, *v.* to rive, S2; see **ryven**.

rift, *sb.* veil, curtain; **rifft**, S.—AS. *rift*; cf. Icel. *ript*, *ripti*.

riften, *v.* eructare, H (Ps. 18. 2); **rift**, to belch, Manip.—Icel. *rypta*.

riht, *adj.* and *sb.* right, S; see **ryght**[2].

rihten, *v.* to direct, correct, S; **rigten**, to set straight, S; **riȝti**, S2; **rightid**, *pt. s.*, S2.—AS. *rihtan*.

rihtlecen, *v.* to direct, set right, S; **riȝtleche**, S2, HD; **ryȝtlokede**, *pp.*, S3.—AS. *rihtlécan*.

rihtwis, *adj.* righteous, S; see **ryght**[2].

rike, *sb.* kingdom, S2; see **riche**[2].

rikenare, *sb.* reckoner, S.

rikenen, *v.* to reckon, S, PP; see **rekenen**.

rin, *v.* to run, S3; see **rennen**.

ring, *v.* to reign, S3; see **regnen**.

riot, *v.* to revel, live dissolutely, gluttonously, WW; **ryot**, B; **riotte**, to be dissolute, *luxuriare*, Manip.

riote, *sb.* uproar, SkD; **riot**, dissolute, luxurious living, WW; **riotte**, Manip.; **ryot**, depredation, B.—AF. *riote* (*ryot*), confusion, OF. *riote*, quarrelling (Bartsch), also feasting (Ducange); cf. ODu. *revot*, 'caterva nebulonum, luxuria'; see SkD.

riotour[1], *sb.* rioter, rioter, glutton, WW; **ryotoures**, *pl.*, C3.—AF. *riotour*, OF. *riotheir* (Ps. 36. 1).

riotour[2], *adj.* luxurious, dissolute, WW. Cf. Low Lat. *riotosus* (Ducange).

ripe, *adj.* fit for reaping, mature, S; **rype**, C2.

174

ripen

ripen[1], *v.* to become ripe, Prompt.; **ripede**, *pt. s.*, S.—AS. *rípian.*

ripen[2], *v.* to divide by tearing open, to rip, to search diligently, examine, HD, JD, SkD (s.v. *rip*); **rype**, Palsg.; **riped**, *pt. s.*, S2.— Cf. Swed. *repa*, to scratch.

ripple, *sb.* an instrument for *ripping* off the flax-seeds, JD. *Comb.*: **repylle-stok**, an implement for cleaning flax, Voc.

ripplen, *v.* to ripple flax, JD; **rypelen**, SkD, Prompt.

rishe, *sb.* rush, S3; see **rusche**.

rist, *pr. s.* riseth, rises, C3; see **rysen**.

rit, *pr. s.* rides, C3; see **riden**.

riuelic, *adv.* frequently, S2. See **ryfe**.

riveling, *sb.* a kind of shoe, SD, HD; **rullion,** JD; **rewlyngis,** *pl.*, S3; **rowlyng-is,** JD.—AS. *rifelingas*, 'obstrigelli' (Voc.); cf. AF. *rivelinges, rivelins.*

rixan, *v.* to reign, S.—AS. *rícsian* (*ríxian*); cf. OHG. *ríhhisôn* (Tatian), see Sievers, 411. See **riche**[2].

rixlien, *v.* to reign, S. See **rixan**.

riȝt, *sb.* right, justice, S2; see **ryght**[2].

ro, *sb.* quiet, S2; see **roo**[2].

robben, *v.* to plunder, spoil, rob, SkD, PP; **robby**, S2.—AF. *robber*; cf. It. *robbare*, to rob (Florio).

robbeour, *sb.* robber, PP; **robbour**, PP.— AF. *robeöur*, OF. *robeör*; Low Lat. *robatorem*; cf. It. *robbatore*, robber (Florio).

robe, *sb.* robe, PP; **robes**, *pl.*, clothes, PP; **robis**, PP.—AF. *robe*; cf. It. *róbba*, gown, robe, goods (Florio).

roberie, *sb.* robbery, S.—AF. *roberie.*

roche, *sb.* rock, S, S3, C2, H; **rooch**, S2, W2. *Comb.*: **roche-wall**, rock-wall, S.— AF. *roche.*

rod, *pt. s.* rode, S, S2; see **riden**.

rode[1], *sb.* a road, a riding, SkD, WW, Sh.; **rade**, S2, JD; **roade**, WW; **roode**, place where vessels ride at anchor, *bitalassum*, Prompt.—AS. *rád.*

rode[2], *sb.* red complexion, C2, S2; see **rude**[1].

rody, *adj.* ruddy, S2, C2, PP; **rodi**, W.

roggen, *v.* to shake, PP, HD, S2, Prompt.; **rug,** JD.—Icel. *rugga*, to rock a cradle.

rohten, *pt. pl.* recked, S; see **rechen**[1].

roial, *adj.* royal, CM; see **real**[2].

roialtee, *sb.* royalty, C3; see **realte**.

rokke, *sb.* a distaff, Prompt., Cath., HD; **rok**, S3; **roche**, Manip.; **rocks**, *pl.*, S3, HD.— Icel. *rokkr.*

rokken, *v.* to rock, Prompt.; **y-rokked**, *pp.*, S2.

romblen, *v.* to ramble; **romblynge**, *pr. p.*, PP.

romen, *v.* to rove about, to ramble, wander, roam, C2, C3, PP, SkD; **rame**, HD;

rote

raymen, PP, S2; **rowme**, PP; **rombe**, PP. Cf. OS. *rómón*, OHG. *râmên*, to strive after (Otfrid).

romere, *sb.* roamer, wanderer, PP; **rowmer**, PP; **romares**, *pl.*, PP; **romberis**, PP.

rome-renneres, *sb. pl.* agents at the court of Rome, PP.

ron, *pt. s.* ran, S2; see **rennen**.

rong, *pt. s.* rang, C3; see **ryngen**.

roo[1], *sb.* roe, deer, S2, Prompt.; **ro**, S2; **ra**, JD; **rays**, *pl.*, S3.—AS. *ráh* (Voc.), also *ráha* (Voc.), see Sievers, 117.

roo[2], *sb.* rest, quiet, S2, HD; **ro**, HD, S2.— Icel. *ró* AS. *rów*: OHG. *ruowa* (G. *ruhe*).

rood, *pt. s.* rode, C2; see **riden**.

roode, *sb.* the rood, cross, gallows, PP, G, Prompt.; **rode**, PP, S, S2, S3; **rude**, B; **roid**, B; **rod**, a rod, SkD. *Phr.*: **rule the rod**, to bear sway, NQ (6. 3. 169); *Comb.*: **rode-tre**, the cross, S2; **rude evyn**, eve of the Rood (Sept. 13), B.—AS. *ród*: OS. *róda*; cf. OHG. *ruoda* (G. *rute*).

roof, *sb.* roof, W, Prompt.; **rhof**, SkD; **roff**, PP; **roue**, S3; **rofe**, PP; **roouys**, *pl.*, W2.—AS. *hróf.*

roomth, *sb.* room, space, ND. See **rowm**.

roomthie, *adj.* spacious, Cotg. (s.v. *large*).

roomthsome, *adj.* spacious, DG.

rop, *sb.* a rope, PP; **rapes**, *pl.*, S.—AS. *ráp*; cf. Icel. *reip.*

rope, *pt. pl.* reaped, W2; see **repen**.

ropere, *sb.* rope-maker or rope-seller, PP.

roploch, *adj.* coarse, applied to woollen stuffs, JD; **ro**. coarse woollen cloth, S3 **raplach, raplock, reploch,** JD.

roren, *v.* to roar, C, PP; **roorin**, Prompt.; **rarin**, H (Ps. 76. i); **rar**, B; **rair**, S3, B.— AS. *rárian*, to lament loudly, to bellow.

ros, *pt. s.* rose, S, C2; see **rysen**.

rose, *sb.* rose, Prompt.; **roose**, W2; **rois**, S; **ross**, S3 (11 a. 6); **rosen**, *pl.*, SkD; **roosis**, W2. *Comb.*: **rose-reed**, red as a rose, C3.—OProv. *rose*; Lat. *rosa*; cf. AS. *róse.*

rosen, *v.* to praise, *reflex.* to boast, H; **roose**, JD; **ruse,** JD; **roysen**, H; **rees,** JD.—Icel. *hrósa*, to praise, *reflex.* to boast, from *hróðr*, praise, fame.

rospen, *v.* to scrape, S; see **raspen**.

rost, *sb.* roast (meat), PP; **roste**, PP. *Phr.*: **rules the rost**, takes the lead, domineers, S3, ND, NQ (6. 3. 170), HD (s.v. *rule-stone*), SPD (s.v. *roast*).—AF. *rost, roste.*

roste, *v.* to roast, C; **y-rosted**, *pp.*, S3.—OF. *rostir.*

rote[1], *sb.* root, W2, PP, S2, C2; **rot**, S2; **roote**, (*in astrology*) the data for a given time or period used as the basis for a horoscope, S2, C3; foot, C2; **rutis**, *pl.*, S3; **rotes**, PP.—Icel. *rót*; the same word as AS. *wrót*, snout, 'bruncus'; see Voc. (cf. *wrótan*, to grub up).

rote[2], *sb.* a musical instrument, C, HD, ND, SkD; **roote**, HD.—AF. *rote*; OHG. *hrota*; cf. Low Lat. *chrotta*, OIr. *crot* (Windisch). Cf. **crowde**[1].

rote[3], *v.* to rot, H (Ps. 15. 10). *Der.*: **rotyng**, rotting, S2.—AS. *rotian*.

rote[4], *in phr.* **by rote**; see **route**[1].

roten, *adj.* rotten, C3; **rotyn**, HD; **rotun**, W2; **rottyn**, B.—Cf. Icel. *rotinn*, perhaps a *pp.* form.

roðer[1], *sb.* a paddle for rowing, used also as a rudder, S, S2; **rothyr**, Prompt.; **rodyr**, Voc., Prompt.; **rudyr**, oar, Cath.; **rither**, rudder, DG. See **rowen**.

roðer[2], *sb.* an ox, SD, HD; **reðer**, SD; **reoðer**, SD; **reoðeren**, *pl.*, SD; **reðeren**, SD; **roðeren**, S3; **roðeron**, S2; **riðeren**, SD; **ruðeren**, SD. *Phr.*: **rule the rother**, ND. *Comb.*: **rother-soyl**, manure, HD, ND; **retherne-tounge**, the herb bugloss, HD.—AS. *hreoðer*: *hríðer*, OFris. *hríðer*: OHG. *hrind* (pl. *hrindir*); cf. G. *rind*.

roþun, *sb.* a driving storm, S2.—Cf. Icel. *róði*, the wind, tempest.

rouken, *v.* to lie close, cower down, CM, C, HD, JD.

rouncle, *v.* to wrinkle, S2; see **runkylle**[2].

rouncy, *sb.* a horse, C, CM; **rounsy**, HD; **rownsy**, HD.—AF. *runcin* (Roland); cf. OF. *roucin* (F. *roussin*), Sp. *rocin*, whence *rocinante*, see Diez, p. 277.

rounde, *adj.* round, PP.—AF. *rounde*, OF. *reont, roont*; Lat. *rotundum* (acc.).

roundel, *sb.* a kind of ballad, C.—OF. *rondel*.

roune, *sb.* a secret, a mystery, S2; **rune**, a secret, S; **roun**, song, S2; **runen**, *pl.*, secret discourses, S; **runes**, SD; **rounes**, S2.—AS. *rún*: OS. and Goth. *rúna*, a secret, counsel.

rounen, *v.* to talk secretly, whisper, PP, C2; **runien**, S; **rownen**, H, PP, Cath., S3, C2, C3; **rounden**, PP, ND, Sh., SPD.—AS. *rúnian*, to whisper.

rouning, *sb.* secret conference, S; **rowning**, B; **runinge**, S; **rouninges**, *pl.*, S; **ronenen**, whisperings, S.

roussat, *sb.* russet, S3; see **russet**.

route[1], *sb.* a rout, overthrow, troop, throng, company, S2, PP, S3, C2, C3; **rout**, S2; **rowtes**, *pl.*, S2; **rute**, a route, rut, way, path, SkD. *Phr.*: **by rote**, C2, C3, SkD; **by roote**, C.—AF. *route, rute*, a band of men, a way, OF. *rote*; Late Lat. *rupta*, a *broken* mass of flying men, a defeat, a company in *broken* ranks, a disorderly array, a way *broken* through a country.

route[2], *v.* to put to flight, Manip.; to assemble in a company, S2, C3.

rouþe, *sb.* pity, S; see **rewþe**.

rouȝte, *pt. s.* recked, C2; see **rechen**[1].

roue, *sb.* roof, S3; see **roof.**

row, *adj.* rough, C3, SkD; **rogh**, SkD; **roȝe**, S2; **rouch**, S3, JD; **ruh**, SD.—AS. *rúh* (gen. *rúwes*); cf. G. *rauh*.

rowen, *v.* to row, S, PP.—AS. *rówan*.

rowle, *v.* to roll, S3; **rele**, S3; **rollyn**, Prompt.; **rueled**, *pt. s.*, S2.—AF. *rouler, roler*; Late Lat. *rotulare*. Cf. **royle**[1].

rowm, *sb.* space, Prompt., B; **rowme**, cell, room, Prompt., S3, SkD; **rome**, S3.—AS. *rúm*, space, Goth. *rums*.

rowme, *adj.* spacious, roomy, H; **roume**, S2.

rowste, *sb.* voice, WA.—Icel. *raust.*

rowt, *sb.* a stunning blow, S2, B; **rout**, B.

rowte, *sb.* noise, snoring, CM.

rowten, *v.* to make a great noise, to bellow, to snore, H, S2, S3, Prompt.; **routen**, B, CM, JD, SD; **rowtande**, *pr. p.*, roaring, noisy, S2; **routte**, *pt. s.*, PP; **rutte**, PP; **routit**, S2.—AS. *hrútan*, to snore.

royle[1], *v.* to rove about, Manip.; **roile**, HD, PP; **roule**, PP. Notes (p. 94), CM.—OF. *roiller, roller* (Ducange), AF. *rouler*; Late Lat. *rotulare*. See **rowle**.

royle[2], *sb.* a stumbling horse, S3, PP. Notes (p. 94); *oblongula mulier*, Manip.

royn, *sb.* scurf; *as adj.*, rough, scurfy, S3.—OF. *roigne* (Cotg.); Lat. *robiginem*, rust, scab.

roynish, *adj.* scabby, ND, Sh.; **roinish**, HD.

royster, *sb.* a bully, swaggerer, saucy fellow, S3; **roister**, ND. *Comb.*: **roister-doister**, S3 (p. 262).—OF. *rustre*, royster, swaggerer (Cotg.), also *roiste* (Ducange), *ruiste* (BH), *ruste*; Lat. *rusticum*, a countryman.

roȝe, *adj.* rough, S2; see **row**.

roȝte, *pt. s.* cared, S; see **rechen**[1].

ruddocke, *sb.* the robin redbreast, Manip.; **ruddok**, CM.

rude[1], *sb.* redness, S; **ruddes**, *pl.*, S3.—AS. *rudu* (Voc.).

rude[2], *adj.* rough, undressed (of cloth) (= Lat. *rudis* = ἀγνάφος) S2; **ruyd**, B; **roid**, B.—OF. *rude*; Lat. *rudem.*

rudelyche, *adv.* rudely, C; **ruydly**, B; **roydly**, B; **rudly**, B.

ruffle, *v.* to bluster, to be noisy and turbulent, S3, Sh., ND; **ruffelynge**, *pr. p.*, S3.—ODu. *roffelen*, to pander.

ruffler, *sb.* a cheating bully, ND, HD.

rug, *sb.* back, S; **rugge**, S, S2; see **rygge**.

ruggy, *adj.* rough, C, CM.—Cf. Swed. *ruggig*, rough, hairy. See **row**.

ruke, *sb.* a heap, S; **ruck**, JD; **ruken**, *pl.*, S. Cf. OSwed. *rúka*, 'acervus'.

rukelen, *v.* to heap up, SD, S.

rummeis, *v.* to bellow, S3; **rummes**, JD; **rowmyss**, JD; **reimis**, JD.—See SkD (s.v. *rumble*). The word *rummeis* is no doubt of Romance origin, an inchoative in *-sco* from Lat. **rumare*, found in *ad-rumare*, to make a lowing noise; cf. OF. *roumant*, a murmur (Ducange).

rummiss, *sb.* a loud, rattling, or rumbling noise, JD; **reimis**, JD; **reemish**, JD; **rummage**, an obstreperous din, JD.

runagate, *sb.* renegade, WW; see **renegat**.

rune, *sb.* a secret, S; **runen**, *pl.* secret discourses, S; see **roune**.

runien, *v.* to discourse, S; see **rounen**.

runge, *pt. pl.* rang; see **ryngen**.

runkylle[1], *sb.* a wrinkle, Cath.; **runkill**, JD.—Cf. Dan. *rynke*.

runkylle[2], *v.* to wrinkle, Cath.; **runkle**, JD; **rouncle**, S2; **rouncled**, *pp.*, Cath. (*n*); **roncled**, HD.—Cf. Swed. *rynka*.

rurd, *sb.* cry, noise, S2; see **rerd**.

rusche, *sb.* rush, PP; **rische**, PP; **resshe**, PP; **rishe**, S3; **rish**, Manip.; **ryshes**, *pl.*, S3.—AS. *risce, resce* (Voc.).

rusien, *v.* to shake, SD, C (*n*); **rese**, C; **resye**, C (*n*); **rused**, *pt. s.*, PP.—AS. *hrysian*, Goth. *hrisjan*.

russet, *adj.* russet, PP, Prompt.; **roussat**, S3; **russets**, *sb. pl.*, clothes of a russet colour, ND.—AF. *russet*, OF. *rousset*; cf. Low Lat. *roussetum* (Ducange).

russetting, *sb.* coarse cloth of russet colour, HD; a kind of apple, ND.

rutis, *sb. pl.* roots, S3; see **rote**[1].

ruþe, *sb.* ruth, pity, S; see **rewþe**.

rwly, *adv.* ruefully, S2; see **rewliche**.

rybybe, *sb.* a kind of fiddle, *uetella, vitula*, Voc., Prompt.; [**ribibe**, an old woman, CM, ND]; **rebeke**, Manip.; **rebekke**, **rebeck**, SkD; **rebecke**, ND.—It. *ribebba* (also *ribecca*); Arab. *rabāba*, a fiddle with one or two strings, Steingass, p. 397.

rybybour, *sb.* a player on the *ribibe*, PP. See **rybybe**.

rydder, *sb.* a sieve, *cribrum*, Voc.—AS. *hrider* (Voc.). Cf. *ridil*.

rydel, *sb.* riddle, Prompt.; see **redels**.

ryfe, *adj.* abundant, numerous, frequent, openly known, S3; **ryyf**, Prompt.; **ryff**, PP; **ryue**, G.—Icel. *rīfr*, munificent.

ryfelen, *v.* to rob, plunder, Prompt. **y-rifled**, *pp.*, PP.—OF. *rifler* (Cotg.).

ryflowre, *sb.* robber, plunderer, Prompt.

ryflynge, *sb.* plunder, PP.

ryge, *sb.* stormy rain, S2; **rig**, HD.—Icel. *hregg*, storm and rain.

rygge, *sb.* back, ridge, HD, PP; **ryg**, B, PP; **rugge**, S, PP, S2; **rug**, S; **rugges**, *pl.*, HD; **rigge**, S, HD, G; **rig**, S2. *Comb.*: **rygge-**bon, *spondile*, Voc.; **ryg-bone**, *spina*, Voc., PP; **rygboon**, HD; **riggebon**, PP, G.—AS. *hrycg*; cf. OHG. *ruggi* (Otfrid).

ryght[1], *adv.* exactly, very, PP; **riht**, right, close, S, S2; **rihht**, S; **rihte**, S; **rict**, S; **rigt**, S; **riȝt**, S, S2. *Phr.*: **ryȝt now late**, only lately, S2.

ryght[2], *adj.* right, Prompt.; **ryht**, S2; **riȝt**, S2, W; **rihte**, S; **rigte**, S; **riȝte**, S; **rict**, S. *Comb.*: **riȝt-ful**, straight (= Lat. *rectus*), S2, W; **ryȝtfol**, S2; **ryȝtuolle**, S2; **riȝtful-nesse**, righteousness, W; **riht-half**, right side, S; **riȝthalf**, W2; **riȝtnesse**, justice, S2; **riht-wis**, righteous; S; **richtwise**, S; **ryȝtwys**, S2; **rightwis**, *v.* to justify, H; **rihtwisnesse**, righteousness, S; **ryȝttwis-nesse**, S2; **riȝtwisnesse**, W; **rightwise-nes**, S2; **ryghtwisnesse**, C3.—AS. *riht*.

ryghte, *sb.* right, law, equity, Cath.; **riȝt**, S2; **riȝte**, S, S2; **riȝtes**, *pl.*, S2; **ryȝtez**, *gen.* as *adv.*, rightly, immediately, S2; **riȝttes**, S2. *Phr.*: **to þe riȝttes**, exactly, S; **at alle rightes**, C; **mid rihte**, rightly, S; **mid rihten**, S; **wiþþ rihhte**, S.

ryme[1], *sb.* hoar-frost, H, Prompt. *Comb.*: **ryme-frost**, hoar-frost, HD.—AS. *hrím*.

ryme[2], *sb.* rime, verse, poetry, Prompt., S, PP; **rym**, C2, C3; **rime**, S; **rymes**, *pl.*, rimes, ballads, PP, C2. *Phr.*: **on his rime**, in his turn, S.—OF. *rime, rym*; OHG. *rím*, number; cf. AS. *rím*.

rymen, *v.* to rime. Prompt., S3, C2, C3.—AF. *rimer* (*rymer*).

ryming, *sb.* the art of riming, C2.

rymthe, *sb.* room, leisure, Prompt. See **rowm**.

rynen, *v.* to touch, H. *Der.*: **riner**, the quoit that touches the mark, HD.—AS. *hrínan*, OS. *hrínan*; cf. OHG. *rínan* (Otfrid).

rynge, *sb.* a circle, *annulus*, Prompt.; **rynges**, *pl.*, PP; **ringes**, C3. *Comb.*: **ring-leader**, *praesultor*, Manip.; the person who opens a ball, HD, NQ (5. 1. 146); **ryng-sangis**, songs adapted for circular dances, S3.—AS. *hring*, Icel. *hringr*.

ryngen, *v.* to ring, Prompt.; **ringes**, *pr. pl.*, S; **rong**, *pt. s.*, C3; **runge**, *pl.*, S (19. 1273); **i-runge**, *pp.*, S.—AS. *ringan*, pt. s. *rang* (pl. *rungon*), pp. *rungen*.

ryngis[1], *sb. pl.* reigns, S3; see **regne**.

ryngis[2], *pr. pl.* reigns, S3; see **regnen**.

rys, *sb.* twig, branch, branches, S2, G (s.v. *woode*), CM; **ris**, S, CM; **ryss**, S3; **ryse**. Cath., S3. *Comb.*: **rise-bushes**, sticks cut for burning, DG.—AS. *hrís*; cf. Icel. *hrís*, G. *reis*.

rysen, *v.* to rise, PP, C2; **riss**, B; **risand**, *pr. p.*, S2; **riseand**, S2; **ris**, *imp.*, S; **rist**, *pr. s.*, C3; **ros**, *pt. s.*, S, C2; **roos**, C2, W; **raiss**,

S2, B; **rass**, B; **risen**, *pl.*, W; **rysen**, W;
rise, C2; **rysed**, *pt. s. (weak)*, S2.—AS.
rísan, pt. s. *rás* (pl. *rison*), pp. *risen*.
ryshe, *sb.* rush, S3; see **rusche**.
rysp, *sb.* coarse grass, S3; **risp**, JD. Cf. G.
rispe, see Weigand.
ryue[1], *sb.* shore, S.—OF. *rive*; Lat. *ripa*.
ryue[2], *adj.* abundant, G; see **ryfe**.
ryuel, *sb.* a wrinkle, SD.
ryuelen, *v.* to wrinkle, HD, PP; **ryueleden**,
pt. pl., PP; **riueld**, *pp.*, S3.—Cf. AS. *rifelede*

(Lat. *rugosus*), Eng. Studien, xi. 66; and Du.
ruifelen.
ryueling, *sb.* a wrinkling, W; **ryuelynges**,
pl., wrinkles, W2.
ryuen, *v.* to tear, rive, S2, C2, C3; **rif**, S2;
ryfe, H.—Icel. *rífa*.
ryuer, *sb.* river, PP; **ryuere**, Prompt., CM;
riuere, S.—AF. *rivere*; Late Lat. *riparia*,
seashore, bank, river. See **ryve**[1].

S

sa, so, as, S, S2; see **swa.**

saaf, *adj.* healed, S2; see **sauf.**

sabat, *sb.* sabbath, W; **sabot**, W; **sabote**, S2; **sabothis**, *pl.*, S2.—Lat. *sabbatum* (Vulg.); Gr. σάββατον; Heb. *shabbâth*, rest, sabbath.

sabeline, *sb.* the sable, also the fur of the sable, S; **sablyne**, S.—OF. *sabeline*, from *sable*; Russ. *соболе*; cf. G. *zobel.*

sac, *sb.* crime, S2; see **sak**[2].

saccles, *adj.* guiltless, S2; see **sakles.**

sachel, *sb.* wallet, satchel, W, H (p. 144).—OF. *sachel*; Lat. *saccellum* (acc.), dimin. of *saccus.* See **sak**[1].

sacren, *v.* to consecrate, hallow, S, Prompt.; **y-sacred**, *pp.*, S3.—OF. *sacrer*; Lat. *sacrare.*

sacristane, *sb.* sacristan, Cath.; **secristoun**, Voc.; **sexteyne**, Prompt.; **sexteyn**, C2.—AF. *secrestein*, OF. *sacristain*, sexton (Cotg.); from Church Lat. *sacrista* (Voc.).

sad, *adj.* sated, over full, weary, satisfied, serious, firm, sober, discreet, grave, PP, S2, S3, C, C2, C3, W; **sead**, S; **sæd**, S; **sadde**, *adv.*, S3; **sadder**, *comp.*, more soundly (of sleep), PP.—AS. *sæd*: OS. *sad*, sated; cf. OHG. *sat* (Tatian): Goth. *saþs*; cf. Lat. *satis*; see Brugmann, § 109.

sadel, *sb.* saddle, C3; **sadyl**, Prompt. *Comb.*: **sadel-bowe**, saddle-bow, S.—AS. *sadol.*

sadelien, *v.* to saddle; **sadelede**, *pt. s.*, S; **sadeled**, *pp.*, G.—AS. *sadelian.*

sadly, *adv.* seriously, S3, C, C2, C3; **sadlier**, *comp.*, more heavily, PP; **sadloker**, more soundly, S2, PP.

sadnes, *sb.* stedfastness, soberness, discreetness, S3, WA; **sadnesse**, C2, P, W, W2.

sæ, *sb.* sea, S; see **see**[1].

sæclian, *v.* to sicken; **sæclede**, *pt. s.*, S. See **sek**[2].

sæd, *adj.* satcd, S; scc **sad.**

sæht, sæhte; see **saht, sahte.**

sæhtleden, *pt. pl.* reconciled, S; see **sahtlien.**

særes, *pl.* shears, S; see **schere**[1].

særi, *adj.* sorry, S; see **sory.**

sætte, *pt. s.* set, S; see **setten.**

sæw, *sb.* juice, S; see **sewe.**

safferes, safiris; see **saphir.**

saffren, *v.* to tinge with saffron, C3.

saffroun, *sb.* saffron, C2; **safrun**, Prompt.; **saffran**, SkD; **safforne**, S3.—AF. *saffran.*

safte, *sb. pl.* creatures, S; see **schaft.**

sag, sagh, saw; see **seon.**

saghe, *sb.* saw, saying, H; see **sawe**[1].

saghtel, *1 p. pr. pl.* become reconciled, S2; see **sahtlien.**

saht, *adj.* at peace, reconciled; **sæht**, S; **sehte**, S; **saut**, HD; **sahhte**, *pl.*, S.—AS. *sæht*; cf. Icel. *sáttr.*

sahte, *sb.* peace, reconciliation, S; **sæhte**, concord, S; **saughte**, HD.—Cf. Icel. *sátt*, concord.

sahtlien, *v.* to reconcile, to be reconciled, S, SkD (s.v. *settle*); **saʒtlen**, SkD; **sauʒtlen**, SkD; **saghtel**, S2; **sæhtlien**, S; **saʒtill**, WA; **saghetylle**, HD.—AS. *sahtlian.*

sahtling, *sb.* reconciliation; **saʒtlyng**, S2; **sauʒtelyng**, HD; **saughtelynge**, HD. See **sahtlien.**

sahtnen, *v.* to reconcile, to be reconciled, S; **sauhtne**, PP; **sauʒtne**, P.

sahtnesse, *sb.* peace, reconciliation, S; **sehtnesse**, S; **seihtnesse**, S.—AS. *sahtnis.*

sair; see **sore**[2].

saiʒ, saw; see **seon.**

sak[1], *sb.* sack, sackcloth, PP, W2; **sek**, S2; **seck**, S; **seckes**, *pl.*, S; **sakkes**, PP.—AS. *sacc*; Lat. *saccus* (Vulg.); Gr. σάκκος (LXX); Heb. *saq*, probably of Egyptian origin.

sak[2], *sb.* guilt, crime, cause, sake, S2, B; **sake**, S; **sac**, S2; **sakess**, *pl.*, crimes, S2.—Icel. *sök* (stem *saka-*), a cause, charge, guilt, crime: Goth. *sakjo* (= μάχη); cf. AS. *sacu*, OHG. *sahha*, 'causa' (Tatian).

sakeð, *pr. s.* shakes, S; see **schaken.**

sakles, *adj.* guiltless, S2; **sakless**, B; **saccles**, S2; **sacclesli**, *adv.*, **guiltlessly**, S2.—AS. *sacléas*; cf. Icel. *saklauss.*

sal, *sb.* salt. *Comb.*: **sal-armoniak**, sal ammoniac, C3; **sal-peter**, saltpetre, C3; **sal-preparat**, prepared salt, C3; **sal-tartre**, salt of tartar, C3.—Lat. *sal.*

salad, *sb.* helmet, CM; **sallet**, ND, Sh.; **salettes**, *pl.*, RD (p. 1663).—OF. *salade* (Cotg.); cf. Low Lat. *salada* (Ducange), Sp. *celada* (Minsheu).

sald, *pt. s.* sold, S2; see **sellen.**

sale[1], *sb.* hall, WA, S, HD.—Icel. *salr*; cf. AS. *sæl* (gen. *sales*).

sale[2], *sb.* basket of willow-twigs for catching eels, etc., S3. See **salwe.**

salewis, *sb. pl.* willows, W2; see **salwe.**

salm, *sb.* psalm, S2, W2; **psalme**, H; **psalmes**, *pl.*, PP; **salmes**, S2. Church Lat. *psalmus* (Vulg.); Gr. ψαλμός (LXX).

salme, *v.* to sing psalms, S2.

salt[1], *sb.* salt, Voc., S; **sealte**, *dat.*, S2. *Comb.*: **salt-cote**, a salt-pit, *salina*, Voc.; **saltecote**, Cath., Voc.—AS. *sealt.*

179

salt², *adj.* salted, salt, *salsus*, SD; **sealte**, S2; **salte**, *pl.*, C2.

salue (**salūe**), *v.* to salute, C2, C3.—OF. *saluer*; Lat. *salutare*.

saluyng (**salūyng**), *sb.* salutation, C.

salue (**salve**), *sb.* salve, ointment, C2, PP; **sallfe**, H (p. 184).—AS. *sealf*; cf. G. *salbe*.

salwe, *sb.* a kind of willow, a sallow, SkD, Voc.; **salwhe**, Prompt.; **salghe**, HD; **salewis**, *pl.*, W2.—AS. *sealh* (Voc.): OHG. *salahá*; cf. Lat. *salic-em*, Ir. *sail*, Gr. ἑλίκη, W. *helyg*.

sam ... sam, *conj.* whether ... or, S.

same¹, *adj.* same, SkD; **samyn**, S3, B; **sammyn**, *dat.*, S2, B.—Icel. *samr*.

same², *sb.* shame, S; see **schame**.

samed, *adv.* together, SD; **somed**, S; **somet**, S.—AS. *samod*.

samen, *adv.* together, PP, S, S2, H; **samenn**, S; **samyn**, H, B; **sammyn**, B.—Icel. *saman*; cf. OHG. *saman* (Tatian).

samet, *sb.* a rich silk stuff, CM; **samyte**, SkD; **samite**, ND.—OF. *samit*; Late Lat. *examitum*; Late Gr. ἑξάμιτον; cf. G. *samt*, velvet, It. *sciamito* (Florio).

samie, *v.* to be ashamed, S; see **schamien**.

samm-tale, *adj. pl.* in harmony, S.

samnien, *v.* to unite; **somnen**, S; **sammnesst**, *2 pr. s.*, S; **i-somned**, *pp.*, S; **samned**, S2; **samened**, S2; **samynd**, H.—AS. *samnian*.

samon, *sb.* salmon, S2; see **saumon**.

sand¹, *sb.* sand, PP; see **sond**¹.

sand², *sb.* a gift, S2; see **sond**².

sanderbodes, *sb. pl.* messengers, S; see **sonder**.

sang¹, *sb.* song, S, S3; see **songe**.

sang², *sb.* blood. *Comb.*: **sank royall**, blood royal, S3 (14. 490).—OF. *sanc, sang*; Lat. *sanguinem*.

sangwine, *adj.* blood-red, S3; **sangwin**, C; **sangwane**, blood colour (in heraldry), S3.—AF. *sanguine*; Lat. *sanguineum*.

sans, *prep.* without, C3; **sanz**, S2, PP; **saun**, HD. *Comb.*: **saun fail**, without fail, HD.—OF. *sans, senz*; Lat. *sine*, see BH, § 50.

sant, *adj.* and *sb.* holy, saint, S2; **sante**, S; **sanct**, B.—Lat. *sanctus*. Cf. **seint**.

sanyt, *pt. s.* crossed himself, S2; see **seynen**.

sape, *sb.* soap, S; see **soope**.

saphir, *sb.* sapphire; **safiris**, W (Apoc. 21. 19); **saphires**, *pl.*, C2, PP; **safferes**, P.—AF. *safir, saphire*; Lat. *sapphirum* (acc.); Gr. σάπφειρος; Heb. *sappîr*.

sapience, *sb.* Wisdom, i.e. the book so called, C2, P; wisdom, C3; **sapiences**, *pl.*, kinds of intelligence, C3.—OF. *sapience*; Lat. *sapientia*.

sar; see **sore**², **sore**³.

sarce¹, *sb.* sieve, Cath., Palsg.; **searce**, Cotg. (s.v. *tamis*); **sarse**, Cath. (*n*); **sars**, Cath. (*n*).—OF. *sas*, a searce (Cotg.), *saas*: Sp. *cedázo* (Minsheu); Lat. *setaceum*, from *seta*, hair on an animal. See **say**².

sarce², *v.* to sift, Palsg.; **searse**, Cath. (*n*).—OF. *sasser*.

sare; see **sore**².

sari, *adj.* sorry, S; see **sory**.

sark, *sb.* shirt, S3; see **serk**.

sarmoun, *sb.* sermon, P; see **sermoun**.

Sateres-dai. Saturday. See **Saturne**.

sattel, *v.* to subside, S2, S3; see **setlen**.

Saturne, *sb.* the Roman god Saturn, SD. *Comb.*: **Sateres-dai**, Saturday, S; **Saterdei**, S; **Seterday**, PP; **Sætterdæi**, S; **Saterday**, PP; **Seturday**, PP.

sauf, *adj.* safe, healed, made whole, S2, C3, P; **sauff**, S2; **saf**, S2; **saaf**, S2, W; **sauf**, *prep.*, save, except, C; **saue**, C2, C3; **saulfe**, S3; **saufliche**, *adv.*, safely, S2; **saufly**, C, C2, PP; **sauely**, H. *Comb.*: **saulfe-garde**, safe-keeping, S3; **salfgard**, S3.—AF. *sauf*, OF. *salf*; Lat. *saluum*.

saugh, saw; see **seon**.

saughte, *v.* to be reconciled, G. See **saht**.

saule, *sb.* soul, S; **sawl**, S; **saull**, S3; **saulen**, *pl.*, S; see **soule**.

saumon, *sb.* salmon, Voc.; **salmond**, B; **samon**, S2; **samowne**, Prompt.—OF. *saumun, salmon*; Lat. *salmonem*.

saumplarie, *sb.* example, instructor, PP.

saumple, *sb.* example, PP, W2, HD.

saumpler, *sb.* exemplar, pattern, W.

saundyuer, *sb.* the fatty substance floating on glass when it is red-hot in the furnace, S2; **sawndevere**, HD; **sandiver**, Cotg.—OF. *suin de verre*, the sweating of glass (Cotg.); *suin* or *suint*, from *suinter*, to sweat, as stones in moist weather; nasalized from OTeut. base **swit-*, whence G. *schwitzen*, to sweat.

sausefleme, *sb.* the scab, *salsum flegma*, C (p. 140). *Der.*: **sausefleming**, *adj.*, having pimples on the face; HD; **sawceflem**, pimpled, C, CM.—Late Lat. *salsum flegma*.

saut, *sb.* assault, H, PP; **saute**, H; **sawt**, B.—OF. *saut*, a leap; Lat. *saltum*.

saute, *v.* to leap, PP.—OF. *sauter, saulter*; Lat. *saltare*.

sauter, *sb.* a musical instrument, psalter, psalms, S2; **sawter**, Voc.; **sawtre**, Voc.; **sautre**, W2; **psauter**, PP; **psautere**, H (p. 3). *Comb.*: **sawtere-boke**, Voc.—OF. *sautier* (Bartsch), *psaultier*; Church Lat. *psalterium*; Gr. ψαλτήριον.

sauvacioun, *sb.* salvation, S2, S3, C3, P.—AF. *salvacioun*; Lat. *salvationem*.

sauȝtne, *v.* become reconciled, P; see **sahtnen**.

saue[1], *prep.* save, C2; see **sauf**.

save[2], *sb.* the herb sage, C; see **sawge**.

saueine, *sb.* savin, sabine, SkD; **sewane**, S3.—AS. *safine*; Lat. *sabina*; cf. OF. *sabine*, *savinier*, the savine-tree (Cotg.).

sauetè, *sb.* safety, PP; **sauyte**, S2; **safte**, P.—AF. *sauvete*; Late Lat. *salvitatem*.

savour, *sb.* savour, smell, pleasantness, pleasure, P, C2, C3, WW.—OF. *saveur*; Lat. *saporem*.

savouren, *v.* to have a pleasant taste, to give an appetite to, S2, P; **sauere** (= Lat. *sapere*), to have a taste, perception, W; **sauer**, S2, WW, CM.—AF. *savourer*.

sawe[1], *sb.* a saw, saying, S2, C, C3; **saghe**, H; **saghes**, *pl.*, H; **saghs**, S2; **sawes**, S2, P.—AS. *sagu*.

sawe[2], *v.* to sow, S; see **sowen**.

sawge, *sb.* the herb sage, Prompt.; **salge**, Cath.; **save**, C, HD.—OF. *sauge*; Lat. *saluia*; cf. Low Lat. *salgia* (Cath.).

say[1], *pt. s.* saw; see **seon**.

say[2], *sb.* silk, WA.—OF. *seie*; Sp. *seda*; Lat. *sēta*, bristle. Cf. **sarce**[1].

sayne, *sb.* a net, WA.—OF. *seine*; Lat. *sagēna*; Gr. σαγήνη; cf. OIr. *sén*.

sayntuaryes, *sb. pl.* relics, S3; see **seintuarie**.

saȝ, *pt. s.* saw; see **seon**.

saȝtled, *pt. s.* settled, S2; see **setlen**.

saȝtlyng, *sb.* reconciliation, S2; see **sahtling**.

sc-. For many words beginning with **sc-** (as well as words beginning with **sh-** and **ss-**) see **sch-**.

scæ, she, S; see **sheo**.

scærp, *adj.* sharp, S; see **scharp**.

scandlic, *adj.* disgraceful, S. See **schonde**.

scaplorye, *sb.* a kind of scarf, Prompt.; **scaplory**, scapelory, Cath., S; **scaplorey**, Voc.; **scapelary**, Prompt.; **chapolory**, S3; **scaplery**, Cath. (*n*); **scapularye**, Cath. (*n*); **scopelarie**, Cath. (*n*).—Church Lat. *scapulare*, from *scapula*, shoulder (Vulg.).

scarl, *sb.* scare-crow, bugbear, HD; **scarle**, Cath.

scarren, *v.* to scare, SD; see **skerren**.

scars, *adj.* scarce, SD; **scarce**, Prompt.; **scarsliche**, *adv.*, scarcely, SD; **scarslych**, sparingly, S2; **scarsly**, parsimoniously, C, Prompt.; **scarseli**, W.—AF. *escars*; Late Lat. *excarpsum*.

scarsetè, *sb.* scarcity, C3; **scarste**, S2.—OF. *scharseté* (Ducange).

scarsnesse, *sb.* scarceness, Prompt.

scarth, *sb.* sherd, H; **skarth**, JD.—Icel. *skarð*. Cf. **scherde**.

scat, *sb.* treasure, S.—AS. *sceat*: OS. *skat*; cf. OHG. *scaz* (Tatian).

scaðe, *sb.* harm, S, C2; **schathe**, S2; **skaith**, S3; **skathe**, C, G; **scath**, WA; **skath**, H.—Icel. *skaði*; cf. OHG. *scado* (Otfrid).

scean, *pt. s.* shone, S; see **schynen**.

sceappend, *sb.* creator, S; see **scheppende**.

scel, shall, S; see **schal**.

sceolde, should, S; see **scholde**.

scewie, *imp. pl.* let us see, S; see **schewen**.

schade, *sb.* shade, shadow, WA; **schadowe**, Prompt.; **schadewe**, S; **shadwe**, C2, C3. *Phr.*: **in ssede**, darkly, S2.—AS. *sceadu* (stem *sceadwa*): OS. *skado*; cf. OHG. *scato* (Tatian).

schaft, *sb.* shape, make, form, creature, S, S2; **schafte**, PP; **shafte**, PP; **scepþe**, S2; **schafte**, *pl.*, S; **safte**, S; **sseþþes**, S2.—AS. *(ge)sceaft*.

schakaris, *sb. pl.* drops of dew hanging down, S3.

schaken, *v.* to shake, Prompt.; **ssake**, S2; **sakeð**, *pr. s.*, S; **schok**, *pt. s.*, S, S2; **schake**, *pp.*, C.—AS. *sceacan*, pt. *scóc*, pp. *scacen*.

schal, *1, 3 pt. pr. s.* shall, S; **sceal**, S; **scal**, S; **sceol**, S; **scel**, S; **schel**, S2; **ssel**, S2; **shal**, S, S2, C2, C3; **sal**, S, S2; **sall**, H; **sale**, S2; **xal**, HD; **salt**, *2 pr. s.*, S2; **ssalt**, S2; **xalt**, HD; **schulen**, *pl.*, S; **schullen**, S. S2; **schulle**, S; **schulleþ**, S; **schule**, S; **sculen**, S; **schuln**, C; **scullen**, S; **scule**, S; **shulen**, S; **shullen**, C3; **shulle**, S; **shul**, S2, C3; **shule**, S2; **sulen**, S; **sule**, S; **sullen**, S; **sulle**, S; **scholle**, S2; **sholen**, S; **shole**, S; **ssolle**, S2; **solle**, S; **salle**, S2; **schaltow**, **saltou**, shalt thou, S2. Cf. **scholde**.

schalk, *sb.* servant, man, WA; **schalke**, S2.—AS. *scealc* (Grein): Goth. *skalks*; cf. OHG. *scalc* (Tatian).

schame, *sb.* shame, S, PP; **schome**, S; **shome**, S2; **scheome**, S; **scome**, S; **ssame**, S2; **same**, S.—AS. *sceamu*.

schamefast, *adj.* modest, C.

schamefastnesse, *sb.* modesty, C, W.

schamelich, *adj.* shameful; **schomelich**, S, S2; **shameliche**, *adv.*, S; **shamlic**, S2.

schamien, *v.* to shame, to be ashamed, S, W; **shame**, S2; **ssame**, S2; **samie**, S.

schamylle, *sb.* stool, Cath. (= Lat. *scabellum*), H; **schamel**, Cath. (*n*); **schambylle**, *macellum*, Cath.; **shambles**, *pl.*, Sh.—AS. *scamel* (Mt. 5. 35), *scamol*, *sceamul* (Voc.); Lat. *scamellum*; cf. OF. *scamel* (Ps. 109. 1), also Lat. *scabellum*, from stem *scam-* in *scamnum*. See NQ (5. 5. 261).

schap, *sb.* shape, PP, C, W2; **shap**, S, C2; **schapp**, S2; **schappe**, PP; **scheape**, S; **shappe**, PP.—AS. *(ge)sceap*.

schapen   schere

schapen, v. to form, create, ordain, *refl.* to
dispose oneself, endeavour, S, C, PP, S3;
shape, PP; **schop**, *pt. s.*, S, S2; **shop**, S;
shoop, C2; **scop**, S; **sop**, S; **schope**, S2;
shope, S2, H; **schapen**, *pp.*, C; **shapen**,
S, S2, C2; **shape**, C2; **y-schape**, S2;
yshapen, C2; **yshape**, C3.—AS. *sceapan*,
pt. *scóp (scéop)*, pp. *sceapen*.
schapien, v. to create, form; **schepien**, 197
S; **schapide**, *pt. s.*, W; **shaped**, *pp.*, S. Cf.
scheppen.
schaply, *adj.* fit, C.
schaplynesse, *sb.* beauty, W2.
scharp, *adj.* sharp; **scharpe**, S; **scherpe**, S;
scærp, S; **scharpe**, *adv.*, S; **sharpe**,
C2.—AS. *scearp*.
scharpin, v. to make sharp; **scherpit**, *pt. s.*,
S3.
schaven, v. to shave, scrape, PP; **schauyde**,
pt. s., W2; **shauen**, *pp.*, S; **schave**, C; **y-
schaue**, S2; **y-shaue**, C2; **ischaven**, S.
Der.: **shauing**, a thin slice, C3.—AS.
sceafan, pt. *scóf*, pp. *scafen*.
schawe, *sb.* a shaw, wood, grove, S2, G, S3,
HD, Cath.; **schaw**, WA, B; **schowe**, HD;
shawes, *pl.*, PP.—AS. *scaga*; cf. Icel. *skógr*.
schawen, v. to show, S, S2, S3; see
schewen.
schawere, *sb.* a veil, S; **scawere**, mirror, S;
sseawere, S2; **schewere**, WA.
schawles, *sb.* scare-crow, an appearance, S;
schewelles, ND; **sewell**, HD.—From the
same root as G. *scheuche*. See **schey**.
sche, she, C; see **sheo**.
scheawen, v. to appear, S2; see **schewen**.
schede, *sb.* the parting of a man's hair,
Cath.; see **schode**.
scheden, v. to separate, to part the hair, to
shed, pour, S, PP, W2; **shædenn**, S;
sheden, PP; **shode**, HD; **schedde**, *pt. s.*,
PP; **shedde**, C2; **shadde**, C2; **ssedde**,
S2; **i-sched**, *pp.*, S; **shad**, S.—AS. *scéadan*,
pt. *scéod*, pp. *scéaden*; cf. OHG. *skeidan*
(Tatian), G. *scheiten*.
scheef, *sb.* sheaf, Prompt.; **shef**, C; **schof**,
Prompt.; **scheffe**, Prompt.; **shæfess**, *pl.*,
S.—AS. *scéaf*.
scheep[1], *sb.* sheep, Prompt.; **shep**, S;
schepe, Cath.; *pl.*, S2; **shep**, S; **sep**, S.—
AS. *scéap*.
scheep[2], *sb.* shepherd, S2, PP; **shepe**, P;
shep, PP; **chep**, PP, Notes (p. 458).—AS.
scéapa (scépa).
scheld, *sb.* shield, S, C, W2; **sheld**, S;
sseld, S2; **scheeld**, C; **shel**, S; **scheelde**,
Prompt.—AS. *scield*, *scyld*.
schelden, v. to shield, PP; **shilden**, S, G;
shilden, C2; **silden**, S.
schelder, *sb.* shielder, S2.

scheltroun, *sb.* shelter, defence, a strong
shield, also a body of troops, battalion, PP;
scheltron, Prompt.; **scheltrone**, *acies*,
Voc.; **scheltrom**, PP, S2; **scheltrun**, W2;
shultrom, PP; **schiltrum**, B; **child-
rome**, B; **jeltron**, shield, shelter, SkD (s.v.
shelter).—AS. *scild-truma*, a shield-troop
(Leo); cf. AF. *chiltron*.
schench, *sb.* draught of beer or wine, SD;
senche, S; **schenche**, *dat.*, S.—Icel. *skenkr*,
the serving of drink.
schenchen, v. to pour out beer or wine, to
offer a good thing, S, CM; **shenchen**, S2;
schenkyn, Prompt.—AS. *scencan*, to pour
out drink (Grein); cf. OHG. *scenken* (Otfrid),
Icel. *skenkja*; from AS. *sceanc*, shank, a hollow
bone used for drawing off liquor. See SkD
(s.v. *nunchion*).
schenden, v. to harm, ruin, disgrace, PP, S,
S2, W2, S3; **shenden**, PP, C2, H;
scenden, S; **ssende**, S2; **sende**, S;
shende, *pt. s.*, S; **schente**, S; **schent**, *pp.*,
S, S2, C, W2, G; **shent**, PP, C2.—AS.
scendan. See **schonde**.
schendful, *adj.* disgraceful, SD; **schend-
fulliche**, *adv.*, PP; **shendfulliche**, PP.
schendlac, *sb.* disgrace, S.
schendschip, *sb.* disgrace, hurt, ruin; **schen-
schip**, W, W2; **schenship**, H; **schen-
shepe**, PP.
schene, *adj.* bright, S, S2, S3, C; **scene**, S2;
scheyn, S3; **shene**, C2, S3; **sheene**, S2,
S3, C3; **schenre**, *comp.*, S.—AS. *scéne*: OS.
skóni; cf. OHG. *scóni* (Otfrid).
scheome, *sb.* shame, S; see **schame**.
scheot, *pr. s.* shoots, S; see **scheten**.
schepieð, *imp. pl.* shape, S; see **schapien**.
schepne, *sb.* shed, stall, stable, C; **schepyn**,
bostar, Voc.; **shippen**, HD; **schyppune**,
Voc.; **shepnes**, *pl.*, CM.—AS. *scypen*,
'bovile' (Voc.). Cf. **schoppe**.
scheppen, v. to create, form, SD; **schupte**,
pt. s., S.—AS. *sceppan*, *scyppan*.
scheppende, *sb.* creator; **sceppende**, S;
sceppend, S; **sceappend**, S; **sheppen-
des**, *pl.*, S.
scheppere, *sb.* creator; **schuppere**, S;
shepper, PP.—Cf. OHG. *sceppheri* (Otfrid)
G. *schöpfer*.
scherald, *adj.* cut by the plough-share, S3.
scherde, *sb.* sherd, Prompt.
schere[1], *sb.* shears, C; **shere**, C2, PP;
særes, *pl.*, S.
schere[2], v. to shear, S3, S2; **schæren**, S;
sheren, to reap, cut, S, C2; **scorn**, *pp.*, S2;
soren, S; **y-schore**, S2.—AS. *sceran*
(*scieran*), pt. *scear* (pl. *scéaron*), pp. *scoren*.
schere[3], *adj.* pure, bright, clear, SD; **skere**,
adv., SD; **sker**, clean, entirely, S. *Comb.*:

182

Shere Þursdai, the Thursday in Holy Week, S.—Icel. *skærr*; *skíri-þórsdagr*, *skírdagr*, names for Maundy Thursday. See **schyre**².

scherpit, *pt. s.* sharpened, S3; see **scharpin**.

scherreue, *sb.* sheriff, G; see **schyre**¹.

scherte, *sb.* shirt, C, C2, PP, Voc.; **sherte**, PP; **shurte**, SkD; **schyrt**, Voc.; **shirte**, SkD.—Icel. *skyrta*.

schete, *sb.* sheet, Prompt., P; **shete**, C3.— AS. *scéte*, for *scýte*, see SkD.

scheten, *v.* to shoot, rush, S, W2, Prompt.; **scheete**, G; **ssete**, S2; **schut**, S2; **schute**, B; **scheot**, *pr. s.*, S; **schot**, *pt. s.*, S2, B; **sscet**, S2; **shote**, *pp.*, S2; **ishote**, S; **iscote**, S; **issote**, S2.—AS. *scéotan*, pt. *scéat* (pl. *scuton*), pp. *scoten*.

scheter, *sb.* shooter, SD; **schetare**, Prompt.; **ssetar**, S2.

schetten, *v.* to shut, C3, Prompt.; **schitte**, G, W2; **schitte**, *pt. s.*, W; **shette**, G, P; *pl.*, C2, C3; **schet**, *pp.*, C, W; **shet**, C3; **schit**, W; **ischet**, G; **y-schette**, S2, C3.—AS. *scyttan*.

schethe, *sb.* sheath, W (Jo. 15. 11), Cath.; **shethe**, C2.—AS. *scéað*; cf. OHG. *skeidâ* (Tatian).

schewen, *v.* to show, appear, S, PP, S3; **scheawen**, S2; **scheauwen**, S; **schewi**, S, S2; **schaw**, S2, S3, S; **sceawen**, S; **sceu**, S2; **scawen**, S; **shewe**, PP; **shæwenn**, S; **sseawy**, S2; **seawen**, S.—AS. *scéawian*, to see, also to make to see, show: OS. *skáwon*, to look, see.

schey, *adj.* timid, shy, Prompt.; **sceouh**, SkD.—AS. *scéoh*. Cf. **eschewen, schawles**.

schide, *sb.* a splinter, WA.—AS. *scíde*; cf. G. *scheit*, see Kluge.

schift, *sb.* shift, change; **shift**, Sh. *Phr.*: **at a schift**, on a sudden, in a moment, S2.

schiften, *v.* to change, shift, to part asunder, to divide, to discern, SkD; **schyftyn**, Prompt.; **shifte**, C3; **scyft**, *pr. s.*, S; **shifte him**, *pt. s.*, removed himself, PP.—AS. *sciftan* (*scyftan*), to divide.

schilden, *v.* to shield, S; see **schelden**.

schip, *sb.* ship, S; **schup**, S; **scipen**, *dat.*, S; **schupe**, S; **sipe**, S; **schupes**, *gen.*, S; **schipes**, *pl.*, S; **schippes**, S; **scipen**, S; **sipes**, S; **ssipes**, S2. *Comb.*: **schip-bord**; *phr.*: **on schipbord**, on board a ship, S2; **ship-breche**, shipwreck, W; **schip-man**, shipman, C; **shipman**, C2; **scipen-monnen**, *pl. dat.*, S; **ssip-uol**, shipful, S2; **schupeward**, shipward, S; **ship-wracke**, shipwreck, S3.—AS. *scip*.

schirchen, *v.* to shriek, S; see **schrychen**.

schirmen, *v.* to skirmish, fence, S; **skirmen**, S; **skyrmez**, *pr. s.*, glides swiftly on

flapping wings, S2.—Cf. Du. *schermen*, to fence, from *scherm*, screen, protection, OHG. *scirm*, protection (Otfrid).

schitte, *v.* to shut, G; see **schetten**.

scho¹, *sb.* shoe, W2; **schoo**, C, Prompt.; **schon**, *pl.*, S2, S3; **schone**, S, W; **schoon**, S2, W, G; **shoon**, C2, W; **shon**, PP.—AS. *scéoh*, pl. *scéos*, gen. pl. *scéona*.

scho², she, S3; see **sheo**.

schod, *pp.* shod, W, Prompt.; **shodde**, P.

schode, *sb.* the parting of a man's hair, the temple or top of the head, C; **schood**, CM.—AS. *scáde*, 'vertex capilli' (Grein); cf. G. *scheitel*. See **scheden**.

schoggyn, *v.* to shake, toss, Prompt.; **schogs**, *pr. s.*, WA; **schoggid**, *pp.*, W.

scholde, *pt. s.* should, S, S2; **scolde**, S; **sceolde**, S; **sholde**, S, C2, C3; **sculde**, S; **schulde**, S; **shulde**, S, C2, C3; **sulde**, S; **suld**, S2; **shuld**, S2; **solde**, S; **scholte**, S; **scolden**, S; **ssolde**, S2; **suld**, S2; **xuld**, HD.—AS. *scolde*. See **schal**.

scholle, shall, S2; see **schal**.

schome, *sb.* shame, S; see **schame**.

schomelich, *adj.* shameful, S; see **schamelich**.

schon¹, *pl.* of **scho**¹.

schon², *pt. s.* shone, C, G; see **schynen**.

schonde, *sb.* disgrace, S; **shonde**, C2.—AS. *scand* (*sceand*), *scond* (OET).

schonye, *v.* shun, P; see **schunien**.

schop, *pt. s.* created, S; see **schapen**.

schoppe, *sb.* shop, S2, Prompt., SkD. Cf. **schepne**.

schore, *sb.* a notch or line cut, a number, score, twenty, S2, PP; **score**, G, Prompt., PP.—AS. *scor*; cf. Icel. *skor*, an incision. See **schere**².

schort, *adj.* short, Prompt.; **schorte**, S2; **scort**, S, S2.—AS. *sceort*; cf. OHG. *scurz*.

schorteliche, *adv.* briefly, C.

schorten, *v.* to make short, C, Prompt.

schot, *pt. s.* rushed, S2; see **scheten**.

schouel, *sb.* shovel, Prompt.; **showell**, S3.—AS. *scofl* (Voc.).

schowpe, *sb.* a hip, *cornum*, Cath. *Comb.*: **schowpe-tre**, the briar, Cath.; **scopetre**, Cath. (*n*).

schowre, *sb.* shower, Prompt.; **schur**, SD; **shoures**, *pl.*, PP, C2; **sures**, S.—AS. *scúr*: Goth. *skura*.

schowwyn, *v.* to shove, Prompt.; **schowued**, *pp.*, S2.—AS. *scofian*.

schowynge, *sb.* pushing, Prompt.; **showuing**, C3.

schraf, *pt. s.* shrove, S3; see **schriven**.

schrapen, *v.* to scrape, PP.—Icel. *skrapa*.

schreden¹, *v.* to clothe, S; see **schrouden**.

schreden — sclavyne

schreden[2], *v.* to cut, Prompt.; **shredde**, *pt. s.*, C2.—AS. *scréadian*.

schredynge, *sb.* a cutting of herbs, Prompt.; **schridyng**, W2.

schrenchen, *v.* to make to fall, to deceive, S; **screnche**, S; **scrennkenn**, S.—AS. *(ge)screncan*, 'supplantare', Ps. 17. 40 (VP); cf. OHG. *screnken* (Otfrid).

schrewe, *adj.* and *sb.* wicked, bad, a wicked one, sinner, peevish woman, the devil, G, W2, S2, P, S, CM; **shrewe**, C2, P; **shrew**, S3, H, S2, C3; **screwe**, PP. Cf. AS. *scréawa*, a shrew-mouse (Voc.).

schrewen, *v.* to curse, CM, C.

schrewid, *adj.* cursed, bad, W, W2.

schrewidnesse, *sb.* wickedness, W2; **shrewednesse**, P.

schrift, *sb.* shrift, confession, S2; **scrift**, S; **schrifte**, *dat.*, S2; **shrifte**, S.—AS. *scrift*.

schrifte, *sb.* confessor, S; **shrifte**, S; **scrifte**, S.

schrippe, *sb.* scrip, bag, S2, PP; **shrippe**, PP; **scrippe**, S, S2, W; **scryppe**, Prompt.

schriuen, *v.* to prescribe penance, to confess, S; **schryue**, S2; **shriue**, S; **shrife**, S2; **schraf**, *pt. s.*, S2; **schrof**, PP; **ssriue**, *pl.*, S2; **shriuen**, *pp.*, S; **shryuen**, P; **scriuen**, S2; **y-shryue**, PP.—AS. *scrífan*, to prescribe penance, to receive confessions; Lat. *scribere*.

schroud, *sb.* dress, garment, PP; **scrud**, S; **shrud**, S; **srud**, S; **schroude**, WA, S2; **shroudes**, *pl.*, rough outer clothes, P.—AS. *scrúd* (Voc.).

schrouden, *v.* to clothe; **scruden**, S; **schruden**, S; **schreden**, S; **shrut**, *pr. s.*, S; **scred**, S; **schrowdis**, S3; **schredde**, *pt. s.*; S, CM; **srid**, S; **schred**, 2 *pt. s.*, S2; **schrudde**, *pl.*, S; **y-schrowdyt**, *pp.*, S3; **ischrud**, S; **iscrud**, S.—AS. *scrýdan*, also *scrédan*.

schrychen, *v.* to shriek, screech, Prompt.; **schriken**, SkD; **scriken**, SkD; **shriken**, SkD; **schirchen**, S; **shryghte**, *pt. s.*, C2; **schrighte**, C; **shryght**, S3; **shryched**, *pl.*, S3; **schrykede**, C.—Cf. Swed. *skrika*.

schulde, should; see **scholde**.

schuldere, *sb.* shoulder, Voc., W, S, C; **shulder**, Voc.; **ssoldren**, *pl.*, S2.—AS. *sculdor*.

schulen[1], shall; see **schal**.

schulen[2], *v.* to squint, S; **skoul**, SkD (s.v. *scowl*).—Cf. Dan. *skule*, to scowl.

schulle, *adv.* shrilly, S; see **schylle**.

schunchen, *v.* to cause to shun, to frighten, S.

schunien, *v.* to shun, S; **schonye**, S; **shonye**, P; **sunen**, S.—AS. *scúnian*.

schup, *sb.* ship, S; see **schip**.

schuppere, *sb.* creator, S; see **scheppere**.

schupte, *pt. s.* created, S; see **scheppen**.

schur, *sb.* shower; see **schowre**.

schurge, *sb.* scourge, S; see **scorge**.

schurten, *v.* *reflex.* to amuse (oneself), S.

schut, *v.* to shoot, S2; see **scheten**.

schylle, *adj.* sonorous, shrill, Prompt., Cath.; **schille**, S, S2; **schill**, S3; **schille**, *adv.*, S, S2; **schulle**, S; **shulle**, PP.

schylly, *adv.* sharply, Prompt.

schyllynge, *sb.* shilling, Prompt.; **schilling**, *pl.*, S2; *solidus*, Cath.—AS. *scilling*.

schyne, *sb.* shin, C; **schynne**, Prompt. *Comb.*: **schyn-bone**, Voc.—AS. *scina* (Voc.).

schynen, *v.* to shine, Prompt.; **sinen**, S; **schinen**, S; **ssynen**, S2; **scean**, *pt. s.*, S; **schon**, C, G; **shoon**, C2 **schane**, *pl.*, S3, H; **sinen**, *pp.*, S.—AS. *scínan*, pt. *scán* (pl. *scinon*), pp. *scinen*.

schynyng, *sb.* lightning, W2.

schynyngli, *adv.* splendidly, W.

schyre[1], *sb.* a shire, PP; **ssire**, S2. *Comb.*: **schir-reue**, shire-reeve, sheriff, S, C; **scherreue**, G; **schyreue**, P; **syrreue**, S; **schirreues**, *pl.*, S2, PP; **shriues**, S3; **shireues**, P.—AS. *scír*.

schyre[2], *adj.* bright, clear, Prompt.; **schire**, S2; **shire**, H; **shir**, S; **shyrest**, *superl.*, H. *Der.*: **shyrnes**, clearness, purity, H.—AS. *scír*; cf. Goth. *skeirs*. Cf. **schere**[3].

schytel, *sb.* shuttle, used for *shooting* the thread of the woof between the threads of the warp, SkD; **schutylle**, Cath.; **schetyl**, Prompt. (p. 470). *Comb.*: **shyttel-cocke**, shuttle-cock, S3. See **scheten**.

schyue, *sb.* a slice, small piece, Prompt.; **shive**, Sh., ND; **sheeve**, ND, JD; **schyfes**, bits of tow, Cath.—Cf. Icel. *skífa*.

schyuere, *sb.* a shiver, piece of wood, slice, Prompt.; **shiuer**, SkD; **scifren**, *pl.*, SkD; **sciuren**, SkD. See **schyve**.

schyueren, *v.* to break into shivers, splinters, C.

scipen, *pl.* ships, S; see **schip**.

scite, *sb.* city, S; see **citee**.

sclate, *sb.* slate, Prompt.; **sklat**, Prompt.

sclattis, *pl.*, *tegulae*, W.—OF. *esclat*, a shiver, splinter, something broken off with violence (Cotg.), F. *éclat*.

sclaundre[1], *sb.* scandal, slander, C2, PP; **sclauder**, Prompt.; **sklaundre**, PP; **slaunder**, Prompt.—AF. *esclaundre*, OF. *escandle*; Lat. *scandalum* (Vulg.); Gr. σκάνδαλον.

sclaundre[2], *v.* to scandalize, to slander, W, C3; **slaunderyd**, *pp.*, Prompt.

sclauyne, *sb.* pilgrim's cloak, S, Cath. (*n*); **slaveyne**, a garment, Prompt., HD; **slavyn**, Cath.; **sklavyn**, HD; **sclauayn**, Voc.; **sclavene**, Voc.; **slaueyn**, PP.—Low

184

Lat. *sclavina*, a long garment like that worn in Slavonic countries (Ducange); cf. AF. *esclavine*; from the people called *Slav*, a name said to be connected with Russ. *слово* 'a word', and to mean 'the speaking, the intelligible'. See SkD (p. 828).

sclender, *adj.* slender, C, SkD; **sklendre**, C, C2; **slendyr**, Prompt.—OF. *esclendre* (Palsg.); of Teutonic origin; cf. ODu. *slinder*; see BH, § 50.

scleyre, *sb.* veil, PP; see **sklayre**.

sco, she, S; see **sheo**.

scolden, should; see **scholde**.

scole[1], *sb.* the bowl of a balance, a bowl, Prompt.; **scoale**, S; **scale**, Cath.—Icel. *skál*, a bowl.

scole[2], *sb.* school, S, C, C2, Prompt. *Comb.*: **scol-meistre**, schoolmistress, S (*meistre*; OF. *meistre*; Lat. *magistra*, see BH).—Lat. *schola*; Gr. σχολή, leisure.

scoler, *sb.* scholar, C.

scoleye, *v.* to attend school, to study, C.

scop, *pt. s.* made, S; see **schapen**.

scorclen, *v.* to scorch, SkD (p. 826); **scorkelyn**, Prompt.; **scorklyd**, *pp.*, Prompt.

scorcnen, *v.* to scorch, S.

scorge, *sb.* scourge, Prompt.; **scourge**, W (Jo. 2. 15); **schurge**, S.—AF. *escorge*, OF. *escurge*; cf. It. *scoreggia* (Florio); Lat. *ex* + *corrigia*, a thong, rein, girdle (Ducange), see Diez, p. 109. Derived from this Lat. *corrigia* is AF. *escurgie*, OF. *escourgee* (Cotg.): It. *scoreggiáta* (Florio); Late Lat. *excorrigiata*, see Diez, p. 289, and Brachet.

scorn, *pp.* shorn, S2; see **schere**[2].

scoute, *sb.* scout, spy, SkD.—OF. *escoute* (Cotg.).

scouten, *v.* to scout, pry; **skowtez**, *pr. s.*, S2.—AF. *escouter*, to listen; OF. *ascouter*, *escolter*; Lat. *auscultare*.

scowkyng, *sb.* sculking, ambush, S2, B.— Cf. Dan. *skulke*, to slink.

scred, *pr. s.* clothes, S; see **schrouden**.

scrippe, *sb.* scrip, bag, S, S2, W; see **schrippe**.

scriptour, *sb.* pencase, S3.—OF. *escriptoire*, a penner (Cotg.); Late Lat. *scriptorium*, pencase (Ducange).

scrit, *sb.* writing, document, S2; **scrip**, Sh.; **script**, SkD.—OF. *escrit*, *escript*; Lat. *scriptum*.

scrud, *sb.* dress, S; see **schroud**.

scruden, *v.* to clothe, S; see **schrouden**.

sculde, should; see **scholde**.

sculptilis, *sb. pl.* idols, W2.—Lat. *sculptile*, a carved image (Vulg.).

---

se[1], *pron. dem. m.* and *def. art. m.* that, the, S. *Comb.*: **se þe**, that man that, he who, S; **se þet**, he that, S.—AS. *se*. Cf. **sheo**.

se[2], so, as, S; see **swa**.

se[3], *sb.* sea; see **see**[1].

se[4], *sb.* see; see **see**[2].

sead, *adj.* satiated, S; see **sad**.

sealte[1], *sb. dat.* salt, S2; see **salt**[1].

sealte[2], *adj.* salt, S2; see **salt**[2].

searce; see **sarce**[1].

seare, *adj.* sere, S3; see **seere**.

searse; see **sarce**[2].

seawede, *pt. s.* showed, S; see **schewen**.

sechen, *v.* to seek, S, S2, C, PP; **sekyn**, Prompt.; **seke**, PP, S, S2; **schechen**, S; **sohte**, *pt. s.*, S, S2; **soȝte**, S; **soȝt**, S2; **soght**, *pt.*, S2; **socht**, S3; **y-soht**, *pp.*, S2. *Phr.*: **to seke**, at a loss, S3.—AS. *sécan* (*pt. sóhte*, pp. *gesóht*): OS. *sókian*.

seck, *sb.* sack, S; see **sak**[1].

secre, *adj.* secret, S2, C, C3; **secree**, C2. *Comb.*: **Secre of Secrees**, Secreta Secretorum (name of a book), C3.—OF. *secre*; Lat. *secretum*.

secrely, *adv.* secretly, C2.

secrenesse, *sb.* secrecy, C3.

secte, *sb.* a suite, following, sect, religion, suit, apparel, PP, C2.—OF. *secte* (Cotg.); Late Lat. *secta*, a set of people, a following, a suit of clothes, a suit in law; Lat. *secta*, a faction, from *sec-* base of *sequi*, to follow.

sectour, *sb.* executor of a will, PP, S3, Cath.; **secatour**, HD; **secture**, HD; **seketowre**, Prompt.; **secutour**, PP.—AF. *executour*; Lat. *executorem*, executor of a will.

sed, *sb.* seed, PP, S, S2; **seed**, PP; **seod**; PP; **seð**, S. *Comb.*: **seed-leep**, seed-basket, PP.—AS. *séd*: Goth. *sēþs*; cf. OHG. *sát* (Tatian); see Brugmann, § 75.

sede, *pt. s.* said; see **seggen**.

see[1], *sb.* sea, Prompt., S, C2; **se**, S, S2; **sey**, S3; **sæ**, S; **sa**, S; **sees**, *pl.*, S2. *Comb.*: **sebare**, sea-wave, surge, S2; **se-calues**, sea-calves, seals, S2; **se-halues**, sea-coasts, S2.—AS. *sé*: Goth. *saiws*.

see[2], *sb.* see, seat, S3, C2, PP, S.— OF. *se*, *sed*; Lat. *sedem*.

seek, *adj.* sick, C; see **sek**[2].

seel, *sb.* seal, C3, P, Prompt.; **sehel**, PP.— OF. *séel*; Lat. *sigillum*.

seeled, *pp.* cieled, WW (s.v. *cieled*); see **ceelen**.

seelen, *v.* to seal, PP; **selen**, P; **seled**, *pp.*, C3.

seeling, *sb.* a sealing, W2.

seere, *adj.* sere, dry, withered, SkD, Prompt.; **seare**, S3.—AS. *séar*; cf. Low G. *soor*, dry.

seeryn, *v.* to become dry, Prompt.—AS. *séarian*. Cf. **soyr**.

seet[1], *pt. s.* sat, C, G; see **sitten**.

seet[2], *sb.* seat, G; see **sete**[1].

seeth, *pt. s.* boiled, C2; see **seþen**.

seg, *sb.* a man, lad, *nuncius, vir*, S2, PP; **segge**, P, WA, HD; **sege**, HD.—AS. *secg*: OTeut. **sagjoz*, see Sievers, 130.

sege, *sb.* seat, siege, S3, W, C, C2, Prompt.; **segys**, *pl.*, H.—AF. *sege*; Late Lat. **sedicum*, from Lat. *sedes*; see BH, § 133. See **see**[2].

segen on, *v.* to make to sink, to cast down, S.—AS. *on-ségan*, 'prosternere' (Grein).

segge, *sb.* sedge, S, Prompt., Voc.—AS. *secg*, sedge, also sword, see Sievers, 258.

seggen, *v.* to say, S, S2, S3, P; **segen**, S; **sægen**, S; **seigen**, S; **siggen**, S, S2; **sygge**, S2, S3; **sayn**, S2, C; **zigge**, S2; **seien**, S; **seie**, S3, C; **sei**, P; **sæin**, S; **seyen**, S; **seyn**, S2, C2; **seȝe**, S; **seiȝ**, S2; **zay**, S2; **sehð**, *pr. s.*, S; **seiþ**, S2; **seyþ**, S2; **zayþ**, S2; **seistow**, sayest thou, C3; **seien**, *pr. pl.*, S2; **sæde**, *pt. s.*, S; **sade**, S; **sede**, S, S2; **sæide**, S; **sayde**, C2; **seyde**, C2; **seide**, S2, C; **seidestow**, saidst thou, S2; **sugge**, *2 pr. s. subj.*, S; **ȝe-sed**, *pp.*, S; **i-said**, S; **i-segd**, S; **i-seid**, S; **ised**, S, S2; **seyd**, C2; **yzed**, S2; **iset**, S; **iseit**, S (3 b. 14); **seyne**, *gerund.*, C2.—AS. *secgan*, pt. *sáde*, pp. *geséd*.

sehte, *adj.* reconciled, S; see **saht**.

sehtnesse, *sb.* peace, reconciliation, S; see **sahtnesse**.

sei, seih, saw; see **seon**.

seily, *adj.* simple, humble, S3; see **sely**.

sein, *pp.* seen; see **seon**.

seint, *adj. and sb.* holy, saint, S, S2, C2; **seynt**, PP; **sein**, S, S2; **seintes**, *pl.*, C2; **seyntis**, W2.—OF. *seint, saint*; Lat. *sanctum*. Cf. **sant**.

seintuarie, *sb.* sanctuary, SD; **seyntewarie**, PP; **sayntuaryes**, *pl.*, holy things, relics of saints, S3.—AF. *saintuarie*, also *seintuarye*, holy relics; Lat. *sanctuarium*.

seir, *adj.* separate, S3; see **ser**.

seirse, *v.* to search; **seirsand**, *pr. p.*, S3. See **cerchen**.

seise, *v.* to seize, possess, SkD; **sese**, PP, B; **seised**, *pp.*, possessed of, S2.—OF. *seisir, sesir, sazir*, to put in possession; Low Lat. *sacire* (Ducange); OHG. *sazjan*, to set, *sezzan* (Tatian); see Brachet (s.v. *saisir*).

seisine, *sb.* possession, S2; **seysyne**, SkD.—AF. *seisine*.

sek[1], *sb.* sack, S2; see **sak**[1].

sek[2], *adj.* sick, S, S2; **seek**, PP, C; **sik**, S, G; **syk**, G; **sic**, S; **seke**, S; **sike**, S, C; **zyke**, S2; **sijke**, W; **sikly**, *adv.*, with ill-will, C2.—AS. *séoc*: Goth. *siuks*.

seke, *v.* to seek, S, S2; see **sechen**.

sekir, *adj.* sure, WA; see **siker**.

seknesse, *sb.* sickness, S2, C; **secnesse**, S; **siknesse**, C2; **sykenesse**, P; **sekenesse**, S2.—AS. *séocnes*.

sel[1], *sb.* happiness, occasion, time, S; **seel**, Prompt.; **sele**, S2.—AS. *sél*.

sel[2], *adj.* timely, good, S.—AS. *sél* (Grein): Goth. *sels*.

selde, *adj. pl.* few, C2; *adv.*, seldom, S, S2, C, C2, G, PP; **selden**, S2, P; **seldene**, S2; **seldum**, S. *Comb.*: **seld-hwonne**, seldom, S; **seld-sene**, rarely seen, SD; **seld-speche**, taciturnity, SD.—AS. *seld*; see Sweet.

self, *pron.* self, *ipse*, S; **seolf**, S; **silf**, W; **selue**, S; **sulf**, S, S2; **sulve**, S, S2; **zelue**, S2; **seolue**, *acc.*, S; **seoluen**, *pl.*, S; **sielfe**, S; **sulf**, S.—AS. *self*.

selke, *sb.* silk, P; **silke**, P; **seolke**, S.—AS. *seolc* (Voc.); Russ. *шелк*; Lat. *sericum*; cf. Icel. *silki*; see SkD (p. 828).

selkouth, *adj. and sb.* wonderful, a wonder, S2, H, PP; **selcouth**, S2, S3, PP; **selcuth**, S, S2, WA; **selkow**, Prompt.—AS. *seld-cúð*.

selkouth, *v.* to make wonderful, H.

selle, *sb.* cell, C, P; see **celle**.

sellen, *v.* to give, sell, Prompt., C; **sullen**, S, S2; **sylle**, S2; **selde**, *pt. s.*, W; **seelde**, W; **sald**, S2; **seeld**, *pp.*, W, W2; **seld**, W; **sald**, S2.—AS. *sellan* (*syllan*): OS. *sellian*: Goth. *saljan*.

seller[1], *sb.* seller, dealer, PP; **suller**, S2; **siller**, W2.

seller[2], *sb.* cellar, G; **seler**, W2; see **celer**.

sellich, *adj.* wonderful, illustrious, S; **sellic**, S; **seollich**, S; **sulliche**, *adv.*, S; **selli**, S2.—AS. *sellic*: OS. *seldlik*; cf. Goth. *sildaleiks*.

selðe, *sb.* happiness, advantage, HD; **selhðe**, S.—AS. (*ge*)*sélð*. See **sel**[1].

selure, *sb.* canopy, ceiling, S3; **seloure**, HD; **selour**, EETS (78); **celure**, EETS (78); **silour**, EETS (78); **sylure**, *celatura*, Prompt.; **siloure**, WA; **syllure**, MD.—OF. **celeüre*; Late Lat. *caelatura* (Ducange).

seluer, *sb.* silver, S, S2; see **silver**.

sely, *adj.* happy, blessed, simple, humble, S2, S3, C, C2, C3; **seely**, S3; **seilye**, S3; **seli**, S.—AS. *sélig*: OHG. *sálig* (Tatian).

selyn, *v.* to line the inner roof of a room, Prompt. See **ceelen**.

semblable, *adj.* like, S3, PP.—OF. *semblable*.

semblably, *adv.* similarly, S3.

semblance, *sb.* appearance, S2.—AF. *semblance*.

sembland, *adj.* like, PP.

semblant, *sb.* appearance, countenance, S, S2, C2; **semblaunt**, S, W, PP; **sembland**, S2.—AF. *semblant*.

semble[1], *v.* to seem; **sembles**, *pr. s.*, S2.—
OF. *sembler*; Lat. *simulare*.
semble[2], *v.* to assemble, PP; **sembled**, *pt. s.*,
S2; **semblyt**, S3; **semblyde**, *pl.*, S3.—
OF. *asembler*; Late Lat. *assimulare*.
semble[3], *sb.* assembly, S2, PP; **semblee**,
S2.—AF. *assemble, assemblee*.
seme, *sb.* load, S, P; **seem**, Prompt., P.—
AS. *séam*: Low Lat. *sauma (salma), sagma*; Gr.
σάγμα, a pack-saddle; see ZRP (2. 537), cf.
Kluge (s.v. *saum*).
semen[1], *v.* to load, to be a weight, S.—AS.
séman, from *séam*; see **seme**.
semen[2], *v.* to make two parties the *same*, to
conciliate, hence to suit, to appear suitable
or seemly, later, to seem, S; **seme**, S2;
seme, to reconcile, S; **semet**, *pr. s.*, seems
fitting, S. *Phr.*: **to my seminge**, as it
appears to me, C2.—AS. *séman, ge-séman*.
See **some**.
semi-, *adj.* half. *Comb.*: **semy-cope**, a short
cope, C.
semliche, *adj.* seemly, S2; **semeliche**, PP;
semely, C, C2, WA; **semlike**, S; **semly**,
S2; **semeli**, W2; **semlokest**, *superl.*, S2.—
AS. **sémelic*; cf. Icel. *sæmiligr*.
sen[1], afterwards, since, H, S2, S3, WA; see
siþþen.
sen[2], seven, H; see **seven**.
sen[3], *pp.* seen; see **seon**.
sence, *sb.* incense; see **sens**[2].
senche, *sb.* draught, S; see **schench**.
senchen, *v.* to cause to sink; **senchtest**, *2 pt.
s.*, S.—AS. *sencan*, causal of *sincan*.
sendal, *sb.* a fine stuff, C; **sendel**, H; see
cendal.
senden[1], *v.* to send, S; **sende**, S2; **send**, *pr.
s.*, S; **sent**, S, S2, C2; **zent**, S2; **sendes**, S;
sent, *imp. s.*, S2; **sende**, *pt. s.*, S, S2; **send**,
S3; *pl.*, S2; **senten**, S2; **send**, *pp.*, S;
y-sent, S2, C3; **i-sent**, S; **i-send**, S;
i-sende, S.—AS. *sendan*: OS. *sendian*: Goth.
sandjan.
senden[2], are; see **sinden**.
senden[3], *v.* to reproach, S; see **schenden**.
sene[1], *adj.* evident, S, S2, C2.—AS. *(ge)sýne*.
sene[2], *pp.* provided. *Phr.*: **well sene**, well
furnished, S3, HD. See **seon**.
seneuey, *sb.* mustard, W; **seneueye**, W;
seneuei, W.—OF. *senevé*, mustard (Cotg.);
an adjectival form from *senve*; Lat. *sinapi*
(Vulg.); Gr. σίναπι; see Brachet (s.v. *sanve*).
seneȝen, *v.* to sin; see **sunegen**.
senged, *pp.* sun-burnt, S3 (p. 364, l. 29); see
sengin.
sengin, *v.* to singe, burn on the surface;
seengyn, Prompt.; **seynd**, *pp.*, C; **seynkt**,
Prompt.; **sengt**, Prompt.—AS. *sengan* (in
be-sengan), causal of *singan*, to sing.

senne, *sb.* sin, S; see **sunne**[2].
sens[1], since, S3; see **siþþen**.
sens[2], *sb.* incense, S3; **sence**, Prompt., Cath.;
sense, PP.—AF. *ensens, encens*; Lat. *incensum*,
lit. what is burned (Vulg.).
sensing, *sb.* use of incense, S3; **sencynge**,
Prompt.
sentence, *sb.* sense, meaning, opinion,
matter of a story, verdict, C, C2, C3;
sentens, PP.—AF. *sentence*; Lat. *sententia*.
seofe, seven, S; see **seven**.
seolf, self, S; see **self**.
seolke, *sb.* silk, S; see **selke**.
seollich, *adj.* wonderful, S; see **sellich**.
seoluer, *sb.* silver, S; see **silver**.
seon, *v.* to see, S, PP; **seo**, S, S2; **seen**, S;
sen, S; **se**, S2, W2; *imp. s.*, S; *pl.*, W; **see**,
may (God) see, S2; **sest**, *2 pr. s.*, S; **sist**, S,
S2; **sixt**, S2; **seð**, *pr. s.*, S; **seoþ**, *pl.*, S2;
seð, S2, P; **sei**, *2 pt. s.*, S2; **sæh**, *pt. s.*, S;
seh, S, S2; **sih**, S2; **siȝ**, S2, W; **syȝ**, S2;
sye, S3; **sy**, C3; **seȝ**, S, S2; **sey**, S2, C2, G;
seiȝ, S2, S3; **seigh**, C; **seih**, G; **seyh**, G;
sag, S; **sagh**, S2; **saugh**, S3, C, G; **saȝ**, S;
sauȝ, S; **sawh**, S2; **say**, S2, S3, C, W, G;
sayȝ, S2; **saye**, W; **saie**, S; **saiȝ**, W;
sawȝ, W; **sihen**, *pl.*, S2; **syȝen**, S2; **seien**,
W; **seiȝen**, W; **seen**, W; **siȝen**, W; **sien**,
W; **syen**, W; **saien**, W; **sayn**, W; **saye**,
W; **seye**, S2; **seand**, *pr. p.*, S3; **seynge**,
W2; **seyn**, *pp.*, S2, C, W; **seȝen**, S2; **sein**,
S2; **sen**, S; **seie**, S2; **sien**, W2; **siȝ**, W;
say, W; **y-seiȝen**, PP; **y-sein**, PP; **seen**,
ger., S3; **zyenne**, S2.—AS. *séon*, pt. *seah* (pl.
sáwon, ségon), pp. *sewen (sawen)*, also *ge-segen*.
AS. *séon* (for **sehwon*): Goth. *saihvan*; cf. Lat.
sequ-or, I follow; see Brugmann, § 419.
seoð, are, S; see **sinden**.
seouen, seven, S; see **seven**.
seowen, *v.* to sew, S; see **sewen**[1].
sep, *pl.* sheep, S; see **scheep**[1].
septemtrioun, *sb.* the North, C2.—OF.
septentrion; Late Lat. *septentrionem* (Voc.); from
Lat. *septemtriones*, a name for the constella-
tion of the Great Bear.
sepulture, *sb.* tomb, S3, C3; **sepultures**,
pl., burials, S3.—AF. *sepulture*; Lat. *sepultura*.
ser, *adj.* separate, several, different, various,
S2, B; **sere**, S2, H, WA; **seir**, S3, B. *Der.*:
sernes, variety, H; **sernessis**, *pl.*, H;
sernesis, H; **serelepy** separate, WA;
serelepes, separately, PP.—Cf. usages of
Icel. *sér*, to himself, used in many compounds, as *sér-liga*, apart, particularly.
sercle, *sb.* circle, W2; see **cercle**.
serewe, *sb.* sorrow, S; see **sorwe**.
serge, *sb.* a taper, Cath.; see **cerge**.
sergeant, *sb.* servant, serjeant, C, C2, C3;
seriaunt, P; **serganȝ**, *pl.*, S; **seriauntes**,

S2; **seriauntz**, P; **seriauns**, S2, PP.—AF. *serjant*; Lat. *seruientem*; see BH, § 162.

serk, *sb.* sark, shirt, PP, S, S3, G; **sark**, S3; **serke**, P.—Icel. *serkr*.

sermone, *v.* to preach, speak, C3.

sermonyng, *sb.* preaching, C.

sermoun, *sb.* sermon, writing, C2; **sarmoun**, P.—AF. *sermoun*; Lat. *sermonem*.

sertes, *adv.* certainly, S2; see **certes**.

seruage, *sb.* servitude, thraldrom, S2, C, C2, C3, W, Prompt.—OF. *servage*.

seruin, *v.* to serve, to deserve, S, S2; **sarui**, S; **serue**, H, PP; **serwis**, *2 pr. s.*, S3; **serwit**, *pt. s.*, S3; **y-served**, *pp.*, C, P; **i-serued**, S.—AF. *servir*; Lat. *seruire*.

seruisable, *adj.* serviceable, C3.

seruise, *sb.* service, S; **seruyse**, C2.—OF. *servise*; Lat. *seruitium*; see BH, § 129.

seruitute, *sb.* servitude, C2.—OF. *servitute*; Lat. *seruitutem*; see Constans.

serwe, *sb.* sorrow, S; see **sorwe**.

serwish, *adj. imperiosus*, Manip.

serye, *sb.* series, C, CM.—Lat. *seriem*.

seryows, *adj.* 'sad and feythefulle', Prompt.; **seriouse**, *seriosus*, Manip.; **seryouse**, earnest, Palsg.—Late Lat. *seriosus*; from Lat. *serius*, grave, earnest.

seryowsly, *adv.* seriously; **ceriously**, minutely, with full details, S2, C3.—Late Lat. *seriose*, 'fuse, minutatim' (Ducange).

sese, *v.* to seize; see **seise**.

sesoun, *sb.* season, C3; **cesoun**, W2.—AF. *seson*, OF. *saison*; Lat. *sationem*, a sowing.

set, *pt. s.* sat, S; see **sitten**.

sete[1], *sb.* seat, Cath., S, C2, PP; **seet**, G.—AS. *seto, seotu* (OET).

sete[2], *adj.* suitable, H (p. xxv).—Icel. *sætt*, endurable, from *sitja*, to sit.

setel, *sb.* seat, SD; **seotel**, S; **settle**, S. *Comb.*: **setel-gang**, sunset, S2.—AS. *setl*; cf. Goth. *sitls*.

Seterday, Saturday, P; see **Saturne**.

setlen, *v.* to cause to rest, also to sink to rest, subside, settle, SkD; **sattel**, S2, S3, SkD; **satelyn**, Prompt.; **saʒtled**, *pt. s.*, S2 [see SkD s.v. *settle*].—AS. *setlan*, to fix, settle (Grein).

setnesse, *sb.* an appointed order, institute, SD.—AS. *(ge)setnis*. Cf. **asetnesse**.

sette,—*sb.* a young plant, a shoot; **settys**, *pl.*, S3.

setten, *v.* to set, place, appoint, S; **sett**, to set, watch game, S2; **setis**, *pr. s.*, S; **settes**, *2 pr. s.*, S2; **sette**, *pt. s.*, S, S2, S3; **zette** S2; **sætte**, S; **set**, *2 pt. s.*, W; **settide**, *pt. s.*, W; **settiden**, *pl.*, W; **sette**, G; **settand**, *pr. p.*, S2; **set**, *pp.*, S; **i-set**, S, S2; **i-sett**, S; **i-sette**, S; **y-set**, S2, S3, C2, C3.—AS.

settan: Goth. *satjan*, to cause to sit; see Douse, p. 113. See **sitten**.

seð, *sb.* seed, S; see **sed**.

sethen, *v.* to seethe, Prompt.; **seeth**, *pt. s.*, seethed, boiled, C2; **y-sode**, *pp.*, S2.—AS. *séoðan*, pt. s., *séað*, pp. *soden*. Cf. **swiþen**.

seððen, afterwards, since, S, S2, G; **seðen**, S, S2; **seþþe**, S2; see **siþþen**.

seurte, *sb.* surety, C; see **surety**.

seuen, *num.* seven, PP; **seue**, PP, S; **seouen**, S; **seove**, S; **seofe**, S; **seuene**, PP; **seouene**, S; **sen**, H; **zeue**, S2; **seofen**, S.—AS. *seofon*; cf. Goth. *sibun*, Lat. *septem*; Gr. ἑπτά. For the Goth. termination *-un*, see Brugmann, §§ 223, 224.

seuend, *num. ord.* seventh, S2.

seue-niht, *sb.* sennight, week, S; **souenyht**, S.

seuen-tene, *num.* seventeen, Prompt.; **sewintine**, S3.

seueþe, *num. ord.* seventh, S2, PP; **seoueðe**, S; **soueþe**, S; **seofeþe**, S.

sew, *pt. s.* sowed, H; see **sowen**.

sewane, *sb.* savin (a herb), S3. See **saveine**.

sewe, *sb.* juice, broth, gravy, delicacy, C2, Cath., HD; **sew**, HD; **sæw**, S.—AS. *séaw*.

sewen[1], *v.* to sew, *suere*, W2; **seowen**, S; **sewide**, *pt. s.*, W2; **y-sewed**, *pp.*, S3.—AS. *siwian*: Goth. *siujan*; see Brugmann, § 120.

sewen[2], *v.* to follow, PP, C, S2. *Der.*: **sewyngly**, in order, S2. See **suen**.

sewen[3], *v. in phr.*: **to sewe at yᵉ mete**, *deponere*, *apponere*, to set upon the table, Cath., Prompt. See **sewer**.

sewer, *sb.* bearer of dishes, *dapifer*, S2, Voc.; **seware**, s., Prompt.; **asseour**, NED; **assewer**, NED.—AF. *asséour*, he who sets the table (Ducange); from OF. *asséoir*, to set, to place; Late Lat. *adsedēre*.

sewintene, seventeen, S3; see **seventene**.

sexe, six, S; see **sixe**.

sexte, sixth; see **sixte**.

sexteyn, *sb.* sacristan, sexton, C2; see **sacristane**.

seych, *sb.* sigh, S3; see **syke**.

seyed, *pp.* passed, lit. swayed, S2; see **sweyen**[1].

seyen, *v.* to say; see **seggen**.

seyl, *sb.* sail, Prompt., S, C; **seil**, S; **seiies**, *pl.*, S2; **seales**, S3.—AS. *segl*.

seylen, *v.* to sail, Prompt.; **sayle**, C2; **saland**, *pr. p.*, S3.—AS. *(ge)seglian*.

seyn, *pp.* seen; see **seon**.

seynen, *v.* to make a sign, esp. the sign of the cross, PP; **saine**, to bless, HD; **seyned**, *pt. s.*, P; **sanyt**, S2.—OF. *seigner* (Bartsch); Lat. *signare*.

seynd, *pp.* singed, C; see **sengin**.

seynt, *sb.* girdle, C; see **ceinte**.

seȝen, *v.* to say, S; see **seggen**.

sh-. For many words beginning with **sh-** (as well as words beginning with **sc-** and **ss-**), see **sch-**.

shadde, *pt. s.* shed, poured, C2; see **scheden**.

shæd, *sb.* discretion, S.—AS. *(ge)scéad*. See **scheden**.

shæfess, *pl.* sheaves, S; see **scheef**.

shæwen, *v.* to show, S; see **schewen**.

sheeuering, *pr. p.* shivering, S3; see **chiveren**.

sheo, *pron. dem., def. art., pron. pers. f.*, illa, that, the, she, PP; **scheo**, SD; **scho**, S3, PP; **sho**, S, H; **sco**, S2; **seo**, S; **sche**, C, PP; **che**, S2; **si**, S; **scæ**, S. *Comb.*: **zi þet**, she that, SD (s.v. *se*).—AS. *séo*; cf. OHG. *siu* (Tatian).

sherch, *v.* to search, S3; see **cerchen**.

sho, she, S; see **sheo**.

shode; see **scheden**.

shriues, *pl.* sheriffs, S2; see **schyre**[1].

si[1], she, S; see **sheo**.

si[2], let there be, S; see **sinden**.

sibbe, *sb.* and *adj.* peace, relationship, *affinis*, related, SD, S, P; **sybbe**, Prompt.; **sib**, S; **syb**, P. *Comb.*: **sib-man**, 'affinis', HD; **sib-nesse**, affinity, SD; **sib-reden**, relationship, SD; **sibrede**, HD; **sybrede**, banns of matrimony, Prompt.; **cybrede**, Prompt.; **sib-sum**, peaceable, SD; **sib-sumnesse**, friendship, SD.—AS. *sib(b)*, peace, relationship: Goth. *sibja*; cf. OHG. *sibba*, peace (Tatian), relationship (Otfrid). See Sievers, 257.

sic, *adj.* sick, S; see **sek**[2].

sicer, *sb.* strong drink, C2; **siser**, C2 (*n*); **ciser**, C2 (*n*), MD.—Low Lat. *sicera* (Vulg.); Gr. σίκερα (LXX); Heb. *shēkar* (Deut. 29. 6). Cf. **sidir**.

siche, *adj.* such, W; see **swyche**.

sicht, *pt. s.* sighed, S3; see **syken**.

siclatoun, *sb.* a costly silk texture, CM; **sicladoun**, CM; see **ciclatun**.

sidir, *sb.* strong drink, cider, S3, W, MD; **sidur**, W2; **sider**, MD; **sydyr**, Prompt.; **sedyr**, Prompt.; **cyder**, C2 (*n*); **cedyr**, Prompt.; **syther**, Cath., S2; **sythir**, C2 (*n*).—OF. *sidre (cidre)*, *sisdre*; Low Lat. *sicera* (Voc.); Gr. σίκερα (Luke 1. 15); cf. Sp. *sidra* (Deut. 29. 6). See **sicer**.

sigaldren, *sb. pl.* sorceries, S.—Icel. *seiðgaldr*, enchantment by spells. See Grimm, Teut. M. pp. 1035-1043.

sigaldrie, *sb.* enchantment, SD; **sigaldry**, HD.

sigaldrien, *v.* to bewitch; **sygaldryd**, *pt. s.*, HD.

siggen, *v.* to say; see **seggen**.

sighte, *sb.* sight, providence, appearance, PP, C; **sihðe**, S; **syhte**, S; **syȝt**, S2; **zygþe**, S2; **zyȝþe**, S2; **sihte**, S; **siȝte**, S.—AS. *(ge)sihð (gesiht)*.

signe, *sb.* sign, portent, PP; see **syng**.

signefiance, *sb.* meaning, S.—OF. *signefiance*.

signefien, *v.* to signify, mean, S.—AF. *signefier*.

sihen, *pt. pl.* saw, S2; see **seon**.

sik, *adj.* sick, S; see **sek**[2].

sike, *adj.* such, S3; see **swyche**.

siker, *adj.* secure, sure, trusty, S, S2, C3, P; **sikir**, W; **sekir**, B; **zykere**, S2; **zikere**, S2; **syker**, S3, P; *adv.*, truly, S3; **sikerer**, *comp.*, S3, C; **sikerere**, P; **sikerest**, *superl.*, S2. *Comb.*: **sikerhede**, security, SD; **sikerlec**, surety, pledge, SD; **sikerliche**, surely, certainly, S; **sykerlych**, S2; **sikerlike**, S; **sikerly**, S3, C, C2, P; **sykerly**, H; **sekirly**, B; **sikernesse**, security, S, S2, C2, C3; **sicernesse**, S; **sykernes**, S2; **sikirnesse**, W; **sykirnes**, H; **sekirnes**, B.—OS. *sikor*; Late Lat. *sēcurus* (with accent on the first syllable); cf. OHG. *sichor* (Otfrid). Cf. **sure**.

siklewe, *adj.* sickly, Trevisa; see **-lewe**. Cf. **sek**[2].

siknesse, *sb.* sickness, C2; see **seknesse**.

sikul, *sb.* sickle, P; **sykel**, PP; **sykyl**, Prompt.—AS. *sicel* (Voc.); Lat. *secula*.

silc, *adj.* such, S2; see **swyche**.

silden, *v.* to shield, S; see **schelden**.

silke, *sb.* silk, P; see **selke**.

silour; see **selure**.

siluer, *sb.* silver, S, C3; **seoluer**, S; **suluer**, S2; **seluer**, S, S2; **siluere**, *dat.*, S; **selure**, S.—OMerc. *sylfur*, AS. *silfor (seolfor)*: OS. *silubar*, Goth. *silubr*; see Sievers, 107.

simle, *adv.* ever, for ever, S.—AS. *simle (symle)* for *simble*: OS. *simbla*; cf. OHG. *simbulum* (Tatian).

sinden, *pr. pl.* are; **sinndenn**, S; **senden**, S; **seoð**, S; **si**, *pr. s. subj.*, let (there) be, S; **seon**, *subj. pl.*, may be, S.—AS. *syndun*, pr. pl., *sí*, pr. s. subj., *síen*, pl., see Sievers, 427.

sinegen, *v.* to sin, S; see **sunegen**.

sinen, *pp.* shone, S; see **schynen**.

sinne, *sb.* sin, S; see **sunne**[2].

siouns, *sb. pl.* branches, W2; see **syon**.

sipes, *pl.* ships, S; see **schip**.

si-quar; see **siþ**.

sire, *sb.* a prince, king, lord, father, master, a term used in addressing knights, kings, S, S2, P, G; **syr**, Prompt.—AF. *sire* (for **se'ior*); Lat. *senior*, older; so F. *pire*; Lat. *peior*, worse.

sis, six, C2; see **sixe**.

siser, *sb.* strong drink; see **sicer**.

sisour, *sb.* juror, PP; **sysour**, P; see **asisour**.

sisoure

sisoure, *sb.* a person deputed to hold assizes, juryman, P, S2, G; **sisour**, PP; **sysour**, PP.—Low Lat. *assisorem* (Ducange), from OF. *a(s)sise*, a sitting down, also a settlement, pp. fem. of *aseeir*; Lat. *assidēre*, to sit at.

sist, seest; see **seon**.

siste, sixth, S; see **sixte**.

sistren, *pl.* sisters, C; see **suster**.

site, *sb.* grief, S2; **syte**, WA, HD.—Icel. *sút*; AS. *suht*; cf. OHG. *suht* (Otfrid), Goth. *sauhts*, sickness.

siten, *v.* to grieve, S2. See **site**.

sitten, *v.* to sit, cost, befit, S, P; **sytte**, PP, S3; **zitte**, S2; **sit**, *pr. s.*, C, S2, G, PP; **sitt**, PP; **sits**, S3; **set**, *pt. s.*, S; **seet**, C, G; **sæt**, S; **setten**, *pl.*, S; **sete**, S, G; **seten**, C2, W; **seeten**, C; **saten**, G; **seten**, *pp.*, S, C; **syttyn**, S2.—AS. *sittan*, pt. *sæt* (pl. *sǽton*), pp. *seten*.

sið, *sb.* time, SD; **siðe**, *dat.*, S; **sith**, *pl.*, H; **syth**, H; **siðe**, C, S2, PP; **sythe**, H, C2, C3; **sythes**, S2, PP; **sithis**, W, S3; **sithes**, PP; **zyþe**, S2; **ziþe**, S2 (9. 72). *Comb.*: **oftsith** (= Lat. *sæpe*), H; **si-quar** (for **siðquar**), time when, S2.—AS. *síð*, journey, turn, time: Goth. *sinþs*; cf. OHG. *sind*, 'via' (Otfrid), Icel. *sinn*.

siððen, *adv. and conj.* afterwards, since, S, C, G; **siþþe**, S2, S3; **siðen**, S, S3, C; **siðe**, S, S3; **sith**, S2, S3, C; **seoðða**n, S; **seoððen**, S; **seoððe**, S; **seððen**, S, S2, G; **seðen**, S, S2; **seðe**, S; **syth**, S3, C; **seþþe**, S2; **suþþe**, S, S2; **syþþen**, S2; **sythen**, S2, S3; **sen**, H, S2, S3; **syn**, S2, S3; **syne**, S2, S3; **sens**, S3.—AS. *síððan*.

sixe, *num.* six, S, PP; **sexe**, S; **sax**, S3; **sis**, C2; **sys**, C2.—AS. *six*.

sixt, seest; see **seon**.

sixte, *ord.* sixth, S; **syxte**, PP; **sexte**, S, S2; **sæxte**, S; **siste**, S.—AS. *sixta*.

siȝe, *sb.* victory, SD; **si**, SD; **sy**, S.—AS. *sige*: Goth. *sigis*; cf. OHG. *sig* (Tatian).

siȝe-craft, *sb.* magic art, SD. See **sigaldren**.

siȝede, *pt. s.* sighed, S3; see **syken**.

siȝen, *pt. pl.* saw; see **seon**.

skaffaut, *sb.* an engine of war used by besiegers, CM; **scafalde**, *procestrium*, Cath.; **scafold**, stage, Prompt., SkD; **scaffould**, *theatrum, scena*, Manip.; **schaffalde**, stage, Cath. (*n*); **skaffold**, Cath. (*n*).—OF. *escafaut* (*eschafaut*); cf. OF. *chafaut* (*chaffaut*), Low Lat. *chaqfallum, chaufaudus*, a wooden tower used against besiegers; cf. also It. *catafalco*. The origin of this word of various forms is absolutely unknown.

skaith, *sb.* harm, S3; see **scaþe**.

skalk, *sb.* scalp, H; **skalke**, H; **skalkys**, *pl.*, H.

slak

skalle, *sb.* scabbiness on the head, scall, SkD.

skalled, *adj.* scabby, C.

skalp, *sb.* scalp, H (Ps. 7. 17); **scalp**, SkD.

skarrit, *1 pt. s.* was scared, S3; see **skerren**.

skathe, *sb.* harm, C, G; **skath**, H; see **scaþe**.

skeet, *adj.* swift; *adv.* soon, quickly, G; **skete**, HD; **sket**, S, HD.—Icel. *skjótr*, swift; adv. *skjótt*.

skele, *sb.* reason, S2; see **skyl**.

skenten, *v.* to amuse, SD.—Icel. *skemta*, to amuse, to shorten, from *skamr*, short.

skentinge, *sb.* amusement, S, SD.

sker, *adv.* clean, entirely, S; see **schere**[3].

skerren, *v.* to scare, frighten, to be frightened, SD; **skeren**, Prompt.; **scarren**, SD; **skarrit**, *1 pt. s.*, S3; **skerrit**, SD.—Icel. *skirra*, to prevent, *reflex.* to shrink from.

skewe, *sb.* sky, S2; see **skye**.

skey, *adj.* shy (as a horse), Prompt.; see **schey**.

skeymowse, *adj.* disdainful, scornful, *abhominativus*, Prompt.; **queymows**, Prompt.; **sweymows**, Prompt.; **squaymous**, CM; **squeamous**, CM; **squaymose**, *verecundus*, Cath.; **skoymus**, disdainful, Cath. (*n*); **squeamish**, coy, precise (of a young girl), Cotg. (s.v. *sucrée*); fastidious, Baret.

skil, *sb.* reason, H; see **skyl**.

skilwise, *adj.* reasonable, discreet, H; **scilwis**, H; **skilwisly**, *adv.*, H.

skinden, *v.* to hasten, S.—Icel. *skynda*; cf. AS. *scyndan*.

sklayre, *sb.* a veil, P; **scleyre**, PP; **skleire**, PP; **skleir**, PP.—Cf. G. *schleier*, Du. *sluijer*.

sklither, *adj.* slippery (= Lat. *lubricus*), H; cf. **slider**.

sklythirynge, *sb.* liability to fall, H.

skowtez, *pr. s.* pries, looks, S2; see **scouten**.

skye, *sb.* cloud, sky, Prompt.; **skewe**, S2; **skwe**, S2; **schew**, WA; **skyes**, *pl.*, PP.—Icel. *ský*, cloud.

skyl, *sb.* discernment, reason, skill, Prompt.; **skil**, H; **skill**, S; **skyle**, S2; **skile**, S, C2, W; **skille**, S2; **skele**, S2; **skiles**, *pl.*, reasons, C2, H; **skilles**, S2, H.—Icel. *skil*, distinction, discernment.

skylfulle, *adj.* reasonable, discerning, Prompt.; **skilful**, W2, C3.

skylly, *perhaps* dispersing (?), S2.

skyualde, *perhaps* scramble (?), S2.

sla, *v.* to slay, S2; see **sleen**.

slade, *sb.* a valley, Manip., ND.—AS. *slǽd*.

slagen, *pp.* slain, S; see **sleen**.

slaht, *sb.* slaughter, SD; **slaȝt**, S2.—AS. *sleaht*.

slaine; see **sleen**.

slak[1], *sb.* ravine, a hollow, depression, gap or pass between two hills, S3, B; **slack**, the

190

low ground, HD; a common (in Yorkshire), NQ (1. 10. 400).
slak², *adj.* slack, Prompt.; **slac**, S2; **slake**, *dat.*, C.—AS. *sleac:* OS. *slak.*
slakien, *v.* to be slack, to make loose, S, W; **slake**, to become less grievous, S2; to slacken, cease, C2; **slakeþ**, *pr. s.*, burns low, S2; assuages, C2.—AS. *slacian.*
slape, *sb.* sleep, S; see **slepe.**
slatten, *v.* to throw down, to slap; **slat**, HD; **sleateð**, *pr. pl.*, S.
slaunder; see **sclaundre**[1].
slaueren, *v.* to slaver, to let the saliva fall from the mouth, S2.
slawe, *adj.* slow, S3; see **slowe.**
slawen; see **sleen.**
sla3t, *sb.* slaughter, S2; see **slaht.**
sle, *adj.* sly, cunning, S3; see **sly.**
sleen, *v.* to slay, PP, C2; **slee**, PP, S3, W, G; **sle**, S, S3, PP; **slen**, PP; **slean**, S; **slæn**, S; **slon**, S; **slo**, S; **sla**, S2; **sleað**, *pr. s.*, S; **sleth**, S3; **sleeth**, C; **sleað**, *pl.*, S; **sla3eð**, S; **slage**, S; **sloh**, *pt. s.*, S; **slo3**, S; **slou**, S, S2; **slow**, S2, S3; **slowe**, W; **slouh**, S2; **slou3**, S2; **slough**, S3, C; **sloghen**, *pl.*, S; **slo3en**, S; **slowe**, S2; **slowen**, W; **slo3e**, S; **slogh**, S2; **sloughe**, S3; **slo**, *pr. subj.*, 2 *p.*, S2; **slen**, *pl.*, S; **slagen**, *pp.*, S; **slaine**, S; **slawen**, C2; **slayn**, C2; **sleie**, S2; **slawe**, S3, C; **slean**, S3; **y-slayn**, C3; **i-slawe**, S2; **y-slawe**, C3; **i-sleiene**, *pl.*, S.—AS. *sléan* (for *slahan*), pt. *slóh* (pl. *slógon*), pp. *slægen*, also *slegen.*
sleet, *sb.* sleet, Prompt.; **slet**, SD.—Cf. G. *schlosse.*
slegh, *adj.* cunning, S2; **sleh**, S; see **sly.**
sleght, *sb.* cunning, S2; **sleht**, S; see **sleyþe.**
slendyr; see **sclender.**
slepe, *sb.* sleep, S, S2, Prompt.; **slape**, S; **slep**, S.—AS. *slép:* OS. *sláp;* cf. OFris. *slép.*
slepen, *v.* to sleep, S; **slep**, *pt. s.*, S, S3; **slepte**, *(weak form)*, C2, PP; **slepen**, *pl.*, PP.—AS. *slépan*, pt. *slép;* a reduplicating verb, see Douse, p. 48.
slepyng, *sb.* sleep, S2.
sleðrende, *pr. p.* falling like snow, S.
sleuth, *sb.* track, trail, slot, S2, B; **sluth**, B; **slewth**, B; **sloð**, S, SkD. *Comb.*: **sleuth-hund**, a sleuth-hound, S2.—Icel. *slóð.*
sleuþe, *sb.* sloth, S2, P; **sleuth**, H; see **slouþe.**
sleue, *sb.* sleeve, C3, Prompt.—AS. *sléfe.*
sleueles, *adj.* sleeveless, useless, HD.
sley, *adj.* sly, S2; see **sly.**
sleythe, *sb.* cunning, skill, falsehood, trick, Prompt., PP; **sleithe**, PP; **sle3þe**, S2; **slehþe**, SD, PP; **slithe**, PP; **slyþe**, PP; **sleighte**, PP, C, C2, C3; **sleht**, S; **sleght**, S2.—Icel. *slægð* (for *slægð*). See **sly.**

sliden, *v.* to slide, PP; **slit**, *pr. s.*, C3; **slod**, *pt. s.*, S2; **slode**, *pl.*, PP; **slide**, *pp.*, W2.—AS. *slídan*, pt. *slád*, pp. *sliden.*
slider, *adj.* slippery, C; **slidir**, W2; **slydyr**, Prompt. See **skliþer.**
slidernesse, *sb.* slipperyness; **slydirnesse**, W2; **slydyrnesse**, Prompt.
slih, *adj.* cunning, experienced, S2; see **sly.**
slike, *adj.* such, H.—Icel. *slíkr.*
slikien, *v.* to smoothe, to polish, SD; **slyken**, P; **slicke**, S3; **isliked**, S.
sliper, *adj.* slippery, SD; **slipper**, S3, Sh.—AS. *slipor* (Leo).
slitten, *v.* to slit, pierce, SD; **slytyn**, Prompt.; **slyttyng**, *pr. p.*, piercing (of language), S2; **islit**, *pp.*, S.—AS. *slítan.*
slo, *vb.* to slay, S; **slon**, S; **sloh**, *pt. s.*, S; see **sleen.**
slod, *pt. s.* slid, S2; see **sliden.**
slogardye, *sb.* sloth, C3; see **sluggardy.**
sloh, *sb.* slough, PP; **slough**, C2, C3.—AS. *slóh.*
slokyn, *v.* to slake, quench, H, Cath.; **slokin**, S3; **slokke**, PP; **slokynd**, *pp.*, H; **slekynd**, H.—Cf. Icel. *slökva.* Cf. **slakien.**
slomeren, *v.* to slumber, Cath., Prompt.; **slumeren**, SD; **slombred**, *pt. s.*, P.
slomering, *sb.* slumbering, S3.
slong, *pp.* cast away, S3; see **slyngen.**
sloppar, *adj.* slippery, S3.
sloterin, *v.* maculare, SD; **sloterd**, *pp.*, bespattered, S2.
sloð, *sb.* track, trail, S; see **sleuþ.**
slough; see **sloh.**
slouthe, *sb.* sloth, S2, C3, PP; **slouhðe**, S; **sleu3þe**, S2, PP; **sleuþe**, S2, P; **slewthe**, C3, PP; **sleuth**, H, PP.—AS. *slǽwð.* See **slowe.**
slow; see **sleen.**
slowe, *adj.* and *sb.* slow, sluggish, a lazy man, PP, S; **slow**, W2; **slouh**, S; **slawe**, S3; **slaw**, S2.—AS. *sláw.*
slo3e; see **sleen.**
sluggardy, *sb.* sloth, S3; **slogardye**, C3; **sloggardye**, C.
slugge, *adj.* slothful, Prompt.
sluggen, *v.* to slug, to be inactive, SkD.
sluggy, *adj.* slothful, Prompt.
sly, *adj.* sly, cunning, skilful, Prompt.; **sli3**, W; **slih**, S2; **sley**, S2; **slegh**, S2; **sleh**, S; **sle3**, S2; **sle**, S3.—Icel. *slægr* (for *slægr*).
slyly, *adv.* cunningly, Prompt.; **sleighly**, prudently, C.
slynge, *sb.* sling, Prompt.
slyngen, *v.* to sling, hurl, throw away, PP, Prompt.; **slonge**, *pt. pl.*, S2; **slong**, *pp.*, S3; **slungin**, S3.—AS. *slingan*, pl. slang, pp. *slungen.*

smak, *sb.* taste, flavour, Prompt.; **smacc**, S; **smach**, S2.—AS. *smæc*, taste, flavour (Voc.).

smaken, to have a savour, scent, S, Prompt.; **smacky**, to imagine, perceive, taste, relish, understand, S2; **smachande**, *pr. p.*, S2; **smauhte**, *pt. s.*, PP; **smauȝte**, *pl.*, PP.—AS. *smæcian*, see Grein (s.v. *smæc*).

smalle, *adj.* small, narrow, Prompt.; **smal**, S, S2; **smaill**, S3.—AS. *smæl*, narrow: Goth. *smals*.

smart, *adj.* bitter, S2; see **smerte**[1].

smatte, *pt. s.* smote, S; see **smiten**.

smec, *sb.* smoke, S; **smech**, S; **smeke**, Prompt.—AS. *sméc*.

smechunge, *sb.* taste, S. See **smak**.

smell, *sb.* smell, S; **smul**, S.

smellen, *v.* to smell, S, PP; **smylle**, PP; **smolte**, *pt. s.*, S2.—Cf. Low G. *smelen*, to smoulder.

smeorten, *v.* to smart, S; see **smerten**.

smerien, *v.* to smear, anoint; **smeren**, S; **smurieð**, *pr. pl.*, S; **smered**, *pp.*, S.—AS. *smerian, smyrian*, from *smeru*, fat, *smero* (Voc.).

smerl, *sb.* ointment, S2.

smerld, *pp.* anointed, S2.

smerte[1], *adj.* and *adv.* painful, sharp, sharply, quick, quickly, C, S, PP; **smert**, S2; **smart**, S2, C3; **smertely**, *adv.*, G.—AS. *smeart*.

smerte[2], *sb.* smart, pain, C2; **smierte**, S; **smert**, C3.

smerten, *v.* to smart, to be pained, PP, S, S2, C2; **smeorten**, S; **smerte**, *pt. s.*, C; **smerted**, S3.—AS. *smeortan* (EETS. 79, p. 36).

smiten, *v.* to smite; **smyten**, PP; **smit**, *pr. s.*, C2, PP; **smot**, *pt. s.*, S, S2, PP; **smette**, S3; **smatte**, S; **smiten**, *pl.*, S; **smyten**, W; **smiten**, *pp.*, PP.—AS. *smítan*, pt. *smát* (pl. *smiton*), pp. *smiten*.

smok, *sb.* smock, C2, PP, Prompt.

smok-les, *adj.* without a smock, C2.

smolder, *sb.* smoke from smouldering wood, PP.

smolderen, *v.* to smoulder; **smolderande**, *pr. p.*, S2.

smorðer, *sb.* suffocating smoke, S; **smorþre**, PP.

smorðren, *v.* to smother, suffocate, SD.

smot, *pt. s.* smote; see **smiten**.

smul, *sb.* smell, S; see **smell**.

smurieð, *pr. pl.* smear, S; see **smerien**.

smyðien, *v.* to forge; **smythye**, P; **smytheth**, *pr. s.*, P.—AS. *smiðian*.

smyþþe, *sb.* smithy, forge, S2; **smythy**, Prompt.—AS. *smiððe* (Voc.).

snapere, *v.* to trip, to stumble, W2, SD; **snapper**, HD; **snapirs**, *pr. s.*, WA.

snað, *pt. s.* cut, S; see **sniþen**.

snaw, *sb.* snow, S; see **snow**.

snelle, *adj.* quick, sharp, S, S2; **snell**, S3; **snel**, S.—AS. *snell*: OHG. *snel* (Otfrid).

snepe, *adj.* foolish, S.

snesien, *v.* to strike, S.—AS. *snǽsan* (in *ásnǽsan*, BT), to put on a spit; from *snás*, a spit (Voc.); cf. Icel. *sneisa* from *sneis*.

sniðen, *v.* to cut; **snað**, *pt. s.*, S.—AS. *sníðan*, pt. *snáð* (pl. *snidon*); cf. OHG. *snídan* (Tatian).

sniwen, *v.* to snow; **snewen**, SD; **sniuþ**, *pr. s.*, S; **sniweþ**, SD; **snew**, *pt. s.*, SD; **snewede**, C.—AS. *sníwan*.

snorkil, *sb.* wrinkle, H.—Cf. North.E. *snurkle*, to run into knots, JD, *snurl*, to wrinkle, JD; cf. OHG. *snuor*, string, see Fick, 7. 351.

snow, *sb.* snow, Prompt., PP; **snouȝ**, PP; **snou**, S; **snaw**, S.—AS. *snáw*: Goth. *snaiws*.

snowte, *sb.* snout, Prompt.; **snute**, S.—Cf. G. *schnauze*.

snybbyn, *v.* to rebuke, Prompt., C; **snube**, H; **snybid**, *pt. pl.*, H; **snyband**, *pr. p.*, H; **snibbed**, *pp.*, C2.

snybbynge, *sb.* rebuke, Prompt.; **snybynge**, H; **snibbing**, S2; **snybyngis**, *pl.*, H.

snytyn, *v.* to clear the nose, Prompt.; **snytte**, *pt. s.*, S2; **y-snyt**, *pp.*, S2.

sobre, *adj.* sober, sedate, C2; **sobur**, Prompt.—OF. *sobre*; Lat. *sobrium*.

sobreliche, *adj.* and *adv.* sedate, soberly, CM; **soburly**, CM; **soberly**, C.

soburnesse, *sb.* soberness, Prompt.

soche, *adj.* such, S; see **swyche**.

socht, *pt. pl.* sought, went, S3; see **sechen**.

socour, *v.* to succour, C2, C3; **socowre**, Prompt.—AF. *sucur, soccour*, OF. *socors*; Late Lat. *succursus* (Ducange).

sodeyn, *adj.* sudden, C2, C3; **sodeynly**, *adv.* suddenly, S3, C2; **sodeynliche**, S2.—AF. *sodeyne*; Late Lat. *subitanum*, see BH, § 122.

softe, *adj.* soft, warm, mild, gentle, S, S2, C3; *adv.* gently, luxuriously, S2, S, C3; **softe-liche**, gently, S; **softely**, C3. *Comb.*: **zoft-hede**, *sb.* softness, S2.—AS. *sófte*.

sohte, *pt. s.* sought, S, S2; see **sechen**.

soke, *sb.* the exercise of judicial power, PP, SkD. *Der.*: **soken**, the territory or precinct in which public privileges were exercised, SkD; **sokne**, PP; **(Rotland)-sokene**, (Rutland-)shire, P.—AS. *sóc*, the exercise of judicial power; *sócn, sócen*, an enquiry; see Schmid.

sokelynge[1], *sb.* suckling, Prompt.

sokelynge[2], *sb.* a herb, *locusta*, Prompt.

sokyl-blome, *sb. locusta*, Voc.—From a form *sokel*, that which sucks. Cf. **hony-souke**.

solas, *sb.* rest, solace, pleasure, merriment, G, C2, PP, SkD.—AF. *solas*, OF. *solaz*, Lat. *solatium*; see BH, § 143.

solde, should; see **scholde**.

solempne, *adj.* solemn, grand, festive, magnificent, C2, C3, Prompt.; **solempnely**, *adv.* with pomp, S2, C2, C3; **solenliche**, PP.—AF. *solempne*; Lat. *solemnem*.

solempnite, *sb.* festivity, C, Prompt.—AF. *sollempnitee*; Lat. *solemnitatem*.

solere, *sb.* an upper room, loft, Prompt., Voc., HD; throne, H; **soler**, W, Voc., HD; **soller**, Palsg.; stage of a house, ND; **sollar**, HD, Palsg.—AF. *soler, solair*, OF. *solier*; Late Lat. *solarium* (Voc.); cf. AS. *solere* (Grein), OS. *soleri*. OHG. *soleri* (Tatian), *solári*, the prætorium of Pilate, also a guest-chamber (Otfrid), Du. *zolder*.

soleyne, *adj.* solitary, hating company, sullen, PP, Prompt.; **soleyn**, PP, W2; **sollein**, S3.—OF. *solain*, solitary, pertaining to one alone: Late Lat. **solanum*, from Lat. *solus*.

somdel *pron.* something, S, S2; see **sum**[1].

some, *sb.* concord, S.—AS. *sóme*.

somed, *adv.* together, S; **somet**, S; see **samed**.

somer, *sb.* summer, C; **sumer**, S; **someres**, *gen. s.*, C2, C3. *Comb.*: **somer-game**, summer-game, P.—AS. *sumor*: OS. *sumar*; cf. OHG. *sumar* (Tatian).

somme, *sb.* sum, S3, C3; **some**, S3; **summe**, Prompt.—AF. *summe (sume)*; Lat. *summa*.

somnen, *v.* to join, S; see **samnien**.

sompne, *v.* to summon, PP, CM; **someny**, PP; **somony**, S2; **somoni**, S; **somownyn**, Prompt.; **somondis**, *pr. s.*, H; **sumundis**, H; **somened**, *pp.*, W.—AF. *somoundre* (pr. p. *somonant*), OF. *semondre*; Late Lat. *submŏnēre*; Lat. *sub* + *mŏnēre*.

sompnour, *sb.* summoner, one who cites before an ecclesiastical court, C, PP; **sumpnour**, S2; **somnour**, PP; **somner**, PP; **somenour**, PP; **sumnowre**, Prompt.—AF. *sumenour*.

somwat, *adj.* somewhat, S2; see **sum**[1].

sond[1], *sb.* sand, S, S2, C, PP; **sand**, PP; **sonde**, *dat.*, S.—AS. *sand*.

sond[2], *sb.* a dish or mess of food; **sand**, gift, S2; **sonde**, *dat.*, S; **sonden**, *pl.*, S; **sandon**, S.—AS. *sand*, 'ferculum' (Voc.).

sonde, *sb.* a sending, message, gift sent, also mission, embassy, messenger, S, S2, C3, P, G, H (p. 497); **sonden**, *pl.*, S; **sondes**, S. *Comb.*: **sondezmon**, messenger, S2; **sandesman**, SD; **sandismene**, *pl.*, HD.

sonder. *Comb.*: **sonderemen**, messengers, S; **sanderbodes**, messengers, S.—AS. *sander* in *sandermen* (Chron. ann. 1123).

sondry, separate, C2; see **sunder**.

sone[1], *sb.* son, S, S2, C2, G; **sune**, S; **zone**, S2; **sun**, S2. *Comb.*: **sone in lawe**, son-in-law, C2.—AS. *sunu*: Goth. *sunus*.

sone[2], *adv.* forthwith, quickly, soon, S, G, S2, C2, PP; **soune**, S3; **son**, S2; **soyn**, S2; **sonest**, *superl.*, C2; **sonnest**, P.—AS. *sóna*, see Sievers, 317.

song, *pt. s.* sang, C2; see **syngen**.

songe, *sb.* song, Prompt.; **sang**, S, S3; **zang**, S2; **songes**, *pl.*, S.—AS. *sang*.

songe-warie, *sb.* the observation of dreams, P.—OF. *songe*; Lat. *somnium*, dream.

sonne, *sb.* sun, S, S2, C2, P; **sunne**, S, S2, Prompt. *Comb.*: **sunne-bem**, sunbeam, S; **Sunnen-dæi**, Sunday, S; **Sunne-dei**, S; **Sunedai**, S; **Sunedei**, S; **Sone-dæi**, S; **Soneday**, S, G; **Sonendayes**, *pl.*, S2; **sunne-risindde**, sun-rising, S.—AS. *sunne*: OS. *sunna*.

soop, *pt. s.* supped; see **sup**.

soope, *sb.* soap, Prompt.; **sape**, S.—AS. *sápe*; Lat. *sāpo*.

soot, soote, *adj.* sweet, S3; see **swete**.

sooth, soothly; see **soþ**.

sop, *pt. s.* created, S; see **schapen**.

sope, *pp.* supped; see **sup**.

soper, *sb.* supper, C, C2, G; see **souper**.

sophyme, *sb.* a sophism, C2; **sophimes**, *pl.*, subtleties, C2.—OF. *sophisme* (Cotg.); Gr. σόφισμα.

soppe, *sb.* a sop, Cath., PP; **sop**, C; **soppis**, *pl.*, S3.

sopun, *pp.* supped; see **sup**.

sore[1], *v.* to soar, mount aloft, C2, CM.—OF. *essorer* (Cotg.); Late Lat. **exaurare*, to expose to the *air* (Lat. *aura*).

sore[2], *adj.* and *adv.* sore, painful, S, C2, G; **sare**, S2, S; **sar**, S, S3, S2; **soore**, Prompt.; **sair**, B.—AS. *sár*.

sore[3], *sb.* sore, misery, C2; **sor**, S; **sar**, S; **soore**, Prompt.—AS. *sár*.

soren, *pp.* shorn, S; see **schere**[2].

sort, *sb.* destiny, chance, lot, C, W; **sorte**, turn (= Lat. *vice*), W.—AF. *sort*; Lat. *sortem*.

sorwe, *sb.* sorrow, S, S2, CM, C2; **sorȝe**, S; **zorȝe**, S2; **soriȝe**, S; **soreȝe**, S; **sareȝe**, S; **soreghe**, S2; **seorewe**, S; **serewe**, S; **seoruwe**, S; **serwe**, S2; **soru**, S2; **sorhe**, S; **sorewe**, S, S2.—AS. *sorh*: OS. *sorga*.

sorwe-ful, *adj.* sorrowful, C; **sorful**, S; **sorwefully**, *adv.* sorrowfully, C2.

sorwen, *v.* to sorrow, CM; **serrȝheþþ**, *pr. s.*, S.—AS. *sorgian*.

sorwynge, *sb.* sorrowing, CM; **sorewyngis**, *pl.*, W.

sory, *adj.* sorry, wretched, painful, grievous, Prompt., S2, C, C2, PP, G; **sori**, S, S2, PP; **sari**, S; **særi**, S; **sariliche**, *adv.*, S; **soryly**,

Prompt. *Comb.*: **sorymod**, sad in mind, S.—AS. *sárig*.

sorynesse, *sb.* sadness, Prompt.; **sorinesse**, S.—AS. *sárignes*.

soster, *sb.* sister, S2; see **suster**.

sote, *adj.* sweet, C2, C3; see **swete**.

sotte, *sb.* fool, S, Prompt., PP; **sot**, S, S2; **sottes**, *gen.*, S, S2. *Der.*: **sotlice**, foolishly, S; **sotschipe**, folly, S; **sotted**, besotted, C3.—OF. *sot*.

sotyle[1], *adj.* subtle, fine-wrought, crafty, ingenious, Prompt.; **sotyl**, PP; **sotil**, PP, C; **sotel**, PP; **sutelle**, Cath.; **sutaille**, S3; **sotely**, *adv.*, PP; **suteli**, W.—AF. *sotil, sutil*; Lat. *subtilem*.

sotyle[2], *v.* to reason subtly, to make use of cunning, PP; **sotilen**, PP; **sutils**, *pr. s.*, makes subtle, H.

sotylte, *sb.* skill, Prompt.; **sotilte**, C3.—AF. *sotiltee*; Lat. *subtilitatem*.

soth, *adj.* and *sb.* true, truth, sooth, soothsaying, S, S2, C3, P, H; **sooth**, C2; **suth**, S2; **sothe**, W, S2, S3, P; **soothe**, S3; **zoþe**, S2; **sothely**, *adv.*, verily, PP, W; **soothly**, C2. *Comb.*: **soðfast**, true, S, S3, H; **sothefast**, W; **soothfastnesse**, truth, C2, C3, H; **sothnes**, truth, S2, H; **sothnesse**, S2, P; **sothriht**, truly, S.—AS. *sóð* (for *sonð, *sanð*); cf. Icel. *sannr* (for *sanðr*); cf. Dan. *sand*.

sothe, *adj.* south, S3; see **sowþe**.

sothien, *v.* to verify, SD, SkD (s.v. *soothe*); **i-soðet**, *pp.*, S.—AS. *ge-sóðian*.

sothroun, *adj.* southern, S3; see **sowþerne**.

souchen, *v.* to suspect, SD, HD; **souches**, *pr. s.*, S2.—OF. *suscher*; Late Lat. **suspicare*, for Lat. *suspicari*, see Diez, p. 681, and BH, § 152.

souden, *v.* to pay, PP. See **sowde**[2].

soudly, *adj.* dirty, S3.—Cf. Northern E. *suddill*, to dirty (JD), also G. *sudeln*, to do dirty work.

souerty, *sb.* surety, S3; see **surety**.

soufre, *sb.* sulphur, S2; **soulfre**, CM.—OF. *soufre, soulfre* (Cotg.); Late Lat. *sulfurem*.

souken, *v.* to suck, C2, S2, W2; **sowken**, S3. *Comb.*: **soukynge-fere**, foster-brother, W.—AS. *súcan*, pt. *séac*, pp. *socen*.

soule, *sb.* soul, PP, S, S2; **sowle**, S, C; **saule**, S, S2, H; **sawle**, S; **saull**, S3; **soulen**, *pl.*, S, S2; **saulen**, S; **sawless**, S; **sowle**, S; **zaulen**, S2, *Comb.*; **soule hele**, soul's salvation, PP; **sawel hel**, S2.—AS. *sáwol, sáwle*: Goth. *saiwala*.

soun, *sb.* sound, S2, S3, C2, W2, H: **sown**, H, W, W2; **sowne**, S2; **son**, S2; **sownde**, Prompt.—AF. *soun*, OF. *son*; Lat. *sonum*.

sound, *sb.* a swoon, S3; see **swowne**.

sounen, *v.* to sound, C2, PP; **sownen**, C2, S2, W2, PP; **sowndyn**, Prompt.; **sunen**, S.—AF. *suner, soner*; Lat. *sonare*.

sounyng, *sb.* sounding, S2.

soupen, *v.* to sup, drink gradually, to eat supper, P, W, C2; **sowpen**, S3.—OF. *souper*. Of Teutonic origin. Cf. **sup**.

souper, *sb.* supper, C; **soper**, C, C2, G.—OF. *souper*, AF. *soper*.

souple, *adj.* supple, pliant, C, C2.—OF. *souple*, beaten, defeated (Bartsch); Lat. *supplicem*, submissive.

soure, *adj.* sour, acid, PP; **sur**, S; **soure**, *adv.* sourly, C2, P. *Comb.*: **sourdouȝ**, leaven, W; **sourdow**, W; **sourdowȝ**, W.—AS. *súr*; cf. Icel. *súrr* and *súrdegi* (Matt. 13. 33).

souren, *v.* to sour; **sowrid**, *pp.*, made sour, W.

sours, *sb.* source, origin, C2; soaring, CM.—OF. *sourse*, a spring of water; Late Lat. *sursa*, a late pp. f. form from Lat. *surgere* (OF. *sordre*, pp. *sors, sours*).

souse[1], *v.* to strike, dash, RD, SkD; **souce**, Spenser 1. See **souse**[2].

souse[2], *sb.* the downward plunge of a bird of prey, RD. (Originally the same as **sours**, used of a hawk's flight.—W.W.S.)

soutere, *sb.* cobbler, S3; **souter**, PP; **sowter**, Cath., ND.—AS. *sútere* (Voc.); Lat. *sutor*.

souteresse, *sb.* a woman shoe-seller, P.

souenaunce, *sb.* remembrance, S3.—OF. *sovenance*, also *souvenance* (Cotg.), from *sovenir*; Lat. *subuenire*.

souerentè, *sb.* sovereignty, Prompt.; **soueràyntee**, C2.—AF. *soverainte*.

souereyn, *adj.* and *sb.* supreme, sovereign, C, C2, C3; **souereynes**, *pl.*, superiors, P, W; **sufrayns**, H; **souereyneste**, *superl.*, W2; **soueraignly**, *adv.*, C.—AF. *soverein*; Late Lat. **superanum*.

sowdan, *sb.* sultan, S2, C3.—OF. *soudan, souldan*; Arab. *sultân*.

sowdanesse, *sb.* sultaness, C2, S2.

sowde[1], *v.* to strengthen; **sowdid**, *pp.* (= Lat. *consolidatae*), W.—OF. *souder* (Cotg.): It. *soldare*; Lat. *solidare*, see SkD (s.v. *solder*).

sowde[2], *sb.* stipend, pay, W; **sowd**, Prompt.; **sowdis**, *pl.*, W.—OF. *soude*; Lat. *soldum*, a sum of money, from *solidus*.

sowdyowre, *sb.* one that fights for pay, soldier, Prompt.; **soudiour**, S3.—Cf. OF. *soudoier* (Ducange).

sowen, *v.* to sow, S, PP; **sawe**, S; **souwen**, PP; **sewe**, *pt. s.*, W; **sew**, H; **sewen**, *pl.*, S; **seowe**, *pt. s. subj.*, S; **sowun**, *pp.*, W; **sowe**, G; **ȝe-sawen**, S.—AS. *sáwan*.

sowse[1], *v.* to immerse in brine, to plunge in water, to drench with rain, Palsg., S3;

soused, *pp.*, pickled, Sh.; **soust**, drenched, Spenser 1.—From OF. *sause*, sauce; Lat. *salsa*, salted.

sowse[2], *sb.* a dish of pickled food, *succidium*, Voc.

sowthe, *adj.* south, Prompt.; **sothe**, S3; **suð**, S. *Comb.*: **Souþ-hamtessire**, Hampshire, S2; **Suð-sæxe**, Sussex, SD.—AS. *súð*: OHG. *sund-ana*, from the south (Tatian).

sowtherne, *adj.* southern, Prompt.; **souþeron**, S2; **southren**, C3; **sothroun**, S3; **suthroun**, S3.

soyr, *adj.* brown (as of withered leaves), S3.—OF. *sor* (Roland); cf. F. *saure*. Of Teutonic origin. See **seere**.

spæc, *pt. s.* spoke; see **speken**.

spæche, *sb.* speech, S; see **speche**.

spak, *adj.* wise, prudent, quiet, gentle, SD; **spake**, HD; **spakliche**, *adv.*, SD; **spakli**, S2.—Icel. *spakr*, quiet, gentle, wise.

spale, *sb.* a chip of wood, splinter, S, SD; **spalle**, Prompt.; **spolle**, Prompt.; **spole**, Voc.—Icel. *spölr* (*spala*, gen. pl.).

spang, *sb.* a metal fastening, brooch, clasp, buckle; **spangs**, *pl.*, S3.—AS. *spange* (Grein).

spangele, *sb.* a small plate of shining metal used to ornament a bridle, *lorale*, Prompt.

spanyn, *v.* to wean, Prompt.; **spane**, HD; **spaned**, H, Cath.—Cf. G. *spänen*, OHG. (*bi*)*spenjan*, Du. *spenen*, see Weigand; cf. also AS. *spana*, 'ubera' (Voc.).

spanynge, *sb.* a weaning, *ablactacio*, Cath., Prompt.

sparkle, *sb.* spark. Prompt. *Comb.*: **deedsparcle** (= Lat. *fauilla*), W2.

sparlire, *sb.* the calf of the leg, HD; **sparlyuer**, *sura*, Trevisa (5. 355); **sperlyuer**, *musculus*, Voc.—AS. *spear-líra*, 'sura' (Deut. 28. 35), *speoru-líra* (OET.).

sparre, *sb.* a beam, bar, spar, C, S3, Prompt., Cath.—AS. *speoru* (Voc.); cf. Icel. *sparri*.

sparthe, *sb.* axe, battle-axe, Prompt., Cath.; **sparth**, C, WA.—Icel. *sparða*.

sparwe, *sb.* sparrow, C, S2; **sparowe**, Prompt. *Comb.*: **spar-hauk**, sparrow-hawk, C2; **sperhauke**, P.—AS. *spearwa*.

spatel, *sb.* spittle, S; see **spotil**.

spateling, *sb.* spitting, S.

spealie, *v.* to tell, S; see **spellien**.

spec, *pt. s.* spoke; see **speken**.

spece, *sb.* species, kind, S, Prompt.—Lat. *speciem*. Cf. **spice**.

speche, *sb.* speech, S, S2, PP; **spæche**, S; **spek**, S2.—AS. *spéc* (Voc.). See **speken**.

sped, *sb.* success, speed, S; **speed**, Prompt.—AS. *spéd*.

spede-ful, *adj.* profitable, W; **speedful**, C3; **spedfullest**, *superl.*, S3.

speden, *v.* to succeed, prosper, speed, S, S2, S3; **spet**, *pr. s.*, speeds, goes on, G; **spedith**, profits, S3, W2; **spedde**, *pt. s.*, S, C2; **sped**, *pp.*, S3.—AS. *spédan*.

speir, *sb.* sphere, S3; see **spere**[1].

speken, *v.* to speak, S, S2; **spæken**, S; **spece**, *1 pr. s.*, S; **specð**, *pr. s.*, S; **spæc**, *pt. s.*, S; **spac**, S, S2; **spak**, S, S2; **spec**, S, spek, S; **spake**, *2 pt. s.*, S, G; **speke**, S; **spækenn**, *pl.*, S; **speken**, S; **speke**, S2; **speeke**, S2; **spekene**, *ger.*, S; **speokene**, S; **i-speken**, *pp.*, S; **ispeke**, S.—AS. *specan* (for *sprecan*), pt. *spæc*, pp. *specen*.

spell, *sb.* a discourse, story, S; **spelle**, *dat.*, S, S2, C2.—AS. *spell*.

spellien, *v.* to relate, speak; **spellen**, S, PP; **spealie**, S; **spilien**, S.—AS. *spellian*.

spellinge, *sb.* recital, Prompt., S2.

spence, *sb.* provision-room, larder, G, Prompt.; **spense**, Voc.; expense, G, W.—OF. *despense* (Constans); Late Lat. *dispensa* (Voc.).

spencer, *sb.* officer having charge of the provisions, G; **spenser**, G; **sponcere**, Prompt.—OF. *despensier*; Late Lat. *dispensarium* (acc.).

spenden, *v.* to use, spend, Prompt., PP; **spene**, S, PP; **spende**, *pt. pl.*, S2; **i-spend**, *pp.*, S; **spendid**, W; **sponded**, G. *Comb.*: **spending-siluer**, money to spend, S.— AS. *spendan* (in compounds); Lat. *dispendere*.

spennen, *v.* to stretch, embrace, grasp, SD; **spendyd**, *pt. s.*, grasped, S3; **spend**, *pp.*, SD.—Icel. *spenna*; cf. AS. *spannan*, to bind, OHG. (*gi*)*spannan* (Otfrid); see Weigand.

spercled, *pp.* scattered, flung abroad, S3 (24. 67).

sperd, *pt. s.* enquired; see **spiren**.

spere[1], *sb.* sphere, Prompt., CM; **speir**, S3.—OF. *espere*; Late Lat. *spera*, *sphera*; Gr. σφαῖρα.

spere[2], *sb.* spear, S, C, Prompt.—AS. *spere*; cf. OHG. *sper* (Tatian).

speren, *v.* to fasten with a spar, to close, S, Cath.; **sperre**, Cath.; **speride**, *pt. s.*, S2; **sperd**, *pp.*, S, H; **sperrid**, H.—AS. *sparrian*. See **sparre**.

sperhauke, *sb.* sparrow-hawk, P; see **sparwe**.

sperling, *sb.* a small fish, S2; **sperlynge**, Cath., Voc.; **sparlynge**, Cath. (*n*); **spurling**, Cath. (*n*).—OF. *esperlan*, smelt (Cotg.).

spet, *pr. s.* speeds; see **speden**.

speten, *v.* to spit, S, W2, Prompt., CM; **spette**, *pt. s.*, W, SD; **spete**, W; **speten**, *pl.*, W; **spetide**, *pt. s.*, W.—AS. *spétan*, pt. *spǽtte*.

spewen, *v.* to vomit, Cath.; **spue**, W2.—
AS. *spiwan*, pt. *spáw*, pp. *spiwen*.

spice, *sb.* species, kind, spice, W; **spyce**,
Voc.; **spices**, *pl.*, S, P. *Comb.*: **spicelike**,
with spices, S; **spices ware**, spicery, S.—
OF. *espice*; Late Lat. *spēcia* (for Lat.
spĕciem), see BH, § 32. See **spece**.

spicer, *sb.* dealer in spices, P, S2; **spyserez**,
pl., S2.

spicerye, *sb.* spicery, S2, C2, C3.—AF.
spicerie.

spie, *sb.* spy, PP; see **aspie**.

spien, *v.* to spy, to look after, to watch, S; see
espye.

spilen, *v.* to play, S; **spilede**, *pt. s.*, S.—Icel.
spila; cf. G. *spielen.*

spilien, *v.* to speak, S; see **spellien**.

spillen, *v.* to perish, also to destroy, S, S2,
C2, C3, P; **spyllen**, S2; **spill**, S3; **spilt**,
pp., killed, C3; **y-spilte**, PP.—AS. *spillan*, to
destroy (Grein).

spire, *sb.* shoot, scion, blade, tall grass, reed,
PP, S, G, CM; **spyre**, Prompt., PP, Palsg.;
spier, W2.

spiren, *v.* to enquire, speer, PP; **speren**, PP;
speoren, PP; **spuren**, PP; **spirs**, *imp. pl.*,
S2; **spird**, *pt. pl.*, S2; **sperd**, *pt. s.*, S3.—
AS. *spyrian*, to make a track, from *spor*, track,
see SkD (s.v. *spur*).

splene, *sb.* the spleen, Prompt.; **splen**, SkD.
Phr.: **on the splene**, suddenly, S3; **fro the
splene**, with sudden fervour, rapidly,
S3.—Lat. *splen.*

spoile, *sb.* booty, SkD; **spuylis**, *pl.*, W2. See
spoilen.

spoilen, *v.* to plunder, W (Mk. 3. 27);
spuyle, W; **spuylid**, *pp.*, W2.—OF. *spolier*
(Cotg.); Lat. *spoliare*; see BH, § 64.

spone, *sb.* a chip, splinter of wood, spoon,
C3, Prompt.; **spoon**, C2. *Comb.*: **span-
newe**, span new, SkD; **spon-neowe**,
SkD.—AS. *spón*; cf. Icel. *spónn*, also *spánn*; cf.
G. *spannen* (Weigand).

spore, *sb.* spur, PP, Prompt., C, G.—AS.
spora.

spotil, *sb.* spittle, W; **spotele**, W2; **spatel**,
S.—AS. *spátl.*

spousaille, *sb.* wedding, C2; **spousail**, C2;
sposailis, *pl.*, W.—OF. *espousailles.*

spouse, *sb.* spouse, bridegroom, bride, W;
spuse, S; **spowse**, Prompt. *Comb.*: **spous-
breche**, adulterer, SD; **spusbruche**,
adultery, SD; **spousebrekere**, adulterer,
W; **spoushod**, marriage, S2.—AF. *espouse*
(*espuse*); Lat. *sponsam*; also OF. *espos*, *spous*;
Lat. *sponsum*; see BH, § 169.

spousen, *v.* to espouse, W, S2, C2; **spousi**,
S2; **i-spoused**, *pp.*, S2; **y-spoused**, S2;
i-spused, S.—OF. *espouser*; Lat. *sponsare.*

sprangis, *sb. pl.* diffused rays of various
colours, S3.

spraulin, *v.* to sprawl, SD; **sprawel**, S2;
sprauleden, *pt. pl.*, S.—AS. *spréawlian*
(cited by Zupitza from *Bouloneser Glossen*, see
Studium der neueren Sprachen, July, 1886).

sprayngis, *sb. pl.* sprinklings, S3. See
sprengen[1].

spreden, *v.* to spread, PP, S, S2; **spradde**, *pt.
s.*, C2; **spredd**, *pp.*, S; **sprad**, C; **y-sprad**,
C2.—AS. *sprǽdan.*

spreit, *sb.* spirit, S3; **spyryte**, Prompt.—
Lat. *spiritus.*

sprengen[1], *v.* to sprinkle, W, G; **sprente**,
pt. s., S3; **spreynten**, *pl.*, W2; **spreynd**,
pp., S2, C2, C3, W; **spreind**, W; **spreynt**,
W; **y-spreynd**, C.—AS. *sprengan*, causal of
springan.

sprengen[2], *v.* to spring, to be diffused;
sprent, *pt. s.*, S3.—AS. *sprengan*, to spring
(Sweet).

sprenkelin, *v.* to sprinkle, to dart, Prompt.;
sprynkland, *pr. p.*, darting in various directions (of fish in the water), S3.

spring, *sb.* a rod, sprig, PP; **sprynge**, P;
sprenges, *pl.*, W2.

springen[1], *v.* to spring, to arise, to dawn, PP,
S, C2; **sprynge**, PP; **sprenge**, *pr. s. subj.*,
W; **sprang**, *pt. s.*, S; **sprong**, S; **sprung-
en**, *pp.*, S2; **sprunge**, S; **sprongen**, S3;
spronge, C; **i-sprunge**, S. *Der.*: **spring-
ing**, beginning, source, C2.—AS. *springan*,
pt. *sprang* (pl. *sprungon*), pp. *sprungen.*

springen[2], *v.* to make to spring, rouse;
sprange, *pt. pl.*, S3. See **springen**[3].

springen[3], *v.* to sprinkle, C2; **y-spronge**,
pp., S2. *Der.*: **springyng**, sprinkling, W.
See **sprengen**[1].

sprutlyt, *pp.* speckled, S3. See SkD (s.v.
sprout).

sprynkland; see **sprenkelin.**

spurn, *sb.* a kick, S3.

spurnen, *v.* to kick, Prompt., C2, SkD;
spurnde, *pt. s.*, S2.—AS. *speornan.*

spuyle, *v.* to plunder, W; see **spoilen.**

spuylis, *pl.* spoils, W; see **spoile.**

spynke, *sb.* finch, *rostellus*, Voc.; **spink**,
Cotg., JD, HD; **spynk**, S3 (s.v. *gold*). Cf.
Gr. σπίγγος, and OF. *pinçon* (BH), F. *pinson.*

spynnare, *sb.* spinner, spider, Prompt.;
spinner, Sh., HD.

spynnen, *v.* to spin, Prompt.

spynstere, *sb.* a woman who spins, Prompt.;
spynnester, PP; **spinster**, S2, PP, Sh.

spyrakle, *sb.* the breath of life, S2.—Lat.
spiraculum uitae, Gen. 7. 22 (Vulg.).

squames, *sb. pl.* scales, C3.—Lat. *squama.*

squaymous, *adj.* loth, fastidious, CM;
skeymowse.

squier, *sb.* squire, S, C2; **squyer**, C2, S2.—
OF. *esquïer, escuier*; Late Lat. *scutarium*, from
Lat. *scutum*, shield; cf. It. *scudíere*.

squyler, *sb.* dish-washer, S2; **sqwyllare**,
Prompt., SkD (s.v. *scullery*); **swyllere**,
Voc.—OF. *sculier* (Ducange); Late Lat.
scutelarium, one in charge of the dishes
(Ducange); from Lat. *scutella*. (It seems to
have been confused with *swiller*; see SkD,
s.v. *scullery*.—W.W.S.)

squylerey, *sb.* room for washing dishes in, a
scullery, SkD.—Cf. OF. *esculier*; Late Lat.
scutellarium, 'locus ubi reponuntur scutellae'
(Ducange). See **squyler**.

sqware, *adj.* square, Prompt.; **sware**, S2.—
OF. *esquarre*; Lat. *ex + quadram*; cf. It. *squadra*.

srid, *pt. s.* clothed, S; see **schrouden**.

srud, *sb.* dress, S; see **schroud**.

ss-. For many words beginning with **ss-** (as
well as words beginning with **sc-** and **sh-**),
see **sch-**.

sseawere, *sb.* a mirror, S2; see **schawere**.

sseawy, *v.* to show, S2; see **schewen**.

ssedde, *pt. s.* shed; see **scheden**.

ssede, *sb.* shade; see **schade**.

ssolde, should; see **scholde**.

ssoldren, *pl.* shoulders, S2; see **schuldere**.

stable[1], *adj.* constant, firm, fixed, C2, W, PP;
stabli, *adv.*, W.—AF. *estable*; Lat. *stabilem*.

stable[2], *v.* to establish, confirm, to cause to
rest, S3, W, P, C; **y-stabled**, S3.—OF.
establir.

stablischen, *v.* to establish, W; **stablisse**,
PP.—OF. *establiss-*, stem of *establissant*, pp.
of *establir*.

stac, *pt. s.* closed up, S2; see **steken**.

stad, *pp.* bestead, circumstanced, beset, WA,
S2.—Icel. *staddr*, circumstanced, Swed.
stadd.

staf, *sb.* a staff, stick, a letter of the alphabet,
PP, SD; **staffe**, Prompt.; **staues**, *pl.*, S2,
PP. *Comb.*: **stef-creft**, the art of grammar,
S; **staf-slinge**, staff-sling, C2; **staff-
slynge**, HD; **staff-slyngere**, staff-slinger,
HD.—AS. *stæf*, staff, stick, twig, letter
written on a twig, see Weigand (s.v.
buchstab); cf. Icel. *stafr*, OHG. *stab, buohstab*
(Tatian).

staire[1], *adj.* steep, WA; **stayre**, WA (*n*).

staire[2], *sb.* stair, ladder, WA.—AS. *stǽger*.
See **stien**.

stal, **stall**, *pt. s.* stole; see **stelen**.

stale, *sb.* stealing, S.—AS. *stalu*.

stalken, *v.* to step slowly, C, G; **stalkyn**,
Prompt.; **stalked him**, *pt. s. refl.*, C2.—AS.
stealcian; see Sweet, *Anglo-Saxon Primer*, 83.
37.

stalle, *sb.* place, state, station, prison, stall,
booth, PP, Prompt.; **steal**, S; **stal**, Prompt.;
stale, S3.—AS. *steal*: OHG. *stal* (Otfrid).

stallit, *pp.* placed, S3.

stallyn, *v.* to enthrone prelates, Prompt.

stalworðe, *adj.* stout, strong, sturdy, S2, G;
stalworth, PP, H (pp. 26, 87); **stalword**,
S2; **stalworthy**, S3, Prompt.; **stalworþ-
est**, *superl.*, S2; **stalwortly**, *adv.* sturdily,
S2. *Comb.*: **stalworth-hede**, stalwartness,
S2.—AS. *stælwurð* (Chron. ann. 896).

stamyn[1], *sb.* stamine, linsey-woolsey cloth, a
garment made of that material, Prompt.,
Cath. (*n*); **stamin**, S; **stamine**, HD.—OF.
estamine, tamine, also a strainer (Cotg.).

stamyn[2], *sb.* the stem, bows of a vessel, S2;
stamyne, Cath. (*n*).—Icel. *stafn, stamn*, a
post, prow-post, also stern-post; cf. It.
stamine, the upright ribs or pieces of timber
of the inside of a ship, of our shipwrights
called foot-stocks (Florio).

standen, *v.* to stand, to cost, be valid, S;
stonden, S, S2, C2, W; **stant**, *pr. s.*, S, S2,
S3; **stont**, S; **stand**, S2; **stonte**, S2;
stode, *pt. s.*, S2; *pl.*, S2; **stoden**, S2, C2;
stude, S3; **i-stonde**, *pp.*, S.—AS. *standan*,
pt. *stód*, pp. *ge-standen*.

stane, *sb. dat.* stone, S; see **stoon**.

stang, *sb.* stagnant pool; **stanc**, S2; **stank**,
HD; **stangis**, *pl.*, H; **stangeȝ**, S2;
staunkis, H.—OF. *estang, estan (estanc)*; Lat.
stagnum.

stangen, *v.* to prick, to throb, HD, H. *Der.*:
stangynge, torment, H.

stannyris, *sb. pl.* the small stones and gravel
at the side of a river, S3. See **stoon**.

staple, *sb.* a loop of iron in a wall used for
fastening chains, S3 (p. 472).—AS. *stapul*
(Voc.).

starf, *pt. s.* died, S2, C2; see **sterven**.

starin, *v.* to stare, also to shine, glitter, SD;
stare, C2, S3, PP; **starinde**, *pr. p.*, S;
stareand, S2.—AS. *starian*.

stark, *adj.* strong, firm, severe, S, S3; **starrc**,
S; **starke**, *pl.*, C2.—AS. *stearc*: OS. *starc*.

starnys, *pl.* stars, S3; see **sterne**[1].

stat, *sb.* state, condition, S2; **staat**, existence
(= Lat. *status*), W. Cf. **estat**.

statut, *sb.* statute, PP; **statute**, PP; **statutes**,
pl., S2, PP. *Comb.*: **statute-staple**, the
staple to which a prisoner is by law attached,
S3.—AF. *statut (estatut)*; Lat. *statutum*.

staþelien, to establish; **ȝe-staþeled**, *pp.*,
S.—AS. *ge-staðelod*.

staþelnesse, *sb.* stability, SD; **staþelnes**,
S2.—AS. *staðolnes*.

stauez, *pr. s.* stows away, S2; **stawed**, *pp.*,
S2; see **stowyn**.

steal, *sb.* place, state, S; see **stalle**.

steapre, *adj.* steeper; see **stepe**.

stea3, *pt. s.* ascended; see **stien**.

stede[1], *sb.* steed, horse, S, C2, PP, WA. *Comb.*: **stede-bac**, horseback, PP.—AS. *stéda*, from *stód*, a collection of horses, a stud.

stede[2], *sb.* place, PP, S, S2, S3; **stude**, S; **stide**, W, W2; **stud**, S2; **sted**, S3. *Comb.*: **stedefast**, steadfast, S; **stedefastliche**, steadfastly, S; **stedfastly**, C2; **stedefastnesse**, firmness, C2.—AS. *stede*: OS. *stedi*: Goth. *stadi-* (stem of *staþs*).

stee, *sb.* a ladder, WA, HD; **sties**, *pl.*, HD. See **stien**.

steef, stef; see **styf**.

steer, *sb.* a young ox, C, PP.—AS. *stéor*; cf. Lat. *taurus*, see Curtius, No. 232.

stef-creft, *sb.* the art of grammar, S; see **staf**.

stefne, *sb.* voice, S; see **stevene**.

steghe, *v.* to ascend, H; see **stien**.

steghere, *sb.* rider, H.

steir, *v.* to stir, S3; see **stiren**.

steken, *v.* to fasten, SD, WA; **stekye**, *v.*, to be fastened up, P; **stekez**, *imp. pl.*, S2; **stac**, *pt. s.*, S2; **stak**, SkD (s.v. *stick*); **stoken**, *pp.*, S2; **y-steke**, G; **i-steke**, G.—Cf. OHG. *stechan*, to fix, pierce, pt. *stáh* (pl. *stáchun*), pp. *gi-stochan*, see Otfrid.

stelen, *v.* to steal, to go stealthily, PP; **stæl**, *pt. s.*, S; **stal**, C2, W; **stall**, S3; **stalen**, *pl.*, S; **stelen**, G; **stole**, *pp.*, C. *Comb.*: **stæl ut**, stole out, S; **stal ut**, S.—AS. *stelan*, pt. *stæl* (pl. *stélon*), pp. *stolen*.

stelðe, *sb.* stealth, PP; **stalthe**, SkD. Cf. **stouþ**.

stem, *sb.* vapour, ray of light, flame, S; **steem**, Prompt.—AS. *stéam*.

stemin, *v.* to steam, shine, gleam, C, S3, CM.—AS. *stéman* (SkD).

stene, *sb.* a stone jar, SD, Trevisa 4. 115; **steenes**, *pl.*, S2. See **stenen**.

stenen, *adj.* made of stone, S.—AS. *sténen* (Voc.). See **stoon**.

stent, *sb.* stopping-place, S3.

stenten, *v.* to cease, pause, CM; see **stynten**.

steoren[1], *v.* to perfume with incense, S.—Cf. AS. *stéran* (Leo). See **stor**.

steoren[2], *v.* lead, direct, S; see **steren**[1].

steorren, *pl.* stars, S; see **sterre**.

step-barn, *sb.* orphan, H.—Cf. AS. *step-cild*, orphan, Ps 67 6 (VP); AS. *stéop*, orphaned; cf. OHG. *stiuf*.

stepe[1], *adj.* steep, WA, SkD.—AS. *stéap*.

stepe[2], *adj.* bright, shining (of eyes), CM, C, S3, HD; **steapre**, *comp.*, S3 (p. 426).

stere[1], *adj.* strong, stout, firm, S, HD. See **store**.

stere[2], *sb.* tiller, helm, rudder, steering-gear, the stern of a ship, C3, S; **steere**, W2; **stiere**, PP. *Comb.*: **sterelees**, without a rudder, S2, C3; **sterman**, steersman. Voc.—Icel. *stýri*, rudder.

stere[3], *sb.* helmsman, C3, S2.

steren[1], *v.* to lead, direct, steer, S, S3, PP; **steir**, B; **steoren**, S.—AS. *stéoran, stýran*.

steren[2], *v.* to stir, to move, S2, WA, PP; see **stiren**.

sterlinge, *sb.* coin, penny of standard currency, C3, PP, SkD.—Cf. Low Lat. *sterlingus* (Ducange).

sterne[1], *sb.* star, WA, H, S2; **stern**, S2, B; **starnys**, *pl.*, S3.—Icel. *stjarna*. Cf. **sterre**.

sterne[2], *adj.* stern, Prompt.; **sturne**, S, S2; **steryn**, WA; **sterin**, HD; **steryne**, HD; **stiarne**, *pl.*, S; *adv.*, S; **sterne**, PP; **sternelich**, CM, PP. *Der.*: **sturnhede**, sternness, S2.—AS. *styrne*.

sterre, *sb.* star, S, S2, S3, C2, C3, W, PP; **storre**, S; **steorren**, *pl.*, S; **steores**, S; **sterris**, W, PP; **sterren**, S, S2. *Comb.*: **sterre-liht**, starlight, S2. *Der.*: **i-stirret**, starred, S; **stirrede**, SD.—AS. *steorra*: OS. *sterro*; cf. OHG. *sterro* (Tatian).

stert[1], *sb.* tail, plough-handle, S, Prompt., Palsg., HD; the stalk of fruit, HD, Palsg.; **sterte**, Voc. *Comb.*: **steort-naket**, quite naked, S.—AS. *steort*; cf. Icel. *stertr*.

stert[2], *sb.* a start, quick movement, C.

sterten, *v.* to start, S2, C, B, PP; **stirt**, *imp. s.*, S; **stirte**, *pt. s.*, S; **stirt**, S; **sterte**, C, G; **stert**, S2; **stert**, *pp.*, C2; **y-stert**, C.

steruen, *v.* to die, S2, S3, C2; **sterfeð**, *pr. s.*, S; **starf**, *pt. s.*, S2, C2; **sturuen**, *pl.*, S; **sturfe**, S; **storuen**, C3; **storue**, *pt. subj. s.*, S; **i-storue**, *pp.*, S; **y-storue**, C; **staruen**, S3.—AS. *steorfan*, pt. *stérf* (pl. *sturfon*), pp. *storfen*.

steruing, *sb.* dying, S2.

steuene, *sb.* voice, command, note, C2, S; **steuen**, S2; time of performing any action, CM; **stefne**, S; **stevynnys**, *pl.*, S3.—AS. *stefn*: Goth. *stibna*; cf. OHG. *stemna* (Tatian). G. *stimme*.

stew, *sb.* vapour, mist, B; **stovys**, *pl.*, S3.—Cf. Dan. *støv*, Du. *stof*, dust, *stofregen*, drizzling rain, G. *staub*, dust, whence *Staubbach*, 'spray-beck'.

steward; see **sty**[2].

stewe[1], *sb.* fish-pond, *vivarium*, C, HD, SD, CM, Prompt.; **stwe**, Prompt.

stewe[2], *sb.* bath, Cath.; **stue**, Cath. (*n*); **stwe**, Prompt.; **stewes**, *pl.* brothels, PP; **stywes**, CM; **stues**, P.

stiarne, *adj. pl.* stern, S; see **sterne**[2].

sticchen, *v.* to prick, stitch, SD; **stiȝte**, *pt. s.*, SD; **stiȝt**, *pp.*, SD; **i-stihd**, S; **i-sticched**, S (p. 119).

stien, *v.* to ascend, HD, PP, S2, W, W2; **styȝen**, S2; **stiȝen**, W, S2; **steȝen**, S2; **steghe**, H, S2; **steaȝ**, *pt. s.*, S2; **steiȝ**, S3; **stegh**, S2, H; **styh**, S2.—AS. *stígan*, pt. *stáh* (pl. *stigon*), pp. *stigen*.

sties, *pl.* paths, S2; **stighes**, H; see **sty**[1].

stikien, *v.* to stick, to pierce, stab, S, S2, C2, C3; **styken**, S2; **steek**, S3; **stekit**, *pt. s.*, B; **stekyt**, S3; **y-styked**, *pp.*, S2.—AS. *stician*. See **steken**.

stikke, *sb.* stick, C3; **stykke**, Prompt.

stillatorie, *sb.* vessel used in distillation, C3, CM; **stillatory**, a place where distillations are performed, ND.—Late Lat. *stillatorium*, from Lat. (*di*)*stillare*.

stingen, *v.* to sting; **stonge**, *pt. pl.*, S; **stongen**, *pp.*, C, H; **y-stongen**, S3; **y-stonge**, C3; **stungen**, H.—AS. *stingan*, pt. *stang* (pl. *stungon*), pp. *stungen*.

stiren, *v.* to stir, to move, to instigate, PP, C3, W2, S, S2; **stere**, PP, S2, G; **sturen**, S, W; **styren**, S; **steir**, S3, B.—AS. *styrian*.

stiring, *sb.* stirring, commotion, W, W2.

stirte, *pt. s.* started; see **sterten**.

stith, *sb.* anvil, C, CM, Sh.; **stythe**, Prompt.—Icel. *steði*.

stiward; see **sty**[2].

stobil, *sb.* stubble, W2; **stobul**, Prompt.—AF. *stuble* (Ps. 82. 12, Oxford Psalter): Prov. *estobla*; OTeut. **stuppula*; cf. OF. *estoulle* (Ps. 82. 13), F. *éteule*; see Kluge (s.v. *stoppel*), and BH, § 153.

stok, *sb.* stock, stem, trap, the stocks, PP, W2; **stoc**, S; **stokke**, PP; **stocke**, S3; **stoke**, S2; **stokkes**, *pl.*, PP; **stockis**, S2; **stokess**, S.—AS. *stocc*. {Professor Napier maintains that the **stokess** of the Ormulum cannot be identified with AS. *stocc*, as the gemination of the consonant persists in the Ormulum. He suggests that **stokess** means 'places', comparing the use of *stoke* in place-names, e.g. *Wude stoke* in Chron. (Earle, p. 249), He also cites in illustration AS. *stoc-weard*, 'oppidanus', see Leo, p. 206.}

stoken, *v.* to stab, SkD, C.—OF. *estoquer* (Ducange).

stole[1], *sb.* stool, P; **stool**, PP, Prompt.; **stoule**, PP.—AS. *stól*.

stole[2], *sb.* a robe, W, Prompt.; **stoole** (= Lat. *stola*), W; **stolis**, *pl.*, W.—Lat. *stola*.

stonden; see **standen**.

stonge, *pt. pl.* stung, S; see **stingen**.

stonien, *v.* to stun, to make a loud din, to amaze with a blow, SD; **stunay**, H;

stunayd, *pp.*, H; **stoynde**, S3. See **astonen**.

stoniynge, *sb.* astonishment, W; **stonying**, W; **stoneyinge**, S2; **stoynynge**, Prompt.

stont, *pr. s.* stands; see **standen**.

stony, *adj.* rocky, Prompt. *Comb.*: **stony see**, Adria, the Adriatic Sea, W.—Cf. Ducange '*adria*, petra; *adriaticus*, petrosus, lapidosus portus'.

stoon, *sb.* stone, PP, W2; **ston**, PP, S, S3; **stane**, *dat.*, S; **stanes**, *pl.*, S. *Comb.*: **stoonstille**, still as a stone, G.—AS. *stán*: Goth. *stains*.

stoor, *sb.* store, stock, provision, Prompt., C, C2, C3, G; **store**, PP. *Phr.*: **telle no store**, set no store by, set no value upon, C.—OF. *estore* (Bartsch).

stope, *pp.* advanced, C; **stopen**, CM, SkD (s.v. *step*).—AS. *stapen*, pp. of *stapan* (pt. *stóp*).

stor, *sb.* incense, S; **store**, *dat.*, S.—AS. *stór*, incense, storax; Lat. *storacem*, acc. of *storax* (Vulg.), also *styrax*; Gr. στύραξ.

stordy, *adj.* rash, reckless, S; see **sturdy**.

store, *adj.* strong, powerful, large, HD, Prompt.; **stoor**, Prompt.—Icel. *stórr*.

storour, *sb.* restorer, S3.

storuen, *pt. pl.* died, C3; see **sterven**.

stot, *sb.* stallion, bullock, stoat, SkD, SD; *caballus*, Prompt., C; **stott**, *buculus*, WA, Voc.; **stot**, stoat, CM; **stotte**, bullock, Cath., Palsg.; **stottis**, *pl.*, PP.—Cf. Icel. *stútr*, bull.

stounde, *sb.* time, occasion, instant, period, S, S2, S3, C, C2, C3, G, PP; **stund**, S, S2; **stunt**, H; **stundum**, *dat. pl.* as *adv.*, at times, H. *Comb.*: **stound-mele**, at times, S3.—AS. *stund*: OS. *stunda*; cf. OHG. *stunta*, 'tempus, hora' (Tatian).

stounden, *v.* to be for a time; **stounded**, *pt. s.*, SD; **stunden**, *pl.* (= **stundeden**), S.

stoupen, *v.* to stoop, W (John 20. 5), C3; **stowpen**, CM, HD.—AS. *stúpian*.

stour[1], *sb.* conflict, commotion, agitation, S2, B, JD; **stowre**, S3; **stoure**, HD; **stoures**, *pl.*, C2; **stowres**, S2.—OF. *estour, estor, estur* (Roland); cf. Icel. *styrr*, a stir, tumult, battle.

stour[2], *v.* to move quickly, JD; **stowrand**, *pr. p.*, S3.

stouth, *sb.* stealth, S3.—Icel. *stuldr*.—Cf. **stelþe**.

stovys, *sb. pl.* vapours, S3; see **stew**.

stowyn, *v.* to stow, bring together, Prompt.; **stauez**, *pr. s.*, S2; **stouwet**, *pp.*, PP; **stawed**, S2; **staued**, S2; **stewed**, PP.—AS. *stówigan* (OET).

stra, *sb.* straw, S; see **strawe**.

straight (for **strait**), *adj.* close-fitting, tight, S3; see **streyt**.

strain, *v.* to distrain, S3.—AF. *destreindre* (pr. p. *destreignant*). See **streynen**.

strand, *sb.* stream, torrent, S2, S3, H; **stronde**, W2; **strynd**, JD.

strande, *sb.* bank, shore, WA.

strang, *adj.* strong, S; see **stronge**.

strangelyn, *v.* to suffocate, Prompt.; **estrangle**, NED; **astrangle**, NED, MD; **astrangeled**, *pp.*, S2.—AF. *estrangler*; Lat. *strangulare*, of Gr. origin; cf. στραγγάλη, halter.

strapeles, *sb. pl.* fastenings of breeches, S; **strapuls**, Voc.; **strapils**, Cath.—AS. *strapulas* (Voc.).

strate, *sb.* way, street, S; see **strete**.

stratly, *adv.* closely, S2; see **streyt**.

straunge[1], *adj.* strange, foreign, C, Prompt.; **strange**, C.—AF. *estrange*; Lat. *extraneum*.

straunge[2], *v.* to become strange; **strangeþ**, *pr. s.*, S2; **straungid**, *pp.*, HD.

strawe, *sb.* straw, Prompt.; **stra**, S, Cath.; **stree**, C, Prompt. *Comb.*: **strauberi**, strawberry, SD; **strabery**, Cath.; **strawberywyse**, strawberry plant, Prompt.; **straberi-wythe**, Cath.—AS. *stréaw*, *stréa*; cf. Icel. *strá*, see Sievers, 250.

strayny, *pr. s. subj.* restrain, S2; see **streynen**.

strayues, *sb. pl.* escheats, goods of strangers dead without English-born issue, and of bastards dead intestate, PP; **streyues**, P.— Cf. OF. *estrahiere* (Godefroy), also *estrayere* (see Cotg.), Low Lat. *estraeria*: Late Lat. *extrateria*; cf. *extrates* (Ducange). For the intrusive *v*, see **parvis**.

strecchen, *v.* to stretch, PP; **streke**, H; **strecche on**, to exert (one self), S2; **strekis**, *pr. s.*, H; **strau3te**, *pt. s.*, W; **strei3te**, W; **strei3t**, S2; **strei3ten**, *pl.*, W; **strekid**, H; **strekand**, *pr. p.*, S2, H; **strekyng**, S3; **strekid**, *pp.*, H; **strahte**, *pl.*, S; **straughte**, C.—AS. *streccan*, pt. *strehte*, pp. *streht*.

stree, *sb.* straw, C; see **strawe**.

strem, *sb.* stream, ray, beam, S, S2, C2, Voc.; **streem**, C.—AS. *stréam*: Icel. *straumr*; see Douse, p. 61.

stren, *sb.* race, progeny, HD; **streen**, C2; **streones**, *pl.*, S.—AS. *stréon*, a getting, possession (Leo).

strend, *sb.* generation, S2; **strinds**, *pl.*, sons, children, WA.—AS. *strýnd*, stock, race.

strenen, *v.* to get, beget, HD; **3e-strenð**, *pr. s.*, S; **i-streoned**, *pp.*, S; **i-striened**, S — AS. *stréonan*, *ge-stréonan*; cf. OHG. *(gi)striunen*, to gain (Tatian).

strenge, *sb.* string, S3, H (p. 367); **strynge**, Prompt.—AS. *streng*.

strengen, *v.* to strengthen, SD; **streng**, *imp. s.*, S.—AS. *strangian*. See **stronge**.

strengðe, *sb.* strength, violence, S, S2; **strencðe**, S; **strenðe**, S, S2; **strengthes**, *pl.*, sources of strength, C2; **strenthis**, strong places, S3.—AS. *strengðu*.

strengðen, *v.* to strengthen, SD; **strengðeð him**, *pr. s. reflex.*, S; **strenghþed**, *pt. s.*, S2; *pp.*, S2; **i-strengþed**, S.

strengthy, *adj.* strong; **strenthie**, JD; **strenghthi**, H.

strenken, *v.* to sprinkle, S.

strenkil, *v.* to sprinkle about, H; **strenkelyn**, Prompt.; **strenkle**, S2; **strinkle**, HD; **strenkild**, *pp.*, H.

strenkyl, *sb.* a sprinkling, a holy-water stick, Prompt.; **strenkle**, HD; **strinkle**, HD; **strenncless**, *pl.*, S.

streones, *sb. pl.* progeny, S; see **stren**.

strepen, *v.* to strip, C2, CM; **streepe**, C; **strupen**, S.—AS. *strýpan* (in *be-strýpan*).

strete, *sb.* way, street, PP, S; **strate**, S; **stret**, S.—AS. *strét*: OS. *stráta*; Lat. *stráta* (*uia*); see Sievers, 17.

streynen, *v.* to draw tight, C2, W, W2, PP; **strayny**, *pr. s. subj.*, S2.—AF. *streign-* base of *streignant*, pr. p. of *streindre* (*straindre*); Lat. *stringere*.

streyt, *pp.* and *adj.* pressed tightly, narrow, strict, S2, C; **streite**, S3, C; **straight**, S3; **strayte**, *pl.*, S2; **streyte**, *adv.* closely, S2, C; **streitliche**, S2; **stratly**, S2; **streatly**, S3.—AF. *estreit* (*estrait*); Lat. *strictum*.

strif, *sb.* strife, S; **stryf**, C.—AF. *estrif*; of Teutonic origin; see **strifen**.

strifen, *v.* to strive, S2; **stryvyn**, Prompt.; **strof**, *pt. s.*, C.—OF. *estriver*; Prov. *estribar*; OHG. *stríbhan*; cf. G. *streben*; see Kluge (s.v.), and Mackel, *Germ. Elemente*.

strike, *sb.* hank of flax, C, HD.

striken, *v.* to strike, to rub, to let down, to advance, to move quickly, to flow, S2, SkD; **stryke**, PP, Palsg.; **strok**, *pt. s.*, PP; **stroke**, P, WW; **strake**, S3, WW; **strook**, Sh.; **strek**, SkD; **strike**, *pl.*, S; **strake**, S2; **strocke**, S3; **striked**, *pp.*, PP, WW; **striken**, WW; **stricken**, WW; **strooke**, Sh.—AS. *strícan*, pt. *strác* (pl. *stricon*), pp. *stricen*.

strogelen, *v.* to struggle, C3, SkD.

strogelynge, *sb.* struggling, Prompt.

stronde[1], *sb.* shore, strand, Prompt., S, C, C3, HD.—AS. *strand*. Cf. **strande**.

stronde[2], *sb.* stream, torrent, W2; see **strand**.

stronge, *adj.* strong, hard, severe, Prompt., S2; **strong**, S; **strang**, S, S2; **stronge**, *adv.*, S, G; **strengre**, *comp.*, S; **strengeste**, S, S2, W2; **strenger**, C2; **strengeste**, *superl.*, S; **strengest**, G.—AS. *strang*, comp. *strengor*, superl. *strengest*.

strook, *sb.* stroke, C2. See **striken**.

stroyen, *v.* to destroy, PP, G, S3; **struyen**, P; **stroy**, S2, Sh.; **struen**, *pr. pl.*, PP; **stryede**, *pt. s.*, S2.—AF. *destruy-* base of *destruyant*, pr. p. of *destruire*; Late Lat. *destrūgere; formed on Lat. *destructus*, pp. of *destruere*.

strupen, *v.* to strip, S; see **strepen**.

stuard, *sb.* steward, S; see **sty**[2].

stubbe, *sb.* stump, trunk, C; **stub**, Cath.

stucche, *sb.* piece, S; **steche**, S.—AS. *stycce*: OHG. *stuki* (Tatian).

stude, *sb.* place, S; see **stede**[2].

stues, *sb. pl.* stews, baths, brothels, P; see **stewe**[2].

stund, *sb.* time, occasion, period, instant, S; see **stounde**.

stunt, *adj.* blunt, not sharp, obtuse, foolish, SD, HD, SkD; **stuntlic**, *adv.*, foolishly, SD. *Der.*: **stuntnesse**, foolishness, SD.—Cf. OSwed. *stunt*, cut short.

sturdy, *adj.* obstinate, stern, cruel, rash, Prompt., C2; **stordy**, CM, S; **stourdy**, SD.—OF. *estourdi*, amazed, rash (Cotg.), *estordi*, pp. of *estordir*; from Lat. *turdus*, a thrush; see Förster, ZRP, x. 84.

sturdynesse, *sb.* sternness, disobedience, Prompt., C2.

sturioun, *sb.* sturgeon, S2, HD.—AF. *sturioun*; Low Lat. *sturionem*; from OHG. *sturio*.

sturne, sturn-hede; see **sterne**[2].

sturuen, *pt. pl.* died, S; see **sterven**.

sty[1], *sb.* path, S2, Prompt.; **stighe**, *dat.*, H; **stighes**, *pl.*, H; **stihes**, S2; **sties**, S2; **styes**, H; **steghes**, H.—AS. *stíg*. See **stien**.

sty[2], *sb.* sty, *porcarium*, Prompt. *Comb.*: **styward**, steward, *senescallus*, Prompt., C2, C3; **stiward**, S, C; **steward**, PP; **stuward**, P; **stuard**, S.—AS. *stígu*, a sty, whence *stigweard*. Cf. **ward**[1].

styf, *adj.* stiff, strong, violent, PP, S2; **stif**, S, S2, PP; **steef**, W2; **stef**, PP. *Der.*: **stefhede**, sturdiness, S2.—AS. *stíf*; see SkD.

styh, *pt. s.* mounted, S2; see **stien**.

stynten, *v.* to stint, cease, pause, PP, S2, H; **stinten**, C2, C3, S2, S; **stunten**, PP; **stente**, C2, S3; *pt. s.*, C2; **stint**, S2; **stynted**, *pl.*, S3; **stent**, *pp.*, C.—AS. *styntan*, to make short. See **stunt**.

sty-rop, *sb.* stirrup, Prompt., G; **stirop**, S, C2; **stiroppe**, S3.—AS. *stíg-ráp* (Voc.). See **stien**.

su-; see also words beginning in **sv-** and in **sw-**.

sublymatorie, *sb.* vessels for sublimation, C3.—Late Lat. *sublimatorium*.

sublymen, *v.* to sublimate, C3.—Lat. *sublimare*.

sublyming, *sb.* sublimation, C3.

succinis, *sb.* amber, S2.—From Lat. *succinum* (Voc.).

sudarie, *sb.* napkin, W; **sudary**, HD.—Lat. *sudarium* (Vulg.).

sudekene, *sb.* sub-deacon, HD.

sudene, *sb.* sub-dean, PP; **suddene**, PP.

suen (**sūen**), *v.* to follow, attend on, persecute, PP, W, W2, S2, S3; **suwen**, S2, W, PP; **sewen**, PP, S2, C; **swe**, S3, W.—OF. *siw-*, pr. p. base of *sivre*: Late Lat. *sĕquere* (for Lat. *sequi*); see BH, § 32.

suere (**sūere**), *sb.* follower, W.

suffisance, *sb.* sufficiency, C2.—AF. *suffisance*.

suffisant, *adj.* sufficient, S2, C2, C3.—AF. *suffisant*.

suffragane, *sb.* assistant, deputy, properly of a bishop, S3.—Late Lat. *suffraganeus*.

suffraunce, *sb.* endurance, patience, C2; **soffraunce**, PP; **suffrance**, P.—AF. *suffraunce*.

suffren, *v.* to suffer, C2, PP; **suffri**, S; **soffren**, PP.—OF. *suffrir*.

sufrayn; see **sovereyn**.

suget, *sb.* subject, H (p. 361).—AF. *suget*; Lat. *subiectum*.

sugetin, *v.* to subject; **sugetide**, *pt. s.*, W; **suget**, *pp.*, W, W2.

sugge, *2 pr. s. subj.* say, S; see **seggen**.

suggestioun, *sb.* criminal charge, reason, P, C2.—AF. *suggestioun*; Lat. *suggestionem*.

suhien, *v.* to sough, sound harsh; **suhiende**, *pr. p. pl.*, S (9. 336); **suinde**, S.—From AS. *swógan*. See **swowen**.

suld, should; see **scholde**.

sulf, self, S; see **self**.

sulien, *v.* to bemire, to sully, SkD, SD; **y-suled**, *pp.*, S3.—AS. *sylian*: OHG. *sulian* (in *bi-sulian*), see Grein, p. 95; cf. AS. *sol*, mire (Voc.).

sullen, *v.* to sell, S, S2; see **sellen**.

suller, *sb.* seller, S2; see **seller**[1].

sulliche, *adv.* strangely, S; see **sellich**.

suluer, *sb.* silver, S2; see **silver**.

sulȝart, *adj.* (perhaps) bright, shining, S3.—(Cf. Gael. *soilleir*, bright, shining, OIr. *sollus*, bright.—W.W.S.)

sulȝe, *sb.* soil, earth, S3; **soyle**, Prompt. *Comb.*: **sule erthe**, soil, Prompt.—AF. *soyl*; Late Lat. *solea* for Lat. *solum*, ground, see Ducange.

sum[1], *adj.* and *pron.* some, a certain one, S; **zom**, S2; **sumere**, *dat.*; **sume**, *pl.*, S. *Comb.*: **sume we**, some of us, S; **alle and some**, one and all, S2; **sum ... sum**, one ... one, S; **sum-chere**, some time, S; **sumdel**, something, S, S2; **somdel**, S2, C2; **sumdeale**, S3; **sumdeill**, S3; **sumdeel**,

W2; **some dele**, P; **sumhwet**, somewhat, S; **somwat**, S2; **summehwile**, for some time, S; **sumewile**, sometimes, S; **sum-wile**, formerly, S; **somtym**, sometimes, C3; **summes-weis**, in some wise, S.

sum[2], *conj.* as. *Comb.*: **swa summ**, so as, S.

sumer, *sb.* summer, S; see **somer**.

sumundis, *pr. s.* summonses, H; see **sompne**.

sund, *adj.* sound, S; **sound**, PP.—AS. (*ge*)*sund*; cf. OHG. *gi-sunt* (Otfrid).

sunder, *adv.* apart; **sonder**, S2. *Comb.*: **sunder-bleo**, diverse colour, SD; **sunder-halƷe**, Pharisee, SD; **sunder-liche**, separately, S; **sundirly**, severally, H; **sunder-lipes**, severally, SD; **sunder-lepes**, S; **sunder-ling**, separately, SD. *Der.*: **sundren**, to separate, S; **i-sundred**, *pp.*, S; **sundri**, separate, S; **sondry**, C2.

sunegen, *v.* to sin, S; **sinegen**, S; **sungið**, *pl.*, S; **sunegeden**, *pt. pl.*, S; **sinegeden**, S; **seneƷden**, S; **seneƷeden**, S; **sineged**, *pp.*, S; **i-suneged**, S.—AS. *syngian*; cf. Icel. *syndga*.

sunen, *v.* to sound, S; see **sounen**.

sungen, *pt. pl.* sang, S; see **syngen**.

sunne[1], *sb.* sun, S. S2; see **sonne**.

sunne[2], *sb.* sin, S, S2, PP; **senne**, S; **sinne**, S; **synne**, PP; **zenne**, S2; **sunnen**, *pl.*, S; **sennenn**; **sinne**, S; **zennen**, S2. *Comb.*: **sun-bend**, sin-bond, S; **sinne-bendes**, *pl.*, S; **sun-bote**, penance, S; **sinbote**, S; **sunful**, sinful, S; **senfulle**, S; **sinfule**, S.—AS. *synn*: OS. *sundea*; cf. OHG. *santa* (Tatian).

sup, *v.* to sup, drink gradually, eat supper, S3; **soop**, *pt. s.*, W; **sopun**, *pp.*, W; **sope**, W.—AS. *súpan*, pt. *séap* (pl. *supon*), pp. *sopen*. Cf. **soupen**.

superflue, *adj.* superfluous, HD; **super-fluli**, *adv.*, W2.—OF. *superflu* (Cotg.); Lat. *superfluum*.

supplement, *sb.* new piece, patch, S2.—Lat. *supplementum*.

supposinge, *sb.* supposition, C2.

supposs, *conj.* supposing, although, S3.

supprioure, *sb.* sub-prior, P.

sur[1], *sb.* shower; **sures**, *pl.*, S; see **schowre**.

sur[2], *adj.* sour, S; see **soure**.

sure, *adj.* sure, PP.—AF. *seür*; Lat. *securum*.

suren, *v.* to give security to, PP, S3.

surety, *sb.* surety; **seurtee**, C3, S2; **seurte**, C; **souerte**, S3.—AF. *seürte*; Lat. *securitatem*.

surfait, *sb.* surfeit, excess, P; **surfet**, PP.—AF. *surfait, surfet*, outrage, annoyance.

surplys, *sb.* surplice, C3.—OF. *surplis*; Late Lat. *superpelliceum*.

surquidry, *sb.* pride, arrogance, WA; **surquedry**, ND, Spenser 2; **surquidrie**,

CM; **succudry**, B.—OF. *surcuiderie*, from *surcuider*; Lat. *super* + *cogitare*, to think.

surrye, *sb.* Syria, S2.

surryen, *adj.* Syrian, S2.

suspect[1], *sb.* suspicion, C2, HD.—Late Lat. *suspectus*, suspicion (Ducange).

suspect[2], *adj.* open to suspicion, C2.—Lat. *suspectus*, pp. of *suspicere*, to suspect.

sustene, *v.* to sustain, C2; **susteene**, C3; **susteyne**, PP; **sustened**, *pp.*, C2; **i-susteined**, S2; **i-sousteined**, S2.—AF. *sustener*, OF. *sostenir*; Lat. *sustinēre*.

suster, *sb.* sister, S, C2, C3, PP; **soster**, S2; **sustre**, P; **sustren**, *pl.*, S, P; **sostren**, S2; **zostren**, S2; **sistren**, C; **sistris**, W.—AS. *swuster, sweostor*; cf. Goth. *swistar* (Icel. *systir*), cognate with Lat. *soror* (for **sosor*), Skt. *svasr*. On the Teutonic intrusive *t*, see Douse, p. 61.

sute, *sb.* suit of clothes, clothing of human flesh, also train, suite, PP, Cath., Prompt.—AF. *suyte*; from *suivre, sivre*, to follow. See **suen**.

sutel, *adj.* manifest, SD; **suteliche**, *adv.* plainly, S.—AS. *sweotol* (*swutol*), see OET; from *sweot*, an assembly; cf. Icel. *sveit*.

suteli, *adv.* subtly, W; see **sotyle**[1].

sutelin, *v.* to be manifest, S.—AS. (*ge*)*sweotulian*.

suð, *adj.* south, S; see **sowþe**.

suþe, *adv.* very, S; see **swiþe**.

suþþe, afterwards, since, S, S2; see **siþþen**.

suthroun, *adj.* southern, S3; see **sowþerne**.

suwed, *pp.* followed, S2; see **suen**.

sua (**sva**), so, as, S, S2; see **swa**.

sual, *sb.* swell (as of the sea), H. See **swellen**.

suank, *pt. pl.* toiled, S2; see **swinken**.

suein, *sb.* servant, S2; see **sweyne**.

suenchen, *pt. pl.* afflicted, S; see **swenchen**.

suik, *sb.* deceit, S2; see **swike**[1].

suor, *pt. t.* swore; see **sweren**.

suun, *sb.* a swoon, S2; see **swowne**.

swa, *adv.* and *conj.* so, as, S, S2; **swo**, S; **sa**, S, S2; **so**, S, S2; **se**, S; **sua**, S, S2; **zuo**, S2. *Comb.*: **se-forð**, so far, S; **so-gat**, in such a way, S2.—AS. *swá*.

swage, *v.* to assuage, diminish, W, W2, H, S3. See **aswagen**.

swaliden, *pt. pl.* dried up, W; see **swelen**.

swamish, *adj.* timorous, *inaudaculus*, Manip. See **sweem**.

swappe, *sb.* a stroke, HD.

swappen, *v.* to strike, slash, to fall suddenly, C2; **swap**, *imp. s.*, C3; **swapte**, *pt. s.*, C2; *pl.*, S3.

swarde, *sb.* covering, skin, turfy surface, sward, Prompt.; **swarth**, Cath. (*n.* p. 373); **swarthe**, HD; **swart**, HD; **sweard**, HD. *Der.*: **swardit**, *pp.*, grass-covered, S3.—AS.

sweard, skin (Voc.); cf. Icel. *svörðr* (base *svarða-*), skin of the head, also the sward, surface of the earth.

sware, *adj.* square, S2; see **sqware**.

swart, *adj.* black, S, HD; **swarte**, S.—AS. *sweart*: OS. *swart*; cf. OHG. *suarz* (Tatian).

swarve, *v.* to swerve, S3; see **swerven**.

swat[1]; see **swot**.

swat[2], **swatte**; see **sweten**[2].

swe, *v.* to follow, S3; see **suen**.

sweande; see **sweyen**[1].

sweem, *sb.* a swoon, trance, grief, Prompt., SkD (s.v. *squeamish*); **sweam**, 'subita aegrotatio', SkD; **swaim**, Prompt. (*n*); **swem**, S; **sweme**, SkD, HD; **sume**, S2.—Icel. *sveimr*, a bustle, stir.

sweigh, *sb.* sway, motion, S2, C3. See **sweyen**[1].

swele, *v.* to wash, S2; see **swilien**.

swelen, *v.* to sweal, to waste away under the action of fire, SkD, Trevisa, 3. 325; **swale**, HD; **swaliden**, *pt. pl.*, dried up, W.—AS. *swélan*; from *swól*, heat (OET).

swellen, *v.* to swell; **swal**, *pt. s.*, S, S2, C2, PP; **swollen**, *pp.*, C2.—AS. *swellan*, pt. *sweall*, pp. *swollen*.

swelten[1], *v.* to faint, to die, PP; **swalt**, *pt. s.*, SD; **swulten**, *pl.*, SD; **swelte**, *pt. s.* (*weak*), C, HD.—AS. *sweltan*, to die, pt. *swealt* (pl. *swulton*); cf. Icel. *svelta*.

swelten[2], *v.* to destroy, to cause to perish, S2; **swelt**, *pp.*, SD.—Icel. *svelta*, to put to death (causal of the above).

swelth, *sb.* offscouring, filth, S3, HD, ND. See **swilien**.

swelwen, *v.* to swallow, C2; see **swolowen**.

swem, *sb.* a grief, S; see **sweem**.

swenchen, *v.* to distress, afflict, S; **suencten**, *pt. pl.*, S; **i-swechte**, *pp.*, S.—AS. *swencan* (causal of *swincan*). See **swinken**.

sweore, *sb.* neck, S; see **swere**.

sweote, *adj.* sweet, S; see **swete**.

swep, *sb.* drift, meaning, S. See **swopen**.

swepe, *sb.* whip, SD; **swepen**, *pl.*, S; **swupen**, S; **swepes**, S.

swepen, *v.* to sweep, SkD; **y-sweped**, *pp.*, C3. See **swopen**.

swerde, *sb.* sword, Prompt., PP; **swerd**, PP, S, C2; **sweord**, S; **suerd**, S, S2; **zuord**, S2.—AS. *sweord*: OS. *swerd*; cf. OHG. *swert* (Tatian).

swere, *sb.* neck, S; **sweere**, G; see **swire**.

sweren, *v.* to swear, S, S2, C2; **swerien**, S; **sueren**, S; **swor**, *pt. s.*, S: **suor**, S, S2; **sware**, S2; **sweren**, *pl.*, S; **sworen**, S, C2; **suoren**, S; **suore**, S2; **sworen**, *pp.*, S; **swore**, C2, G; **y-swore**, S2, C2; **i-suore**, S2.—AS. *swerian*, pt. *swór*, pp. *sworen*.

swering, *sb.* swearing, C3.

sweruen, *v.* to swerve, SkD; **swarve**, S3; **suaruing**, *pr. p.*, S3; **swarued**, *pp.*, S3.—AS. *sweorfan*, to rub, pt. *swearf*, pp. *sworfen*.

swete, *adj.* sweet, S, C; **sweote**, S; **suete**, S, S2; **suote**, S2; **sote**, C2, C3; **swete**, *adv.*, S; **swote**, S, C; **soote**, S3; **soot**, S3; **swettere**, *comp.*, W2; **sweteliche**, *adv.*, sweetly, S; **swetlike**, S; **swetterly**, *comp.* more sweetly, H. *Der.*: **swetnesse**, sweetness, S; **swotnesse**, S.—AS. *swéte*: OS. *swóti* cf. OHG. *suozi* (Tatian).

sweten[1], *v.* to make sweet, S.—AS. *swétan*.

sweten[2], *v.* to sweat, S, P; **swatte**, *pt. s.*, S, C2, C3, W2; **swattes**, *2 pt. s.*, S; **swat**, *pl.*, S3.—AS. *swétan*, pt. *swétte*. See **swot**.

sweuen, *sb.* dream, S, C2; **sweuene**, S, S2, P, W; **swefnes**, *pl.*, S.—AS. *swefen*: OS. *sweban*.

sweuenen, *v.* to dream, SD.

sweuening, *sb.* dreaming, S, S2.

sweuien, *v.* to send to sleep; **sweueð**, *pr. s.*, S.—Icel. *svefja*, to lull to sleep.

sweyen[1], *v.* to sway, to go, walk, pass, SkD, HD; **sweiȝen**, SD; **sweȝen**, SkD; **sweande**, *pr. p.*, S2; **swe**, *pr. pl.*, S2; **seyed**, *pp.*, S2.—Cf. Swed. *sviga*, to bend.

sweyen[2], *v.* to sound, PP; **sweien**, S.—AS. *swégan* (causal of *swógan*). See **swowen**.

sweyne, *sb.* servant, *armiger*, Prompt., S; **swayn**, C2, G; **swein**, S; **sueyn**, S; **suein**, S2.—Icel. *sveinn*, a boy, lad, servant; cf. AS. *swán*.

swi-, *prefix*, silent. *Comb.*: **swi-dages**, still days, days of silence, S; **swi-messe**, the Canon of the Mass, the silent Mass, S; **swi-wike**, the still week, SD.—AS. *swíge*, silence.

swien, *v.* to be silent; **swigeð**, *pr. s.*, S; **swiede**, *pt. s.*, S.—AS. *swían*, *swígian*; cf. OHG. *suñgén* (Tatian), G. *schweigen*.

swiere, *sb.* neck, S; see **swire**.

swike[1], *sb.* traitor, deceiver, S; **suikes**, *pl.*, S.—AS. *swica*.

swike[1], *sb.* mouse-trap, S; **swyke**, Voc.; **suik**, deceit, S2.—AS. *swice*, 'scandalum' (Grein).

swike[1], *adj.* deceitful, SD. *Comb.*: **swikedom**, treachery, S, S2; **suikedom**, S2; **swicful**, treachery, S; **swikfull**, H.—AS. *swice*.

swikel, *adj.* treacherous, S, H; **sikil**, H; **swikilly**, *adv.*, H. *Comb.*: **swikeldom**, treachery, S; **swikeldome**, S2; **swikelhede**, treachery, S; **swikelede**, S; **suikelhede**, S2.—AS. *swicol*.

swiken, *v.* to cease, fail, deceive, S; **swyken**, H; **suyken**, *pt. pl.*, S.—AS. *swícan*, pt. *swác* (pl. *swicon*), pp. *swicen*.

swilien, *v.* to wash, SkD; **swele**, S2.—AS. *swilian.*

swilk, *adj.* such, H, S; see **swyche.**

swin, *sb.* pig, *porcus*, SD; **swyne**, Voc.; *pl.*, S.—AS. *swín.*

swinden, *v.* to perish, dwindle away, S; **swynde**, S.—AS. *swindan*, pt. *swand* (pl. *swundon*), pp. *swunden.*

swing, *sb.* bias, inclination, sway, HD; free course of behaviour, S3; **swinge**, sway, S3.

swingen, *v.* to swing, beat, whip, scourge; **swyngen**, H; **swungen**, *pp.*, S; **swongen**, H; **swongyn**, H.—AS. *swingan*, pt. *swang* (pl. *swungon*), pp. *swungen.*

swink, *sb.* toil, S, C3; **swynk**, S2; **swinc**, S; **suinc**, S; **swinch**, S; **swunche**, S.—AS. *(ge)swinc.*

swinken, *v.* to toil, S, C3, ND; **swynke**, S2, C; **swincke**, S3; **swanc**, *pt. s.*, S; **swonc**, S; **swunken**, *pl.*, S; **swonken**, S2; **suank**, S2.—AS. *swincan*, pt. *swanc* (pl. *swuncon*), pp. *swuncen.*

swinkere, *sb.* labourer, C.

swippen, *v.* to move violently; **swipte**, *pt. s.*, tossed, S.—AS. *swipian.*

swire, *sb.* neck, CM; **swyre**, S2, HD; **sweore**, S; **swere**, S; **sweere**, G; **swiere** S; **swyer**, HD.—AS. *sweora.*

swirk[1], *v.* to dart swiftly away, S3.

swirk[2], *sb.* a jerk, a blow, HD.

swithe, *adv.* very, greatly, much, quickly, S, S2, P, W, G; **swythe**, S, S2, C3; **swuðe**, S; **suiðe**, S, S2; **suyðe**, S, S2; **suþe**, S; **swith**, S2; **swiðeliche**, exceedingly, S.—AS. *swíðe*, adv. from *swíð*, strong: Goth. *swinþs.*

swiðen, *v.* to scorch, burn, SD; **swideð**, *pr. s.*, S.—Icel. *svíða.*

swo, so, as, S; see **swa.**

swogh, *sb.* a swoon; see **swough.**

swolowe, *sb.* gulf, W2.

swolowen, *v.* to swallow, W2; **swolwen**, C3; **swelwen**, C2, Prompt.; **swolgen**, *pp.*, S; **i-swolʒe**, S; **swolewid**, *pt. s.* weak, W2.—From AS. *swelgan*, pt. *swealh* (pl. *swulgon*), pp. *swolgen.*

swongen, *pp.* beaten, H; see **swingen.**

swonken, *pt. pl.* toiled (to get), S2; see **swinken.**

swopen, *v.* to sweep, cleanse, S2, PP, HD, SkD (s.v. *swoop*).—AS. *swápan*, pt. *swéop*, pp. *swápen.*

swor, *pt. s.* swore; see **sweren.**

swot, *sb.* sweat, PP, W; **swat**, S; **swote**, dat., C3.—AS. *swát.*

swote, *adj.* sweet, S, C; see **swete.**

swouch, *v.* to make a rustling sound, S3.—AS. *swógan.* See **swowen.**

swough, *sb.* the sound of the wind, a sighing, swoon, C, C2, CM, HD; **swogh**, S3, HD; **swowe**, S2, HD. See **swouch.**

swowe, *sb.* swoon, S2; see **swough.**

swowen, *v.* to faint, swoon, PP; **i-swoʒe**, *pp.*, S; **y-swoʒe**, S.—AS. *swógan*, to make a noise like the wind, to sough, sigh. Cf. **swouch, swough, suhien.**

swowne, *sb.* swoon; **sowne**, S3; **suun**, S2; **swownde**, HD; **sound**, S3.

swownen, *v.* to swoon, C, C2, C3, Prompt., Cath.; **swoune**, PP.

swunche, *sb.* toil, S; see **swink.**

swungen, *pp.* beaten, scourged, S; see **swingen.**

swunken, *pt. pl.* worked, toiled, S; see **swinken.**

swupen, *pl.* whips, scourges, S; see **swepe.**

swuðe, *adv.* very, quickly, S; see **swiþe.**

swyche, *adj.* such, PP, S2; **swiche**, S, C2, PP; **swuch**, S; **suich**, S2; **soche**, S; **zuyche**, S2; **siche**, W; **swice**, S; **swulche**, S; **swilch**, S; **swulc**, S; **swilc**, S; **swilk**, H, S; **suilc**, S; **suilk**, S, S2; **silc**, S2; **sike**, S3.—AS. *swilc* (= *swá* + *líc*).

swymbel, *sb.* a giddy motion, C.—Cf. Dan. *svimmel*, giddiness.

swyme, *sb.* dizziness, vertigo, HD (s.v. *swime*), SkD (s.v. *swim*, 2); **swym**, SkD.—AS. *swíma*; see SkD (s.v. *squeamish*).

sy, *sb.* victory, S; see **siʒe.**

syde, *adj.* and *adv.* wide, long, far, Cath.; **side**, S, PP, S2, Cotg. (s.v. *robon*); **syd**, Prompt. (*n*); **syyd**, Prompt.; **cyyd**, Prompt.; **sydder**, *comp.*, P.—AS. *síd*, wide, *síde*, far.

syen, *pt. pl.* saw; see **seon.**

syke, *sb.* sigh, C; **syk**, C2; **seych**, S3.

syken, *v.* to sigh, C, C3, PP; **siken**, S, S2, PP; **syghte**, *pt. s.*, C3; **sicht**, S3; **sykede**, PP; **syked**, C2; **siʒede**, S3.—AS. *sícan.*

syment, *sb.* cement, MD; **cyment**, MD.—OF. *ciment*; Lat. *caementum*; see BH, § 39.

symented, *pp.* cemented, S2.

symulacris, *sb. pl.* images, idols, W; **simylacris**, W; **symelacris**, W.—Lat. *simulacrum* (Vulg.).

syn, since, S2, S3; see **siþþen.**

synewe, *sb.* sinew, Prompt.; **synow**, Voc.; **synoghe**, S2.—AS. *sinu* (gen. *sinwe*), see Sievers, 259.

syng, *sb.* sign, S3; **singne**, W; **sygne**, PP; **signe**, PP.—AF. *signe*; Lat. *signum.*

syngabil, *adj. pl.* things to sing (= Lat. *cantabiles*), H.

syngen, *v.* to sing, PP; **singen**, S; **song**, *pt. s.*, S, S3, C2; *pl.*, S3; **songe**, S3; **sungen**, *pl.*, S; **sunge**, *pp.*, S; **songe**, C2.—AS. *singan.*

synguler, *adj.* sole, alone, excelling all, PP; **singuler**, S2, C3, W2; relating to one

person, S3; **singulare**, individual, S3;
syngulerli, only, W2.—Lat. *singularis*.

synnamome, *sb.* cinnamon, S3; **cyna-
mome**, MD; **synamome**, MD; **syna-
mon**, MD.—OF. *cinamome*; Lat. *cinnamomum*
(Vulg.); Gr. κινάμωμον; Heb. *qinnāmōn*.

synopyr, *sb.* a pigment of reddish and
greenish colour, Prompt.; **synopar**, S3;
cynoper, MD; **cinoper**, ND; **cynope**,
green, in heraldry, SkD (s.v. *sinople*).—Cf.
OF. *sinople*, green colour in blazon (Cotg.),
also *sinope*; Late Lat. *sinopidem*, red ochre;
from Gr. σινωπίς, a red earth; from
Σινώπη, Sinope, a port on the Black Sea.

syon, *sb.* scion, a cutting for grafting, a young
shoot, S3, Palsg.; **cyun**, Prompt.; **cion**,

SkD; **sioun**, SD; **siouns**, *pl.*, branches (=
Lat. *palmites*), W2.—OF. *cion*.

syrupe, *sb.* syrup, Cath.; **sirop**, SkD;
soryp, Prompt.; **seroppes**, *pl.* syrups,
S3.—OF. *syrop* (Cotg.); Arab. *shuráb*, syrup,
a beverage.

sythe, *sb.* scythe, PP, Voc., Prompt.; **sithe**,
P.—AS. *síðe* (Voc.), *sigdi* (OET); cf. Icel.
sigðr.

syue, *sb.* sieve, C3, Prompt.—AS. *sife* (Voc.),
sibi (OET), see Sievers, 262.

sy3en, *pt. pl.* saw; see **seon**.

sy3t, *sb.* sight, S2; see **sighte**.

T

ta, *v.* to take, S2, S3; see **taken**[1].

taa[1], *Comb.*: **the taa**, the one, HD.

taa[2], *sb.* toe, S2; see **too**.

tabard, *sb.* a short coat or mantle, usually sleeveless, formerly worn by ploughmen, noblemen, and heralds, now by heralds only, HD, SkD, C; **tabart**, S2, PP; **tabarde**, PP, Voc.; **tabbard**, *collobium*, Prompt.; **taberd**, Voc.; **taberde**, Voc.; **tabare**, Voc.—OF. *tabard, tabart*, also *tabarre* (Cotg.); cf. It. *tabarro*.

tabarder, *sb.* a name for scholars at Queen's College, Oxford, ND.

tabernacle, *sb.* a place in which some holy thing is deposited, WA; **tabernacles**, *pl.*, niches of a lofty cross, S3; ornamental niches, HD; shrines, S3 (1. 181).—Lat. *tabernaculum* (Vulg.); cf. OF. *tabernacle* (Cotg.).

table, *sb.* in palmistry, a space between certain lines on the hand, HD; **tables**, *pl.*, a game, now called backgammon, CM. See **tavel**.

tabour, *sb.* a small drum, SkD; **tabur**, WA; **taber**, Voc.—OF. *tabor, thabour*.

taburne, *sb.* a drum, *tympanum*, WA, Voc., Cath.; **taburn**, H.

taburner, *sb.* a player on the tabor, *timpanista*, Cath.; **taberner**, *timpanizator*, Voc.

taburnystir, *sb.* female tabor player (= *tympanistria*), H.

tache[1], *sb.* a mark, sign, quality, stain, blemish, fault, HD; **tacche**, HD; **tacches**, *pl.*, PP; **tacchis**, HD; **teches**, S2. *Der.*: **tached**, *pp.*, tainted, stained; **tachyd**, PP.—OF. *tache, teche*, and OF. *tacher*, to spot, to stain.

tache[2], *sb.* a clasp, brooch, *fibula*, Cath. (*n*), Voc. Cf. **takke**.

tachen, *v.* to fasten, Cath. (*n*). Cf. **takken**.

tacne, *sb.* token, S; see **tokne**.

tacnen, *v.* to betoken, S; **takened**, *pp.*, S2.—AS. (*ge*)*tácnian*.

tade, *sb.* toad, *bufo*, Voc., Cath., S2; **tadde**, S. *Comb.*: **tadde-chese**, *tubera*, Voc.; **tadde-pol**, *brucus*, Voc.; **tadpolle**, *lumbricus*, Voc.; **tade-stole**, *boletus, fungus*, Cath.—Cf. AS. *tádige* (*tádie*).

taffata, *sb.* a thin glossy silk stuff, C, WA, Cotg.; **tafata**, Palsg.; **taffaty**, HD.—Low Lat. *taffata* (Ducange); cf. OF. *taffetas* (Cotg.).

tahte, tagte, *pt. s.* taught; see **techen**.

tai, they, S; see **þei**.

taille, *sb.* a tally, an account scored on a piece of wood, C, P; **taile**, CM, P; **tayle**, Cath., Prompt.; **taly**, Prompt.—OF. *taille*, a cut, a notch, a tally (Cotg.), from *tailler*, to cut.

taillour, *sb.* tailor, S2, PP; **tayleȝour**, Voc.; **taylȝor**, Voc.; **taylours**, PP.—AF. *taillour*. See **taille**.

takel, *sb.* implement, tackle, arrow, C, SkD; **tacle**, Prompt.; **takil**, B. *Der.*: **takild**, *pp.*, caught, seized, H.—Cf. Du. *takel*.

taken[1], *v.* to take, to deliver, yield up, hand over, to hit, *reflex.*, to betake oneself, S, S2, S3, G, PP, W; **tæcen**, S; **ta**, S2, S3, B; **toc**, *pt. s.*, S: **tok**, S, S2; **tuk**, S3; **toke**, *2 pt. s.*, S; **token**, *pl.*, S, W2; **taken**, *pp.*, S3; **take**, S2, C, C2; **y-take**, S2, C2; **i-take**, S; **tane**, S2, S3; **tan**, S2. *Phr.*: **taken with**, to endure, accept, S; **taken to**, to take to, S (s.v. *tok*); **taken kepe**, to take heed, C2; **taken tome**, to vacate, H.—Icel. *taka*.

taken[2], *sb.* token, S2; see **tokne**.

taking, *sb.* snare; **takyng**, W2.

takke, *sb.* button, clasp, Prompt. Cf. **tache**[2].

takken, *v.* to fasten, to sew together, Prompt. Cf. **tachen**.

takning, *sb.* signification, S2; see **toknynge**.

tal, *adj.* seemly, Prompt.

talde, *pt. s.* told; see **tellen**.

tale, *sb.* account, reckoning, tale, narrative, talk, the gospel narrative, S, S2, C2, PP. *Comb.*: **tale-tellour**, tale-bearer, PP; **talewys**, slanderous, PP; **tal-wis**, PP.—AS. *talu*, 'numerus, narratio'; cf. OHG. *zala* 'numerus' (Tatian).

talen, *v.* to speak, C, S2.—AS. *talian*, to reckon (Grein).

talent, *sb.* desire, inclination, appetite, B, Prompt., C3, HD.—OF. *talent*, desire (BH); Late Lat. *talentum* (Ducange).

talvace, *sb.* a kind of buckler or shield, HD; **talvas**, HD.—OF. *talevas, talvas* (Ducange), also *tallevas* (Cotg.); cf. Low Lat. *talavacius* (Ducange).

talyage, *sb.* a taxing, Prompt. (s.v. *taske*).

tallage, flavour, S3; **talage**, HD.—Low Lat. *talliagium*, a taxing, testing public weights and measures (Ducange).

tan, *pp.* taken, S2; see **taken**[1].

tancrit, *adj.* transcribed; **tancrete**, S3.—OF. *tancrit*; Lat. *transcriptum* (Ducange).

tang, *sb.* sea-weed, SkD, JD. *Comb.*: **tang-fish**, the seal, JD.—Icel. *þang*.

tangle, *sb.* sea-weed, HD, JD.—Icel. *þöngull*.

tangle, *v.* to twist confusedly; **tangell**, Palsg.; **tangild**, *pp.*, ensnared, H (p. 149).

tapecer, *sb.* a maker of tapestry, Prompt.; **tapicer**, C; **tapesere**, Prompt.—OF. *tapissier*, from *tapis*, *tapiz*; Late Gr. ταπίτιον, for ταπήτιον. Cf. **tapet**.

tapecerye, *sb.* tapestry, HD.—OF. *tapisserie*.

tapet, *sb.* cloth, hangings, tapestry, Prompt., ND; **tappet**, HD; **tapite**, S3; **tapyt**, Voc.; **tapett**, Cath.; **tapetis**, *pl.* (= Lat. *tapetes*), W2; **tapites**, HD; **tapets**, S3. *Der.*: **tapiter**, a maker of tapestry, HD.—Lat. *tapete*, from Gr. ταπήτιον Cf. **tapecer**.

tapinage, *sb.* secret sculking, HD.—OF. *tapinage* (Ducange); cf. *tapir*, to hide (Cotg.).

tapissynge, *sb.* hangings, H.

tappe, *sb.* a tap, *clipsidra*, Prompt.; **teppe**, SD. *Comb.*: **tap-tre**, *clipsidra*, HD, Cath.

tappestere, *sb.* a tapster (a woman who tapped or drew ale or other liquor for sale in an inn), C; **tapstare**, *propinaria*. Prompt.

tarette, *sb.* ship of heavy burden, S2.—Low Lat. *tareta*, also *tarida* (Ducange); cf. OF. *taride*.

targe[1], *sb.* a charter, Prompt.

targe[2], *sb.* a small shield, C, S2, Voc.—OF. *targe* (BH); cf. *targue* (Cotg.).

target, *sb.* a small targe, Prompt.; **targett**, Voc.; **tergate**, S3; **targattes**, *pl.*, SkD.—Low Lat. *targeta*; cf. It. *targhetta* (Florio).

tarien, *v.* to delay, to hinder, C2; to tarry, W2, S3; see **terien**[2].

tarne[1], *sb.* a girl, HD.—Icel. *þerna*; cf. OHG. *thiarna* (Otfrid); see Kluge (s.v. *dirne*). See **þerne**.

tarne[2], *sb.* a tarn; see **terne**.

tas, *sb.* heap, C; **taas**, C; **tasse**, Prompt., HD.—OF. *tas*, stack, heap (BH); cf. Du. *tas*, Low Lat. *tassis* (Voc.), *tassus* (Ducange).

taske, *sb.* a taxing, Prompt.; a task, HD, Palsg.—Cf. Late Lat. *tasca* for *taxa*, a tax. See **taxen**.

tasker, *sb.* a thrasher, Voc., HD; **taskar**, B; **taskur**, Bardsley.

tassel, *sb.* male hawk; see **tercel**.

tast, *sb.* taste, S3, PP; **taast**, Prompt.

tasten, *v.* to feel, touch, kiss, taste, C3, PP; **taasten**, Prompt.; **tast**, *pt. s.*, probed, HD.—OF. *taster*, to feel by touch, to taste (F. *tâter*); Late Lat. *taxitare*, frequent. of Lat. *taxare*, to handle.

tatter, a shred, loose-hanging rag, a ragged person, ND, SkD; **totters**, *pl.*, rags, Sh. *Der.*: **tatered**, *adj.*, jagged, S3.—Icel. *tötturr* (for *tölturr*), *töturr*.

tauny, *adj.* tawny, P; **tanny**, Prompt.—AF. *taune*, OF. *tanne*, tawny, tanned, pp. of *taner*, to tan (BH).

tavel, *sb.* the game of 'tables', backgammon, SD. *Comb.*: **tævel-bred**, backgammon-board, SD.—AS. *tæfel*, 'alea' (Voc.); Lat. *tabula*. See **table**.

tavelen, *v.* to play at 'tables', S.

taverne, *sb.* an inn, Prompt., Voc.—AF. *taverne*; Lat. *taberna*.

taverner, *sb.* inn-keeper, C2, HD, P, Voc.; **tavernere**, Prompt.—AF. *taverner*; Late Lat. *tabernarium*.

tawen, *v.* to prepare leather, SkD; **tewen**, Prompt.; **taw**, to dress hemp, HD; **tawed**, *pp.*, hardened with labour, S3; **i-tauwed**, S.—AS. *tawian*, to prepare, dress leather, to scourge.

tawer, *sb.* a tanner, SD, SkD.

tawnen, *v.* to show, S; **taunede**, *pt. s.*, SD.—Cf. ODu. *toonen* and MHG. *zounen* for *zougenen*, from OHG. *zougjan* for *azougjan* (see Lexer); cf. AS. *æt-ýwan*. See **awnen**.

taxen, *v.* to tax, SkD, PP.—AF. *taxer*; Lat. *taxare*.

taxoure, *sb.* a taxer, P.

tayl, *sb.* tail, a retinue, train of followers, S2, C2, PP; **taile**, S2, PP; **tayle**, Cath.—AS. *tægl*: Goth. *tagl*, hair.

tayt, *adj.* glad, cheerful, brisk, S3; **teyte**, *pl.*, HD.—Icel. *teitr*.

te-, *prefix*; same as **to-** (2).

teald, *pp.* of **tellen**.

teares, *pl.* tears, S; see **tere**.

techen, *v.* to teach, S, C2, S2; **teachen**, S; **tache**, S; **tahte**, *pt. s.*, S; **taihte**, S; **tagte**, S; **tahtes**, 2 *pt. s.*, S; **tehten**, *pl.*, S; **taucht**, *pp.*, S3; **y-ta3t**, S2; **y-taught**, C2.—AS. *tǽcan*, pt. *tǽhte*, pp. *tǽht*.

teches, *sb. pl.* marks, signs, S2; see **tache**[1].

teer, *sb.* tear, C2; see **tere**.

teise, *sb.* a fathom, HD.—AF. *teise* (OF. *toise*); Late Lat. *tensa*. Cf. **tese**.

tei3en, *v.* to tie, bind, S2; see **ti3en**.

teld, *sb.* a covering, tent, SkD (s.v. *tilt*); **telde**, S2, HD; **telte**, Prompt.; **tilde**, PP (p. 779).—AS. (*ge*)*teld*, a tent; cf. Icel. *tjald*.

telden, *v.* to pitch a tent, to erect a building, to dwell, PP; **tilden**, S3; **tilde**, *pt. s.*, PP; **tulde**, PP; **telt**, HD; **teldit**, *pp.*, PP; **tyld**, S3.

tele, *sb.* sorcery, magic, HD.

telen, *v.* to reprove, to scoff at, S; **tælen**, S.—ONorth. *telan* (Luke 7. 30), AS. *tǽlan* to blame, from *tálu*, 'calumnia' (Grein).

telie, *v.* to till, cultivate, PP; see **tilien**.

telinge, *sb.* husbandry, culture, study, practice of magic; **telynge**, HD; **tulyinge**, PP; **teolunges** *pl.*, S.—AS. *teolung*, *tilung*, tilling, culture, study.

tellen, *v.* to tell, count, esteem, S, S2; **telst**, 2 *pr. s.*, S; **telð**, *pr. s.*, S, S2; **tellus**, *pl.*, S2;

teme

talde, *pt. s.*, S; tolde, S2, PP; telld, S2; tolden, *pl.*, S; talden to, accounted, S; telden, W; teald, *pp.*, S; talde, S2; ytold, C2, S2; i-told, S; told, S2.—AS. *tellan*, pt. *tealde*, pp. *ge-teald*. See tale.

teme[1], *sb.* theme, subject, text, PP; teeme, S2, PP.—OF. *theme*; Lat. *thema*; Gr. θέμα.

teme[2], *v.* to tame, H; temyd, *pp.* H.—AS. *temian* (Voc.): Goth. (*ga*)*tamjan*.

temen[1], *v.* to bring forward as witness, S.—AS. *téman*, *týman* (Schmid), from *téam*, a summoning for warranty (Schmid).

temen[2], *v.* to make empty, to pour out, HD, Prompt., Cath., H; tume, JD; teym, JD.—Icel. *tœma*, to empty; from *tómr*, empty. See tome[1].

temp, *v.* to tempt, H; tent, to probe, Sh.; temped, *pp.*, HD.—OF. *tempter* (F. *tenter*); Lat. *tentare*.

temporal, *adj.* lasting but for a short time, S2.—OF. *temporel*; Lat. *temporalem* (Vulg.).

temporalite, *sb.* temporal power, PP; temperaltes, temporalities, PP.—AF. *temporalitee*.

tempre[1], *v.* to temper, moderate, restrain, PP, C2; temperid, *pp.*, directed, W2; tempred, fitted, attuned, S2, PP.—OF. *temprer* (F. *tremper*); Lat. *temperare*.

tempre[1], *adj.* tempered, modified, temperate, H.—OF. *tempre*.

ten, *v.* to draw, pull, train, also to go, mount, *reflex.* to conduct oneself, S; teon, S; tuen, HD; te, HD; teð, *pr. s.*, S; tuhen, *pt. pl.*, S; i-toȝen, *pp.*, S; i-tohen, S. *Comb.*: fulitohe, badly trained, S.—AS. *téon*, pt. *téah* (pl. *tugon*), pp. *togen*: Goth. *tiuhan*; cf. Lat. *ducere*; see Brugmann, § 65.

tend, *adj. ord.* tenth, S2, B; tende, HD.

tende[1], *sb.* a tenth, HD; teind, tithe, S3; tendis, *pl.*, H.—Icel. *tíund*, a tenth.

tende[2], *v.* to tithe, Cath.

tenden, *v.* to kindle, set fire to, S2, W; teenden, W; tind, HD; tendeden, *pt. pl.*, PP; tenden, PP; tendyn, PP; tende, S2; y-tend, *pp.*, S2.—AS. *tendan* (in *on-tendan*): Goth. *tandjan*, causal of **tindan*, to burn.

tene, *sb.* grief, vexation, injury, S, S2, S3, PP, B; teene, PP; teone, S, S2, PP; teyne, B; tyene, S2.—AS. *téona*.

tenen, *v.* to vex, trouble, injure, PP; teene, PP; teonen, PP.—AS. *týnan*.

tennes, *sb.* tennis, S3; see tenyse.

tenserie, *sb.* an extraordinary impost, robbery, S (2. 42).—OF. *tenserie*; Late Lat. *tensaria*.

tente[1], *sb.* a tent, C2, PP.—OF. *tente* (Bartsch); Late Lat. *tenta*, cloth stretched.

teste

tente[2], *sb.* intention, purpose, PP; tent, attention, care, heed, S2, JD, W, W2, H.—OF. *atente* (BH).

tentyf, *adj.* attentive, CM; tentifly, *adv.*, attentively, C2.—OF. *attentif*.

tenyse, *sb.* tennis, Palsg.; teneys, *tenisia*, Prompt.; tennes, S3, SkD.

teolung, *sb.* magical practice, S; see telinge.

teon, *v.* to draw, S; see ten.

teone, *sb.* grief, S; see tene.

terce, *adj.* a third, SkD; tierce, the third hour (canonical), SkD; tyerse, SkD.—AF. *terce*, *tierce*, OF. *terc*, *tiers*, *tierce*; Lat. *tertia*.

tercel, *sb.* the male of any kind of hawk, CM, Prompt., Sh.; tercelle, Voc.; terselle, Cath.; tassel, Sh.; tassell, Cotg.—AF. *tercel*, from OF. *terce*.

tercelet, *sb.* a small hawk, C2.—AF. *tercelet*, OF. *tiercelet* (Cotg.).

tere, *sb.* tear, S, C2; teer, C2; teares, *pl.*, S.—AS. *téar*, also *teagor*, OHG. *zahar* (Tatian); cf. Gr. δάκρυ; see Douse, p. 94.

teren[1], *v.* to tear, S.—AS. *teran*, cf. Goth. (*ga*)*tairan*.

teren[2], *v.* to tar, S. See terre[1].

tergate, *sb.* a small shield, S3; see target.

terien[1], *v.* to vex, irritate, to make weary, to delay, hinder, *irritare*, *fatigare*; teryyn, Prompt.; terwin, Prompt.; terre, W, W2; tarien, C2; y-taryed, *pp.*, S2.—AS. *tergan*, to vex.

terien[2], *v.* to tarry, to delay; teryyn, Prompt.; taryen, CM; tarien, W2, S3.—The same word as above; for change of sense cf. AS. *dreccan*, to vex, with the equivalent ME. See drecchen, to tarry.

terme, *sb.* term, period, S, C2; termes, *pl.*, expressions, examples, PP, C2; limits, ends, W, W2.—AF. *terme*; Lat. *terminum*.

terminen, *v.* to determine, limit, W; itermynet, *pp.*, S2; y-termyned, PP.—AF. *terminer*, to determine.

terne, *sb.* a tarn, small lake, S2; tarne, Manip.—Icel. *tjörn* (*tjarn-*).

terre[1], *sb.* tar, Prompt.; tarre, PP; teer, HD; ter, B.—AS. *teoru* (Voc.).

terre[2], *v.* to provoke, W, W2; see terien[1].

terryng, *sb.* a provoking, W2.

Teruagant, *sb.* one of the seven gods of Hengest, S; Termagant, a supposed god of the Saracens, ND; one of the characters in the old moralities, ND, Sh., TG; Trivigant, ND.—OF. *Tervagant*, also *Tervagan*, one of the three gods of the Saracens (Roland); cf. It. *Trivigante* (Ariosto).

teste, *sb.* a pot in which metals are tried, HD, SkD, C3; teest, HD. *Phr.*: to bring to the test, lit. to bring to the refiner's vessel, Sh.—OF. *teste*, a refiner's vessel; Lat.

testa, a vessel used in alchemy, orig. a piece of baked earthenware, also shell of fish, skull, head. Cf. OF. *test* (F. *têt*), a test in chemistry, orig. a potsherd, see Bartsch.

testere, *sb.* a head-piece, helmet, tester for a bed, SkD, HD; **teester**, Prompt.; **tester**, C; **testar**, Palsg.—OF. *testiere*, head-piece (Cotg.).

testif, *adj.* headstrong, testy, CM; **testie**, S3.—OF. *testif* (Palsg.).

te-tealte, *adj.* quite unstable, in jeopardy, S2. (**to-**².)

teð, *pr. s.*; **teð up**, mounts, S; see **ten**.

tewelle, *sb.* the pipe of a chimney, HD; **tuel**, a pipe, HD.—OF. *tuel, tuyel* (F. *tuyau*): Sp. *tudel*; of Teutonic origin; see Kluge (s.v. *düte*), and Weigand (s.v. *zotte*).

texte, *sb.* text, scripture, SkD; **text**, Cath., C2; **tixte**, PP, S2; **tixt**, PP; **tyxte**, PP; **tyxt**, PP.—OF. *texte*; Lat. *textum*.

textuel, *adj.* literal, C3.

teye, *sb.* a coffer, Prompt.—OF. *teie* (*toie*); Lat. *thēca*; cf. F. *taie*.

teyne, *sb.* a thin plate of metal, C3.

teyrre, of them, S; see **þei**.

teyse, *v.* to poise for shooting, HD; **tasit**, *pt. s.*, B; **taisand**, *pr. p.*, HD.—OF. *toiser*, to measure (Cotg.). See **teise**.

teyte, *adj. pl.* cheerful, HD; see **tayt**.

ti, *pron. poss.* thy, S; see **þou**.

tid¹, *sb.* time, season, hour, *hora canonica*, S, S2, S3; **tide**, S2; **tyde**, S2, C3, PP. *Comb.*: **tideful**, seasonable (= Lat. *opportunus*), H; **tydfulnes**, needfulness, H.—AS. *tíd*, time, hour; cf. Icel. *tíð*, time, 'hora canonica'.

tid², *adv.* quickly, PP; **tyd**, PP. See **tit**.

tiden, *v.* to happen, S; **tyden**, S2, C3; **tid**, *pr. s.*, PP; **tit**, PP; **tydde**, *pt. s.*, PP; **tidde**, S2.—AS. *tídan*.

tidi, *adj.* seasonable, honest, respectable, S; **tidy**, PP; **tydy**, PP, Prompt.

tidif, *sb.* the name of some very small bird, C2; **tydy**, a sort of singing bird, ND.

tiding, *sb.* an event, tidings, S; **tyding**, C2, C3; **tidinge**, *pl.*, S2; **tydinge**, S; **tydinges**, C2. See **tiþing**.

tiffen, *v.* to trick out, trim, adorn, SkD.—OF. *tiffer*, to trim, adorn.

tiffung, *sb.* adornment, finery, S.

til, *prep.* and *conj.* to, till, S, PP, S2, C3; **tyl**, S, PP; **till**, S, S3.—Icel. *til*.

tilden, *v.* to set a trap, S; **tildeþ**, *2 pr. pl.*, set up, S3; see **telden**.

tilien, *v.* to till, cultivate, earn, gain, PP; **tilen**, S, PP; **tylie**, PP; **tulien**, PP; **telie**, PP; **tolie**, S; **tylle**, S2.—AS. *tilian*, to aim at, to till land; cf. OHG. *zilón*, to attempt (Tatian).

tilier, *sb.* tiller, husbandman, W.

tillen, *v.* to draw, entice, S, H, PP; see **tollen**².

tilðe, *sb.* labour, toil, tilth, S; **tulthe**, PP; **telðe**, PP.—AS. *tilð*. See **tilien**.

timen, *v.* to prosper, S.—Icel. *tíma* (reflex.), to happen.

tin, *pron. poss.* thy, thine, S; see **þou**.

tinsel, *sb.* a stuff made partly of silk and partly of silver, S3, TG, SkD.—OF. *estincelle*, a spark, a flash (BH).

tintreȝe, *sb.* torment; **tintreow**, S; **tintreohe**, S; **tintreohen**, *pl.*, S.—AS. *tintreg* (Grein).

tirannye, *sb.* tyranny, C2, C3; **tirandye**, HD.

tiraunt, *sb.* tyrant, C2, PP; **tyraunt**, PP, W; **tirant**, S2; **tyrauns**, *pl.*, oppressors, PP.—AF. and OF. *tirant, tiranz*; Lat. *tyrannus*; see Constans, Supplement, p. 57, and BH, § 72.

tirauntrie, *sb.* tyranny, W2; **tyrauntrye**, HD.

Tis-dæi, *sb.* Tuesday, S; **Tisdei**, S.—AS. *Tiwes-dæg*, the day of the Teutonic god Tiw; cf. OHG. *Zio*, Icel. *Týr*; see Grimm, *Teut. M.*, cap. ix, and Kluge (s.v. *dienstag*).

tit, *adv.* quickly, PP; **tyt**, S2; **tyte**, PP, S2, H; **tite**, PP, S2, H; **tiȝt**, S2; **tiȝtly**, S2; **titere**, *comp.*, H; **titter**, S2.—Icel. *títt*, neut. of *tíðr*. See **tid**².

tiðende, *sb. pl.* tidings, news, customs, S; **tiðenden**, S; **tiðand**, S2; **tiðandes**, S2.—Icel. *tíðindi*, pl., tidings, news; from *tíða*, to happen; cf. *tíðska*, a custom, *tíðr*, customary, frequent.

tiðing, *sb.* tidings, news, S, S2; **tyðyng**, S2; **tiðinge**, *pl.*, S; **tiðinges**, S2.—Cf. **tiding**.

titill, *sb.* an epistle, WA.

titmose, *sb.* titmouse, S3, Manip.; **tyte-mose**, Prompt.; **tytmase**, Voc.—AS. *máse*, a word forming the second element of the names of many kinds of small birds, see SkD.

titte¹, *sb.* a quick pull, S2.

titte², *v.* to pull tightly, HD; **tytted**, HD.

tixt, *sb.* text, PP; see **texte**.

tiȝen, *v.* to tie, PP, S2; **teiȝen**, S2; **tey**, B; **te**, B; **teien**, *pr. pl.*, SkD; **teyd**, *pp.*, C2; **y-teyd**, C.—AS. *tígan* (**tégan*).

tiȝt, *adv.* quickly, S2; see **tit**.

to-¹, *prefix*; the preposition *to* in composition.

to-², *prefix*, in twain, asunder, to pieces.—AS. *tó-*; cf. OHG. *zi-* (Tatian), Lat. *dis-*.

to¹, *prep.* to, at, in, upon, for, with reference to, by, against, after, as, until, PP, S, S2; **te**, S, S2. *Comb.*, *as though* **t'**: **tabide**, to abide, S; **tacord**, C3; **taffraye**, C2; **tallege**, C; **talyghte**, C2; **tamenden**, S2, C2; **tanoyen**, S2; **tapese**, S3; **tariue**, S;

tarraye, C2; tassaile, C2; tassaye, C2; taswage, S3; tembrace, C2; tencombre, S3; tendure, S3; tenforme, S3; tenrage, S3; tespye, C2; texpounden, C2.

to², *adv.* too, S, PP; te, S.

to³, *num.* two, S, S2; see tuo.

to-belimpen, *v.* to belong to, S. (to-¹.)

to-bellen, *v.* to swell extremely; tobolle, *pp.*, PP. (to-².)

to-beren, *v.* to part; tobar, *pt. s.*, S. (to-².)

to-beten, *v.* to beat in pieces, C3. (to-².)

to-breden, *v.* to spread out; tobreddest, *2 pt. s.*, S2. (to-².)

to-breiden, *v.* to tear asunder, *distorquere*; tobreidynge, *pr. p.*, W; debreidynge, W; tobraidide, *pt. s.*, W. (to-².)

to-breken, *v.* to break in pieces, S, C3, W; to-brac, *pt. s.*, PP; to-brak, G; to-brake, *pt. s. subj.*, S; to-broken, *pp.*, PP, G; to-broke, PP, S2, W. (to-².)

to-bresten, *v.* to burst asunder, C; to-bersteð, *pr. s.*, S: to-barst, *pt. s.*, S2, G; to-brast, W; to-brosten, *pp.*, C. (to-².)

to-brisen, *v.* to break to pieces; tobrisid, *pp.*, W. (to-².)

to-cleue, *v.* to cleave asunder, to fall to pieces, PP; to-cleef, *pt. s.*, PP; to-clief, PP. (to-².)

to-comen, *v.* to come together; to-comen, *pt. pl.*, PP. (to-¹.)

to-comyng, *adj.* future, W2. (to-¹.)

to-cweme, *adv.* agreeably, S. (to-¹.)

to-cyme, *sb.* advent, S. (to-¹.)

tod¹, *sb.* a fox, JD, ND, HD, SkD; toddis, *pl.*, S3. *Comb.*: todman, Bardsley.—The word is common in Mid Yorkshire and Cumberland, see EDS (Ser. C).

tod², *sb.* a bush, generally of ivy, HD; todde, SkD.

to-dasht, *pt. s.* dashed (herself) in pieces, S3. (to-².)

to-delen, *v.* to divide, S, S2; to-dælen, S; to-dealen, S. (to-².)

to-drawen, *v.* to draw asunder, S2, W; to-draȝen, S; to-drowe, *pt. pl.*, PP; to-droȝe, S; to-drawun, *pp.*, W; to-drahen, S. (to-².)

to-dreuen, *v.* to trouble; to-dreued, *pp.*, S2, (to-².)

to-driuen, *v.* to drive asunder; to-dryue, PP; to-drif, *imp. s.*, S. (to-².)

to-dunet, *pp.* struck with a sounding blow, S. (to-².)

to-fallen, *v.* to fall in pieces, SD. (to-².)

to-flight, *sb.* refuge, S2. (to-¹.)

to-foren, *prep.* and *adv.* before, SD; toforn, PP, S3; tofore, S, PP, S2; touore, S, S2; tofor, S, PP, S2, W. (to-¹.)

to-forrow, *adv.* previously, S3. (to-¹.)

toft, *sb.* hillock, eminence, a slightly elevated and exposed site, PP, S2; *campus*, Prompt.—Cf. OSwed. *tomt*, a cleared space (Dan. *tomt*, a toft); from Icel. *tómr*, empty. See tome¹.

to-gadere, *adv.* together, S, S2; tegædere S; togedere, S, PP; togedre, PP; togeddre, S; togidere, PP; togider, S, C2; togederes, PP, S; togideres, PP; togidres, PP, C3; togederis, PP; togeders, PP; to-gedders, S2. (to-¹.)

to-gan, *v.* to go asunder, SD; togað, *pr. pl.*, S. (to-².)

to-genes, *prep.* towards, S; togeines, S; toȝeines, S; toȝenes, S. (to-¹.)

toggen, *v.* to draw, allure, sport, S, Prompt.

to-grinden, *v.* to grind in pieces; togrynt, *pr. s.*, PP. (to-².)

to-hewen, *v.* to hew in pieces, S, S2, C3. (to-².)

to-hope, *sb.* hope, S. (to-¹.)

to-hurren, *v.* to hurry apart, S. (to-².)

tokker, *sb.* fuller, one who thickens cloth, S2, PP; towker, PP; toucher, PP; tucker, HD; touker, Bardsley; tuker, Bardsley. See tuken.

tokne, *sb.* token, PP; tocne, S; tacne, S; taken, PP, S2; takun, W; takens, *pl.*, S2.—AS. *tácn*: Goth. *taikns*; cf. OHG. *zeichan* (Tatian).

toknynge, *sb.* signification, PP; tocninge, S; toknyng, PP; takning, S2; takeninge, S2; tokening, C3.—AS. *tácnung.*

tolie, *v.* to till, S; see tilien.

to-liggen, *v.* to pertain to; toliỗ, *pr. s.*, S. (to-¹.)

tolke, *sb.* a man, S2; see tulke.

tolle, *sb.* toll, custom, Voc.; tol, PP, Prompt. *Comb.*: tol-bothe, toll-booth (= Lat. *telonium*), S2, W, Voc.—AS. *toll*: OFris. *tolen*, *tolne*; Lat. *telonium* (Vulg.); Gr. τελώνιον. Note that the *n* of the stem appears in AS. *tolnere*, 'teloniarius', Voc.; see Weigand (s.v. *zoll*).

tollen¹, *v.* to take toll, C. *Der.*: tollere, tax-gatherer, usurer, S2, PP; toller, Voc.

tollen², *v.* to draw, allure, entice, Prompt., PP, ND, SkD; tole, ND; tullen, CM, SD; tillen, S, H, PP.—AS. *tyllan* (in *for-tyllan*).

to-loggen, *v.* to drag hither and thither, S2, PP; to-lugged, *pp.*, PP.

tolter, *adv.* unsteadily, totteringly, S3, SkD (s.v. *totter*).

to-luken, *v.* to rend asunder, S; tolokon, *pp.*, S. (to-².)

toly, *sb.* scarlet colour, WA; tuly, Prompt., HD; tuely, SkD (s.v. *trap*, 2).—Heb. *tōlā'*, crimson (Isaiah 1. 18), properly a worm.

tombestere, *sb.* female dancer, C3; see tumbestere.

tome[1], *adj.* empty, void, unoccupied, H, HD; **toom**, Prompt.; **tume**, JD.—Icel. *tómr*, vacant, empty. Cf. **toft.**

tome[2], *sb.* leisure, S2, PP, H (p. 169); **toym**, B; **tume**, B; Icel. *tóm*, leisure. See **tome**[1].

to-morwen, *adv.* to-morrow, S; **tomorwe**, PP; **tomoreȝe**, S; **tomorn**, C. (**to-**[1].)

to-name, *sb.* cognomen, PP; **towname**, PP. (**to-**[1].)

tonge[1], *sb.* tongue, S2, C2, C3, PP; **tunge**, S, C, PP, W2; **tounge**, PP; **tong**, S3; **tung**, S2. *Der.*: **tongede**, tongued, talkative, PP.—AS. *tunge.*

tonge[2], *sb.* pair of tongs, *forceps*, S, S2, Prompt.; **tange**, Voc.—AS. *tange* (Voc.).

tonne, *sb.* tun, PP, S3, C2, G; **tunne**, S, PP. *Comb.*: **tonne-greet**, as large round as a tun, C.—AS. *tunne.*

too, *sb.* toe, C; **taa**, S2, HD; **toon**, *pl.*, C; **ton**, C; **tas**, S2; **taes**, S2.—AS. *tá* (pl. *tán*).

tool, *sb.* tool, weapon, C, Prompt.; **toles**, *pl.*, PP; **tooles**, PP.—AS. *tól.*

toom, *adj.* empty; see **tome**[1].

toord, *sb. stercus*, W2, Prompt.

topase, *sb.* topaz, Cotg.; **topace**, S3; **tupace**, SkD; **topacius**, W (Apoc. 21. 20); **thopas**, C2 (p. 151).—OF. *topase*; Lat. *topazum* (acc.); Gr. τόπαζος.

toppe, *sb.* tuft of hair, P, S; **top**, top of the head, Prompt.

to-quassen, *v.* to shake asunder, PP; **to-quashte**, *pt. s.*, PP. (**to-**[2].)

to-quaȝte, *pt. s.* quaked, PP. (**to-**[2].)

to-racen, *v.* to scrape to pieces, C2. (**to-**[2].)

to-renden, *v.* to rend in pieces, PP; **torente**, *pt. s.*, C2, W; **to-rent**, *pp.*, S, C2, W. (**to-**[2].)

toret[1], *sb.* ring on a dog's collar, through which the leash was passed, CM; **torettz**, *pl.*, C; **turrets**, DG.—OF. *touret*, the chain which is at the end of the check of a bit, also the little ring whereby a hawk's lune is fastened to the jesses (Cotg.).

toret[2], *sb.* turret, G, C, Prompt.; **touret**, SkD.—OF. *tourette* (Cotg.).

to-reuen, *v.* to completely take away, PP. (**to-**[2].)

torf, *sb.* turf, S2; **turf**, Voc.; **turues**, *pl.*, S2.—AS. *turf* (Voc.).

torfare, *sb.* hardship, misery, peril, WA.—Icel. *torfœra.*

to-rightes, *adv.* to rights, aright, G. (**to-**[1].)

to-riven, *v.* to rend in twain; **to-rof** (*intrans.*), *pt. s.*, was riven in twain, S2.

torment, *sb.* a tempest, torment, suffering, SkD, C3, Prompt.; **tourment**, SkD.—AF. *torment*, a tempest, *turment* (Roland), OF. *torment, tourment*, a tempest, torture (Bartsch), *tormente*, a tempest (Cotg.).

tormenten, *v.* to torment, SkD.—OF. *tormenter.*

tormentour, *sb.* executioner, C3, WW; **tormentoures**, *pl.*, C3.—AF. *tormenter*, executioner.

tormentynge, *sb.* torture, C2.

tormentyse, *sb.* torture, C2.

torne, *sb.* a turn, trick, wile, G.

tornen, *v.* to turn, PP; see **tournen**.

to-rof, *pt. s.* rent in twain; see **toriven.**

tortuous, *adj.* oblique (a term used in astrology), C3.—Lat. *tortuosus*, crooked.

to-samen, *adv.* together, S. (**to-**[1].)

to-schaken, *v.* to shake asunder, S. (**to-**[2].)

to-scheden, *v.* to part asunder; **tosched**, *pp.*, S2. (**to-**[2].)

to-schellen, *v.* to shell, peel; **toshullen**, *pp.*, PP. (**to-**[2].)

to-schreden, *v.* to cut to pieces, C. (**to-**[2].)

to-spreden, *v.* to scatter; **to-sprad**, *pp.*, S2. (**to-**[2].)

to-swellen, *v.* to swell greatly; **toswolle**, *pp.*, S, PP. (**to-**[2].)

to-swinken, *v.* to labour greatly, C3. (**to-**[2].)

to-tasen, *v.* to pull to pieces; **to-tose**, S. (**to-**[2].)

toten, *v.* to peep, look about, PP, S3; **tutand**, *pr. p.*, projecting, pushing out, S3; **totede**, *pt. s.*, S3; **y-toted**, *pp.*, S3. *Comb.*: **totehylle**, *specula*, Prompt.—AS. *tótian*; see SkD (s.v. *tout*).

to-teren, *v.* to tear to pieces, C3; **toteoren**, S; **toteore**, S; **totorne**, *pp.*, PP; **totorn**, S; **totore**, C3. (**to-**[2].)

to-turn, *sb.* refuge, SD. (**to-**[1].)

to-twicchen, *v.* to pull apart; **totwichet**, *pr. pl.*, S. (**to-**[2].)

toun, *sb.* an enclosure, farm-stead, town, S2, C, W; **toune**, PP; **tun**, S, S2; **toune**, *dat.*, S2, C2. *Comb.*: **toune-men**, men of the town, not rustics, PP; **tun-scipe**, the people of the farm-stead, S. *Der.*: **townish**, belonging to the town, S3.—AS. *tún*, enclosure, farm, town; cf. OHG. *zún*, hedge (Tatian).

tour, *sb.* tower, S, S2, C2, PP, W2; **tur**, S; **torres**, *pl.*, S2.—OF. *tur, tor, tour*: Lat. *turrem.*

tournen, *v.* to turn, PP; **turnen**, S, S2, PP; **tornen**, S2, PP; **teornen**, S2; **tirnen**, S; **y-tornd**, *pp.*, S2; **i-turnd**, S, S2.—AF. *turner*; Lat. *tornare*, from *tornus*, a lathe.

tourneyment, *sb.* tournament, C2.—OF. *tornoiement.*

towaille, *sb.* towel, C2; **towayle**, Prompt., Voc.; **twaly**, Prompt.; **towelle**, Voc.; **towylle**, Voc.—AF. *towaille* (*tuaille*), OF. *touaile* (Bartsch); Low Lat. *toacula*; of Teutonic origin, cf. OHG. *duáhila*, washing-cloth;

from *duahan*, also *thuahan*, to wash (Tatian). See SkD, also Kluge (s.v. *zwehle*).

to-walten, *v.* to roll with violence; *pt. pl.*, overflowed, S2. (**to-**².)

to-ward, *prep.* towards, against, S, PP; **touward**, S; **towart**, S. (**to-**¹.)

to-warde, *adj.* present, as a guard or protection, PP. (**to-**¹.)

to-wawe, *v.* to move about near, S2. (**to-**¹.)

towker, *sb.* a fuller; see **tokker**.

to-wringen, *v.* to distort; **towrong**, *pt. s.*, S. (**to-**².)

to-wrye, *v.* to cause to go on one side, S3 (4. 164) (**to-**².)

toȝeines, *prep.* towards, S; see **togenes**.

to-ȝere, *adv.* this year, Cath. (**to-**¹.)

to-ȝesceoden, *v.* to separate, S. (**to-**².)

trace, *sb.* track of a way over a field, **trace**, Prompt., C, SkD; **tras**, PP; **trass**, S2.

tracen, *v.* to trace, to draw a picture, to trace one's way, to conduct oneself, Prompt., CM, S3; **trasen**, S3.—OF. *tracer* (*trasser*); Late Lat. *tractiare, from Lat. *tract-*, base of pp. of *trahere*; see BH, § 131.

trade, *sb.* a trodden path, S3, TG, SkD, HD. See **treden**.

tradicion, *sb.* surrender, S3.—Lat. *traditionem*. Cf. **tresoun**.

traitorye, *sb.* treachery, C3, CM.

traitour, *sb.* traitor, S; **traytour**, S; **treitur**, S.—AF. *traitur*; Lat. *traditorem*.

tram, *sb.* engine, machine, WA; **trammys**, *pl.*, B.

trappe, *sb.* the trappings of a horse, SkD; **trappys**, *pl.*, SkD.

trapped, *adj.* adorned with trappings, C, Prompt.

trappings, *sb. pl.* ornaments, Sh.

trappure, *sb.* trappings of a horse, Prompt.; **trappures**, *pl.*, C.

trauail, *sb.* work, labour, toil, trouble, S2, PP; **trauaille**, C2; **trawayle**, S2; **trauell**, S2; **trauel**, W, W2, H (Ps. 108. 10).—AF. *travail*, *travaille*; Late Lat. *trabaculum; from Lat. *trabem*, a beam; cf. It. *traváglio*, a frame for confining unruly horses. See **trave**.

trauaille, *v.* to work, toil, travel, trouble, vex, torment, PP; **traueilen**, W, S2; **trauele**, W, W2.—AF. *travai(l)ler*, to work, to vex. See **travail**.

trauailous, *adj.* laborious, W2.

trave, *sb.* a frame in which farriers confine unruly horses, CM. See **travail**.

trawed, *pt. pl.* trowed, expected, S2; see **trowen**.

tray, *sb.* vexation; see **treȝe**.

trays, *sb. pl.* traces, horse-harness, C; **trayce**, Prompt.; **trayse**, Cath.—OF. *trays*, horse-harness (Palsg.) for *traits*, pl., of *traict* a trace for horses (Cotg.); Lat. *tractum*, pp. of *trahere*.

trayste, *v.* to trust, S2; **traste**, PP, S2.— Icel. *treysta*, from *traust*. See **trist**.

traystly, *adv.* confidently, H.

traystnes, *sb.* confidence, H.

traystynge, *sb.* confidence, H.

traytyse, *sb.* treaty, truce, S3; see **tretis**³.

tre, *sb.* tree, wood, *lignum*. Prompt., S2, PP, W, W2; **treo**, S, PP; **treowe**, *dat.*, S; **treuwe**, *pl.*, S; **tren**, S2; **treen**, S3; **treon**, S; **trewes**, S; **trowes**, PP. *Comb.*: **tre tymus** (*lignum thyinum*), W.—AS. *tréow* (*tréo*), dat. *tréowe*, pl. *tréowu* (*tréo*), see Sievers, 250; cf. Goth. *triu*.

treatise, *sb.* a passage (lit. a treatise), S3; see **tretis**².

treatyce, *sb.* treaty, truce, S3; see **tretis**³.

trechery, *sb.* treachery, trickery, S; see **tricherie**.

trechoure, *sb.* a cheat, HD.—OF. *trichëor* (Bartsch); Late Lat. *tricatorem*.

trechurly, *adv.* treacherously, S3.

tred, *sb.* a foot-mark. SkD (s.v. *trade*).

treden, *v.* to tread, C, Prompt., PP; *pt. pl.*, W, PP; **tret**, *pr. s.* CM; **troden**, PP; **trade**, H (Ps. 55. 2); **troden**, *pp.*, C3; **trodun**, W2; **treddede**, *pt. s.* (*weak*), S3.—AS. *tredan*, pt. *træd* (pl. *trédon*), pp. *treden*.

treget, *sb.* guile, trickery, CM.

tregetrie, *sb.* a piece of trickery, CM.

tregettowre, *sb.* a juggler, *joculator*, Prompt.; **tregetour**, Prompt. (*n*), CM, HD.

tregettyn, *v.* to juggle, Prompt.—OF. *tresgeter* (Ducange); Lat. *trans* + *iactare*.

treien, *v.* to betray, P; **trayet**, *pp.*, HD.— OF. *traïr*; Late Lat. *tradïre for Lat. *tradere*.

treilȝis, *sb.* trellis, S3; **trelys**, *cancellus*, Prompt.—OF. *treillis*, from *treille*, a vine, arbour (Bartsch); Late Lat. *tricla; Lat. *trichila*; see BH, § 98.

tremlen, *v.* to tremble, stagger, PP; **tremelyn**, Prompt.; **trimlen**, HD; **trymlen**, S3; **tremblen**, W, PP; **trimble**, Manip.— Picard F. *tremler* (AF. *trembler*); Late Lat. *tremulare*.

tremlynge, *sb.* trembling; **tremelynge**, Prompt.; **trimlyng**, S3; **trymlinge**, HD.

trental, *sb.* a set of thirty masses for the dead, SkD, ND, PP; **trentall**, money paid for a trental, S3; a month's mind, ND.— OF. *trental*, *trentel*; Church Lat. *trigintalem* (Ducange).

treo, *sb.* tree, S; **treon**, *pl.*, S; see **tre**.

treowe, *adj.* true, S; see **trewe**¹.

trepeget, *sb.* a military engine, HD, CM; **trebget**, Prompt.; **trebgot**, an instrument for catching birds, Prompt.

全

tresor, *sb.* treasure, S, S2, C3; **tresour**, PP; S2, S3, C2; **treosor**, S; **tresores**, *pl.*, PP; **tresures**, S.—AF. *tresor*; Lat. *thesaurum*.

tresorere, *sb.* treasurer, PP; **treserour**, PP.—AF. *tresorer*.

tresorie, *sb.* treasury, S2; **tresory**, WA.—AF. *tresorye*.

tresoun, *sb.* treason, craft, C, PP; **tresun**, Prompt., S; **treson**, WA, C2, H; **treison**, PP; **trayson**, S.—AF. *treson, traïson*; Lat. *traditionem*.

trespas, *sb.* trespass, PP; **trespace**, PP, C.

trespassen, *v.* to trespass, PP, WW; **trespace**, C2; **trespasside**, *pt. s.*, W (Acts 1:25).—AF. *trespasser*, to cross over, to disobey.

tretee, *sb.* treaty, C2, C3; **trete**, C.—OF. *traite*; Late Lat. *tracta*. See **tretis**[3].

tretis[1], *adj.* well made, pretty; **tretys**, CM, C; **treitys**, CM.—OF. *tretis, treitis, traitis*, nicely made (Bartsch); from *traitier*; Lat. *tractare*.

tretis[2], *sb.* treatise, short poem, PP, C2, WA; **treatise**, S3. See **tretis**[3].

tretis[3], *sb.* treaty, B, CM; **tretys**, S2, C2, C3; **treatyce**, S3; **traytyse**, S3.—AF. *tretiz*; Late Lat. **tracticium*.

trewage, *sb.* tribute, S, JD; **truage**, Voc., S2, WA; **trouage**, WA.—OF. *treüage* (*truage*), toll, tax, from *treü, treüd*, tribute; Lat. *tribūtum*; see Constans (s.v.).

trewe[1], *adj.* true, S, PP, S2, C2; **treowe**, S; **trywe**, PP; **triwe**, S2; **trew**, S2, C2, **tru**, S2.—AS. *tréowe*: OS. *triuwi*.

trewe[2], *sb.* fidelity, trust, agreement, truce, PP; **treowe**, SkD; **treowes**, *pl.*, truce, SkD; **trewes**, PP; **trewis**, B; **treuwes**, PP; **triwes**, SkD; **truwys**, Prompt.; **trewysse**, Cath.

trewehede, *sb.* truth, uprightness, S2.

treweliche, *adv.* truly, PP, C2; **trewely**, C2.

trewen, *v.* to think to be true, to trow, believe, S.—AS. *tréowan*. See **trowen**.

trewes[1], *pl.* trees, S; see **tre**.

trewes[2], *sb. pl.* truce; see **trewe**[2].

trewðe, *sb.* truth, troth, S, C2, PP; **treuðe**, S, S2, PP; **trouthe**, S2, C3; **trouth**, H; **tryuðe**, PP; **trowwðe**, S; **trawðe**, S2; **treothes**, *pl.*, S; **truthes**, pledges, S2.—AS. *tréowðu*.

trey, *sb.* a throw at dice, viz. three, SkD; **treye**, C3. *Comb.*: **trey-ace**, the throw of three and one; a quick exclamation, S3.—OF. *trei, treis*; Lat. *trēs*.

treȝe, *sb.* affliction, grief, SD; **treiȝe**, S; **treie**, S; **treye**, S2; **tray**, vexation, B.—AS. *trega*; cf. Icel. *tregi*, Goth. *trigo*.

treȝen, *v.* to afflict, SD.

triacle, *sb.* a remedy, healing medicine, S2, PP, C3, NQ (6. 1. 308); **tryacle**, Voc., PP, NQ; **treacle**, TG, Prompt.; **tryakill**, S3.—OF. *triacle* (Bartsch); Lat. *theriaca*, lit. an antidote against the bite of serpents; cf. Gr. θηριακὰ φάρμακα. For examples of the intrusive *l*, see **cronicle**.

triblen, *v.* to trouble, H; see **trublen**.

tricherie, *sb.* treachery, trickery, S, PP, S2; **trecherie**, PP; **trechery**, S; **treccherie**, C.—AF. *tricherie*; from OF. *tricher, trecher*, to cheat; Late Lat. *tricare* for Lat. *tricari*.

trick, *adj.* neat, elegant, ND; **trig**, JD.—For the voicing of the guttural in North.E. cf. *prigmedainty* (JD), with *prickmedainty* or *prickmedenty* (HD); see SkD (s.vv. *prig, trigger*).

trien, *v.* to try, PP; **triȝede**, *pp.*, S2, PP; **i-triȝed**, S2; **itriȝet**, S2; **y-tried**, PP; **y-tryed**, PP; **tried**, *pp.* as *adj.*, choice, PP; **trye**, PP, C2; **triedest**, *superl.*, S2, PP; **trieste**, PP; **tryest**, PP; **triedliche**, *adv.*, excellently, PP; **triȝely**, PP, S2; **trielich**, P.—AF. *trier*; Late Lat. *tritare*, to thresh corn.

triennels, *sb. pl.* masses said for three years, PP; **triennales**, P.—OF. *triennal*; Church Lat. *triennale*.

trillen, *v.* to turn round and round, to trickle, CM, Prompt., C2, S3, Sh., SkD; **tryll**, Palsg.; **tril**, Manip.—Cf. Swed. *trilla*, to roll.

trinal, *adj.* threefold, RD; **trinall**, Spenser, 1. *Comb.*: **trinal triplicities**, SkD.—Late Lat. *trinalis*.

trine, *adj.* taken three at a time, ND. *Comb.*: **trine aspect** (in astrology), SkD, ND; **tryne compas**, the round world containing earth, sea, and heaven, C3—OF. *trine*; Lat. *trinum*.

Trinite, *sb.* Trinity, S2, PP; **Trinitee**, PP.—AF. *Trinite, Trinitet*; Church Lat. *Trinitatem*.

trisen, *v.* to hoist up, to trice, to pull off, SkD; **tryce**, C2; **trice**, CM. *Der.*: **tryyste, tryys**, windlass, Prompt.—Cf. Dan. *tridse*, to haul up; to **trice**, Swed. *trissa*, a pulley. The final *-se* is the same as in E. *cleanse*.

trist, *sb.* trust, a tryst, meeting-place, B, W, W2, PP, S2; station in hunting, HD; **trust**, PP.—Icel. *traust*. For E. *ī* = Icel. *au*, cf. ME. *mire* = Icel. *maurr*; see SkD (s.v. *pismire*).

tristen, *v.* to trust, S2, C3, W, W2, PP; **trysten**, S2, PP; **truste**, C3; **trosten**, S3, S2, PP; **truste**, *pt. s.*, S, S2. *Der.*: **tristyng**, a trust, W. See **trist**.

tristili, *adv.* confidently, W, W2.

tristnen, *v.* to trust, W. *Der.*: **tristenyng**, a trust, W.

triuials, *sb. pl.* studies connected with the *trivium*, the initiatory course taught in the schools, comprising grammar, rhetoric, and

dialectic, S3; **trivial**, *adj.*, initiatory, ND.—
Schol. Lat. *trivialem*.

troblen, *v.* to trouble, W; **troubild**, *pp.*,
WA; see **trublen**.

trod, *sb.* a trodden path, SkD (s.v. *trade*), HD.
See **treden**.

troden, *pp.* trodden; see **treden**.

trofle, *sb.* a trifle, S3; see **trufle**.

trompe[1], *sb.* a trump, trumpet, C3; **trumpe**,
C.—AF. *trompe*.

trompe[2], *v.* to play the trumpet, PP;
trumpe, W, Prompt.—AF. *trumper*.

tronchoun, *sb.* a truncheon, broken piece of
a spear-shaft. C; **trunchone**, Prompt.—
OF. *tronchon, tronçon*.

trone, *sb.* throne, S, PP, S3, C2, C3, W;
trones, *pl.*, S; one of the nine orders of
angels, WA; **tronen**, S2.—OF. *trone*; Lat.
thronum; from Gr. θρόνος.

tronen, *v.* to enthrone, PP.—OF. *troner*.

trost, *subj. pr. s.* trust, S2; see **tristen**.

trotevale, *sb.* a trifling thing, HD.

trouble, *adj.* troubled, S2, C2.—AF. *truble*,
pp. of *trubler*; see **trublen**.

trouthe, *sb.* truth, S.2, C3; see **trewþe**.

trowabile, *adj.* credible, H.

trowen, *v.* to believe, S, S2, S3, C2, C3, H,
PP; **tru**, S2; **trawed**, *pt. pl.*, expected,
S2.—Icel. *trúa*; Swed. *tro*. See **trewen**.

trowyng, *sb.* belief, S2.

truage, *sb.* tribute, S2; see **trewage**.

trublen, *v.* to trouble, W; **troblen**, W;
triblen, H.—AF. *trubler*; Late Lat. *turbulare*.

trufle, *sb.* nonsense, absurd tale, trifle, PP,
SkD; **trofle**, S3, SkD; **trefele**, PP; **triful**,
PP; **trifle**, PP.—AF. *trufle, trofle*, mockery,
OF. *truffe*, a jest, a flout, also a truffle
(Cotg.); Lat. *tubera*, truffles; see SkD (s.v.
truffle). For the intrusive *l*, cf. **triacle**.

truflen, *v.* to beguile, SkD; **trofle**, SkD;
trifelyn, Prompt.; **treoflynge**, *pr. p.*,
S2.—OF. *truffler, truffer*, to mock (Cotg.).

trukenen, *v.* to fail, S.

trukien, *v.* to fail, S.—AS. *trucian*, to fail,
deceive.

trusse, *sb.* a bundle, Manip., CM.

trussen, *v.* to pack, to pack off, C, S2, PP,
Manip.; **turss**, B.—OF. *trusser, trosser, torser*;
Late Lat. **tortiare*.

truste, *pt. s.* trusted, S; see **tristen**.

tryce, *v.* to trice, to hoist up, C2; see **trisen**.

tryg, *adj.* trusty, secure, S3.—Icel. *tryggr*.

trymlyt, *pt. pl.* trembled, S3; see **tremlen**.

tryst, *adj.* sad, S3. *Der.*: **tristes**, sadness,
S3.—OF. *trist*; Lat. *tristem*; and OF. *tristesse*;
Lat. *tristitia*.

tua, *num.* two, S2; see **tuo**.

tuhen, *pt. pl.* of **ten**.

tuht, *sb.* discipline, S.—AS. *tyht*; cf. OHG.
zuht (Otfrid). See **ten**.

tuhten, *v.* to draw, persuade, discipline, S;
tihte, *pt. s.*, S.—AS. *tyhtan*.

tuin, *num.* two, S2; see **twinne**.

tuken, *v.* to pluck, vex, S; **tuke up**, *succingere*,
Cath.; **tukkyn up**, Prompt.; **y-touked**,
pp., tucked, fulled, PP.—AS. *tucian (twiccan)*;
cf. OHG. *zukken* (Otfrid).

tuker, *sb.* a fuller; see **tokker**.

tulke, *sb.* a man, soldier, knight, WA, EETS
(56); **tolke**, S2; **tulk**, WA, SkD (s.v. *talk*).—
Icel. *túlkr*, interpreter; Lithuan. *tulkas*,
interpreter; cf. Dan. *tolk*.

tullen, *v.* to draw, entice, CM, SD; see
tollen[2].

tumben, *v.* to leap, tumble, dance; **tom-
bede**, *pt. s.*, SD.—AS. *tumbian* (Mk. 6. 22);
cf. OF. *tumber*, to fall.

tumbestere, *sb.* a female dancer, HD;
tombester, SD; **tumbesteris**, *pl.*, SD,
C3 (p. 151); **tombesteres**, C3.

tumblen, *v.* to leap, dance, SD, SkD; to
tumble, PP; **tombly**, PP; **tumlyn**, *volutare*,
Prompt.

tumbler, *sb.* a tumbler, a female dancer,
Voc.; **tumlare**, *volutator*, Prompt.

tun, *sb.* enclosure, farm-stead, town, S, S2;
see **toun**.

tunen, *v.* to enclose, S; see **tynen**.

tunge, *sb.* tongue, S, C, W2; see **tonge**[1].

tunne, *sb.* tun, S; see **tonne**.

tuo, *num.* two, S2, C, PP; **tua**, S2; **two**, S;
twa, S, S2; **to**, S, S2; **towe** S3.—AS. *twá*
(neuter).

tur, *sb.* tower, S; see **tour**.

turnen, *v.* to turn, S; see **tournen**.

turss, *v.* to pack; see **trussen**.

turues, *sb. pl.* pieces of turf, S2; see **torf**.

tus, for **thus**, S; see **þus**.

tutand, *pr. p.* projecting, pushing out, S2; see
toten.

tute[1], *sb.* a horn, *cornu, os*, SD.—For Teutonic cognates see Weigand (s.v. *zotte*). See
tewelle.

tute[2], *v.* 'to tute in a horne', Manip.—Cf.
Swed. *tuta*, to blow a horn.

tutel, *sb.* beak, mouth (?), S.

tutelen, *v.* to whisper, S.

tuteler, *sb.* tittler, tattler, PP.

tutlyng, *sb.* noise of a horn, B. See **tute**[2].

tutour, *sb.* guardian, warden, keeper, P,
WW, TG.—OF. *tuteur*; Lat. *tutorem*.

twa, *num.* two, S, S2; see **tuo**.

tweamen, *v.* to separate, S.—AS. *(ge)twéman*.

tweire, *num. gen.* of twain, S.—AS. *twegra*
(gen.).

twelf, *num.* twelve, S, C2; **tuelf**, S2; **tuelue**,
S2. *Comb.*: **twelfmoneth**, twelvemonth,

PP; **tuelmonth**, S2.—AS. *twelf.* Goth. *twalif.*

twengen, *v.* to press tightly, tweak, S; **tuengde**, *pt. s.*, S2.—Cf. **twingen**.

twestis, *pl.* twigs, S3; see **twyste**[1].

tweye[1], *num.* twain, PP, C, C2; **tweie**, S; **tueie**, S; **twey**, S3, PP; **twei**, PP. *Comb.*: **twey-fold**, twofold, C3.—AS. *twega* (gen.). See **tuo**.

tweye[2], *adv.* twice, PP; **twye**, HD; **twie**, S.—AS. *twíwa.*

tweyne, *num.* twain, G, PP; **tueyne**, S2; **twene**, S; **tweien**, S; **twe33enn**, S.—AS. *twegen.*

twi- (*prefix*). *Comb.*: **twi-bil**, an axe, *bipennis*, Voc., Prompt., H; **twi-feald**, twofold, SD; **twye-lyghte**, twilight, Prompt.; **twi-ræd**, of diverse opinion, SD.

twichand, *pres. pt.* touching, regarding, S3 (13. 271).

twie, *adv.* twice, S; see **tweye**[2].

twikken, *v.* to twitch, snatch, pull slightly but quickly, Prompt.; **twychyn**, Prompt.; **twyghte**, *pt. s.*, CM; **twight**, *pp.*, CM.

twine, *sb.* doubled thread; **twines**, *gen.*, S.—AS. *twín.*

twinen, *v.* to twist, S; **twined**, *pp.*, S; **twyned**, PP.

twingen, *v.* to pain, afflict, SkD; **twungen**, *pp.*, SkD.—Cf. G. *zwingen.*

twinging, *sb.* affliction, S2.

twinken, *v.* to wink, Prompt., G.

twinklen, *v.* to twinkle, Prompt.

twinne, *num.* two apiece, two at a time, S; **twynne**, S2; **tuin**, S2.—Icel. *twinnr.*

twinnen, *v.* to separate, C2; **twynnen**, S2, S3, H; **twyne**, S3; **twyn**, S2, H; **tuyn**, H; **twynned**, *pt. pl.*, PP, S3.

twyes, *adv.* twice, S2, C2, C3, PP.—Formed with suffix *-es* on AS. *twíwa*. See **tweye**[2].

twyste[1], *sb.* bough, Cath., S3; **twist**, B, S2, C2, CM; **twest**, S3.—Cf. ODu. *twist.*

twyste[2], *v.* to strip the boughs, *defrondare*, Cath.

twyster (of trees), *sb.* a stripper of boughs, *defrondator*, Cath.

tycement, *sb.* enticement, HD.

tycen, *v.* to entice, instigate, provoke, Prompt., Manip., S; **tisen**, PP; **tyse**, HD (s.v. *tise*). See **atisen**.

tykel, *adj.* unsteady, uncertain, CM.

tyle, *sb.* tile, Prompt.; **tyil**, Prompt.; **tyyl**, S2. *Comb.*: **tyle-stone**, tile, brick, Prompt.; **tiyl-stoon** (= Lat. *testa*), W2.—AS. *tigele*; Lat. *tegula.*

tymber, *sb.* timber, wood for building, Voc., PP; **tymbre**, PP.—AS. *timber.*

tymbre[1], *v.* to frame, build, PP; **timbrin**, S, S2.—AS. *timbrian*: Goth. *timrjan*; cf. OHG. *zimbrón* (Tatian).

tymbre[2], *sb.* the crest of a helmet, also a helmet, WA; **timber**, Cotg.; **tymbrys**, *pl.*, B.—OF. *timbre* (Cotg.); Lat. *tympanum*; Gr. τύμπανον; cf. SkD (s.v. *timbrel*).

tyme, *sb.* time, due season, S, C2, C3, PP; **tyme**, *pl.*, C2; **tymes**, C2. *Comb.*: **tymeful**, seasonable, early, W; **timliche**, quickly, S.—AS. *tíma*; cf. Icel. *tími.*

tymen, *v.* to betide, S2.—AS. (*ge*)*tímian.*

tynd, *sb.* the tine or prong of a deer's horn, the spike of a harrow, JD, SkD; **tyndis**, S3.—AS. *tind* (Voc.); cf. Icel. *tindr.*

tyne[1], *adj.* tiny, WA.

tyne[2], *sb.* prickle, Prompt.

tyne[3], *v.* to lose, S2, PP, H; **tine**, S2, H; **tynt**, *pp.*, S2, PP, H. *Der.*: **tynsil**, loss, ruin, H; **tinsill**, H.—Icel. *týna*, to lose, to destroy, *týnask*, to perish, from *tjón*, loss, damage.

tynen, *v.* to enclose, S2; **tinen**, S; **tunen**, S.—AS. *týnan*, from *tún*. See **toun**.

tynken, *v.* to ring, tinkle, W.

tynkere, *sb.* tinker, PP.

tynsale, *sb.* loss, harm, B. See **tyne**[3].

tyred, *pp.* attired, dressed, S2; see **atyren**.

tysane, *sb.* a drink, Prompt.—OF. *tisane*, barley-water; Lat. *ptisana*, pearl-barley, also barley-water; Gr. πτισάνη.

tysyk, *sb.* consumption, S2, Prompt.; **tysike**, Cath.—OF. *tisique* (Bartsch); Lat. *phthisica*, consumptive disease; from Gr. φθίσις decay; cf. It. *tisica.*

tyyl, *sb.* tile, S2; see **tyle**.

Þ

The letters þ *and* ð *and the digraph* th *are interfiled here.*

th, an abbreviation of the article **the**, ND. *Combined, as though* **th'**: **thair**, S2; **thangel**, C2; **tharmes**, C; **tharray**, S2, C2; **thassemblee**, S2, C3; **thavys**, the advice, C; **theffect**, C2; **theffusion**, S3; **thegle**, C2; **thembatel**, S3; **themperice**, S; **themperour**, S2, C3; **thencens**, C; **thenchauntement**, C; **thencres**, C; **thende**, S, S2, S3; **thentencioun**, C3; **therle**, S3; **thestat**, C; **thimage**, C2; **thingot**, C3; **thold**, S3; **thorient**, C2; **thorisoun**, C; **thothre**, S, S3. See **þe**¹.

þa¹, *art. def. fem.* the, S; *dat. masc.*, S; *pl.*, S; see **þe**¹.

þa², *pron. pl.*, who, S; see **þe**².

þam, *art. dat. s.* and *pl.* the, S; see **þe**¹. And see **þei**.

þan¹, *art. dat.* and *acc.* the, S; see **þe**¹.

þan², *adv.* then; see **þanne**¹.

þane¹, *art. acc. masc.* the, S; see **þe**¹.

þane², *adv.* then, S; see **þanne**¹.

þane³, *sb.* thane, S2; see **þeyn**¹.

þanen, *adv.* thence, S; **þanene**, S2.—AS. *þanon.*

þank, *sb.* a thought, a thank, gratitude, grace; **þanc**, S; **þonc**, S; **þonk**, S, PP; **þance**, *dat.*, S; **þonke**, S, S2; **þankes**, *pl.*, PP; **thonkes**, PP, S2. *Phr.*: **can þanc, con þonk**, is thankful, S; **here þankes**, *gen.* as *adv.*, of their own thought, spontaneously, S, C.—AS. *þanc*; cf. OHG. *thanc* (Otfrid).

þanken, *v.* to thank, PP, S; **þonken**, PP, S, S2.—AS. *þancian.*

þanne¹, *adv.* then, when, S, PP, S2, C; **þann**, S; **þane**, S; **þan**, S, S2, C2; **þenne**, S, PP, S2; **þene**, S, PP; **þen**, S; **þeonne**, S.—AS. *þænne.*

þanne², *conj.* than, S; **þane**, S; **þan**, S2; **þenne**, S; **þenn**, S; **þene**, S; **þen**, S, PP.—AS. *þænne.*

þanne³, *adv.* thence, S2; see **þenne**³.

þar-, *prefix*; see **þer-**.

þar, *pt. pr. s. impers.* it needs, *opus est*, B, H; **thare**, H; **þarf**, S; **tharst**, *2 pt. pr. s.*, PP; **thart**, *pt. pr. s.*, HD. *Comb.*: **thardestow**, thou wouldst need, PP; see **þurfen**.

þare, *art. dat. f.* to the, S; see **þe**¹.

þarmes, *sb. pl.* entrails, HD.—AS. *þearm* (Voc.); for cognates see Kluge (s.v. *darm*).

þarne, *v.* to lack, want, HD, H; **tharn**, H; **tharnys**, *pr. s.*, H; **tharnyd**, *pt. s.*, H.—Icel. *þarnask* (for *þarfnask*), to lack.

þas, *pron. dem. pl.* those, S, S2; see **þes**.

þat, *pron. dem., pron. rel.* and *conj.* that, S, S2; **þet**, S, S2; **at**, S2, S3, H, NED.—AS. *þæt.* See **þe**².

þauien, *v.* to permit, SD; **þeauien**, S; **thave**, HD.—AS. *þafian.*

þe¹, *pron. dem.* and *def. art. m.* that man, the, S; **þæ**, S; **te**, S; **to**, S; **þat**, *n.*, S, S2; **þet**, S, S2; **tat**, S; **tatt**, S; **þes**, *gen. m.*, S; **þes þe**, so much the (more), S; **þas**, S; **þane**, *acc. m.*, S, S2; **þan**, S, S2; **þene**, S; **þenne**, S; **þen**, S, S2; **þam**, *dat. m.*, S; **þan**, S; **þen**, S, S2; **þon**, S; **þo**, S; **þa**, S; **þeo**, *nom. f.*, S; **þære**, *dat. f.* and *gen. f.*; **þare**, S; **þere**, S; **þar**, S; **þer**, S; **þa**, *acc. f.*, S; **þo**, S; **þeo**, S; **þie**, S; **þe**, *inst.* as in **þe bet**, the better, PP. *Comb.*: **the self**, itself, H.—ONorth. *ðé*, see Sievers, 337.

þe², *pron. rel.* who, which, S.—AS. *ðe* (the indeclinable relative pronoun). See **þe**¹.

þe³, *conj.* than, S.—AS. *ðe*, 'quam'.

þeaw, *sb.* habit, virtue, S; see **þew**.

þedam, *sb.* prosperity, Prompt., HD. See **þeen**.

þede, *sb. pl.* nations, S2 (3. 29); see **þeode**.

þeden, *adv.* thence, S; see **þeþen**.

þeder, *adv.* thither, S2; see **þider**.

þeef, *sb.* thief, C2; see **þeof**.

þeen, *v.* to thrive, *vigere*, Prompt.; **thee**, S3, C2, C3, Spenser (2), HD; **the**, C, HD; **the**, *1 pr. s. subj.*, PP; **theech** (**thee** + **ich**), may I thrive, C3; **theich**, PP; **þeagh**, *pt. s.*, SD; **i-þeȝ**, S2.—AS. *(ge)þéon*: **þíhan*; cf. Goth. *þeihan*; see Sievers, 383, Douse, p. 40.

þefe, *sb.* leafy branch, twig; **theve**, Prompt. *Comb.*: **thefethorn**, buckthorn, Alph. (*n.* p. 156), Voc.; **thefthorne**, H; **thewethorn-ys**, *pl.*, *morus*, Voc.; **thethorne**, *ramnus*, Prompt.; **the thorntre**, Voc.—AS. *þýfe* (*þéfe*), *þefe-þorn*, 'ramnus' (Voc.), *ðeofeðorn* (Voc.); cf. AS. *þúfian*, 'frutescere' (Voc.).

þei, *pron. pl.* they, S, PP, C; **þeȝȝ**, S; **teȝȝ**, S; **þai**, S, PP, S2; **tai**, S; **the**, S3; **þeȝȝre**, *gen.*, S; **teȝȝre**, S; **thair**, S2; **thayr**, PP; **þar**, S2, S3; **þeȝȝm**, *dat. acc.*, S; **thaim**, S2; **thaym**, PP; **tham**, S2. *Comb.*: **þamselue**, themselves, S2.—Icel. *þeir*, they (Dan. *de*), *gen. þeirra*, *dat. þeim*; cf. AS. *ðá*, those. See **þe**¹.

þein, *sb.* thane, S; see **þeyn**¹.

þellyche, *pron.* such, S2; see **þulli**.

þenchen, *v.* to think, to intend, S, S2; **þenken**, PP, S; **þohte**, *pt. s.*, S, S2; **þoȝte**, S; **þoght**, S2; **thoucte**, S; **þouhten**, *pl.*, S; **þoght**, *pp.*, S2; **þouht**, PP; **thouct**, S.—

þene

þider

AS. *þencan*, pt. *þóhte*, pp. *(ge)þóht*. See **þynken**.

þene, *art. acc. masc.* the, S; **þen**, S; see **þe**[1].
þenien, *v.* to serve; **þeniÞ**, *pr. pl.*, S. *Der.*:
þeninge, services, S.—AS. *þénian, þegnian*, from *þegn*. See **þeyn**[1].
þenne[1], than; see **þanne**[1].
þenne[2], then; see **þanne**[2].
þenne[3], *adv.* thence, S; **þanne**, S2; **þonne**, S; **þeonne**, S2, PP. See **þanen**.
þennes, *adv.* thence, PP, S2, C2, C3; **thennus**, W. *Comb.*: **thennes-forth**, thenceforth, C2.
þeode, *sb.* people, nation, S; **þiode**, S; **þeode**, *pl.*, orders (of angels), S; nations, S2; **þede**, S2; **þeden**, *dat.*, S.—AS. *þéod*; cf. Goth. *þiuda*, OHG. *thiota* (Tatian).
þeof, *sb.* thief, S, PP; **thef**, PP; **þyef**, S2; **theef**, C2, Prompt.; **þeue**, *dat.*, S; **þieue**, S; **þeofes**, *pl.*, S; **þeoues**, S, PP; **theues**, W2; **theueli**, in a thief-like manner, W2; **þeofte**, theft, S; **þefte**, PP, Prompt.—AS. *þéof*: Goth. *þiubs*; cf. OHG. *thiob* (Tatian).
þeorrf, *adj.* unleavened, S; see **þerf**.
þeos, *pron. dem. f.* this, S; see **þes**.
þeoster, *sb.* darkness, S.—AS. *þéostru*: OS. *thiustri*.
þeostre, *adj.* dark, S; see **þester**.
þeow, *sb.* servant; **þeoww**, S. *Der.*: **þeoudom**, bondage; **þeoudome**, *dat.*, S.—AS. *þéow*: Goth. *þius*; cf. OHG. *thiu*, 'ancilla' (Otfrid).
þeowten, *v.* to serve; **þeowwtenn**, S.—From AS. *þéowet*, service.
þer-, *prefix*, SkD (s.v. *there-*). *Comb.*: **þerfore**, for it, for that cause, PP, S, C2; **þerfor**, S, S2; **þeruore**, S2; **þereuore**, S; **þarfore**, S, S2; **þaruore**, S; **þareuore**, S; **þærfore**, S; **þerinne**, therein, S, S2, C2; **þærinne**, S; **þarinne**, S; **þrinne**, S, S2; **thrynne**, G; **þarin**, S, S2; **þerin**, S; **þerwiÞ**, therewith, S, C2; **þarwiÞ**, S, S2; **þerwiȝt**, S2; **þærwiÞÞ**, S; **þermide**, therewith, S; **þeremyde**, P; **þarmid**, S; **þerof**, thereof, S, C2; **þrof**, S.—AS. *ðǽre*, pron. dem. dat. f.; see **þe**[1].
þer, *pron. dem. pl.* these, S2, HD; **there**, H; **þir**, S2, H. S3, JD; those, B.—Icel. *þeir*, they. See **þei**.
þere[1], *adv.* there, where, S, S2, S3; **þare**, S; **þore**, S, S2; **þer**, S, S2, S3; **þar**, S, S2; **þor**, S; **þear**, S; **þiar**, S; **þær**, S; **tær**, S (in Ormulum). *Comb.*: **þer aboute**, thereabouts, S2; **þare amang**, at various times, S2; **þer an under**, there beneath, S2; **þere as**, where that, S3; **þer biuore**, before then, S2; **þer before**, S; **þer efter**, thereafter, S; **ther on**, thereon, C2; **þron**, S; **þrute**, thereout, S; **þer oȝeines**, in comparison therewith, S; **þare ogayne**, S2; **þorquiles**, meanwhile, S; **þere whiles**, P; **þertil**, thereto, S; **þortil**, S; **þerto**, thereto, S, S2, C2, C3; **þarto**, S2; **þer towart**, against it, S; **þer uppe**, besides, S; **þruppe**, thereupon, S.—AS. *þǽr*: Goth. *þar*.
þere[1], *art. gen.* and *dat. f.* of the, to the, S; see **þe**[1].
þerf, *adj.* unleavened, W, S2, PP; **þeorrf**, S. *Comb.*: **therf looues**, unleavened bread, W; **therf breed**, HD.—AS. *þeorf*; cf. Icel. *þjarfr*.
þerfling, *adj.* unleavened; **þerrflinng**, S.
þerne, *sb.* a girl, SD (Havelok, 298); see **tarne**[1].
þes, *pron. dem. m.* this, S; **þis**, S; **þis**, *n.*, S; **þeos**, *f.*, S; **teos**, S; **þesses**, *gen. m.*, S; **þisse**, *gen. f.*, S; **þissen**, *dat. m.*, S; **þisse**, *dat. f.*, S; **þisser**, S; **þesser**, S; **þeser**, S; **þas**, *acc. f.*, S; **þas**, *pl.*, S, S2; **þos**, S; **þeos**, S; **þes**, C, W2; **these**, W2; **þues**, S2; **þis**, S2; **þies**, S3; **þisse**, *dat. pl.*, S; **þise**, S2, C2; **þyse**, S2; **þesen**, S.—AS. *þes*, see Sievers, 338, and SkD (s.v. *this*).
þester, *adj.* dark, HD; **þyester**, S2; **þeostre**, S, **þuster**, S.—AS. *þéostre*: OS. *thiustri*.
þesternesse, *sb.* darkness, S, PP; **þyesternesse**, S2; **þiesternesse**, S; **þeosternesse**, S.—AS. *þéosternis*.
þestrien, *v.* to become dark, S.—AS. *þystrian*.
þet, *pron.* that; see **þat**, **þe**[1].
þeþen, *adv.* thence; **þeþenn**, S; **þeden**, S; **thethyn**, H.—Icel. *þeðan, þaðan* (Dan. *deden*).
þeues, *sb. pl.* thieves, W2; see **þeof**.
þew, *sb.* habit, practice, virtue, S2; **þeaw**, S; **þeawes**, *pl.*, manners, virtues, S; **þæwess**, S; **þewes**, PP, S2, C2, C3; **thewis**, W; **thewys**, H. *Comb.*: **þeauful**, moral, virtuous; **þeaufule**, *pl.*, S.—AS. *þéaw*, habit.
þewed, *adj.* mannered; **thewde**, S3. *Phr.*: **wel þewed**, S.
þeyn[1], *sb.* thane, warrior, attendant at a king's court, S; **þein**, SkD; **thane**, S2, Sh.—AS. *þegn* (*þén*), Icel. *þegn*: OS. *thegan*, a youth, disciple, knight, warrior; cf. OHG. *thegan* (Otfrid).
þeyn[2], *sb.* service (?), S2.
þi, *pron. poss.* thy, S; see **þou**.
þicke[1], *adj.* thick, S; **þikke**, S2, C2; **thykke**, Prompt.; **thicke**, *adv.*, S; **þikke**, S, PP; **þicce**, S.—AS. *þicce*, adj. and adv.: OS. *thikki*.
þicke[2], *sb.* thicket, S3.
þider, *adv.* thither, S, PP, S2, C3; **þuder**, S, PP; **þeder**, S2; **þedyr**, S2, PP. *Comb.*:

217

þider-ward, thitherward, S, S2; **þuder-ward**, S2.—AS. *þider*.

þie, *art. f.* the, S; see **þe**[1].

þies, *pron. dem. pl.* these, S3; see **þes**.

þiesternesse, *sb.* darkness, S; see **þesternesse**.

þild, *sb.* patience, S.—AS. *(ge)þyld*: OS. *githuld*. See **þolien**.

þildili3, *adv.* patiently, S.

þilk, *adj.* that, that very, that sort of, such, W; **thylke**, S3; **thilke**, C2, C3, W2, S; **þulke**, *pl.*, S2, PP.—AS. *þylc*; cf. Icel. *þvílíkr*, such.

þin, *pron. poss.* thy, thine, S; see **þou**.

þing, *sb.* thing, affair, property, S; *pl.*, S, C3; **þyng**, PP; **þinge**, S, PP; **þynge**, S2; **þinges**, S, C2; **þinkes**, S; **þenges**, S; **þynges**, PP.—AS. *þing*.

þiode, *sb.* people, S; see **þeode**.

þir, *pron. dem. pl.* those, these, S2, H, S3, JD, B; see **þer**.

þire, *pron. poss. dat. f.* thy, S; see **þou**.

þirlen, *v.* to pierce, C, S2, H; see **þurlen**.

þis, þise, þisse, etc.; see **þes**.

þistel, *sb.* thistle, Voc.; **thystell**, Voc.; **thystylle**, Voc., Prompt.; **thrissil**, S3. *Comb.*: **thistle-finch**, linnet, HD.—AS. *þistel* (Voc.): OHG. *thistila* (Tatian); cf. Icel. *þistill*.

þit, *put for* **þe it**, who it, S; see **þe**[1].

þo[1], *pron. dem. and def. art. pl.* those, they, them, the, S, S2, C, PP, W2; **þoo**, S2, S3, W2, PP; **þa**, S, S2, H; **þaa**, S2; **þeo**, S; **þe**, S; **þam**, *dat.*, S; **þan**, S, S2; **þa**, S.—AS. *þá*, dat. *þém* (*þám*). See **þe**[1].

þo[2], *adv.* then, when, S, S2, S3, C, C2, C3, PP; **þoo**, PP; **þa**, S.—AS. *ðá*.

þo[3], *art. acc. f.* the, S; see **þe**[1].

þoght, *sb.* thought, anxiety, S2, C2; **þohht**, S; **þogt**, S; *þouht*, S, PP; **thought**, C2; **þo3te**, *dat.*, S; **þu3te**, S; **þohtes**, *pl.*, S; **þo3tes**, S2. *Der.*: **þoghtful**, thoughtful; **þoghtfulest**, *superl.*, S2.—AS. *(ge)þóht*. See **þenchen**.

þohte, *pt. s.* thought; see **þenchen**.

þolemode, *adj.* patient, H, HD; **tholemodely**, *adv.*, H.

þolemodnes, *sb.* patience, H, HD, S2.

þolien, *v.* to suffer, S, S2; **þolyen** S, S2; **þolen**, S, S2, H, PP, HD; **þoland**, *pr. p.*, B; **þolede**, *pt. s.*, S, S2, S3; **þaleð**, *pr. s.*, S.—AS. *þolian*; cf. OHG. *tholén* (Tatian).

þombe, *sb.* thumb, PP, C, C2; **thome**, HD.—AS. *þúma* (Voc.); cf. G. *daumen*; see Kluge.

þonc, *sb.* thought, mind, S; see **þank**.

þondringe, *sb.* thundering, S2.

þoner, *sb.* thunder, S2, S; **thonur**, H; **þunre**, S; **thonder**, C, C2; **þunder**, S2. *Comb.*: **þunder-þrast**, stroke of thunder, S2.—AS. *þunor*, thunder, also Thor or

Thunor, the thunder-god; cf. OHG. *thonar* (Tatian). Cf. **Þorr** and **Þunre**.

þoneren, *v.* to thunder, S2; **thonord**, H (Ps. 17. 15).—AS. *þunrian*.

þonken, *v.* to thank, S, S2; see **þanken**.

þonwanges, *sb. pl.* the temples, HD.—Icel. *þunn-vangi*, the thin cheek (CV.).

þong, *sb.* a slip of leather, S; see **þwong**.

þorn, *sb.* thorn, SD; **thorne**, Prompt. *Comb.*: **thorne-garthis**, hedges (= Lat. *sepes*), H (Ps. 88. 39).—AS. *þorn*.

þorp, *sb.* a village, hamlet, farm, SkD; **þrop**, S, C2; **thropes**, *gen.*, C3; **thrope**, *dat.*, C2; **þorpes**, *pl.*, PP; **þropes**, PP; **þroupes**, PP.—AS. *þorp*, Icel. *þorp*; cf. OHG. *thorph* (Tatian).

Þorr, *sb.* the Teutonic god Thor, the god of thunder. *Comb.*: **Þors-day**, Thor's day, Thursday, PP; **Þorisdai**, S.—Icel. *þórr*, *þórsdagr*.

þoru, *prep.* through, S; **þorw**, S; **þor3**, S2; see **þurgh**.

þos, *pron. dem. pl.* these, S; see **þes**.

þou, *pron.* thou, SD; **þu**, S, PP; **tu**, S; **þe**, *dat. and acc.*, S, S2, C2; **þei**, S2; **te**, S; **þin**, *gen. and poss.*, S, S2; **þi**, S; **tin**, S; **ti**, S; **þire**, *poss. dat. f.*, S; **þina**, S; **tine**, *pl. dat.*, S. *Comb.*: **þut** (= **þu + it**), S; **þeself**, thyself, S; **þesellf**, S; **þe-selue**, S; **þe-suluen**, S; **þe-seoluen**, S.—AS. *þú*.

thoue, *v.* to say 'thou'; **thowis**, *2 pr. s.*, S3.

þouht, *sb.* thought, S; see **þoght**.

thowe, *sb.* thaw, Prompt.

thowen, *v.* to thaw, CM, Prompt.—AS. *þáwan*.

þo3, *conj.* though, nevertheless, PP; **þow3**, PP; **þowgh**, PP; **þou3e**, PP; **þoh**, SD; **þohh**, S; **thocht**, S3; **thoucht**, S3; **thofe**, HD; **þof**, S2, WA; **of**, WA; **þauh**, S, PP; **þah**, S, S2; **þa3**, S2; **þa3t**, S2; **þeh**, S; **þeih**, S; **þei3**, PP; **þey3**, S2; **þeigh**, PP; **þei3e**, PP; **þe3**, S; **þei**, S2; **þey**, S2, G. *Comb.*: **þah-hweðer**, nevertheless, S; **þeih-hweþere**, S; **þoþwæthere**, S; **þof-queþer**, S; **þa3les**, nevertheless, S2; **þahles yef**, unless, S2.—AS. *þéah* (*þéh*): Goth. *þauh*.

þo3te[1], *sb. dat.* thought, S; see **þoght**.

þo3te[2], *pt. s.* thought; see **þenchen**. See also **þynken**.

þra, *adj.* eager, B; see **þro**.

þral, *sb.* servant, slave, thrall, S, C2, C3; **thrall**, S3; **þralle**, *dat.*, S; **threllis**, *pl.*, B; **þralles**, S, PP. *Comb.*: **eorðe-þrelles**, slaves upon earth, S; **þral-dom**, slavery, S, PP, C3; **þrildome**, B; **þral-hod**, slavery, S; **þral-shipe**, slavery, S; **þral-sipe**, S; **þrel-weorkes**, thrall-works, S.—ONorth. *þræl*; Icel. *þræll*.

þrallen, *v.* to put into bondage; **thralled**, *pt. s.*, S2.

þrasten, *v.* to oppress, afflict, S.—AS. *(ge)þræstan*, to twist, hurt, torment.

þraw, *sb.* space of time, S2; see **þrowe**[1].

þreaten, *v.* to threaten, S; see **þreten**.

þred, *ord.* third, S2; see **þridde**.

threed, *sb.* thread, C, SkD; **þred**, S; **þræd**, S; **threde**, Prompt. *Comb.*: **þredbare**, threadbare, C, PP, SkD.—AS. *þréd*, a dental derivative from *þráwan*, to twist; cf. OHG. *drát* (G. *draht*), from *dráian*; see Kluge (s.v.), and Douse, p. 101. See **þrowen**[1].

þrelles, *sb. pl.* thralls, slaves, S; see **þral**.

þrengen, *v.* to press, SD; **þrengde**, *pt. s.*, S. Causal of **þringen**.

þreo, *num.* three, S, S2, PP; **þre**, S, PP; **þree**, PP; **þri**, S; **þrie**, S. *Comb.*: **Þreohad**, Trinity, S; **þreottene**, thirteen, S; **þrettene**, S2, PP; **þrettyne**, PP; **þretend**, thirteenth, S2; **thritteind**, S2; **þretti**, thirty, PP; **þrette**, S2; **þritty**, PP; **þritti**, S2; **Þrines**, Trinity; **Þrunnesse**, S; **thresum**, with three at a time, B.—AS. *þréo*.

þrep, *sb.* controversy, contradiction, S2; **threpe**, JD.

þrepen, *v.* to maintain a point obstinately in contradiction to another, to assert, C3, CM, JD; **threape**, HD.—AS. *þréapian*.

þreschen, *v.* to thresh, beat, PP; **thresshe**, S, C; **þrosshenn**, *pp.*, S; **y-þorsse**, S2.—AS. *þerscan*; see Douse, p. 112.

þrescwolde, *sb.* threshold, PP; **threschwolde**, Prompt.; **thresshewolde**, P; **threshfold**, C2; **threshfod**, HD.—AS. *þrescold*, Icel. *þreskoldr*; cf. OHG. *driscufli*; see Douse, p. 110.

þrestelcoc, *sb.* throstle, S2; see **þrustel**.

þrete, *sb.* threat, S.—AS. *þréat*, pressure.

þreten, *v.* to menace, S2, Prompt., HD; **þreaten**, S.—AS. *þréatian*, to reprove.

threting, *sb.* menace, C3; **thretynges**, *pl.*, W.

thretnen, *v.* to threaten, W2; **thretenede**, *pt. s.*, W.

þrette, *num.* thirty, S2; see **þreo**.

þrettene, *num.* thirteen, S2; see **þreo**.

þridde, *ord.* third, S, S2, PP; **þrydde**, S2, PP; **þryd**, S2; **thrid**, S3; **þred**, S2.—AS. *þridda*.

þrië[1], *num.* three, S; see **þreo**.

þrië[2], *adv.* three times, S; **þrien**, S.—AS. *þríwa*.

þriës, *adv.* thrice, S, S2; **þriȝess**, S; **thryes**, C2. The form is due to analogy; cf. AS. *ánes*, E. *once*.

þrift, *sb.* prosperity, success in life, C3, PP; **þruft**, PP; **þryft**, fertilising power, S2.—Icel. *þrift*. See **þriven**.

thrifty, *adj.* serviceable, cheap, S2, C2, C3.

thrill, *v.* to pierce, H; see **þurlen**.

thrillage, *sb.* thraldom, B; see **þral**.

þrim-setel, *sb.* throne, SD. See **þrum**.

þringen, *v.* to press, S, HD; **dringan**, S; **þrungen**, *pt. pl.*, PP; **þrongen**, S2, PP; **i-þrunge**, *pp.*, S; **thrungun**, W; **y-thrungin**, S3.—AS. *þringan*, *pt. þrang* (pl. *þrungon*), *pp. þrungen*.

þrinne[1], *adv.* three at a time, S.—Cf. Icel. *þrinnr*.

þrinne[2], *adv.* therein, S, S2; see **þer-**, *prefix*.

þrist[1], *sb.* thirst, S, S2, PP; **þurst**, S, C2, PP. *Comb.*: **þurstlew**, thirsty, HD.—AS. *þyrst* (*þirst*), *þurst*.

þrist[2], *pt. pl.* thrust, S; see **þrusten**.

þriste, *adj.* bold, S.—AS. *þríste*: OS. *thrísti*; cf. G. *dreist*.

þristen, *v.* to thirst, W, S; **thresten**, S2; **þursten**, SD; **thursted him**, *pt. s. impers.*, C2.—AS. *þyrstan*: OHG. *thursten* (Tatian).

þriuen, *v.* to thrive, S, PP; **þryue**, PP; **þroff**, *pt. s.*, PP; **þriuen**, *pp.*, grown up, PP; **þryuen**, well grown, S2.—Icel. *þrífa*, to seize, *þrífask*, to thrive.

þro, *adj.* eager, earnest, vehement, HD; **þra**, B; **þraa**, HD; **þroo**, sharp, HD; **throw**, *adv.*, S3; **þroliche**, *adv.*, vehemently, S2; **þroly**, quickly, resolutely, S2, HD, PP.—Icel. *þrá-r*, stubborn, also frequent.

þrof, *adv.* thereof, S; see **þer-**.

þroh, *sb.* coffin; see **þruh**.

þrop, *sb.* a village, S, C2; see **þorp**.

þrosshen, *pp.* threshed, S; see **þreschen**.

þrote, *sb.* throat, S, PP.—AS. *þrotu* (Voc.); cf. OHG. *drozza* (whence G. *drossel*); related to Du. *stroot*; cf. It. *strozza* (Diez). See Kluge (s.v. *drossel*).

þrowe[1], *sb.* a little while, course, time, moment, Prompt., PP, S2, C2, C3, HD; **throw**, HD; **þroȝe**, S; **thrawe**, S2; **thraw**, S2, B.—AS. *þrág*.

þrowe[2], *sb.* suffering, *ærumna*, SD, Prompt.

þrowen[1], *v.* to throw, S; **þreu**, *pt. s.*, S; **þrewe**, threw himself, P; *2 pt. s.*, S; **þrowe**, PP; **þrawen**, *pp.*, S2; **þrowen**, S2; **y-throwe**, C2.—AS. *þráwan*, to twist, to whirl, *pt. þréow*, *pp. þráwen*.

þrowen[2], *v.* to suffer, S; **þrowede**, *pt. s.*, S.—AS. *þrowian*; cf. OHG. *thruoén* (Tatian).

þrowunge, *sb.* suffering, passion; **þroweunge**, *dat.*, S; **þrowenge**, S; **þroweinge**, S.—AS. *þrowung*.

þrublen, *v.* to press, crowd; **þrublande**, *pr. p.*, S2.

þruh, *sb.* coffin, S.—AS. *þruh*.

þrum, *sb.* strength, a crowd, glory, SD; **þrom**, SD. *Comb.*: **þrim-setel**, *tronus*, SD; **þrimsettles**, *pl.*, S.—AS. *þrymm*, *þrymsetl*.

Þrunnesse, *sb.* Trinity, S; see **þreo**.

þruppe, *adv.* thereupon, S; see **þer-**.

þrusche, *sb.* a thrush, S.—AS. *þrysce*.

þrustel, *sb.* the song-thrush, S; **þrostle**, S. *Comb.*: **þrustel-cock**, thrustlecock, C2; **þrestelcoc**, S2.—AS. *þrostle* (Voc.).

þrusten, *v.* to thrust, SD; **þreste**, C; **þristen**, W; **þruste**, *pt. s.*, W; **þrist**, S; **þriste**, *pp.*, S.—Icel. *þrýsta*.

þu, *pron.* thou, S; see **þou**.

þues, *pron. dem. pl.* these, S2; see **þes**.

þuften, *sb.* handmaid, S; **þuhten**, S.—A fem. deriv. of AS. *(ge)þofta*, a comrade, properly one who sits on the same rowing-bench; from *þofta* 'transtra' (Voc.); cf. Icel. *þopta*.

þulke, *adj.* that, those, S2; see **þilk**.

þulli, *adj.* such, S, SD; **þellich**, SD; **þellyche**, S2.—AS. *þullic, þyllic,* also *þuslic, þyslic,* from *þus*; see Sievers, 349. See **þus**.

þuncheð, þuncð; see **þynken**.

Þunre¹, *sb.* the Teutonic god Thor, S; *Comb.*: **Þunres dæi**, the day of Thor, Thursday, S. Cf. **þoner** and **Þorr**.

þunre², *sb.* thunder, S; see **þoner**.

þurfen, *v.* to need; **þarf**, *pt. pr. s.*, need, *ei opus est*, S; **þare**, H; **þar**, H; **þarst**, *2 pt. pr. s.*, PP; **þurt**, *pt. s.*, needed, S2, H, B. *Comb.*: **thardestow**, thou wouldst need, PP.—AS. *þurfan*, pt. pr. *þearf*; pt. *þorfte* (*þurfte*), Icel. *þurfa*, pt. pr. *þarf*; pt. *þurfum*; cf. OHG. *thurfan*, to need (Tatian).

þurgh, *prep.* through, S2, C2; **þur3**, S2, W2; **þure3**, S; **þurh**, S; **þurch**, S; **þuruh**, S; **þor3**, S2; **þoru3**, S2, W2; **þorw**, S; **þoru**, S, S2; **thorou**, W; **thurght**, H; **þurð** S, S2; **þurf**, S2, HD; **þoru3like**, *adv.*, thoroughly, S. *Comb.*: **thurghfare**, thoroughfare, C; **þurhfaren**, to pass through; **thurghfare**, S2; **thurgh-girt**, pierced through, C; **thurchhurt**, thoroughly hurt, S3; **þurh-lefien**, to live through; **þurhlefede**, *pt. s.*, S; **þurh-seon**, to perceive; **þurhsihð**, *pr. s.*, S; **þuruh-ut**, wholly, S; **thurghout**, C2; **þuruhtut**, throughout, S; **þoru-out**, S2.—AS. *þurh*; cf. OHG. *thuruh* (Tatian).

þurl, *sb.* an aperture for admitting light, a hole, S; **thurles**, *pl.*, HD.—AS. *þyrel*, hole,

from *þurh*, through; so (with different suffix) Goth. *þairko*, hole, the eye of a needle, from *þairh*, through; see Kluge (s.v. *durch*). See **þurgh**.

þurlen, *v.* to pierce, S, S2, PP; **þirlen**, C, S2, PP, H; **thrill**, H.—AS. *þyrlian* (*þirlian*).

þurst, *sb.* thirst, S, C2; see **þrist¹**.

þurstlew, *adj.* thirsty, HD; see **-lewe**. Cf. **þrist¹**.

þus, *adv.* thus, S; **tus**, S (in Ormulum). *Comb.*: **þusgate**, in this way, PP; **þusgates**, HD, PP.—AS. *þus*, OS. *thus*.

þuster, *adj.* dark, S; see **þester**.

þut, for **þu it**, S; see **þou**.

þuvele, *sb. pl.* twigs, S.—AS. *þýfel*, 'frutex' (Voc.). See **þefe**.

þwang, *sb.* thong, S; see **þwong**.

þwert, *adv.* thwart, SD. *Comb.*: **þwert-ut**, throughout, S.—Icel. *þvert*, neuter of *þverr*, transverse; cf. AS. *þweorh*, Goth. *þwairhs*, angry, cross.

þwong, *sb.* strip of leather, thong, S, S2, W; **þwang** S; **þong** S.—AS. *þwang*.

þwytel, *sb.* a knife, whittle; **thwitel**, SkD; **thewtill**, S3. See **þwyten**.

þwyten, *v.* to cut, to whittle, Voc., Prompt., Palsg. *Der.*: **thwytynge**, cutting, whittling, PP.—AS. *þwitan*.

þy, *sb.* thigh, Prompt.; **þe**, SkD, HD; **þee**, HD; **þy3**, S2; **þih**, SkD; **þei3**, SkD.—AS. *þéo, þéoh*.

þyester, *adj.* dark, S2; see **þester**.

þyesternesse, *sb.* darkness, S2; see **þester-nesse**.

þyht, *adj.* close, compact, tight. Prompt.; **thite**, HD; **ti3t**, SkD.—Cf. G. *dicht*, Icel. *þéttr*; see Kluge (s.v.).

þyhtyn, *v.* to make tight, Prompt.; **y-ti3t**, *pp.*, S3.

þynken, *v.* to seem; **þynkeþ**, *pr. s. impers.*, PP; **þuncð**, S; **þunchð**, S; **þincheð**, S; **þinkð**, S; **þingð**, S2; **þenkeð**, PP; **þuhte**, *pt. s.*, S; **þu3te**, S; **þo3te**, S2; **thoughte**, C3; **þout**, S2.—AS. *þyncan*, pt. *þúhte*, pp. *(ge)þúht*. See **þenchen**.

U

For words in which initial **u-** *or* **v-** *has the sound of* **v-**, *see under* **V** *below.*

uggen, *v.* to dread, to shudder at, HD; **ug**, H; **huge**, H; **uggis**, *pr. s.*, H; **uggid**, *pt. s.*, H.—Icel. *ugga.*

uggynge, *sb.* shuddering, horror, H.

ugly, *adv.* dreadful, horrible, H, SkD; **uglike**, SkD.—Icel. *uggligr.*

ugsom, *adj.* frightful, SkD (s.v. *ugly*).

uhte, *sb.* the part of the night before daybreak; **uȝten**, *dat.*, S, SD.—AS. *úhte*: OS. *uhta*: Goth. *uhtwo*; cf. OHG. *uohta*, Icel. *ótta*, see Weigand (s.v. *ucht*), and Fick, 7. 9.

uhten-tid, *sb.* early morning-time, SD.

uht-song, *sb.* morning-chant, matins, SD.—AS. *uht-sang.*

ulke, *adj.* the same, S; see **ilke**.

umbe, *prep.* about, around, WA, S; **umm-benn**, S; **embe**, S.—AS. *ymbe (embe)*: OHG. *umbi* (Otfrid), OS. *umbi.*

vmbe-cast, *v.* to cast about, consider, ponder, B; **umbekestez**, *pr. s.*, S2.

umbe-grouen, *pp.* grown all round, S2.

umbelappe, *v.* to surround, WA. See **umlap.**

vmbe-set, *v.* to beset, B; **umbeset**, *pt. s.*, B; **vmset**, S2; **umbeset**, *pp.*, B; **umsett**, H, HD; **vmset**, S2.—AS. *ymb-sittan.*

vmbe-stount, *adv.* sometimes, B; **umstunt**, H.—AS. *ymbe + stund.*

umbe-þenken, *v.* to bethink, meditate, S; **umthink**, H; **vmbethinkis ȝow**, *imp. pl. refl.*, B; **umbithoghte**, *pt. s.*, HD; **vmbethoucht**, B.—AS. *ymb-þencan.*

umbe-weround, *pp.* environed, B.

umbe-while, *adv.* sometime, at times, S; **umwhile**, H, HD; **umwile**, S; **vmquhile**, B; **umquile**, WA.

um-ga, *v.* to go about, H.

um-gang, *sb.* circuit, S2, H.—AS. *ymb-gang.*

um-gifen, *v.* to surround, H; **vmgaf**, *pt. pl.*, S2, H.

um-gripen, *v.* to surround; **vm-griped**, *pt. pl.*, S2.

um-hilen, *v.* to cover up; **umhild**, *pt. s.*, H.

um-lap, *v.* to wrap around, comprehendere, to embrace, WA, S2; **umlappe**, H, HD; **vmlapped**, *pp.*, S2. See **umbelappe.**

um-louke, *v.* to lock in, H.

um-sege, *v.* to besiege, H.

um-set, *pp.* beset all round, S2; see **umbeset.**

um-shadow, *v.* to shadow round, protect, H.

um-stride, *v.* to bestride, S2; **umstrode**, *pt. s.*, HD.

um-writhen, *v.* to wind round, H; **umwrithyn**, *pp.*, H.

um-ȝede, *pt. s.* went about, H.

un-[1], *prefix*, has a negative force and is used before substantives, adjectives, and past participles; **on-**, B.—Goth. *un-*; cf. Gr. ἀν-.

un-[2], *prefix*, expresses the reversal of an action, and is used before verbs; **on-**, S3.—Goth. *and-*; cf. Gr. ἀντι-.

un-[3], *prefix*, until.—OS. *und-*. Cf. **oþ**[1].

un-aneomned, *pp.* unnamed, innumerable, S. Cf. **nemnen.**

un-auanced, *pp.* unpromoted, S2.

un-bermed, *pp.* unleavened; **unberrmedd**, S.

un-bicumlich, *adj.* unbecoming, S; **unbicomelich**, S.

un-biheue, *adj.* unprofitable; **unbihefre**, *comp.*, S.

un-bileue, *sb.* unbelief, W.

un-bileueful, *adj.* unbelieving, W; **unbileful**, S.

un-binden, *v.* to unbind, S2; **unbind**, *pr. s.*, S; **unbint**, S; **unbond**, *pt. s.*, S; **unbounden**, *pl.*, S; *pp.*, C2.—Cf. OHG. *inbintan* (Otfrid). (**un-**[2].)

un-bischoped, *pp.* unconfirmed; **unbishped**, S.

un-bisorȝeliche, *adv.* piteously, S.

un-bliðe, *adj.* joyless; **unblyþe**, S2.

un-boht, *pp.* unatoned for, S; **unbouht**, S.

un-bokelen, *v.* to unbuckle, C2, C3. (**un-**[2].)

un-brosten, *pp.* unburst, S2.

un-buhsum, *adj.* disobedient, S; **vnboxome**, P.

un-buxsumnes, *sb.* disobedience, H.

unce, *sb.* ounce, SkD, C, Cath. See **ounce** and cf. **inche.**

un-chargid, *pp.* unladen, W. (**un-**[2].)

un-cofre, *v.* to take out of a coffer, S3. (**un-**[2].)

un-conabil, *adj.* unsuitable; **unkonnabil**, H; **vncunable**, H.—Cf. OF. *covenable* (BH. 153. 43).

un-conabilly, *adv.* unsuitably, H.

un-conabilnes, *sb.* misbehaviour, H.

un-conabiltes, *sb. pl.* incongruities, H.

vn-conand, *adj.* ignorant, HD, H; **vnkunand**, H.

vn-conandly, *adv.* ignorantly, H.

un-corrupcioun, *sb.* incorruption, W.

uncuð, *adj.* strange, unknown, S2; see **unkouþ.**

un-cweme, *adj.* displeasing, SD: **unn-cweme**, S. See **unyqueme**.

undampned, *pp.* uncondemned, W.

un-deedli, *adj.* immortal, W; **vndedly**, H.

un-deedlynesse, *sb.* immortality, W; **un-dedlynes**, WA.

un-defoulid, *pp.* undefiled (= *impollutus, immaculatus*), W, WA.

un-dep, *adj.* not deep, S.

under[1], *prep., adv.* during, between, under, underneath, S; **onder**, SD; **undur**, W; **undir**, B. *Phr.*: **vnder þan**, during these things, *interea*, meanwhile, S.—AS. *under*: Goth. *undar*; cf. OHG. *untar*.

under[2], *sb.* afternoon, CM; see **undern**.

under[3], *v.* to subject, S2.

under-crien, *v.* to cry out; **undurcrieden**, *pt. pl.* (= *succlamabant*), W.

under-fangen, *v.* to receive, S; **underfonge**, S; **onderuonge**, S2; **underuongen**, S; **onderfang**, *imp. s.*, S; **undurfong**, *pt. s.*, S2; **underueng**, S2; **underfangen**, *pp.*, S; **underuonge**, S; **underfongen**, P; **undurfongun**, W.

under-fon, *v.* to receive, S; **underfo**, S; **under-uon**, S; **underfon**, *pp.*, S.—AS. *under-fón*.

under-giten, *v.* to perceive, understand; **underȝiten**, SD; **underȝeite**, S; **undergæton**, *pt. pl.*, S.—AS. *under-gitan*.

under-leggen, *v.* to subject; **under-laide**, *2 pt. s.*, S2.

under-ling, *sb.* a subject, inferior, S, PP.

under-lout, *adj.* subject, H.

under-master, *sb.* usher; **undurmaistir** (= *paedagogus*), W.

under-mel, *sb.* the afternoon-meal, SD, CM. See **undern**.

undern, *sb.* the time between, the time between sunrise and noon, between noon and sunset, a mealtime, S2, C, C2, CM, Voc.; **undorne**, WA; **vndren**, S, HD, SD; **under**, S2; **undur**, HD; **aunder**, HD.—AS. *undern*, OS. *undorn*, Icel. *undorn*; cf. OHG. *untorn* (G. *untern*).

undern-time, *sb.* SD; **undrentime**, S; **undirtime**, SD.

under-nymen, *v.* to receive, perceive, reprove, PP; **undirnyme**, W2; **under-nimen**, S; **underneme**, *reprehendo*, Prompt.; **undernom**, *pt. s.*, C3; **undernumen**, *pp.*, S; **undirnommen**, W; **undernome**, PP,

under-picchen, *v.* to fix underneath; **underpyghte**, *pt. s.*, C3.

under-preost, *sb.* under-priest; **unnderrpreost**, S.

under-sette, *v.* to place beneath, support, prop up; **undursette**, W2.

under-standen, *v.* to understand, S; **onderstanden**, S2; **understonden**, S, S2; **undyrstonde**, S2; **understant**, *pr. s.*, S; **understont**, S; **undyrstode**, *pt. s.*, S2 **understoden**, *pt. pl.*, S; **undurstoden**, stood under, W2; **understande**, *pp.*, S; **understonde**, S2; **onderstonde**, S2. **under-stondingnesse**, *sb.* faculty of understanding, S.

under-take, *v.* to undertake, agree, SD; **undertoc**, *pt. s.*, S2; **undertok**, S.

under-þeod, *sb.* subject, S; **underþeoden**, *pl.*, S; **underþiede**, S.—AS. *under-þéod*.

under-uon, *v.* to receive, S; see **underfon**.

under-ȝeite, *v.* to learn, discover, S; see **undergiten**.

un-digne, *adj.* unworthy, C2.—OF. *undigne*.

un-discreet, *adj.* undiscerning, C2.—OF. *undiscret*.

un-don[1], *v.* to undo, open, disclose, SD, W; **undo**, WA; **undede**, *pt. s.*, S2; **undude**, S, PP; **undone**, *pp.*, S.—AS. *un-dón*. (**un-**[2].)

undon[2], *v.* to undo, destroy, PP.

undoubtabili, *adv.* without doubt, S3.

un-dreh, *adj.* impatient, out of patience, S2.

un-duhtiȝ, *adj.* unworthy; **unduhti**, S.

un-eað, *adj.* uneasy; **uneaðe**, S.

un-eaðe, *adv.* scarcely, S; **unneðe**, S, S2, C2, C3, W; **onneaþe**, S2; **oneþe**, S3; **uneth**, S3, P, WA; **unneth**, S3.

un-eðes, *adv.* scarcely, W, S; **unnethes**, S2, C2, W, H; **vnneths**, H; **vnees**, PP.

un-faȝen, *adj.* displeased; **unfeyn**, S2.

un-fest, *adj.* unstable, S2.

un-festlich, *adj.* unfestive, C2.

un-fete, *adj.* ill-made, bad, S2. (**un-**[1].)

un-filabil, *adj.* insatiable, H. (**un-**[1].)

un-filed, *pp.* undefiled, S2.

un-flichand, *pp.* unflinching, H. (**un-**[1].)

un-forȝolden, *pp.* unrequited, S; **unvorgulde**, S.

un-freme, *sb.* disadvantage, S.—AS. *unnfremu*.

un-fruytouse, *adj.* unfruitful, W.

un-gert, *pp.* ungirt, G.

un-glad, *adj.* unhappy, S2.

un-happe, *sb.* ill-luck, WA.

un-happy, *adj.* unlucky, S2.

un-hardy, *adj.* not bold, PP.

un-hele, *sb.* sickness, S; misfortune, CM.

un-heled, *pp.* uncovered, WA, PP.—AS. *helian*; OHG. *haljan*. (**un-**[2].)

un-helðe, *sb.* sickness, S; **unhalðe**, S.

un-hersumnesse, *sb.* disobedience, S.—AS. *unhýrsumnis*.

un-hillen, *v.* to disclose, S; **unhilen**, S2, W; **onhillin**, Prompt.; **unhulien**, SD, MD; **unhiled**, *pp.*, CM, G, SD, PP; **unhuled**,

S2.—Cf. Goth. *huljan*, OHG. *huljan, hullan*. (**un-**².)

un-hol, *adj.* sick, S.—AS. *un-hál*.

un-hold, *adj.* ungracious, S.

un-ifoȝ, *adj.* innumerable; **unnifoȝe**, *pl.*, S.—AS. *un-gefóg*.

un-imeað, *sb.* want of moderation, S (8 b. 12).

un-imet, *adj.* immense, immeasurable, S; **onimete**, S.—AS. *un-gemet*.

un-imete, *adv.* immensely, S.—AS. *ungemete*.

un-imeteliche, *adv.* infinitely, S.—AS. *ungemetlice*.

un-iredlice, *adv.* sharply, roughly, S; **unrideli**, S.—AS. *un-gerýdelice*.

un-isalðe, *sb.* unhappiness, S.—AS. *ungesǽlð*.

un-iseli, *adj.* unhappy, S.—AS. *un-gesǽlig*.

un-itald, *pp.* unnumbered, S.—AS. *ungeteald*.

universite, *sb.* universe, world, W.—OF. *universite*; Lat. *universitatem* (Vulg.).

un-iwasse, *pp.* unwashen, S.

unk, *pron. dual.* us both, S; **unker**, of us both, S.—AS. *unc*, dat. and acc., *uncer*, gen.: Goth. *ugk*, acc., *ugkis*, dat., *ugkara*, gen.

un-kempt, *pp.* uncombed, rough, S3.

un-keulen, *v.* to ungag, S. (**un-**².)

un-kouth, *adj.* unknown, strange, PP; **unkuð**, S; **uncuð**, S2; **uncouthe**, *pl.*, S2, C2; **uncuðe**, S; **uncoðe**, S.—AS. *un-cúð*.

vn-kunnyng, *sb.* ignorance, W; **vnkunnyngis**, *pl.*, W2.

vn-kunnynge, *adj.* unskilful, ignorant, S2, W, W2; **unkonnyng**, C; **vnkonnynge**, PP.

un-kunnyngenesse, *sb.* ignorance, W.

un-kynde, *adj.* unnatural, unkind, C2, PP; **uncunde**, SD.

un-kyndenesse, *sb.* unkindness, C3, PP.

un-kyth, *v.* to hide, S2. (**un-**².)

un-lace, *v.* to unbind, W. (**un-**².)

un-lappe, *v.* to unfold; **onlappyt**, *pt. s.*, S3. (**un-**².)

un-lede, *adj.* miserable, wretched, S, SD.—AS. *un-lǽd*: Goth. *un-léds*.

un-leueful, *adj.* not permissible, W; **onleefful**, *illicitus*, Prompt.

un-leuesum, *adj.* not permissible; **onlesum**, S3.

un-liche, *adj.* unlike, S.

un-louken, *v.* to unlock, PP; **vnloke**, *pp.*, G. (**un-**².)

un-lust, *sb.* lack of pleasure, displeasure, SD.

un-lusti, *adj.* unlusty, idle, SD; **onlosti**, S2.

un-lykynge, *adj.* unfit, improper, scandalous, PP.

un-mayte, *adj.* unmeet, H. *Phr.*: **in unmayte**, unfittingly, H.

un-meoð, *sb.* want of moderation, S; **unmeð**, S (8 a. 10). See **meþ**².

un-meuable, *adj.* immovable, W.

un-moebles, *sb. pl.* immovable property, PP.—Cf. OF. *muebles* (BH); pl. of *mueble*; Late Lat. *mõbilem*.

un-mylde, *adj.* cruel, W; **unmyld**, H.

un-nait, *adj.* useless, S2, H.

unnen, *v.* to grant, S; **hunne**, S; **an**, *1 pr. s.*, S; **on**, *pr. s.*, S; **i-unne**, *pp.*, S.—AS. *unnan*, 1 and 3 pr. s. *ann*, opt. *unne*, pt. *úðe*, pp. *geunnen*. Cf. Icel. *unna*, OS. *gi-unnan*, OHG. *gi-unnan*, pt. *onda* (Otfrid), G. *gönnen*.

unneðe, *adv.* scarcely, S, S2, C2, C3, W; **unneth**, S3; see **uneaþe**.

unnethes, *adv.* scarcely, S2, C2, W, H; **vnneths**, H; see **uneþes**.

un-nit, *adj.* useless, S; **unnet**, S; **unnut**, S.—AS. *un-nytt*.

un-noble, *adj.* ignoble, W2.

un-noblei, *sb.* ignobleness, W.

un-noyandnes, *sb.* harmlessness, H.

un-obedience, *sb.* disobedience, W.

un-onest, *adj.* dishonourable, W.

un-orne, *adj.* old, worn out, S; **unorn**, S; **unourne**, HD.—AS. *un-orne* (Grein).

un-perfit, *adj.* imperfect, W2; **unparfit**, PP.

un-pesible, *adj.* unquiet, W.

un-pined, *pp.* untouched by pain, S.

un-pitè, *sb.* want of feeling, W, W2.

un-profit, *sb.* unprofitableness, W.

un-quaynt, *adj.* imprudent, unwise, H.

un-rede, *sb.* bad counsel, folly, mischief, S.—AS. *un-réd*.

un-redi, *adj.* not prepared, W; **unredy**, improvident, PP.

un-repreuable, *adj.* not to be reproved, W.

un-rest, *sb.* restlessness, S3; **vnreste**, *dat.*, C2.

un-resty, *adj.* restless, H; **unristy**, H.

un-ride, *adj.* harsh, cruel, WA, HD, SD.—AS. *un-(ge)ryde* (Luke, 3. 5).

un-rideli, *adv.* sharply, vehemently, roughly, S; **unridly**, fiercely, WA; see **uniredlice**.

un-riȝt, *adj.* injustice, wrong, S2; **unryht**, S; **vnright**, PP, S2; **unriht**, S.—AS. *unriht*.

un-riȝtfulnesse, *sb.* unrighteousness, unlawfulness, W2; **unrihtfulnesse**, S.

un-riȝtwisnesse, *sb.* unrighteousness, W.

un-sad, *adj.* unsteady, C2.

un-sadnesse, *sb.* instability, W2.

un-saht, *adj.* unreconciled, discontented, S2.

un-schape, *pp.* unshapen, outlandish, S2.

un-schutten, *v.* to open, SD; **unschette**, *pt. s.*, SD; **onschet**, S3; **vnshette**, *pp.*, S3. (**un-**².)

un-scilwis, *adj.* unwise, H.

un-scilwisly, *adv.* unwisely, H.

un-sehelich, *adj.* invisible, S.
un-seill, *sb.* misfortune, B.—AS. *unsél.*
un-sele, *adj.* unhappy, S, S2.
un-selð, *sb.* unhappiness; **unselðe**, S; **unnsellðe**, S; **unnseolðe**, S.—AS. *un-sélð.*
un-sely, *adj.* unhappy, C2; **vnceli**, W.
un-sete, *sb.* unsettledness, S2.
un-skaþeful, *adj.* harmless; **unnskaþefull**, S.
un-skaþiȝnesse, *sb.* harmlessness, S.
un-skilful, *adj.* unreasonable, outrageous, unprofitable, PP; **unschilful**, S2.
un-slekked, *pp.* unslacked, C3.
un-soote, *adj.* unsweet, bitter, S3.
un-sounded, *pp.* unhealed, S3.
un-souerable, *adj.* insufferable, S3.
un-sowen, *v.* to slit open what has been sewn, PP; **unsouwen**, PP. (**un-**[2].)
un-spedful, *adj.* unsuccessful, H; **onschet**, S3.
un-sperren, *v.* to unfasten, unbar, PP. (**un-**[2].)
un-spurne, *v.* to kick open, S. (**un-**[2].)
un-staðeluest, *adj.* without a firm foundation, S.
un-stedefast, *adj.* not firm in one's place, unsteady, S, PP; **unstudeueste**, S.—AS. *unstedefæst.*
un-stirabil, *adj.* immovable, H.
un-strong, *adj.* feeble, S.—AS. *un-strang.*
un-suget, *pp.* not subject, W.
un-tellendlic, *adj.* indescribable, S.
un-tiffed, *pp.* unadorned, S.
until, *conj.*, *prep.* until, unto, S2, PP, SkD; **ontill**, B. (**un-**[3].)
un-tiled, *pp.* untilled, PP; **untuled**, S2.
un-to, *prep.* unto, SkD.—OS. *untó* for *undt +* *ó*; cf. OS. *unte*, until, Goth. *unte*, for, OHG. *unz* (Tatian). (**un-**[3].)
un-todealet, *pp.* undivided, S. (**un-**[1].)
un-toheliche, *adv.* unrestrainedly, S.
un-tohen, *pp.* undisciplined, S; **untowun**, SkD (p. 695), **untohe**, S.—Cf. AS. *téon*. See **ten.**
un-trewe, *adj.* untrue, not straight, S, PP, C2.—AS. *un-tréowe.*
un-trewnesse, *sb.* untruth, S.
un-trewthe, *sb.* untruth, C3.
un-trist, *sb.* disbelief, W.
un-þanc, *sb.* dislike; **unþonkes**, *gen.*, S. *Phr.*: **hares unþances**, against their will, S.—AS. *un-þanc.*
un-thende, *small, out of season, unprosper-ous*, PP, HD. Cf. **þeen.**
un-thewe, *sb.* immorality, S; **un-þeu**, S; **unþewe**, *dat.*, S; **unþewes**, *pl.*, S2.—AS. *un-péaw.*
un-tholemodnes, *sb.* impatience, H.
un-þrift, *sb.* unprofitableness; **unþryfte**, S2.

un-thryftyly, *adv.* unprofitably, improperly, S2, C3.
un-vysible, *adj.* invisible, W.
un-war, *adj.* unexpected, unexpecting, SD, S2, C2, C3.
un-ware, *adv.* unwarily, S2.
un-warly, *adv.* at unawares, S3.
un-way, *sb.* wrong path, H.
un-weawed, *pp.* unveiled, S.—Cf. AS. *wǽfels*, a covering, veil.
un-welde, *adj.* impotent, weak, SD, S; **vnweldy**, S3, C3.
un-wemmed, *pp.* unstained, unspotted, S, S2, C3, W2; **unwemmyd**, W, H; **unwemmet**, S; **unweommet**, S.—AS. *un(ge)-wemmed.*
un-werȝed, *pp.* unwearied; **unwerget**, S.—AS. *un(ge)wériged.*
un-wiht, *sb.* monster, an uncanny creature, evil spirit, S; **unwiȝt**, S; *adj.*, S; **unwiȝtes**, *pl.*, S.
un-wille, *sb.* unwillingness, displeasure, S. *Phr.*: **hire unwilles**, against her will, S.—AS. *un-willa.*
un-willich, *adj.* unwilling, S.
un-wine, *sb.* enemy, S; **unwines**, *pl.*, S.
un-wis, *adj.* unwise, S2.—AS. *un-wís.*
un-wisdom, *sb.* folly, W.
un-wist, *pp.* unknown, C.
un-wit, *sb.* want of wit, C3, H.
un-witti, *adj.* unwise, W.
un-wityng[1], *pr. p.* unknowing, C3.
un-wityng[2], *sb.* ignorance, W.
un-wiȝt, *adj.* uncanny, S. See **unwiht.**
un-worschip, *v.* to dishonour, W.
un-wrappen, *v.* to disclose, C2. (**un-**[2].)
un-wrast, *adj.* infirm, weak, base, bad, S, PP; **unwreast**, S; **unwraste**, *pl.*, S; **unwreste**, *dat. s.*, S.—AS. *un-wrǽst.*
un-wrenc, *sb.* evil design; **unwrenche**, *dat.*, S.—AS. *unwrenc.*
un-wréon, *v.* to discover, to reveal, SD; **unwreo**, S; **unwroȝen**, S; **unwroȝe**, S.—AS. *un-wréon.* (**un-**[2].)
un-wrien, *v.* to uncover, SD; *pp.*, S.—From AS. *wríhan.* (**un-**[2].)
un-wunne, *sb.* sadness, S, SD; **unwinne**, S; **unwenne**, S.
un-wurð, *adj.* unworthy, S; **unwurðe**, *pl.*, S; **unwurðere**, *comp.*, S; **unwurðeste**, *superl.*, S.—AS. *un-wurð.*
un-wurði, *adj.* unworthy, S, SD; **onwurþi**, Prompt.
un-wurðlich, *adj.* unworthy, base; **un-worþelych**, S2; **unwurðliche**, *adv.*, S.—AS. *un-wurðlic, -lice.*
un-yliche, *adj.* unlike, S; **unilich**, S.—AS. *un-gelíc.*

un-yqueme, *adj.* displeasing, S. See **un-cweme**, **icweme**.

up, *adv. and prep.* up, S2, S3, G; **op**, S, S2.
Phr.: **up so doun**, upside down, C, C3, W, PP; **up se doun**, W, W2; **up soo doune**, S3.—AS. *up, upp*; cf. OHG. *úf* (Otfrid).

up-braiding, *sb.* reproach, S2.

up-breiden, *v.* to reproach, S, W.

up-breyd, *sb.* reproach, S2.

up-cumen, *v.* to ascend; **uppcumenn**, S.

up-heuen, *v.* to raise, S2; **uphaf**, *pt. s.*, C; **uphouen**, *pp.*, S2; **upe-houen**, S2.

up-holdere, *sb.* seller of second-hand things, P.

up-londisch, *adj.* rustic, countrified, S2; **oplondysch**, S2.

vppe, *adv.* up, PP, S; **upe**, S, S2; **ope**, S2.

vppon, *prep.* upon, PP; **uppen**, S; **apon**, S2.
Phr.: **vpon lofte**, above, S2.

up-right, *adv.* on one's back, C, C2; **upryghte**, C2.

up-risen, *v.* to rise up; **up-rist**, *pr. s.* CM.

up-risinge, *sb.* resurrection, S2.

up-rist, *sb.* rising, SD, S3; **upriste**, *dat.*, S, C.

up-set, *pp.* set up, S2.

up-sterten, *v.* to start up; **upsterte**, *pt. s.*, S2, C.

up-sti3e, *sb.* ascension, S.

up-sti3en, *v.* to ascend, SD; **upsteghes**, *pr. pl.*, S2; **upstegh**, *pt. s.*, S2.

up-stowr, *v.* to be stirred up, S3.

up-take, *v.* to take up, receive; **uptoke**, *pt. s.*, S2.

up-ward, *adv.* upward; **uppard**, S.

up-warp, *v.* to throw up, S3.

up-wauen, *v.* to move upward with an undulating motion; **up-wafte**, *pt. pl.*, S2.

up-3elden, *v.* to deliver up, S2.

vrchun, *sb.* hedgehog, H; see **irchon**.

ure[1], *sb.* practice, work, operation, ND, Manip., SkD.—OF. *eure, uevre*; Lat. *ŏpera*.

ure[2], *sb.* fate, luck, good luck, B, CM.—OF. *eur, eür*: Prov. *agur*; Late Lat. **agurium* for Lat. *augurium*; see BH, § 27.

urnen, *v.* to run, S; see **rennen**.

urre, *sb.* anger, S; see **eorre**.

vrþe, *sb.* earth, S2; see **erþe**[2].

usage, *sb.* custom, C2, C3.—AF. *usage*.

usaunce, *sb.* custom, HD, CM.—OF. *usance* (Cotg.).

use, *sb.* use, usury, HD; **us**, S2, SD; **vce**, S3; **oyss**, B.—AF. *us*; Lat. *usum*.

usen, *v.* to use, to be accustomed, PP, S3, C2; **usede**, *pt. s.*, SD, PP; **usiden**, *pl.*, dealt with, W; **yvsed**, *pp.*, S2; **uset**, customary, PP; **used**, C3; **vsyt**, S3; **oysit**, B; **wsyt**, S3.—AF. *user*.

ussher, *sb.* usher, door-keeper, C2, SkD; **uschere**, Prompt.; **usshere**, PP.—AF. *ussher, usser*, OF. *ussier*; Lat. *ostiarium*, door-keeper, from *ostium*, door.

usure, *sb.* usury, C2, P; **vsuris**, *pl.*, W.—AF. *usure*; Lat. *usura*.

utas, *sb.* the octave of a festival, HD, ND, SkD, Palsg.—AF. *utaves*; Lat. *octavas*. For the *s* = *v's* cf. in Old French *vis* = *vivus* (BH).

ute, *adv.* out, S.—AS. *úte*.

uten, *prep.* away from, S.—AS. *útan*; cf. Goth. *utana*.

ut-la3e, *sb.* outlaw, S.—Icel. *útlaga*, outlawed, *útlagi*, an outlaw. See **outlawe**.

uttring, *sb.* circulating, S3. See **outren**.

uthe, *sb.* wave, S; **yþez**, *pl.*, S2, HD.—AS. *ýð*: Lat. *unda*.

u3ten, *sb.* early morning, S; see **uhte**.

V

For words in which initial **v-** *or* **u-** *has the sound of* **u-**, *see under* **U** *above. For some words of Teutonic origin beginning with* **v-**, *see* **F** *above; see also in some cases* **W** *below.*

vacherye, *sb.* a dairy, Prompt.—OF. *vacherie*, a cow-house (Cotg.); Late Lat. *vaccaria*, from Lat. *uacca*, a cow.

vader, *sb.* father, S, S2; see **fader**.

uæin, *adj.* fain, S; see **fayn**[2].

uair, *adj.* fair, S2; see **fayre**[1].

uale[1], *adj.* many, S; see **fele**.

vale[2], *v.* to descend, S3.—Cf. OF. *avaler*, to descend. Cf. **avalen**.

vale[3], *sb.* vale, PP.—AF. *val*; Lat. *vallem*.

valè, *sb.* valley, S2, B; **valeie**, S2; **valeye**, PP; **valayis**, *pl.*, B.—OF. *valee*; cf. It. *vallata*.

valuwen, *v.* to become yellow, S; see **falwe**.

vampies, **vampett**; see **vaumpe**.

vane, *sb.* a vane, C2; see **fane**.

vanishen, *v.* to vanish, C2; **vanshe**, Voc.; **vanshede**, *pt. s.*, PP; **vanyschiden**, *pl.*, became vain, W; **vanyssht**, *pp.*, S2.—Cf. OF. *esvanuïss-*, base of pr. p. of *esvanuïr*; Lat. *ex* + *uanescere*, from *uanus*.

vant, *v.* to vaunt, WA.—OF. *vanter*; Late Lat. *vanitare*, from Lat. *uanus*.

vantwarde, *sb.* vanguard, S2; see **vauntwarde**.

uaren, *v.* to fare, S; see **faren**.

variaunt, *adj.* changing, fickle, C2.

varien, *v.* to vary, Prompt.; **wariande**, *pr. p.*, S2; **variand**, S2, S3; **variant**, S3.—AF. *varier*; Lat. *uariare*.

varlet, *sb.* a young vassal, servant, squire, SkD, Sh.; *verna*, Manip.; **verlet**, S3.—OF. *varlet, vaslet*, dimin. of *vassal*. See **vassal**.

vassal, *sb.* a servant, subject.—AF. *vassal*; Low Lat. *vassallum* (acc.), from *vassus*, a man, a subject (of Celtic origin); cf. Wel. *gwas*, a youth, servant.

vassalage, *sb.* good service, prowess in arms, courage, B; **vasselage**, C, CM.—AF. *vasselage* (Roland).

vath[1], *sb.* danger, B.—Icel. *váði*.

vath[2], *interj.* fie! (= *vah*), W.

uaumpe, *sb.* the fore part of the foot, the vamp, Prompt., S; **vampies**, ND; **wampe**, *pedana, pedium, ante pedale,* Voc.; **wampay**, *pedana*, Voc.; **vauntpe**, Palsg.; **vampett**, Cath.—OF. *uantpie* (Palsg.), *avant-pied*, the fore part of the foot (Cotg.).

vaunte, *sb.* a boast, WA. See **vant**.

vaunten, *v.* to vault, S3; **vant**, S3 (s.v. *vaut*). Probably for *vauut, vaut*.

vauntwarde, *sb.* vanguard, PP; **vantwarde**, S2; **vaward**, B, WA.—AF. *avauntgarde*, OF. *avantwarde, avantgarde*.

vauntynge, *sb.* vaulting, S3.

vavasour, *sb.* a sub-vassal, C, HD.—AF. *vavasour*; OF. *vavassor*, a gen. pl. form, see Bartsch, p. 500; Low Lat. *vassus vassorum*, vassal of vassals (Diez, p. 338).

vaylen, *v.* to avail; **vaille**, PP; **vayleth**, *pr. s.*, S3; **vayls**, H. See **availen**.

vayn, *sb.* vein, S3; see **veyne**.

ueale, *adj.* many, S; see **vele**.

ueat, *sb.* vessel, S; see **fat**[1].

veaw, *adj.* few, S2; see **fewe**.

veder, *sb.* father, S; see **fader**.

veel, *sb.* veal, SkD; **veale**, calf, Manip.; **veal**, Manip.; **veilys**, *pl.*, calves, S3.—OF. *veël* (Ps. 28. 6): Prov. *vedel*; Lat. *uitellum* (acc.).

veer-tyme, *sb.* spring-time, W2. See **ver**[1].

veille, *sb.* watcher, P; **veil**, PP.—OF. *veile*; Lat. *uigilia*, a vigil, a watch.

ueir[1], *adj.* fair, MD; see **fayre**[1].

ueir[2], *sb.* beauty, S. See **veir**[1].

vekke, *sb.* an old woman, CM.

uelaʒ-rede, *sb.* fellowship, S2; see **felaw-rede**.

uele, *adj.* many, S, S2; **ueole**, S; **ueale**, S; see **fele**.

uelen, *v.* to feel, MD; see **felen**.

veluet, *sb.* velvet, *sericum villosum*, Manip., Prompt.; **velwet**, Prompt.; **velouette**, C2; **vellet**, HD.—It. *veluto* (Florio); Late Lat. **villutum*; from Lat. *uillus*, shaggy hair; cf. OF. *velu*, shaggy (Cotg.).

vendage, *sb.* vintage, PP.—OF. *vendange*; Lat. *uindēmia*; see BH, § 167.

venerie, *sb.* hunting, C; **venery**, game, DG.—OF. *venerie* (Cotg.), from *vener*, to hunt; Lat. *uenari*.

venesoun, *sb.* venison, P, Voc.; **venysoun**, PP.—AF. *venesoun, venysoun*, OF. *venison*; Lat. *uenationem*, hunting, see Apfelstedt (Introd. xxx), BH, § 28.

venge, *v.* to avenge, PP, ND, W; **wenge**, S2; **vengide**, *pt. s.*, W.—OF. *venger, vengier*; Lat. *uindicare*.

vengeable, *adj.* full of vengeance, S3, ND.

vengeaunce, *sb.* vengeance, PP; **vengance**, WA; **veniaunce**, PP, W, W2; **vengeans**, B; **veniauncis**, *pl.*, W.—OF. *venjance* (BH).

uenie, *sb.* supplication for pardon on one's knees, S.—Church Lat. *venia* (Ducange).

venkisen, *v.* to vanquish, PP; **vencuss**, B; **venkquyst**, *pt. s.*, S2; **venquysshed**, *pp.*, S2, C3; **venkised**, PP; **vencust**, B.—AF.

226

venquiss-, base of pr. p. of *venquir*, an inchoative form of OF. *veincre*; Lat. *uincere*.

uenne, *sb. dat.* mud, S; see **fen**[2].

ventose, *sb.* cupping-glass.—OF. *ventose* (*ventouse*), cupping-glass (Cotg.); Late Lat. *uentosa*.

ventouse, *v.* to cup, HD.—OF. *ventouser* (BH).

ventusynge, *sb.* cupping, C.

venust, *adj.* beautiful, S3.—Lat. *uenustus*.

venym, *sb.* poison, PP, C; **venim**, C2, C3, PP, Manip.—OF. *venin* (Ps. 139, 3). Lat. *uenēnum*; see BH, § 44.

venym-makere, *sb.* poisoner, W2, H.

venymous, *adj.* venomous, CM.—AF. *venymouse*, OF. *venemouse*.

venymous-heede, *sb.* venom, PP.

ueole, *adj.* many, S; see **vele**.

ueond, *sb.* enemy, S; see **feend**.

ueor, *adv.* far, S; see **fer**[2].

ver[1], *sb.* spring, JD, H (Ps. 73. 18). *Comb.*: **veer-tyme**, spring-time, W2.—Lat. *uer*.

ver[2], *sb.* glass, W2; **verre**, HD.—OF. *verre* (*voirre*); Lat. *uitrum*.

uerd, *sb.* army, MD; **uerden**, *pl. dat.*, S; see **ferd**[1].

uerden, *pt. pl.* fared, S; see **faren**.

verdegrese, *sb.* verdigris, PP; **verdegrece**, *viride grecum*, Voc.; **verdegrees**, C3.—OF. *vert de gris*, verdigrease (Cotg.); OF. *Gris*, Greeks (Ducange), pl. of *gri*; Late Lat. *grēcum*; Lat. *graecum*; see Constans, Notes, p. 25, and BH, § 32.

verdite, *sb.* verdict, C; **verdyte**, Palsg.—AF. *veirdit*; Lat. *uere dictum*.

uere, *sb.* companion, S; see **fere**[2].

vergere, *sb.* an orchard, CM.—OF. *vergier* (BH); Late Lat. *viridiarium*; see BH, § 134.

verlet, *sb.* a young servant, S3; see **varlet**.

vermel, *adj.* vermilion-coloured, S3; **vermayle**, CM.—OF. *vermeil*; Lat. *uermiculus*, scarlet (Vulg.).

vermiloun, *sb.* vermilion; **vermyloun**, Voc.; **vermylion**, WA; **vermeon**, WA.—AF. *vermiloun*.

vernage, *sb.* an Italian white wine, Prompt., CM, HD.—AF. *vernage*; It. *vernaccia*, 'a kind of winter wine in Italy very strong like Malmezy', so Florio, cf. Dante, Purg. 24, 24; from It. *vernaccio*, a severe winter, from *verno*, winter; Lat. *hibernum*, belonging to winter. Cf. Low Lat. *vernachia* (Ducange).

vernicle, *sb.* a copy of the handkerchief of St Veronica, S2, PP, C; **vernakylle**, Cath.; **vernacle**, HD.—Church Lat. *veronicula*, also *veronica* from *Veronica*, the traditional name of the woman who wiped the Saviour's face (the word being popularly connected with *uera icon*, true likeness); *Veronica* is a form of Bernice, the traditional

name of the woman who was cured of an issue of blood. *Bernice* or *Berenice* is a Macedonian form of Φερενίκη, bearer of victory. See F. *veronique* in Cotg.

vernisch, *sb.* varnish, S2, PP; **vernysche**, Prompt.; **vernysh**, *bernix*, Voc.; *viridium*, *virificum*, Voc.; **vernish**, *encaustum*, Manip.—OF. *vernis*, varnish, Cotg.; from OF. *vernir*; Late Lat. **vitrinire*, from *uitrinus*, from *uitrum*, glass (Diez, p. 339).

vernish, *v.* encaustare, Manip.—OF. *vernisser*, to varnish, to sleek, or glaze over with varnish (Cotg.).

verony, *sb.* a vernacle, HD.—OF. *veronie*; Low Lat. *veronica* (Ducange). See **vernicle**.

verraily, *adv.* verily, C2, C; **verralyest**, *superl.*, H.

verray, *adj.* true, S, S2, C2, C3, B; **verrey**, G, HD; **very**, W. *Phr.*: **verray force**, main force, C2.—AF. *verrai*, *verai*; Late Lat. **verācum* (whence F. *vrai*), from Lat. *uerus*.

verrayment, *adv.* verily, C2; **verament**, S3, HD.

vers, *sb.* verse, PP.—AF. *vers*; Lat. *uersus*.

versifie, *v.* to compose verses, PP.

versifyour, *sb.* versifier; **vercefyour**, S2.

vertu, *sb.* power, healing power, miracle, virtue, kindness, S2, PP, W, C2; **vertues**, *pl.*, S2. *Phr.*: **the Lord of vertues**, the Lord of hosts, W2, H.—OF. *vertu*, *virtud*; Lat. *uirtutem*.

verveine, *sb.* vervain, SkD; **verueyne**, S2; **verveyn**, Voc.—OF. *verveine*; Lat. *uerbēna*; see BH, § 44.

very, *adj.* true, W; see **verray**.

vese[1], *v.* to drive away, HD; see **fesien**.

vese[2], *sb.* a rush of wind, C.—Cf. Icel. *fýsi*, impulse. See **vese**[1].

vestiment, *sb.* vestment, C2; **uestimenz**, *pl.*, S, C.—OF. *vestiment* (Bartsch); Lat. *uestimentum*.

vewe, *adj.* few, S2; see **fewe**.

veyne, *sb.* vein, C; **veine**, SkD; **vaine**, S3; **vayn**, S3; **vanys**, *pl.*, S2; **waynys**, S3.—AF. *veine*; Lat. *uēna*; see BH, § 44.

viage, *sb.* voyage, journey, S2, S3, C, C3, CM, B; **vyage**, S2.—OF. *viage*, (BH); Lat. *uiaticum*, provisions for a journey, from *uia*.

vicarie, *sb.* vicar, PP; **vicary**, C2; **vicorie**, PP; **vikery**, PP; **vickery**, PP; **vecory**, Voc.—AF. *vicaire* (F. *viquier*); Lat. *uicarium*, a substitute.

vilanye, *sb.* villainy, C2, C3, PP; **villanie**, *violentia*, Manip.; **vilonye**, disgrace, G.—AF. *vilanie*, OF. *vilenie* (*vilonie*), from *vilain*, peasant, farm-servant, also bad, villainous (BH); Late Lat. *villanus*, farm-servant, from Lat. *uilla*, farm-stead, country-house.

vile

vile, *adj.* vile; **vyle**, PP; **vil**, PP.—AF. *vil*; Lat. *uilem*.

villiche, *adv.* vilely, S2.

vilte, *sb.* vileness, H (Ps. 49. 22); **vylte**, HD; **vilete**, HD.—OF. *vilté*; Lat. *uilitatem*.

viole[1], *v.* to violate; **violid**, *pp.*, S3.—OF. *violer*; Lat. *uiolare*.

viole[2], *sb.* vial; **violis**, *pl.*, W (Rev. 5. 8); **violes**, C3.—OF. *viole*; AF. *fyole*; Lat. *phiala*; Gr. φιάλη.

virelay, *sb.* a sort of rondeau, ND; **virelayes**, *pi.*, S3, CM; **virolais**, HD.—OF. *virelay* (Cotg.); OF. *virer* + *lai*; OF. *virer*; Late Lat. *virare*; Lat. *uibrare* (Diez, p. 736). Cf. **vyre**.

visage, *sb.* face, PP, C2; **vysege**, S2.—AF. *visage*; Late Lat. **visaticum*, from Lat. *uisum*, acc. of *uisus*, sight.

vitaille, *sb.* food, S2, C2, C3; **vitaile**, PP, WW; **vitayle**, S3; **victual**, WW; **vitalis**, *pl.*, B.—AF. *vitaille*; Lat. *uictuālia*, provisions; see BH, § 6.

vitailled, *pp.* provisioned, C3; **vitailid**, W.

vitailler, *sb.* victualler, PP; **vittelleris**, *pi.*, foragers, B.

vitremyte, *sb.* woman's cap, C2.—Lat. *uitream mitram*, glass head-dress (?). Cf. Sp. *mitra*, a sort of cap made of pasteboard, which was put on the heads of witches when led to punishment (Stevens). For the loss of *r* in -*myte* cf. F. *marte* for *martre*, a marten, also OF. *feneste* for *fenestre*, and *terreste* for *terrestre*; see Apfelstedt (p. xxxviii).

voide, *adj.* void, empty, W2.—AF. *voide* (F. *vide*), OF. *vuide*, fem. of *vuit*; Late Lat. **vocitum*, from stem *voc-*; [cf. Lat. *uacare*; see BH, § 63, and Constans (s.v. *vuit*).—A.L.M.]

voiden, *v.* to empty; **voyden**, to get rid of, C2; to expel, C; **voidis**, *pr. s.*, S3; **voyde**, *imp. pl.*, make room, S3; depart from, C2; **voydeth**, send away, C3; **voyded**, *pt. s.*, S2; **voidid**, *pp.*, made void, W.—AF. *voider*, to leave, OF. *vuidier* (Bartsch). See **voide**.

vokyte, *sb.* an advocate, Voc.; **vocates**, *pl.*, PP.—Lat. *aduocatus*.

vyre

volage, *adj.* light of conduct, giddy, CM.—OF. *volage*, light (BH); Lat. *uolaticum*.

volageouss, *adj.* light of conduct, B. See **volage**.

volatilis, *sb. pl.* birds (a misrendering of Lat. *altilia*). W; so in the AS. version *altilia* is rendered by 'fugelas'; birds (= Lat. *uolatilia*), W2; **volatils**, HD.—Lat. *uolatilia*, poultry (hence F. *volaille*), pl. of *uolatilis* (Voc.); from *uolare*, to fly.

voluntè, *sb.* will, CM.—OF. *volonta*, *voluntet*; Lat. *uoluntatem*.

voluper, *sb.* a woman's cap, CM; **volyper**, Cath.—Cf. OF. *envoluper*, to wrap round (BH).

uor-zwelȝe, *v.* to swallow up, S2; see **for-swelȝen**.

vouches, *pr. s.* avouches, S3; see **vowchen**.

vow, *sb.* vow, PP; **vowes**, *pl.*, PP; **vouwes**, S2.—OF. *vou* (Ps. 21); Lat. *uotum*. Cf. **avowe** (p. 18).

vowchen, *v.* to vouch, cite, call, HD; **vouchen**, to avouch, S3. *Phr.*: **vouchen saf**, to guarantee, vouchsafe, PP, HD; **vouche sauf**, C2.—AF. *voucher*, *vocher*; Lat. *uocare*; see BH, § 96.

vowtres, *sb. pl.* vultures, WA.—OF. *voutre*; Lat. *uultur*.

vowtriere, *sb.* adultress, WA. See **avoutrie**.

voys, *sb.* voice, S2, S3, C2, C3; **woice**, S2; **voce**, B; **vois**, PP.—OF. *vois*; Lat. *uōcem*; see BH, § 74.

vyne, *sb.* vine, PP.

vyner[1], *sb.* vineyard, W2; **vynere**, H; **vyneris**, *pl.*, W2; **vyners**, H.—OF. *vinier* (BH); Late Lat. *vinarium*, vineyard, from Lat. *uinum*.

vyner[2], *sb.* vine-dresser, Manip.—OF. *vinier* (Ducange); Late Lat. *vinarium* (acc.).

vynour, *sb.* vine-dresser, Bardsley.—OF. *vineir*; Lat. *uinitorem*.

vyre, *sb.* a crossbow-bolt, B.—OF. *vire* (Ducange). Cf. **virelay**.

228

W

For some words of Teutonic origin beginning with **w-**, see **F** and **V** above.

wa[1], *sb.* woe, WA, B; **waa**, WA, HD; see **wo**[2].

wa[2], *pron.* who, S; see **who**.

waast, *sb.* waist, C2; see **waste**[3].

wacche, *sb.* vigil, watch, PP, HD; **wecche**, S; **wach**, one who keeps a lookout; **wecche**, *pl.*, S; **wecchess**, S; **wacchis**, WA; **wachis**, sentinels, S3.—AS. *wæcce*.

wacchen, *v.* to watch, SkD; **vachit**, *pp.*, S2.—AS. *wacian*.

wachet, *sb.* a sort of blue cloth, CM. See Philolog. Soc. Trans. 1885, p. 329.

waden, *v.* to wade, PP; **vayd**, S2. *Der.*: **vading**, wading, S2.—AS. *wadan*, pt. s. *wód*, pp. *gewaden*.

wæs[1], *imp. s.* be, S, *Comb.*: **wæs hail**, be hale, S; **wæs hæil**, S; **wassail**, S; **wassayl**, S.—ONorth. *wæs*, AS. *wes*, imp. s. of *wesan*, to be.

wæs[2], *pt. s.* was, S; see **was**.

waff, *v.* to waft, lift up, raise, bear, SkD, JD; **wafte**, *pt. s.*, S2.—Icel. *váfa*, to wave, vibrate.

wafre, *sb.* a thin small cake, wafer, CM, PP; **wafur**, Prompt., Voc.—AF. *wafre* (F. *gaufre*); ODutch *wafel* (see Kilian); cf. OHG. *waba*, honey-comb (Tatian); see Weigand (s.v. *waffel*).

wafrere, *sb.* a maker of wafer-cakes, confectioner, PP; **wafereres**, *pl.*, C3.

wafrestre, *sb.* a female maker or seller of wafer-cakes, PP.

wage, *sb.* a gage, pledge, pay for service, WA, Prompt.; **wages**, *pl.*, PP.—AF. *wage*, *gage*; Low Lat. *wadium*, a pledge; Goth. *wadi*; cf. Lat. *uas* (*uadi-*). Cf. **wed**.

wagen, *v.* to engage, to go bail, P, Prompt.—OF. *gagier*; Low. Lat. *wadiare*, from *wadium*. See **wage**.

waggen, *v.* to shake to and fro, Prompt., CM, PP; **waggid**, *pp.*, W.

waghe, *sb.* wall, H; **wah**, S; see **wowe**[1].

waille, *v.* to wail, C2; see **weilen**.

wait, *pr. s.* knows, S3; see **witen**[1].

waith[1], *sb.* danger, peril, B, JD; **wathe**, WA; **vath**, B.—Icel. *váði*.

waith[2], *v.* to hunt, fish.—Icel. *veiða*, to catch, hunt; cf. AS. *wæðan*, to hunt, to wander (Grein). Related to F. *gagner* (see Brachet). See **gaignage**.

waith[3], *sb.* game, sport, a 'take', S3, JD.—Icel. *veiðr*; cf. OHG. *weida* (Otfrid), see Weigand (s.v. *weide*).

waithing, *sb.* what is taken in hunting or fishing, JD, S3.

wak, *adj.* wet, moist, S3, SkD (s.v. *wake*). *Der.*: **waknes**, moistness, JD.—Cf. Du. *wak*, Icel. *vökr*; cf. Icel. *vök* (*vaka-*), a hole in ice.

wake, *sb.* a watch, *vigilia*, Cath. *Comb.*: **wakepleyes**, ceremonies attending the vigils for the dead, C.

waken, *v.* to be awake, to wake, cease from sleep, S, PP, S2; **woc**, *pt. s.*, S; **wok**, S; **wook**, S2, C3.—AS. *wacan*, pt. *wóc*, pp. *wacen*.

wakien, *v.* to watch, to awake, S, PP; **waky**, S2; **wakede**, *pt. s.*, S, PP; **waked**, *pp.*, S.—AS. *wacian*, pt. *wacede*.

waking, *sb.* a watch, S2, C2; **wakynge**, W.

waknen, *v.* to be aroused from sleep, SkD, PP.—AS. *wæcnan*.

wal, *sb.* wall, *murus*, *paries*, Prompt., S, S2, C2; **wall** (= Lat. *maceria*), H, WA; **walles**, *pl.*, S; **wallen**, S.—AS. *weall*, wall, rampart; Lat. *uallum*.

wald, *sb.* wold, wood, WA.—AS. *weald*; cf. OHG. *wald*.

wald-eʒed, *adj.* wall-eyed, WA.—Icel. *vald-eygðr*.

wale, *v.* to choose, WA.—Cf. Goth. *waljan*.

walette, *sb.* bag, wallet, Prompt.; **walet**, C.—Perhaps a corruption of **watel**; see SkD.

walk (**valk**), *v.* to watch, S2, S3, B.—So written for *wakk* (*vakk*). See **wakien**.

walke, *sb.* a walk, WA.

walken, *v.* to roll, walk, S; **welk**, *pt. s.*, SkD; **welke**, HD; **walke**, *pp.*, S.

wallare, *sb.* stone-mason, *murator*, Prompt. See **wal**.

walle, *sb.* a spring of water, HD. *Comb.*: **walle-heued**, a springhead, S2.

wallen, *v.* to boil, to well, to turn about, S, S2, PP; **weallen**, S. *Comb.*: **wal-hat**, boiling hot, S. *Der.*: **wally**, surging, S3.—AS. *weallan*, pt. *wéol*, pp. *weallen*.

walme, *sb.* a bubble in boiling, HD.

walshe, *adj.* and *sb.* foreign, a foreigner, Welshman, PP. *Comb.*: **walshe note**, walnut, CM.—AS. *wælisc*, foreign, Welsh (SkD); from *wealh*, a foreigner, a Welshman.

walt, *pt. s.* possessed, S2; see **welden**[2].

walten, *v.* to roll, to roll over, overturn, to fall, to well out, S2; **welt**, *pt. s.*, SkD (s.v. *welter*); **welte**, HD; **walt**, S2.—AS. *wealtan*.

walter, *sb.* water, S3; see **water**.

walteren, *v.* to roll about, welter, S2, S3, PP; **weltyn**, Prompt. *Der.*: **waltrynge**, a

229

walwen

weltering, Prompt.; **weltering**, a turning over, S3.

walwen, v. to roll, CM, PP; **welwyn**, Prompt.; **walowand**, pr. p., WA; **walewide**, pt. s., W.—AS. wealwian: Goth. walwjan (in compounds).

walwyng, sb. a rolling, W.

wambe, sb. belly, womb, WA; **wame**, WA.

wan-, prefix, expressing lack, deficiency. Comb.: **wan-beleue**, perfidia, Prompt.; **wan-hope**, despair, S2, C, P, H, Voc.; **wan-towen**, untrained, wanton; **wantown**, C; **wantoun**, C2; **wanton**, WA; **wantowe**, Prompt.; **wanton-nes**, want of discretion, S3; **wantownesse**, C; **wantruce**, fail, failure, S; **wan-trukien**, to fail, SD; **wan-trokiynge**, abatement, S2; **wan-trust**, distrust, CM.—Cf. Du. wan-, prefix.

wan, adj. wan, pale, C3, W; **wanne**, Prompt.; **won**, S2. Comb.: **wannesse**, lividness (= Lat. liuor), W2.—AS. wann (wonn).

wand[1], sb. a rod (= Lat. uirga), H (Ps. 109. 3), WA; **wande**, H (Ps. 44. 8).—Cf. OSwed. wand.

wand[2], sb. hesitation, S2. See **wonden**.

wandren, v. to wander, to walk, S2, PP, W; **wondren**, S2, PP.—AS. wandrian.

wand-reðe, sb. misery, S, HD; **wandreth**, peril, S2, WA; **wontreaðe**, S; **wondrede**, S; **wanrede**, S.—Icel. vand-ræði, difficulty, from vandr, difficult.

wane[1], sb. weening, thought, judgement, B; **wan**, S2; **vayn**, S2, B; **veyn**, doubt, B.—AS. wén. See **wenen**[1].

wane[2], sb. a quantity, a number, S2, S3; see **woon**.

wane[3], sb. want, deficiency, misery, S, S2, WA; **wone**, S.—AS. wana.

wanelasour, sb. one who rouses and drives game, alator, Voc. See HD (s.v. wanlace).

wanen, v. to wane, to fail, to grow less, C, C2, S2; **wanye**, P; **wanne**, to ebb, S3; **woned**, pp., S2.—AS. wanian (wonian).

wanene, adv. whence, S; see **whanene**.

wangeliste, sb. evangelist, S2.—Church Lat. euangelista (Vulg.).

wangtooth, sb. molar tooth, C2; see **wonge**[2].

wankel, adj. tottery, unstable; **wankyll**, S2.—AS. wancol (SkD, s.v. wench); cf. OHG. wank, tottering (Otfrid).

wanne, adv., conj. when, S, S2; see **whan**.

wannes, adv. whence, S3; see **whannes**.

want, adj. deficient; **wannt**, SkD; **wonte**, sb. deficiency, SkD.—Icel. vant, n. of vanr, deficient.

wanten, v. to be lacking, carere, Cath.; **wonte**, S, S2; **wantede**, pt. s., S; **wayntyt**, pl., S3.—Icel. vanta.

wareyne

wapne, sb. weapon, S; see **wepne**.

wapnid, pp. armed, S2; see **wepnen**.

wappen, v. to lap, wap (said of water), to yelp, S3, Prompt.

wappynge, sb. barking of hounds, Prompt.

war[1], adj. cautious, wary, S, S2, C2, G, W, W2, PP; **wear**, S; **warliche**, adv. cautiously, S; **wearliche**, S; **warly**, H; **warli**, W. Der.: **warschipe**, prudence, S.—AS. (ge)wær: OHG. gi-war (Otfrid). See **iwar** (p. 123).

war[2], pt. s. subj. were, S2; **war ... ne**, unless, S2; see **was**.

war[3], adv. where, S; see **wher**[1].

warant, sb. a warrant, guarantee, SkD; protector, Prompt.—AF. warant, OF. garant, Low Lat. warentem (Diez, p. 177); OHG. werento, pr. p. of weren, warjan, to protect, to take heed. Cf. **warice**.

waranten, v. to warrant, C3.

ward[1], sb. a guard, SD; **wardes**, pl., SD.—AS. weard (m.), 'custos'.

ward[2], sb. world (Lancelot of the Laik, E.E.T.S. No. 6). See **werd**[2].

warde, sb. ward, custodia, S; **ward**, care, heed, regard, S2; keeping, Prompt.—AS. weard (f.), 'custodia'. Comb.: **warde-motes**, meetings of a ward, P.

warden, v. to guard, S; **warded**, pp., S2.—AS. weardian.

wardeyne, sb. warden, Prompt.; **wardeyn**, CM, Voc.; **wardane**, B; **wardeynes**, pl., umpires, G.—AF. wardein.

wardone, sb. a kind of pear, volemum, Prompt.

wardrobe, sb. a house of office, CM.

ware[1], sb. merchandise, S2, C3, G, SkD.—Icel. vara; cf. AS. waru, care, custody, (Grein).

ware[2], sb. host, collection, S2. Comb.: **helleware**, the host of hell, SD; **watres ware**, waters, S2; **windes ware**, winds, S2.—AS. -waru (Grein), see Fick, 7. 291. Cf. **were**[2].

ware[3], sb. spring, H; **wayr**, ver, Cath.; **were**, B.—Icel. vár.

ware[4], sb. weir, dam, HD; **wore**, S2; **were**, CM.—AS. wer (SkD); cf. Icel. vörr.

ware[5], adj. comp. worse, H; see **werre**[1].

ware[6], v. to lay out, to spend, S2, HD, JD, Palsg. (p. 452); **wayr**, commutare, Cath., JD; **war**, JD,—Icel. verja, to clothe, to invest money, to spend. See **werien**[2].

wareyne, sb. a warren, Prompt.; **warrayne**, HD. Der.: **warnere**, warrener, Prompt.; **warner**, P, HD, Bardsley.—AF. warenne (garenne, garreyne); Low Lat. warenna; from OHG. war- in warjan. See **warant**.

warh (*in compounds*), an outlawed felon.
Comb.: **warh-treo**, the felon's tree, the
gallows (used of the cross of Christ), S.—
AS. *wearh*, an outlawed felon, a wolf; cf.
Icel. *vargr*, a wolf, an outlaw. With *warh-tréo*
cf. OS. *warag-treo*, Icel. *varg-tré*, also AS.
wearh-ród (Voc.).

wari-angel, *sb.* a butcher-bird, a small
woodpecker, WA (p. 469); **wary-angle**,
Cotg. (s.v. *pie*).

warice, *v.* to heal, cure, to be cured, C3;
warschyn, *convalesco*, Prompt.; **warisch**,
WA; **warysshe**, Palsg.; **warisshed**, *pp.*,
Prompt. (*n*).—OF. *wariss*-, pr. p. stem of
warir, *garir* (F. *guérir*), of Teut. origin; OHG.
warjan, to protect. Cf. **warant**.

warien[1], *v.* to curse, S, S2, S3, W, H (Ps.
108. 27), C3; **werien**, H; **varyit**, *pt. s.*, S2;
wereged, *pp.*, S.—AS. *wergian*; cf. OHG.
(*fur*)*wergen* (Tatian). AS. *wergian*, from *wearh*,
an accursed person, an outlawed felon. See
warh.

warien[2], *v.* to be on the watch, S (9. 132);
waren, S; **ware þe**, *imp. s.*, PP; **war yow**,
pl., C2.—AS. *warian*, to take heed.

warke, *sb.* work, S2; see **werke**[1].

warlaȝe, *sb.* a warlock, sorcerer, deceiver,
WA.—AS. *wérloga*, covenant-breaker, often
used of the devil (Grein).

warnin, *v.* to warn, *moneo*, S, C2; **warnon**,
Prompt.; **warnyt**, *pt. s.*, B; **warnede**,
PP.—AS. *wearnian*, from *wearn*, a denial,
refusal. Cf. **wernen**.

warnishen, *v.* to fortify, protect, SkD (s.v.
garnish); **warenyss**, H; **warnist**, **warnyst**,
warnyscht, *pp.*, H; **warnised**, HD. *Der.*:
warnysynge, protection, defence, H;
warnyshynge, H.—AF. *warniss*-, pr. p.
stem of *warnir*, of Teut. origin. See **warnin**.

warpen, *v.* to throw, cast, utter, to lay (eggs),
PP, S2, S, Cath.; **werpen**, S, H; **worpen**,
S; **warp**, *pt. s.*, S, PP; **warpe**, PP; **werp**,
S2; **worpen**, *pp.*, S.—AS. *weorpan*, pt.
wearp, pp. *worpen*: OS. *werpan*; cf. OHG.
werphan (Tatian).

warrok[1], *v.* to fasten with a girth, PP;
warrick, HD.

warrok[2], *sb.* a girth, Voc.

warysone, *sb.* reward, *donativum*, *possessio*,
Prompt.; **waryson**, WA; **warison**, CM;
warysoun, S2, B; **waresun**, Voc.;
warisoune, B.—OF. *warison*, help, protection, from *warir* (*guarir*, *garir*). See **warice**.

was, *pt. s.* was; **wæs**, S; **wees**, S2; **wes**, S,
S2; **watz**, S2; **was**, *2 pt. s.*, S; **wes**, S;
were, S, W2; **wæren**, *pl.*, S; **wærenn**, S;
waren, S; **weren**, S; **wer**, S; **war**, S2;
weoren, S; **woren**, S; **wern**, S2; **wore**, S;
ware, S; **wear**, S; **ware**, S3; **ware**, *pt. s. subj.*, S;

war, S2; **war ... ne**, were ... not, unless,
S2, H; **were**, S2.—AS. *wæs*, 1 and 3 pt.,
wére, 2 pt. (pl. *wéron*), subj. *wére* (pl. *wéren*).
See **wæs**[2].

waschen, *v.* to wash, S; **waische**, W2;
wasshen, S; **weschen**, S; **wessche**, S2;
wassen, S; **wasse**, S; **wesch**, *pt. s.*, S;
wessh, S, S2; **wesh**, C2, C3; **weis**, S;
waischide, W, W2; **wesse**, *pl.*, S;
wosschen, S2; **wisschen**, G; **wesshen**,
P; **wasshe**, *pp.*, C3; **wasschen**, G;
waischun, W; **ȝe-wasse**, S.—AS. *wascan*,
pt. *wósc* (*wóx*), pp. *wascen* (*wæscen*).

waselen, *v.* to wade in mire; **waseled**, *pt. s.*,
S3.—Icel. *vasla*, to wade in ooze, from *vás*,
wetness, cf. AS. *wós* (*wór*). See **wose**,
worie.

wassail, a salutation used in drinking, S,
ND; **wassel**, ND; **wassayl**, S; **wæshail**,
S. See **wæs**[1].

wast, *sb.* wasteful expenditure, C3 (p. 48).

waste[1], *adj.* solitary, S; **vast**, S2.—AF.
wast.—OF. *guaste*. See **waste**[2].

waste[2], *v.* to waste away, C2; **vast**, to waste,
S2.—OF. *waster* (*gaster*); cf. MHG. *wasten*;
Lat. *uastare*; see Mackel, Germ. Elemente, p.
72.

waste[3], *sb.* waist, a man's middle, Prompt.;
wast, Prompt.; **waast**, C2.—Probably a
deriv. from **wexen** (to grow); see SkD.

wastel, *sb.* a cake made of the finest flour, P,
Prompt.; **wastell**, *libum*, Voc.; **wastelle**,
Voc., Cath. *Comb.*: **wastel breed**, cake-
bread, CM, C.—AF. *wastel*, *gastel* (F. *gâteau*).

wastme, *sb.* growth, form, personal appearance, S, SkD (s.v. *waist*); **westm**, fruit, S.—
AS. *wæstm*. See **wexen**.

wastoure, *sb.* a destroyer, WA; a wasteful
person, P.

wat[1], *pron.* what, S, S2; see **what**[1].

wat[2], *1 and 3 pr. s.* know, knows, S, S2, S3;
see **witen**[1].

wat[3], *pt. s.* quoth, S; see **queþen**.

wate, *sb.* chance, luck, S; see **whate**.

watel, *sb.* a hurdle woven with twigs, a bag of
woven stuff, the baggy flesh on a bird's
neck, wattle, SkD. *Comb.*: **watelful**, wallet-
full, PP.—AS. *watel*, hurdle, covering. Cf.
walette.

watelen, *v.* to wattle, to strengthen with
hurdles, SkD; **watelide**, *pt. s.*, PP.

water, *sb.* water, S2; **weater**, S; **vattir**, S2;
walter, S3; **watres**, *pl.*, S2. *Comb.*: **watir-
bank**, shore, W; **waterles**, without water,
C. *Der.*: **watrand**, watering, S2.—AS.
wæter: OS. *watar*; cf. OHG. *wazzar* (Tatian).

watloker, *adv. comp.* sooner, S2; see **what**[3].

wattri, *adj.* venomous, S2; see **attri**.

waueren, *v.* to waver, to wander, Prompt.; **waverand**, *pr. p.*, B; **vauerand**, S2, B; **wawerand**, B; **waweryt**, *pt. s.*, B; **vaueryt**, S2.—Icel. *vafra.*

wawe[1], *sb.* wall, WA; **waghe**, WA.—AS. *wáh*; cf. Goth. *waddjus.* See **wowe**[1].

wawe[2], *sb.* wave, S2, C3, W, PP, Prompt.; **wawes**, *pl.*, WA, S2, S3, C3; **waweȝ**, S2; **waȝeȝ**, S2; **quawes**, S2.—Icel. *vágr*; cf. AS. *wég*: Goth. *wegs*; see Kluge (s.v. *woge*).

wawen, *v.* to move from side to side, P; **wawid**, *pp.*, shaken, SkD (s.v. *wag*).—AS. *wagian* (Grein).

wax, *sb.* wax, Prompt.; **wex**, C, C3; **wexe**, W2. *Comb.*: **wax-bred**, a board covered with wax, a writing-tablet, S; **wax-lokes**, wax-flakes, S2.—AS. *weax*, wax; *wæxbred*, a board covered with wax.

waxen, *v.* to grow, S, S2; see **wexen**.

way, *interj.* wo!, S; see **wo**[1].

wayke, *adj.* weak, Cath., S2, C, C3, PP; **wayk**, S2, C2; **waik**, PP, B; **waiker**, *comp.*, S3.—Icel. *veikr*; cf. AS. *wác.* Cf. **woc**[1].

waykely, *adv.* watchfully, carefully, S3.—AS. *wacollice*, adv. from *wacol* (Voc.). See **waken.**

waymenten, *v.* to lament, Prompt., Spenser (2).—AF. *weimenter, guaimenter.*

waymentynge, *sb.* lamentation, C, CM, H; **weymentynge**, C.

wayne, *sb.* wain, cart, Prompt., G; **waines**, *pl.*, S.—AS. *wægn*: OHG. *wagan* (Otfrid).

wayowre, *sb.* a wager, Prompt.; **waiour**, S2.—OF. *wageure* (F. *gageure*), from *wage* (*gage*). See **wage.**

wayryngle, *sb.* a little villain, WA.

wayte, *sb.* watchman, waker, spy, Prompt.; **waites**, *pl.*, S2. See **wayten.**

wayten, *v.* to watch, expect, C2, S2, PP; **waiten**, S, S2, S3, C2, PP; **i-wayted**, *pp.*, S2.—AF. *wayter*, OF. *guaiter* (Roland): OHG. *wahten*, to watch (Otfrid).

wayue, *v.* to send, put away, WA; **wayfe**, WA.—Cf. Low Lat. *wayviare*; see Ducange (s.v. *wayf*). Cf. **weyven.**

we, *sb.* way, S2; see **wey.**

weaden, *sb. pl.* garments, S; see **wede.**

wealden, *v.* to govern, S; see **welden**[1].

wealdent, *sb.* ruler, S; **walden**, S.—AS. *wealdend.*

wealden, *v.* to govern, rule, control, possess, S; see **welden**[1].

weallen, *v.* to boil, S; see **wallen.**

wear, *adj.* wary, cautious, S; see **war**[1].

weater, *sb.* water, S; see **water.**

web, *sb.* that which is woven, S2, W2 (Job 7. 6); **webbe**, P; **wobbys**, *pl.*, S3.—AS. *webb.*

webbare, *sb.* maker of woollen or linen cloth, Prompt.

webbe, *sb.* a weaver, Bardsley, CM, C; a female weaver, P.

webster, *sb.* a female weaver, Voc.; *textor*, Voc.; **webstere**, *textor*, Voc., W2 (Job 7. 6); **websteris**, *pl.*, S2.—AS. *webbestre.*

wecche, *sb.* vigil, watch, S; see **wacche.**

wed, *sb.* a pledge, W2; **wedde**, P; *dat.*, S, S3, C. *Comb.*: **wed-lac**, wedlock, S; **wedlak**, S; **wedlock**, C2; **wedlackes**, *gen.*, S; **wedlakes**, S.—AS. *wedd*: Goth. *wadi.* Cf. **wage.**

wedden, *v.* to engage by a pledge, to marry, S, C; **i-weddet**, *pp.*, S; **y-wedde**, S; **y-wedded**, C2.—AS. *weddian*, to pledge.

wede, *sb.* weed, garment, S, C2, PP, WA; **weid**, S3; **weyd**, S3; **weden**, *pl.*, S; **weaden**, S; **wedes**, S, S2, P; **wedis**, S3, B.—AS. *wéde*: OS. *wádi.*

weden, *v.* to be mad, to go mad, S2, WA; **weide**, S3 (6. 438); **wedde**, *pt. s.*, S.—AS. *wédan*, from *wód.* See **wode**[3].

weder[1], *sb.* wether, Voc.; **wedyr**, Prompt.; **weddir**, S2; **veddir**, S2; **wether**, S2.—AS. *weðer*: cf. Goth. *wiþrus*, lamb.

weder[2], *sb.* weather, S, S2, C2; **wedirs**, *pl.*, S2, WA; **vedirs**, S2; **wedereȝ**, storms, S2; **wederes**, P.—AS. *weder*; cf. G. *wetter.*

wederen, *v.* to expose to the weather; **wederyn**, *auro*, Prompt.; **widren**, to wither, SkD; **wydder**, S3. *Der.*: **wethering**, weathering, seasoning from exposure to the weather, S3.

Wednes dai, *sb.* Wednesday, SD; see **Wodnesdei.**

wedous, *sb. pl.* widows, S3; see **widewe.**

wee, *sb.* a man, WA; **we**, WA. See **wye.**

weed, *sb.* weed, wild herb, Prompt.; **wed**, S; **weode**, *dat.*, S.—AS. *wéod, wíod*: cf. OS. *wiod.*

weep, *pt. s.* wept, C1, C3; see **wepen.**

weet, *adj.* wet, PP; **wete**, C.—AS. *wét.*

weete, *sb.* wet, perspiration, S2, PP; **wete**, S2, C3; **weet**, C2, PP.—AS. *wéta.*

weeten, *v.* to wet, W2; **wette**, *pt. s.*, C.—AS. *wétan.*

wei, *interj.* wo! S; see **wo**[1].

weilen, *v.* to lament, W, W2, S2; **weylen**, C; **waille**, C2. *Der.*: **weilyng**, lamentation, W.—Cf. Icel. *væla.*

weir[1], *sb.* war, S3; see **werre**[2].

weir[2], *sb.* doubt, B; **weyr**, B, S2; **were**, CM, S2, JD; **wyre**, Digby Myst.

weird, *sb.* fate, S3; see **werd**[1].

weiȝh, *sb.* man, S2; see **wye.**

wel[1], *adv.* well, very, S, S2, PP; **wæl**, S; **weyl**, S2; **weill**, S3; **wiel**, S3; **wol**, S; **wele**, S2; **welle**, S. *Comb.*: **wel-bigoon**, joyous, CM; **welcomen**, welcome, PP; **welcume**, S; **welcome**, to welcome, PP; **wolcumen**, S;

wilcweme, content, S; **wel dede**, good deed, PP; *pl.*, S; **welfaring**, prosperous, C2.—AS. *wel*; cf. OHG. *wuola* (Tatian). Cf. AS. *weldéd*, a benefit (Bosworth).

wel², *1 pr. s.* will, desire, S2; see **wille**¹.

welde, *sb.* weld, dyer's weed, Prompt., CM, SkD; **wolde**, Prompt.; **wald**, JD.—Cf. Low Lat. *gualdum* (Ducange). Cf. **gaude**¹. 'Weld, *Reseda luteola, Genista tinctoria*', Britten (Plant-names).

welden¹, *v.* to have power over, govern, possess, SD (s.v. *walden*); **wealden**, S; **wolde**, S; **wald**, *pr. s.*, S; **wolde**, *pt. subj.*, SD.—AS. *wealdan*, pt. *wéold*, pp. *wealden*.

welden², *v.* to wield, possess, S, S2, W2; **weld**, S3; **welt**, *pt. s.*, S2; **welte**, C2; **welde**, C2; **walt**, S2; **welded**, C2; **weldide**, established, W2; **weldiden**, *pl.*, obtained, W2.—AS. *(ge)weldan*.

weldere, *sb.* possessor, W2.

weldynge, *sb.* possession, H.

wele, *sb.* weal, prosperity, S, S2, S3, C2, PP; **weole**, S, S2, PP; **welle**, PP; **well**, PP; **weolen**, *pl.*, benefits, S. *Comb.*: **weleful**, blessed, joyous, S; **weoleful**, S; **welful**, S2, C3; **welefully**, prosperously, W.—AS. *wela, weola*.

welewen, *v.* to fade, to become yellow, W, HD; **welwen**, S2; **welyen**, S2; **welowe**, Cath., HD; **wilowe**, H (Ps. 72. 17); **walows**, *pr. s.*, WA; **wellowd**, *pp.*, Cath.—AS. *wealowian* (Bosworth).

welk, *pt. s.* walked; see **walken**.

welken, *v.* to fade, wither, Prompt., S, S2, S3, C3, H, HD; **wealked**, *pp.*, S3.—Cf. Du. *welken*.

welkene, *sb.* welkin, sky, PP; **welken**, WA; **welkne**, C2, HD; **weolcne**, S; **wolcne**, S.—AS. *wolcnu*, pl. of *wolcen*, cloud, OS. *wolkan*.

welle, *sb.* spring, fountain, S, C2, S2; **well**, S3; **wel**, S; **weeles**, *pl.* (= Lat. *torrentes*), S2. *Comb.*: **welsprung**, wellspring, S.—AS. *wella*, also *well*, *wyll*, from *weallan*, to boil up. See **wallen**.

wellen¹, *v.* to well, S2, PP.—AS. *wellan, wyllan*.

wellen², *v.* to weld; *fundo*, Prompt.; **wellid**, *pp.*, W2. *Comb.*: **wellyng-place**, a smelting-place (= Lat. *conflatorium*), W2.—Cf. Swed. *välla*, to weld.

welt, *pt. s.* overturned; see **walten**.

welðe, *sb.* wealth, riches, S, PP; **weolthe**, PP. See **wele**.

welwen, *v.* to fade, S2; see **welewen**.

wem, *sb.* spot, blemish, S2, PP, C2, W, W2, H; **wemme**, Prompt., W; **wembe**, H. *Comb.*: **wemles**, spotless, S, WA; **wemmeles**,

S2; **wemmelees**, C3.—AS. *wamm*, Goth. *wamm*, OS. *wam*, crime, wickedness.

wemmen, *v.* to stain, blemish, SD.—AS. *wemman*: Goth. *(ana)wammjan*.

wenche, *sb.* a girl, maiden, maid-servant, S2, C2, WA, Prompt., SkD; **wench**, B, S2, WW.

wenchel, *sb.* an infant (boy or girl), SkD (s.v. *wench*).—AS. *wencel*, weak, tottery; cf. OHG. *wankón*, to totter (Otfrid). See **wankel**.

wenden, *v.* to turn (*act.*), to turn oneself, to turn, to go, depart, S, S2, C2; **went**, S3; **wend**, *imp. s.*, S; **went**, S; *pr. s.*, turns (*act.*), S; **wend**, *pl.*, C2; **wende**, *pt. s.*, S, S2; **wenden**, *pl.*, S; **wenten**, S; **wente hym**, turned him (*reflex.*), S3, C3; **went**, *pp.*, S, S2, C2, C3; **wente**, W; **iwent**, S; **iwente**, S. *Der.*: **wendynge**, departure, H.—AS. *wendan*, pt. *wende*: Goth. *wandjan*, causal of *windan*. See **winden**.

Wendes dei, *sb.* Wednesday, S; see **Wodnesdei**.

wenen¹, *v.* to ween, suppose, S, S2, C2, C3, PP; **weene**, PP, S3; **wanst**, *2 pr. s.*, S; **wende**, *pt. s.*, S, S3, C2, PP; **wente**, *pp.*, S3; **wend**, C2.—AS. *wénan*, (pt. *wénde*): Goth. *wênjan*, from *wêns*, hope; cf. OS. *wánian*, OHG. *wánen* (Tatian).

wenen², *v.* to disaccustom, to wean, *ablacto*, Prompt., W2, H.—AS. *á-wenian*, to disaccustom, to wean (VP. Ps. 130. 2), cf. *wenian* (*wennan*), to accustom, Icel. *venja*: Goth. **wanjan*; cf. Icel. *vanr*, accustomed.

wenge, *sb.* wing, PP, Cath.; **wenges**, *pl.*, S2, S3; **winges**, C2; **whynges**, S2; **wengis**, W2; **wyngis**, W2; **wengen**, *dat.*, S. *Der.*: **wenged**, winged, C.—Icel. *vengr*.

went, *sb.* passage, road, pathway; **wente**, *dat.*, CM.

weod, *sb.* weed, S; see **weed**.

weole, *sb.* weal, S, S2, PP; see **wele**.

weoli, *adj.* powerful, S.—AS. *welig*, rich. See **wele**.

weorc, *sb.* work, S; see **werke**¹.

weored, *sb.* a host, cohort; **weordes**, *pl.*, S; **wordes**, S.—AS. *weorod*: OS. *werod*.

weoren, *pt. pl.* were, S; see **was**.

weorld, *sb.* world, S; see **werld**.

weorren, *v.* to war, S.—AS. *werrian* (*uerrien* in Chron. ann. 1135).

wepe, *sb.* weeping, S2; **wep**, S.

wepen, *v.* to weep, S, P, C3; **weopen**, S; **wep**, *pt. s.*, S, S2, C; **weep**, C2, C3; **wepe**, P; **wep**, S; **wepen**, *pl.*, S; **wepte**, *pt. s.*, C3; **wepten**, *pl.*, P; **wopen**, *pp.*, C2.—AS. *wépan* (pt. *wéop*): OS. *wópian*, Goth. *wopjan*. See **wop**.

wep-man, *sb.* a man, a male, SD; **weop-mon**, S; **wepmen**, *pl.*, S.—AS. *wǽpman* (Voc.), *wǽpnedman* (Grein). See **wepne**.

wepne, *sb.* weapon, *membrum virile*, PP, S, Prompt.; **wepen**, C2; **wapne**, S; **wapyn-nys**, *pl.*, S3, B; **wapnys**, B; **wapen**, WA.—AS. *wǽpen*: Goth. *wēpna*, pl. weapons; see Sievers, 17, and Cosijn, p. 41.

wepnen, *v.* to arm, SD; **wapnid**, *pp.*, S2; **wapened**, WA; **wopnede**, *pl.*, S.

wer, *sb.* war, B; see **werre**[2].

werble, *sb.* warble; **wrablis**, *pl.*, S3.

werblen, *v.* to warble (of trumpets), WA, SkD; **werbelen**, SkD; **wrabil**, to move in an undulating manner, JD.—OF. *werbler*; of Teut. origin, cf. G. *wirblen*, to whirl, to warble.

werchen; see **werke**[2], **werken**.

werd[1], *sb.* fate, destiny, S3, B; **weird**, S3; **werðe**, S2; **wurde**, SD; **werdis**, *pl.*, S3, H, B; **wierde**, HD, CM; **wordis**, H; **wurðes**, S.—AS. *wyrd.* See **worþen**.

werd[2], *sb.* world, WA, S2; see **werld**, **ward**[2].

were[1], *sb.* a man, husband, S. *Comb.*: **wer-wolf**, wer-wolf, S2; **werwolues**, *pl.*, S3.—AS. *wer*, OS. *wer*; cf. Goth. *wair*, Lat. *uir*, OIr. *fer*.

were[2], *sb.* company, host, S.—Cf. MHG. *wer*, *were*: OHG. *warí*, see Weigand (s.v. *wehr*). Cf. **ware**[2].

were[3], *sb.* war, H; see **werre**[2].

were[4], *sb.* doubt, S2; see **weir**[2].

wereged, *pp.* accursed, S; see **warien**[1].

wereld, *sb.* world, S; see **werld**.

weren, *pt. pl.* were, S; **were**, S; **wer**, S; see **was**.

werien[1], *v.* to weary, C3. See **wery**.

werien[2], *v.* to wear, PP, S; **were**, S2, C2; **wer**, S3; **werede**, *pt. s.*, C; **wered**, PP, C2, C3; **wered**, *pp.*, C2, C3, PP; **worne**, spent, past, S3.—AS. *werian*: Goth. *wasjan*; cf. Icel. *verja*, to clothe, to invest money, to spend.

werien[3], *v.* to defend, to keep off, S; **weren**, S, S2, C; **werede**, *pt. s.*, S2.—AS. *werian*, OS. *werian*; cf. OHG. *werren*, to defend, forbid (Otfrid), *weren*, to forbid (Tatian).

werke[1], *sb.* work, a work of defence, WA; **werk**, S, S2, C2, Prompt.; **were**, S; **weorc**, S; **worc**, S2; **worke**, S2; **warke**, S3; **weorkes**, *pl.*, S. *Comb.*: **werk-beeste**, *jumentum*, W2.—AS. *(ge)weorc*: OS. *werk*; cf. Icel. *virki*, an entrenchment.

werke[2], *v.* to work, Prompt.; **wirken**, S2; **werchen**, S, S3, C3; **wirchen**, S; **wurchen**, S, S2; **worchen**, W, S2; **wrohte**, *pt. s.*, S; **wroȝte**, S, S2; **wroght**, S2; **wraht**, S2; **wrahtes**, 2 *pt. s.*, S; **wrogt**, *pp.*, S; **wrocht**, S3; **wroght**, S2; **wroughte**, S3; **i-wraht**,

S; **i-wrouhte**, S; **y-wrouȝte**, P; **y-wroght**, C2.—AS. *wyrcan*, pt. *worhte*, pp. *geworht.*

werke[3], *sb.* pain, HD.—AS. *wærc* (Grein); cf. Icel. *verkr.*

werken, *v.* to ache, WA; **werkyn**, Prompt.; **werchen**, S3.—Icel. *verkja.*

werkinge, *sb.* aching; **werkynge**, H; headache, Prompt.; **warkynge**, H; **werk-yngis**, *pl.*, H.

werld, *sb.* world, S, S2; **weorld**, S; **woreld**, S; **worlde**, PP; **world**, S; **wereld**, S; **wurld**, S; **worlt**, S; **wordle**, S2, PP; **word**, S2, PP; **werd**, WA, S2; **werde**, Prompt.; **weorldes**, *gen.*, S; **woreldes**, S; **wereldes**, S; **werldes**, S; **werdes**, S2; **wordles**, *pl.*, S2. *Comb.*: **weoreldliche**, worldly; **weorelldlike**, S; **worldlich**, S; **wurldlic**, S; **worltliche**, S; **wordliche**, S; **werdliche**, S3; **weoreldschipe**, worldliness; **weorelldshipess**, *gen.*, S.—AS. *weoruld*: OS. *werold*; cf. OHG. *weralt* (Tatian).

wermod, *sb.* wormwood, Voc.; **wermode**, SB; **wormod** (= Lat. *absinthium*), W; **wormode**, Voc.; **wormwod**, Voc.—AS. *wermód*, (OET.); cf. G. *wermuth.*

wern, *pt. pl.* were, S; see **was**.

wernard, *sb.* a deceiver, liar, P; **wernardes**, *pl.*, P.—OF. *guernart*. See **wernen**.

wernen, *v.* to refuse, PP, S, S2, G, HD; **wurne**, S2; **warn**, H, B, S2, HD; **wornde**, *pt. s.*, S2.—AS. *wyrnan*, to refuse (Grein); cf. OS. *wernian*. See **warnin**.

werpen, *v.* to throw, to bring forth, S; see **warpen**.

werrayour, *sb.* warrior, B.—OF. *guerreier* (BH).

werre[1], *adj. comp.* worse, H, HD; **were**, JD; **wer**, B; **ware**, H, JD, B; **war**, JD, B; **waur**, JD.—Icel. *verri.*

werre[2], *sb.* war, S, C, C2, H, Cath.; **worre**, S2; **were**, H; **wer**, B; **war**, B; **weir**, B, S3. *Der.*: **werely**, warlike, S3, JD.—OF. *werre* (F. *guerre*); OHG. *werra*, strife, cf. *gi-werri*, a tumult (Otfrid).

werreyen, *v.* to make war, C2; **werray**, H, B; **warray**, B.—OF. *werreier, guerroier.*

werrien, *v.* to make war, SD; **weorren**, S; **worri**, S2; **waryed**, *pt. pl.*, H; **werid**, H (Ps. 108. 2).—AS. *werrian*; OF. *guerrier* (BH). See **werreyen**.

werse, *adj. comp.* worse, S; see **wurse**.

werte, *sb.* a wart, C, Prompt., Voc.; **warte**, Cath.; **wrette**, Prompt.; **wrot**, Prompt. (*n*). *Comb.*: **wrot-wort**, *uerrucaria*, Prompt. (*n*).—AS. *wearte* (Voc.).

werwolf, *sb.* man-wolf; see **were**[1].

wery, *adj.* turbid, dirty, S2 (4 a. 38); weary, C2; **weri**, *adv.*, S. *Der.*: **werinisse**, weariness, S2.—AS. *wérig*, weary. See **worie.**

wes, *pt. s.* was, S, S2; see **was.**

weschen, *v.* to wash, S; **wessche**, S2; **wesch**, *pt. s.*, S; see **waschen.**

weste, *adj.* desolate; **wesste**, *sb.*, wilderness, S.—AS. *wéste*, desolate (*wésten*, a desert): OS. *wósti*; cf. OHG. *wuosti* (Tatian). Cf. **waste**[1].

westi, *adj.* desolate, S.

westm, *sb.* fruit, S; see **wastme.**

wet, *pron.* what, S; see **what**[1].

wette, *pt. s.* wetted, C; see **weeten.**

wether, *sb.* wether, S2; see **weder**[1].

weued, *sb.* altar, S2.—AS. *weofod* (for *wihbedd*), idol-table, altar (Voc.), *wigbed* (Grein), *wibed* (VP). AS. *wíh* (*wig*), idol, sacred place, altar (Grein); cf. Goth. *weihs*, holy, and G. *weih-* in *weih-nacht*, *weih-rauch*.

wexen, *v.* to wax, to grow, S, S2, C3, W, W2; **waxen**, S, S2; **walxis**, *pr. pl.*, S3; **wex**, *pt. s.*, S, S2, S3; **weex**, C3; **wæx**, S; **wax**, S2; **wox**, S2; **wexe**, W; **wexen**, *pl.*, S; **wexe**, C2; **woxen**, W; **wolx**, S3; **wexide**, *pt. s.* (weak form), W2; **waxen**, *pp.*, S; **woxen**, C2, C3, W; **woxe**, G; **wox**, S2.—AS. *weaxan*, pt. *wéox*, pp. *weaxen*.

wey, *sb.* way, S, S2, C2; **wei**, S, S2; **weg**, S; **weie**, S; **weye**, S; **we**, S2; **weies**, *gen.*, S; **vayis**, S2. *Comb.*: **weybrede**, plantain, Prompt., Voc. (see Grimm, p. 1215). *Phr.*: a **litill we**, a little bit, S2; **a wei**, a little time, S2 (see SkD, s.v. *wee*, p. 833).—AS. *weg*; cf. Goth. *wigs*.

weyd, *sb.* garment, S3; see **wede.**

weye[1], *sb.* creature, person, wight, man, PP; **wye**, PP; **wy**, PP.—AS. *wíga*, warrior, man.

weye[2], *sb.* a wey, a weight so called, PP.

weyen, *v.* to weigh, to move, PP, C2, S, S2; **weie**, S2; **wei3en**, S; **weyen**, *pp.*, S2, P; **weyede**, *pt. s.* (weak form), S2; **wey3ed**, P.—AS. *wegan*, to bear, to move, pt. *wæg* (pl. *wégon*), pp. *wegen*.

weyuen, *v.* to swing about, to set aside, remove, push aside, waive, C2, C3, G, S2.—AF. *weiver*; Icel. *veifa*, to vibrate. Cf. **wayve.**

weyues, *sb. pl.* men or things found astray without an owner, P.—AF. *waif*; *weifs* (pl.). See **weyven.**

wha, *pron.* who, S2; see **who.**

whær, *adv.* where, S; see **wher**[1].

whal, *sb.* whale, W2.—AS. *hwæl* (Voc.). Cf. **qual.**

whan, *adv. interrog.*, *conj.* when, S2, C2; **whane**, S; **whanne**, S, W; **hwanne**, S; **huanne**, S2; **hwenne**, S; **hwan**, S; **hwen**, S; **hwon**, S; **wanne**, S, S2; **wonne**, S; **wane**, S, S2; **wone**, S; **wan**, S; **won**, S;

quanne, S; **quane**, S; **quan**, S; **quuan**, S; **quen**, S2; **quene**, S. *Comb.*: **whannse**, whensoever, S.—AS. *hwanne.*

whanene, *adv.* whence, S; **wanene**, S; **wenene**, S2; **whænnenen**, S; **whenne**, S2, C2.—AS. *hwanon.*

whannes, *adv.* whence, S, S2; **huannes**, S2; **whannus**, W2; **whennys**, W; **wannes**, S2; **whennes**, C3, P.

what[1], *pron. interrog.*, *adj. n.*, and *adv.* what, why, wherefore, S, S3, W; **whæt**, S, S2; **whatt**, S; **whaut**, S2; **hwat**, S; **hwet**, S; **huet**, S2; **wat**, S, S2; **wet**, S, S2; **quat**, S, S2. *Comb.*: **hwat … wat**, both … and, S; **wat … wat**, S; **what swa**, whatsoever, S; **quat so**, S; **quat kin**, what kind, S2; **quat als euer**, whatsoever, S2.—AS. *hwæt.* **what**[2], *conj.* what time, until; **wat**, S.—Cf. **alwat.**

what[3], *adj.* quick, keen, sharp, strenuous, MD; **whæt**, MD; **hwat**, MD; **wat**, MD; *adv.*, S; **wate**, MD; **whate**, MD, HD; **hwatliche**, S; **watloker**, *comp.*, S2.—AS. *hwæt*: OS. *hwat*; cf. Icel. *hvatr*, OHG. *was*, sharp (Otfrid).

[**whate**], *sb.* chance, luck; **hwate**, S, MD; **wate**, S; **quate**, HD.—AS. *hwat*, omen, augury, *incitamentum*; cf. Icel. *hvöt* (*hvata-*). See **what**[3], *adj.*

whaup, *sb.* the larger curlew, HD, JD; **whaap**, JD; **whap**, JD; **quhaup**, JD; **quhaip**, JD; **awp**, JD; **awppis**, *pl.*, S3.

wheen, *sb.* a number, a quantity, JD; **quhene**, JD.—Cf. AS. *hwéne* inst. of *hwón*, see Sievers, 237. See **woon.**

wheene, *adj. pl.* few, B.

whele[1], *sb.* wheel, Voc., W2; **whiel**, CM; **whel**, C; **quhele**, S3; **hweoles**, *pl.*, S. *Comb.*: **quheill-rym**, wheel-rim, S3.—AS. *hwéol*; cf. Gr. κύκλος; see Douse, p. 37.

whele[2], *sb.* a pimple, Prompt., Voc. (790. 27); **wheal**, SkD; **wheale**, 'pupula', Manip.; **queale**, Manip.

whelen, *v.* to putrefy, Prompt.—AS. *hwelian* (BT).

whelke, *sb.* a pimple, Voc., Prompt., MD; **whelk**, Sh.; **whelkes**, *pl.*, CM, C, SkD (s.v. *wheal*).

whelp, *sb.* a whelp, dog, C2, C3, Prompt.; **welp**, MD; **quelpe** MD; **quilpe**, MD; **qwelpe**, Voc.—AS. *hwelp.*

whene, *v.* to lament, MD.—AS. *hwénan*. See **quain.**

whennes, *adv.* whence, C3, P; see **whannes.**

wher[1], *adv. interrog.* and *rel.* where, S, C2; **whare**, S2; **whær**, S; **hwer**, S; **hwar**, S; **huer**, S2; **wer**, S; **war**, S; **quar**, S2 (s.v. *si-quar*); **quhare**; **quuor**, S. *Comb.*: **wheras**, where, S3, C2; **werbi**, whereby,

235

wher

S; **werefore**, wherefore, S; **hwerfore**, S; **warevore**, S, S2; **werinne**, wherein, S2; **huermyde**, wherewith, S2; **quor-of**, whereof, S; **whærswa**, wheresoever, S; **wherso**, C2; **hwarse**, S; **hwerse**, S; **warso**, S2; **whærsitt**, S; **quhair-to**, wherefore, S3; **whærwiþþ**, wherewith, S; **wareþoru**, wherethrough, S2.—AS. *hwǽr*. **wher²**, *pron.* and *conj.* whether of the two, whether, S2, C, C2, G, PP; **where**, PP; **whar**, S; **hwere**, S; **wer**, S2; **quer**, S2; **quhidder**, S3; **whether**, S; **hweðer**, S. *Comb.*: **wher so**, whethersoever, S; **queðer so**, S.—AS. *hwæðer*. Cf. **oþer¹**, **eiþer**. **whete**, *sb.* wheat, Voc., C3; **hwete**, S; **wete**, S; **quete**, S2; **quet**, S2.—AS. *hwǽte*: Goth. *hvaiteis*. **whetten**, *v.* to sharpen, CM, Prompt., S3; **whætte**, *pt. s.*, S, MD; **wette**, MD. *Comb.*: **whet-stone**, Prompt.; **whestone**, Prompt.; **wheston**, Voc.; **whestones**, *pl.*, S2.—AS. *hwettan*: Icel. *hvetja*. See **what³**. **whethen**, *adv.* whence, HD, H; **whythyne**, HD (p. 929).—Icel. *hvaðan*. **whi**, *adv. interrog.* why, S; **wi**, S; **wy**, S; **hwi**, S; **qui**, S2.—AS. *hwí*, inst. of *hwá*. See **who**. **whicche**, a chest, trunk, box; **whucche**, PP; **whyche**, Prompt.; **hoche**, Prompt.—AS. *hwicce*; 'Clustella, *hwicce*'; Engl. Studien, xi. 65. **which**, *pron. interrog.* and *rel.*, *adj.* which, S2; **whilk**, S2; **whillc**, S; **whulche**, S; **hwilc**, S; **hwilch**, S; **hwich**, S; **hwuch**, S; **huych**, S; **huyche**, S2; **wulc**, S; **wilk**, S2; **wulche**, S; **woche**, S; **wuch**, S2; **wic**, S; **quilc**, S; **quilk**, S2 (*squilk*) H; **quhilk**, S3. *Comb.*: **wilc so**, whichsoever, S; **hwychso**, S.—AS. *hwilc* (for *hwí-líc*). **whider**, *adv.* whither, PP, C2, C; **whidir**, SkD; **whyder**, PP; **hwider**, S; **wider**, S; **quhethir**, S2. *Comb.*: **hwiderse**, whitherso, S; **whider-ward**, whitherward, S2; **whederward**, S2; **whydyrward**, S2; **whederwarde-so**, whithersoever, S2.—AS. *hwider*. **while**, *sb.* a while, duration of time, PP; **whyl**, C2; **hwile**, S; **hwule**, S; **wile**, S; **wyle**, S2; **wule**, S2; **quhyle**, S3; **whyle**, *adv.*, for a time, sometimes, formerly, S2; **wile**, S; **wil**, S3; **quile**, *conj.*, S; **quhill**, S2, S3; **wile**, S. *Comb.*: **whyle-ere**, formerly, S3; **whyler**, C3.—AS. *hwíl*, a time, space. cf. Goth. *hveila*. **whiles**, *adv.* and *conj.* whiles, whilst, S2, PP; **wiles**, S; **whyls**, C3; **hwils**, S. **whilk**, *pron.* which, S2; see **which**. **whilom**, *adv.* sometimes, formerly, C, S2, PP; **whilum**, PP; **whylom**, C2; **hwilem**,

wicke

S; **hwylem**, S; **wylem**, S; **quilum**, S; **quhilum**, S3.—AS. *hwílum*, at times. **whipling**, *sb.* a murmuring, S3. **whippe**, *sb.* whip, scourge, SkD; **quippe**, Voc.; **quhyp**, S3. **whippen**, *v.* to move suddenly and quickly, SkD; **whypt**, *pt. s.*, S3. **whit**, *sb.* a wight, man, S3; see **wight²**. **whitely**, *adv.* quite, H; see **quytly**. **who**, *pron. interrog.* and *rel.* who, any one, SD, PP; **wha**, S2; **hwo**, S; **huo**, S2; **hwa**, S; **ho**, S2; **wo**, S, S2; **wa**, S; **quho**, S3; **quha**, S2; **ʒwo**, SD; **qva**, SD; **qvo**, SD; **qwo**, SD. *Comb.*: **who se**, who so, S2, PP; **hwo se**, S; **ho se**, S2; **ho so**, P; **wo so**, S, S2; **hwa se**, S.—AS. *hwá*, *hwá-swá*; cf. Lat. *quo-d*; see Douse, p. 71. **whom**, *pron. interrog.* and *rel. dat.* to whom, C2; **wham**, S; **wam**, S; **hwom**, S; **hwam**, S; **quam**, S.—AS. *hwám*, *hwém* (dat.). **whon**, *pron. interrog.* and *rel. acc.* (also *dat.*), S; **whan**, SD; **hwan**, S; **wan**, S, S2.—AS. *hwone* (acc.). **whos**, *pron. interrog.* and *rel. gen.* whose, C2, W; **whas**, SD, P; **whes**, SD; **quhais**, S3; **quhois**, S3.—AS. *hwæs* (gen.). **whough**, *interj.* whew!, S3; **wough**, S3. **whulche**, *pron.* which, S; see **which**. **whyppyltre**, *sb.* cornel-tree, C; see **wyppyltre**. **whyrle**, *sb.* whirl, *giraculum*, Cath. (*n*). *Comb.*: **whirl-bon**, *vertebra*, SD; **whyrlebone**, Voc.; **whorlebone**, Cath.; **whyrle-wynde**, *turbo*, Prompt. **whyrlyn**, *v.* to whirl, Prompt.; **whirlen**, C2; **wyrle**, S2; **quhyrl**, S3. *Comb.*: **whirlinge wyndys**, whirlwinds, W.—Icel. *hvirfla*, to whirl. **whyte¹**, *sb.* white wine, C3. **whyte²**, *adj.* white, PP, C2; **whit**, S, C, PP; **hwit**, S; **wit**, S; **quhite**, S3; **quhyt**, S3; **quite**, S2; **huyter**, *comp.*, S2; **whittore**, S2. *Der.*: **whytnesse**, whiteness, C3. *Comb.*: **Witsunnedei**, Whitsunday, S; **Witesone-tid**, Whitsuntide, S2.—AS. *hwít*: cf. Goth. *hveits*. **wi**, *adv.* why, S; see **whi**. **wicche**, *sb.* sorcerer, *magus*, *sortilegus*, also witch, PP; **wyche**, *magus*, Prompt., Cath., Voc.; **witch**, Cath. *Comb.*: **wicchecrafte**, PP; **wychecraft**, Cath., Voc.; **wichche-creftes**, *pl.*, S.—AS. *wicca* (m). **wicht**, *adj.* active, vigorous, S3; see **wight¹**. **wicke**, *adj.* bad, false, S, S2, PP; **wicce**, S; **wycke**, S2; **wikke**, P, C2, C3; **wike**, S, S2; **wic**, S2; **wik**, S2, H. *Der.*: **wickenesse**, iniquity, SD; **wickenes**, S2; **wiknes**, S2; **wickenesses**, *pl.*, S2.

236

wicked, *adj.* depraved, Cath.; **wykkyd**, Prompt.; **wykkid**, H (p. 360); **wykked**, S2; **wikked**, C2, P; **wikkedly**, *adv.*, wickedly, C2.

wid[1], *adj.* wide, S; **wide**, *adv.*, S, PP; **wyde**, C2, PP; **wydder**, *comp.*, PP. *Der.*: **wydene**, wide, far, S2, PP. *Comb.*: **wydewhere**, far and wide, S2, PP; **wydewher**, C3, G.—AS. *wíd*; cf. OHG. *wît* (Tatian).

wid[2], *prep.* against, with, S2; see **wiþ**.

widewe, *sb.* widow, PP; **wydewe**, PP; **widwe**, C2, C3; **wodewe**, PP; **wedous**, *pl.*, S3.—AS. *widwe* (*weoduwe*): Goth. *widuwo*; cf. OHG. *wituwá* (Tatian).

wif, *sb.* woman, wife, S, S2, PP; **wyf**, C3, PP; **wiues**, *gen.*, S2, C2; **wiue**, *dat.*, S; **wif**, *pl.*, S; **wyf**, G; **wifes**, S; **wiues**, S2, C2. *Comb.*: **wyfhood**, womanhood, C2; **wifman**, woman, S; **wimman**, S; **wymman**, S; **wiman**, S; **womman**, S, PP; **wummon**, S; **wommanhede**, womanhood, C2, C2.—AS. *wíf*: OHG. *wîb* (Tatian).

wig, *sb.* a beast of burden, a horse, S.—AS. *wicg*; cf. Icel. *viggr* (*viggja-*), also *vigg*, see Sievers, 247.

wigelen, *v.* to reel, stagger, S.

wight[1], *adj.* active, swift, strong, S2, PP, CM, G; **wyght**, S2; **wiȝt**, PP; **wiht**, PP; **wyht**, Prompt.; **wicht**, S3; **wycht**, S3; **wict**, S; **vicht**, S2; **wyte**, Prompt.; **wightly**, *adv.*, H; **wiȝtli**, S2; **wiȝtliche**, S2, P; **wihtliche**, S2; **witly**, S2. *Der.*: **wightnesse**, alacrity, Cath.

wight[2], *sb.* wight, creature, being, PP, S2, C3; **wyght**, PP, S2, C3; **wiȝt**, PP, S; **wijȝt**, S3; **wiht**, S, S2; **wyht**, S2; **whit**, S3; **whiȝt**, S3.—AS. *wiht*, see SkD.

wiht, *sb.* a thing, S; **wiȝt**, S; **whit**, WW.—AS. *wiht* (*wuht*), thing, *f.* and *n.*

wihte, *sb. dat.* weight, S; see **wyghte**.

wik, *sb.* a dwelling; **wike**, *pl.*, S. *Comb.*: **wike-tun**, court; **wiketunes**, *pl.*, S.—AS. *wíc*; Lat. *uicum* (acc.).

wike[1], *sb.* week, S, S2, GS, CM, PP; **wyke**, PP, C, S2; **weke**, PP, Cath.; **woke**, W, S2, PP, Prompt., Cath.; **wouke**, W; **wowke**, Cath.—AS. *wice* (*wucu*); Lat. *uicem*.

wike[2], *sb.* office, service, SD; *pl.*, S.—Cf. Goth. *wiko*; Lat. *uicem*, change, regular succession, office, service.

wike[3], *sb. pl.* the corners of the mouth, S (4 a. 49).—Cf. Icel. *munnvik*, pl., the corners of the mouth; see CV (s.v. *munnr*). The word *wikes* is still in use in this sense at Whitby. See Whitby Glossary (EDS).

wiken, *sb.* office, charge; **wikenn**, S (5. 1113), SD.

wikenere, *sb.* officer, SD.

wiket, *sb.* a small gate, S, P, CM; **wickett**, PP; **wykett**, *valva*, gate, Cath.; little window, *fenestrella*, Prompt.; **viket**, *lodium*, a lover-window, Cath. (*n*).—OF. *wiket* (*viquet*); cf. ODu. *wicket*.

wikke, *adj.* bad, C2, C3; see **wicke**.

wikked, *adj.* depraved, bad, C2; see **wicked**.

wil, *sb.* will, joy, S; *Comb.*: **wilful**, desirous, gracious, willing, W, W2; **wilfull**, S3; **wilfulliche**, willingly, S; **wilfulli**, W; **wilfully**, C3.—AS. (*ge*)*will*. Cf. **wille**[2].

wild, *adj.* self-willed, untamed, uncultivated, desert, S; **wielde**, W2; **wylde**, *sb. pl.*, wild animals, S2. *Der.*: **wilderne**, wilderness, SkD; **wildrin**, desert, belonging to a wilderness, S2; **wildernesse**, wilderness, SkD; **wyldernys**, Voc.—AS. *wild*.

wile, *sb.* a while, S; see **while**.

wilk, *pron.* which, S2; see **which**.

will, *adj.* at a loss, astray, bewildered, B, S2; **wil**, H; **vill**, B; **wille**, *adv.*, S. *Phr.*: **will of red**, at a loss in counsel, B; **will of wane**, at a loss in thought, B; **will of wan**, S2; **vill of vayn**, S2.—Icel. *villr* (for *wildr*), wild.

wille[1], *1 pr. s.* will, S, S2; **wel**, S2; **wule**, S; **wulle**, S; **wile**, *pr. s.*, S, S2; **wole**, S; **wol**, S2, C2; **wult**, *2 pr. s.*, S; **wolt**, S, S2, C2; **willen**, *pl.*, S; **willeð**, S; **wulleð**, S; **wulle**, S; **wilen**, S; **wiln**, S; **wolleð**, S; **wole**, C2; **woln**, C. *Comb.*: **ichulle** (ich + wulle), S; **ich chulle**, S; **ich chule**, S; **wiltu** (wilt + ðu), S; **wilte**, S; **woltow**, C, PP.—AS. *wille*, 1 and 3 pr. s., *wilt*, 2 pr. s. See **wolde**[2].

wille[2], *sb.* will, joy, pleasure, S, S2, C2, PP; **wylle**, PP; **willes**, *gen.* as *adv.* willingly, S; **willeliche**, *adv.*, willingly, S. *Comb.*: **willesful**, wilful, S; **willesfol**, S2; **wylles uol**, S2; **wylsfully**, wilfully, S2. *Phr.*: **mid guode wylle**, willingly, S2; **in good wille**, anxious, G.—AS. *willa*: Goth. *wilja*. Cf. **wil**.

willing, *sb.* desire, C2.

wilnen, *v.* to desire, S, S2, S3, C, C2, W, P; **wilnien**, S; **wylny**, S2. *Der.*: **wylnynge**, desire, S2.—AS. *wilnian*.

wilwe, *sb.* willow-tree, C, Prompt.—AS. *welig* (Voc.).

wimman, *sb.* woman, S; see **wif**.

wimpel, *sb.* a nun's veil, S; **wympel**, C. *Comb.*: **wimpel-leas**, wimple-less, S.—Icel. *vimpill*; cf. AF. *guimple*.

wimplin, *v.* to cover with a wimple, S; **y-wimpled**, *pp.*, C; **i-wimplet**; S; **y-wympled**, C.

wimplunge, *sb.* wimpling, S; **wimlunge**, *dat.*, S.

winden, *v.* to wind, twist, turn; **wynde**, PP; **wand**, *pt. s.*, SD; **wonden**, *pl.*, P; **wounden**,

PP; **wunden**, *pp.*, S; **wounden**, S; **wounde**, PP; **y-wounden**, PP.—AS. *windan*, pt. *wand* (pl. *wundon*), pp. *wunden*.

wine, *sb.* friend; **wines**, *pl.*, S. *Comb.*: **wine-maies**, kinsmen, S.—AS. *wine, wine-mǽg*.

winne, *sb.* joy, S; **wynne**, HD (p. 933); **wunne**, S, S2; **win**, S. *Der.*: **winli**, pleasant, S2; **winsom**, S2.—AS. *wynn*.

winnen, *v.* to win, S, S2, C2; **wynne**, S2; **wyn**, S3; **vyn**, S2; **wunien**, S; **wan**, *pt. s.*, S, S2, C2, C3, P; **van**, S2; **wonne**, *pl.*, PP, S2; **wonnen**, *pp.*, C; **wonne**, C; **y-wonne**, P; **i-wonne**, S2; **wonen**, S2; **wune**, S2. *Der.*: **wynnyng**, gain, W.—AS. *(ge)winnan*, pt. *wan* (pl. *wunnon*), pp. *wunnen*.

wirken, *v.* to work, S2; see **werke**[2].

wis, *adv.* indeed, S; **wisly**, *adv.*, certainly, surely, C, C2, C3.—AS. *(ge)wiss*. See **iwis**.

wissen, *v.* to direct, guide, S, S2, S3, CM, P; **wyssen**, S2; **wyssye**, S; **wisi**, S. *Der.*: **wissunge**, instruction, S; **wissinge**, *dat.*, S; **wissenge**, S.—AS. *wissian, wisian*: OHG. *wísjan*, also *uuîsen* (Otfrid).

wiste, *pt. s.* knew, S, C2, G; **wist**, *pp.* known, S3, C2, G; see **witen**[1].

wistynge, *sb.* learning, H.

wit[1], *sb.* wisdom, intelligence, S, C2; **wyt**, S; **wittes**, *pl.*, senses, S, S2, C2; **wites**, S.—AS. *(ge)witt*.

wit[2], *prep.* with, S; see **wiþ**.

wite, *sb.* blame, S2, H; **wyte**, C3. See **witen**[3].

witen[1], *v.* to know, S, S2, W, PP; **wyten**, S, S2; **witte**, S2; **witt**, S3; **witt**, *imp. s.*, S; **wittow, witow**, know thou, S2; **wute**, *pl.*, S; **wytene**, *ger.*, S2; **witynge**, *pr. p.*, S2, W; **wat**, *1* and *3 pr. s.*, S, S2, S3; **wate**, H; **wait**, S3; **wot**, S, S2, C2; **woot**, S2, W; **wote**, S3; **woȝt**, S2; **wost**, *2 pr. s.*, S, C2; **wostu**, knowest thou, S; **wostow**, C2; **witen**, *pl.*, S, W; **wyteð**, S2; **wate**, S2; **wiste**, *pt. s.*, S, C2, G; **wisten**, *pl.*, S, W; **wist**, S2, S3; **wyst**, S2, S3; **wuste**, *pt. s.*, S, S2; **wust**, S2; **wist**, *pp.*, S3, C2, G.—AS. *witan*, 2 pr. *wást*, 3 pr. s., *wát* (pl. *witon*), pt. *wiste (wisse)*, pp. *witen*.

witen[2], *v.* to observe, keep, guard, S, P, S2; **wiste**, *pt. s.*, S; **wistest**, *2 pt. s.*, S; **i-wist**, *pp.*, S. See **witen**[1].

witen[3], *v.* to impute, blame, S, S2; **wyte**, C2.—AS. *wítan*, to see, to blame (Grein).

witen[4], *v.* to depart, to disappear, to dwindle, S, H; **wyte**, H; **wit**, S2; **ute**, let us, S. AS. *(ge)witan*; see Grein. See **witen**[3].

witerliche, *adv.* truly, S; **witerlike**, S; see **witter**.

witien, *v.* to keep, S2; **wited**, *pt. s.*, S2. *Der.*: **witunge**, care-taking, S.—AS. *witian*, 'providere' (Grein).

witing, *sb.* knowledge, C2. See **witen**[1].

witȝe, *sb.* seer, prophet, S; **witeȝe**, S.—AS. *witiga*, from *witan*, to see; cf. OHG. *wízago* (Tatian) from *wízan*, to see (Otfrid). See **witen**[3].

witter, *adj.* wise, skilful, S; **wyter**, S2; **witerliche**, *adv.*, truly, wisely, S; **witerlike**, S; **witterly**, clearly, P, HD; **witerrlike**, S; **witterlike**, S; **witerli** S2; **witirly**, H.—Icel. *vitr, vitrliga*.

witti, *adj.* skilful, W2.—AS. *wittig*.

wit-word, *sb.* covenant, H; **witeword**, S2.

wið, *prep.* against, towards, by, with, S, S2; **wid**, S, S2; **wit**, S, S2; **wiȝth**, S2. *Comb.*: **wiðinnen**, within, S; **wiðinneforð**, inwardly, S3, W; **wiððan**, provided that, S; **wiððat**, S, S2; **wiðouten**, without, S2, S3, W; **wiðuten**, S; **wiðoutenforth**, outside, S2; **wiðouteforð**, S3, W; **withoutforth**, S2.—AS. *wið*.

with-clepin, *v.* to recall, *revocare*, Prompt.

with-draȝen, *v.* to withdraw, S; **wyðdraȝen**, S2; **wiðdroȝe**, *pt. s.*, S; **withdrow**, S.

wiðer, *prep.* against, SD; *adj.*, hostile, S; *sb.*, resistance, SD. *Comb.*: **wiðerling**, adversary, S; **wiðerward**, contrary, SD; **wider-wardnesse**, opposition, S; **wiðerwin**, adversary, HD, S2.—AS. *wiðer*, against.

wiðeren, *v.* to resist; **wiððreðð**, *pr. s.*, S.—AS. *wiðerian*.

wiði, *sb.* a willow, a flexible twig, a withy, SD, SkD; **wythy**, Voc.; **widdie**, a rope made of twigs of willows, a halter, a whip made of twigs, JD. *Comb.*: **wythe-bonde**, *boia*, chain for prisoners, Prompt.; **weðe-bondes**, *gen.*, S2; **wið-winde**, *convolvulus*, SD; **withe-wyndes**, *gen.*, S2 (p. 334), P.—AS. *wiðig*, willow, *wiðwinde*, 'viticella', Voc.; cf. ODu. *wedewinde*.

with-seye, *v.* to contradict, renounce; **wythsay**, HD (p. 935); **wiðseggen**, S, S2.

wið-stod, *pt. s.* stood beside, S2; **withstode**, *pl.*, resisted, PP.

with-take, *v.* to reprove, H; **withtoke**, *pt. s.*, H.

with-takere, *sb.* reprover, H.

wiȝt, *sb.* creature, thing, S; see **wight**[2].

wlaffyng, *sb.* babbling, S2.

wlanc, *adj.* proud, fine, grand, S2; **wlonk**, S2; **wlonke**, fine woman, HD.—AS. *wlanc* (OET).

wlappen, *v.* to wrap, W, W2; **lappen**, W, II, Cath., SkD, HD.

wlatien, *v.* to feel disgust, to abominate, W, W2, S2, HD; **wlathid**, *pt. s.* H.—AS. *wlǽtian*.

wlat-some, *adj.* disgusting, abominable, S2, HD; **wlatsom**, C; **wlatsum**, S2; **latsom**, S2; **wlathsum**, H.

wlatunge, *sb.* disgust, SD; **wlathyngis**, *pl.*, abominations, H.—AS. *wlátung*, nausea (OET).

wlech, *adj.* warm, S.—AS. *wlæc.*

wlite, *sb.* beauty, splendour, form, hue, face, S.—AS. *white* (OET).

wliten, *v.* to see, SD; **wlyteð**, *pr. pl.*, S2.—AS. *wlítan*; cf. Icel. *líta.*

wlonk, *adj.* fine, grand, S2; see **wlanc.**

wluine, *sb.* she-wolf, S. See **wolf.**

wo[1], *interj.*, woe!, SD; **way**, S; **wei**, S; **wi**, S. *Comb.*: **wo la wo**, an exclamation of sorrow, S; **weylaway**, S2, C3; **weilawei**, S; **wailawai**, S; **wayloway**, G; **walawai**, S; **wele away**, S3.—AS. *wá*: Goth. *wai*; cf. OHG. *wê* (Otfrid), Icel. *vei.*—AS. *wá lá wá.*

wo[2], *sb.* also used as *adj.* woe, sorrowful, S, S2, C2, C3; **wa**, S, S2, B. *Phr.*: **wo begon**, surrounded with woe, SkD; **wa worth**, B; **wo worthe**, SD.—AS. *wéa.*

woc[1], *adj.* weak, S; **wooc**, SkD.—AS. *wác.* See **wayke.**

woc[2], *pt. s.* woke, S; see **waken.**

woche, *pron.* which, S; see **which.**

wode[1], *sb.* wood, tree, S, S2, C2, PP; **wod**, S2; **vod**, S2; **wude**, S. *Comb.*: **wode-bynde**, woodbine, SkD; **woode-bynde**, *caprifolium*, Prompt., C; **wod-bynde**, S2 (p. 476); **woode-lynde**, linden-tree in a wood, G; **wode-roue**, woodruff, S2; **wooderys**, brushwood, G; **woode-schawe**, thicket of the wood, G; **wude-side**, wood-side, S; **vode-syde**, S2; **wode-wale**, the name of a bird, also called wit-wall, Prompt., HD; **wude-wale**, S; **wode-wose**, a satyr, faun, SD, Voc., Prompt. (*n*); **wode-wese**, Prompt.; **wod-wose**, WA.—AS. *wudu*; cf. OIr. *fid* (Windisch).

wode[2], *sb.* woad, S, Prompt.; **wod**, SkD; **wad**, *gaudo* Prompt.—AS. *wád.*

wode[3], *adj.* mad, raging, S, S2, S3, C; **wod**, S, S2, H; **wood**, C2, C3, S3; **woode**, W; **wodly**, *adv.*, madly, C. *Der.*: **wodnes**, madness, S2, H; **wodenesse**, S2; **woodnesse**, C3, W. *Comb.*: **wodewrothe**, madly angry, S3.—AS. *wód*: Goth. *wods*; cf. OHG. *wuot.*

Woden, *sb.* the Teutonic god Woden, S2.—AS. *Wóden*; cf. OHG. *Wuotan*, Icel. *Óðinn.* See **Wodnes-dei.**

Wodnes-dei, *sb.* Wednesday, SD; **Wednes dai**, SD; **Wendes dei**, S.—AS. *Wódnesdæg*, the day of the Teutonic god Woden; cf. OHG. *Wuotan*, Icel. *Óðinn.*

woh[1], *adj.* crooked, wrong; **woȝe**, S; **woȝhe**, *pl.*, S. *Adv. phr.*: **mid wohe**, wrongfully, S; **mid gret wou**, S2; **wiðð woȝhe**, S; **wið wou**, S2; **on wowe**, S.—AS. *wóh*, crooked.

woh[2], *sb.* wrong, S; **wouche**, S3; **wowe**, *pl.*, S2.—AS. *wóh*, iniquity.

woke, *sb.* week, W, S2; see **wike**[1].

wol[1], *pr. s.* will, S2; see **wille**[1].

wol[2], *adv.* well, very, S; see **wel**[1].

wolcne, *sb. pl.* clouds, the sky, S; see **welkene.**

wold, *sb.* power, meaning, force, S, S2.—AS. *(ge)weald.*

wolde[1], *sb.* wold, open country, country, S, Prompt.—AS. *weald*, wood, forest: OS. *wald.*

wolde[2], *pt. s.* was desirous, was willing, would, S, S2, C2; **wulde**, S; **walde**, S; **wald**, S2, B; **wlde**, S2; **woldes**, *2 pt. s.*, S; **wolden**, *pl.*, S; **wolde**, S, C2; **wulde**, S; **wuld**, S2; **walden**, S; **vald**, S2, B.—AS. *wolde*, pt. s. of *willan.* See **wille**[1].

wolf, *sb.* wolf, PP; **wlf**, S; **wlfe**, Voc.; **wolwes**, *pl.*, S2; **wulues**, *gen.*, S. *Comb.*: **wolues-heed**, wolf's head, outlaw, G.—AS. *wulf*; cf. Icel. *úlfr.*

wolle, *sb.* wool, S, S2, C3, P. *Comb.*: **wolleward**, with the skin against the wool, SkD; **wolward**, S3; **woolward**, ND; **wollewebsteres**, wool-weavers, P.—AS. *wull*: Goth. *wulla.*

wollen, *adj.* woollen, P.

wolt, *2 pr. s.* wilt, S; see **wille**[1].

wolx, *pt. s.* grew, S3; see **wexen.**

wombe, *sb. venter, alvus, uterus*, Prompt., S, S2, S3, C2, C3, P; **wambe**, S3.—AS. *wamb*: Goth. *wamba*, the belly.

won, *adj.* wan, S2; see **wan.**

wonden, *v.* to turn aside, to fear, to hesitate, S, S2; **wayndyt**, *pt. s.*, S3.—AS. *wandian.*

wonder, *adj.* fearful, wonderful, S, S2, C2; *adv.*, C3; **wounder**, S2; **vounder**, S2; **wondir**, S3, H; **wunder**, *sb.*, a wonder, S; **wounder**, S2; **wunder**, *pl.*, awful wickednesses, S. *Der.*: **wunderlice**, wonderful, S; **wunderliche**, *adv.*, S; **wonderlyche**, S2; **wonderly**, C; **wunderlicheste**, *superl.*, S; **wunderlukeste**, S. *Phr.*: **to wundre**, wrong, S.

wondrien, *v.* to wonder; **wondrye**, S2; **wondre**, C; **wundrien**, S.—AS. *wundrian.*

wondringe, *pres. p.* wandering, S2; see **wandren.**

wone[1], *sb.* dwelling, PP, S2, S3; **won**, S2; **woon**, S3; **wun**, S3; **woanes**, *pl.*, S; **wanes**, S, S2. See **wonen**[1].

wone[2], *sb.* custom, habit, PP, S, S2; **wune**, S.—AS. *(ge)wuna.*

wone[3], *sb.* want, loss, misery, S; see **wane**[3].

wone[4], *adj.* one, S3 (7. 97); see **oon.**

woned, *pp.* accustomed, S, S3; see **iwoned.**

wonen[1], *v.* to dwell, PP, S, S2; **wonien**, S, S2, PP; **wunien**, S; **wonyand**, *pr. p.*, S2;

wonnand, S2; **wounnand**, S3.—*Der.*: **wonynge**, dwelling, PP, S; **woning**, C, S2; **wonyinge**, S2; **wunienge**, *pl.*, S.—AS. *wunian*.

wonen[2], *v.* to weep, lament, SD; **wanen**, SD. *Der.*: **wonyng**, lamentation, S.—AS. *wánian*; cf. OHG. *weinón* (Tatian).

wonge[1], *sb.* *territorium*, Prompt.; **wong**, low land, HD; **wonges**, *pl.*, meadows, S.—AS. *wang*, a plain, field; cf. Goth. *waggs*, a field, paradise.

wonge[2], *sb.* a cheek, SD, JD; **wonges**, *pl.*, S2. *Comb.*: **wange-toothe**, molar tooth, *molaris*, Prompt.; **wongtothe**, Voc.; **wangtooth**, C2; **wank-teeth**, *pl.*, W2; **wangtotht**, *geminus*, *molaris*, Voc.—AS. *wange* (*wonge*); cf. OHG. *wanga* (Tatian).

wonger, *sb.* pillow, C2, CM. See **wonge**[2].

wonne[1], *adv.*, *conj.* when, S; see **whan**.

wonne[2], **wonnen**, *pp.* of **winnen**.

wonteð, *pr. s.* is lacking, S; see **wanten**.

wonung, *sb.* waning, S.—AS. *wonung*, *wanung*. See **wanen**.

wood, *adj.* mad, C2, C3, S3; see **wode**[3].

wooden, *v.* to be mad, to look madly, CM, C3.

woon, *sb.* a small quantity, a few, a quantity, a number, S2, G, PP; **wone**, S2; **woone**, Prompt.; **wane**, S2, S3; **won**, PP; **quhone**, B. *Comb.*: **good woon**, abundantly, G; **good won**, PP.—AS. *hwón* (adj. used as sb.). Cf. **wheen**.

wop, *sb.* crying, loud lament, S, S2.—AS. *wóp*.

wopen, *pp.* wept, C2; see **wepen**.

wopne, *sb.* urine, HD, Prompt. See **wepne**.

wopnede, *pp.* armed, S; see **wepnen**.

worc, *sb.* work, S2; see **werke**[1].

worchen, *v.* to work, W, S2; see **werke**[2].

word, *sb.* beginning, CM (3. 224); see **ord**.

worde, *sb.* word, Prompt.; **word**, *pl.*, S; **weord**, S; **weordes**, S; **wordes**, S.—AS. *word*; cf. OHG. *wort* (Tatian).

wore, *pt. pl.* were, S2; see **was**.

woreld, *sb.* world, S; **wordle**, S2; see **werld**.

worie, *adj.* turbid, dirty, S; **wori**, S.—From AS. *wór*, a swampy place, perhaps identical with *wós*, mire, see SkD (s.v. *weary*). Cf. **wose**.

worm, *sb.* reptile, worm, snake, S, S2, C3; **wurm**, S; **werm**, S; **wirm**, insect, S.—AS. *wyrm*; OHG. *wurm* (Tatian), cf. Goth. *waurms*; see Douse, p. 56.

wormod, *sb.* wormwood, W; see **wermod**.

worne, *pp.* spent, past, lit. worn, S3; see **werien**[2].

worowen, *v.* to choke, strangle, worry, Prompt., Cath., S2, SkD; **worry**, HD;

wyrry, S3; **wirry**, SkD.—AS. *wyrgan*, to strangle, worry (in compounds): OHG. *wurgan*. Cf. **warh**.

worpare, *sb.* thrower, S.

worpen, *v.* to throw, S; see **warpen**.

worre, *sb.* war, S2; see **werre**[2].

worri, *v.* to make war, S2; see **werrien**.

worschipen, *v.* to honour, S2; **worshepen**, PP; **wurschepen**, S2. See **worþ**[1].

wort, *sb.* a plant, vegetable; **wortes**, *pl.*, S2, S3, C; **wortis**, S2, S3, W, W2.—AS. *wyrt*: OS. *wurt*; cf. Goth. *waurts*, root, and Lat. *rādix*; see Brugmann, § 306, and Douse, p. 56.

worth[1], *adj.* worth, esteemed, worthy, PP; **wurth**, S; **wurthe**, S, S2. *Der.*: **worthi**, PP; **wurðy**, S2; **worþly**, worthy, PP, S2; **worðely**, S3; **wurðliche**, honourably, S; **worðliche**, S; **wurthmint**, honour, S; **wurðscipe**, worship, honour, S; **worðssipe**, S2; **worschupe**, S2; **worsipe**, S; **wurschipe**, S.—AS. *weorð*; cf. Goth. *wairþs*.

worth[2], *sb.* value, worth, honour, PP; **wurrþe**, *dat.*, S.—AS. *weorð*.

worthen, *v.* to become, to be, to dwell, PP, S2, S3, G; **wurðen**, S; **weorðen**, S2; **worst**, *2 pr. s.*, PP; **wurstow**, thou shalt be, PP; **wurstu**, S; **worth**, *pr. s.*, S2, PP; **wurð**, S; **wrþ**, S; **vorthis**, S2; **wurðeð**, S; **worthe**, *pt. s.*, PP; **worth**, S2, PP; **worthed**, S3; **vorthit**, S2; **warð**, S; **wart**, S; **ward**, S; **wærd**, S.—AS. *weorðan*, *pt. s. wearð* (pl. *wurdon*), *pp. (ge)worden*; cf. Goth. *wairþan*.

wose, *sb.* ooze, slime, PP, Prompt.; **woose**, Cath. (*n*); **wase**, *alga*, Cath.—AS. *wáse* (SkD. s.v. *ooze*), and *wase* (OET): OHG. *waso*; whence OF. *wason*, *gason* (F. *gazon*); see Kluge (s.v. *wasen*).

wot, *1 and 3 pr. s.* know, knows, S, S2; **wost**, *2 pr. s.* knowest, S, C2; see **witen**[1].

wouke, *sb.* week, W; see **wike**[1].

wound, *sb.* wound, PP, C2; **wund**, S.—AS. *wund*.

wounden, *v.* to wound, S3; **wowndyn**, Prompt.; **y-wounded**, *pp.*, S3; **i-wundet**, S.—AS. *wundian*.

wout, *sb.* a vault, Voc., HD.—OF. *voute* (BH); Late Lat. *uolta*.

wowe[1], *sb.* wall, *paries*, *murus*, Prompt., PP; **woȝe**, S; **waghe**, HD, H; **waȝhe**, S; **wawe**, S; **wah**, S. *Comb.*: **waheles**, wall-less, S; **waȝherifft**, veil of the temple, S.—AS. *wáh*; cf. ODu. *waeg*, see SkD (s.v. *wainscot*, p. 833); cf. also Goth. *waddjus*.

wowe[2], *sb. pl.* wrongs, S2; see **woh**[2].

wowen, *v.* to incline any one to one's own wishes, to woo, S2, C3, P, W2, S3; **woȝe**,

wower

S.—AS. *wógian* (SkD, s.v. *woo*), from *wóh*. See **woh**[1].

wower, *sb.* wooer, S3; **wowar,** S3; **wouw-ere,** PP; **woweres,** *pl.*, PP.—AS. *wógere* (Voc.).

wox, *pt. s.* grew, S2; see **wexen**.

wrablis, *sb. pl.* warblings, S2; see **werble**.

wraht, *pt. s.* wrought; see **werke**[2].

wrak, *sb.* that which is driven ashore, wreck, S2, S3, C3; **rac,** driven vapour, rack, S2, SkD; **rack,** Sh.—AS. *wræc*. Cf. **wreche** and **wreken**.

wranne, *sb.* wren, S; see **wrenne**.

wrastlen, *v.* to wrestle, C, S2, G, PP; **wraskle,** PP; **wrastylle,** Cath.; **wraxle,** Voc. *Der.*: **wrastling,** wrestling, C2, G; **wrastelyng,** G.—AS. *wréstlian* (oftener *wráxlian*), from *wréstan*, to wrest, from *wrést*, firm, strong. *Wrést* is for *wréðt*, from *wráð*, pt. of *wríðan*, see Sievers, 232. See **wryþen**.

wrað, *adj.* wroth, S; see **wroþ**[2].

wraðði, *v.* to get angry, S; see **wreþþen**.

wraw, *adj.* perverse, angry, fierce, SD, Prompt., C3, CM, HD; **wrau,** SD. Cf. **wro**.

wrawid, *pp.* perverse, peevish, WA.

wrawnesse, *sb.* fierceness, Prompt., CM.

wrecche, *sb.* also as *adj.* wretch, miserable, S, S2, C, PP; **wreche,** S, S2, CM; **wrecce,** S. *Comb.*: **wreccehed,** wretchedness, S; **wrecchede,** S2.—AS. *wrecca*, an outcast, exile. See **wreken**.

wrecched, *adj.* wretched, S, PP; **wriched,** S. *Comb.*: **wrecchednesse,** misery, C2, C3, PP.

wreche, *sb.* vengeance, misery, S, S2, C2, C3; **wrache,** S; **wræche,** S; **wreke,** S2; **wrake,** S2, PP; **wrac,** S2; **wrick,** S2. *Comb.*: **wrakful,** full of vengeance, S2.—AS. *wracu*, vengeance, misery, also *wræc*, exile, misery. See **wreken**.

wreken, *v.* to urge, wreak, drive, punish, avenge, S, S2, C2, C3, PP; **wræken,** S; **wrak,** *pt. s.*, G; **wreken,** *pp.*, S2, PP; **wreke,** G, PP; **wroken,** PP, WA; **wroke,** PP, HD; **i-wroken,** G.—AS. *wrecan*, pt. *wræc* (pl. *wrécon*), pp. *wrecen*; cf. Goth. *wrikan*, to persecute.

wreker, *sb.* avenger, S2.

wrenche, *sb.* a twist, trick, deceit, S, S2, S3, C3; **wrink,** S3; **wrenkis,** *pl.*, WA.—AS. *wrenc* (*wrence*).

wrenchen, *v.* to turn, twist, S. *Der.*: **wrinch-ing,** wrenching, struggling, S3.—AS. *wrencan*.

wrengðe, *sb.* distortion, S. See **wringen**.

wrenne, *sb.* wren, Voc.; **wranne,** S.—AS. *wrenna, wrénna*.

wreon, *v.* to cover; **wre,** CM; **wreo,** *pr. s. subj.*, S.—AS. *wréon*, pt. *wréah* (pl. *wrugon*), pp. *wrogen*, see Sievers, 383. Cf. **wrihen**.

wreten, *pp.* of **wryten**.

wreth, *sb.* wrath, S2, H; **wraþþe,** PP, S. *Comb.*: **wreðful,** wrathful, S, S2; **wraððe-lees,** S2.—ONorth. *wréððo*. See **wroþ**[2].

wrethe, *sb.* wreath, C.—AS. *wréð*. See **wryþen**.

wreððen, *v.* to become angry, to make angry, S; **wreaððin,** S; **wraððin,** S, S2, G; **wreðen,** S, S2, H. *Der.*: **wrath-thing,** provocation, W.

wrien, *v.* to twist, bend, CM, SkD (s.v. *wry*); **wrye,** S3, PP.—AS. *wrigian*, to drive, bend.

wrigt (*in compounds*), an accusation. *Comb.*: **wrigtful,** guilty, S; **wrigteles,** without an accusation; **wrigteslike,** causelessly, S.—Cf. AS. *wróht*, an accusation, from the pt. of (*ge*)*wrégan*, to accuse (cf. *sécan*, pt. *sóhte*).

wrihels, *sb.* a covering, veil; **wriheles,** S; **wriels,** SD.—AS. *wrígels*.

wrihen, *v.* to cover; S; **wrie,** CM; **wrien,** *pr. pl.*, S.—AS. **wríhan*, pt. *wráh* (pl. *wrigon*), pp. *wrigen*; cf. OHG. *rîhan* (Tatian). Cf. **wreon**.

wrikken, *v.* to twist to and fro, to move about, SkD (s.v. *wriggle*); **wrickede,** *pt. s.*, S2.

wringen, *v.* to wring, press, S, S2, C2; **wrang,** *pt. s.*, S; **wrong,** S, S2, S3, C3; **wronge,** P; **wrongen,** *pl.*, S2; **wrong,** *pp.*, S.—AS. *wringan*, pt. *wrang* (pl. *wrungon*), pp. *wrungen*.

writelinge, *sb.* trilling (of a nightingale), S.

wro, *sb.* that which is crooked, a corner, HD; **wroo,** HD; **wra,** WA; **wraa,** WA; **wray,** WA, NQ (6. 12. 252).—Cf. Icel. *rá* (for *vrá*). See **wraw**.

wrohte, *pt. s.* wrought, worked; see **werke**[2].

wrong, *pp., adj.* and *sb.* twisted awry, wrong, a wrong, S, PP; **wrang,** PP. *Comb.*: **wrong-wis,** unjust, wicked, H, S; **wrangwis,** S2; **wrangwislie,** wrongly, S2; **wrongwisly,** PP; **wrangwisnes,** iniquity, S2. See **wringen**.

wroot, wrot, *pt. s.* wrote; see **wryten**.

wroth[1], *pt. s.* writhed; see **wryþen**.

wroth[2], *adj.* wroth, fearful, S, C3, PP; **wrað,** S, S2, H; **wroþer,** *comp.*, PP, HD; **wrothe,** *adv.*, angrily, evilly, S, G; **wroðliche,** wrathfully, S2; **wroðly,** S2; **wroðely,** S2; **wrathly,** H. *Comb.*: **wrothirhaile,** calamity, WA. *Phr.*: **to wraðer heale,** to evil fortune, bad luck, S; **to wroþer hele,** PP.—AS. *wráth*.

wryt, *sb.* writing, S; **writ;** S; **writte,** S2.—AS. (*ge*)*writ*.

wryten, *v.* to write, C2; **writen;** S; **wright,** S3; **wrot,** *pt. s.*, S, S2, PP; **wroot,** C2, C3; **wrate,** S, H; **wroten,** *pl.*, W; **writen,** C2;

241

wryten, *pp.*, PP; **writen**, S, C2, C3; **write**,
S; **wryte**, S2; **wreten**, S2; **y-writen**, S2;
y-write, S2; **i-wryten**, S; **i-writen**, S.—
AS. *wrítan*, pt. *wrát* (pl. *wríton*), pp. *writen*.

wrythen, *v.* to writhe, twist, Prompt., S2;
wroth, *pt. s.*, PP; **writhen**, *pl.*, W; **wryth-
en**, S; *pp.*, PP; **writhun**, W; **i-wriþen**, S2.
Der.: **wrything**, turning, C2.—AS. *wríðan*,
pt. *wráð* (pl. *wriðon*), pp. *wriðen*.

wu-; see also words beginning in **wo-** and
wou-.

wuch, *pron.* which, S2; **wulc**, S; see **which**.

wude, *sb.* wood, tree, S; see **wode**[1].

wule[1], *sb.* while, S2; see **while**.

wule[2], *1 pr. s.* will, S; see **wille**[1].

wundi, *adj.* rid of, S; **windi**, S.

wune, *adj.* accustomed, S.

wunien, *v.* to dwell, S; see **wonen**[1].

wunne, *sb.* joy, S, S2; see **winne**.

wurne, *v.* to refuse; see **wernen**.

wurse, *adj., adv. comp.* worse, S; **wurs**, S, G;
werse, S; **wers**, CM, S, H (p. 269);
wærse, S; **wrse**, S; **wurse**, *sb.*, the devil,
S; **worse**, S.—AS. *wyrs*.

wursien, *v.* to become worse, take hurt, S;
i-wursed, *pp.*, S.—AS. *wyrsian*.

wurst, *adv. superl.* worst, S; **wurste**, *adj.* S;
werste, S; **werst**, W2; **warst**, H (p. 269);
werest, S; **wrst**, S. **worste** (= Lat.
nequissimi = Gr. τοῦ πονηροῦ, i.e. the
devil), W.—AS. *wyrst*.

wurstu; see **worþen**.

wurð, wurðen; see **worþen**.

wurðien, *v.* to honour, S; **wurrþenn**, S;
wurðeð, *pr. s.*, S; **wurðeden**, *pt. pl.*, S.
Der.: **wurðing**, honour, S.—AS. *wurðian*,
weorðian, from *weorð*. See **worþ**[1].

wurthmint, *sb.* honour, S; see **worþ**[1].

wuschen, *v.* to wish, S2, PP; **wusshen**, PP;
wisshen, PP.—AS. *wýscan*, from *wúsc*:
OHG. *wunsc*, a wish; see Sievers, 185.

wute, *imp. pl.* know, S; see **witen**[1].

wy, *adv.* why, S; see **whi**.

wydder, *v.* to wither, S3; see **wederen**.

wye, *sb.* a man, PP; **wy**, S3, P; **wyʒe**, S2;
weiʒh, S2; **wiʒes**, *pl.*, S2; **wies**, S2.—AS.
wíga, warrior, man. See **weye**[1].

wygge, *sb.* a small cake or bun, Prompt.;
wigg, HD.

wyghte, *sb.* weight, HD, PP, C3; **wyhte**, S;
wiʒte, PP; **wihte**, S.—AS. *(ge)wiht*.

wylem, *adv.* formerly, S; see **whilom**.

wyn, *sb.* wine, S, C; **wyne**, *dat.*, S. *Comb.*:
wyn-ape, ape-wine, *vin de singe*, C3; **win-
iærd**, vineyard, S; **wynʒord**, S2; **win-tre**,
vine, S.—AS. *wín*; Lat. *uinum*.

wynd, *sb.* wind, S; **wynt**, S2.—AS. *wind*:
Goth. *winds*: Lat. *uentus*; see Curtius, No.
587.

wyndas, *sb.* windlass, Prompt., C2.—Icel.
vind-áss, a pole which can be wound round.

wyndewen, *v.* to winnow, W2; **wyndowen**,
S2; **windwen**, S; **wynewen**, W. *Comb.*:
wynwe-schete, winnowing-sheet, S3.—
AS. *windwian* (OET). See **wynd**.

wyne-grapis, *sb. pl.* vine-grapes, S3 (13. 99).

wynk, *sb.* sleep, nap, PP; **wink**, PP, S2.

wynken, *v.* to wink, nod, sleep, PP, Prompt.;
winke, C2; **vynke**, S2. *Der.*: **wynkynge**,
fit of sleepiness, PP.

wyppyl-tre, *sb.* the cornel-tree, CM (2. 90);
whyppyltre, C.—Cf. MLG. *wipel-bom*, the
cornel-tree (Pritzel).

wyrle, *v.* to whirl, S2; see **whyrlyn**.

wys, *adj.* wise, PP; **wis**, S, S2; **viss**, S2;
wisliche, *adv.*, S. *Der.*: **wisdom**, learning,
S.—AS. *wís*, Goth. *weis*.

wyse, *sb.* mode, manner, C2, S2; **wise**, S,
S2; **wis**, S; **wes**, S; **viss**, S2. *Comb.*:
ryghtwis, righteous, PP; **wrongwis**,
PP.—AS. *wise*.

wyue, *v.* to take to wife, C2; **wiuen**, S;
wyued, *pp.*, married, PP.—AS. *wífian*.

wyuere, *sb.* a serpent, CM.—OF. *wivre, vivre*
(F. *givre*); Lat. *uipera*; see BH, § 150.

wywere, *sb.* a fishpond, Voc.; **wayowre**,
piscina, Prompt.—OF. *vivier*; Lat. *uiuarium*;
cf. OHG. *wîwâri* (Tatian), G. *weiher*; see
Kluge.

X

x is written in some MSS. for **sh**. It constantly occurs in the Coventry Mysteries, as
in **xal, xalt, xuld**, etc.; see HD. See **schal**,
scholde.

Y

For words in which initial **y-** *represents an older* **ʒ-**, *see also under* **ʒ** *below.*

y-, *prefix*; see **ʒe-**.
yald, *pt. s.* yielded; see **ʒelden**.
yane, *v.* to yawn, HD, Palsg.; see **ganien**.
yare, *adv.* soon, S2, Sh.; see **ʒare**[2].
yate, *sb.* gate, C2, S3; see **gate**[2].
yawle, *v.* to howl, HD; see **ʒoulen**.
ychan, each one, HD; **ychone**, HD; see **eche**[1].
yche, *adj.* the same, S2; see **ilke**.
ydolastre, *sb.* idolater, C2.—Cf. OF. *idolâtre* (Cotg.); Church Lat. *idolatra* (Vulg.).
ydolatrie, *sb.* idolatry, PP.—Church Lat. *idolatria* (Vulg.).
ydole, *sb.* idol, C3; **ydoles**, *pl.*, C3.— Church Lat. *idōlum* (Vulg.); Gr. εἴδωλον (LXX); cf. OF. *idle, ydle* (Roland); Late Lat. *ídolum* (accented as in Greek).
ydre, *sb.* hydra, water-snake, WA.—OF. *ydre*; Lat. *hydra*; Gr. ὕδρα.
ydres, *sb. pl.* water-pots (= Lat. *hydriae*), S.— Gr. ὑδρίαι; cf. OF. *ydrie* (Ducange).
ye, *sb.* eye, Voc., HD; see **eʒe**[2].
yeant, *sb.* giant, HD; see **geaunt**.
yeddinges, *pl.* romances, songs, C; see **ʒeddynge**.
yede, *pt. s.* went, S, S2, S3, C3; see **eode**, **ʒeode**.
yeer, *sb.* year, C2; see **ʒeer**.
yef, if, S, S2; see **ʒif**.
yefte, *sb.* a gift, S; see **ʒift**.
yeir, *pl.* years, S2; see **ʒeer**.
yelde, *sb.* a payment, S; see **ʒeld**.
yelde-halle, *sb.* guild-hall, CM, C.
yelden, *v.* to yield, pay, C2; see **ʒelden**.
yelderes, *sb. pl.* debtors, S2.
yeldinges, *sb. pl.* payments, debts, S2.
yelleden, *pt. pl.* yelled, C; see **ʒellen**.
yelpe, *v.* to boast, C; see **ʒelpen**.
yelwe, *adj.* yellow, C; see **ʒelow**.
yeman, *sb.* retainer, C; see **ʒoman**.
yeme, *sb.* an uncle, HD; see **eem**.
yemen, *v.* to heed, S; see **ʒemen**.
yemer, *adj.* sad, S; see **ʒemer**.
yemernesse, *sb.* sadness, S.
yen, *sb. pl.* eyes, HL; see **eʒe**[2].
yep, *adj.* prompt, quick, HD; **yepe**, HD; see **ʒape**.
yer, *conj.* ere, before, S3; see **er**[2].
yerd, *sb.* an enclosure, S, C; see **ʒerd**.
yerde, *sb.* rod, C2; **yeorde**, S; see **ʒerde**.
yere, *sb.* ear, HD; see **ere**[1].
yerle, *sb.* earl, S3; see **erl**.

yerly, *adv.* early, S3; see **erly**.
yerne, *adj.* desirous, CM; see **ʒerne**[2].
yerthe, *sb.* earth, S3; see **erþe**[2].
yeste, *sb.* gest, tale, HD; see **geste**[1].
yete, *conj.* yet, S; **yet**, C3; see **ʒet**.
yeuen, *v.* to give, S; see **ʒiven**.
yftles, *adj.* giftless, HD. See **ʒift**.
yh- is written in some MSS. for **y-**; see HD.
yheden, *pt. pl.* went, S2; see **eode**.
yhode, went, S2; see **eode**.
ying, *adj.* young, S3, G, B; see **ʒong**.
yis, *adv.* yes, C2; see **ʒis**.
yistirday, yesterday, PP; see **ʒister-**.
yit, *conj.* yet, C2, C3; see **ʒet**.
y-kuenct, *pp.* quenched, S2; see **quenchen**.
ylaste, *pt. s.* lasted; see **ʒe-lesten**.
y-leuen, *v.* to believe, S2.—AS. *ge-lýfan.* See **leven**[2].
y-liche, *adv.* alike, C2; see **iliche**[1].
ylk-oon, each one, HD; see **eche**[1].
ylonde, *sb.* island, S2; **ilond**, SkD.—AS. *íg-land*; *íg*, watery land, island, from OTeut. stem **auja*, see Sievers, 99.
y-mone, *sb.* company, S.—AS. *ge-mána*, 'societas' (Voc.).
ympe, *sb.* a graft, scion, offspring, HD, PP, H; **impe**, Prompt., ND; **imp**, S3, TG.— AS. *impe* (BT); Low Lat. *impotus*, a graft; Gr. ἔμφυτος engrafted; cf. F. *ente.*
ympen, *v.* to graft, PP; **ympyd**, *pp.*, H, Prompt. *Der.*: **ympynge**, graft, scion, H; **impynge**, Prompt.
ympne, *sb.* hymn, CM, HD.—OF. *ymne*; Church Lat. *hymnum* (Vulg.); Gr. ὕμνος see Brugmann, § 131. See **impne**.
ynkirly, *adv.* particularly, B; see **enkerly**.
ynow, *adj.*, *sb.*, and *adv.* enough, S2, C2, W, PP; **ye-noughe**, S3; **inoh**, S; **ynoh**, S2; **ynou**, S2, S; **ynow**, S3; **ynouʒ**, S2; **innoh**, S; **inow**, S; **inouh**, S; **inou**, S2; **inoʒe**, S; **inoʒh**, S; **ynouh**, S; **ynowʒ**, W; **innoghe**, S2; **ynough**, C2; **inough**, C; **onoh**, S; **anough**, CM; **ynewe**, HD; **anew**, S3; **ynewch**, S3; **eneuch**, S3; **inouwe**, *pl.*, S2.—AS. *genóh*; cf. OHG. *gi-nuht*, abundance (Tatian).
ynwyt, *sb.* understanding, conscience, HD; see **inwyt**.
yod, *pt. s.* went, S2; see **eode**, **ʒeode**.
yolden, *pp.* yielded; see **ʒelden**.
yolle, *v.* to yell, C; see **ʒellen**.
yollyng, *sb.* yelling, clamour, C; see **ʒellen**.
yond, *adv.* yonder, S2, C2; see **ʒond**[2].
yonge, *adj.* young, C2; see **ʒong**.
yonghede, *sb.* youth, S; see **ʒonghede**.

yore, *adv.* formerly, S2, S3, C2; see **ʒore**.

yornyng, *sb.* desire, S3; see **ʒerning**.

youngth, *sb.* youth, S3; see **ʒongþe**.

youngthly, *adj.* youthful, S3. See **ʒongþe**.

youthe, *sb.* youth, C2; **yowthe**, S2; see **ʒouþe**.

yow[1], *pron. pl. acc.* and *dat.* you, S, C2; see **ʒou**.

yow[2], *sb.* ewe, CM.—AS. *eowu*: Goth. *awi*; see Sievers, 106.

yoye, *v.* to joy, HD; see **joien**.

ypocrysie, *sb.* hypocrisy, PP; **ypocrisye**, C3.—AF. *ipocrisie*.

ypocryte, *sb.* hypocrite, C2.—OF. *ypocrite*; Lat. *hypocrita* (Vulg.); Gr. ὑποκριτής.

y-rayled, *pp.* covered, S3. See **reʒel**.

yre, *sb.* anger, H; **iris**, *pl.*, W2.—Lat. *ira*.

yreyne, *sb.* spider, W2; see **aranye**.

yrk[1], *v.* to make tired, to become tired, H: **irkyn**, *fastidior*, Prompt.; **erke**, SD; **irkyt**, *1 pt. s.*, S3; **irked**, *pt. s.*, SD.—Swed. *yrka*; cf. Lat. *urgere*.

yrk[2], *adj.* oppressed, tired, S3; **irke**, SkD. *Comb.*: **irkesum**, *fastidiosus*, Prompt.; **irke-sumnesse**, *fastidium*, Prompt.

yrous, *adj.* angry, H.

ysche, *v.* to issue, to go forth, B; see **ische**.

yse, *sb.* ice, CM, H (Ps. 148. 8); **iys**, W2; **ijs**, S3; **yse**, *dat.*, S2.—AS. *ís*.

ysels, *sb. pl.* ashes, HD.—AS. *ysle* (Grein); see Curtius, No. 610. See **isle**.

ysope, *sb.* hyssop, W2, Voc.; **ysoop**, HD; **ysoppe**, Voc.—OF. *ysoppe* (Ps. 50. 7); Lat. *hyssopum* (Vulg.); Gr. ὕσσωπος.

ysue, *sb.* issue, P; **issue**, PP.—AF. *issue*, pp. f. of *issir*; Lat. *ex-ire*. See **ische**.

y-tiʒt, *pp.* made tight, S3; see **þyhtyn**.

ythen, *adj.* busy, B; **ythand**, B.—Icel. *iðinn*.

yþez, *sb. pl.* waves, S2, HD; **ythes**, WA; see **uþe**.

yugement, *sb.* judgement, HD; see **jugement**.

yuel, *adj.* and *sb.* evil, S, S2, W, W2, C3; **uuel**, S2, S; **iuel**, S, W2, S2; **euel**, S, W2, S2; **eueyl**, S2; **ufel**, S; **yuels**, *pl.*, S2; **the yuele** (= malignus, i.e. the devil), W.—AS. *yfel*: OS. *ubil* (Tatian).

yuele, *adv.* evilly, W; **uuele**, S2; **euele**, S.

yuer, *sb.* ivory, W, W2; **yuor**, HD; **yuour**, HD; see **evour**.

yuory, *sb.* ivory, Prompt.; see **evorye**.

yʒe, *sb.* eye, HD; see **eʒe**[2].

yzed, *v. pp.*, said, S2; see **seggen**.

y-zi, *v.* to see, S2; **y-zy**, S2; **i-zeʒ**, *1 pt. s.*, S2; **y-zeʒen**, *pl.*, S2; **y-zoʒe**, *pp.*, S2; see **iseon**.

3

3a, *adv.* yea, S, PP, S2, H; see **3ea**.
3æn, *prep.* against, in comparison with, S; see **3eyn**.
3af, *pt. s.* gave S, S2; see **3iven**.
3aik, *v.* ached, NED; see **aken**.
3al, *pt. s.* yelled, S2; see **3ellen**.
3ape, *adj.* vigorous, strong, keen, bold, WA.—AS. *geap*, astute, bold (BT).
3are¹, *adv.* formerly, S; see **3ore**.
3are², *adj.* ready, S, S2, G; **yare**, HD; **3aru**, S; **3arowe**, S; **3are**, *adv.*, soon, S, G; **yare**, S2, Sh.—AS. *gearo*.
3arken, *v.* to prepare, S, S2, WA; **3arrkenn**, S; **gerken**, S; **giarkien**, S; **3earceon**, S; **3eirken**, S; **3arketh hym**, *pr. s. reflex.*, P; **3æarced**, *pp.*, S; **i-garcket**, S; **i3arked**, S; **giarked**, S.—AS. *gearcian*.
3arm, *sb.* cry, S2.—Icel. *jarmr*, a crying.
3arme, *v.* to scream, yell, bellow, WA, HD.
3arowe¹, *sb.* milfoil, *millefolium*, herb for nose-bleeding, Prompt.; **yarowe**, Palsg., Manip.; **3arow**, Voc.; **3arrow**, S3.—AS. *gearwe* (Voc.): OHG. *garawa, garwa*.
3arowe², *adj.* ready, S; **3aru**, S; see **3are²**.
3ate, *sb.* gate, S2, G, H, WA; **yat**, HD; see **gate²**.
3e-, a prefix before verbs and substantives.—AS. *ge-*. [In ME. the equivalents of *ge-*, viz. **3e-, i-, y-, hi-, a-, e-**, are often found prefixed to past participles. For words beginning with this particle see in many cases the uncompounded form.]
3e, *pron.* ye, S, S2, PP; **ye**, C2; **ge**, S; **yhe**, S2; **3eo**, S; **3ie**, S.—AS. *ge*. See also **3ou**, **3oure**.
3ea, *adv.* yea, PP: **3a**, S, S2, PP, H; **3e**, S, S2, PP, G; **3he**, W; **ye**, S2, PP, C2; **3ie**, S; **3ha**, S2; **3o**, S2.—AS. *géa*; cf. Goth. *já*, Icel. *já*.
3e-arnen, *v.* to earn, S.—AS. *ge-earnian*. See **ernen¹**.
3eat, *pt. s.* poured, S; see **3eten¹**.
3e-bugon, *pt. pl.* were obedient, S.—AS. *ge-bugon*, from *ge-búgan*. See **bowen**.
3e-cende, *adj.* natural, S; **i-cundur**, *comp.*, S.—AS. *ge-cynde*. See **kynde¹**.
3e-ceosen, *v.* to choose, MD; **3e-cas**, *pt. s.*, S.—AS. *ge-céosan*.
3ed, *sb.* a word; **3eddes**, *pl.*, MD.—AS. *gied*, *gid, gyd*, song, poem, saying.
3eddien, *v.* to speak, MD; **3edde**, to sing, S2.—AS. *geddian, giddian*, to sing, to speak.
3eddynge, *sb.* a gest or romance, Prompt.; **3eddyngis**, *pl.*, HD; **yeddynges**, songs, C. See **3eddien**.
3ede, *pt. s.* went, S, S2; see **3eode**.

3edire, *adj.* vehement, WA; **3ederly**, *adv.* quickly, S2, HD.—Cf. AS. *ædre*, (*edre*), quickly, at once: OS. *adro*, quick.
3eer, *sb.* year, S3; **3er**, S, S2; **gær**, S; **yeer**, C2; **3ere**, PP, S2; **yere**, S2, C2; **yeire**, S2; **3er**, *pl.*, PP, S, S2, S3; **yer**, S; **yeer**, C2; **ger**, S; **3eir**, S3; **yeir**, S2; **3ere**, PP; **yere**, S2; **yhere**, S2; **3eres**, S, PP; **geres**, S.—AS. *gér*, *géar*: OS. *jer*, *jar*; cf. Gr. ὥρα; see Brugmann, § 118.
3eerli, *adv.* yearly, S3.
3ef, *conj.* if, S, S2; see **3if**.
3e-fered, *sb.* company, *societas*, S; **i-ferred**, MD; **ifereden**, MD.—AS. *ge-férǽden*, companionship.
3eft, *sb.* gift, S; see **3ift**.
3e-fo, *sb.* foe, MD; **ifo**, MD; **y-uo**, MD; **ivo**, S; **3efo**, *pl.*, S; **ifo**, MD.—AS. *ge-fá*. See **foo**.
3e-geng, *sb.* company, S.—AS. *gegang*.
3eid, *pt. s.* went, S2; see **3eode**.
3eien, *v.* to cry out, S, MD; **3eide**, *pt. s.*, MD.—Icel. *geyja*, to bark (a strong vb.).
3eir, *pl.* years, S3; see **3eer**.
3e-laðien, *v.* to invite, S.—AS. *ge-laðian*.
3e-laðiere, *sb.* inviter, S.
3eld, *sb.* payment; **yelde**, S; **3ielde**, S; **gildes**, *pl.*, S; **gæildes**, S.—AS. *gild*.
3elden, *v.* to pay, yield, S, PP, S2, G, W; **yelden**, C2; **3ulde**, PP; **yhelde**, S2; **yheld**, S2; **3elt**, *pr. s.*, PP; **3ilt**, PP; **3ald**, *pt. s.*, PP, S2, S3; **yald**, PP, S2; **yalt**, HD; **3elde**, PP, S2; **3elte**, PP; **3elt**, PP; **geld**, S; **3eldide**, W; **yolden**, *pp.*, C; **3oldun**, W; **3olde**, W; **i3olde**, S, S2.—AS. *geldan*, pt. *geald* (pl. *guldon*), pp. *golden*: cf. Goth. *gildan*.
3eldingus, *sb. pl.* payments, debts, S3.
3e-lesten, *v.* to fulfil, to perform, to continue, last, extend, S; **i-leste**, S; **i-lest**, *pr. s.*, S; **i-lested**, S; **gelest**, *pr. s.*, S; **y-laste**, S2; **i-laste**, S, S2.—AS. *ge-léstan*.
3e-limpen, *v.* to happen, MD; **3elamp**, *pt. s.*, S; **ilomp**, S.—AS. *ge-limpan*. See **limpen**.
3elke, *sb.* yolk of an egg, Prompt.
3ellen, *v.* to yell, MD; **yolle**, C; **3olle**, S; **3ellynge**, *pr. p.*, howling, W; **3al**, *pt. s.*, MD, S2; **3ulle**, *pl.*, MD; **3elliden**, MD; **yelleden**, C.—AS. *gellan* (*giellan*), pt. *geall* (pl. *gullon*), pp. *gollen*.
3ellynge, *sb.* yelling, MD; **yollyng**, C; **3ollinge**, S.
3elow, *adj.* yellow, MD; **3eoluwe**, S; **3eolewe**; **3eluwe**, S; **3olewe**, S; **yelwe**, C; **yalu**, HD.—AS. *geolw-* stem of *geolu* (*geolo*); see Sievers, 300; cf. G. *gelb*.

245

ȝelpe, *sb.* boasting, S.
ȝelpen, *v.* to boast, S; **yelpe**, C; **yalp**, *pt. s.*, MD; **yelp**, MD.—AS. *gilpan* (*gielpan*), pt. *gealp* (pl. *gulpon*), pp. *golpen*.
ȝelpynge, *sb.* boasting, Prompt.
ȝeman, *sb.* youth, servant, MD; see **ȝoman**.
ȝemanry, *sb.* yeomanry, B.
ȝeme, *sb.* care, S, S2, G; **yeme**, HD; **geme**, S.—AS. *géme* (in compounds), *gýme*.
ȝeme-leas, *adj.* careless, S: **ȝemeles**, S.—AS. *gémeléas*.
ȝemeleaste, *sb.* carelessness, S; **ȝemeleste**, S; **ȝemeles**, S.—AS. *gémelést, gýmeléast*.
ȝemen, *v.* to care for, to heed, S, HD, S2, S3; **yemen**, S, G; **yem**, S2; **ȝiemeð**, *pr. s.*, S; **yhemes**, *pl.*, S2; **ȝemed**, *pt. s.*, S2; **ȝemedd**, *pp.*, S; **ȝemmde**, *pl.*, S.—AS. *géman*, (*gýman*); cf. Icel. *geyma*, mutated form from Icel. *gaumr*, heed, attention; see Sievers, 21. See **gome**².
ȝemer, *adj.* sad, MD; **yemer**, S; **ȝeomer**, S; **ȝomere**, *adv.*, S.—AS. *géomer*.
ȝe-meten, *v.* to meet, S; **i-meten**, to find, S: **y-mete**, S; **ȝe-met**, *pr. s.*, S; **i-metten**, *pt. pl.*, S; **y-mette**, *pp.*, C2, PP.—AS. *ge-métan*, pt. s. *gemétte*. See **meten**³.
ȝemsall, *sb.* keeping, B. See **ȝemen**.
ȝene, *v.* to reply, S; see **ȝeȝnen**.
ȝeode, *pt. s.* went, S, PP; **ȝede**, PP, S, S2; **ȝeid**, S2, S3; **ȝude**, S2; **yede**, S, S2, S3, C3; **yhode**, S2; **yod**, S2; **yheden**, *pl.*, S2 (s.v. *forth-*).—AS. *ge-éode*. See **eode**.
ȝeolewe, *adj.* yellow, S; see **ȝelow**.
ȝeomer, *adj.* sad, S; see **ȝemer**.
ȝeorne, *adv.* eagerly, S, S2; see **ȝerne**².
ȝeornen, *v.* to yearn, desire, S; see **ȝernen**.
ȝeoten, *v.* to pour, S; see **ȝeten**¹.
ȝep, *adj.* prompt, HD; see **ȝape**.
ȝer, *sb.* year, S, S2; see **ȝeer**.
ȝerd, *sb.* an enclosure, court, field, garden, W; **yerd**, S, C; **ȝerde**, G; **ȝard**, S3.—AS. *geard*: Goth. *gards*, house; cf. Lat. *hortus*; see Douse, p. 73. See **garþ**.
ȝerde, *sb.* rod, stick, yard, staff, Prompt., W, S, S2, P; **yerde**, C2; **yeorde**, S; **ȝerd**, S2; **ȝerdis**, *pl.*, W; **ȝerden**, *dat. pl.*, S.—OMerc. *gerd* (VP): Goth. *gazds*; cf. Lat. *hasta*; see Douse, p. 73.
ȝe-redie, *adj.* ready, S; **iredy**, S2; **ireadi**, *adv.*, S. See **redi**.
ȝerne¹, *v.* to run, S.—AS. *ge-ærnan*. See **rennen**.
ȝerne², *adv.* eagerly, S, S2, S3, PP; **yerne**, C2, ȝeȝȝrne, S, S2; ȝorne HD; ȝierne S; ȝern, S2.—AS. *georne*.
ȝernen, *v.* to yearn, S, S2, PP; **ȝeornen**, S, S2; **ȝirnen**, S; **ȝarnand**, *pr. p.*, S2; **ȝirnde**, *pt. s.*, S; **ȝornde**, S; **ȝyrnden**, *pl.*, S2; **i-ȝirnd**, *pp.*, S; **yȝyrned**, S2.—AS. *geornan*, also *gyrnan*; see Sievers, 79.

ȝernful, *adj.* desirous, MD: **ȝeornful**, S.
ȝerning, *sb.* desire, MD; **yornyng**, S3; **yherninges**, *pl.*, S2.—AS. *geornung*.
ȝernliche, *adv.* diligently, MD; **ȝeornliche**, S.—AS. *geornlice*.
ȝerre, *sb.* outcry, loud lament, WA.—Cf. AS. *georran*, to make a noise.
ȝe-sceaft, *sb.* creature; **ȝesceafte**, *dat.*, S.—AS. *ge-sceaft*. Cf. **schaft**.
ȝe-sceapen, *v.* to create, MD; **ȝescop**, *pt. s.*, S; **ȝesceop**, S; **ȝescepe**, *pp.*, S.
ȝe-sceod, *sb.* distinction, difference, discrimination, reason, S; **ȝescod**, S.—AS. *ge-scéad*, *ge-scád*. See **scheden**.
ȝescung, *sb.* covetousness, S; see **ȝiscunge**.
ȝe-secðe, *sb.* sight, S; see **isihþe**.
ȝet, *conj.* yet, S, S2; **giet**, S; **gæt**, S; **ȝiet**, S; **yete**, S; **ȝeiet**, S; **ȝut**, S, S2, P; **ȝete**, S; **ȝette**, S; **ȝute**, S, S2; **yhit**, S2; **ȝit**, W; **ȝhit**, S3; **yit**, C2, C3; **yet**, C3; **ȝyt**, S2; **get**, S.—AS. *get*.
ȝeten¹, *v.* to pour, MD; **ȝeoten**, MD, S; **ȝett**, WA, Cath.; **ȝeat**, *pt. s.*, S; **ȝet**, S; **ȝoten**, *pp.*, PP; **ȝotun**, molten, W2; **ȝeten**, PP.—AS. *géotan*, pt. *géat* (pl. *guton*), pp. *goten*: Goth. *giutan*; cf. Lat. *fundo* (for *fu-d-no*); see Douse, p. 112.
ȝeten², *v.* to say yea, to grant, S; **ȝaten**, MD; **ȝettien**, S, MD; **ȝettede**, *pt. s.*, S; **ȝetede**, S; **ȝette**, S; **i-ȝette**, S; **gatte**, S, MD; **gat**, MD; **gatten**, *pl.*, S; **gett**, *pp.*, S2.—AS. *géatan*, pt. s. *géatte* (pl. *géatton*); cf. Icel. *játa*, to say yea, confess, grant, see Fick, 7. 243. See **ȝea**.
ȝett, *sb.* gate, S3; **ȝet**, B; see **gate**².
ȝeu, ȝew, *pron.* you, S; see **ȝou**.
ȝe-wealden, *v.* to control, MD; **ȝe-wold**, *pt. subj. pl.*, S.—AS. *ge-wealdan*. See **welden**¹.
ȝe-wer, *adv.* everywhere, S.—AS. *ge-hwǽr*.
ȝe-winne, *v.* to contend, S.—AS. *ge-winnan*.
ȝeyn, *prep.* and *prefix*, against, in comparison with; **ȝæn**, S.—AS. *gegn*; cf. Icel. *gegn*.
ȝeynbowght, *pt. s.* redeemed, HD; **biggen**².
ȝeyncome, *sb.* return, HD.
ȝeynsey, *v.* to gainsay; **ȝeinseye**, SkD.
ȝha, *adv.* yea, S3: **ȝhe**, W; see **ȝea**.
ȝhis, *adv.* yes, W; see **ȝis**.
ȝicchen, *v.* to itch, MD; **ȝitchinge**, *pr. p.*, W.—AS. *giccan*, also *gyccan* (see OET): OHG. *juochen*: OTeut. **jukkjan*.
ȝielde, *sb.* a payment, S; see **ȝeld**.
ȝierne, *adv.* eagerly, S; see ȝerne²
ȝiet, *conj.* yet, S; see **ȝet**.
ȝif, *conj.* if, S, S2, G, H; **ȝiff**, S; **ȝyf**, S2; **yif**, S; **gif**, S2; **yf**, S; **gief**, S; **ȝief**, S; **gef**, S; **ȝef**, S, S2; **yef**, S, S2; **ef**, S, C2; **geue**, S3; **gife**, S3, H.—AS. *gif* = *ge* + *if* (cf. Icel. *ef*, and OIcel. *if*, if): Goth. *jabai*; see Brugmann, §123.

ȝife, *sb.* gift, grace, S; giue, S; gyue, S; gife, S; ȝieue, S; gief, S.—AS. *gifu.*

ȝift, *sb.* gift, PP; ȝyft, S2; yefte, S; yifte, C3; ȝiftes, *pl.*, PP; ȝeftes, S; yeftes, S; ȝiftus, S2; yiftes, C3.—Icel. *gipt.*

ȝimmes, *sb. pl.* gems, jewels, S; ȝymmes, WA.—AS. *gim;* Lat. *gemma;* see Sievers, 69. See gemme.

ȝim-stones, *sb. pl.* jewels, S.—AS. *gim-stán.*

ȝing, *adj.* young, S3, G; see ȝong.

ȝirnan, *v.* to desire, S; see ȝernen.

ȝis, *adv.* yes, MD; ȝys, Prompt.; yis, C2; ȝus, PP, S2; ȝhis, W.—AS. *gese* for *géa* + the particle *-se, -si* (for Goth. *sai,* OHG. *sé,* behold); see Sievers, 338.

ȝiscare, *sb.* covetous person, S; ȝitsere, MD; ȝietceres, *pl.*, S.—AS. *gítsere.*

ȝiscen, *v.* to covet, desire, MD.—AS. *gítsian, gídsian;* cf. Goth. *gaidw,* want; see Sievers, 198, 205.

ȝiscunge, *sb.* covetousness, S; ȝescung, S; ȝitsunge, MD.—AS. *gítsung.*

ȝister-, *adj.* yester-, MD.—AS. *geostra, gystra:* Goth. *gistra.*

ȝister-dai, yesterday, W2; yistirday, PP.

ȝister-evin, yester-eve, S3.

ȝit, *conj.* yet, W; see ȝet.

ȝiu, you, S; see ȝou.

ȝiuen, *v.* to give, S, S2, PP; ȝifenn, S; ȝyue, W, S2; gyuen, S; geuen, S; ȝeuen, S, S2, S3; ȝefen, S; yiuen, C2; yeuen, S; ȝeouen, S; ȝieuen, S; ȝefue, S; ȝiefe, S; ȝief, S; geyff, S3; yef, *imp. s.*, S; yif, S, S2; gif, S2; ȝeueþ, *pl.*, S2; gifð, *pr. s.*, S; yeft, S; yefþ, S2; gaf, *pt. s.*, S2; ȝaf, S, S2, G; ȝæf, S; ȝifuen, *pl.*, S; yaf, S, C2; iaf, S; ȝiaf, S; gef, S; ȝef, S, S2; gaiff, S3; yafe, S3; ȝaue, S2; ȝeue, *pl.*, S2; ȝauen, W; iafen, S; iauen, S; geuen, *pp.*, S; gyuen, S; ȝiuen, S; yiuen, C2; iiuen, S; iȝiue, S; yeuen, S2, C2; y-ȝeue, S2, G; ȝouen, S2; ȝouun, S2, W; iȝiue, S, S2.—AS. *gifan,* pt. *geaf* (pl. *géafon*), pp. *gifen;* see Sievers, 391.

ȝiuer, *adj.* greedy, MD; ȝiure, S.—AS. *gífre;* cf. G. *geifer,* drivel.

ȝoill-euen, *sb.* Yule-even, Christmas eve, B. See ȝole.

ȝok, *sb.* yoke, W, W2; ȝockis, *pl.*, W, W2.— AS. *geoc:* Goth. *juk;* cf. Lat. *iŭgum,* Gr. ζυγόν; see Brugmann, § 133.

ȝolde, *pp.* paid, W; see ȝelden.

ȝole, *sb.* Yule, Christmas, HD, SkD.—AS. *géola;* cf. Goth. *jiuleis,* Grimm, p. 702; see Sievers, 220.

ȝoman, *sb.* a youth, MD, Cath.; ȝeman, MD; yeman, servant, retainer, C; ȝemen, *pl.*, HD, PP; ȝoumen, PP.

ȝomere, *adv.* sadly, S; see ȝemer.

ȝomerly, *adj.* sad, S2.—AS. *géomorlic.*

ȝon, *adj.* yon, MD, PP; ȝone, PP, S2.—AS. *geon,* (SkD); cf. Goth. *jains;* see Sievers, 338, and Brugmann, § 123.

ȝond[1], *prep.* through, MD; ȝeond, S; ȝont, S; ȝeon, S.

ȝond[2], *adv.* yonder, there, MD, S3; yond, S2, C2; ȝonde, PP.

ȝonde, *used as adj.* yon, PP; yond, S2, S3, Sh.—AS. *geond,* through, also yonder.

ȝonder, *adv.* yonder, G; *used as adj.*, PP.

ȝong, *adj.* young, S, S2, S3, W, PP; ȝung, S; ȝonge, G; yonge, S, C2; yunge, S; ȝyng, S3; gunge, S; iunge, S; yhung, S2; ying, S3, G; ȝing, S3, G; yonger, *comp.*, S; ȝeunger, S; ȝungre, S; gungest, *superl.*, S; gunkeste, S; ȝongost, S2; ȝongest, G.—AS. *geong:* Goth. *juggs* (for *jungs*); cf. Lat. *iuuencus;* see Kluge (s.v. *jugend*).

ȝonghede, *sb.* youth, MD; yonghede, S, CM; ȝunghede, MD.

ȝonglyng, *sb.* young man, disciple, MD, W; iunglenges, *pl.*, S.

ȝongthe, *sb.* youth, W; ȝungthe, HD, Prompt.; youngth, S3.

ȝop, *adj.* bold, HD; see ȝape.

ȝore, *adv.* formerly, S2, G; yore, S2, S3, C2: ȝare, S.—AS. *geára,* for *géara,* gen. pl. of *géar.* See ȝeer.

ȝorle, *sb.* earl, HD; see erl.

ȝornde, *pt. s.* yearned, S; see ȝernen.

ȝoskinge, *sb.* sobbing, WA; ȝyxynge, Prompt.—Cf. AS. *giscian* (BT).

ȝotun, *pp.* molten, W2; see ȝeten[1].

ȝou, *pron. pl. acc.* and *dat.* you, S, S2, W, PP; ȝow, S2, G, PP; yow, S, C2; ȝew, S; ȝeu, S; ȝuw, S; ȝiu, S; giu, S; gu, S; ow, S, S2; ou, S, S2; eu, S; eou, S; eow, S.—AS. *éow.* See also ȝe.

ȝoulen, *v.* to howl, cry, MD; goulen, S2; ȝaulen, MD; yawle, HD; gowland, *pr. p.*, S3.—Icel. *gaula.*

ȝoure, *pron. pl. gen.* of you (also *poss. pron.*, your), S; eouwer, S; æoure, S; ȝure, S; ȝiure, S; ȝowre, PP; eure, S; gur, S; ȝeur, S; ower, S; oure, S2; our, S; ore, S2; or, S2; youres, C2.—AS. *éowre,* gen. of *éow,* you. See ȝe.

ȝou-selue, yourselves, S; ȝou-silf, W; ȝow-seluen, PP; ȝow-self, PP; ow-seolf, S; ow-seoluen, S; ou-suluen, S.

ȝouthe, *sb.* youth, PP, S2; youthe, C2; ȝowthe, PP; yowthe, S2; yhouthe, S2; yhowthe, S2; ȝieuð, S; ȝuheðe, S; ȝuȝeðe.—AS. *geoguð, guguð, iuguð;* Sievers, 74.

ȝouthede, *sb.* youth, MD; youthede, MD; guðhede, S.—AS. *geoguðhád.*

ȝouen, *pp.* given, S2; see ȝiven.

ȝowle, *sb.* Yule, HD; see ȝole.

303elinge, *sb.* guggling noise, S.

3ude, *pt. s.* went, S2; see **3eode**.

3uheðe, *sb.* youth, S; see **3ouþe**.

3us, *adv.* yes, S2; see **3is**.

3ut, *conj.* yet, S, S2, P; see **3et**.

3yng, *adj.* young, S3; see **3ong**.

Z

zalmes, *sb. pl.* psalms, S2; see **salm**.

zang, *sb.* song, S2; see **songe**.

zaulen, *sb. pl.*, souls, S2; see **soule**.

zay, *v.* to say, S2; **zayþ**, *pr. s.*, S2; see **seggen**.

zedewale, *sb.* zedoary, a root resembling ginger, Alph.; see **cetewale**.

zelue, *pron.* self, S2; see **self**.

zenne, *sb.* sin, S2; **zennen**, *pl.*, S2; see **sunne**[2].

zent, *v. pr. s.*, send, S2; see **senden**[1].

zette, *v. pt. s.*, set, placed, appointed, S2; see **setten**.

zeue, *num.* seven, S2; see **seven**.

zigge, *v.* to say, S2; see **seggen**.

zikere, *adj.* secure, sure, trusty, S2; see **siker**.

zinzebrum, *sb.* ginger, Cath.; see **gingivere**.

zitte, *v.* to sit, cost, befit, S2; see **sitten**.

zoft-hede, *sb.* softness, S2; see **softe**.

zom, *adj.* and *pron.* some, a certain one, S2; see **sum**.

zone, *sb.* son, S2; see **sone**[1].

zorȝe, *sb.* sorrow, S2; see **sorwe**.

zostren, *sb. pl.*, sisters, S2; see **suster**.

zoþe, *adj.* and *sb.* true, truth, sooth, soothsaying, S2; see **soþ**.

zuo, *adv.* and *conj.* so, as, S2; see **swa**.

zuord, *sb.* sword, S2; see **swerde**.

zuyche, *adj.* such, S2; see **swyche**.

zyenne, *v. ger.*, seen, S3; see **seon**.

zygþe, *sb.* sight, providence, appearance, S2; **zyȝþe**, S2; see **sighte**.

zyke, *adj.* sick, S2; see **sek**[2].

zykere, *adj.* secure, sure, trusty, S2; see **siker**.

zyþe, *sb. pl.*, time, S2; **ziþe**, S2; see **siþ**.

CPSIA information can be obtained
at www.ICGtesting.com
Printed in the USA
BVHW030302110821
614127BV00001B/17

9 781904 808237